CONSUMER BEHAVIOR

CONSUMER BEHAVIOR

Thomas S. Robertson

Joan Zielinski

Scott Ward

The Wharton School
University of Pennsylvania

Scott, Foresman Series in Marketing
Consulting Editor
Thomas C. Kinnear, University of Michigan

Scott, Foresman and Company
Glenview, Illinois
Dallas, Texas
Oakland, New Jersey
Palo Alto, California
Tucker, Georgia
London, England

To Diana Robertson
Ken Gross
Larry and Betty Ward

Acknowledgments
Acknowledgments for literary selections, charts and graphs, and illustrations appear
in a section at the back of the book beginning on pp. 609 which is an extension of the
copyright page.

Library of Congress Cataloging in Publication Data
Robertson, Thomas S.
  Consumer behavior.
  (Scott, Foresman series in marketing)
  Includes index.
  1. Consumers. 2. Motivation research (Marketing) I. Zielinski, Joan, 1948–
II. Ward, Scott, 1942–   . III. Title. IV. Series.
HF5415.3.R57 1984   658.8'342   83-20423
ISBN 0-673-15841-1

PREFACE

Our primary objective in this book is to present a comprehensive account of consumer behavior from a multitheoretical perspective and to relate this perspective to the development of marketing plans and actions. Our secondary objective is to show the value of consumer behavior theory for social policy decision-making. The "market segments" for whom the book is written are MBAs and advanced undergraduates.

It is perhaps equally important to say what the book is not. The book does not proceed from the point of view of any one model or conception of consumer behavior, nor does it adhere to any one theoretical perspective. We believe that the robustness of the field today lies in the multitheoretical perspectives pursued by scholars, researchers, and managers.

This book differs from other consumer behavior texts in three significant ways. First, we attempt to show the relevance of consumer behavior concepts, theories, and research methods to strategic and tactical problems of both marketers and social policy decision-makers. Second, in each chapter we attempt to show the historical development of a particular theoretical domain of consumer behavior from early studies to the most recent investigations. Third, we attempt to develop new conceptualizations in several areas and to include topics not found in other consumer behavior texts.

Our academic colleagues will notice a more systematic focus on cognitive processes (Chapters 4–6), as well as a greater emphasis on consumer socialization and cognitive development (Chapter 7) and on communication theory (Chapter 10). Topics unlikely to be covered in other books include behavioral methodology (Chapter 3), psychological economics (Chapter 13), and organizational buying behavior (Chapter 19). Knowledgeable readers will find new conceptualizations within some individual chapters, as in Chapter 20, on social class, Chapter 18, on family behavior, and Chapter 21, on subcultures, which develops the consumer behavior of the Hispanic market in some detail.

As we have suggested, this book approaches the application of consumer behavior to marketing problems in depth. This is accomplished in an integrated fashion throughout each chapter and not as an "add-on" at the end of the chapters. The practice of marketing is an essential component of this book. We have also included interviews with marketing practitioners and abstracts of relevant application materials to further show the value of consumer behavior to marketing practice.

ACKNOWLEDGMENTS

This book has benefited from the help of many. We are most indebted to our colleagues who helped in the writing of a number of chapters—Victor J. Cook, Jr. (Tulane), Elizabeth Dunn (Towers, Perrin, Forster and Crosby), John Deighton (Dartmouth), and Barton Weitz (Wharton). This project also bears the imprint of Harold H. Kassarjian (UCLA), since the several editions of his and Thomas S. Robertson's readings book, *Perspectives in Consumer Behavior* (Scott, Foresman, 1968, 1973, 1981), have contributed intellectually to the development of the book.

A number of reviewers offered invaluable critiques of various drafts of the manuscript: Luis V. Dominguez (University of Miami), G. Ray Funkhouser (Rutgers), Harold H. Kassarjian (UCLA), George P. Moschis (Georgia State), Richard L. Oliver (Washington University), John R. Rossiter (New South Wales), John L. Swasy (Pennsylvania State), and George M. Zinkhan (Houston). Reviews of particular chapters were also provided by our colleagues at Wharton—Raymond Burke, Barton Weitz, and Yoram Wind.

Our research assistants did much of the library work and manuscript editing: Cynthia Biondi, Deborah Bowman, Paula Breger, Timothy Choate, Lisa D'Esposito, Darriel Hoffman, Gretchen Marks, Esther Mills, Prakash Nedungadi, and Susan Snyder. Finally, our secretaries Sue Chotiwani and Jean Kristie provided stellar support in manuscript typing and editing.

Thomas S. Robertson
Joan Zielinski
Scott Ward

CONTENTS

PART
I

Foundations

1 The Developing Field of Consumer Behavior

Consumer behavior is an interdisciplinary field of study that focuses on how and why consumers behave as they do. Its objective is to understand, explain, and predict consumer actions under given circumstances.

Consumer can refer either to the "ultimate" consumer or the "organizational" consumer. The ultimate consumer is the end user of products and services, frequently referred to as the "household" consumer. The organizational consumer is also involved in the consumption of goods and services, but not for personal use. Industrial firms, government agencies, universities, charitable groups, and so forth are all organizations that consume goods and services.

A significant amount of human activity is consumer behavior. We play a consumer role whenever we engage in economic transactions, although we may be more conscious of this role and more involved in it when we purchase an expensive durable good, such as a new car, than when we buy an inexpensive, routinely purchased item, such as toothpaste. Nonetheless, both transactions involve consumer behavior, although the amount of information processed and the complexity of the decision process may be different for each.

In this chapter we examine the field of study of consumer behavior and how it has developed as a source of knowledge that can be useful in decision-making by managers and public policymakers. We begin by taking a broad look at the nature of consumption. What are the consumer behaviors—literally—that marketers seek to understand and influence? Then we examine consumer behavior as a developing interdisciplinary field of study that seeks to understand, explain, and predict consumer behavior based on theory and empirical research. In the next chapter we examine how managers and policymakers use consumer-behavior research and how they integrate it with other sources of knowledge to make strategic and tactical decisions.

THE SCOPE OF CONSUMER BEHAVIOR

Consumer behavior involves a sequence of decisions and activities. Although much of the focus of this book is on decisions about brands, a number of other decisions precede or follow brand selection. It is useful to think of consumer behavior in five phases of decision-making (see Exhibit 1–1):

1. decisions about whether to consume (or to save),
2. decisions about what categories of goods and services to consume,
3. decisions about what brands to consume,
4. decisions about buying and shopping behavior, and
5. decisions about how products will be used and discarded.

Whether to Consume

In this early phase consumers decide whether to consume and how much to consume. The decision depends, in part, on economic and demographic variables—variables on which it is possible to characterize every family. The amount and type of goods a family consumes will depend in large measure upon its *income* level. In fact, income alone has a major impact on consumer behavior, determining to a significant extent whether the consumer buys a

EXHIBIT 1–1
CONSUMER DECISION HIERARCHY

Phase	Decisions
1. Whether to Consume	• Whether to consume or save • Amount of goods and services to consume • Timing of consumption, depending on such factors as the state of the economy
2. Product Category Spending	• Allocation of funds to different product categories • Priority patterns in consumption (for example, what household goods to buy first, second, etc.)
3. Brand Selection	• What brands to choose, depending on factors such as the following: Brand preferences Brand loyalty patterns Decision rules or product benefits sought (for example, price, status, reputation)
4. Buying/Shopping Behavior	• What channel of distribution to select • Whether to comparison shop • What information to seek in-store • How organizations or families gather, evaluate, and use information to make purchase decisions
5. Usage and Disposition	• When to use the product and in what situations • When to dispose of the product

Mercedes or a Toyota, a vacation in Martinique or in Atlantic City, or an education at a private college or at a state college.

Yet, as economists have discovered, there is not a simple causal relationship between income and consumption; other factors must be considered. One factor is the consumer's **marginal propensity to consume** versus the **marginal propensity to save.** What proportion of an additional dollar of income will a consumer spend, and what will be saved? Consumers in different countries vary in their propensities to consume and to save. Americans, for example, save considerably less than Japanese. Similarly, segments within the American population have varying levels of consumption versus savings; black consumers, for example, save more than whites at equivalent income levels.

Some economists propose the concept of *relative income* to help explain the proportion of income devoted to consumption. This concept suggests that not only income at a particular time is important, but also the consumer's sense of what the family's *permanent income* will be over the family life cycle.

Finally, in the tradition of *psychological economics*, George Katona and others have suggested that consumer attitudes play a major role in determining levels of consumption.[1] In particular, **consumer confidence** is an important intervening variable between income and consumption. At constant income levels, consumers may or may not buy durable goods such as automobiles and appliances, depending on how "confident" they are about the economy. The Consumer Confidence Index, in fact, is used by many firms manufacturing durable goods as a factor in sales forecasting (see Chapter 13).

Economics is not the only discipline that contributes to our understanding of whether or how much people will consume. Anthropologists who study different cultures and sociologists who study social classes and subcultures within a society provide further insight into consumption behavior. Consumption may be used as a ritualistic means of exhibiting social prestige, for example. In some societies, articles of adornment specify a certain status in society. On the other hand, deliberately not consuming may be a symbol of atonement in certain religious subcultures.

One of the most dramatic uses of consumption to assert social prestige is the ritual of the *potlatch* in some tribes. In this ritual tribal leaders demonstrate their wealth by trying to outdo each other in burning possessions. Perhaps equally dramatic was Gandhi's nonconsumption, or fasting, to achieve very different social ends. In everyday society consumption is a visible aspect of self presentation and an important attribute in understanding a society.

Product-Category Spending

Given a predisposition to spend, consumers next decide from what *product categories* to consume. Different categories of goods and services are consumed by different demographic segments of consumers. Demographic characteristics are easily quantifiable factors—like income or age. The incidence of vacation travel and vacation-home ownership, for example, is positively related to income, as is the incidence of participation in skiing, golf, and tennis. Alternatively, skiing is more likely to interest younger people, and golf, older people. Both males and females participate in skiing, whereas many more males than females play golf.

An interesting aspect of product-category spending is the order in which goods from various categories are acquired and how this pattern changes from one generation to another. Exhibit 1–2 shows an inventory of durable goods acquired and the rank order of acquisition for three generations. A sewing machine, for example, was the first purchase by grandparents, but it was fifth by parents and ninth by children. By contrast, washers and vacuum cleaners were acquired earlier by succeeding generations.[2]

An important factor that influences product-category spending is *lifestyle*, which denotes the consumer's pattern of interests. Lifestyle may be characterized on a number of dimensions, including the following:

- *active* versus *passive* (for example, participating in sports and attending live concerts versus watching television and listening to records);
- *ostentatious* versus *private* (for example, acquiring public symbols of success versus acquiring private goods);
- *family* versus *career* (for example, having children and spending time on family activities versus having no children and spending time on career advancement); and
- *local* versus *cosmopolitan* (for example, orientation to the local community versus orientation to the broader world).

**EXHIBIT 1–2
RANK ORDER OF PRODUCTS ACQUIRED
ACROSS GENERATIONS**

Grandparents	Parents	Children
1. Sewing machine	1. Cooking Range (gas)	1. Cooking Range (gas)
2. Cooking Range	2. Refrigerator	2. Refrigerator
3. Dining table	3. Sofa	3. Washer
4. Refrigerator	4. Washer	4. Radio
5. Washer	5. Sewing machine	5. Sofa
6. Sofa	6. Dining table	6. Vacuum cleaner
7. Radio	7. Radio	7. Television
8. Carpeting	8. Vacuum cleaner	8. Carpeting
9. Vacuum cleaner	9. Carpeting	9. Sewing machine
10. Television	10. Television	10. Coffeemaker
	11. Coffeemaker	11. Dining table
	12. Musical instrument	12. Electric frypan
	13. Electric frypan	

SOURCE: Reuben Hill (1970), *Family Development in Three Generations* (Cambridge, Mass.: Schenkman), p. 154.

The individual's lifestyle is a major determinant of the inventory of goods and services that he or she will consume. If we hold income levels constant, we can still find people consuming quite differently because of lifestyle. Whether consumers buy skis and tennis rackets or a new television may well be related to lifestyle. Whether they buy designer clothing or sheets and towels may be related to lifestyle. And so may whether they attend a university close to home or a university some distance away.

Lifestyle and demographic factors are particularly important in explaining *primary demand*, that is, the sales of a whole *product category* of goods and services. It might be suggested, for example, that the rise in primary demand for skiing is associated with greater affluence (income) and a greater concern with physical fitness and the active life. The rise in primary demand for fast-food outlets, microwave ovens, and convenience foods is associated with the increase in dual-income households together with an increase in the value of time for the working woman.

From the point of view of business firms, analyses of demographics and lifestyle are critical in forecasting primary demand and deciding whether to enter new product categories, as well as whether to continue selling within existing product categories. Consider the following decisions:

- Should a firm enter the household-moving business? (not certain, since there is some evidence of a change in lifestyle whereby people refuse to allow their careers to dictate constant moving)[3]
- Should a firm specializing in medical care introduce a new nursing-home concept? (yes, because the demographics are favorable—the population is aging)
- Should a firm consider the design of a new product line with particular appeal to Hispanics? (possibly, given the rapid growth of the Hispanic population in the United States)

Of course, other variables, such as the firm's capabilities and the nature of competition, are important for firms making decisions about which product categories to emphasize.

Brand Selection

Brand selection is the most important phase of consumer behavior from the viewpoint of the marketing manager, selling a particular brand. Consequently, it has been the focus of most research in consumer behavior (and it receives the most attention in this book). Many theories and models of consumer information-processing explicitly focus on how individual consumers select, evaluate, and use information in making brand decisions.

The process of brand selection varies considerably depending on the consumer's involvement with the product category. For *high-involvement* products—usually those that are socially visible or ego-related—consumers often go through fairly complex processes of brand selection based on extensive information-seeking. Alternatively, for *low-involvement* products—those that are not socially visible and not ego-related—the process of brand selection may be quite simple and based on limited information. For both types of products, however, consumers frequently form reasonably stable brand preferences as an alternative to having to make decisions every time a product is purchased.[4]

An important concept in brand-selection research is the consumer's response to brand **positioning**, or how the consumer perceives the brand relative to other brands. Exhibit 1-3, for example, shows a perceptual map of how some consumers might view a limited set of automobiles on two key dimensions—*sportiness* and *cost*. We would expect that consumers would select brands from the positions they prefer—for example, Mercedes in the expensive/low sportiness positioning or Volkswagen in the economy/low sportiness positioning.

Brand selection of cars, in fact, may be based as much on the symbolic meanings of different brands, such as *high status* (Mercedes), *virile* (Corvette), or *conservative* (Buick), as on the primary function, that is, to provide transportation. Levy, who coined the term "brand image,"[5] suggests that ". . . people buy things not only for what they do but also for what they mean."[6] This depends, of course, on the product and how much symbolic meaning the product carries—cars carry more than canned peas. Even for canned peas, however, a gourmet brand of "petite pois" means something different from a generic brand. People often buy more than the basic function of the product. Among industrial buyers of computers, for example, a majority buys IBM, although the actual product performance is generally not superior to competitors. But IBM symbolizes high service, reliability, and reassurance.

EXHIBIT 1–3
A PERCEPTUAL MAP FOR CARS

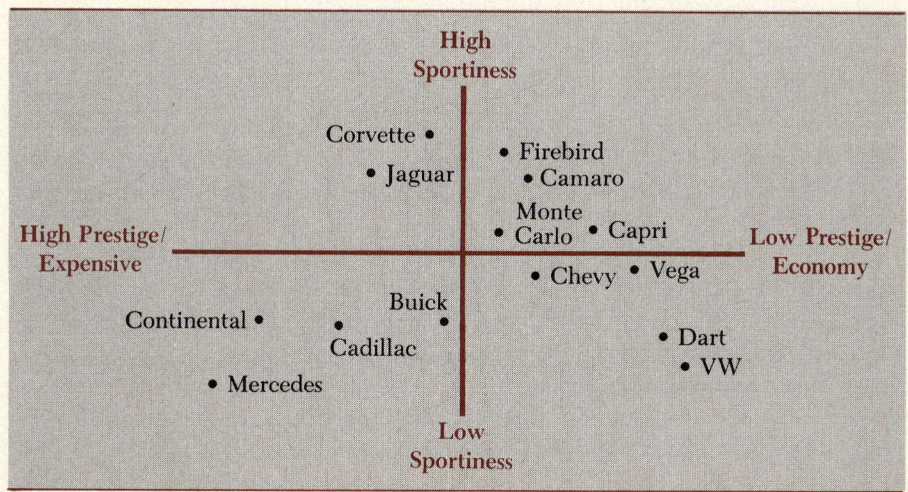

SOURCE: Yoram J. Wind (1982), *Product Policy* (Reading, Mass.: Addison-Wesley), p. 87.

Buying/Shopping Behavior

The actual buying or shopping process is the next phase in the hierarchy of consumer behavior. Note that phases may occur simultaneously. For example, while shopping, consumers may select brands in response to a store display or a reduced price rather than deciding on brands before shopping.

At this stage household consumers must select a channel (for example, direct mail or a store) and decide on the amount of effort to devote to buying. These decisions depend on the product and the consumer's "involvement" level (see Chapter 6). For high-involvement products, such as fashion items, consumers may engage in extensive shopping and information-processing. They may select stores on the basis of image or positioning. Saks Fifth Avenue's positioning is quite different from K-mart's. For low-involvement products, such as many grocery products, consumers may engage in a shopping routine, characterized by little in-store processing of information.

The kinds, amounts, and sources of information consumers utilize when they shop is of considerable interest. How much information do people acquire from the store in making a brand decision? What kinds of information do people seek? What kinds of people seek what kinds of information? How important a source of information is the store versus other sources, such as friends and advertising? How much do consumers use unit-pricing or nutritional labeling information? What types of consumers use such information, and for what products?[7]

Consumer buying may be conducted on a "team" basis, often in a family context. The following pattern is quite typical.

- One family member may *initiate* the idea of buying a product.
- Another family member may seek *information*.
- Another may actually *buy* the product. (The buyer, however, may not be the *decision-maker* but only the *purchasing agent*.)
- Another member of the family may have *veto power*. (Much of children's influence, for example, comes from the veto power of refusing to eat certain foods.)

Thus, for any product or service it is important to study the buying process within the family and the roles that various family members play in that process.

Similarly, organizational buying of goods and services may involve a number of participants, who may play different roles. For example, when a firm buys a computer, the president, the controller, the information-systems department, and the purchasing department may all be involved. Much as in family consumer decision-making, the people in the organizational decision process play such varying roles as information-seeker, decision-maker, advisor, actual buyer, and user. The role of the purchasing department, for example, may be limited to buying and may not include decision-making about the computer to buy.

Product Usage and Disposition

The final phase of consumer behavior involves the actual use (and disposition) of products. Of interest here are the various ways people use the same product—for example, cereal as a snack food and as a breakfast item—and the differences between individuals who make heavy use of products and those who make light use. Also of interest are the factors that determine when and in what situations people dispose of products. For example, why do some people keep cars for two or three years, while others keep them for nine or ten?

The situational nature of product usage has been studied in some depth.[8] The selection of a beverage, for example, varies situationally by time of day (coffee versus soft drinks) and by location (home versus restaurant). The brand selected may also vary situationally, as when people serve premium brands when guests are present but inexpensive brands to the family.

The topic of *disposition* has received only limited attention from researchers in consumer behavior.[9] They have tended to study why people consume but not why they dispose of products. Yet, interest in disposition has risen recently because of consumers' increased willingness to hold on to older cars, thus limiting new-car sales. It may be that in order to sell a new product marketers must know whether consumers are willing to dispose of old products.

THE DEVELOPING DISCIPLINE OF CONSUMER BEHAVIOR

The **discipline of consumer behavior** is still developing, as we shall see in this chapter. *Discipline* refers to a defined area of study in which basic research is conducted. Theoretical and scientific studies of consumer behavior contribute to the development of consumer behavior as a discipline. Studies within a discipline are conducted according to the rather strict criteria for scientific inquiry. For example, in contrast to commercial marketing research studies (which are generally proprietary—private to a company), discipline-oriented research in consumer behavior (and other scientific fields) can be subjected to scrutiny by peers through publication in journals and made available for reanalysis and replication by other researchers.

In a discipline it is believed that predictable patterns of relationships exist among concepts and variables. That is, consumer behavior is nonrandom and may be reliably predicted if we can discover and measure the causal relationships among variables. Thus, consumer-behavior researchers seek to discover general *laws* of consumer behavior, in much the same way that psychologists and sociologists seek to discover general laws of such phenomena as learning, personality, child development, and social interaction processes.[10]

Using the Concepts and Research of Consumer Behavior

Scientific knowledge of consumer behavior is needed by managers, who otherwise would have to rely on intuitive descriptive analysis of consumers in order to formulate and implement marketing strategies. It is also needed by public policymakers as a basis for regulating marketing activities, by educators, and by consumers themselves, as they seek to improve their consumption practices.

The concepts and research of consumer behavior can be used by managers or social policymakers to help answer particular questions—whether to introduce a new product (is there a consumer need?), whether to increase the price of a product (are consumers price sensitive?), or whether to require nutritional labeling (will consumers use the information?). However, management problems are always specific, and there is not a direct relationship between the discipline of consumer behavior and the manager's decisions. As Raymond Bauer aptly summarizes the matter,

> *The action problems of marketing are engineering problems, not scientific ones. By this I mean marketing action demands a specific rather than a generalized solution of its problems. Thus, while many scientific principles are involved in the design of a bridge, each bridge demands its specific solution to its specific problems.*[11]

Thus, whereas the discipline-based researcher is interested in explaining general patterns of consumer behavior across situations, the manager is necessarily more interested in describing specific consumer behaviors. The consumer-behavior researcher is often less concerned with how knowledge is applied to managerial decisions than with how particular studies contribute to the body of knowledge about consumers. The researcher seeks to add to knowledge in the quest for general laws or regularities in human behavior. Although managers may believe that such laws exist, their needs dictate that research should address specific problems rather than seek general patterns.

THE HISTORY OF THE CONSUMER BEHAVIOR DISCIPLINE

As a field of study, consumer behavior is at an embryonic stage. Consider, for example, that

- courses in consumer behavior did not appear until the 1960s;
- the first textbook on consumer behavior was published in 1968; and
- the first professional journal of consumer-behavior research began in 1974.

Nevertheless, understanding consumer behavior has been an issue of concern for perhaps thousands of years. Since the first time that someone tried to persuade someone else to barter one good for another, people have had conceptions, at least implicitly, of why consumers behave as they do. The major locus of theory and research on consumer behavior has been within the discipline of marketing, and marketing managers have been the major users of consumer-behavior research. However, most theories of consumer behavior *borrow* from the more general theories of the behavioral sciences. Consumer behavior is simply one particular type of behavior, and it may sometimes be understood by reference to many of the same theories that explain other types of behavior.

Current attempts to explain and predict consumer behavior rest on many theoretical foundations. The general perspective is that of the behavioral sciences—psychology, sociology, social psychology, and anthropology. But consumer behavior also has deep roots in economics, and uses many of the concepts of this science for their explanatory power. All of these disciplines are, in some sense, concerned with behavior, but their units of analysis differ. **Psychology** is the study of individual behavior; **sociology** is the study of group and subcultural behavior; **social psychology** is the study of interpersonal behavior (that is, how the individual's behavior is mediated by the group); **anthropology** is the study of societies and cultures; and **economics** is the study of a society's material well-being.

EXHIBIT 1–5
A 1930s
ADVERTISEMENT
BASED ON AN
EMOTIONAL
"PSYCHOANALYTICAL"
MODEL OF
CONSUMER BEHAVIOR

— May They Never Be In Want —
ADEQUATE PROTECTION FOR YOUR LOVED ONES
ASSURED BY
THE PRUDENTIAL INSURANCE COMPANY OF AMERICA
EDWARD D. DUFFIELD, President   HOME OFFICE, Newark, N.J.

Our brief history of the development of the field of consumer behavior begins with early traditions and proceeds to the current multitheoretical approach.

Early Traditions

Our earliest conceptions of consumer behavior were shaped by economics because of its focus on demand for products and services. Early in this century economics was the only "behavioral" science being pursued by academic researchers and also receiving attention from business managers. Traditional theories focused on aggregate-demand trends, which were based on two crucial assumptions about individual consumers, who make up the overall demand functions: first, that individuals possess complete and "perfect" information about alternatives, that is, products and brands to buy; and second, that all such information is used in economic decisions. Given these assumptions, it is hardly surprising that early marketing appeals contained enormous amounts of information, even for the most insignificant, routinely purchased items. A model developed of the "economic man," whose consumer decisions were completely "rational"—that is, based on complete and perfect information. Consequently, advertisers attempted to provide consumers all possible information, assuming that people would read and digest it all (see Exhibit 1–4).

By the 1930s the psychoanalytic theories of Freud and his followers began to change markedly our conception of consumers, as reflected in the marketing appeals and advertising of the period. "Emotional" appeals became the order of the day, reflecting a new view of consumers as emotional beings, rather than as perfect and complete information processors (see Exhibit 1–5).

Since then our views of consumer behavior have changed; we feel that no single discipline, such as economics or psychology, is adequate to explain the range and complexity of consumer behavior. Instead, virtually all disciplines, or fields of study, involving human behavior are viewed as relevant to understanding and predicting the subset of behavior that is the focus of this text: consumption. In the following sections, we briefly examine the viewpoints of these various disciplines, tracing their value to our developing knowledge of consumer behavior.

Microeconomics

The first discipline that exerted a major influence on our views of consumer behavior was microeconomics. The basic microeconomic model posits that consumers seek to maximize **utility,** or more generally, *satisfaction*, from consuming any particular product. Consumers will purchase quantities of products to the point at which the *marginal utility* (the amount of additional satisfaction derived from consuming one more unit) per dollar's worth of any one product equals the marginal utility per dollar's worth of any other product for a given period of time. The microeconomic model is based on important assumptions: first, that consumers seek to *maximize overall satisfaction* for a certain income level and a given set of prices for products, and second, as we have seen, that consumers *act rationally,* meaning that they gather and act upon full and complete knowledge of product alternatives.

This microeconomic model, although useful to a degree, falls short of satisfactorily explaining consumer behavior, because it is difficult to measure utility and because other factors affecting consumer decisions are not included. Nor are the assumptions beyond dispute. For example, does the consumer truly seek to maximize satisfaction? Research on organizational and individual decision-making has indicated that *satisfactory* alternatives, rather than *optimal* ones, are generally the goal. Does the consumer act rationally? What is *rational behavior*? Is it rational to buy a high-status car, such as a Cadillac or a Mercedes? One could argue that such a purchase is rational if it is important to a consumer's self-concept and if the consumer obtains more satisfaction from owning a prestigious car than a lower-status car. Research on pricing indicates that consumers are not always sensitive to prices or knowledgeable about them; they may even buy the more expensive of two products under the assumption that a price-quality relationship exists—"If it costs more it must be of higher quality."

Finally, the microeconomics perspective is concerned only with aggregate patterns of consumer behavior. That is, predictions about consumer behavior from economic models are applied equally to all consumers who make up the economist's demand curves. Thus, the model is more useful for predicting aggregate trends in behavior than it is for considering an individual consumer's choice of brands or the behavior of market segments.

Some economists have recognized the limitations of microeconomic theory in explaining consumer actions. Katona, for example, proposed the study of "economic psychology," which takes into account various factors that affect consumer decisions, such as motives and attitudes.[12] These factors may influence and alter patterns of such consumer behaviors as spending, savings, and investment decisions which would be predicted from a traditional economics perspective. Recently, other scholars have proposed new theories of consumer economic behavior that take into account consumer perceptions of brands and allow some relaxation of the rigorous assumptions imposed by the traditional model.[13] (See Chapter 13.)

Motivation Research

If the economic model proved disappointing because of its limiting assumptions of rational behavior and its focus on aggregate demand rather than individual consumer behavior, just the opposite problems characterized another early development in the discipline of consumer behavior—**motivation research.** Perhaps in response to the kinds of difficulties posed in utilizing microeconomics for management decisions, some researchers went to the other extreme of assessing uniquely individual consumer behaviors in terms of Freudian psychoanalytic concepts.

Essentially, motivation research posited that particular consumption behaviors (such as product selection and brand choice) are a direct function of their *psychological* meanings to individual consumers. These meanings are related to basic motivational and personality components of human beings, such as the constructs of the id, ego, and superego proposed by Freud (see Chapter 12). Exhibit 1–6 describes a motivation-research interpretation of the "meaning of soup." Early motivation researchers relied on individual *depth interviews* (extensive open-ended questioning) to probe these dimensions, although today's researchers usually conduct *focus group* interviews—the main differences being the group rather than an individual, and less focus on subconscious motivations.

Motivation research caused considerable reaction among both academics and marketing practitioners. Initially, reaction was quite positive, perhaps because it caused managers to consider aspects of products and customers they had not previously thought much about. The novelty soon wore off, however, as many questioned whether a limited set of psychoanalytic concepts was adequate to explain all aspects of consumer behavior. Also, questions were raised about the generalizability of motivation-research results, since small numbers of clinical interviews were the basis of results such as those given in Exhibit 1–6. Many noted varying interpretations of results from analyst to analyst. Finally, questions were raised about the predictive ability and practical value of motivation research; that is, could the explanations suggested lead to better prediction of who would buy what products?

But motivation research leaves the discipline of consumer behavior two important legacies. First, as we have seen, the concepts and findings of motivation research helped managers view products from the consumer perspective; managers began to understand the importance of the symbolic significance of products, which derives from individual feelings and perceptions and relates to buying behavior. Second, the research methods used by motivation researchers are commonly used today, as an informal, quick, and inexpensive way to gain relatively deep information about product concepts, advertising executions, decision-making processes, and the like. Skillful managers do not assume that such information is necessarily valid and reliable for all consumers, but it can be useful in augmenting thinking and testing *a priori* judgments.

Later Developments

By the 1960s consumer-behavior researchers had begun to pay greater attention to a broader range of basic behavioral sciences, and had "borrowed" concepts pertinent to consumption behavior from each of these sciences.

The efforts of consumer-behavior researchers to find personality correlates of product- and brand-purchasing behavior provide an illustration of how the discipline progressed during this era. Early attempts to find such relationships were stimulated by a classic motivation-research study by Mason Haire that explored the "personality" characteristics of women who use instant

the classic coffee study

coffee and of those who use ground coffee.[14] Conducted in 1950, the study involved showing different groups of respondents two housewives' shopping lists that were identical, except that one list contained "Nescafé Instant Coffee" and the other, "Maxwell House Coffee (drip grind)." Compared with the drip-grind buyer, the instant-coffee buyer was viewed as being lazy, "not a good wife," and a poor planner. Obviously, the meanings of these products and the role of women in society have changed considerably in the ensuing years.

standardized personality tests

Nearly ten years later, other researchers used standardized personality inventories to investigate whether personality differences do indeed predict consumer behavior. The early studies found weak relationships between personality-test scores and purchase behaviors,[15] probably because the traits measured were developed for psychological testing and counseling and were not intended to be linked to purchase motivations.[16]

Other researchers developed measures of personality more specifically related to motivations for purchase behavior.[17] For example, one study found that consumers who scored high on personality characteristics such as "compliance" (a need to comply with the perceived wishes of others) were more

**EXHIBIT 1–6
A MOTIVATION-RESEARCH PERSPECTIVE**

THE MEANING OF SOUP

Ernest Dichter, one of the pioneers of motivation research, wrote extensively on the meanings of products. Here is an illustration of how he viewed soup from a motivation-research perspective.

Soup is endowed with magic power in the folklore of many countries. It is the brew of the good fairy, satisfying a hunger that is not merely of the body. It protects, heals, and gives strength, courage, and the feeling of belonging. Magic arises from the brewing together of special ingredients. Similarly, it is the complex distillation of kitchen magic that produces soup. Herbs have traditionally been associated with a more than earthly power. And the skillful blending of various herbs lends to soup the transcendent properties of legendary potions. Even a clear soup represents the extract, the quintessence of the strength of flesh and bone. As an elixir formed of all the nourishing virtues of the original foods, it is akin to blood or marrow.

Magic power often expresses itself as having immediate efficacy. Thus, part of the magic of soup resides in the fact that as concentrated liquid food it can be absorbed so quickly. Soup is magical as a quick physiological stimulant, the supreme "pepper-upper." The infusion of strength provided by soup is similar in its effect to a blood transfusion; many stories and ritual practices among peoples throughout the world likely than others to use deodorant soaps and mouthwashes.[18] In recent years, consumer-behavior researchers have gone beyond the standardized personality measures, developing tests called "psychographics" that are explicitly linked to desired product benefits and brand usage.[19]

psychographics

Consumer-behavior researchers have borrowed concepts from sociology. For example, sociologists had studied the diffusion of agricultural innovations throughout populations of farmers[20] and the pattern of personal influence affecting how physicians adopt new prescription drugs.[21] Consumer-behavior researchers borrowed conceptualizations from these sociological studies and applied them to consumer-behavior phenomena, such as the adoption of new fashions, instant coffees, and telephone equipment.[22] Similarly, consumer-behavior researchers applied concepts and methods from basic studies of group dynamics to such topics as peer-group influence and purchase decisions,[23] family consumer behavior,[24] and organizational buying behavior.[25]

Consumer-behavior researchers also have explored the cognitive processes intervening between exposure to marketing stimuli and purchase decision-making and behavior. Initially, they devoted much attention to the concept of *attitude*, which has long been studied in communication research and psy-

cognitive processes

---

show soup playing the role of reviving and restoring health. In many countries, farmers drink soup for breakfast to gain strength for the heavy tasks of the day.

Soup is a profoundly emotion-charged food. It has become identified with the positive symbols of abundance, security, warmth, comfort, and friendliness. Moods of nostalgic reverie characterize the way respondents recall the soups of their childhood. Highly emotional associations with soup center around family ties, especially mother's love. Soup evokes images of the warmth of the family dining room, the familiar sights and smells of the kitchen. . . .

Sick people, especially, crave soup. Illness is usually accompanied by tendencies to infantile regression. When we are ill, we become children again and we want mother love. Soup, like milk, is the perfect symbol of that mother love. In the case of soup, we are dealing with a relationship involving both genders. The mother-love symbolism of soup is directed towards essentially masculine acceptance. The gift of soup is a form of the woman's gift of love to the man as protector and defender of the home. Accordingly, soup is for the father and son much more than for the daughter. There are, of course, some soups that have more masculine appeal than others, such as mulligatawny (an East Indian curry soup), oxtail soup, and split pea soup. All these are represented as bearers of energy, health, strength, and virility.

SOURCE: Ernest Dichter (1964), *Handbook of Consumer Motivations* (New York: McGraw-Hill), pp. 67–68.

chology, as a construct intervening between stimulus and response.[26] For example, communication researchers during World War II studied the persuasiveness of different communicators and messages on audiences. In those studies, the interest was in how the mass media could be used to further the war effort, by encouraging people to observe "meatless" days, to conserve gasoline, and to contribute money to the armed forces.[27] Consumer-behavior researchers in later years studied how marketing stimuli, such as advertising, influence consumer attitudes, that may, in turn, influence purchase behavior. Fishbein and others greatly elaborated the concept of attitudes and explored how attitudes are formed, changed, and related to purchase decision-making.[28]

By the 1970s consumer-behavior researchers were beginning to develop conceptualizations of consumption processes *per se,* rather than simply borrowing concepts from basic disciplines and applying them (uncritically, in some cases) to consumption behavior. For example, many researchers reasoned that the processes leading to purchase decisions are far more complex than earlier attitude studies had revealed. The broader concept of *information-processing* formed the basis for an important tradition of studies concerning these complex processes. Researchers in this tradition examine how consumers acquire information, how it is stored in memory, and how it is used in decision-making.[29]

models   Another major development in the emerging discipline of consumer behavior in the 1970s was the appearance of relatively complete models of consumer behavior.[30] Such models vary in the particular aspect of consumer behavior each seeks to explain, in the scope and nature of variables included, and in the level of specificity. Each uses a flow chart portraying hypothetical relationships among variables relating to purchase behavior.

Efforts to validate these models (particularly the Howard and Sheth model) have been undertaken with limited success.[31] The actual application of the models to management decisions is limited by several obstacles. Data requirements are extensive and exacting, and the quantity and quality of data called for are rarely available. Some of the variables specified in the models are difficult to measure. Finally, it is exceedingly difficult to conduct a simultaneous statistical analysis of the great many variables portrayed. Nonetheless, the models have usefully applied theoretical perspectives from basic disciplines, and have done much to pull together the various streams of research that had been developed separately in the past.

methodologies   In recent years consumer-behavior researchers also have devoted considerable effort to improving methodologies and measurements used in consumer research. Attention has been focused on the need to improve the reliability and validity of consumer-research measures.[32] New methodologies for assessing consumer preferences and behaviors have been developed.[33] Some researchers have suggested that predictions based on consumer research can be improved if the situation in which consumer decisions occur is taken into account more explicitly.[34] Others have suggested that precise prediction of how an individual will behave is not possible. Rather, consumer behavior is a *stochastic* process, meaning that only *probabilities* of behaviors can be determined.[35]

Some research has been conducted on public policy issues. For example, research has examined questions surrounding whether federal or state regulations should require nutritional and other kinds of disclosures in advertising,[36] and whether advertising practices affecting children should be modified.[37] Some investigators have examined the utility of research in public-policy debates,[38] and the broader question of how and why consumers experience varying levels of satisfaction or dissatisfaction with various products.[39]

Although other areas have been explored in the developing discipline of consumer behavior, the ones we have discussed represent some of the most important. The field has developed from early "borrowing" to explicit models and conceptualizations of specific consumption phenomena. Even though researchers have not developed complete theories or discovered laws or invariant relationships among variables (as have natural scientists), the goals remain the same: to develop concepts and theories accurately explaining and predicting consumer behaviors.

A MULTITHEORETICAL APPROACH

No single theory in the study of consumer behavior is sufficient both to contribute to the theoretical development of the field and to solve practical problems of marketing managers. Rather, a **multitheoretical approach** is necessary. Consumer-behavior phenomena can best be understood by examining the major theories and concepts that underlie any consumption phenomenon.

Although theories may be drawn from various basic disciplines, we have seen that they usually cannot simply be "borrowed" and applied to consumption phenomena without modification and evaluation of their relevance. Personality measures, for example, became more useful in predicting consumer behavior when they were modified to be more relevant to consumption. Nonetheless, concepts and theories from many of the basic disciplines provide a useful basis for explaining particular aspects of consumer behavior. For example, consumer-behavior research in the area of advertising's effects on children has usefully drawn from child-development theories in psychology, as well as from sociological concepts of family life.

Factors studied in three major disciplines influence consumer actions.

- *Psychological factors*—cognition, perception, learning, personality, motivation, and attitudes. These are essentially psychological and social-psychological variables.
- *Sociological factors*—family, group membership, and social influence. These are basically sociological and social-psychological variables.
- *Sociocultural factors*—social class, subcultures, and cultures. These are sociological and cultural-anthropological variables.

The amount of influence exerted by each of these categories of factors differs for different types of products. Some forms of consumer behavior, such as the consumption of alcohol, are subject to high levels of social and cultural influence, and others, such as the use of detergents, are subject to very little.

Psychological Factors

The psychological approach focuses attention on the individual as a psychological unit. The individual's values, attitudes, opinions, perceptions, experiences, and learning—in short, *cognitions*—help govern responses and actions, including behavior as a consumer.

Psychological theories of behavior each contribute to our overall understanding of the consumer, and they should be viewed as complementary. For example, *learning theory,* which views behavior as the result of patterns of rewards and punishments associated with various actions, forms the basis for analyzing patterns of repeat buying and brand loyalty. Learning theory is also highly relevant to the study of advertising effects—how many advertisements are necessary to achieve brand recall and learning of the message, for example. A complementary psychological approach is *attitude theory,* which focuses on the beliefs that consumers hold about brands; marketing managers seek to create attitudes favorable to new brands, to reinforce positive attitudes toward established brands, or to change unfavorable attitudes. *Perception theory* builds our understanding of what consumers see and how meaning is attached to products and services. For example, some advertisements are noticed and retained by consumers, whereas others fail to gain attention. And although one spokesperson is perceived as trustworthy and reliable, another is unable to generate consumer confidence.

Another psychological field of inquiry of value to consumer behavior is *information-processing,* a field that dominates contemporary consumer research. Information-processing essentially portrays the consumer as first perceiving and attending to various marketing stimuli (becoming aware of brands within product groups), then selecting and evaluating information pertaining to products and brands (internally "weighing" the importance of various attributes or characteristics used to compare different brands of a product), and finally using information to reach decisions such as whether or not to buy, how to buy, and which brand to buy.

Related to information-processing is the notion of *low-involvement.* Although some consumer decisions are very important, highly salient, and psychologically involving, other decisions are unimportant, nonsalient, and noninvolving. When a purchase decision is highly involving, consumers often seek and carefully evaluate information about product alternatives. But when a decision arouses only low consumer involvement—as for most paper goods or canned foods—then the information search and evaluation are not extensive. How, then, do consumers choose among alternatives? Can brand loyalty be generated for low-involvement products? Consumer-behavior research sheds light on these managerially relevant questions.

Each of these psychological theories represents an important school of thought and builds the researcher's knowledge of how and why consumers behave as they do. Knowledge of these approaches and an appreciation of their compatability and interdependence also enables managers and social policymakers to develop a thorough understanding of consumers' preferences, purchasing habits, and brand decisions.

Sociological Factors

Sociology takes as its basic unit of concern the structure and functioning of groups, that is, sets of people who interact over time. For consumer-behavior analysis, the *group* is an important concept, because it is often more accurate to think of consumers as buying groups (such as families) rather than as individuals. Similarly, in organizational marketing, the customer is actually a group of individuals who play distinct roles in the purchase process. **the group**

The family group is also relevant to consumer behavior since it engages in *consumer socialization* of the child. How children learn to be consumers, to respond to advertising, and to seek and evaluate information about products and brands is a function of family role structure, values, and interaction patterns.

Social factors also play a role in the form of *personal influence*. Other people exert considerable influence on the individual's purchase of products, particularly socially visible products. The concept of the *opinion leader* is also relevant, since influence seems often to be transmitted from mass media to opinion leaders to followers. These concepts have particular relevance in the marketing of new products and the study of how new products "diffuse" or spread within a social system.

Thus, a number of sociological concepts improve our ability to explain consumer behavior. We should recognize that social factors also provide an overlay on the psychological factors already discussed. The attitudes of individuals, for example, tend to be consistent with the attitudes of the groups to which they belong. The child's attitude toward the Republican party is likely to be essentially the same as the parents' attitude. Similarly, the social nature of perception has been experimentally demonstrated in numerous research efforts. People tend to see things the way their relevant friends or associates see them, or, in the way they have come to "expect" to see things. The concept of the "self" may, in fact, be viewed as a social product, as discussed by such social psychologists as George Herbert Mead:

> *The individual experiences himself as such, not directly, but only indirectly, from the particular standpoints of the individual members of the same group, or from the generalized standpoint of the social group, as a whole, to which he belongs.*[40]

Mead maintains that a "self" cannot come into being without social experience, and that individuals develop their self-concepts and self-perceptions based on the ways in which other people interact with and respond to them.

Sociocultural Factors

Consumer behavior is also governed by sociocultural factors. Included at this level of analysis are social aggregates, which consist of categories of people sharing common attributes. *Social classes*, for example, are categories of people possessing the common attribute of equal social prestige. *Subcultures* are groupings of people with commonly held beliefs, values, and interests. *Cultures* are categories of people sharing a distinctive social heritage.

We can demonstrate how these sociocultural factors govern psychological and sociological factors. The *social class* into which a person is born, for example, whether "upper crust" or "the wrong side of the tracks," influences his or her view of life, attitudes, and personality. Social class also governs the groups to which a person belongs, whether the downtown athletic club or the uptown bowling league. And social class ultimately influences consumer behavior and the inventory of goods a person consumes, as well as the type of home owned, the college attended, and even the location of the television set within the home (likely to be the living room for low social class and in another room for higher social class).

A person's *subculture*—like black, Hispanic, Jewish, or Italian—may also influence attitudes and behavior. The influence of a subculture depends on how much the individual identifies with it. For recent Hispanic immigrants, for example, such influence may be very strong; they may retain Spanish as their dominant language and adhere to the values of their homeland in marriage, family relationships, and religious beliefs. The influence of the subculture also affects their consumer behavior. They may prefer Spanish-language media and Spanish-language stores—and even Hispanic brands of foods.

Finally, the *culture* in which people live also influences their view of life and greatly affects their behavior, including their consumption behavior. Individuals from different cultural backgrounds attach different meanings to common objects, for example. Native and American children living in Lebanon were asked to describe the uses of different objects. In answer to the question, "What are hands used for?" 33 percent of the Lebanese children— but only 6 percent of the American children—said "eating." "Food" was stated as a use for *trees* by 69 percent of the Lebanese—but by only 34 percent of the American children.[41]

Theoretical Interactions

Psychological, sociological, and sociocultural factors form a compatible and interdependent set of influences on consumer behavior.[42] Exhibit 1–7 depicts the relationship of these three behavioral science perspectives to one another and to the processes of consumer behavior. The diagram in Exhibit 1–7 is not intended to be viewed as a formal model of consumer behavior; such a model would specify all of the variables thought to influence consumer behavior and their relationships. Rather, the categories of variables are intended to represent the major theoretical traditions from which consumer researchers have borrowed during the gradual development of consumer behavior as a discipline.

Note that marketing stimuli, such as a product and the advertising for that product, represent only one component affecting behavior. As we have seen, the actual impact of these stimuli is mediated by the consumer's individual and social milieu. If a manager wishes to develop a thorough comprehension of the influences affecting consumer behavior, then knowledge of the social and psychological factors operating in the consumer's environment is essential. The development of valid marketing strategies proceeds from a sound understanding of the consumer's needs and wants, and the factors affecting those needs and wants. The aim of this book is to provide the basis for developing this thorough understanding of consumers and their behaviors.

The structure of the book parallels the preceding discussion. The book opens with a section on the foundations of the field of consumer behavior that sets the stage. Three sections follow, on psychological theories, sociological theories, and sociocultural theories. Throughout the book our objective is to present the most relevant theories and concepts for explaining consumer be-

EXHIBIT 1–7
MAJOR DISCIPLINES AND CONCEPTS IN THE STUDY OF CONSUMER BEHAVIOR

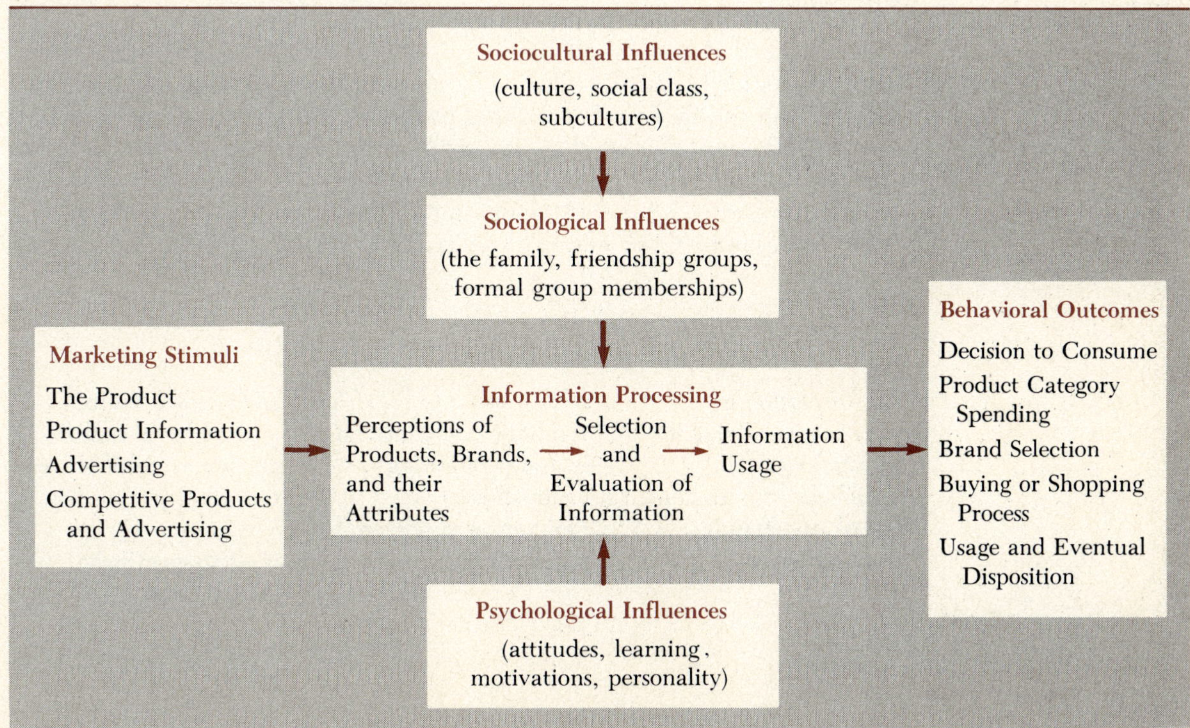

havior, and to relate these theories to the practice of marketing and social policy.

SUMMARY

The emerging discipline of consumer behavior is a field of study that focuses on how consumers behave and why they behave as they do. As a subset of the study of human behavior, the study of consumer behavior borrows concepts largely from the social and behavioral sciences—psychology, economics, sociology, and anthropology.

The discipline today is best characterized as being *multitheoretical*. No simple theory can account for the range and dynamics of consumer behavior. Psychological, sociological, and sociocultural factors are all integrally related in helping to explain consumer actions in the marketplace.

Consumer behavior actually encompasses a number of decisions. A first decision is whether to consume; varying spending and saving levels across cultures and within subcultures affect this decision. Given a decision to consume, the next decisions must be about what product categories to consume and in what order to acquire goods and services. Next are decisions about what brands to consume, a focus of this book. These decisions are followed by how to buy or shop for brands and what levels and kinds of information on products to seek. The final decisions are about how products will be used and in what situations, and when to dispose of products.

Consumer behavior is a field of inquiry with value in its own right. However, consumer behavior is also a key input to the formulation of marketing strategy and the design of marketing programs. Ultimately, a firm's success depends on consumer-needs assessment and the delivery of products designed to satisfy the needs of target market segments. The results of studies in consumer behavior are also important for social policymakers who have a mandate to improve the consumer welfare.

KEY CONCEPTS

the discipline of consumer behavior	economics	sociological factors
psychology	symbolic consumption	sociocultural factors
sociology	brand positioning	consumer confidence
social psychology	utility theory	marginal propensity to consume
anthropology	motivation research	multitheoretical approach
	psychological factors	

DISCUSSION QUESTIONS

1. What are the characteristics of a "discipline"?
2. How might the interests and concerns of marketing managers be different from the interests and concerns of consumer-behavior researchers?
3. What are the contributions of microeconomic theory to the development of consumer-behavior theory? What are the limitations of microeconomic theory?
4. What are the contributions of motivation research to the development of consumer-behavior theory? What are the limitations of motivation theory?
5. Why is a multitheoretical approach necessary for the study of consumer behavior?
6. Discuss the interaction of sociological and sociocultural theories on psychological theories. Provide some examples of how these interactions affect consumption decisions.
7. Must the "hierarchy of consumer behavior" always occur in that order? Could phases be skipped? Could phases occur simultaneously?
8. Recall a significant purchase that you have made, and examine that purchase phase by phase in the hierarchy of consumer behavior.

NOTES

1. George Katona (1975), *Psychological Economics* (New York: Elsevier). See also issues of the *Journal of Economic Psychology*.
2. Reuben Hill (1970), *Family Development in Three Generations* (Cambridge, Mass.: Schenkman).
3. "America's New Immobile Society" (1981), *Business Week* (July 27), pp. 58–62.
4. James R. Bettman (1979), *An Information Processing Theory of Consumer Choice* (Reading, Mass.: Addison-Wesley), Ch. 2.
5. Burleigh B. Gardner and Sidney J. Levy (1955), "The Product and the Brand," *Harvard Business Review*, 33 (March–Apr.), pp. 33–39.
6. Sidney J. Levy (1959), "Symbols for Sale," *Harvard Business Review*, 37 (July–Aug.), p. 118.
7. For background on unit pricing and consumer behavior, see J. Edward Russo, Gene Krieser, and Sally Miyashita (1975), "An Effective Display of Unit Price Information," *Journal of Marketing*, 39 (Apr.), pp. 11–19.
8. Pradeep Kakkar and Richard J. Lutz (1981), "Situational Influence on Consumer Behavior: A Review," in *Perspectives in Consumer Behavior*, ed. Harold H. Kassarjian and Thomas S. Robertson (Glenview, Ill.: Scott, Foresman), pp. 204–15 and Russell W. Belk (1975), "Situational Variables and Consumer Behavior," *Journal of Consumer Research*, 2 (Dec.), pp. 157–64.
9. Jacob Jacoby, Carol K. Berning, and Thomas Dietvorst (1977), "What About Disposition," *Journal of Marketing*, 41 (Apr.), pp. 22–28.
10. For an excellent and thorough assessment of consumer behavior research in terms of scientific criteria, see Gerald Zaltman, Christian R. A. Pinson, and Reinhard Angelmar (1973), *Metatheory and Consumer Research* (New York: Holt, Rinehart & Winston).
11. Raymond A. Bauer (1968), "Application of Behavioral Science," in *Applied Science and Technological Progress*, a report to the Committee on Science and Astronautics, U.S. House of Representatives, by the National Academy of Sciences.
12. George Katona (1974), "Psychology and Consumer Economics," *Journal of Consumer Research*, 1 (June), pp. 1–9 and (1960), *The Powerful Consumer* (New York: McGraw-Hill).
13. See Brian T. Ratchford (1975), "The New Economic Theory of Consumer Behavior: An Interpretive Essay," *Journal of Consumer Research*, 2 (Sept.), pp. 65–75; Kelvin Lancaster (1971), *Consumer Demand: A New Approach* (New York: Columbia Univ. Press); or Kelvin

Lancaster (1966), "A New Approach to Consumer Theory," *Journal of Political Economy*, 74 (Apr.), pp. 132–57.

14. Mason Haire (1950), "Projective Techniques in Marketing Research," *Journal of Marketing*, 14 (Apr.), pp. 649–56.

15. See, for example, Franklin B. Evans (1959), "Psychological and Objective Factors in the Prediction of Brand Choice: Ford Versus Chevrolet," *Journal of Business*, 32 (Oct.), pp. 340–69 or Arthur Koponen (1960), "Personality Characteristics of Purchasers," *Journal of Advertising Research*, 1 (Sept.), pp. 6–12.

16. Harold H. Kassarjian (1971), "Personality and Consumer Behavior: A Review," *Journal of Marketing Research*, 8 (Nov.), pp. 409–18.

17. Harold H. Kassarjian (1965), "Social Character and Differential Preference for Mass Communication," *Journal of Marketing Research*, 2 (May), pp. 146–53.

18. Joel B. Cohen (1967), "An Interpersonal Orientation to the Study of Consumer Behavior," *Journal of Marketing Research*, 4 (Aug.), pp. 270–78.

19. See, for example, William D. Wells, ed. (1974), *Life Style and Psychographics* (Chicago: American Marketing Assn.). Related techniques, such as benefit segmentation, are discussed in Russell I. Haley (1968), "Benefit Segmentation: A Decision-Oriented Research Tool," *Journal of Marketing*, 32 (July), pp. 30–35. See also Yoram Wind (1978), "Issues and Advances in Segmentation Research," *Journal of Marketing Research*, 15 (Aug.), pp. 317–37.

20. Everett M. Rogers (1962), *Diffusion of Innovations* (New York: Free Press). The third edition of this book appeared in 1983.

21. James S. Coleman, Elihu Katz, and Herbert Menzel (1966), *Medical Innovation: A Diffusion Study* (Indianapolis: Bobbs-Merrill).

22. See Johan Arndt (1967), "Role of Product-Related Conversations in the Diffusion of a New Product," *Journal of Marketing Research*, 4 (Aug.), pp. 291–95; Charles King (1963), "Fashion Adoption: A Rebuttal to the 'Trickle-Down' Theory," *Proceedings of the American Marketing Association*, ed. Stephen A. Greyser (Chicago: American Marketing Assn.), pp. 108–25; and Thomas S. Robertson (1971), *Innovative Behavior and Communication* (New York: Holt, Rinehart & Winston).

23. M. Venkatesan (1966), "Experimental Study of Consumer Behavior Conformity and Independence," *Journal of Marketing Research*, 3 (Nov.), pp. 384–87. See also James E. Stafford (1966), "Effects of Group Influences on Consumer Brand Preferences," *Journal of Marketing Research*, 3 (Feb.), pp. 68–75.

24. Harry L. Davis (1976), "Decision-Making Within the Household," *Journal of Consumer Research*, 2 (March), pp. 241–60.

25. Frederick E. Webster and Yoram Wind (1972), *Organizational Buying Behavior* (Englewood Cliffs, N.J.: Prentice-Hall).

26. For a review of attitude research and consumer behavior, see Richard J. Lutz (1981), "The Role of Attitude Theory in Marketing," in *Perspectives in Consumer Behavior*, ed. Harold H. Kassarjian and Thomas S. Robertson (Glenview, Ill.: Scott, Foresman), pp. 233–50.

27. For a summary of the wartime research, see Carl I. Hovland, Irving L. Janis, and Harold H. Kelley (1953), *Communication and Persuasion* (New Haven: Yale Univ. Press).

28. Reviews are provided in Martin Fishbein (1972), "The Search for Attitudinal-Behavioral Consistency," in *Behavioral Science Foundations of Consumer Behavior*, ed. Joel Cohen (New York: Free Press) and William L. Wilkie and Edgar A. Pessemier (1973), "Issues in Marketing's Use of Multiattribute Attitude Models," *Journal of Marketing Research*, 10, pp. 428–41.

29. See Brian Sternthal and C. Samuel Craig (1982), *Consumer Behavior: An Information Processing Perspective* (Englewood Cliffs, N.J.: Prentice-Hall); Jerry Olson, "Theories of Information Encoding and Storage: Implications for Consumer Research," in *The Effect of Information on Consumer and Market Behavior*, ed. Andrew Mitchell (Chicago: American Marketing Assn.); James Bettman (1979), *An Information Processing Theory of Consumer Choice* (Reading, Mass.: Addison-Wesley); and G. David Hughes and Michael L. Ray (1974), *Buyer/Consumer Information Processing* (Chapel Hill, N.C.: Univ. of North Carolina Press).

30. See Francesco Nicosia (1966), *Consumer Decision Processes* (Englewood Cliffs, N.J.: Prentice-Hall); John A. Howard and Jagdish N. Sheth (1969), *The Theory of Buyer Behavior* (New York: Wiley) and James Engel, David Kollat, and Roger Blackwell (1968), *Consumer Behavior* (New York: Holt, Rinehart & Winston).

31. John U. Farley, John A. Howard, and L. Winston Ring (1974), *Consumer Behavior Theory and Application* (Boston: Allyn & Bacon).

32. Jacob Jacoby (1976), "ACR Presidential Address—Consumer Research: Telling It Like It Is," in *Advances in Consumer Research*, 3, ed. Beverlee B. Anderson, pp. 1–11.

33. See, for example, Paul E. Green and Yoram Wind (1975), "New Ways to Measure Consumers' Judgments," *Harvard Business Review* (July–Aug.), pp. 107–17; Barton Weitz and Peter Wright (1979), "Retrospective Self-Insight on Factors Considered in Product Evaluations," *Journal of Consumer Research*, 6 (Dec.), pp. 280–95; and Paul E. Green and Wayne S. DeSarbo (1978), "Additive Decomposition of Perceptions Data via Conjoint Analysis," *Journal of Consumer Research*, 5 (June), pp. 58–66.

34. See Russell W. Belk (1975), "Situational Variables and Consumer Behavior," *Journal of Consumer Research*, 2 (Dec.), pp. 157–64. See also James A. Russell and Albert Mehrabian (1976), "Environmental Variables in Consumer Research," *Journal of Consumer Research*, 3 (June), pp. 62–63.

35. See, for example, Frank M. Bass (1969), "A New Product Growth Model for Consumer Durables," *Management Science*, 15 (Jan.), pp. 215–27. See also Alfred A. Kuehn (1962), "Consumer Brand Choice as a Learning Process," *Journal of Advertising Research*, 2 (Dec.), pp. 10–17.

36. See, for example, Dennis L. McNeill and William L. Wilkie (1979), "Public Policy and Consumer Information: Impact of the New Energy Labels," *Journal of Consumer Research*, 6 (June), pp. 1–11 and Kenneth C. Schneider (1977), "Prevention of Accidental Poisoning Through Package and Label Design," *Journal of Consumer Research*, 4 (Sept.), pp. 67–74.

37. See, for example, Gerald J. Gorn and Marvin E. Goldberg (1977), "The Impact of Television Advertising on Children from Low Income Families," *Journal of Consumer Research*, 4 (Sept.), pp. 86–88 and Terence A. Shimp, Robert F. Dyer, and Salvatore F. Divita (1976), "An Experimental Test of the Harmful Effects of Premium-Oriented Commercials on Children," *Journal of Consumer Research*, 3 (June), pp. 1–11.

38. See, for example, William L. Wilkie and David M. Gardner (1974), "The Role of Marketing Research in Public Policy Decision-Making," *Journal of Marketing*, 38 (Jan.), pp. 38–47. See also William L. Wilkie (1975), *How Consumers Use Product Information: Assessment of Research in Relation to Public Policy Needs* (Washington, D.C.: GPO.)

39. An excellent overview is H. Keith Hunt, ed. (1977), *Conceptualization and Measurement of Consumer Satisfaction and Dissatisfaction* (Cambridge, Mass.: Marketing Science Inst.), Report No. 77–103. See also Richard L. Oliver and Gerald Linda (1981), "Effect of Satisfaction and Its Antecedents on Consumer Preference and Intention," in *Advances in Consumer Research*, 8, ed. Kent B. Monroe, pp. 88–93.

40. George H. Mead (1934), *Mind, Self and Society,* ed. Charles W. Morris (Chicago: Univ. of Chicago Press), p. 23.

41. Wayne Dennis (1957), "Uses of Common Objects as Indicators of Cultural Orientations," *Journal of Abnormal and Social Psychology*, 55 (July), pp. 21–28.

42. For another account of consumer behavior today, see Harold H. Kassarjian (1982), "Consumer Psychology," in *Annual Review of Psychology*, 33, pp. 619–49.

2 The Role of Consumer Behavior in Marketing Management

The major objectives of this text are to show the relationship and the value of consumer-behavior theory and research to the practice of marketing. *The success of the firm or organization depends foremost on the satisfaction of consumer needs. The discipline of consumer behavior provides concepts and methods for the assessment of consumer needs that enables marketers to target appropriate products and services to particular market segments. The design of marketing programs—product positioning, pricing, communication, and distribution—also benefits from the inputs of consumer behavior.*

A secondary objective of this text is to show the value of consumer-behavior theory and research to formulating decisions of social policy. The discipline of consumer behavior can supply information and insight for social-policy decisions involving consumer affairs. The role of regulatory agencies, such as the Federal Trade Commission, the Federal Communication Commission, and the Food and Drug Administration, is to protect and enhance consumer welfare. Managers of these agencies must take actions based on a sound understanding of consumer welfare from the perspective of the consumer. *Only by understanding consumer behavior can they undertake the most appropriate regulatory initiatives. At the same time, marketing managers must also be concerned with social-policy issues, or they risk having no voice in the formulation and implementation of regulations. Both regulators and marketers must address compelling policy questions such as these: Do consumers want unit pricing information? Should advertising for food products contain nutritional information? Should advertising to children be banned?*

In this chapter, we show how the development of marketing strategies depends critically on understanding consumer behavior. We begin by examining the relationship of consumer behavior to the basic mission of marketing: satisfying consumer needs. And we assess the related issue of whether marketers can create needs or simply respond to them. Next we consider the uses of research aimed at understanding consumers. Finally, we illustrate how consumer-behavior concepts and measures can be useful in designing and implementing marketing strategies.

THE LOGIC OF CONSUMER-NEEDS SATISFACTION

The marketing concept reflects a basic premise of American business: that organizations exist in order to satisfy consumer needs. Despite some exceptions—such as the federal government's "bail-out" of the Chrysler Corporation in the early 1980s—Americans generally believe that if a firm fails to meet consumer needs for whatever reasons, the marketplace should operate to replace it with a competitively viable organization.

If a firm is to remain viable, it must continually monitor consumer needs and behavior, and formulate strategies designed to satisfy consumer needs. It was not always so. Within this century, Cornelius Vanderbilt was saying "The public be damned," and Henry Ford offered to give customers any color of car they wanted, "as long as it was black." In the post-World War II economy, however, the production capacity of American business increased, the number of competitors in virtually all markets jumped dramatically, and the marketing concept emerged as a guiding philosophy for business. Social- and behavioral-science concepts and methods simultaneously became more sophisticated and accepted, allowing organizations to employ marketing research in order to assess consumer needs and behavior.

The congruence of these developments has meant that sophisticated organizations realize that satisfying consumer needs is a necessary condition for economic survival. However, the rationale of consumer-needs satisfaction is a relatively recent driving force in the development of business strategy. Many business firms are still technologically or financially driven, making key decisions with a logic that says, "we know what is good for customers" or "if you build a better mousetrap people will beat a path to your door." Needless to say, consumers often reject "superior" technology, from AT&T's Picture Phone to RCA's Videodisc. Most product failures are not due to products of poor quality, but simply to a lack of consumer interest. AT&T's Picture Phone is a classic example of a technology-driven product that works; but people are not willing to pay for the marginal benefit of seeing each other during a telephone conversation. Moreover, it transforms a comfortable and familiar communication transaction into a demanding, unfamiliar one. The benefit is not obvious to consumers.

Ultimately, the only viable business strategy is one that is consistent with consumer needs. Assessment of consumer behavior, therefore, is the most basic input to the formulation of marketing strategy and the design of marketing programs. From a business firm's perspective, it guides the allocation of corporate resources to legitimate market needs, thus serving both the consumer interest (better products and services) and the corporate interest (profits from meeting consumer needs). From a nonprofit organization's perspective, assessing consumer needs also leads to more effective deployment of resources—as in the considered choice of exhibitions for a museum or programs for a public television station. And from a regulator's perspective, consumer-needs analysis can help to identify important policy issues and guide efforts to design regulations to protect and enhance consumer welfare.

CAN MARKETERS CREATE NEEDS?

A question that is frequently discussed is whether marketers can create needs. This turns out to be a complex issue, and the subject of considerable debate between social critics and marketing advocates. Among those often in the critic's role are individuals such as Ralph Nader, organizations such as Action for Children's Television (which seeks to limit advertising to children), and such agencies as the Federal Trade Commission and the Food and Drug Administration (which have consumer protection within their charters).

The critic's viewpoint is that marketing (and particularly advertising) can make people want things that they don't need and that may not be good for them. Marketing practices are considered to be the primary reasons for the success of products that some feel are of dubious value—for example, sugar-coated cereals, gourmet cat foods, and designer jeans. Marketing is viewed as a contributing factor to cigarette addiction, alcoholism, the nutritionally inferior diet of many Americans, and overdependence on prescription and pro-

EXHIBIT 2–1
A LATE 1960s ADVERTISEMENT FOR TRANQUILIZERS: COULD THIS ADVERTISEMENT LEAD TO OVERPRESCRIBING BY PHYSICIANS?

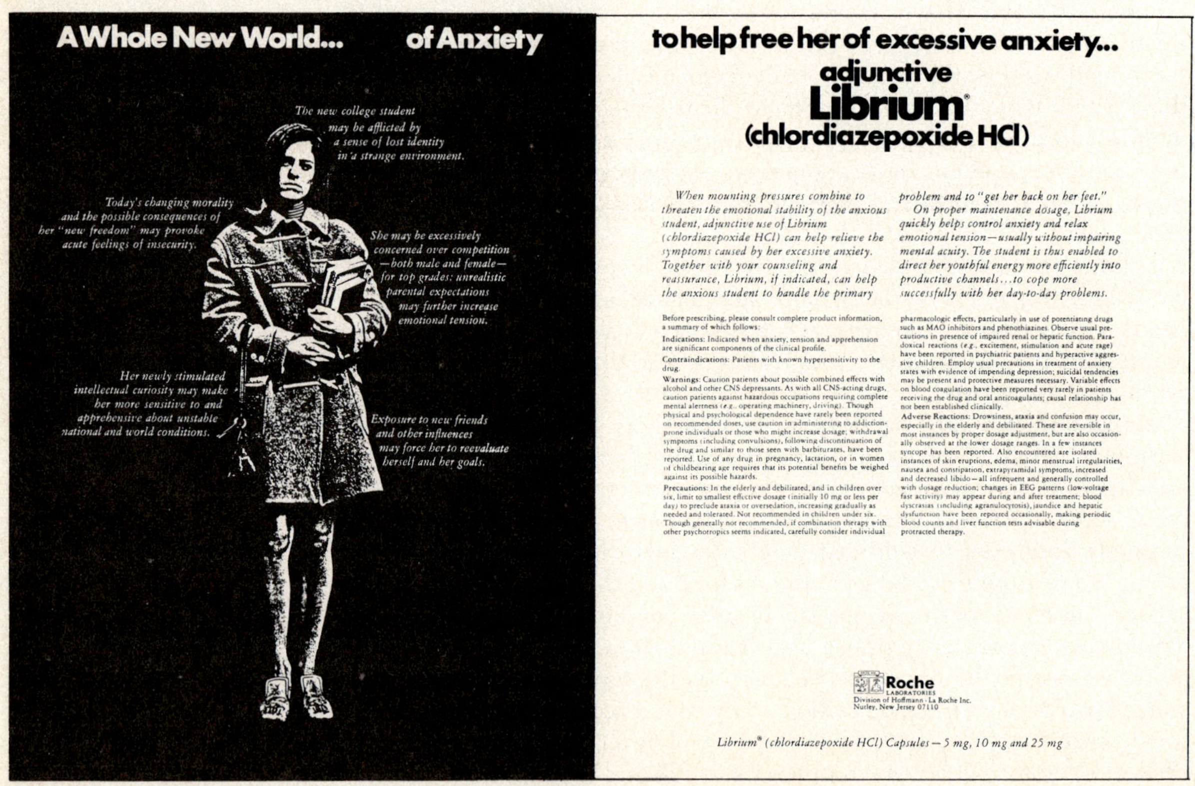

prietary medicines. The late 1960s advertisement for tranquilizers in Exhibit 2–1, for example, which was directed to physicians, would be considered a prime example of many of marketing's abuses according to critics. First, a question may be raised about the product itself—are tranquilizers products that people actually need, or are the needs created by marketing? Second, although the advertisement was directed to physicians, should marketers be using emotional appeals for prescription drugs, or should physicians' decisions be made on the basis of other, nonemotional, "objective" types of information? Finally, the advertisement might be criticized as sexist, portraying a woman as unlikely to be able to cope with the pressures of college life. Does this represent the potential for exploitation—"pacifying" women?

The marketing advocate's viewpoint, on the other hand, is that marketing merely gives people what they want and that consumers vote every day in the marketplace on which products and services will succeed and which will fail. Sugar-coated cereals are purchased because children prefer them; gourmet cat food is bought by consumers who treat their cats as "baby substitutes"; and designer jeans indicate a social affiliation or satisfy a need for conspicuous consumption for some consumers. On such problems as alcoholism, marketers point out that it is more severe in some countries that prohibit advertising of alcohol. The most basic premise of marketers is that business responds to—rather than creates—consumer needs.

Reality, as elusive as it is, may be a mix of these viewpoints, although we believe that marketing *responds* more than it *creates*. The marketplace is littered with products that fail to make profits, indicating that it is folly to introduce a product to the market without research indicating a consumer desire for it. For the most part, marketing identifies consumer needs and then tries to satisfy such needs. Most unsuccessful products are introduced by businesses that have no idea of what consumers want or that assume consumers will "come around" to their ideas.

Products must at least have the potential to meet consumer needs. Following the assessment of needs, the task of marketing is to articulate the product or service offering to attract appropriate market segments. For example, when Federal Express discovered an unfulfilled *need* for reliable overnight delivery service for small packages, it then designed a product to meet that need and engaged in heavy promotion and advertising to convince consumers that it actually could meet the need, thus generating **demand**. The process does not work well in reverse. Despite RCA's heavy promotion of its Videodisc, sales levels have been insignificant, probably because there is no evidence of a consumer need for the product.

It is nevertheless undeniable that marketing and advertising efforts have an effect on and change a society—if only by accentuating existing societal tendencies. Billions of dollars of advertising depicting the American "lifestyle" must be instrumental in making consumers desire that lifestyle. The power of marketing is not so much in changing consumer needs, but in *accentuating* a particular set of these consumer needs. Some scholars might also argue that, although marketing cannot create needs in the *short run* (for a given product or service), it might create needs in the *long run* by heightening the materialistic orientation of a society.

In an advanced economy most products are designed to meet **discretionary needs,** rather than **basic needs** such as food, water, shelter, or reproduction. Consumption of products such as sports cars, designer clothes, or imported bottled water is related more to discretionary needs for status, entertainment, novelty, or self-fulfillment than to the more basic needs for transportation, warmth, or quenching of thirst.

ULTIMATE USES OF THE DISCIPLINE OF CONSUMER BEHAVIOR

Even though consumer-behavior research may be justified as a way of meeting consumer needs, questions can still be raised about the ultimate uses of information about consumers. If researchers discover "laws" of consumer behavior, laws which can be used to explain and predict specific behaviors as a function of specified variables, will consumers not be open to manipulation and exploitation? If researchers construct a model which fully and accurately describes the variables and their interrelationships that lead to purchase of a particular product, might not a marketer use this model to manipulate consumers to buy a particular brand?

The ultimate uses of the research of behavioral sciences are always subjects of controversy. However, although many people have decried the dangers inherent in the research carried out by the behavioral sciences, others have called for the behavioral sciences to be "more relevant," to apply their findings to more human problems. Indeed, many psychologists have devoted themselves to applying abstract concepts from their discipline to actual problems in human behavior. For example, principles of Gestalt psychology have been applied in therapeutic settings, and Skinner's research on conditioning laboratory animals has been extended to behavior-modification programs, from those in mental hospitals to stop-smoking clinics.

To a large extent views on the ultimate uses of the research of the behavioral sciences are determined by individual value positions. Few would object to the contribution of consumer-behavior researchers to "marketing" programs aimed at increasing people's use of seat belts while driving, or to stop-smoking or anti-drug-abuse programs aimed at young people. However, many people are concerned about the application of consumer-behavior research to marketing programs of snack foods or other products that they find objectionable.

It is true that discipline-oriented consumer-behavior researchers seek to discover general patterns of consumer behavior and to construct general laws of human consumption behavior. However, understanding and prediction of behavior do not imply that the behavior can be controlled. Even if a marketer were to possess a model of consumer behavior with high explanatory power, it does not follow that this model could be used to manipulate consumers, since no marketer could control all of the relevant variables.

It is one thing to postulate that consumer personality and attitudes play a role in product purchasing, but it is quite another thing to change or even influence these consumer variables. For example, United Airlines once participated in research to determine the characteristics of people who do not fly and why they do not. The results indicated that nonflyers not only did not fly but did not travel very much by any means of transportation. Furthermore, they were generally more anxious than people who flew.[1] Advertising designed to reach such nonflyers, such as that shown in Exhibit 2–2, was quite unsuccessful, since even strong marketing efforts can do little to change people's basic orientations and predispositions. Encouraging people who are afraid of flying to fly is probably not worth the trouble.

As another example, many attempts have been made to encourage greater consumption of prunes over the years. Various marketing approaches have been tried, from very humorous and memorable advertising to price promotions to nutritional appeals. But these efforts have not been very successful because of the strong stereotypes most individuals have of prunes—that they

EXHIBIT 2–2
AN AIRLINE INDUSTRY ADVERTISING CAMPAIGN TO REACH NONFLYERS

ADVERTISEMENT

What Kind of People FLY   ...and What Kind Don't

Whether or not you normally travel by air seems to say a lot about you. But does it describe the real you?

FOR four months, literally from Maine to California, interviewers questioned 1,600 Americans. All of them earned enough to travel if they wanted to. Some of them flew a lot. Some very little. Some had never been up in an airplane.

Their thousands of answers were fed into computers. And, from it all, Behavior Science Corporation of California could draw some very revealing pictures of the kind of people who fly and those who don't.

Of course, no human being is 100% one kind or another. Someone you think of as adventuresome may, in ways, be quite timid. Deep inside another person everyone calls timid, there may be a spark of adventure that has just never been kindled.

It's only because, in different people, certain traits come out more easily and frequently that we can type them. That's what happened when the Behavior Science researchers talked to people who travel by air and those who don't.

The Flying Type

Here are the traits that bob quickly to the surface among people who travel by air:

They are *venturesome*. They go places and do things that other people only "hope to do someday." Not that they have more time or money. But because they like new experience so much they are willing to risk some time and money to get it.

They are *self-confident*. They feel comfortable with themselves, are sure of their own capabilities and have trust in themselves as people.

They are *involved and interested* in the world around them. They care about what's happening to other people in other places. They have enthusiastic interest in whatever they do.

The Non-Flying Type

They tend to be what the researchers call "territory bounded." If they travel, they don't travel much or go very far. In fact, they don't see much *need* to go anywhere else.

They suffer from what the psychologists term "*generalized anxieties.*" They may not have any more problems than anyone else. Still they spend most of their lives in a state of anxiety, fretting about everything, even when they can't point to any specific problem. They are worry warts.

They feel *powerless* to control their own lives. They are helpless in the hands of fate.

Which Type Are You?

Don't — repeat *don't* — decide you are the non-flying type just because you have never been in an airplane. That might be only the result of circumstances, or opportunities, or even how you grew up. For example, if your parents used airlines and often took you along, you would probably be flying regularly now. Today, you might have no air travel experience simply because you had

none as a child. *Still you might be the flying type!*

In other words, just because you have never flown does not mean you never will. The key is not what you have done so far. Rather, it's what type of person you really are.

are a natural (and powerful) laxative! Similarly, efforts to encourage cranberry consumption at times other than holidays have met with limited success, since most consumers have strongly established habits for the product's use.

USING CONSUMER BEHAVIOR IN MARKETING MANAGEMENT

Marketing managers are responsible for planning and implementing marketing strategies for products or services. In many companies that manufacture consumer goods, managers are responsible for one or more brands and are called **brand managers.** In other consumer-goods companies, and in many industrial companies, managers are responsible for particular markets and are called **market managers.** *Markets* may be defined by demographic characteristics (for example, geographic region) or other characteristics, such as type of industry served (for example, computer industry and hotel/motel business).

In most companies and organizations, marketing managers must prepare an annual "marketing plan," which assesses the current situation for the product and market, and proposes a strategic plan for the coming year. Since the marketing plan sets the agenda of activities for the product, and since plans are typically presented to senior management for approval, preparation of such plans is perhaps a manager's single most important activity.

If companies attempt to operate according to the marketing concept, then, in a sense, every element of a marketing plan is influenced by a manager's understanding of consumer behavior, since marketing planning starts with a focus on the consumer. But how, specifically, does a manager use consumer-behavior theories and concepts? The integral relationship of consumer behavior to the marketing process is shown in Exhibit 2–3. The manager must consider consumer behavior in each stage in this model.

Situation Analysis

Consumer-behavior analysis is the basis for the initial step in marketing planning—assessing consumer and market behavior as part of the overall **situation analysis.** The components of situation analysis are as follows:

- *Consumer/Market Behavior.* Assess consumer demand for the product category as well as examine preference for the company's own brand. Examine factors affecting aggregate demand, such as socio-cultural trends, changing patterns of family decision-making, and changing demographics. Segment the market and conduct needs analysis by segment. Examine the positioning of the company's brand in line with changing consumer-behavior patterns. Assess consumer information needs (for promotion decisions), buying habits and patterns (for sales force and distribution decisions), and product perceptions and expectations (for promotion and price decisions).
- *Internal/Company Factors.* Conduct an analysis of the company's capabilities and weaknesses relevant to marketing the brand. Variables to consider include the financial resources of the company, production capabilities, re-

EXHIBIT 2–3

A SIMPLIFIED MODEL OF THE MARKETING PLANNING PROCESS

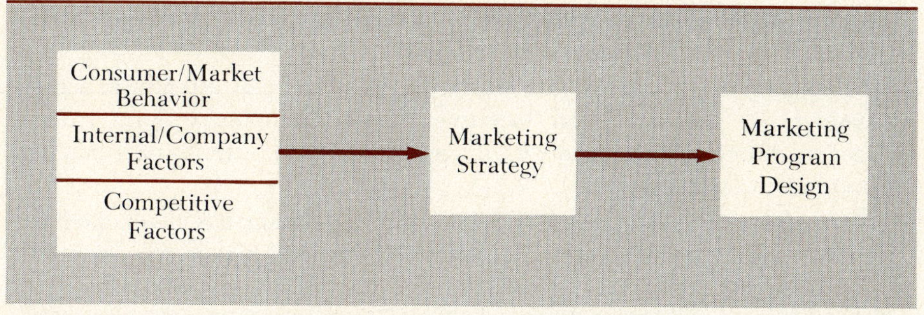

search and development strengths, marketing capabilities, and human-resource capabilities.

- *Competitive Factors.* Analyze the capabilities and weaknesses of the competition; review current and likely future competitive strategies. Develop strategies that achieve competitive differentiation.

Marketing Strategy

Marketing managers next turn their attention to developing a **marketing strategy,** an overall plan of action to achieve business objectives—usually a combination of goals regarding sales, market share, and return on investment. Many writers have described and analyzed marketing strategies.[2] Among the major strategies are the following:

- *Market segmentation.* Pursue only a limited portion of the total market.
- *Product differentiation.* Distinguish a brand by producing, for example, high priced, specialty goods or by producing low-cost, low priced products, such as generic brands of groceries.

- *Innovation.* Introduce new products and brands. (Procter & Gamble and General Foods, for example, continually engage in innovation.)
- *Achieving greater sales volume to present customers.* Intensify current market penetration. (A soft-drink company encourages consumers to buy products in large containers, for example.)
- *Gaining supply or distribution leverage.* (An airline may attempt to achieve competitive dominance on lucrative routes; Campbell's Soup tries to achieve strong relationships with grocery retailers in order to maintain high presence on store shelves.)
- *Diversifying into new markets.* (Yamaha Corporation has diversified into tennis rackets, snowmobiles, stereo equipment, and pianos, for example.)

Marketing Programs

A marketing program must be designed to carry out a firm's strategies. Tactical decisions must be made concerning each of the variables of the marketing mix: product, price, distribution, and promotion.

Marketers give various attributes to *products* in order to identify the products clearly to consumers and to differentiate them from competitive offerings. This is called product or brand *positioning*, and such decisions depend critically on a marketer's strategic objectives and on consumer preferences and behaviors. For example, General Motors' objective is to compete in all segments of the automobile market, and this strategy requires them to produce many models of automobiles within and across the various divisions. Their marketing program calls for them to position Cadillac, for example, as the most luxurious and prestigious of the firm's automobile offerings. As another example, Procter & Gamble positions its several brands of laundry detergent according to consumer applications: some brands are for special problems, such as stains, others are for use in cold water, and still others offer different formulations, such as liquids or powders.

Price decisions require understanding of consumer behavior, since marketers must design marketing programs consistent with consumer price sensitivity for products and services. For example, hotels offer lower-price packages for families on weekend nights, but charge higher rates for less price-sensitive business travelers on weeknights.

Distribution decisions pertain to how a marketer chooses to make product offerings available for purchase. Analysis of how consumers buy is essential in determining distribution alternatives. For example, mail-order firms such as Horchow and L. L. Bean have developed in response to trends such as the increasing numbers of working women and the growing need for shopping convenience. As another example, consider the marked changes in distribution that have paralleled changes in consumer behavior patterns in the stereo component market. Fifteen years ago, early in the product life cycle for stereo equipment, consumers had little familiarity with products and brands. Merchandise was sold primarily through specialty stores that provided consumers with personal contact with knowledgeable salespeople. As consumers became more familiar with stereo components, distribution shifted to a wider range of retail outlets, including department stores, mail-order firms, and discount merchandisers, such as Stereo World and Pacific Stereo. Instead of salespeople, these types of outlets provide wide assortments and low prices—which today's stereo consumers desire.

Decisions regarding *promotion* depend critically on understanding consumer behavior. A marketer must assess consumer information needs, attitudes, and responses to advertising, personal selling, and other forms of product promotion. For example, Procter & Gamble distributed free samples of a new detergent, Solo, in various parts of the country, and followed up with intensive television advertising in order to achieve rapid awareness and trial of the brand. This promotion program was based on P & G's experience as a dominant advertiser in the detergent market.

The various tactical decisions must be coordinated in order to ensure a consistent marketing program. Expensive perfumes are generally not marketed through discount stores, since consumers who shop in those stores are generally an inappropriate market segment for those products. On the other hand, consider Hewlett-Packard's skill at assessing consumer behavior with their marketing program for hand-held calculators. The firm avoids direct competition with Texas Instruments, the market leader, by positioning its relatively expensive calculators to a narrow market segment: scientists and engineers, who have a favorable "brand image" of Hewlett-Packard because of the firm's excellent reputation in high-technology markets. Hewlett-Packard offers a narrow range of technically complex and sophisticated calculators, consistent with the product desires of the target market segment. The firm attempts to limit its distribution of products to college bookstores and related types of outlets patronized by scientists and engineers, and its advertising for calculators usually appears in highly targeted, technically oriented publications. Thus, its entire marketing strategy is internally consistent and demonstrates considerable skill in assessing consumer-behavior patterns and designing marketing programs that "fit" these patterns.

These examples of conducting situation analyses, formulating marketing strategies, and designing marketing programs suggest that products and services offered by a firm are *variables* used to achieve a firm's objectives. Products and services may be part of a broad or narrow product line, expensive or inexpensive, simple or complex. Moreover, successful marketers carefully define markets they wish to serve. The complexity of today's consumer and industrial markets requires marketers to designate carefully those market segments they are best equipped to serve. Both types of decisions—what types of products and services to offer and what markets to serve—depend critically on the marketer's abilities to assess consumer-behavior patterns.

MARKETING STRATEGY FORMULATION: CASE EXAMPLES

In order to provide some sense of the value of consumer-behavior inputs to the formulation of marketing strategy, we shall consider two case examples. The first involves the wine market and the second, the airline market.

Wines

In the late 1970s a number of major corporations entered the wine industry, including the Coca-Cola Company through its acquisition of the Taylor, Great Western, Monterey, and Sterling brands. In 1983 Coca-Cola sold its wine business to Seagrams. It is useful to assess the consumer-behavior analyses behind both the acquisition and the divestiture decisions.

The Coca-Cola Company's consumer/market behavior analyses of the late 1970s showed that the soft-drink market profile was changing. Per capita consumption of soft drinks was projected to level off after many years of growth, and the number of consumers in the primary soft-drink age segment—ten to twenty-four years of age—would decline as the population matured in the 1980s. The median age of the population, which was twenty-five years old in the mid-1960s, would rise to thirty-five years old by the mid-1980s. In its search for new opportunities compatible with company analyses and resources, Coca-Cola found the wine market highly attractive because of wine's high growth in per capita consumption.

Consumer-behavior analysis helps us to understand *why* wine consumption is increasing in the United States and whether the trend will continue. For example, analysis of broad cultural trends reveals a growing concern with health and fitness that, in turn, benefits the sales of "lighter" alcoholic beverages, such as wines. Increased wine consumption may also reflect greater awareness of European customs and products among affluent young adults, who represent a growing segment of the population and who have high per capita consumption of wine.

The acquisition of the flagship Taylor brand name by Coca-Cola was based partly on consumer-behavior analysis. Research showed that next to Gallo, Taylor had the best brand recognition among consumers. The consumer-behavior assumption was that it is easier and less costly to develop and expand the sales of a well-known brand name than to create a new brand name.

Coca-Cola created considerable competitive uproar in the wine industry with comparative advertising that touted Taylor's superiority over its competitors. The company also moved beyond the traditional notions of wines, experimenting with lower calorie wines and packaging innovations, such as wines in cans.

Coca-Cola seemed to have the objective of selling wine by brand name—as with soft drinks—and repositioning the Taylor brand to eventually command a premium price. Many observers were surprised, therefore, when Coca-Cola abruptly sold its wine business in 1983 to Seagrams Distillers.

In the long run, the behavior of wine consumers may not be motivated as

EXHIBIT 2–4A
MIDWAY AIRLINES: A NEW STRATEGY DIRECTION BASED ON CONSUMER/MARKET ANALYSIS

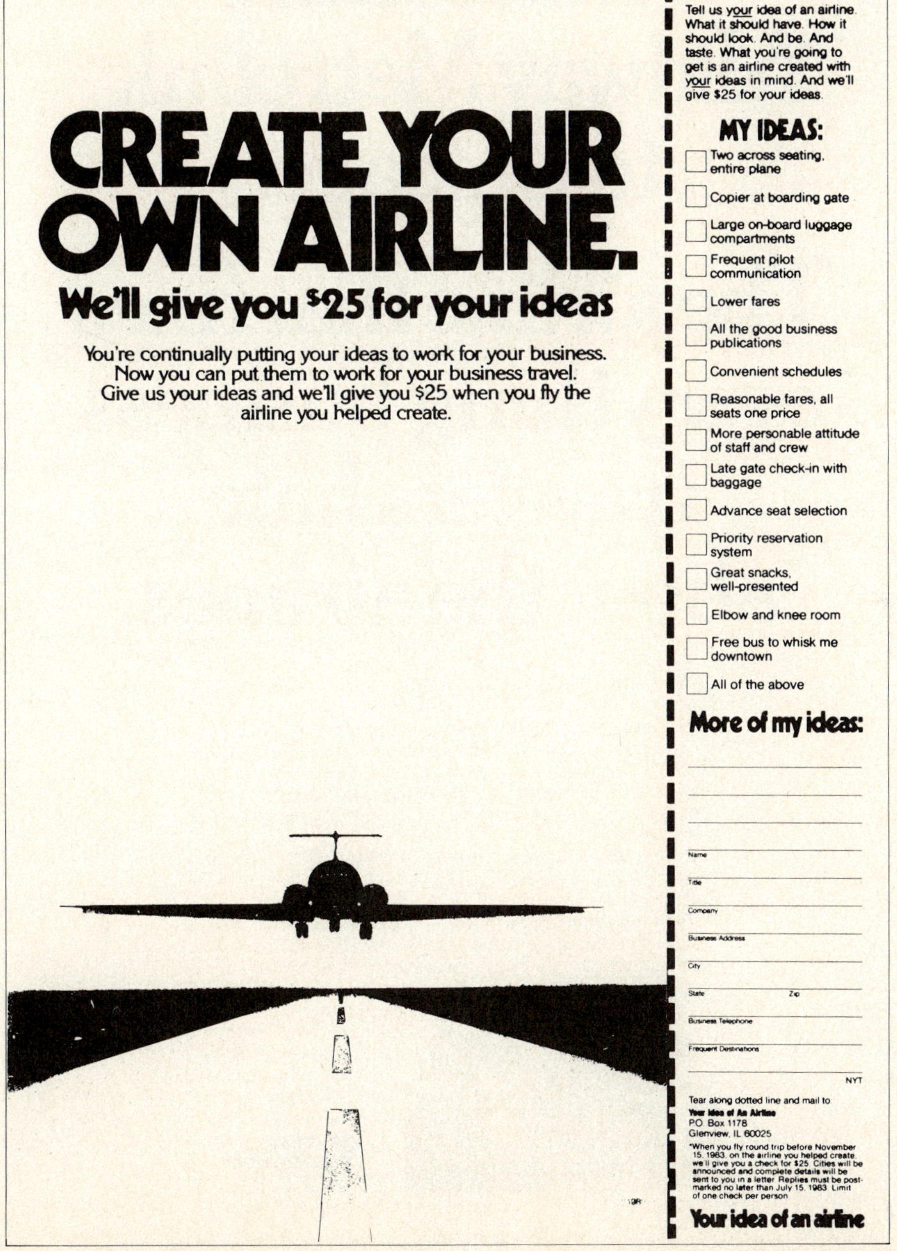

EXHIBIT 2–4B

Announcing Midway Metrolink℠ to Chicago.

The airline that fixes everything business travelers hate about the airlines.

You hate being stuck in middle seats: We've thrown out every middle seat, so every seat could be wider and more comfortable. And every seat is on a window or the aisle.

You hate not having enough carry-on luggage space: We give you enough room for two carry-on bags each.

You hate being served insulting food: We serve you simple snacks, prepared fresh and delicious instead of strange and suspicious.

You hate flying into and out of O'Hare: We fly you into and out of Midway Airport, a full half-hour closer to downtown Chicago. And into and out of LaGuardia.

You hate paying more and getting less: We give you more and charge you as much as 30% less than other airlines' regular coach fare. Call your travel agent or Midway Metrolink at 1-800-621-5536 before your next trip to Chicago. Why continue putting up with airlines you hate, when for less money, you can fly an airline you'll like?

much by brand name as by other factors, particularly price for "jug" wines and taste preference for varietal wines, such as Chardonnay and Chenin Blanc. Furthermore, the oversupply of wine in the early 1980s due to increased California production and an abundance of inexpensive Italian wines drove consumer prices down: Taylor was apparently unable to meet the Coca-Cola Company's profitability objectives. Coca-Cola may also have found it too costly to change consumer perception of the brand name and the packaging. Preferences and habits relating to wine may be resistant to change.

Airlines

The deregulation of the American airline industry in 1979 set considerable change in motion. In particular, a number of new airlines entered the industry and sought to meet the need of many consumers for low fares.

One of the more successful of these new airlines was Midway Airlines. The company began business as a "no frills" airline offering low prices and appealing, to a large extent, to the nonbusiness segment of the market. Despite achieving short-run profitability with this strategy, management analysis revealed that expected long-term profitability was inadequate. In June of 1983, therefore, Midway undertook an interesting change of strategic direction.

The thrust of the problem was revealed in the situation analysis:

1. The consumer/market behavior analysis revealed that most of the market (some 80 percent) was business travelers. Midway, with its focus on low service to accompany low price, was simply not meeting the needs of business travelers. The service positioning for business travelers had to be one of high service, with frequent flights, on-time reliability, and personable in-cabin service. Furthermore, business travelers were not very price sensitive, allowing the potential for higher fares and higher profitability.
2. The internal (company) analysis suggested that, with its cost structure, Midway would have difficulty maintaining low costs as labor rates increased and it had to re-equip its fleet. These uncertainties put its ability to remain a "no frills," low-cost carrier in doubt.

As a consequence of this analysis, Midway changed from a low-service/low-price positioning aimed at nonbusiness travelers to a high-service/competitive-price positioning aimed at business travelers. Exhibit 2–4 shows the advertising preceding the strategic change—an invitation to create your own airline—and the advertising announcing the change. Whether this new strategy will succeed depends on whether Midway can convince business customers of its new high-service profile as well as on the reactions of competitors.

CONSUMER BEHAVIOR'S ROLE IN THE DESIGN OF THE MARKETING PROGRAM

Just as consumer behavior provides important input to the design of marketing *strategy,* it also plays a key role in the **design of the marketing program—** that is, the mix of product, price, promotion, and channels of distribution.

Product Design

What products to offer and what the positioning for these products should be are *strategic* decisions. However, after these, many *tactical* product design decisions remain. These include

- the *breadth of the product line* (that is, number of items or, in the case of Midway, number of flights);
- the actual *product configuration*;
- the *packaging* of the product; and
- the *brand name* to use.

All of these tactical decisions should be responsive to consumer behavior. For example, Coca-Cola retained the Taylor wine name because of its high recognition among consumers, but added "California Cellars" to overcome Taylor's image as a New York-produced wine. Similarly, Midway changed its name to Midway Metrolink to signal to consumers that it was a "new" airline.

The consequences of not using consumer-behavior data may be serious. For example, some time ago a leading cosmetics company introduced a new line of men's cologne. They created a very avant garde packaging which won a number of design awards. But they had neglected to conduct any consumer research on the package design. They found that what wins design awards among professional designers may not be in tune with the taste of the average consumer. Men judged the design to be impersonal and alien.

Consumer-behavior data can also be of value in product redesign. Hoover, for example, was considering redesigning its vacuum cleaners to make them much quieter. In-home tests of the new vacuum cleaner, with a sample of consumers, however, indicated that when the cleaner was quiet, people did not think it worked as well, that it was not as powerful. Although the quiet cleaner was just as powerful, plans for introducing it were abandoned because of the results of this consumer research.

Pricing

The price to be charged for a product or service is a function of a number of factors, including costs of manufacture, competitive pricing practices, and, perhaps most importantly, the price sensitivity of consumers by market segment. Here again consumer research can provide direction for the company's decisions.

Some of the questions to be asked are

- What price will consumers pay?
- Will different market segments pay different prices?
- Is there a belief that a higher price will be associated with higher quality?

The dynamics of pricing are in evidence every day in our competitive economy. The different levels of price sensitivity can be vividly demonstrated for air travel by Midway Airlines: Business travelers may be quite price insensitive (they will travel almost regardless of the price), whereas pleasure travelers may be quite price sensitive (demand will be highly affected by price). Similarly, in the wine market the pricing has varied by segment: The Taylor brand is priced low, for the mass market, whereas the Sterling and Monterey brands are premium priced for the affluent market.

Promotion

The design of the communication program aimed at consumers will also depend on consumer-behavior input. Questions to be considered include the following:

- What is the appropriate mix of advertising, personal selling, merchandising, and other communication vehicles?
- Are consumers sensitive to advertising for this product?
- What is the optimum level of advertising or personal selling direct to consumers?
- What benefits should be stressed in the advertising or selling message?
- What media are most appropriate for advertising?

The most basic decision, concerning the mix of advertising and personal selling, depends heavily on consumer-information needs. If the product is simple—soft drinks or potato chips—then consumers can acquire as much information as they want from advertising. If, however, the product is complex or involves risk—stereos and pharmaceuticals, are examples—then a high component of personal selling will be necessary at the point of purchase.

The levels or weights of advertising to use depend in large measure on how sensitive to advertising the product is. Salt, for example, is not very sensitive to advertising: No matter how much it is advertised, additional sales will be negligible. Dial-A-Joke, in contrast, is the most advertising-sensitive product we have discovered. When it is advertised in the morning newspaper, people call to hear a joke; when it is not advertised, the number of calls plummets.

The content of the advertising message depends on how consumers perceive the product. For example, how would you advertise a decorator telephone? Most people who buy a decorator phone already have one or more phones in the house. You certainly would not advertise by emphasizing its communication benefits—"you can talk to other people with it." In many ways a decorator telephone is not really a telephone at all. Consumers may view it as a novelty, a piece of art, an electronic gadget, a status symbol—but rarely as a means of talking to other people. The benefit stressed in advertising, therefore, is much more likely to be the design, fun, or status value of the product.

Channels of Distribution

Finally, in designing the marketing program, we must select channels of distribution. The channel selected must first be compatible with consumer shopping habits, and the channel must provide consumers with the benefits they need in order to close the purchase. Channel requirements may be simple (salt only has to be on the grocery shelf) or intense. For example, in the purchase of carpeting, consumers may expect the channel of distribution to provide the following benefits:

- display of colors, fabrics, designs;
- information on nylon versus wool versus rayon, and so on;
- some interior decorating help;
- credit (since carpet purchases may involve hundreds of dollars); and
- installation.

The manufacturer of carpeting will select stores that provide these benefits.

Channels also add meaning to the product. Consumers will perceive a coat in Saks Fifth Avenue quite differently from the same coat in Sears. A manufacturer should select stores which are compatible with the image being projected—from high status to inexpensive. In fact, to maintain an image, the product design and the channel of distribution must be complementary and consistent. For Midway Metrolink, travel agents will be an important distribution channel because consumer information requirements are high. Attempts by airlines such as World to use Ticketron have been quite unsuccessful because of these information requirements.

As a whole, the design of the marketing program depends most on consumer needs and consumer patterns of behavior. The field of consumer behavior provides an important input to the managerial decision-making process. The marketing program must be a match between consumer needs and interests and company resources and capabilities.

THE ROLE OF CONSUMER BEHAVIOR IN SOCIAL POLICY

Most modern societies are concerned with the consumer interest, and many have established government agencies to protect and enhance that interest. Such government involvement on behalf of the consumer may be only at the level of public safety, as with the control of drugs. Or it may extend to strict controls over advertising, or even the banning of advertising, and strict control over pricing, or even government setting of prices in some countries.

Within the United States there are many agencies whose mission—directly or indirectly—is to protect and enhance the consumer welfare. These agencies exist at federal, state, and local levels, and have myriad functions, from agricultural grading to advertising regulation to rent control. Consumer-behavior research provides input from the population to be protected to the regulators who do the protecting.

In order to demonstrate the potential value of consumer behavior in guiding regulatory initiatives, let us consider a possible government regulation and ask whether it would truly be in the consumer interest. A proposal by the staff of the Federal Trade Commission suggests that all advertising for food products devote some portion of the space or time to nutritional information. The proposal is based on the assumption that consumers have a "right to know" and that some buyers would use this information wisely, thus making "better" marketplace decisions; that is, they would choose a higher nutritional value per dollar of expenditure for food products. Providing this information, however, could be quite expensive. This suggests the need for a cost-benefit analysis.

Consumer research to help in this decision would address the following questions:

- Do consumers use nutritional information in choosing food products?
- Do consumers want more nutritional information?
- If consumers were provided with additional nutritional information, would they use it?
- If consumers used additional nutritional information, would they make "better" decisions—more nutritional value per dollar expended?

These questions can all be answered through empirical research. Food buying patterns and the extent to which consumers use nutritional information can be ascertained. An experiment could be designed to provide consumers with the proposed additional information to see (1) if they use it and (2) whether it leads to better nutritional decisions. Research could also indicate whether nutritional value or some other benefit, such as taste, is the key benefit sought by consumers.

Providing the additional nutritional information is warranted only if consumers make better decisions, commensurate with the cost of the information. Thus, consumer-behavior data can help in the development of public policy responsive to consumer needs and can help to avoid needless rules that do not benefit the consumer.

SUMMARY

Consumer-behavior analysis can be of value to two primary patrons—business firms and social-policy makers. The firm must take consumer-needs satisfaction as its primary mission much as the regulatory agency must take enhancing the consumer welfare as its primary mission.

Consumer-behavior concepts and research serve as key inputs to the formulation of marketing strategy—what products to sell to what market segments. Consumer behavior also provides an integral perspective in the design of the marketing program—the mix of product, pricing, promotion, and distribution.

For the social-policy maker, consumer-behavior concepts and research are useful in deciding about new regulatory initiatives. Whether unit pricing, nutritional labeling, or allowing pharmaceutical companies to advertise directly to consumers are appropriate depends on whether consumers want the information and whether they would use the information to make more enlightened decisions.

The concept of consumer needs and the question of whether marketing can create needs are both of interest to consumer-behavior researchers. In a well developed economy, discretionary needs, rather than basic needs, are often those satisfied. Food products are often sold not so much for their nutritional value but rather to satisfy such discretionary needs as taste or appearance. Clothing is often sold not so much for warmth as for status or sex appeal.

Although marketing and advertising may influence the inventory of goods consumed in a society, the business firm has very limited ability to create needs. Instead it must respond to consumer needs by introducing products and services in the consumer interest. The failure rates of new products attest to the power of consumers as the ultimate judges in the marketplace.

The results of consumer-behavior research are condemned by critics and welcomed by managers, reflecting their different characterizations of marketing—as either manipulating or satisfying consumer needs and wants. Whatever the case, it is clear that the discipline of consumer behavior, and the body of knowledge it represents, can be used for "good" or "evil," depending on people's values and positions about the nature of consumer needs.

KEY CONCEPTS

basic needs	**brand managers**	**marketing strategy**
discretionary needs	**market managers**	**marketing-program**
demand	**situation analysis**	**design**

DISCUSSION QUESTIONS

1. Can marketers create needs? Take a position and defend it.
2. Distinguish between *basic* needs and *discretionary* needs. Provide examples of each.
3. What role do consumer-behavior theory and research play in marketing?
4. How can consumer-behavior theory and research help social policy decision-makers?
5. Can consumer-behavior theory and research be misused—for purposes not in the society's best interests?
6. How much concern should there be that marketers might manipulate consumers? By understanding consumer behavior, are marketers in a position to take unfair advantage of consumers?

7. Consider the proposal that pharmaceutical companies be allowed to advertise prescription drugs directly to consumers. What possible consumer benefits might result? What problems might result? What questions would you want answered in consumer research before making a decision on this proposal?
8. It has been suggested that much illness in the United States is "lifestyle" related—resulting from smoking, drinking, poor diet, obesity, etc. It has also been suggested that marketing and advertising bear some responsibility because of promoting cigarettes, alcohol, and nutritionally inferior foods. Have marketers caused such lifestyle illness? Discuss.

NOTES

1. Steven L. Diamond, Thomas S. Robertson, and Scott Ward (1970), "United Airlines," a Harvard Business School Case Study.
2. See, for example, Michael E. Porter (1980), *Competitive Strategy* (New York: The Free Press) or Derek F. Abell and John S. Hammond (1979), *Strategic Market Planning* (Englewood Cliffs, N.J.: Prentice-Hall). See also the special issue of the *Journal of Marketing* on marketing strategy, Spring, 1983.

Wines in the United States Today

An interview with Mr. Gil Schy, Executive Vice President, Marketing, General Wine and Spirits Division of Seagram, Inc.

Q *Will the consumption of wine ever equal that of beer?*

A The positioning of wine today is such that it is becoming a "beverage" and a "thirst quencher," similar in some ways to beer. The advertising of beer shows comradery and social get-togethers after a hard day's work. Beer fits in with relaxation and cooling-off. Beer is sold in ballparks and at sporting events; it is readily available.

Until recently wine was something to be drunk at dinner parties or as a cocktail. The marketing and advertising of wine may, in fact, have limited its appeal. Today, however, we see new ideas in advertising and packaging wine. For example, one of the more popular new wine drinks is called the spritzer—which is no more than club soda and wine. A company in Milwaukee, Wisconsin, recently started marketing six packs (12 oz. cans) of wine coolers called Steidl's. They were awarded the franchise in the Milwaukee stadium to sell it along with beer, and it's doing very, very well. If consumers are given an opportunity to consume a wine product in some light form—the lightness of a spritzer, for example—it appears that they will do so. It is a very pleasant drink and offers a variety of tastes. The sales of wine will increase, therefore, as it becomes thought of as a beverage and not just a special-occasion drink.

Q *What accounts for the increasing popularity of wine?*

A There has been an evolutionary change in consumption. Vodka grew substantially in sales because it was easy to drink with orange juice. Much of gin is consumed as a gin and tonic. Consumers told us that they wanted a pleasant drink. Today distilled spirits are consumed in new ways—with mixers, for example. Distilled spirits have become lighter with lower proofs, and liqueurs have become more popular.

Wine benefits from this trend toward lightness. The main factor in its growth is that it is an easy beverage to consume. It also has the prestige of spirits. Wine has been taking the place of cocktails—the pre-dinner activity. It has become the "in" thing to do. People move in peer groups and are influenced by other people. Wine has grown dramatically as it has taken the place of distilled spirits as a lighter, easier-to-drink beverage.

Q *In the United States, will wine ever achieve the levels of consumption that it holds in France and Italy?*

A There must be a biological lid on total beverage consumption: how much can one person consume with one mouth and one stomach? In France they drink more wine but less soft drinks. If wine is to reach the levels of consumption of France or Italy, it will be at the expense of other beverages, such as distilled spirits, beer, or soft drinks. Wine will benefit from the trend toward lighter drinks but whether it will be consumed to the extent it is in some European countries is debatable-or it may take a very long time.

Q *What is the market segmentation for wine? Who drinks wine?*

A If we first look at the differences between males and females, we see that women are more likely to drink wine—both at home and in bars or restaurants. And, whereas men drink red and white wines in equal proportions, women drink twice as much white as they do red wine. Again, I think that this is indicative of the present trend toward lighter alcoholic beverages and women's greater sensitivity to lightness.

Wine drinkers are more likely to be higher than average in income and more likely to be white. The largest wine markets in the United States are California, New York, and Florida.

Q *Can wine be considered a status drink?*

A A product that is consumed by almost two thirds of the population cannot be considered a major status symbol. The most popular wines, such as Gallo, Taylor, and Paul Masson, are not expensive and are drunk with family meals.

But something else is going on here as well. Let's use Chivas Regal as our benchmark, since this is the premiere scotch in the United States. We use Simmons [market research] data to determine the target market for our Chivas Regal scotch [a Seagram brand]. We cross reference what else a Chivas Regal drinker consumes. The second preference, by far, is for wine.

We communicate the superiority of this product compared with all other scotches. If the Chivas Regal user's second preference is wine, that may mean something. Certain classes of wine are consumed for snob appeal or prestige. There is a romance about wine that lends itself to people's need for one-upmanship. Drinking an expensive or prestigious wine gives some people an opportunity to differentiate themselves. Instead of buying a $45,000 Maserati, they're able to buy a $12 bottle of wine—and that gives them the same feeling. Is there a perceived difference among wines? Yes, there is a perceived difference.

Q *Why did Seagrams buy the Coca-Cola wine division?*

A The economies of scale were a major factor. This is our business—wine and spirits; it is all that we do. Here was an opportunity to become a strong number 2, with major lines. We have U.S. produced Paul Masson and Gold Seal wine. We have great expertise in production; we have expertise in marketing and sales. So it is a natural "fit," and not even a question of "why"—it is almost an obvious factor. As consumption increases, which we know it will, we are in an outstanding position for profitability.

Q *Why would a wine division fit better with Seagrams' business definition than it did with Coca-Cola's?*

A This comes into the mentality and understanding of a business. The distilled-spirits mentality is that we're used to the long pull. We don't have all the benefits that you have in other consumer goods of bringing brands to market. There are not as many ways to promote and to advertise open to us in the marketing of liquor or wine products.

So why does it fit? Because we know how to bring these brands to market within the confines of all the laws and regulations that we have to live with. We have federal law, we have state laws, we have county laws, and we have city laws. The laws are totally different, and the ways we market our brands are totally different as well.

Coca-Cola is a very strong consumer-goods marketing company, but with little experience in distilled spirits. The frustrations of what you have to do are so overwhelming that people don't know what to do and don't have the skills for it. We know what to do and how to do it— it's second nature to us.

3 Behavioral Methodology

<U>U</U>nderlying the study of consumer behavior is the belief that identifying and responding to consumer wants and needs is the only reasonable strategy for the firm. Thorough understanding of consumers' needs reduces the amount of risk characterizing managerial decision-making and increases the probability of marketing success. The intent of this chapter is to discuss the marketing research processes and techniques that can be used to investigate consumer wants, needs, attitudes, and behavior.

Gaining knowledge about consumer preferences or behavior can sometimes be a relatively straightforward task. For example, the Pepsi Challenge advertising campaign, initiated in the late 1970s, simply asks consumers to take a blind (unlabeled) taste test involving Coca-Cola and Pepsi-Cola. This test consistently shows that the majority of consumers prefers the taste of Pepsi to the taste of Coke.

But measuring consumers' preferences is not always so readily accomplished. For example, in the late 1970s Citibank developed the concept of the computerized automatic teller machine. Citibank management was, however, hesitant to build and install these units in all the New York City bank branches because managers were unable to assess accurately consumer reactions to the automated teller. Simply asking prospective users to evaluate this radically new product was not considered adequate or reliable because consumers had no experience on which to base their evaluations. The notion of **consumer experience** is a crucial one in consumer behavior because the less experience individuals have had with a product, the less able they are to evaluate the product.

The Pepsi Challenge, for example, provided consumers with the opportunity to experience two familiar cola brands. Similarly, Citibank provided consumers with experience by means of a computerized teller prototype. Over two years, 2500 customers were observed and sometimes interviewed. It was possible, therefore, to obtain meaningful feedback from customers who had actually used the automated facility.[1]

Another example of consumers' inability to make an accurate evaluative judgment involves the motion picture Star Wars, which is one of the top movie money-makers of all time. When consumers were polled by a market researcher before the movie had been released, they unhesitatingly replied that the Star Wars concept did not appeal to them and that they would not be likely to view the movie![2] But Twentieth Century-Fox executives realized that consumers are often unable to evaluate unfamiliar products. Questioning findings generated by non-experienced consumers was the key to a successful product introduction.

The three examples above illustrate the important connection between research results and managerial expertise. The development of sound marketing strategy requires a thorough understanding of consumer behavior. But the process of formulating research goals and directions should begin with managerial expertise, proceed to the actual research process, and then conclude with a managerial interpretation and evaluation of the research findings.

THE FUNCTION OF RESEARCH: REDUCING RISK

In 1979, I–Point, Inc., a small Virginia-based firm, mailed a brochure to 5000 presumed potential customers.[3] The brochure described I–Point's product—a temperature monitoring device which could be affixed to the side of a frozen food package. The device would change color if the temperature rose too high for a long enough period of time to induce food spoilage. The device had been developed by I–Point's Swedish parent company, Kockum's Chemicals. A total of $12 million had been spent on research and development (R&D).

Potential customers were thought to be food-company presidents and vice-presidents who had received the promotional brochure mailed in March 1979. However, the result of the mailing was dismal, generating only a very small number of orders.

Despite the $12 million investment in R&D, no marketing research had been conducted. An I–Point spokesperson identified this lack of research as the major contributing factor to the product's failure. First of all, the spokesperson suggested that the market selected—food companies—was probably not the correct target for the product. Rather, producers of pharmaceutical products, blood, film, and refrigerated (not frozen) food (all of which are characterized by great sensitivity to temperature variations and/or short shelf lives) would probably constitute far more receptive markets. Marketing research could have helped to identify correctly the target market. A second reason suggested for the product failure was the choice of company presidents and vice-presidents as the recipients of the brochure. These individuals, who probably were not especially interested in the product, may have passed on the brochure to quality-control personnel, who were not purchasing agents. Marketing research could have assisted in identifying the individuals involved in the decision-making process. A third problem associated with the product failure was that the brochure itself was concerned with the technical aspects of the product rather than with the benefits to the consumer from product use. Prior discussion with potential consumers would have shed light on this problem as well. I–Point is currently developing a strategy for reintroduction of the product. This time, $350,000 has been budgeted to marketing and consumer research.

The I–Point experience illustrates the major function of research, which is to minimize the degree of uncertainty and, hence, the degree of risk involved in decision-making. Without research, strategy can be developed solely on the basis of managerial judgment. Although managerial experience is certainly a crucially important factor in the development of strategy, the results of research can refine and sharpen that strategy.

Research, then, can help to reduce risk in decision-making by confirming (or failing to confirm) management judgments, by refining those judgments, and by revealing new information about consumer preferences or behaviors.

APPROACHES TO CONSUMER-BEHAVIOR RESEARCH

One of the strongest ties between consumer behavior and other behavioral sciences is their common research methodology. The overall approaches to research, the methods of gathering data from individuals, and even the data-analysis procedures tend to be very similar. Behavioral science attempts to determine why the individual (from a psychological perspective) or the group (from a sociological perspective) behaves in a certain manner, holds certain beliefs, or has developed particular attitudes. Correspondingly, consumer-behavior research is directed toward developing an understanding of why either the individual consumer (psychological orientation) or an aggregate segment of consumers (sociological orientation) develops particular product-specific or brand-specific behaviors, beliefs, and attitudes.

Marketing managers face a series of choices as they consider how to conduct research on consumer behavior. The most important question, of course, is what is it that the manager wants to know? Some aspects of consumer behavior are considerably easier to assess through research than others. For example, research services can readily document the sales of a particular brand sold via retail outlets. However, it is considerably more difficult to assess more subtle aspects of consumer behavior—for example, why people buy one brand instead of another, or how purchase decisions are made within the family.

An initial consideration for the manager is whether to use **secondary research,** that is, existing information sources such as census data or research from syndicated market-research services, or to commission original, or **primary, research.** Typically, to answer more subtle and specific questions requires primary research. Secondary research is applicable to more general questions, such as the demand level for a product category or the demographic structure of particular markets.

secondary versus primary research

If primary research is necessary, the manager must decide on the particular approach to data collection and analysis. The choices here range from small-sample **qualitative research** to a larger-sample **quantitative research.** *Qualitative research* is defined by its methods, such as in-depth individual interviews with consumers (also known as *motivation research)* and focus-group interviews, which involve elaborate discussions of consumer behavior with small groups of consumers. Analysis of data obtained by these methods is qualitative, since sample sizes are small, and the objectives are typically to explore feelings and attitudes about products or brands.

Quantitative research is defined by its research approaches, such as consumer panels and surveys, observational techniques, and experiments. Panel, survey, or observational approaches typically involve large samples and require quantitative analysis of data. Experiments may be conducted in laboratory settings or in the real-world environment. Experiments also require quantitative analysis (although sample sizes may be smaller, at least in laboratory experiments), since the objective is to discover the functional relationships between **independent** (causal) and **dependent** (effects) **variables,** and to measure the relationship with greater precision than would be obtained by the more informal methods of in-depth or group interviews. A marketer's assessment of the extent to which varying levels of advertising affect sales could be an experiment. If advertising levels were actually varied in some comparable cities, and sales effects recorded, the experiment would be called a *field experiment*. If the advertising and sales measures were simulated in a testing facility (as many undergraduates undergo experiments in Psychology 1), the experiment would be a *laboratory experiment*.

Underlying the manager's choices about consumer-behavior research is concern with the *accuracy* of the data to be gathered. The essential concern is to guard against *bias* entering into the research. For example, the phrasing of questions in a survey can introduce bias; similarly, a competitor's actions, such as lowering prices, may bias a consumer-behavior field experiment designed to assess the effects of advertising on the brand's sales. In particular, research accuracy refers to the concepts of **validity** and **reliability.** A valid instrument actually measures what it purports to measure. A classic example from the 1950s and 1960s concerns the administration of intelligence tests to children who were members of minority groups. Many IQ tests presupposed an understanding of white, middle-class, American culture. The poor performance of minority group children on these tests could be attributed to their lack of integration in mainstream America—not to low intelligence levels. These IQ tests were not valid data-collection instruments: They did not accurately measure intelligence.

Reliability is another aspect of data accuracy. In one type, known as *test-retest* reliability, an instrument is said to be *reliable* if it yields consistent and stable results each time it is administered to any given respondent. If a respondent is tested twice and the two sets of results are widely disparate, then the reliability of the instrument should be questioned. Thus, a reliable questionnaire designed to elicit attitudinal information should provide stable and highly correlated measures of attitudes if it is administered to the same respondent on two separate occasions within a relatively short period of time (three to four weeks). *Alternative-forms* reliability is another type. Each respondent is given two equivalent (but not identical) forms of the test instrument. Reliability is estimated by comparing the discrepancy in scores obtained using the two instruments.

Qualitative Research

In-depth Interviews   The personal in-depth interview is sometimes used as the first step in consumer research. Its purpose is to gain insight into the range of a consumer's feelings about a particular product or service. In-depth interviews are conducted by a trained interviewer who asks individual consumers a series of questions about the product or brand under study, the nature of its use, and, usually, the meanings of the product. Typically, ten to twenty such interviews are conducted. Knowledge gained is generally used to generate hypotheses for later testing in quantitative studies. A great advantage of this method is that each consumer's attitudes can be more thoroughly probed than through any other technique.[4] The major disadvantage is that personal interviews cost considerably more than telephone or mail interviews.

In-depth interviews were used by the Canada Dry Corporation in the first part of a two-stage study, when they decided to develop a new advertising campaign for ginger ale. Canada Dry believed that ginger ale had an ambiguous image that caused confusion between perceptions of ginger ale as a soft drink and as a mixer. Thus the aim of the twenty in-depth interviews of adult men and women and of teenagers was to generate a list of phrases describing product attributes and associations which related to the consumption of both ginger ale and other carbonated beverages. A total of 130 different phrases was generated. Using the statistical technique of factor analysis to determine which of the 130 phrases were highly correlated, the original 130 were reduced to 22 uncorrelated phrases or "factors," such as "gives you a lift," "drunk by modern sociable people," and "thirst quenching without filling or bloating you."

Canada Dry utilized the in-depth interviews to generate questionnaire items for stage 2 of the study. In the second stage, a national sample of consumers was asked to rate both Canada Dry and their "ideal beverage" across the 22 identifying factors. The result of the research was that Canada Dry developed two very distinct advertising campaigns: One featured ginger ale distinctly positioned as a soft drink, and the other was oriented toward ginger ale specifically as a mixer.

Focus-Group Interviews[5]   Rather than dealing with one individual at a time, the focus-group interview brings together a small group of consumers to discuss their product-related behaviors and attitudes. Typically, the session lasts for about two hours. The optimum group size is generally taken to be from eight to twelve consumers, although Wells has suggested that size depends on the interviewer and on seating arrangements.[6] Most market-research agencies are equipped with tape-recording facilities and one-way mirrors to allow the research sponsors to observe the group.

The issue of selection of participants is crucial for these small discussion groups. They must conform to two criteria. First, they must all share a common interest, which forms the basis for and focuses the discussion. Second, all participants should be of approximately equal social status to ensure freedom of communication among group members. Consider, for example, the effect that the presence of two or three lower-income people might have on the discussion of high-priced automobiles or home furnishings among a group of upper-income respondents.

There are two main points of difference between the information generated in individual and group interviews. First, the information provided in the individual interview is *unidirectional*; that is, it flows from the respondent to the interviewer. But in the group, information flows *among* the ten or so respondents as well. Thus, latent ideas which might not be verbalized in the individual session may well be sparked in the more dynamic group situation.

The second difference is that opinions and thoughts offered by a member of the group are subject to evaluation and criticism, since the other group members are reacting to ideas. In the individual interview, however, the interviewer plays a noncritical role. The choice between individual and group interviews depends not only on the type of information desired, but also on the type of product under consideration. If social risk or word-of-mouth influence is expected to be involved in deciding on the product, focus-group interviews may be more effective in that they capture these effects. The traditional belief is that a focus group generates more information than a summary of an equal number of individual interviews,[7] but there is some evidence to the contrary.[8] Like the in-depth interview, the focus-group interview can be a highly effective research tool in generating hypotheses about consumer attitudes and behavior, especially when prior information about consumers is limited. The data that emerge from focus groups are rich in depth and scope.

It should be noted, however, that interpreting data from in-depth and focus-group interviews can be difficult. In Chapter 1, we noted that the focus group is a legacy from the era of motivation research. Just as objectively interpreting data was a problem in motivation research, so it is with current qualitative techniques. The interviewer's interpretation of the information can

"You mean this survey took 6 months and $25,000 to find out that our typical consumer is under 21, chases cats and barks?"

**EXHIBIT 3–1
QUANTITATIVE WITHOUT QUALITATIVE RESEARCH**

be quite subjective since there are no formal guidelines to assist in data evaluation.

Another problem which generally characterizes in-depth and focus-group interviews is that because samples are often small for convenience, results cannot be readily generalized to the population as a whole.[9] If the sample sizes were large enough and if the selected respondents were truly representative of the population, results could be generalized.

But these methods are typically used as exploratory research techniques. Ideally, they supplement rather than replace quantitative research. The qualitative results obtained can be used as the basis for formulating survey questionnaires. Managers who rush directly into conducting surveys, without first gaining an understanding of their consumers' basic attitudes and preferences, run the risk of obtaining results similar to those depicted in Exhibit 3–1.

Projective Techniques[10]   A third qualitative type of procedure used to elicit data from consumers is the **projective technique,** which is used extensively in psychology and psychiatry. This technique is designed to uncover motivations that individuals are either unable or unwilling to divulge. They are termed "projective" because respondents are shown and asked to interpret an ambiguous stimulus. Since it is not clearly defined, individuals presumably project their inner thoughts or feelings into their descriptions of the stimulus.

Perhaps the most widely recognized test using a projective technique is the Rorschach inkblot test, developed by Hermann Rorschach.[11] Individuals are shown a number of formless, ambiguous inkblots and asked to describe what they see. An example from the Rorschach test is shown in Exhibit 3–2A. As you can see, the stimulus is truly ambiguous.

Another well-known test using a projective technique is the Thematic Apperception Test (TAT), developed by Henry Murray.[12] This test uses a set of cards depicting individuals engaged in some ambiguous activity or unclear situation. Exhibit 3–2B shows an example of a TAT stimulus. In the TAT, subjects make up a story about the pictured event, describing both the event and the characters involved. The therapist interprets the information by identifying themes (presumably unconscious) which recur frequently.

Although projective techniques are most commonly used in psychoanalysis, consumer research has borrowed the approach on occasion. The rationale for their use is that projective methods will enable the researcher to obtain information which consumers otherwise would not or could not give.

Mason Haire utilized a projective technique in his classic consumer study of 1950[13] (see Chapter 1). In conducting research on the use of instant coffee, Haire noted that when nonusers were asked why they did not use instant coffee, they typically responded, "I don't like the flavor." Haire believed that this was too simple a response, and he suspected that there were other motives. He devised a projective technique to uncover these hidden motivations. The abridged reading in Exhibit 3–3 outlines Haire's research.

Haire's experiment has been the subject of a good deal of debate. Hill[14] and Anderson[15] have both suggested that an interaction effect between the instant coffee and other items on Haire's shopping list might have influenced the results. *Interaction effect* refers to a phenomenon in which a number of independent variables operating together can have a greater effect on the dependent variable than the sum total of the main effect of each single independent variable. But a later replication of the shopping-list study by Webster and von Pechmann again showed a difference between the buyers of instant and of ground coffee. But this time, twenty years later, the instant-coffee buyer was seen as an energetic, friendly, active individual. Over time, then, convenience foods had become an accepted form of consumption.[16]

Projective techniques, though widely regarded in the 1950s, have met with many criticisms, one of which is that the test responses are contaminated by the social desirability factor: respondents tend to give a response that they believe the tester wants to hear rather than a response reflecting their true underlying motivations. Murstein[17] cited research showing that if the respondent believes the tester wants to hear a "pleasant" response, that's the type of response the respondent will give.

Another, more fundamental, criticism of projective techniques has to do with questions about the underlying logic of such techniques. Many social

EXHIBIT 3–2A
A CARD FROM RORSCHACH'S TEST

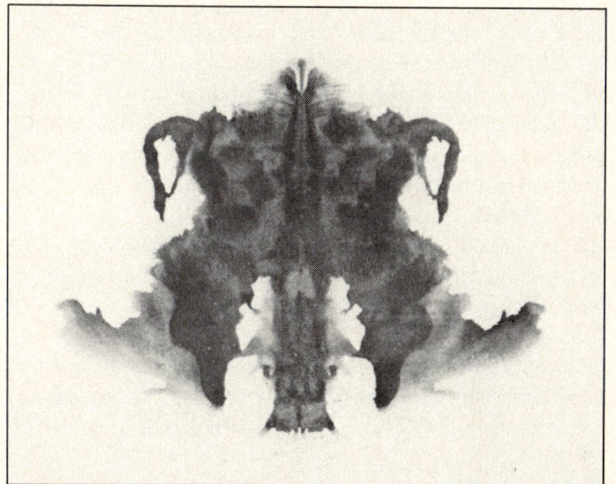

EXHIBIT 3–2B
A CARD FROM THE TAT

scientists do not believe in Freud's concept of projection and thus see no reason to believe that responses to projective stimuli reveal *anything* about the individual respondent. Moreover, we must question the relevance of subconscious motivation and the applicability of projective techniques to con-

EXHIBIT 3–3
A CLASSIC CONSUMER STUDY

PROJECTIVE TECHNIQUES IN MARKETING RESEARCH

The following study selection is an abridgment of a report of a study published in 1950. When you read the selection, try to place yourself in the position of the housewife in this time period. The women's movement had not even begun to form and, for most women, success entailed excelling as a homemaker. Coffee was an important household product, and "making a good cup of coffee" tended to symbolize success in the kitchen. Coffee was invariably percolated, and while it brewed, it filled the kitchen with a very distinctive aroma. Then, with the introduction of instant coffee, the ritual preparation of ground coffee was affected. Instant coffee was among the first of the convenience foods, so its entry into the market represented a real break with tradition.

Through the use of a projective technique, Haire attempted to learn how consumers of the day really reacted to the new, instant coffee.

For the purposes of experiment a conventional survey was made of attitudes toward Nescafé and instant coffee. The questionnaire included the questions "Do you use instant coffee?" (If *no*) "What do you dislike about it?" The bulk of the unfavorable responses fell into the general area "I don't like the flavor." This is such an easy answer to a complex question that one may suspect it is a stereotype, which at once gives a sensible response to get rid of the interviewer and conceals other motives. How can we get behind this facade?

In this case an indirect approach was used. Two shopping lists were prepared. They were identical in all respects, except that one list specified Nescafé and one Maxwell House Coffee. They were administered to alternate subjects, with no subject knowing of the existence of the other list. The instructions were "Read the shopping list below. Try to project yourself into the situation as far as possible until you can more or less characterize the woman who bought the groceries. Then write a brief description of her personality and character. Wherever possible indicate what factors influenced your judgement."

Shopping List I	*Shopping List II*
Pound and a half of hamburger	Pound and a half of hamburger
2 loaves Wonder bread	2 loaves Wonder bread
Bunch of carrots	Bunch of carrots
1 can Rumford's Baking Powder	1 can Rumford's Baking Powder
Nescafé instant coffee	1 lb. Maxwell House Coffee (Drip Ground)
2 cans Del Monte peaches	2 cans Del Monte peaches
5 lbs. potatoes	5 lbs. potatoes

sumer research. Psychological projective methods are diagnostic tools used in psychoanalysis. But as Kassarjian has stated, in consumer research,

One finds problems not related to schizophrenia or incest or a massive inability to cope with the environment, but rather extremely low-intensity

---

Fifty people responded to each of the two shopping lists given above. The responses to these shopping lists provided some very interesting material. The following main characteristics of their descriptions can be given:

1. 48 percent of the people described the woman who bought Nescafé as lazy; 4 percent described the woman who bought Maxwell House as lazy.

2. 48 percent of the people described the woman who bought Nescafé as failing to plan household purchases and schedules well; 12 percent described the woman who bought Maxwell House this way.

3. 4 percent described the Nescafé woman as thrifty; 16 percent described the Maxwell House woman as thrifty. 12 percent described the Nescafé woman as spendthrift; 0 percent described the Maxwell House this way.

4. 16 percent described the Nescafé woman as not a good wife; 0 percent described the Maxwell House woman this way. 4 percent described the Nescafé woman as a good wife; 16 percent described the Maxwell House woman as a good wife.

A clear picture begins to form here. Instant coffee represents a departure from "home-made" coffee, and the traditions with respect to caring for one's family. Coffee-making is taken seriously. . . . Coffee drinking is a form of intimacy and relaxation that gives it a special character. . . .

In this experiment, as a penalty for using "synthetics" the woman who buys Nescafé pays the price of being seen as lazy, spendthrift, a poor wife, and as failing to plan well for her family. The people who rejected instant coffee in the original direct question blamed its flavor. We may well wonder if their dislike of instant coffee was not to a large extent occasioned by a fear of being seen by one's self and others in the role they projected onto the Nescafé woman in the description. When asked directly, however, it is difficult to respond with this. One cannot say, "I don't use Nescafé because people will think I am lazy and not a good wife." Yet we know from these data that the feeling regarding laziness and shiftlessness was there. . . .

Conclusions

There seems to be no question that in the experimental situation described here:

1. Motives exist which are below the level of verbalization because they are socially unacceptable, difficult to verbalize cogently, or unrecognized;

2. These motives are intimately related to the decision to purchase or not to purchase; and

3. It is possible to identify and assess such motives by approaching them indirectly. . . .

SOURCE: Mason Haire (1950), "Projective Techniques in Marketing Research," *Journal of Marketing*, 14 (Apr.), pp. 649–56.

> *forces that determine the purchase of Mobil gasoline rather than Standard,
> the use of cologne rather than after-shave lotion, or the voting preference
> toward one of two equally bland, uninspiring, and uninteresting city coun-
> cilmen.*[18]

Kassarjian concludes that projective techniques can be useful tools for consumer research when the research investigates individuals' beliefs, attitudes, values, or motivations. He suggests, however, that using projective methods raises an additional problem—that of *ethics*. If consumers unwittingly reveal attitudes or motivations that they would prefer not to reveal, then their basic right to privacy is compromised. This differs from the patient-psychiatrist relationship, in which the patient willingly agrees to forego his or her right to privacy. Despite such criticisms, and given an appreciation of ethical issues, projective techniques can assist researchers in identifying some consumer opinions and issues.

Quantitative Research

Unlike qualitative research, which is intended to provide a thorough (and often introductory) understanding of consumers' behaviors or attitudes, quantitative research is intended to estimate the extent to which the consumer population subscribes to specific behaviors or attitudes. There are four main tools of quantitative research used in studies of consumers: **surveys,** which are typically administered once and only once; consumer **panels,** in which respondents participate on an ongoing basis over a period of time ranging anywhere from three to four weeks to several years; **observation,** in which consumer behaviors are observed by researchers (in grocery stores, for example); and **experiments,** which test the relationship between marketing variables and their effects on consumers under controlled conditions.

samples   With any of these methods, the manner in which the *sample* is selected is crucial to the generalizability of the results. One frequently recommended procedure uses statistical sampling to obtain a *random* sample in which each member of the population has the same probability of being included in the sample. Because no particular individual or group is favored for selection, the sample should not be biased in any particular direction. The results obtained from a random sample can be generalized to the entire population from which the sample was drawn. In other words, we can make assumptions and draw inferences about the whole population on the basis of sample findings.

An alternative approach to random sampling is the *stratified* sample. In this case, the sample is selected to conform to the population pattern of relevant variables. For instance, if product usage is thought to be dependent on age, the respondents are screened by age so that the age distribution of the sample matches that of the population.[19]

Very often, primarily because of cost considerations, research commissioned by managers tends to circumvent formal sampling procedures. Much quantitative research involves administering questionnaires to a sample of people intercepted in shopping centers. The inherent bias of such a sample precludes the generalization of results to the entire population. Careful analysis of the nature and direction of the sample bias is crucial in these cases.

Surveys The most common procedure used to gather data from consumers is the *survey questionnaire*, which is intended to tap information such as the extent of consumers' awareness of products or brands, their degree of product usage (the size of heavy- versus medium- versus light-usage segments), frequency of purchase, attitudes toward brands, perceived differences among brands, and/or any other relevant variables. Survey questionnaires can be administered face-to-face or via telephone. Mail surveys using self-administered questionnaires are also common.

Most survey questionnaires use both **closed-ended** and **open-ended questions.**[20] For closed-ended or multiple-choice questions, the range of possible responses is restricted, since respondents select their answers from a list provided by the researcher. For open-ended items, the respondent has the freedom to answer in whatever way he or she chooses.

A major benefit of the use of closed-ended items is that responses may be easily tabulated, thus providing statistical information about issues such as the degree of consumer product usage, dominant attitudes, or the size of various market segments. However, a drawback inherent in the use of closed-ended questions is that there is no guarantee that the set of available answers is exhaustive. This drawback is at its extreme for dichotomous questions. Since consumers are restricted in the types of responses they may make, important information may be miscoded into the available response categories or may be lost altogether. Another drawback is that it is very easy for respondents who do not know an answer or who do not have an opinion to provide an answer nonetheless.

The use of open-ended questions avoids these problems. But the drawbacks in their use include the time, difficulty, and costs involved in the data analysis. Responses to closed-ended questions can be precoded while the questionnaire is being developed. Subsequent analysis of responses is completely computerized and straightforward. Open-ended questions, however, must be individually edited and coded by research assistants, a practice that not only greatly increases costs, but also builds in another possible bias, since not all coders may be using the same definitions and interpretations as a basis for classifying responses.

A final issue of relevance for both open- and closed-ended questions is the manner in which they are generated. Good research procedure involves the use of a qualitative procedure to develop questions, as was done in the Canada Dry example. If survey questionnaire items are constructed without the benefit of knowledge gleaned from consumers, then the resulting questions run the risk of being biased by the preconceived ideas held by the researchers, product managers, or advertising agency personnel.

The general conclusion is that open-ended questions are appropriate for exploratory research,[21] in which the attitudes and beliefs of respondents are not well known or understood. On the other hand, closed-ended questions

closed-ended versus open-ended questions

are considered more appropriate for mail surveys and self-administered questionnaires, since they require fewer instructions than open-ended items and can be completed more quickly.[22]

Most consumer surveys are administered only once. But if a survey is administered two or more times, comparisons can be made among the sets of results. Such studies can be very helpful to managers, because they can measure the impact of changes in various variables on buying patterns. For instance, results of surveys administered both before and after an advertising campaign can be compared to assess the impact of that campaign on consumers' attitudes or preferences.

In recent years, *telephone interviewing*[23] has become increasingly popular among marketing researchers, largely because the costs tend to be substantially lower than the costs associated with personal interviewing,[24] that is, face-to-face interviewing. Care must be taken, however, with the manner in which telephone respondents are selected.[25] Consumer researchers often recruit a sample using telephone books, for example; but this introduces a sample bias, since approximately one fifth of households have unlisted phone numbers.[26] The use of random-digit dialing, although somewhat more costly than telephone-book sampling (because of the inefficiencies in calling unused numbers), creates a more representative sample, since both listed and unlisted telephone numbers are randomly generated and called.[27]

Mail surveys are also a popular data-collection technique.[28] As with telephone interviewing, the response rate to a mail survey is an important consideration. A high response rate helps insure that a representative sample has been reached. But the more people who refuse to participate, the less representative of the population as a whole the sample may be. If a low response rate is obtained, the researcher must ask if nonrespondents differ significantly from respondents. It may be that a certain segment of consumers is consistently refusing to respond, thus introducing bias into the data: respondents may behave quite differently from nonrespondents. Much research has been conducted to determine how to induce a high response rate. The major findings are that response rate increases if respondents are notified (either by telephone[29] or by postcard[30]) of the survey prior to receiving it, if a reminder or follow-up is used,[31] and if monetary incentives are used.[32]

Social Desirability   A problem that survey researchers must be sensitive to is the tendency for some respondents to give **socially desirable** responses.[33] When asked questions about their personal behaviors or habits, consumers sometimes respond so as to portray themselves in the most favorable light in the interviewer's eyes. For example, some consumers tend to understate the number of hours of television they watch, believing that heavy television viewing is not socially desirable behavior. Personal interviews tend to have the largest problem with socially desirable responses. Self-administered surveys have the least problem, and telephone interviews are in the middle.[34]

The researcher can also use a *social desirability scale* to measure the extent or incidence of these responses. Exhibit 3–4 gives the twenty items from the shortened version of the Marlow-Crowne Social Desirability Scale.[35] This scale is administered at the same time as the research interview. Respondents are asked to indicate whether the items are true or false. In fact, most people are "guilty" of all the negative thoughts and acts—at one time or another. To score the scale, the researcher simply adds up the socially desirable responses given by each respondent. If respondents consistently deny the negative actions, then they are completing the Marlow-Crowne scale in a socially desir-

EXHIBIT 3–4
SOCIAL DESIRABILITY SCALE

Indicate "true" or "false" for each item.	True	False
1. I'm always willing to admit when I make a mistake.	___	___
2. I like to gossip at times.	___	___
3. I always try to practice what I preach.	___	___
4. There have been some occasions when I took advantage of someone.	___	___
5. I never resent being asked to return a favor.	___	___
6. I sometimes try to get even rather than forgive and forget.	___	___
7. I have never been irked when people expressed ideas very different from my own.	___	___
8. At times I have really insisted on having my own way.	___	___
9. I have never deliberately said something that hurt someone's feelings.	___	___
10. There have been occasions when I felt like smashing things.	___	___
11. I never hesitate to go out of my way to help someone in trouble.	___	___
12. I sometimes feel resentful when I don't get my way.	___	___
13. I have never intensely disliked anyone.	___	___
14. There have been times when I felt like rebelling against people in authority even though I knew they were right.	___	___
15. When I don't know something I don't at all mind admitting it.	___	___
16. I can remember "playing sick" to get out of something.	___	___
17. I am always courteous, even to people who are disagreeable.	___	___
18. There have been times when I was quite jealous of the good fortune of others.	___	___
19. I would never think of letting someone else be punished for my wrong doings.	___	___
20. I am sometimes irritated by people who ask favors of me.	___	___

SOURCE: R. Strahan and K. Gerbasi (1972), "Short, Homogeneous Versions of the Marlow-Crowne Social Desirability Scale," *Journal of Clinical Psychology*, 28 (Apr.), p. 192.

able manner. The researcher can assume that a similar degree of socially desirable responses affects the other questions being asked.

Of course, the issue of social desirability is not always relevant to consumer research. Questions about brand preferences or incidence of product usage are often unrelated to the images consumers wish to project. But many topics are socially sensitive, such as attitudes toward child-rearing (of relevance to consumer socialization), the use of high-prestige brands, and attitudes toward advertising. In such cases, it is important for the researcher to take account of the issue of social desirability.

Consumer Panels　A second quantitative procedure commonly used to collect data in consumer research is the **panel study.** Once again, a sample of consumers is selected from a defined population. Members of the panel are given consumer "diaries" in which they record all purchases they make of a number of specified products. They also record the brands bought, amounts purchased, where the products were purchased, and so on. Consumer panels are also used by companies such as A. C. Nielsen and Arbitron to determine trends in television viewing among households. The Nielsen organization uses both consumer diaries and television-monitoring devices.

Because consumers record their purchases in sequence and the number and size of units purchased, panel data are especially useful for generating estimates of brand switching, brand loyalty, and market shares of various brands (or services, or television or radio programs).

Panels usually operate over long periods of time. When some consumers drop out of a panel after a period of participation, they are replaced by other individuals, and the overall sample structure of the panel is presumed to remain stable over time.

Panel data offer enormous advantages to managers because the effects of numerous marketing variables can be studied. For example, a manager operating a national panel could increase television advertising in one geographical area and increase magazine or newspaper advertising in another. Advertising in all remaining areas would be held constant; sales from these areas could be used as a benchmark against which to compare any increases resulting in the two test areas. The effects of changes in price, promotion, and competitor activity can also be ascertained through panel data on an ongoing basis.

Panel Studies Versus Surveys　The types of information generated by these two approaches is similar in some respects, since consumers basically report their purchasing patterns in both. But the accuracy of the two types of data has been shown to differ. Panel diary data is generally said to be the most accurate form of purchase data, because of validity checks provided by other data, such as records of factory or warehouse shipments.

Using data collected by the Market Research Corporation of America, Wind and Lerner compared purchase information recorded by a sample of consumers in panel diaries with purchase information provided by the *same* consumers in a survey using a self-completion questionnaire.[36] In the survey, respondents were asked to report the following:

1. the brand of margarine most frequently purchased,
2. other brands purchased, and
3. other brands they would consider buying.

In the analysis, the data from the survey (reported data) and from the purchase diary (recorded data) were compared at two levels: (1) the *aggregate* level, where market-share estimates from the survey were compared with estimates from the panel data, and (2) the *individual* level, where each respondent's responses in the survey were compared with his or her written diary entries.

At the aggregate level, the survey information approximated the diary data quite well. That is, market shares shown by the two approaches were quite similar. However, at the individual level, some very interesting findings emerged. First, 48 percent of respondents who named a given margarine brand as their "most frequently purchased brand" did not record this brand in their diaries. Also, an average of 63 percent of respondents who named a given brand as "brand also bought" did not record this brand in their diaries.

Although these results may seem somewhat surprising, think about the last time you purchased a bar of soap, laundry powder, or paper towels. Are you absolutely sure you can remember the brand you bought? Often, with such frequently purchased, nondurable products, consumers are not really aware of their brand choices. So although they can state the brand usually bought, or the brand most preferred, they cannot recall accurately the specific brand purchased, especially if the last purchase occurred more than a week or two in the past.

We can conclude that consumer surveys measure *recall* of purchases, whereas panel data provide an actual *record* of purchases. Most research is intended to provide knowledge and insight into aggregate market attitudes, preferences, and purchasing patterns. In such instances, consumer surveys are a very acceptable research tool.

Observation One of the most important contributions that direct *observations* of consumers in buying situations can make to consumer research is the provision of a *low-involvement* methodology with which to study consumer dynamics.[37] A low-involvement methodology is one that does not affect the research process. The more standard research procedures suffer from the drawback of possibly influencing a subject's responses. For example, a survey questionnaire may well suggest to a respondent new ways in which to evaluate a product. In this case, the very act of measuring a response could change that response.

The research technique of observation has been applied most frequently in supermarkets. For example, Wells and LoSciuto report a pilot study involving 1500 observations of shopping behavior. In this study, observers were trained to record as much detail as possible about each episode, including conversations between co-shoppers, handling of packages, and so on.[38]

Among their findings were the facts that although most shopping was done by the female shopper alone, in 29 percent of the episodes she was not present, and in 32 percent of the cases, she was accompanied by someone else.

When children accompany her, they influence purchases of a range of products from candy and cereal to detergents. And when adult males accompany the female shopper, not only do they attempt to influence decisions, they almost always succeed! Additionally, it was found that shoppers tend to be price insensitive, with 25 percent or fewer looking at the price for various product categories. Finally, and very importantly for marketing purposes, people spend a good deal of time *handling* packages, seemingly reading labels.

In another observational supermarket study, Atkin observed 516 episodes of parents and children making cereal purchases. His observations were as follows.

1. *Initiation*—The child initiated the interaction in two thirds of the cases, usually by demanding rather than requesting a cereal. One third of the parents took the initiative, generally by inviting the child to select a cereal. Highest levels of child-initiated interaction occurred for children who were younger, white, and middle-class.
2. *Response*—Parents were twice as likely to approve as to refuse proposed purchases, with demands resulting in slightly more acceptance than requests. Success in obtaining the desired cereal increased with age. Children typically made a selection as directed or invited, with little disagreement.
3. *Consequences*—One fourth of all interaction sequences resulted in parent-child conflict, and the child became unhappy in one sixth of all cases. Most problems arose when parents responded negatively to requests or demands; two thirds of these rejections or denials led to conflict, and one half were followed by unhappiness.
4. *Reasons for selection*—The premium accompanying the cereal was explicitly mentioned as the primary purchase motivation by one tenth of the children. This motivation was highest for older, minority, and working-class subgroups. Fewer than 1 percent of the children made reference to nutritional attributes.[39]

In another unobtrusive study, the researchers hypothesized a relationship between attitudes toward an issue and whether or not people discarded a handbill on the issue. Results showed that individuals supporting a political candidate were less likely to discard a flier supporting the preferred candidate than the nonpreferred candidate.[40]

In discussing unobtrusive techniques, Wells and LoSciuto note that two major advantages are that they study *what people do, not what they say,* and that they provide hypotheses that can later be tested (for example, that certain types of packaging attract more shopper attention than other types).[41] Disadvantages include problems in sampling (for example, type of shopper or voter differs with time of day and week) and the lack of experimental control. Also, and importantly, although the method studies what people do, it does not provide a definite explanation of why they are engaging in certain behaviors. Finally, a disadvantage of the observational method is that the interpretation of the results can often be qualitative and judgmental, introducing the possibility of bias.

Experimentation Experimentation is geared toward helping researchers identify cause-and-effect relationships. In an experiment, the researcher attempts to control all the conditions and variables involved in the study.

cause-and-effect relationships

The basic objective of a formal experiment is to measure the impact of various *independent variables* on specified *dependent variables*, while controlling for the effects of other *extraneous variables*. In terms of cause and effect, a dependent variable is equivalent to the *effect*. In marketing research, typical dependent variables are sales, consumers' preferences and attitudes, and levels of awareness and knowledge. Each of these variables can be affected by differences in the levels of independent variables, such as the amount of advertising for a product, the price of that product, and so forth. These independent variables, then, constitute the *cause* in the cause-and-effect relationship.

types of variables

However, cause-and-effect relationships are not always clear-cut. Extraneous variables can influence outcomes. For instance, sales of grocery products are affected not only by advertising, price, and promotional displays, but also by the amount of store traffic, the weather, and any number of other factors.

In a bona fide experiment, the researcher intentionally manipulates one or more independent variables in order to assess their effect on the dependent variable, while controlling for as many extraneous variables as possible. This approach is very different from the other methodologies we have discussed, which do not manipulate independent variables. With survey research, panel studies, projective techniques, and observation, the researcher simply records reports of behavior (effects). And although researchers may speculate about causes, there is no formal attempt to measure cause-and-effect relationships.

Experimental treatments refer to combinations of the various independent variables that are manipulated. For example, a researcher may hypothesize that sales of a laundry detergent (dependent variable) are affected by price (independent variable). Sales at two different price levels (say $1.79 and $2.19) might be measured: each price level constitutes a treatment. If sales were hypothesized as contingent on both price and the presence or absence of a promotional display in a store, then combining two prices with the display variable generates four treatments.

Treatment	Price	Display
1	$1.79	yes
2	$1.79	no
3	$2.19	yes
4	$2.19	no

In this case, the researcher could conduct the experiment using four similar units (stores), each receiving one of the treatments.

The intent of an experiment is to test a specific *null hypothesis* (H_o), which states that there is no difference in the effect each of the treatments has on the dependent variables. This null hypothesis is either "accepted" or "rejected," based on the measurement of the units exposed to each treatment. If

null hypothesis

the arithmetical means of the measurements of each treatment exceed some predetermined difference, the null hypothesis is rejected. If the difference between means does not exceed the standard, H_o is accepted.

Types of Experiments There are two types of experiments—*laboratory experiments* and *field experiments*. As the name suggests, laboratory experiments are conducted in a laboratory, which is an artificial setting. For example, a researcher interested in evaluating the effectiveness of three different television advertisements in transmitting a specific piece of information about a product might expose a different sample of people to each of the three commercials in a laboratory setting. Then the response of each group would be compared to assess the relative effectiveness of each advertisement. Since the setting is artificial, a question arises as to the *external validity* of the results—can the results be projected to real world situations?

external validity

As a general rule, field experiments, which are conducted in natural settings, have greater external validity. But field experiments tend to have lower internal validity. *Internal validity* refers to the ability of the experiment to establish clear relationships between dependent and independent variables. For instance, to evaluate the effectiveness of the three television advertisements, a researcher might air one in Boston, one in Denver, and one in Columbus. A day-after recall test would assess viewer responses in the three cities. In this case, responses may be affected by extraneous variables over which the researcher has no control. Thus, differences in response may be due to factors other than the differences in the advertisements, reflecting the lower level of internal validity associated with field experiments.

internal validity

Experimentation in Marketing Research Although bona fide field experiments tend to be more frequently conducted by academic researchers than by corporate research practitioners, there are some well-known commercial uses of experimentation. Perhaps the best known example is the large-scale experiment conducted by Anheuser-Busch, advertising for Budweiser beer.[42] Actual geographic areas were randomly assigned to experimental and control groups. The levels of advertising for the experimental groups were varied from 100 percent less than that for the control group to 300 percent more. The testing period ranged from one to two years, depending on the region. Anheuser-Busch found that beyond a certain level, sales were insensitive to advertising. That is, advertising tended to increase sales up to a point, but then sales stabilized, despite additional advertising. The result was that Anheuser-Busch was able to *decrease* its advertising budget without suffering a loss in sales at that particular time. This is an example of an experiment designed to determine scientifically the effect of certain independent variables (such as the level of advertising or point-of-sale promotion) on other dependent variables (such as sales). The researcher intentionally varies the levels of independent variables, while controlling for all other variables which could possibly affect the dependent variable under study.

Bona fide experiments are conducted rather infrequently in corporate consumer research. This is due partially to the time and expense involved. In addition, there is some risk that manipulating the levels of variables such as advertising may result in a sales decrease or attitude change among consumers in some regions. Most marketing practitioners believe that the quantitative and qualitative research approaches described above can generally provide a type of information similar to that provided by experimentation.

SUMMARY

The aim of consumer research is to identify consumer needs. Acquiring information about consumer needs can be a relatively straightforward exercise when consumers already have experience with the product class. In the absence of experience, however, the research process is far more complex. Sources of consumer-behavior information include secondary (published) research and primary (original) research directly involving consumers.

The major forms of primary consumer-behavior research can be distinguished as *qualitative* or *quantitative*. Qualitative research is generally conducted with small numbers of consumers on an in-depth basis. Its methods include in-depth interviews, focus groups, and projective techniques. They are a legacy of motivation research, and they are useful for developing hypotheses as to why consumers behave as they do for more rigorous testing by quantitative research methods.

Quantitative approaches include consumer surveys and panels, as well as observation and experimentation techniques. Much of consumer behavior research is based on surveys or interviews with consumers. Panels are used to track behavior over time. Observation has the benefit of its nonintrusive character. Experimentation has the potential to probe cause-and-effect relationships (for example, the effect of advertising on sales). Regardless of the technique used, researchers should be aware of the issues of social desirability (the tendency of consumers to respond in a socially acceptable manner) and data accuracy (validity and reliability). These issues affect both qualitative and quantitative research.

KEY CONCEPTS

data collection	quantitative research	projective techniques
social desirability	in-depth interviews	observation
validity	focus-group interviews	experimentation
reliability	open-ended questions	independent variables
primary research	closed-ended questions	dependent variables
secondary research	surveys	extraneous variables
qualitative research	panel studies	

DISCUSSION QUESTIONS

1. A national manufacturer of frequently purchased food products is considering introducing an innovative product with which consumers have no experience. How might the marketer accurately assess consumers' reactions to the new product?
2. When would qualitative approaches be more suitable than quantitative techniques?

3. When might projective techniques be used in marketing research? What are the problems involved in their use among consumers?
4. Design a study similar to Haire's (on instant coffee), in which you attempt to ascertain consumers' reactions to (a) an innovative product and (b) generic brands.
5. "Experimentation is too costly and too complex to be of any practical value to marketing practitioners." Do you agree with this statement? Defend your position.
6. What types of consumer research do you think are more susceptible to the problem of respondents' giving socially desirable responses?
7. Under what general conditions is it preferable to conduct a laboratory experiment rather than a field experiment?
8. Design an experimental study to measure advertising effectiveness. What extraneous variables will affect your study? What steps can you take to minimize their effects?

NOTES

1. Julie Salamon (1981), "Marketers Start to Help Banks Recognize Gains from Selling," *Wall Street Journal* (Sept. 3), sec. 2, p. 25.
2. "What's in a Name? Ask the Research Department" (1978), *New York Times* (Dec. 24), sec. D, p. 11.
3. "How to Waste $12 Million" (1981), *Inc.* (Dec.), p. 95.
4. Edward F. Fern (1982), "The Use of Focus Groups for Idea Generation: The Effects of Group Size, Acquaintanceship, and Moderator on Response Quantity and Quality," *Journal of Marketing Research*, 19, pp. 1–13.
5. For a discussion of different interviewing approaches in focus groups, see Bobby J. Calder (1977), "Focus Groups and the Nature of Qualitative Marketing Research," *Journal of Marketing Research,* 14, pp. 353–64.
6. William D. Wells (1974), "Group Interviewing," in *Handbook of Marketing Research,* ed. Robert Ferber (New York: McGraw-Hill), pp. 133–46.
7. Alfred E. Goldman (1962), "The Group Depth Interview," *Journal of Marketing,* 26, pp. 61–68 and John M. Hess (1968), "Group Interviewing," in *1968 ACR Fall Conference Proceedings*, ed. Robert L. King (Chicago: American Marketing Assn.), pp. 193–96
8. Edward F. Fern (1982).
9. Keith K. Cox, James B. Higginbotham, and John Burton (1976), "Applications of Focus Group Interviews in Marketing," *Journal of Marketing,* 40, pp. 77–80.
10. For a review of projective techniques and their use in marketing see Harold H. Kassarjian (1974), "Projective Methods," in *Handbook of Marketing Research*, ed. Robert Ferber (New York: McGraw-Hill), pp. 3–85 to 3–100.
11. For a comprehensive discussion of Rorschach tests, see Robert M. Allen (1966), *Student's Rorschach Manual* (New York: International Univ. Press).
12. Henry A. Murray (1938), *Explorations in Personality* (New York: Oxford Univ. Press).
13. Mason Haire (1950), "Projective Techniques in Marketing Research," *Journal of Marketing,* 14 (Apr.), pp. 649–56.
14. Conrad R. Hill (1960), "Another Look at Two Instant Coffee Studies," *Journal of Advertising Research* (Dec.), pp. 18–21 and (1968), "Haire's Classic Instant Coffee Study—18 Years Later," *Journalism Quarterly,* 45 (Aug.), pp. 466–72.
15. James C. Anderson (1978), "The Validity of Haire's Shopping List Projective Techniques," *Journal of Marketing Research*, 15 (Nov.), pp. 644–49.
16. Frederick E. Webster, Jr., and Frederick von Pechmann (1970), "A Replication of the 'Shopping List' Study," *Journal of Marketing*, 34 (Apr.), pp. 61–77.
17. B. Murstein (1963), *Theory and Research in Projective Techniques: Emphasizing the TAT* (New York: Wiley).
18. Harold H. Kassarjian (1974), pp. 3–96.
19. A full consideration of sample selection is beyond the scope of this book. The interested

student may consult William G. Cochran (1977), *Sampling Techniques,* 3rd ed. (New York: Wiley) or Raymond J. Jessen (1978), *Statistical Survey Techniques* (New York: Wiley).

20. A comprehensive discussion of open- and closed-ended questions can be found in Thomas C. Kinnear and James R. Taylor (1979), *Marketing Research: An Applied Approach* (New York: McGraw-Hill), pp. 456–64.

21. Stanley L. Payne (1975), "Are Open-Ended Questions Worth the Effort?" *Journal of Marketing Research,* 2, pp. 417–18.

22. Kenneth D. Bailey (1978), *Methods of Social Research* (New York: Free Press), p. 107.

23. For an excellent treatment of the pros and cons of telephone interviewing, see Tyzoon T. Tybejee (1979), "Telephone Survey Methods, The State of the Art," *Journal of Marketing,* 43, pp. 68–78.

24. Gerald J. Glasser and Gale D. Metzger (1972), "Random Digit Dialing as a Method of Telephone Sampling," *Journal of Marketing Research,* 9, pp. 59–64.

25. Ronald Czaja, Johnny Blair, and Jutta P. Sebestick (1982), "Respondent Selection in a Telephone Survey: A Comparison of Three Techniques," *Journal of Marketing Research,* 19, pp. 381–85 and Frederick Wiseman and Philip McDonald (1979), "Noncontact and Refusal Rates in Consumer Telephone Surveys," *Journal of Marketing Research,* 16, pp. 478–84.

26. Robert M. Groves (1978), "An Empirical Comparison of Two Telephone Sample Designs," *Journal of Marketing Research,* 15, pp. 622–31.

27. William Lyons and Robert F. Durant (1980), "Interviewer Costs Associated with the Use of Random Digit Dialing in Large Area Samples," *Journal of Marketing,* 44, pp. 65–69.

28. Two comprehensive literature reviews of mail survey methodologies are Leslie Kanuk and Conrad Berenson (1975), "Mail Surveys and Response Rates: A Literature Review," *Journal of Marketing Research,* 12, pp. 440–53 and Arnold S. Linsky (1975), "Stimulating Responses to Mailed Questionnaires: A Review," *Public Opinion Quarterly,* 39, pp. 82–101.

29. Marvin A. Jolson (1977), "How to Double or Triple Mail Survey Response Rate," *Journal of Marketing,* 41, pp. 78–81.

30. Bruce J. Walker and Richard K. Burdich (1977), "Advance Correspondence and Error in Mail Surveys," *Journal of Marketing Research,* 14, pp. 379–82.

31. Kanuk and Berenson (1975) and Linsky (1975).

32. Kanuk and Berenson (1975); Linsky (1975); and D. H. Robertson and D. N. Bellenger (1978), "A New Method of Increasing Mail Survey Responses: Contributions to Charity," *Journal of Marketing Research,* 15, pp. 632–33.

33. Allen L. Edwards (1961), "Social Desirability of Acquiescence in the MMPI: A Case Study with the Social Desirability Scale," *Journal of Abnormal and Social Psychology,* 63, pp. 351–59; and F. Wiseman (1972), "Methodological Bias in Public Opinion Surveys," *Public Opinion Quarterly,* 36, pp. 105–8.

34. Tyzoon T. Tybejee (1979).

35. R. Strahan and K. Gerbasi (1972), "Short, Homogeneous Version of the Marlow-Crowne Social Desirability Scale," *Journal of Clinical Psychology,* 28 (Apr.), pp. 191–93.

36. Yoram Wind and David Lerner (1979), "On the Measurement of Purchase Data: Surveys Versus Purchase Diaries," *Journal of Marketing Research,* 16 (Feb.), pp. 39–47.

37. The need for low-involvement methodologies has been long recognized. For a complete discussion, see Eugene J. Sebb, Donald T. Campbell, Richard D. Schwartz, and Lee Sechrest (1965), *Unobtrusive Measures: Non-reactive Research in Social Sciences* (Chicago: Rand McNally).

38. William D. Wells and Leonard A. LoSciuto (1966), "Direct Observation of Purchasing Behavior," *Journal of Marketing Research,* 3 (Aug.), pp. 227–33.

39. Charles K. Atkins (1975), "The Effects of Television Advertising on Children: Parent-Child Communication in Supermarket Breakfast Cereal Selection," Report for the Office of Child Development, U.S. Dept. of Health, Education, and Welfare (Oct.).

40. Robert B. Cialdini and Donald J. Baumann (1981), "Littering: A New Unobtrusive Measure of Attitude," *Social Psychology Quarterly,* 44, pp. 254–59.

41. Wells and LoSciuto (1966).

42. Russell L. Ackoff and James R. Emshoff (1975), "Advertising Research at Anheuser-Busch (1963–68)," *Sloan Management Review,* 16, no. 3 (Winter).

PART

II

Psychological Theories and Applications

4 Cognitive Processes: Information Search and Product Adoption

One of the marketing manager's most fundamental tasks is to inform consumers about products, brands, and services. Companies spend over $100 billion annually in the United States on this task, using a wide variety of communications vehicles. Information is presented in television, radio, newspaper, and magazine ads; on the packaging and labels for products; in point-of-sale displays; and by salespeople. It is estimated that the typical consumer is exposed to between 300 and 600 advertisements per day.[1]

The consumer also is exposed to product-related information over which marketers have no control. Friends talk about their experiences with products and services. Opinions or products are presented in magazine articles and television programs. Consumers see people buying and using products. All of these messages about products compete for the consumer's attention. These product-related messages not only compete among themselves, they also compete with all other environmental stimuli to which the consumer is exposed.

This crowded environment poses a difficult problem for marketing managers. First, the manager must get the consumer's attention. But getting the consumer to notice the message is not enough. The manager also needs to have the message stored in the consumer's memory in a form that is resilient enough to withstand the bombardment of competing messages that the consumer will receive. Finally, when and if the message is recalled at the time of a purchase decision, the impression recalled needs to be sufficiently favorable so that the consumer will purchase the marketer's brand. To develop marketing communications that will solve this difficult problem, marketers need a thorough knowledge of how consumers process, store, and recall information.

In this chapter we describe the adoption process—a series of stages that consumers go through beginning with initial exposure to a message about a product and ending with a commitment to repeatedly buy and use the product. Then we discuss the consumer's search for information in detail. In the next chapter we examine the cognitive activities of consumers as they organize and make sense of the information they have collected.

THE ADOPTION PROCESS

The product **adoption process** includes the various mental and behavioral stages through which consumers must progress if adoption—that is, the acceptance and use of a product—is to occur. These *stages in the adoption process* are shown in Exhibit 4–1.

First the consumer becomes **aware** of the product or brand. At this stage, the consumer has little information about the product and has not developed an attitude or evaluation of the product. During the second stage, the consumer acquires some **knowledge** about the product by searching for additional information. This information search can involve a review of internal sources of information stored in the consumer's memory and an active search for external information sources, such as the experience and opinions of friends or articles in *Consumer Reports*. Based on this information, the consumer **evaluates** the product and forms a positive or negative attitude.

awareness

knowledge

evaluation

EXHIBIT 4–1
STAGES IN THE ADOPTION PROCESS

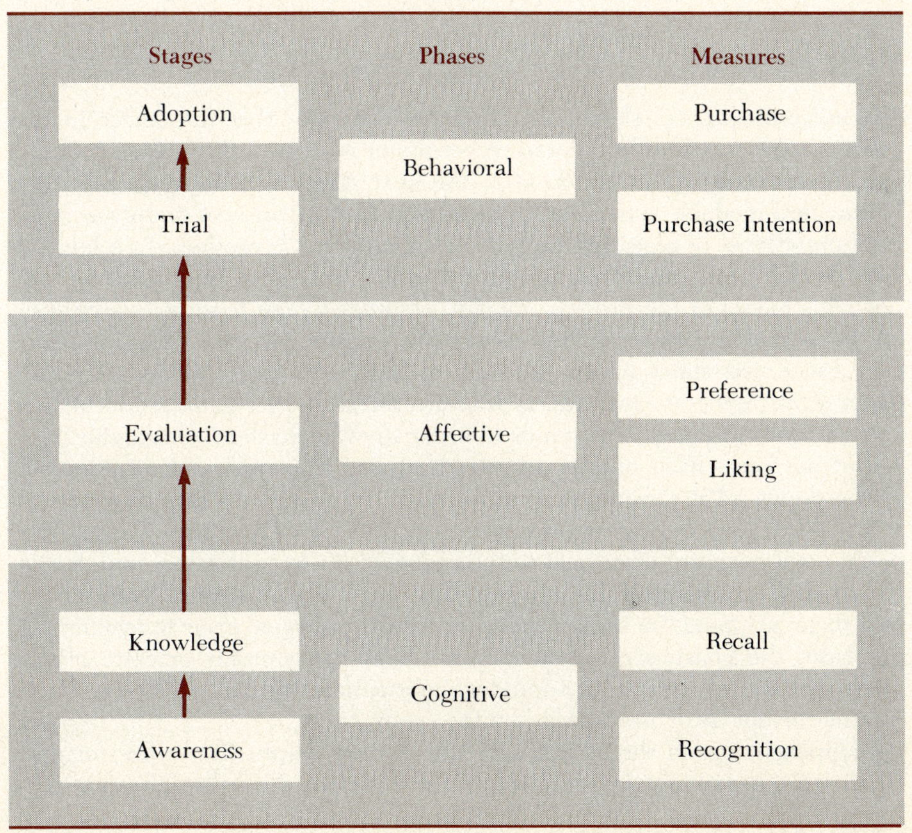

trial

adoption

Following the evaluation stage, the consumer makes a decision either to try or not to try the product. During this **trial** stage, the consumer uses the product on a small scale to determine whether or not the product is useful. Based on the additional information obtained during this trial stage, the consumer decides whether or not to **adopt** the product. *Adoption* is defined as a commitment to use the product regularly.

The adoption process shown in Exhibit 4–1 is one conceptualization, among several different models that have been proposed in the marketing literature. For example, the AIDA model has only four stages: *Awareness, Interest, Desire,* and *Action;*[2] McGuire's information-processing model has six stages: *Presentation of Message, Attention to Message, Comprehension, Yielding to the Conclusion, Retention of the Belief,* and *Behavior on the Basis of the New Belief.*[3] Even though these adoption models have various numbers of stages, they all contain three underlying phases: *cognitive, affective* or *evaluative,* and *behavioral.* In the cognitive phase (*Awareness* and *Knowledge* stages of Exhibit 4–1), the consumer develops a set of beliefs about the characteristics of the product. These beliefs are used to form feelings of liking or disliking toward the product during the affective phase (*Evaluation* stage). Based on these feelings, the consumer undertakes actions in the behavioral phase (*Trial* and *Adoption* stages).

The Hierarchical Nature of the Adoption Process

The adoption process shown in Exhibit 4–1 implies that the stages in the process are hierarchically ordered. A consumer must pass through each of the preceding stages before going on to the next stage. The basic concept of a hierarchical model is appealing. It seems logical to picture consumers as moving from a level of acquiring basic information about a product, to a level of attitude and preference formation, to a decision actually to purchase the product. This model of the process, though, assumes a *high level of involvement* on the part of consumers. This means that consumers are viewed as being very concerned about which products or brands to buy and that they are pictured as deliberate individuals who are interested in gaining information about various products and brands in order to evaluate them thoroughly.

high involvement

But we know from our experiences that the process described does not always depict what consumers actually do. Often consumers skip or return to stages when considering or adopting a product. For example, a consumer might see a new candy bar next to the cash register in a drugstore and decide to buy it. The consumer has gone directly from the awareness stage to the trial stage, skipping the knowledge and evaluation stages. Prior to making the purchase, the consumer had no beliefs about the contents or taste of the candy bar, did not search for additional information, and had no feeling about whether or not he or she would like the candy bar.

low involvement

Skipping stages in the adoption process occurs frequently for *low-involvement* decision-making, in which purchase decisions are relatively unimportant. Most consumers simply do not care about what paper goods or cleaning products to buy. When one considers the massive number of products available to consumers (the average supermarket, for example, stocks over 7500 items) and the number of purchase decisions they make, it becomes obvious that consumers do not have the time to analyze each decision in depth. In fact, these unimportant, low-involvement, purchase decisions occur so often that Chapter 6 is devoted to the behavior of consumers making just these types of decisions.

In addition to skipping stages, consumers may return to stages that they have already passed. In our example, the consumer, after making a trial purchase of the candy bar and eating it, would then decide whether or not it was good, thus going from the trial stage to the evaluation stage. Often, consumers will move back and forth among the knowledge, evaluation, and trial stages. For example, a consumer might read some information about an IBM personal computer, go to a retail store to buy the computer, and then decide to collect more information.

Even though the adoption-process model does not describe the adoption behavior of consumers in all situations, it is a useful framework for organizing knowledge about consumers' responses to marketing information. In addition, the model is helpful for planning and evaluating marketing strategies.

Marketing Communications and the Adoption Process

The stages in the adoption-process model are used for planning and evaluating marketing-communication programs. Different communication programs are directed toward each stage.[4] For example, the marketing communication programs for industrial products use a combination of advertising, personal selling, and demonstrations to move customers through the adoption process. Advertising in trade journals is used primarily to create awareness of the product and to provide a limited amount of information about the product. Then salespeople are used to educate customers further about the benefits of the product and to influence them to make favorable evaluations. Finally, the product is demonstrated to customers and perhaps left with them for trial periods.

These different communication elements are used because the cost effectiveness of the elements differs across stages in the adoption process. Because it is not cost effective to use salespeople at a rate of $178 per sales call to create awareness,[5] advertising is used at this stage. On the other hand, advertisements can convey only a limited amount of information, so salespeople are used to move customers through the knowledge and evaluation stages.[6]

Just as various marketing-communication programs are directed at specific stages of the adoption process, advertising campaigns can be differentially effective across the adoption-process stages. Some advertising campaigns may be very effective in inducing consumers to take one step in the adoption process while simultaneously inhibiting the accomplishment of following steps.

salespeople versus advertising

DAGMAR Approach   Using the idea that advertisements can have different effects at different stages of the adoption process, Russell Colley formalized the process of setting goals for advertising related to adoption stages.[7] This approach, referred to as DAGMAR (*Defining Advertising Goals for Measured Advertising Results*), suggests that an advertising campaign should be evaluated according to the degree to which the campaign moves consumers through the adoption stages. Before Colley's work, most marketers felt that the goal of advertising was to increase sales and thus that advertising should be evaluated in terms of sales generated. Colley argued, however, that advertising is just one communication element in a marketing program directed toward increasing sales. Advertising should be evaluated on the basis of communication goals, such as creating awareness or favorable attitudes, rather than end results or sales.

The DAGMAR approach is based on the premise that consumers progress through a sequence of stages—an adoption process—before awareness of a product or brand is translated into adoption. Since these stages are hierarchical, there is a "hierarchy of effects" for an advertisement.[8]

In addition to defining communication goals for advertising in terms of the adoption process, DAGMAR proposes that these goals should be measurable (that is, through the use of research techniques to assess progress), the specific target market should be defined, and a time period for realizing goals should be established. For example, a marketer of women's hosiery identified the target market as 12 million women who customarily wear hosiery nearly every day. The goals of the company's marketing program as stated in the marketing plan were to establish distribution in 1200 grade-A retail outlets and to achieve an annual sales volume of $15 million in three years. The goals of the advertising, however, were stated in terms of the first two stages of the adoption process: During the first year after introduction, (1) achieve brand awareness among 60 percent of the women in the target market (awareness stage) and (2) have 30 percent of these women know about the anti-fatigue benefits and the "sheer beauty" of the hosiery (knowledge stage).[9]

Measuring Communication Effectiveness

At the different stages of the adoption process marketers use a number of measures to assess communication effectiveness.

Awareness   Recognition and recall tests are two methods for determining whether consumers became aware of a product or brand through an advertisement. In a *recognition test*, consumers are shown a magazine or series of television ads and asked to indicate which ads they recognize as having seen and/or read.

One organization that administers such tests, the Starch Readership Service, regularly measures readership of advertisements that appear in the major newspapers and magazines. The Starch Service uses personal interviews with a sample of readers of various publications to gather information. Readers are asked to indicate whether or not they remember having seen an advertisement that appeared in a specific issue, whether they remember the brand name of the advertised product (these names are blocked out), and how much of the ad they read. The Starch Service summarizes the results of their survey by providing three scores for each ad indicating the percentage of readers who *noted* the ad, who saw the ad and associated it with the advertiser or brand name (*seen/associated*), and who *read most* of the ad.[10] These scores represent various levels of *awareness*, although the *read most* score captures some aspects of the *knowledge* stage.

The publishers of trade publications directed toward industrial customers provide similar measures of readership for ads in their magazines. In addition, they provide readers the opportunity to request additional information about products advertised by circling a number on an inquiry card. The *number* of inquiries generated by an ad, then, indicates the ad's effectiveness at moving readers from the awareness to the knowledge stage.[11]

A widely used procedure for testing the effectiveness of television commercials is the *day-after recall* technique, one version of which is used by Burke Marketing Research. In a study of day-after recall, the day after a new commercial is shown, Burke contacts a sample of consumers who viewed the television program in which the advertisement appeared. These consumers are questioned to ascertain whether or not they saw the portion of the program in which the commercial appeared, and whether or not they recall a commercial for the specific type of product. Next, they are asked to recall the actual content of the commercial. These responses are analyzed to determine if consumers actually saw the commercial and, importantly, if they correctly recall the brand name and advertising content. The commercial's effectiveness is measured in terms of a *day-after-recall score*, which states the proportion of all consumers exposed to the advertisement who are able to recall at least part of it correctly.

day-after recall

The recognition task (as measured by Starch) involves a different set of mental processes from the recall task (as measured by Burke). To *recognize* an advertisement, consumers need only to discriminate among a number of advertisements presented to them. *Recalling* an advertisement is much more difficult, because consumers must reconstruct the content from memory.

recognition versus recall

Knowledge   Recall tests are used to measure knowledge as well as awareness. The knowledge level is determined by asking consumers to indicate the product features of benefits shown in the ad. Again, recall requires consumers to reconstruct information from memory.

Evaluation   Attitude, preference, and purchase-intention measures are used to determine how consumers *evaluate* products or brands. Consumers' attitudes typically are assessed using "bad-good" or "dislike-like" scales. The effects of an ad on consumer attitudes are determined by comparing consumer attitudes before and after exposure or by comparing matched groups of consumers exposed to the ad with those not exposed. The difference between the before-after measures or the measures from the two groups indicates how the advertisement affected consumers' evaluations.

Other measures of evaluation are preference and purchase intention. *Preference* indicates the consumer's evaluation of the product relative to other products. *Purchase intention* is usually assessed by using a "probable-improbable" scale on which consumers indicate the probability that they will purchase a product.

Trial/Adoption   Purchase behavior can be measured by the use of consumer panels which record each purchase, by observing purchases in stores, or by pantry checks.

USING THE ADOPTION PROCESS: A HYPOTHETICAL EXAMPLE

The following example illustrates how the adoption-process model can be used to formulate and evaluate strategic marketing plans for a hypothetical new product. The new-product marketer is often hampered in the early stages of a product's life cycle in arriving at meaningful sales predictions because the sales data base is so small and, frequently, unpredictable. A heavy, early sales rate may indicate either a large potential market or a small potential market that is highly interested in the product and moves rapidly through the adoption process toward trial. However, a large number of trial sales will indicate strong long-term sales only if consumers have a favorable experience during the trial stage and are motivated to make repeat purchases. Slow beginning sales rates may be due to the complexity or lack of communicability of the product and may not reflect long-run sales potential. In other words, *sales* figures in the short-run need not be the best indicator of long-run adoption rates.

EXHIBIT 4–2

CLASSIFICATION OF CONSUMERS BY STAGE OF THE ADOPTION PROCESS FOR A HYPOTHETICAL INNOVATION

Adoption-Process Stage	Cumulative Percentage of Consumers[a]	
	June 1983	December 1983
Awareness	55	85
Knowledge	45	70
Evaluation	25	30
Trial	10	14
Adoption	3	10

[a]*100 percent* is assumed to represent the entire market potential for the product.

In order to interpret the market situation more fully, consumer research could track sales figures but also levels of awareness, knowledge, liking, and preference. Some data illustrating this approach are provided in Exhibit 4–2.

Assume that the new product was introduced to the market on January 1, 1983. Using sales rates only, we see that 3 percent of the potential market has adopted by June, and 10 percent has adopted by December. At this point, management may be plotting sales figures and noting what appears to be the takeoff point on the traditional S-shaped curve (see Exhibit 4–3). The product manager may be a strong contender for a bonus.

If, however, we examine the trends for each of the five stages in the hierarchy of effects scheme, quite a different picture emerges. Although aware-

EXHIBIT 4–3
CHANGES IN GROWTH OF HIERARCHICAL EFFECTS (based on Exhibit 4–2)

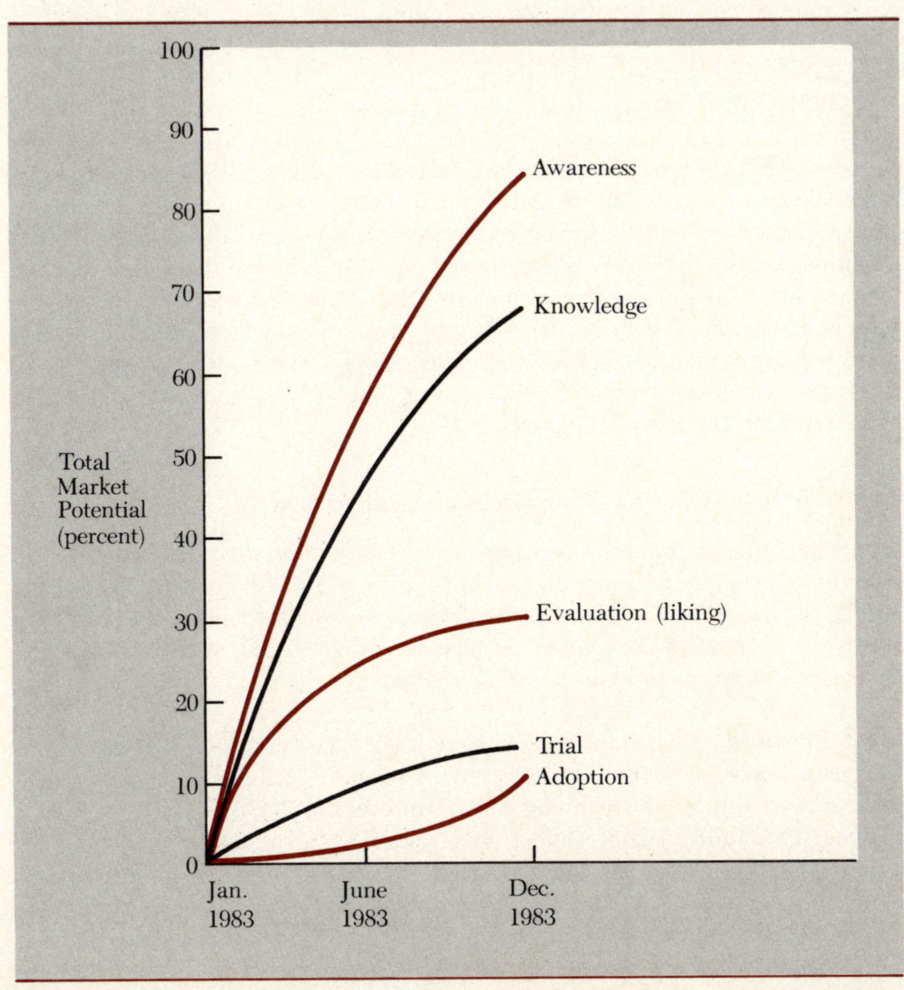

ness and knowledge levels have shown significant gains, the relative percentage increase in numbers of consumers holding favorable attitudes (liking) toward the product is indeed small; and an even smaller relative percentage increase is shown in the number of consumers advancing as far as preference. According to this additional data, sales levels will soon stabilize rapidly since other consumers in the population are not progressing toward purchase.

Since the rate of repeat purchasing is high, the problem is not with the product. Rather, these data would suggest either that the eventual market share for this product is limited and has been achieved quickly, or that promotional efforts are not successfully gaining attitude change—perhaps because they are still focusing on information messages for the new product despite the fact that 85 percent of the consumers are at or beyond the awareness level. Using this approach, the marketer would be able to check these hypotheses in December 1983 rather than many months later when adoption had stabilized after production had been expanded. It could also be possible to attempt to correct the promotional campaign.

INFORMATION SEARCH

As consumers progress through the hierarchical stages to adoption, they acquire more and more information about the product or service being considered. The amount of information required by consumers to move through the adoption process depends upon the nature of the purchase decision and some characteristics of the consumer. In some situations, consumers will actively search for additional information, while in others they will rely on information collected and remembered from their experiences. We shall examine some of the factors affecting the search process. But first we shall consider approaches to research on the information search.

Research Approaches for Examining Information Search

A considerable amount of research has been undertaken to examine the amount and type of information sought by consumers.[12] Before we discuss the results and implications of this research, we shall differentiate between the two major research approaches that have been used in these investigations: field research and laboratory experiments.

Field Research   One approach to examining consumer information search has been to assess the extent and type of search consumers *actually* undertake. For example, Newman and Staelin questioned 653 respondents from a national probability sample about their out-of-store information-seeking for automobile, television, refrigerator, room air conditioner, and washing machine purchases made during the prior thirteen months.[13] Respondents were asked questions about the type and sources of information or advice sought. The results suggested that information-seeking was generally quite limited:

only 53 percent of the sample considered more than one brand for the purchase of automobiles and household appliances.

Laboratory Studies—The Information Display Board   In addition to the field studies of consumers in actual choice situations, studies have been conducted in laboratory settings. In these laboratory studies, consumers (subjects) are exposed to hypothetical choice situations, and their information-search behavior prior to choice is monitored. The information display board, developed by Jacoby and his colleagues, is an innovative approach that has been used in a number of recent studies to examine search behavior in a controlled environment.[14] In this approach, information about products is displayed in a matrix such as that shown in Exhibit 4–4. Each column of the matrix contains information about a characteristic of each brand. The information for each cell is presented on a card, the blank back side of which faces the consumer. Respondents are asked to behave as though they were shopping. They then select as much (or as little) information as they wish by looking at the cards for all desired cells. All cards chosen are placed in a tray, enabling the researcher to know how much information each respondent consulted. This technique has been used to observe how much information consumers seek, the type of information sought, and the order in which information is acquired.

In line with the results of field research, studies using information display boards also suggest that consumer information search is fairly limited. For example, in an experiment using an information display board with 16 brands of breakfast cereal and 35 product characteristics per brand (a total of 560

monitors hypothetical search

EXHIBIT 4–4
AN INFORMATION DISPLAY BOARD (hypothetical) FOR LAUNDRY DETERGENTS

Characteristic	Tide	Fab	Wisk	Era	All
Price					
Cleaning Power					
Form (liquid or powder)					
Concentrated or Nonconcentrated					
Includes Softeners?					
Includes Whiteners?					

pieces of information), consumers selected, on average, only 11 pieces of information—less than 2 percent of information available—before choosing a brand. Also, they selected information concentrated on just 6 of the 35 product characteristics.[15]

Amount of Information Sought

limited search

As we have seen, consumers generally do not engage in extensive external searches for information.[16] Research indicates that even for important, high-involvement decisions such as the purchase of an automobile or appliance, only about one half of consumers visit more than one retail outlet or consider more than one brand.[17] However, the results of this research may understate the amount of search actually undertaken. When traditional self-report, survey measures were compared to unobtrusive, in-store observations of the shoppers, the self-reports understated the amount of search actually observed.[18]

adequate existing information

This limited amount of external information search does not imply that consumers typically make ill-informed or irrational purchase decisions. First, the low level of external search may mean that consumers have collected enough information through past experiences that they can rely on information stored in memory; thus they may not need to search extensively for information. Second, the consumers may feel that the costs of additional external search are greater than the benefits that might be gained. In fact, one

costs

study showed that for four out of five appliances (air conditioner, range, refrigerator, and washer), a comparison of three brands generally provided enough information for the average consumer to make a rational, "near optimal" decision.[19]

Benefits of Information Search

The amount of information sought by consumers depends upon the consumer's perception of the benefits that are likely to be gained from additional information and the perceived costs of undertaking the search. Consumers seek additional information as long as the perceived benefits outweigh the costs.[20] The principal benefit of additional information is the increased satisfaction that is realized by making an appropriate purchase decision. The costs of information search include effort expended, time that might be spent on more rewarding activities, financial costs associated with travel, psychological costs, and so on.

Nature of Existing Information The perceived benefits of information search are affected by the quantity and quality of information presently possessed by consumers. If consumers have extensive knowledge of product alternatives, they are likely to perceive that additional search will not reveal new information that will improve their purchase decision. The more experience a consumer has with a product, the less search activity.[21] Research has shown that the amount of information search is inversely related to both the breadth of experience (the number of different brands purchased in a product category) and the depth of experience (the number of purchase decisions already made in a product category).[22]

The quality of prior experience is even more important than the *quantity* of information. For example, the effects of prior experience are mediated by the consumer's satisfaction with past purchases. Consumers who are satisfied with past purchases engage in less search while unsatisfied consumers will search for information even though they have substantial prior experience.[23] In addition, consumers may feel that prior experience is inapplicable when the purchases were made some time ago and when there have been recent changes in the market offerings. Thus, the amount of information search is directly related to the time that has elapsed since the last purchase and rate of changes in price, style, and new product offerings.[24]

Importance and Riskiness of Purchase Decision The expected benefits of additional information are a function of the degree of uncertainty associated with the decision and the importance of the decision. In general, the greater the uncertainty, the more information is sought; the more important the decision, the greater the information-seeking.[25]

These two factors, uncertainty and importance, combine to form the level of *risk* perceived by consumers. The highest perceived risk occurs when decisions are both uncertain and important. Under these conditions, the expected losses due to a poor decision are greatest, and thus consumers engage in an extensive information search. Locander and Hermann found that under conditions of high perceived risk, more information was sought from both personal sources (such as friends and neighbors) and neutral sources (such as *Consumer Reports*).[26]

Since economic risks are associated with the price of the product, it is not surprising that the amount of information search is directly related to higher priced products.[27] However, physical and social risks can be even more important to consumers than economic risks. For example, purchase decisions for medical products involve physical risks and thus are preceded by extensive information search. Social risks arise when the purchase of a product may affect the way other people view the consumer. Consumers search for more information about products that are socially visible, such as clothing or automobiles.[28]

Product-Related Factors Characteristics related to the actual product can affect the duration of the search process. For example, search increases if the brands under consideration are perceived to be very different from one another.[29] When products are highly differentiated, the perceived benefits offered by the product will differ and the potential loss of satisfaction due to a poor decision will be greater. On the other hand, homogeneous products seem to offer the same degree of potential for satisfaction, and thus there is a minimal degree of risk associated with the purchase decision.

Costs of Information Search

Although information gained through search can assist consumers in making purchases, the costs associated with information-seeking must be taken into account.

Expenditure of Time and Money   Information search often can be expensive. For example, visits to retail outlets can be costly in both time and money (such as costs of transportation and parking). In an era of increasing energy costs, monetary outlays to acquire additional information can dissuade potential consumers from engaging in additional search.[30]

Psychological Costs   In addition to financial costs, consumers incur some psychological costs as they search for information. They may experience frustration and tension when driving through traffic to visit a store, dealing with uncooperative salespeople in the store, and resolving conflicting opinions and facts.

These psychological costs may explain Bettman and Park's finding that even first-time home buyers engaged in a limited amount of information search.[31] Even though extensive information search is typically undertaken for risky decisions (such as purchasing a house) and when prior experience is limited, the combination of high risk and limited experience may create so much tension that the consumers feel overwhelmed and thus do not even attempt to cope with the uncertainty.

Information Overload   The amount of information available to consumers can affect the amount of information search and the quality of decisions. Researchers have argued that as the amount of available information increases, the amount of search will increase at first; however, search will eventually decrease when the information load becomes too high. Several studies[32] have reported this decrease in search at various levels of available information, although one study has found no decline.[33]

Perhaps the most provocative and controversial studies concerning information overload were undertaken by Jacoby, Speller, and Kuhn using the information display-board paradigm.[34] These studies were concerned with the effects of information load on quality of decisions rather than information search. In these studies, consumers (subjects) were presented with display boards describing the characteristics of hypothetical brands of laundry detergents, rice, and prepared dinners. The size of the display boards (the amount of information presented) ranged from four brands with two characteristics per brand to sixteen brands with sixteen characteristics per brand. The consumers were asked to make a choice among the brands displayed. The "quality" of their choices was determined by comparing the products chosen with the consumers' descriptions of their "ideal" products. The researchers concluded that "subjects felt better with more information but actually made poor purchase decisions."[35]

This finding has important implications for marketing managers and public-policy makers. It suggests that more information is not always better. Too much information may increase the psychological cost of acquiring and processing the information to a point at which the information is not used or used erroneously by consumers. Several researchers have challenged the conclusions of these studies, however, and thus the issue of whether increased information helps or hinders consumers is still unresolved.[36]

Information Format and Processing Costs

In many purchase situations, consumers are confronted with a vast array of information that can be acquired very economically. Consider the abundance of information from signs, demonstrations, displays, and packages in the typical supermarket. Although there is little economic cost in acquiring information in this environment, consumers still are selective about the information they collect. While economic costs are not a consideration, psychological costs become critical. In this rich information environment, consumers use information that can be acquired and processed with limited psychological or mental effort.

The format utilized to present information has a significant impact on the amount of processing effort needed to use the information. Although there is considerable information in a supermarket, much of it is not presented in a convenient format for consumers to assimilate, and thus it is not utilized.

Research on the use of unit-price information has demonstrated the effect of information format on usage. *Unit pricing* is the practice of displaying price information in terms of a common denominator for all brands and package sizes in a product category. For example, the price for all containers of coffee is shown in units of dollars per pound, or soft drink prices are shown in cents per ounce. Consumerists have advocated the use of unit pricing because it makes it easier for consumers to make economical choices among different brands and package sizes. However, research indicates that unit-price information is not used by the majority of consumers.[37]

unit pricing

One explanation for the limited use of unit pricing lies in the way the information typically is displayed. To use this information, consumers must look at the unit price under each brand and size, and then mentally compare the prices they can remember. Under these conditions, it still is difficult to make unit-price comparisons across alternatives, even though the prices are standardized. This processing difficulty accounts for the limited use of unit-price information. However, research indicates that when the format of unit-price information is altered to make processing easier, the use of unit pricing increases. When unit prices are displayed in a list ranking all brands and sizes, shoppers can easily make price comparisons between alternatives, and utilization of unit-price information increases.[38] Similar effects of information format have been found for truth-in-lending[39] and nutritional information.[40] Studies have shown that when information on the amount of interest to be paid or on nutritional ingredients is presented to facilitate easy comparisons, use of information increases.

Individual Differences and Information-Seeking Propensity

Clearly, there are significant differences among consumers in their perceptions of the cost benefit associated with information search. The amount of prior experience, the perception of decision importance and risk, and the value placed on time and expenses differ across consumers. In addition, consumers differ in their ability to process information and their desire to make an optimal rather than just satisfactory choice. Consumers who are highly concerned with making optimal purchase decisions tend to engage in more information search.[41]

The sources of individual differences in information search are systematically related to socioeconomic and demographic characteristics of consumers. Bucklin found, for example, that the greater the family wealth and social status, the more the information search for the purchase of food products.[42] Capon and Burke found that members of higher social classes sought more information then their lower-class counterparts for the purchase of microwave ovens, toaster ovens, and steam irons.[43]

social class

A woman's perception of her family role affects the importance she places on decisions about food products and the amount of information search she will undertake when making these decisions. "Liberal women," who have little interest in "typical family chores at home," and "traditionalists," who plan meals the way their parents did, engage in little information search. On the other hand, "mother" types, who are very concerned with child care, engage in extensive information search.[44]

women's roles

Information Search and Marketing Strategy

Information-search activities undertaken by consumers need to be considered in developing marketing programs. Effective marketing programs provide the amount and type of information needed by consumers to make purchase decisions. Thus marketing programs for durables and new products should incorporate a strong information component, since consumers view purchase decisions for these products as risky and thus need more information prior to purchase. In addition, consumers have less experience and internally-stored information about these products that can be used to reduce perceived risk. This information can be conveyed through informational ads, brochures, or trained salespeople in specialty retail outlets. On the other hand, marketing programs for mature package goods do not require a high information content. Purchase decisions for these products are not risky, and consumers have a backlog of experience to draw upon.

In some situations, marketers may wish to encourage information search. The marketer of an innovative product, who wants to interrupt the habitual buying pattern of consumers, would like to encourage consumers to search for new information. Such information search can be encouraged by attempting to differentiate the new product from existing competitors, since search tends to increase when products are perceived as different from one another.

Finally, marketers can increase the probability that their information will be used by reducing the acquisition costs for the consumer. It is not enough to make information readily available at minimal economic costs. The psychological costs of acquiring and processing the information must also be minimized. Information needs to be presented in a format that is compatible with consumer information processing. For example, comparative information such as unit pricing is more frequently used when all information is listed together, simplifying the comparison process.

SOURCES OF INFORMATION

We now consider the impact of various sources of information. A typology of information sources is shown in Exhibit 4–5. The extent to which these information sources are used by consumers varies considerably with the type of product to be purchased and the stage in the adoption process. The survey results shown in Exhibit 4–6 indicate that consumers typically become aware of a product from advertising, a marketer-controlled, impersonal source. However, consumers indicate that nonmarketer-controlled, personal sources of information play the most important role in the eventual purchase decision.

Impersonal Versus Personal Information Sources

In general, personal sources of information, shown in Exhibit 4–5, are reported by consumers to provide more information and to have more impact on consumers than impersonal information sources. Because of this difference

EXHIBIT 4–5
CATEGORIES OF INFORMATION SOURCES

	Personal	Impersonal
Marketer controlled	• salespeople • company seminars • 800-number information lines • trade shows	• media advertising • point-of-purchase displays • packaging • sales promotions
Nonmarketer controlled	• word of mouth from friends, family, and acquaintances • professional advice • personal consumption experiences	• editorial and news material

information flow

tailored information

in effectiveness, marketing managers will pay one dollar for each minute a customer is with a salesperson and less than one cent for each minute a customer views an advertisement on television.

Personal sources are more effective because of the two-way flow of information between the source and the consumer. Salespeople, friends, and family are able to tailor information to satisfy the recipient's needs. They can respond to the specific questions of the person with whom they are talking. If a consumer is interested in the gas mileage of a car, they can provide information about gas mileage. If ride comfort is important, they can provide information about that.

On the other hand, impersonal information sources only provide one-way communications. Information delivered via print or other mass media is developed to satisfy the typical needs of large groups of consumers. Because individual needs cannot be considered, the information provided is not ideally suited for any one customer.

In addition to providing more knowledge and creating more interest, personal sources secure more attention than impersonal sources can. It is quite easy for consumers to disregard an advertisement on television or in a maga-

EXHIBIT 4–6
CONSUMER USAGE OF INFORMATION SOURCES

Channels	Small Appliances			Clothing			Food		
	First[a]	Else[b]	Most Important[c]	First	Else	Most Important	Food	Else	Most Important
Marketer-Controlled									
Advertising	48	23	8	35	27	16	45	25	19
Salesmen	1	1	1	4	1	6	0	0	0
Sales Promotion	9	7	9	19	14	32	26	16	27
Nonmarketer-Controlled									
Personal Influence									
Friends, neighbors, relatives	23	41	53	27	29	33	16	19	29
Immediate family	8	7	11	2	4	0	12	12	21
Professional advice	6	8	13	0	0	0	1	0	0
Editorial and news material	1	0	1	6	6	6	0	0	1
No Mentions	4	13	4	7	19	7	0	28	3
Total ($N = 99$)	100%	100%	100%	100%	100%	100%	100%	100%	100%

Three questions were asked:

[a]"Could you tell me how this product came to your attention for the very first time?"

[b]"How else did you hear about this product before you bought it?"

[c]"Which one of these was your most important source of information in your decision to buy this product?"

SOURCE: Based on Thomas Robertson (1971), *Innovative Behavior and Communication* (New York: Holt, Rinehart and Winston), p. 156.

zine; however, people will generally pay attention to someone talking to them.

Source Properties and Marketing Strategies

Marketers need to consider the properties of information in developing marketing programs. The effectiveness of various information sources varies with the nature of the product and stage of the adoption process. Consumers need significant amounts of information prior to adopting unfamiliar, high-risk, complex products. Since personal information sources are more effective at conveying large amounts of information, marketers of new and of high-risk products rely more on salespeople and favorable word-of-mouth than on advertising. In contrast, low-risk, familiar products and brands rely on more economical, impersonal sources—advertising and point-of-purchase displays, for example—because two-way communication is not needed to adapt the information to individual consumer needs.

The nature of the perceived risks associated with a product must also be considered by marketing managers selecting information sources. Economic and physical risks can be reduced by emphasizing the expertise of the source, and social risks are best reduced through attractive sources.

SUMMARY

Prior to adopting a product or service, consumers generally go through a hierarchical sequence of stages. At first, their attention is directed toward the product. Then they become more knowledgeable about the product, develop an interest in it, evaluate the product's ability to satisfy their needs, and finally try the product. Based on a favorable trial, consumers become adopters and make repeated purchases.

While the actual adoption process may not always follow this hierarchical sequence, the specific stages identified in the process are useful in designing and evaluating marketing programs. The effectiveness of a marketing program can be assessed by determining the number of consumers (potential adopters) who have progressed through the various stages in the process. Specific marketing programs can be developed to encourage consumers to move from one stage to another. For example, free samples can be used to move consumers to the trial stage.

Information is a critical factor associated with the movement of consumers through the adoption process. Consumers typically do not engage in extensive information searches prior to adoption. They rely on information gained through experience to supplement information they have actively acquired before making a specific purchase. The amount of information search depends upon consumer perceptions of the benefits and costs associated with the search. More information is sought when there is little prior information concerning the purchase, when there is high perceived risk, and when the economic and psychological costs of information search are low.

Sources of information can be categorized as marketer controlled or nonmarketer controlled and as personal or impersonal. Typically, marketer-controlled sources have less impact because they are perceived as less trustworthy. Of course, for low-involvement products, trustworthiness may not be an issue because consumers may have confidence in their own judgments. Personal sources have more impact when consumers require a two-way communication process in order to gain information directly relevant to their needs.

KEY CONCEPTS

adoption process	**day-after recall**	**benefits of search**
awareness	**information search**	**information overload**
knowledge	**field research**	**information format**
evaluation	**information display**	**personal sources**
trial	**board**	**impersonal sources**
adoption	**amount of search**	**marketer controlled**
hierarchy of effects	**costs of search**	**sources**
perceived risk	time	**nonmarketer**
recognition tests	money	**controlled sources**
recall tests	psychological costs	

DISCUSSION QUESTIONS

1. What value can the adoption-process model have if it is not an accurate reflection of consumer adoption behavior in all circumstances?
2. How can sales be a misleading indicator of the success or failure of a new product?
3. Discuss the differences in the information search process (a) across individual consumers and (b) across different purchase situations.
4. How could the structure of an advertising campaign intended to generate awareness of a new consumer product differ from a campaign designed to induce trial?
5. How do the costs of information search alter consumer behavior in the decision-making process?
6. Discuss the differences in search behavior that might be expected for purchasing (a) a new car versus a personal computer and (b) a family vacation versus a clothes dryer. Be sure to include a consideration of the benefits and the costs of search, and the types of sources that would be consulted.
7. How does information overload affect information search?
8. Discuss the benefits and drawbacks of (a) personal versus impersonal sources of information and (b) marketer controlled versus nonmarketer controlled information sources.

NOTES

1. Steuart Henderson Britt, Stephen C. Adams, and Alan S. Miller (1972), "How Many Advertising Exposures Per Day?" *Journal of Advertising Research*, 12 (Dec.), pp. 3–10.
2. E. K. Strong (1925), *The Psychology of Selling* (New York: McGraw-Hill), p. 9.
3. William J. McGuire (1978), "An Information Processing Model of Advertising Effectiveness,"

in *Behavior and Management Sciences in Marketing*, ed. H. L. Davis and A. J. Silk (New York: Wiley), pp. 156–80.

4. Michael L. Ray (1982), *Advertising and Communications Management* (Englewood Cliffs, N.J.: Prentice-Hall), pp. 34–55.

5. Estimate based on U.S. Dept. of Labor (1981), Bureau of Labor Statistics, *Monthly Labor Review* (June). See also McGraw-Hill Research Laboratory of Advertising Performance, No. 8013.6 (undated).

6. John E. Morrill (1970), "Industrial Advertising Pays Off," *Harvard Business Review* (March-Apr.), pp. 4–12, 159–68 and William Swinyard and Michael L. Ray (1977), "Advertising-Selling Interactions: An Attribution Theory Experiment," *Journal of Marketing Research*, 14 (Nov.), pp. 509–16.

7. Russell H. Colley (1961), *Defining Advertising Goals for Measured Advertising Results* (New York: Assn. of Natl. Advertisers). See also Robert J. Lavidge and Gary A. Steiner (1961), "A Model for Predictive Measurement of Advertising Effectiveness," *Journal of Marketing*, 25 (Oct.), pp. 59–62.

8. Kristian S. Palda (1966), "The Hypothesis of a Hierarchy of Effects: A Partial Evaluation," *Journal of Marketing Research*, 8 (Aug.), pp. 283–89.

9. Colley (1961).

10. Daniel Starch (1966), *Measuring Advertising Readership and Results* (New York: McGraw-Hill).

11. Dominique M. Hanssens and Barton A. Weitz (1980), "The Effectiveness of Industrial Print Advertisements Across Product Categories," *Journal of Marketing Research*, 17 (Aug.), pp. 294–306.

12. See, for example, Joseph W. Newman (1977), "Consumer External Search: Amount and Determinants," in *Consumer and Industrial Buying Behavior*, ed. A. Woodside and P. Bennett (New York: North Holland), pp. 79–94.

13. Joseph W. Newman and Richard Staelin (1972), "Pre-Purchase Information Seeking for New Cars and Major Household Appliances," *Journal of Marketing Research*, 9 (Aug.), pp. 249–57.

14. Jacob Jacoby, Robert W. Chestnut, Karl C. Weigl, and William Fisher (1976), "Pre-Purchase Information Acquisition: Description of a Process Methodology, Research Paradigm, and Pilot Investigation," in *Advances in Consumer Research,* ed. Beverlee B. Anderson, vol. 3 (Assn. for Consumer Research); Jacob Jacoby, Donald E. Speller, and Carol A. Kuhn (1974), "Brand Choice Behavior as a Function of Information Load," *Journal of Marketing Research*, 11 (Feb.), pp. 63–69; and Jacob Jacoby, George J. Szybillo, and Jacquelline Busato-Schach (1900), "Information Acquisition Behavior in Brand Choice Situations," *Journal of Consumer Research*, 3 (March), pp. 206–16.

15. Jacoby, Chestnut, Weigl, and Fisher (1976).

16. For a comprehensive discussion of this topic, see R. W. Olshavsky and Donald Granbois (1979), "Consumer Decision Making—Fact or Fiction?" *Journal of Consumer Research*, 6 (Sept.), pp. 93–100.

17. Newman and Staelin (1972); and W. P. Dommermuth (1965), "The Shopping Matrix and Marketing Strategy," *Journal of Marketing Research*, 2 (May), pp. 129–32.

18. Joseph E. Newman and Bradley D. Lockeman (1975), "Measuring Prepurchase Information Seeking," *Journal of Consumer Research*, 2 (Dec.), pp. 216–22.

19. Brian T. Ratchford (1980), "The Value of Information for Selected Appliances," *Journal of Marketing Research,* 7 (Feb.), pp. 14–25.

20. For an economic theory of search based on a cost-benefit tradeoff, see George J. Stigler (1961), "The Economics of Information," *Journal of Political Economy*, 69 (June), pp. 213–25. A psychological cost-benefit model of information search based on expectation theory is examined in Robert E. Burnkrant (1976), "A Motivational Model of Information Processing Intensity," *Journal of Consumer Research*, 3 (June), pp. 21–30.

21. Ronald D. Anderson, Jack L. Engledow, and Helmut Becker (1979), "Evaluating the Relationships Among Attitudes Toward Business, Product Satisfaction, Experience, and Search Effort," *Journal of Marketing Research*, 16 (Aug.), pp. 394–400.

22. G. David Hughes, Seha Tinic, and Phillipe Neast (1969), "Analyzing Consumer Information

Processing," in *Marketing Involvement in Society and the Economy* (Chicago: American Marketing Assn.), pp. 235–40 and Paul E. Green, Michael Halbert, and J. Sayer Minas (1964), "An Experiment in Information Buying," *Journal of Marketing Research*, 4 (Sept.), pp. 17–23.

23. Peter Bennett and Robert Mandell (1969), "Prepurchasing Information Seeking of New Car Purchasers—the Learning Hypothesis," *Journal of Marketing Research*, 6 (Nov.), pp. 430–33.

24. George Katona (1964), *The Mass Consumption Society* (New York: McGraw-Hill).

25. Jacob Jacoby, Robert W. Chestnut, and William A. Fisher (1978), "A Behavioral Process Approach to Information Acquisition in Nondurable Purchasing," *Journal of Marketing Research*, 15 (Nov.), pp. 532–44.

26. William B. Locander and Peter W. Hermann (1979), "The Effect of Self-Confidence and Anxiety on Information Seeking in Consumer Risk Reduction," *Journal of Marketing Research*, 16 (May), pp. 268–74.

27. Newman and Staelin (1972).

28. Katona (1964).

29. John D. Claxton, Joseph N. Fry, and Bernard Portis (1974) "A Taxonomy of Prepurchase Information Gathering Patterns," *Journal of Consumer Research*, 1 (Dec.), pp. 35–42.

30. Brian T. Ratchford (1980).

31. James F. Bettman and C. W. Park (1980), "Effects of Prior Knowledge and Experience and Phase of Choice Process on Consumer Decision Processes: A Protocol Analysis," *Journal of Consumer Research*, 7 (Aug.), pp. 234–48.

32. Harold M. Schroder, Michael J. Driver, and Siegfried Streuleit (1967), *Human Information Processing* (New York: Holt, Rinehart & Winston) and Joan E. Sieber and John T. Lanzetta (1964), "Conflict and Conceptual Structure as Determinants of Decision-Making Behavior," *Journal of Personality*, 32, pp. 622–41.

33. Denis A. Lussier and Richard W. Olshavsky (1974), "An Information Processing Approach to Individual Brand Choice Behavior," paper presented at the ORSA/TIMS joint natl. meeting (Puerto Rico).

34. Jacoby, Speller, and Kuhn (Feb. 1974) and (June 1974), "Brand Choice Behavior as a Function of Information Load: Replication and Extension," *Journal of Consumer Research*, 1, pp. 33–42.

35. Jacoby, Speller, and Kuhn (June 1974), p. 69.

36. J. Edward Russo (1974), "More Information Is Better: A Reevaluation of Jacoby, Speller, and Kuhn," *Journal of Consumer Research* (Dec.), pp. 68–72; John O. Summers (1974), "Less Information Is Better?" *Journal of Marketing Research*, 11 (Nov.), pp. 467–8; and William L. Wilkie (1974), "Analysis of Effects of Information Load," *Journal of Marketing Research*, 11 (Nov.), pp. 462–6.

37. James Carmen (1973), "A Summary of Empirical Research on Unit Pricing," *Journal of Retailing*, 48 (Winter), pp. 63–71 and Kent Monroe and Peter LaPlaca (1972), "What Are the Benefits of Unit Pricing?" *Journal of Marketing*, 36 (Jan.), pp. 16–22.

38. Jay Russo (1977), "The Value of Unit Price Information," *Journal of Marketing Research*, 14 (May), pp. 193–201 and Jay Russo, Gene Krieser, and Sally Miyashita (1975), "An Effective Display of Unit Price Information," *Journal of Marketing*, 39 (Apr.), pp. 11–19.

39. George Day and William Brandt (1974), "Consumer Research and the Evaluation of Information Disclosure Requirements: The Case of Truth in Lending," *Journal of Consumer Research*, 1 (June), pp. 71–80.

40. James Bettman (1975), "Issues in Designing Consumer Information Environments," *Journal of Consumer Research*, 2 (Dec.), pp. 169–77.

41. John Swan (1969), "Experimental Analysis of Predecision Information Seeking," *Journal of Marketing Research*, 6 (May), pp. 192–7 and Claxton, Fry, and Portis (1974).

42. Louis Bucklin (1969), "Consumer Search, Role Enactment, and Market Efficiency," *Journal of Business*, 42, pp. 416–38.

43. Noel Capon and Marion Burke (1980), "Individual, Product Class, and Task Related Factors in Consumer Information Processing," *Journal of Consumer Research*, 7 (June), pp. 314–26.

44. Bucklin (1969).

5 Information Processing

Companies, political organizations, and consumer advocate groups all undertake expensive campaigns to provide information to consumers and to influence their decisions. Some advertising campaigns, such as the promotion of Miller Lite beer, are extremely successful in building up sales; but other campaigns, such as the Edsel automobile and Schlitz beer campaigns, fail to alter consumer purchase decisions even though substantial expenditures are incurred. During major election years, hundreds of millions of dollars are spent on advertising by political candidates but research indicates that few voters change their minds because of it.[1]

These examples illustrate that exposing consumers to information is not enough. Consumers must utilize this information if it is to influence their behavior. Thus, to be effective, the marketing manager must influence the information processing undertaken by consumers. The objective of this chapter is to provide an understanding of that process: how consumers receive, transform, store, and recall information that is eventually used to evaluate products and make purchase decisions.

The study of consumer information processing places considerable emphasis on **cognitive analysis**—the study of how information is received and translated into cognitions. Cognitions are the knowledge, opinions, and beliefs that individuals have about objects, people, and events. They take the form of object-attribute associations, such as "Pepsi Free has no caffeine," where Pepsi Free is the object associated with the attribute no caffeine.

After an overview of consumer information processing, we discuss specific elements in the overview in greater detail. First we examine the storage of information in memory. Then we describe the processes that people use to control the flow of information in and out of memory. Thus, the first part of this chapter focuses on the attention stage of the adoption process shown in Exhibit 4–1, Chapter 4, while the latter part of the chapter examines the knowledge stage.

A model of the stages in information processing is shown in Exhibit 5–1: It shows that information processing begins when consumers are *exposed* to information. Consumers can play either a passive or an active role in this stage. **Passive exposure** to controlled marketing information occurs when a consumer is exposed to an advertisement while reading a magazine, watching a television program, or driving along a highway. Marketers attempt to increase the probability of such passive exposure by placing ads in media encountered by consumers in the segment they have targeted.

As we saw in Chapter 4, exposure to information also can be the result of an **active** information-search process undertaken by consumers. To accommodate consumers who are actively searching for information, marketers need to provide relevant information in a readily accessible form. For example, the advertisement on p. 322 presents the redesigned container for Tylenol capsules. Since consumers are very interested in information concerning the safety of this product, the ad emphasizes and illustrates the three safety seals in the new package. This information is presented in an easily accessible format.

But consumers may not receive information, even if they are exposed to it. To receive the information, they need to be first aroused and then they need to pay attention to the information. Drawing an analogy between consumer and computer information processing, *arousal* is similar to the *on-off switch* of the computer. The on-off switch activates the computer's circuits just as arousal activates the central nervous system of the consumer. To continue with the computer analogy, *attention* is similar to *allocating computing capac-*

EXHIBIT 5–1
MODEL OF INFORMATION PROCESSING

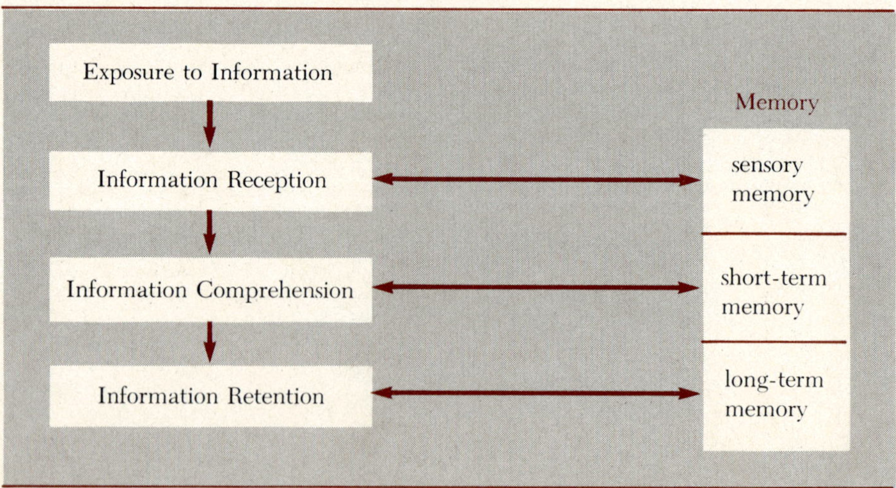

ity, core memory, to process the information. When consumers attend to information, they devote processing effort to the information.[3]

After receiving information, consumers *interpret* the information and assign meaning to it: they relate the incoming information to information gathered in the past and stored in memory. Existing cognitions are reinforced and/or altered by the new information. Research indicates, however, a bias toward processing information that confirms previously held beliefs.[4]

Finally, the information that has been received and processed is *stored* in permanent memory. The information that is retained may be an accurate representation of the incoming information or it may be distorted by the information that was previously in memory. In addition, the cognitions can also have a positive or negative value. Positively valued cognitions, such as good taste, are associated with favorable aspects of the object while negatively valued cognitions, such as high cost, are associated with unfavorable aspects.

Memory functions are intimately related to these information processing stages. Information is received initially in *sensory* memory, held briefly in a temporary storage location, *short-term* memory, during the knowledge phase, and then transferred to a permanent storage location, *long-term* memory. The cognitive processing during the knowledge stage involves an interplay between short-term and long-term memory.

INFORMATION RECEPTION

Before consumers can process and store information, they must first receive it. Even though the consumer is physically exposed to information, there is a strong possibility that the information will not be received. The probability of actually receiving the information depends upon the degree to which the consumer is aroused by the information and pays attention to it.

Arousal

Exposure to novel information initiates internal physiological activity in people which is referred to as **arousal.** This activity signals the brain to prepare to process information. However, the *level* of arousal of physiological activity also affects the attention that consumers pay to incoming information.

Optimal Level   Some minimal level of arousal is needed to initiate information processing; very high levels of arousal, however, may narrow the focus of attention to only a few aspects of the incoming information.[5] In addition, high arousal can bias the internal search for information in memory so that only the most readily available information is utilized.[6] Thus, very high levels of arousal may actually impede the processing of complex messages because highly aroused people cannot pay attention to the nuances of a message and have limited access to information in memory that will help them understand the message.

On the other hand, very low levels of arousal may reduce the amount of information the consumer is interested in processing. Arousal, then, is not a *sufficient* condition for message processing, but it is a *necessary* condition.

Thus, there is an optimal level of arousal that will maximize the amount of information processing undertaken by the consumer. However, this level depends upon the nature of the processing task. A relatively low level of arousal may be sufficient to stimulate processing of a familiar television commercial or information related to the purchase of frozen peas; but a higher level of arousal is probably needed to initiate processing of information about a new type of video system.

Measuring Arousal   A commonly used measure of the arousal level produced by advertisements is the *galvanic skin response* (GSR). GSR measures the electrical resistence of skin between two electrodes placed on the body. Increasing levels of skin resistance indicate higher levels of arousal.[7] However, marketers must be cautious when interpreting GSR. A higher GSR cannot be taken to indicate a more effective ad because, at some point, information processing will begin to decrease as GSR continues to increase. In addition, GSR measures just arousal, not whether a consumer is favorably aroused or unfavorably aroused. Both very pleasing and very irritating ads will produce high arousal.

GRS

Attention

Consumers must pay attention to information in order to receive and process it. Two aspects of attention—intensity and selectivity—are relevant to information processing. *Intensity* refers to the amount of capacity or effort allocated to processing information, and *selectivity* refers to the specific aspects of the information that is processed.

Intensity of Effort   People have a limited capacity for processing information at a given point in time because the temporary storage location, short-term memory, is small. Thus, when the quantity or complexity of incoming information is great, individuals must narrow the range of their attention and consider only limited aspects of the incoming information at that point in time.

Selective Attention   Research indicates that the two principle influences on selective aspects of attention are the *relevance* of the information to the individual's needs and the *novelty* of incoming information.

When selecting among stimuli, consumers are prone to attend to information that is related to their salient needs. A person considering the purchase of a new suit will pay attention to information about suits—ads in the newspaper, articles describing the latest fashions, and so on. Thus, marketers can increase the level of attention directed toward their messages by making them pertinent to consumers' actual needs.

relevance

Novel or unexpected information also attracts attention. For example, people tend to direct their attention to loud noises, movement, vivid colors, and flashes of light. In the consumer context, unexpected events can be unusual packaging, price decreases, unusual advertisements, and extreme positive or negative aspects of a product.

novelty

When the information presented does not require a lot of attention, people are able to divide their attention and process several inputs at once. For example, people are able to attend to simple television commercials at the same time they are watching their children play. However, unless further processing of the "unattended" information is undertaken, this information will not be recalled even a short time later.

Measurement of Attention   Marketers frequently use measures of attention to evaluate television commercials and print advertising.[8] Measures requiring verbal responses are often used to measure attention, on the assumption that respondents could not recall aspects of an ad unless they had paid attention to it. However, these verbal-response measures assess the nature of information processing in addition to the intensity and selectivity of attention.

Two nonverbal methods for measuring the attention and processing effort directed toward a stimuli are *pupillary dilation* and *eye movement*. Attention is assessed by exposing consumers to a stimulus (an ad or package) and using a pupilometer to measure pupil dilation, increases in the size of the pupil. At one time, it was felt that increases in pupil size, like increases in skin resistance (GSR), indicated an increase in arousal. Recent research, however, suggests that pupil dilation measures more than simple arousal: It indicates a combination of arousal level, mental effort, and the amount of information that a subject is processing with respect to the stimulus.[9]

nonverbal measures

In the past, pupil dilation and GSR were considered to be measures of affective response to a stimulus. An increase in GSR or pupil dilation indicated that the observer was favorably disposed toward the stimulus. However, research indicates that these measures assess only *changes* in activation level and not whether those changes are positive or negative. Thus, GSR and pupil dilation will increase when consumers are exposed to very irritating ads as well as when they are exposed to ads that elicit a favorable response.

Krugman describes some interesting research on the use of pupil dilation to determine the amount of attention or processing capability consumers allocate to processing television ads.[10] He found that the greatest pupil dilation occurred during the first ten seconds of a sixty-second commercial. This peak reading was strongly related to the average pupil dilation for the entire commercial. Thus, it appears that the amount of attention consumers pay to a commercial is based on a decision made at the beginning of the commercial.[11]

While pupil dilation assesses attention intensity, *eye movement analysis* is used to examine the selective nature of attention. Advertisers can determine the parts of an ad that attract and hold attention by tracking the eye movements of people exposed to the ad.[12] The summary of an eye-tracking study to pretest an ad for a new liqueur is shown in Exhibit 5–2.

In this study, one hundred consumers were exposed to twelve ads, including the Arrow Pina Colada ad and ads for other liqueurs, cigarettes, cameras, and automobiles. After their eye movements had been monitored, consumers were shown the Arrow Pina Colada ad and each was asked to describe the product to a friend, indicating beliefs, evaluations, and purchase interest in the product. Eye-movement data shows that most respondents focused initially on the headline statement, and moved through the "First . . . . Then" visual, to the bottle, and then to the name at the bottom of the ad. However, only 42 percent actually saw the name and fewer than 40 percent read the headline.

This eye-movement information coupled with other information collected indicated an execution problem with this ad. The *Arrow* name and the primary sales message were not communicated effectively. Most consumers were confused, believing that Arrow Pina Colada was a premixed cocktail rather than a liqueur.

MEMORY AND INFORMATION COMPREHENSION

The **comprehension** stage of information processing follows the exposure and reception stages (see Exhibit 5–1). In the comprehension stage, people draw upon their prior experiences and information stored in the memory to assign

EXHIBIT 5–2
THE SUMMARY OF AN EYE-TRACKING STUDY

Upper Figure = % Noting
Lower Figure = % Reading

Average Viewing Time: 8.9″

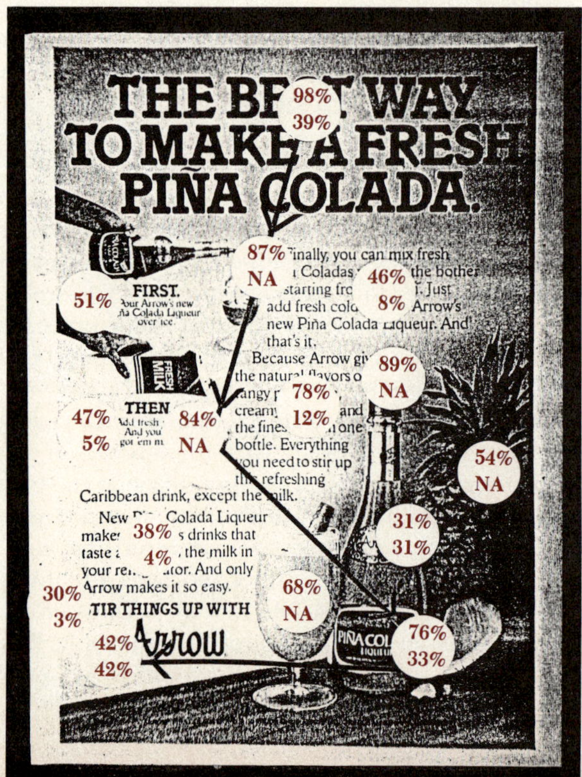

meaning to the recently received information.[13] Since memory is intimately related to the comprehension process, we will first discuss the nature of memory. Then we can examine the interaction between incoming information and memory.

Memory Stores

There are many different theories about the structure of memory and how it works. Perhaps the most influential concept of memory is that memory is composed of multiple stores—a **sensory store** (SS), a **short-term memory store** (STM), and a **long-term memory store** (LTM).[14] Each store serves a different function and has unique properties. A model based on the multiple stores concept is shown in Exhibit 5–1.

Information processing in memory begins when the information passes from the sense organs (eyes, ears, nose, and so on) to an associated sensory store. Information is retained in SS for only a fraction of a second. If the information is unattended, it is lost. However, if attention is directed to the information, the information is processed and transferred to short-term memory store (STM). The processing undertaken in SS is limited to determining the physical properties of the stimulus, such as size, color, or loudness.

The STM is the center of active information-processing activity. Information from the SS and long-term memory stores (LTM) is brought together in the STM to interpret the incoming information. Strategies using information in LTM in combination with information in STM are referred to as *memory control processes*. Based on the results of the processing in STM, the information in STM can be transferred to LTM and permanently stored. LTM is thought to have unlimited capacity to store information permanently.

Short-Term Memory   The short-term memory store has a limited capacity to process information at one point in time. Miller was first to suggest that the capacity of STM is approximately seven chunks of information, where a chunk is a collection of information that is processed as one unit.[15] For example, a nine-digit Social Security number can be processed as nine chunks of information—2–7–1–3–6–7–2–9–1. However, people typically recode these nine chunks into three chunks, 271–36–7291, so that they can be easily recalled and processed in STM.[16]

In a marketing context, information about a product is usually stored as one chunk of information in the form of the product's brand name. This chunk contains a great deal of information concerning the nature of the product— information that could not be processed at one time in STM if it were stored as separate chunks. The packaging of marketing information into chunks represented by symbols such as the Pillsbury *Doughboy* or the *Jolly Green Giant* assists consumers in accessing and using this information.

In addition to its limited capacity to process information, STM's capacity to retain information is limited. Unless information is actively processed, it will be lost from STM in about thirty seconds.[17]

Long-Term Memory The long-term memory store consists of a set of concepts and the associations between these concepts. The concepts stored in LTM include events, objects, characteristics of objects, evaluative information concerning objects, temporal sequences, and rules for processing information such as "check the prices of the various cereal brands." In addition to these semantic concepts, visual images and auditory information are stored in memory.

The semantic concepts are organized into a network of nodes and links between the nodes.[18] Each node is a concept, and a link indicates an association between concepts. An illustration of part of a memory network in one person is shown in Exhibit 5–3. This example shows the interrelation be-

network of nodes and links

EXHIBIT 5–3
EXAMPLE OF MEMORY NETWORK

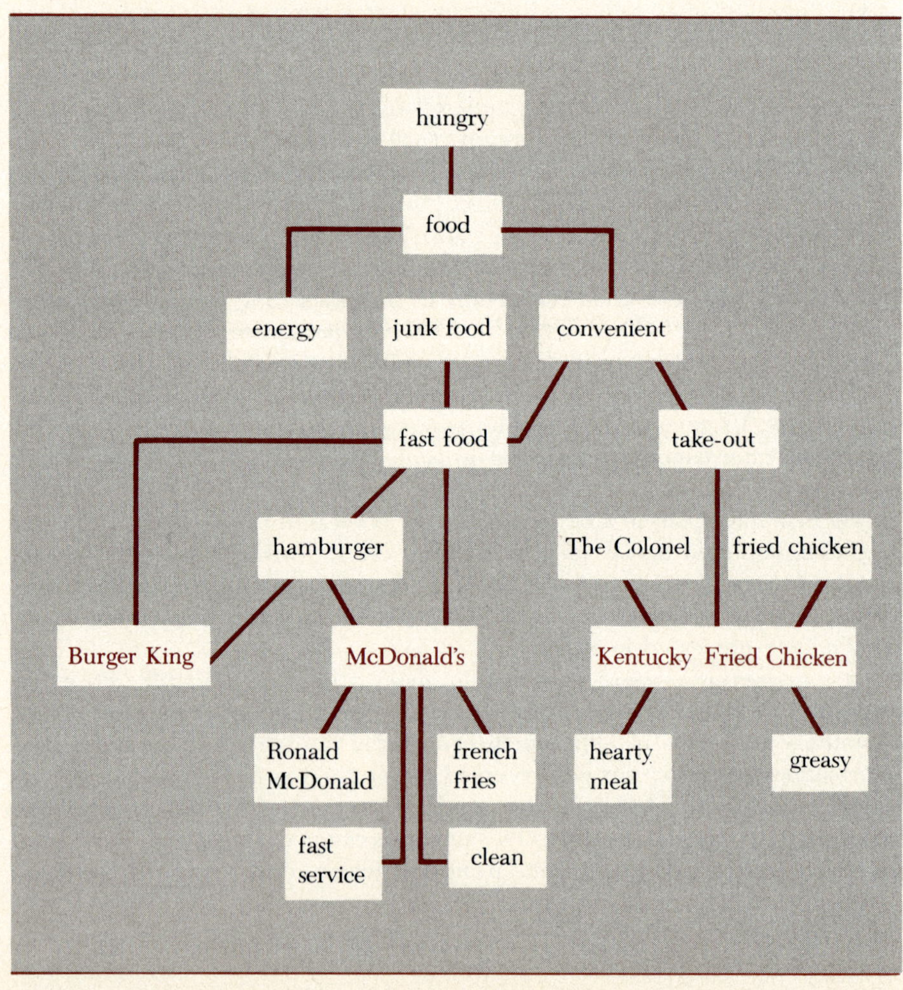

tween the nodes or concepts of *food, fast food, McDonald's,* and *Kentucky Fried Chicken.* Each of these links is a cognition—a product-attribute association. Naturally, the memory structure will be different for each individual.

The activation of a single node leads to the the activation of adjacent nodes. For example, a person driving through a city may see a McDonald's. The sight of the McDonald's might provide some arousal. If the person attends to the McDonald's, the McDonald's node in memory is activated. When this node is activated, the adjacent nodes of *fast food, Ronald McDonald, fast service, french fries,* and *clean* are activated. All of these concepts may be brought into STM as one chunk.

In another situation, a person's internal state of hunger may activate the *food* node. When the *food* node is activated, the *convenient* node may be activated and ultimately the *Kentucky Fried Chicken* concept may be activated and brought into short-term memory.

This example demonstrates that some concepts (nodes) stored in memory can be quite general, such as *food,* while other concepts are quite specific, such as *The Colonel.* In addition, some concepts, such as *McDonald's,* may have many associations with other concepts, while other concepts, such as *Burger King,* may have few associated concepts. Of course, the situation may be just the reverse for another consumer.

The cluster of concepts related to the McDonald's concept can be referred to as the person's *schema* for McDonald's. This represents a person's stereotype of what a McDonald's is like. The illustration in Exhibit 5–3 suggests that this person has a well-developed schema for McDonald's. The schema could have been developed through prior visits to McDonald's, from discussions with friends, or by seeing commercials on television. The poorly elaborated schema for Burger King might be due to lack of exposure to information about Burger King.

schema

Memory Control Processes

Memory control processes[19] are the techniques used to control the flow of information in and out of STM and LTM. In some instances these processes are habitual or "unconscious" processes. However, people can actively or "consciously" use these memory control mechanisms to process information.

Rehearsal When a concept or piece of information is brought into short-term memory, further processing is needed to keep it active in STM and eventually to store the information in long-term memory. **Rehearsal** is the control process used to maintain the concept in STM.

Rehearsal can be thought of as the silent repetition of the concept. The more time the concept is rehearsed, the longer the concept will be active in STM, and the greater will be the retention of the concept when it is eventually stored in LTM. In fact, researchers have observed that speech muscle (lip, chin, and throat) activity increases when people are actively processing information even though they are not actually talking.[20]

However, the retention of a concept is not directly related to simple repetition or rehearsal. Simple rehearsal may be adequate to retain a simple concept such as a street address, but it is not enough to retain a complex concept. To retain a complex concept, the concept must be interconnected with other concepts in memory. Such interconnectors are established by elaborated rehearsal—the new concept is rehearsed together with other concepts stored in memory.

Coding   People use information in long-term memory to develop methods for rehearsing a concept. Images, mnemonics, and association are used to **code** a concept and assist in the rehearsal process. For example, brand names may be associated with images stored in memory that reflect the name.[21] For example, advertising for Marlboro cigarettes has associated the brand with an image of a rugged cowboy. This image is so strong that the mere picture of a cowboy holding a cigarette is sufficient to stimulate the rehearsal of the Marlboro brand name.

Transfer   The **transfer** process governs the selection of information to be stored in LTM. This selection is based on a kind of cost-benefit tradeoff. Information that provides a high benefit related to a person's needs or goals and that can be transferred easily at a low psychological cost is likely to receive a high priority.

Placement   **Placement** refers to where the information is stored in memory—the specific nodes to which it is connected. The placement decision is related to the person's expectations about how the information will be used in the future. If a consumer expects to purchase a food processor soon, information on food processors will have priority over information related to products which do not interest the consumer. Since the consumer plans to use the food-processor information soon, the consumer will attempt to store the information in a form that is accessible when the food-processor node is activated. When a person does not anticipate using information, less effort is spent in storing the information, thus the information may be stored using an easily executed transfer-and-placement mechanism—a mechanism that may make retrieval difficult.

Retrieval   The **retrieval** process is perhaps the most crucial memory-control process. Once information is encoded, transferred, and placed in LTM, it is always available.[22] Physiologically, the central nervous system retains all information unless some profound injury to the brain occurs. However, only a limited amount of this stored information is accessible. Thus, forgetting is not due to a decay or loss of information. It is due to an inability to retrieve the information—a failure of the retrieval mechanism. This notion can be seen intuitively by considering the times that you could not remember something, but when you were confronted with a cue, all of a sudden you could remember. Initially, you were not using the appropriate retrieval mechanism; however, the cue provided you with the correct retrieval mechanism.

The retrieval of information is directly related to how the information was

encoded and placed in LTM. For example, if information about the characteristics of a brand is presented along with a symbol for the brand, the symbol
and brand information will be closely associated and tranferred to LTM together. To facilitate the retrieval of the product-related information, marke-

EXHIBIT 5–4
ILLUSTRATION OF MEMORY PROCESSES

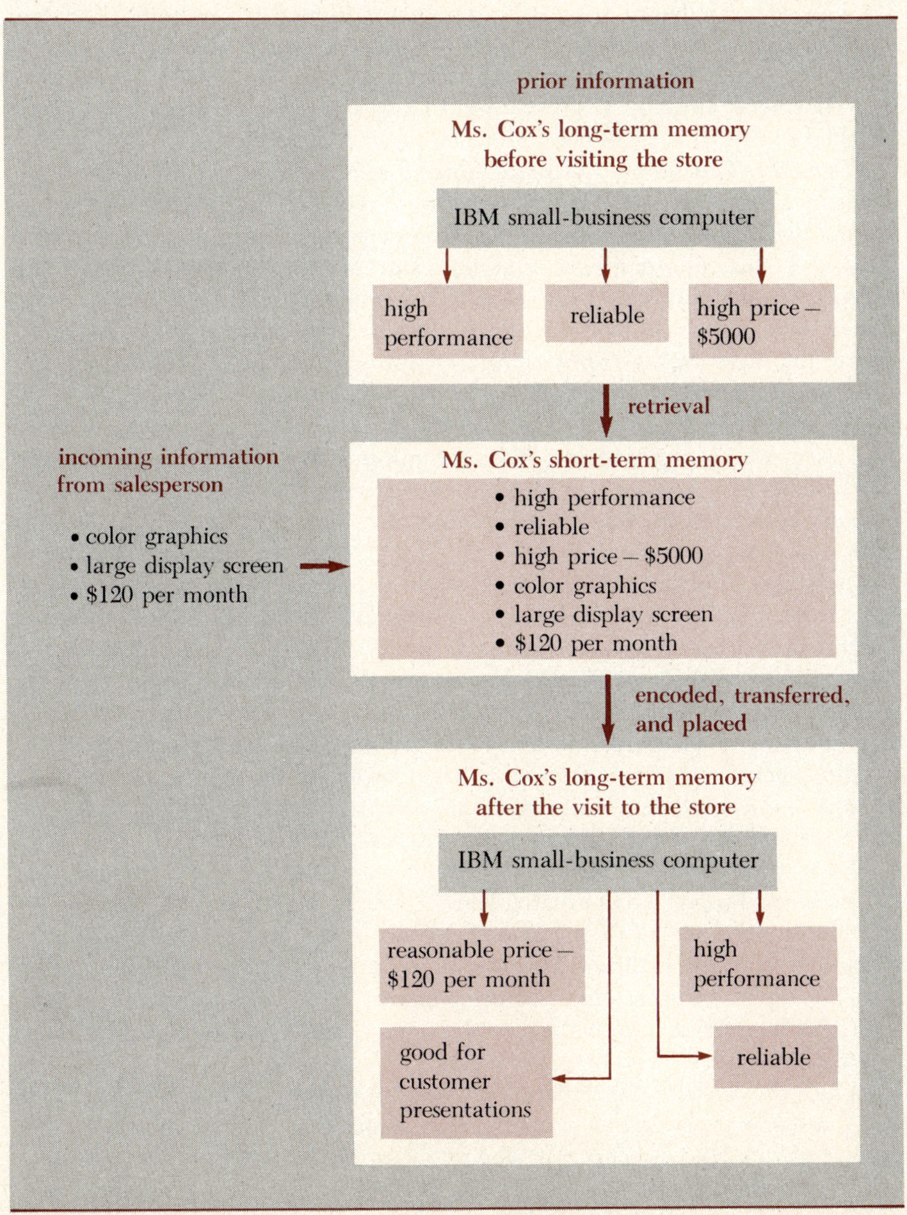

ters may display the symbol at the point of purchase. Thus, "Mikey" in the Life cereal television commercials is on the cereal package to trigger the retrieval of information about Life cereal presented in the ad with "Mikey."

Memory Processes: An Illustration

In order to illustrate the memory stores and control process, consider Ms. Audrey Cox, the owner of a small marketing-research firm, who is interested in purchasing a computer for the business. Prior to entering a computer store, Ms. Cox's knowledge of business computers is limited to the names of a few manufacturers and an image of the IBM computer as reliable and as a good performer but high priced—costing around $5000. This image of the IBM small-business computer is stored in her long-term memory as three concepts attached to the IBM small-computer node (see Exhibit 5–4).

When Ms. Cox enters the retail store, a salesperson greets her, finds out that she is interested in a computer, and demonstrates the IBM computer. During the demonstration, the salesperson emphasizes two unique features of the IBM—the color-graphics capability and the large-screen display. The salesperson mentions that these capabilities will enable Ms. Cox to make effective presentations of market-research data to her clients. Finally, the salesperson indicates that the IBM computer can be purchased for only $120 per month over a five-year period.

The information presented by the salesperson is represented in Exhibit 5–4 as *incoming information*. This incoming information is stored in Ms. Cox's short-term memory. She then retrieves information from long-term memory associated with an IBM computer and adds it to the incoming information in short-term memory.

These six chunks of information are rehearsed, processed, and recoded in short-term memory. The *high price—$5000* and *$120 per month* chunks are combined and coded into a *reasonable price—$120 per month* chunk. The *color graphics* and *large display screen* are also combined, into a *good for customer presentations* chunk. Eventually, this recoded information in short-term memory is transferred to long-term memory and connected to the *IBM small-business computer* node. When Ms. Cox leaves the computer store, the information in her long-term memory concerning an IBM small-business computer is quite different from when she entered the store.

Notice that in this illustration, the information about color graphics and large-screen display is not retained in long-term memory. Ms. Cox retains only the benefit of these two product characteristics and not the specific information about the features. This retention of the results of processing rather than the inputs to processing is quite common. However, the product characteristics could also have been retained, connected to the *good for customer presentation* node.

In this illustration, the structure of long-term memory was not altered by the transfer-and-placement process. The associations between nodes were preserved; just the concepts attached to the *IBM small-business computer* node were changed. However, the transfer-and-placement processes can alter the structure of memory. For example, the sales presentation could have changed Ms. Cox's view of small-business computers. Before entering the store, she had never considered using the computer to make client presentations. Her memory was organized in terms of several brand names emanating from a *small-business computer* node (see Exhibit 5–5). After seeing the demonstration, she felt that a major application of the computer would be client presentations.

This change in perspective about computers could lead to the reorganization of Ms. Cox's memory into two groups of computers—those that are *good for client presentations* and those that are *poor for client presentations*. If this reorganization had occurred, Ms. Cox would have then had difficulty retrieving information about the Atari and Osborne computers because this information would no longer be closely associated with the type of small-business computer she needs.

Product Position and Memory

From an information-processing perspective, the positioning of a brand is determined by the associations between the brand and various concepts in long-

EXHIBIT 5–5
ILLUSTRATION OF A REORGANIZATION OF MEMORY

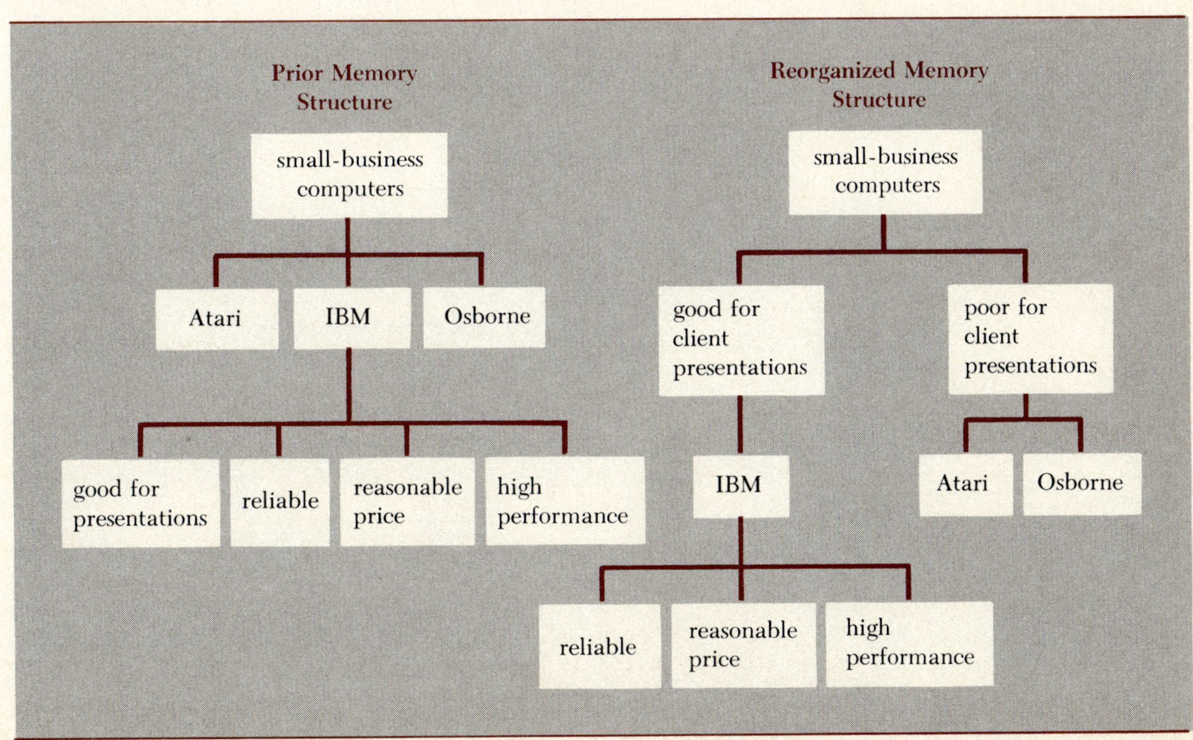

term memory. For example, the reorganization of memory shown in Exhibit 5–5 repositioned the IBM computer from a *small-business computer with several attributes* to the *small-business computer that is good for making client presentations*. The memory-network example in Exhibit 5–3 shows McDonald's and Burger King are positioned as *hamburger, fast-food* facilities, while Kentucky Fried Chicken is positioned as a *fried-chicken, take-out* establishment.

Thus, a positioning *strategy* focuses on establishing a unique set of associations for a brand. Often, these associations are linked to usage situations— using a small-business computer for client presentations or accounting, taking convenient food out or eating it in the restaurant. Some other examples of positioning strategies based on associations with usage situations are provided by Canada Dry ginger ale and Schaeffer beer.

Most people associate ginger ale with mixers for alcoholic beverages. Thus, ginger ale is more closely associated with club soda than with noncola soft drinks such as 7-Up. To increase the usage and sales of ginger ale, Canada Dry has attempted to reposition ginger ale by increasing its association with soft drinks.

The Schaeffer beer campaign focusing on "The beer to have when you're having more than one" can be viewed as an attempt to reorganize long-term memory concerning beers. Rather than organizing beers into *standard, premium, light,* and *super-premium* nodes, this campaign suggests that beers should be organized into *beers to have when you're having one* and *beers to*

EXHIBIT 5–6A
PRODUCT PARTITIONS

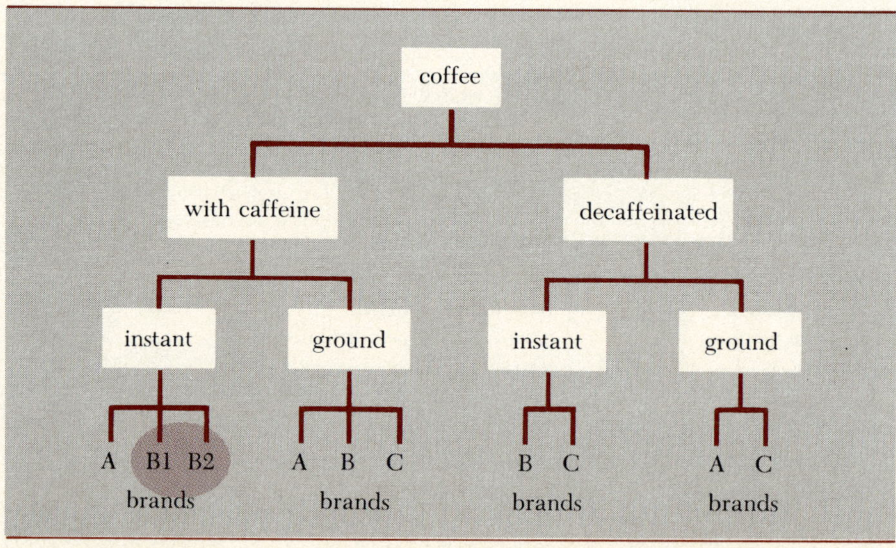

have when you're having more than one nodes. Schaeffer's would be uniquely associated with or positioned in the second category.

Product Partitioning and Memory

Product partitioning refers to the way consumers view a market. Consumers make a number of hierarchically ordered decisions to classify brands into various categories. For example, some consumers may initially divide the coffee market into *with-caffeine* and *decaffeinated* groups. The market can be further subdivided into *ground* and *instant* categories. Within each of these four categories there are several brands available. This view of the coffee market is shown in Exhibit 5–6A. Other consumers may have a totally different view of the market. They may first divide the market on the basis of brands (such as *Maxwell House* and *Folgers*). Within each brand, the market can be subdivided into *with-caffeine* and *decaffeinated* and *instant* and *ground* (see Exhibit 5–6B). Of course, there are many other possible partitions for the coffee market.

Not all consumers perceive the coffee market the same way, so there are probably several market segments, each with a different view. The managerial

EXHIBIT 5–6B
PRODUCT PARTITIONS

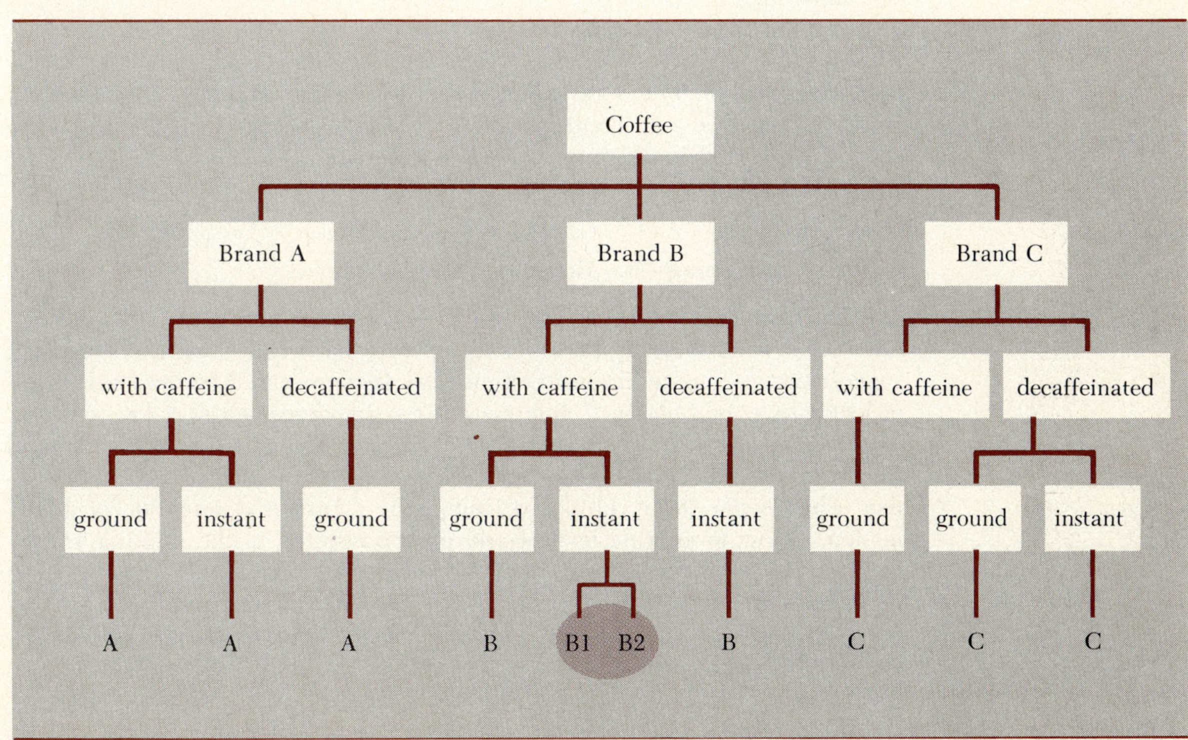

implication of product partitioning is that the partitioning defines the set of alternatives that consumers will consider. If the partitioning shown in Exhibit 5–6A represented the consumer's view of the coffee market, consumers buying a *with-caffeine, instant coffee* would select between Brand A and the two products from Brand B, B1 and B2, because these brands are the only ones grouped under *with-caffeine, instant.* The excitation of the *coffee* node would excite the *with-caffeine* node, which would excite the *instant* node, and, finally, brands A, B1, and B2 would be transferred to short-term memory.

However, if Exhibit 5–6B represented the consumer's view, the selection would be either A or between B1 and B2 because the excitation of the *coffee* node results in the excitation of a brand node before the *with-caffeine* and *instant* nodes are excited. Thus, Brand A would not be considered if the consumer had an overall brand preference for Brand B, since the consumer would have focused on a brand before examining the type. If the consumer had an overall preference for Brand C, the consumer would buy Brand C *with-caffeine, ground* because there is no Brand C *with-caffeine, instant.*

The brands connected to the bottom nodes on the exhibit are the consideration set up by the consumer. There is more loyalty to a brand under the partition in 5–6B. Thus, if company A wanted to introduce a new brand of ground, with-caffeine coffee, it would take a share away from B and C under the partition in 5–6A, but cannibalize from its other brand under the partition in 5–6B.

Thus, knowledge of product partitions is useful for developing product-line strategies. Typically, product partitions are identified using mathematical models to analyze brand-switching data.[23] However, an analysis of memory structures may be a more direct approach. Basically, the product partitions shown in Exhibit 5–6 depict the memory networks of consumers related to the coffee node.

Levels of Processing—An Alternative View of Memory

Our discussion so far has focused on the multiple-stores model of memory; other models for memory have been proposed, however. Craig and Lockhart suggest that the limited capacity of memory is represented by different *levels* of processing information.[24] Information can be processed at a low sensory level, as in noting that a dress is yellow, or at a deeper level, as in relating the style and cost of the dress to what the person who is wearing it must be like. The deeper the level of processing, the greater the retention of information. A low processing level would be represented in the multiple-stores model as information residing in STM with limited rehearsal, while a deep processing level would be represented as extensive rehearsal of information in STM using information in LTM to comprehend the new information. While the multiple-stores model and level-of-processing model differ in many respects, they both are consistent with the idea of limited processing capacity and the need to allocate that capacity to process incoming information.

These descriptions or models of memory multiple stores and level of processing—should not be taken literally. The multiple-stores model does not suggest that there are *physical* areas of the brain in which short-term and long-term memory reside. Similarly, the level-of-processing model does not contend that lightly processed information is on the surface of the brain, whereas heavily processed information is physically stored deeper in the brain. These memory models are just conceptual schemes that are useful for organizing research findings concerning how people process information. The value of these models is determined by the degree to which research findings can be explained by the models and the ability of the models to predict the impact of influence strategies on information processing.

Computers and Human Memory

The description of memory and memory-control processes in this section implies that a person can be viewed as a computer—an IBM with skin. There are some similarities. Both people and computers process information, and the information processing may be organized in a similar fashion. However, there are important differences.[25]

Humans have great input capabilities, unlimited and very efficient permanent memory, but slow and inefficient short-term memory. Computers are just the opposite. They are very limited in information input and permanent memory but they are efficient at making accurate calculations in their computing registers (short-term memory). Thus human information processing is suited for relatively slowly changing information in which good approximations are sufficient. However, human information processing can draw parallels between different events and process several events at one time. On the other hand, computers are designed to process one job (or event) at a time, but to do this job rapidly with perfect accuracy.

COGNITIVE RESPONSES

The information-processing perspective we have discussed assumes that people are not passive receivers of information. They actively process incoming information in short-term memory, drawing on information stored in long-term memory to assign meaning to the incoming information. Based on this active processing, consumers will either integrate the incoming information with their existing memory structure or ignore the information completely. If the information is integrated, it may be represented accurately or distorted.

Assessing Message Impact

Thus, the impact of marketing communication does not depend simply on the information in the message, but on the *interaction* between the thoughts in   **interaction**
the message and the thoughts brought up from the recipient's memory. Since

the knowledge structures of individuals differ, depending upon their experiences, the impact of a marketing communication will not be the same for all consumers exposed to the message.

Cognitive responses provide a method for investigating the active processing of incoming messages. Peter Wright has been a pioneer in using this approach for examining advertising effectiveness.[26] The basic notion behind cognitive-response methodology is that people generate cognitive responses, thoughts, and ideas as they relate their existing knowledge to the incoming information. These cognitive responses determine the impact of the message—whether or not it will be integrated into the existing knowledge structure, and the form in which it will be integrated.

Measuring Cognitive Responses

Cognitive responses are measured using a thought-monitoring approach. Immediately after exposure to an ad, consumers are instructed to list all thoughts or ideas that occurred to them while they were watching the ad. The time that the consumers have to list their thoughts is limited to a few minutes to minimize the probability of collecting thoughts generated after rather than during the message. The group of responses is referred to as a *protocol*.

protocol

After the protocol has been collected, the individual thoughts or cognitive responses are then coded. The principal categories of cognitive responses are shown below.[27]

type of cognitive response	definition	examples
counterarguments	refutation of message claim	"The Polaroid picture quality isn't that good."
support arguments	support of message claim	"The Polaroid looks easy to use.
source derogation	negative characterization of message source	"James Garner doesn't know anything about cameras."

In addition to these cognitive-response categories, protocols typically contain general statements that support or discount the message, such as "I believe it" or "I don't like the product."

Cognitive Responses and Message Acceptance

Research indicates that **counterarguments** are the most prevalent responses and that they are strongly related to message acceptance. Message acceptance decreases when counterarguing is high. The presence of **support arguments** is not as strongly related to message acceptance.[28]

An analysis of cognitive responses provides insights into how people integrate incoming information with information in their long-term memory or cognitive structure. Consider situations in which consumers are favorably disposed toward a product. These consumers have mostly positive concepts related to the product. When they retrieve information from memory to interpret incoming information about the product, it is likely to be favorable. Their cognitive responses reflecting the retrieval and rehearsal processes will be either general statements like "Tide is a good detergent" or support arguments like "The new Tide [described in the ad] is even better at getting tough stains out." A preponderance of *general* cognitive responses reflects a limited amount of rehearsal and suggests that the cognitive structure of the consumers will not be altered by the ad. However, if the ad instigates support arguments, consumers are engaging in more rehearsal, and the information in the message will probably be integrated into long-term memory. On the other hand, when consumers do not like a product, an ad for the product may lead to the generation of a lot of counterarguments. Negative information about the product will be retrieved and rehearsed with the positive incoming information in the ad.

INFORMATION PROCESSING AND MARKETING COMMUNICATIONS

An information-processing perspective provides some interesting insights into the design of marketing-communications programs. In this section, we examine the effects of repetition and mode of communications from an information-processing viewpoint.

Repetition

A basic concept in advertising is that repeating a message increases recall, recognition, and the likelihood of product purchase. For example, in a laboratory study, Ray and Sawyer found that the percentages of subjects recalling an ad increased from 27 percent to 74 percent as the number of repetitions increased from one to six.[29] Although recognition and recall increase as the number of repetitions increases, there are diminishing returns. For additional repetitions, there are smaller and smaller gains in recall and recognition.

Repeating messages increases the probability that the message contents will be stored in long-term memory.[30] Just the sheer number of repetitions insures that the message is stored in a more easily retreived form in memory. But repetition can also have a more active processing effect. On the first exposure, a consumer may begin to develop a plan for using the information in the ad. For example, the consumer may think, "That product is interesting. I'll have to pay more attention next time."[31] The effects of repetition on learning are considered in more detail in Chapter 9.

There are circumstances, however, in which repetitions can have a negative effect on recall and recognition. When consumers have negative attitudes toward a product, increased repetitions appear to result in more negative attitudes.[32] This effect probably arises because each repetition results in the retrieval of negative thoughts. The more repetitions, the greater the rehearsal of negative information.

wearout

In addition, some researchers have observed that message effectiveness actually declines at very high levels of repetition.[33] This phenomenon, termed *wearout*, might arise because consumers learn everything there is to know in ads after a number of repetitions. Beyond this point, consumers no longer process the favorable information in the ad, but instead focus their processing on the information retrieved from long-term memory. It is likely that some negative information about the product is in long-term memory. Thus, a high level of repetition favorable to the mix of information processed shifts from *almost exclusively* to *mostly* favorable.

Mode of Communications

The three major methods or modes for providing information to consumers (outside the store) are *television commercials, radio commercials,* and *print advertisements.* The degree to which consumers utilize information presented via these modes differs because of the unique properties of each mode. Television commercials provide both visual and auditory information, whereas radio commercials provide only auditory. Print ads provide only visual information, but impose fewer processing contraints than television and radio commercials. Consumers can control the amount of time they have to process information in print ads. They can spend more time on specific aspects of the ad that interest them, and ignore information that is not useful. The time allocated to processing radio and television commercials, however, is strictly limited to the length of the commercials.

Because of these differences, messages that are difficult to process are more easily recalled when transmitted in print. The self-pacing nature of the print mode permits consumers to spend enough time to absorb the information. However, the differences in recall between the types of communication are decreased when messages are easily understood.[34]

Visual images have a powerful effect on memory. Studies have shown that people, after being shown 600 pictures, can recognize a specific ad over 87 percent of the time after 7 days and 58 percent of the time after 120 days.[35] These findings would suggest that visual modes, television, and, to a lesser extent, print, would achieve greater information acceptance than radio. However, there may be some unintended consequences of providing complex, visual images. The images may unintentionally trigger the retrieval of some unfavorable thoughts.

SUMMARY

We have examined how consumers process information and incorporate it into long-term memory. Information processing begins with the reception of information. To receive information, the information-processing system needs to be activated and some processing capacity allocated to incoming information. Marketers can determine if stimuli such as product advertising activate the information-processing system of a consumer by measuring the consumer's level of arousal. When activation occurs, the level of arousal increases. The intensity level of attention measures the amount of processing capacity that is allocated to the incoming stimulus. Attention also has a selectivity aspect. *Selectivity* refers to the specific aspect of the stimulus to which attention is directed. Stimuli that are related to a consumer's needs and are novel attract attention.

Memory plays a crucial role in information processing. The permanent store for information is long-term memory, while the active processing of information occurs in short-term memory. In short-term memory, meaning is assigned to incoming information by using information stored in long-term memory. As a result, recoding or restructuring of information stored in long-term memory can occur.

Product positioning and product-line strategies can be directly related to how information is stored in memory. Positioning strategies are directed toward creating unique association between the brand and product attributes. These associations are represented by connections between brand-name nodes and attribute nodes in long-term memory. The organization of brand names and attributes in memory determines which brands will be considered when a consumer contemplates a purchase decision.

Cognitive responses provide a method for assessing how consumers process information. The responses reflect the rehearsal and retrieval processes occurring in short-term memory, and thus can be used by marketers to understand how consumers are processing information about marketing stimuli.

KEY CONCEPTS

cognitive analysis	sensory memory	information coding
attention stage	short-term memory	information transfer
passive exposure	long-term memory	information placement
active exposure	arousal	information retrieval
information reception	selective attention	cognitive response
information comprehension	memory control processes	counterargument
information retention	rehearsal	support argument

DISCUSSION QUESTIONS

1. What determines the probability of a consumer's *receiving* the information to which he or she is exposed?
2. Why should marketers utilize symbols to promote brands?
3. How can evaluation of product partitions and memory structures be used in the formulation of marketing strategy?
4. Why would the effect of a marketer's message be different among the consumers exposed to it?

5. What are the unique properties of the major modes of communication, and what implications do these properties have for advertising strategies?
6. What impact does the difference in information-processing for high-involvement and low-involvement products have on marketing communication?
7. Watch TV for one hour during an evening. One hour later, jot down all the commercials you remember seeing. What is it about these commercials that caused you to remember them? What are the implications for marketing communication?
8. Discuss the relationship between information coding and the retrieval process. How can marketers insure that their information, once communicated, is easily retrievable by consumers?

NOTES

1. Michael Rothschild (1979), "Marketing Communications in Non-Business Situations or Why It's So Hard to Sell Brotherhood like Soap," *Journal of Marketing*, 43 (Spring), pp. 11–20.
2. For a more detailed discussion of information processing see James R. Bettman (1979), *An Information Processing Theory of Consumer Choice* (Reading, Mass.: Addison-Wesley) and John A. Howard (1977), *Consumer Behavior: Application of Theory* (New York: McGraw-Hill).
3. Daniel Kahneman (1973), *Attention and Effect* (Englewood Cliffs, N.J.: Prentice-Hall).
4. John Deighton (1983), *Advertising's Influence on Consumers' Use of Evidence: The Bias of Confirm*, unpublished Ph.D. dissertation, The Wharton School, Univ. of Pennsylvania.
5. Daniel Kahneman (1973), pp. 37–42.
6. Michael Eysenck (1976), "Arousal, Learning, and Memory," *Psychological Bulletin*, 83 (May), pp. 389–404.
7. Paul J. Watson and Robert Gatchel (1979), "Automatic Measure of Advertising," *Journal of Advertising Research*, 19 (June), pp. 15–26 and Werner Kroeber-Riel (1979), "Activation Research: Psycho-Biological Approaches in Consumer Research," *Journal of Consumer Research*, 5 (March), pp. 240–50.
8. David Aaker and James Myer (1982), *Advertising Management*, 2nd ed. (Englewood Cliffs, N.J.: Prentice-Hall).
9. Roger D. Blackwell, James S. Hensel, and Brian Sternthal (1970), "Pupil Dilation: What Does It Measure?" *Journal of Advertising Research*, 10 (Aug.), pp. 15–18 and Michael W. Eysenck (1977), *Human Memory: Theory, Research, and Individual Differences* (Elmsford, N.Y.: Pergamon Press), p. 184.
10. Herbert E. Krugman (1968), "Processes Underlying Exposure to Advertising," *American Psychologist*, 23 (Apr.), pp. 245–53.
11. For other measures of attention and information processing, see John G. Lynch and Thomas K. Srull (1982), "Memory and Attentional Factors in Consumer Choice: Concepts and Research Methods," *Journal of Consumer Research*, 9 (June), pp. 18–37.
12. For an example, see Joan Triesman and John P. Gregs (1979), "Visual, Verbal, and Sales Response to Print Ads," *Journal of Advertising Research*, 19 (Aug.), pp. 41–47.
13. For an excellent treatment of the role of memory in consumer behavior, see James R. Bettman (1979), "Memory Factors in Consumer Choice: A Review," *Journal of Marketing*, 43, pp. 37–53.
14. Richard C. Atkinson and Richard M. Shiffrin (1968), "Human Memory: A Proposed System and Its Control Processes," in *The Psychology of Learning and Motivation: Advances in Research and Theory*, ed. K. W. Stone and J. T. Spence, vol. 2 (New York: Academic Press) and (1971), "The Control of Short-Term Memory," *Scientific American*, 225 (Aug.), pp. 82–90.

15. George A. Miller (1956), "The Magical Number Seven, Plus or Minus Two: Some Limits on Our Capacity to Process Information," *Psychological Review*, 63, pp. 81–97.

16. Herbert A. Simon (1974), "How Big Is a Chunk?" *Science*, 183 (Feb.), pp. 482–88.

17. Richard M. Schiffrin and Richard C. Atkinson (1970), "Storage and Retrieval Processes in Long-Term Memory," *Psychological Review*, 76, pp. 179–83.

18. Nico H. Frijda (1972), "Simulation of Human Long-Term Memory," *Psychological Bulletin*, (Jan.), pp. 1–31.

19. See James Bettman (1979), *An Information Processing Theory*, pp. 143–47.

20. John Cacioppo and Richard Petty (1979), "Attitudes and Cognitive Response: An Electrophysiological Approach," *Journal of Personality and Social Psychology*, 37, pp. 2181–99.

21. See Kathy A. Lutz and Richard J. Lutz (1977), "Effects of Interactive Imagery on Learning: Applications to Advertising," *Journal of Applied Psychology*, 62, pp. 493–98.

22. See Donald J. Lewis (1979), "Psychobiology of Active and Inactive Memory," *Psychological Bulletin*, 86, pp. 1054–83.

23. See Manohar U. Kalwani and Donald G. Morrison (1977), "A Parsimonious Description of the Hendry System," *Management Science*, 23 (Jan.), pp. 467–77.

24. Fergus I. M. Craig and Robert S. Lockhart (1972), "Levels of Processing: A Framework for Memory Research," *Journal of Verbal Learning and Verbal Behavior*, 11, pp. 671–84. See also Jerry C. Olson (1981), "Theories of Information Encoding and Storage: Implications for Consumer Research," in *Effects of Information on Consumer and Market Behavior*, ed. A. Mitchell (Chicago: American Marketing Assn.).

25. James Bettman (1979), *An Information Processing Theory*, p. 151 and Earl B. Hunt and Walter Mackous (1969), "Some Characteristics of Human Information Processing," in *Advances in Information Processing*, ed. J. Tou, vol. 2 (New York: Plenum), pp. 282–335.

26. Peter L. Wright (1973), "Cognitive Processes Mediating Acceptance of Advertising," *Journal of Marketing Research*, 10 (Feb.), pp. 53–62 and (1978), "Cognitive Responses to Mass Media Advocacy and Cognitive Choice Processes," in *Cognitive Responses in Persuasion*, ed. R. Petty, T. Ostrum, and T. Brock (New York: McGraw-Hill).

27. For a more detailed categorization of cognitive responses, see Richard J. Lutz and John L. Swasy (1977), "Integrating Cognitive Structure and Cognitive Response Approaches to Monitoring Communications Effects," in *Advances in Consumer Research*, ed. W. D. Perreault, Jr., vol. 4 (Assn. for Consumer Research), pp. 363–71.

28. Peter L. Wright (1978).

29. Michael L. Ray and Alan G. Sawyer (1971), "Repetition in Media Models: A Laboratory Technique," *Journal of Marketing Research*, 8 (Feb.), pp. 20–29.

30. See Andrew Mitchell and Jerry Olson (1977), "Cognitive Effects of Advertising Repetition," in *Advances in Consumer Research*, ed. W. D. Perreault, Jr., vol. 4 (Assn. for Consumer Research) and Alan Sawyer (1980) "Repetition and Cognitive Responses," in *Cognitive Responses to Persuasion*, ed. R. Petty, T. Ostrum, and T. Brock (New York: McGraw-Hill).

31. Herbert E. Krugman (1972), "Why Three Exposures May Be Enough?" *Journal of Advertising Research*, 17 (Dec.), pp. 7–12.

32. See S. Saegert, W. Swap, and R. Zajonc (1973), "Exposure, Contact, and Interpersonal Attraction," *Journal of Personality and Social Psychology*, 25, pp. 234–42.

33. C. Samuel Craig, Brian Sternthal, and Clark Leavitt (1976), "Advertising Wearout: An Experimental Analysis," *Journal of Marketing Research*, 13 (Aug.), pp. 365–72 and Bobby Calder and Brian Sternthal (1980), "Television Advertising Wearout: An Information Processing View," *Journal of Marketing Research*, 17 (May), pp. 173–86.

34. S. Chaiken and A. H. Eagley (1976), "Communication Modality as a Determinant of Message Persuasion and Message Comprehensibility," *Journal of Personality and Social Psychology*, 34, pp. 605–14.

35. Lionel Standing (1975), "Learning 10,000 Pictures," *Quarterly Journal of Experimental Psychology*, 25, pp. 353–78.

6 Low-Involvement Cognitive Processes

A considerable proportion of all consumer behavior is of a "low-involvement" nature. Most consumers simply do not care very much about what facial tissues to buy, what gasoline to buy, or what coffee to buy. Cognitive energies are likely to be conserved in these purchase decisions, often by using simple heuristics, such as brand loyalty or brands on sale. High cognitive involvement does characterize some forms of consumer behavior, such as the selection of a car or a college to attend, and it is for these decisions that considerable information-seeking and information-processing often occur.

By **involvement** we mean the level of identification and personal relevance the purchase decision holds for the consumer. Under high-involvement conditions (as in buying cars or clothing), the purchase-decision process is characterized by considerable identification and personal relevance. But under low-involvement conditions (as in buying paper towels or detergents), the purchase-decision process is characterized by a lack of identification and personal relevance. We expect that the nature and level of cognitive processing will be quite different under these high- and low-involvement conditions.

This chapter develops a conceptualization of cognitive involvement with a particular focus on low-involvement consumer behavior. We shall review theory and research on low involvement with special relevance to consumer decision processes. Then we shall consider the implications for marketing strategy; that is, how will the marketing program differ for high- versus low-involvement products?

PRODUCT VERSUS BRAND INVOLVEMENT

Involvement varies by *product category*. One research study among college students developed the following continuum, which indicates the involvement levels which students have with a number of products, from automobiles (high involvement) to facial tissues (low involvement).[1]

High Involvement — Automobile — Blue Jeans — Stereo Speakers — Beer — Blanket — Toothbrush — Soap — Facial Tissue — **Low Involvement**

Involvement also varies by *brand*. Even in low-involvement product categories, there may be high-involvement brands: Perrier in water or Gucci in shoes, for example. Such high-involvement brands, however, may account for only a limited proportion of total consumption in the product category. Conversely, for high-involvement products, there may not be high involvement for all brands. Exhibit 6–1, for example, shows an advertisement for a low-involvement, generic cigarette. This advertisement was run by Ligget and Myers, the tobacco company that is dominant in the manufacture of "no-name" brand cigarettes. Research by Traylor also has shown that for some high-involvement durable goods, such as refrigerators and furniture, there may not be much brand involvement.[2]

Exhibit 6–2 shows the relationships between product and brand involvement. Some purchase decisions (such as choosing a car) are high on both product and brand involvement, whereas other purchase decisions (such as choosing paper towels) are low on both product and brand involvement. However, there can be purchase decisions in which product involvement is low and brand involvement is high (Perrier in water) or in which product involvement is high and brand involvement is low (such as furniture).

Factors Affecting Involvement Level

Consumer involvement level in the purchase-decision process depends on a number of factors, the most important of which are *cost, interest, perceived risk, situation*, and *social visibility*.

Cost Most research on involvement indicates that involvement increases with the cost of the good being purchased, as we have seen in the involve-

ment continuum—although there are some exceptions. Similarly, research among households finds that automobiles, appliances, and furniture are higher in involvement than packaged goods and food products.[3] This is hardly surprising and, in some ways, it is the exceptions that are interesting. One such exception is the high involvement among college students with blue jeans, as indicated in the involvement continuum, perhaps because of their social visibility.

Interest Involvement is highly related to consumer interests. Consumers seem to have domains of interest, such as entertainment, food, clothing, cars, or electronics, but they are not interested in all product categories. For example, although toothpaste is a reasonably low-involvement product category, it is highly important for some people—the market segment that is very concerned with self-presentation and social acceptance. This segment includes many teenagers and young adults.

Perceived Risk Involvement is likely to increase with the consumer's **perceived risk** in making a purchase. The level of risk perceived for a purchase decision is a function of the possible *consequences* in purchase and the *likeli-*

hood of these consequences. Thus, some products, although relatively inexpensive, may be high in perceived risk and involvement—for example, the wine for a dinner party, since there are perceived social consequences of choosing the wrong wine.

Situation   Involvement in the purchase-decision process also varies by situation; that is, with how the product will be used. The selection of a particular brand, for example, may be low in involvement for family consumption but high in involvement for consumption with guests. A company which bottles Bubble-Up once told us that the brand sold well for weekday consumption but that consumers switched to the more socially acceptable 7-Up for weekend consumption.

New situational conditions may also heighten people's involvement in consumer decision processes and lead to greater information processing. Newlyweds, newly divorced, and those moving to a new community are in such situations. For these people involvement in purchase decision-making will tend to be high until learning occurs and habits are established.

Social Visibility   Finally, involvement seems to increase with the extent to which the product is socially visible. This may help account for the high involvement with jeans among college students. In general, products which are on "social display," such as clothes, cars, and furniture, have high involvement levels.

EXHIBIT 6–2
PRODUCT/BRAND-INVOLVEMENT RELATIONSHIPS

		Brand Involvement	
		High	**Low**
Product Involvement	**High**	• Cars • Some clothing (especially designer labels)	• Furniture • Appliances
	Low	• Water (Perrier) • Shoes (Gucci)	• Many grocery items, especially paper goods and cleaning products

SOURCE: Based on Mark B. Traylor (1981), "Product Involvement and Brand Commitment," *Journal of Advertising Research,* 21 (Dec.), pp. 51–56.

THEORY AND RESEARCH ON LOW INVOLVEMENT

Krugman's Low-Involvement Learning Theory

A number of research streams in psychology and consumer behavior have found distinctions between high and low involvement. Particularly influential is the work of H. E. Krugman who, nearly twenty years ago, articulated a high/low-involvement distinction which is regularly cited in contemporary marketing.

Krugman's main focus was on advertising, and he suggested that consumers were not involved in most advertising, particularly television advertising. He likened television advertising's effects to the learning of trivia[4] and suggested a fairly passive, rather than active, learning process. By *involvement*, Krugman meant the number of conscious, bridging experiences or "connections" between the advertising communication and the viewer's own life; the more the connections, the greater the involvement.

In later work, Krugman distinguished involvement in *print media* (newspapers and magazines) from involvement in *broadcast media* (television and radio).[5] Print media create higher involvement since they require more thinking and concentration, whereas broadcast media tend to ask little of the viewer or listener and therefore frequently create only low involvement (especially radio, which is frequently "background"). This distinction has been validated in recent research on television viewing by Csikszentmihalyi and Kubey, who conclude, "Television viewing was found to be a relatively unchallenging activity requiring little cognitive investment and consistently tied to feelings of relaxation, passivity, and drowsiness."[6]

The importance of Krugman's work is that he proposed an alternative model of the purchase-decision process to the traditional model discussed in Chapter 4. Instead of the usual decision process which proceeds from information to attitude change to behavior, Krugman suggested that under low-involvement conditions, the decision process might proceed from information to behavior (purchase) and then attitude change. The effect of advertising under low involvement, according to Krugman, is that it acts gradually on perceptions at some less conscious level, without the audience's thinking very much nor recognizing that the advertising is influential. Alternatively, under high-involvement conditions, advertising acts on the consumer's conscious opinions about the brand by offering persuasive evidence.

Incidental Learning

The effects of advertising under low-involvement conditions might be equated to *incidental learning*[7] rather than to *intentional learning*. When we attend to material with the goal of learning or memorizing it, we exhibit *intentional learning*. This mental set is, however, relatively uncommon. Most of what we attend to in the world does not need to be recalled verbatim. Yet we find some recall to be the unintended by-product of even casual attention. This is termed **incidental learning**—as, for example, when children sing a commercial to which they have been exposed again and again.

Incidental learning may be rather passive and uncritical. Similarly, a great deal of advertising is incidental to the audience at the time it is received. The audience may process it uncritically and, given enough repetition, the low-involvement hierarchy of effects may operate; that is, exposure leads to purchase which then leads to attitude change.

Some evidence for the high- versus low-involvement modes can be found in a program of research by Ray[8] and his co-workers. Ray and Sawyer, for example, found in some experiments that repetitions shifted recall and attitude first, then intention to purchase, findings which support the high-involvement mode.[9] Other experiments in this program found shifts in recall and intention to purchase without a shift in attitude, supporting the low-involvement mode. Silk and Vavra reported a similar result, in which advertising affected recall of the brand, but not attitude toward the brand.[10] A study by Kapferer also provides evidence that persuasion can affect behavior without affecting attitude.[11] He mailed either one *or* three letters to students urging them to go to the Student Health Service for a free blood-pressure check-up. Repetition (the three letters) increased response from 4.9 percent to 15.2 percent. It had no effect on recall, recognition, or attitude toward getting such a test or intention to do so. Because the letters were not carefully read, the content of the argument did not seem to be important.

Sherif's Social Judgment Theory

An alternative theory in the low-involvement tradition is Sherif's **theory of social judgment.** Sherif's concept of involvement is tied to a person's acceptance or rejection of persuasion, including advertising.

The thesis is that a highly ego-involved individual will have a narrower **latitude of acceptance** regarding persuasion than a less involved person. For example, if a person's ego is involved in ownership of a car, the tendency will be to reject competing advertisements. A less involved person, in contrast, will tend to be less resistant to competing advertisements. *Ego-involvement* is defined as the proximity of a persuasive attempt (such as an advertisement) to attitudes which "define a person's status or give him some relative role with respect to other individuals, groups, or institutions."[12]

Social-judgment theory suggests three possible outcomes to a persuasive attempt, such as advertising. The advertising may fall within the latitude of acceptance, of noncommitment, or of rejection. Advertising advocating an opinion consistent with an individual's beliefs will fall within the latitude of acceptance and be assimilated, evaluated as fair, and produce positive attitude change. Advertising counter to an individual's beliefs will fall within the latitude of rejection and be resisted, evaluated as biased, and may produce attitude change opposite to what is intended. Advertising that is not relevant to any existing beliefs (low involvement) will fall within the latitude of noncommitment and is less subject to either assimilation or rejection.[13]

Involvement, then, is an important concept mediating advertising effectiveness. Involved consumers interpret advertising in line with existing attitudes and opinions and, therefore, have narrow latitudes of acceptance and wide latitudes of rejection. The uninvolved consumer, however, brings fewer attitudes to bear and has a wider latitude of acceptance in response to advertising.

HIGH- VERSUS LOW-INVOLVEMENT CONSUMER DECISION PROCESSES

Now we shall explore the contrast between high- and low-involvement consumer decision processes. You should remember, however, that this distinction overstates the case and that a *range* of involvement has actually been found. Exhibit 6–3 specifies a set of cognitive dimensions on which high- and low-involvement decision processes can be distinguished. We shall examine each in turn.

Information Seeking

As might be surmised, under high-involvement conditions the consumer actively engages in **information seeking** about products and services. Under low-involvement conditions, in contrast, the consumer is not highly motivated and seeks little information. Olshavsky and Granbois, for example, in a review of consumers' prepurchase information seeking, put the low-involvement view this way:

> A *significant proportion of purchases may not be preceded by a decision process. . . . How then does purchasing occur. . .? Purchases can occur out of necessity; they can be derived from culturally-mandated lifestyles. . . ; they can reflect preferences acquired in early childhood; they can result from a simple conformity to group norms or from imitation of others; purchases can be made exclusively on recommendations from personal or non-personal sources; they can be made on the basis of surrogates of various types; or they can even occur on a random or superficial basis.*[14]

Indeed, there is even some debate as to how much information consumers acquire for high-involvement products. Olshavsky and Granbois conclude that, even when prepurchase information seeking occurs, it is limited: "It typically involves the evaluation of few alternatives, little external search, few evaluative criteria, and simple evaluation process models."[15] Some sense of the levels of information seeking that consumers conduct is reflected in the following findings:

limited information search

- A study by Granbois found that many consumers visited only one store before making a purchase—22 percent of furniture buyers, 50 percent of color-television buyers, and 75 to 80 percent of soft-goods (e.g., towels and sheets) buyers.[16]

- Research by Bucklin found that only 10 percent of shoppers for shoes and personal-care accessories sought advertising information; only 5 percent of appliance and furniture shoppers sought advertising information.[17]

After considerable research on consumer decision processes for appliances, Katona and Mueller concluded, "Any notion that careful planning and choosing, thorough consideration of alternatives, and information seeking accompanied every major purchase was contradicted by the data; . . . many purchases were made in a state of ignorance, or at least indifference."[18]

In order to gain a more balanced perspective on information-seeking levels, consider two points. First, it is necessary to maintain cognizance of the costs

EXHIBIT 6–3
HIGH- VERSUS LOW-INVOLVEMENT CONSUMER DECISION PROCESSES

Behavioral Dimension	High-Involvement View	Low-Involvement View
Information Seeking	• Consumers actively seek product and brand information	• Consumers seek limited product and brand information
Cognitive Response	• Consumers resist discrepant information and utilize counterarguments	• Consumers may passively receive discrepant information with limited counterarguments
Information Processing	• Consumers process information in a hierarchy-of-effects decision sequence	• Consumers process information in a simplified awareness to trial-decision sequence
Attitude Change	• Attitude change is difficult and rare	• Attitude change is frequent but transient
Repetition	• Sheer number of messages will be less important than message content in achieving persuasion	• Sheer number of messages may result in persuasion
Brand Preference	• Brand loyalty is common	• Consumers may routinely buy the same brands but may not be "loyal"
Cognitive Dissonance	• Post-purchase dissonance is common	• Postpurchase dissonance is uncommon
Personal Influence	• Other people are used for information and social-imitation purposes.	• Other people exert little personal influence

involved in information seeking—time, money, and possible frustration. Many consumers obviously do not find the rewards to be greater than the costs incurred. Especially for low-involvement products, there is an unwillingness to commit cognitive energy to extensive information seeking. Second, consumers may have different information-seeking styles and preferences for varying kinds of information sources. Research by Westbrook and Fornell, for example, suggests that appliance buyers can be classified by the information sources they use: Some use the store as an information source; some use neutral sources (such as *Consumer Reports*); and some use personal sources (such as friends and neighbors).[19] Few consumers, however, will make heavy use of all sources.

Cognitive Response

A further distinction between the high- and low-involvement views of consumer decision processes is in the consumer's **cognitive response** to persuasion, especially advertising. Consistent with social judgment theory, the high-involvement view is that consumers resist discrepant information (such as advertising for a brand that they don't use) and counterargue against the discrepant advertisement. The low-involvement view is that consumers may passively receive discrepant information, since there is no commitment to an existing brand. Thus, consumers will have limited cognitive defenses or counterarguments to advertising for low-involvement products.

Indeed, evidence supports the view that when involvement is low, discrepant messages are less likely to arouse counterargument than when involvement is high. Wright and Weitz[20] manipulated involvement toward birth-control methods by varying the time before a purchase decision would have to be made. When involvement was assumed to be low (long time period before decision), counterargument was less likely than when involvement was assumed to be high (short time period). In a similar vein, Ray has found that respondents have greater interest in reading information which is opposed to their views when the subject is noncontroversial.[21]

We might now ask whether a greater number of messages "get through" to the consumer in low-involvement conditions. Most advertising research assumes that a message gets through if it achieves recall on a short-term basis. At least that is the operational measure on which most advertising-research funds are expended and on which most advertising decisions are based. If this is what we mean by *message reception*, then most messages don't get through. But what if a message gains consumer *exposure*, although not short-term recall? Could not exposure alone be a sufficient cause of purchase under conditions of low-involvement consumer behavior when the amount of learning necessary is often totally minimal? We would then argue that *impact may correlate highly with exposure* under low-involvement conditions.

This is a critical point. Despite the popular myth that viewers head for the kitchen or the bathroom during commercials, the research evidence doesn't bear this out—most viewers stay put. Steiner, for example, found that 89 percent of those viewing television remain in the room at the time of the commercial; that is, they are "exposed" to the commercial.[22] Ward, Robertson, and Wackman, in research with children replicating the Steiner study, found that 92 percent of the children remained in the room and were exposed to commercials.[23]

Thus, whether the consumer pays explicit attention or not, and whether some learning, as measured by recall, occurs or not may be irrelevant for low-involvement products. Since the learning requirement is often so minimal, frequency of exposure may be the key to impact. This is not unlike Krugman's analogy between advertising and nonsense syllables and his conclusion that "exposure to mass media content is persuasive per se!"[24]

Information Processing

Another contrast between high and low involvement occurs in the consumer's **information processing.** The high-involvement view is that consumers process information in a "hierarchy of effects" adoption process (see Exhibit 6–4). The consumer is assumed to progress through a sequence of steps from awareness, to interest, evaluation, trial, and adoption (repeat purchase). The low-involve-

EXHIBIT 6–4
THE ADOPTION PROCESS UNDER HIGH- AND LOW-INVOLVEMENT CONDITIONS

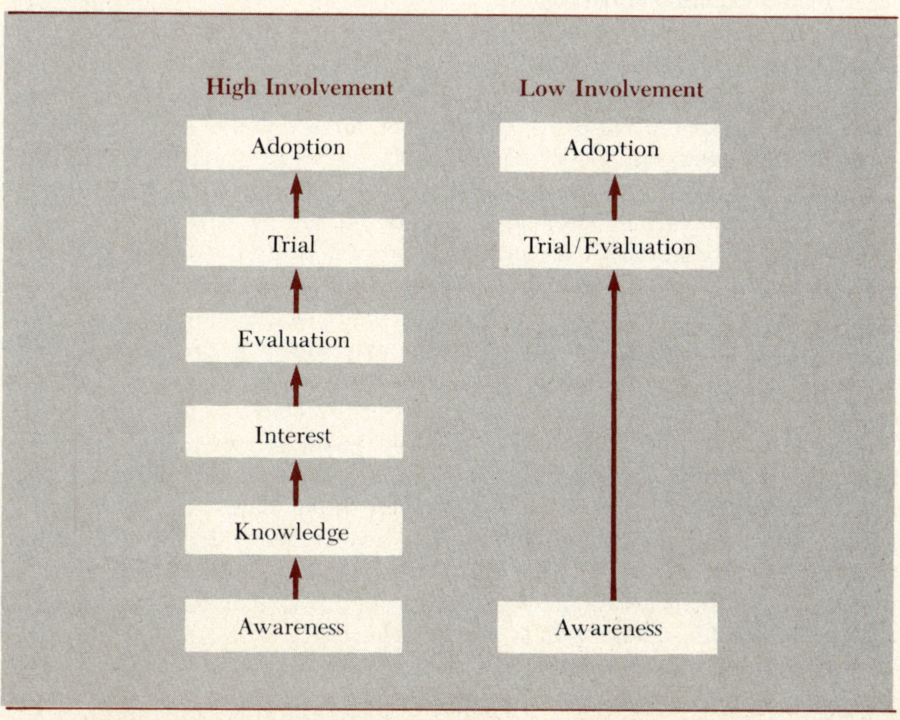

ment model does not reject this intuitively appealing hypothetical framework. Instead, it suggests that the hierarchy may often be collapsed and that awareness and trial followed by evaluation are the only *necessary* stages preceding adoption. For example, the response to an advertisement for a new packaged food may be trial, which is often the simplest way to test the product, rather than information seeking and processing.

In research on information processing, Ray and his colleagues found the low-involvement hierarchy to hold true somewhat more often than the high-involvement hierarchy—referred to as the "learning hierarchy" by these researchers.[25] The low-involvement hierarchy was particularly prevalent for convenience goods. The implication is that consumer information processing varies by involvement level.

Attitude Change

The process of bringing about **attitude change** may be different under high than under low involvement. The thesis is that attitude change occurs more easily, but is more transient, under low-involvement conditions. This thesis derives from attitude theory (to be discussed in Chapter 11), which suggests that attitudes under low involvement have less intensity and less knowledge to support them. They are, therefore, more susceptible to change when exposed to counterpropaganda (competing brand advertising, for example), although this change will be fairly unstable, and the attitude may change again for yet another brand's advertising.

A highly involved consumer, however, may be more motivated to think about the information presented in an advertising message—as long as the message "gets through." Therefore, an advertising message based on strong arguments and sound logic may have more impact under high- than low-involvement conditions. Thus, the advertising message is much more critical if the attitude change is to be achieved under high-involvement conditions.

Several researchers in the field of attitude change have used involvement level to suggest differences in persuasion strategies. Early work at Yale suggested that involvement level determines whether or not a communicator should draw explicit conclusions. Hovland, Janis, and Kelley proposed that explicit conclusions should be drawn when involvement is low, but not when it is high. They hypothesized that on low-involvement issues, an audience might be willing to "borrow" the opinions of the communicator, but when involvement is high, an explicit conclusion would be resisted.[26] Hovland, Janis, and Kelley also considered whether a communication should present its most powerful arguments first or last. When the audience is initially minimally interested in the communication (low involvement), they proposed that strongest arguments should come first. When audiences have enough curiosity to pay attention to the opening statements (high involvement), strongest arguments should be held back to create a climax.

Sherif and Sherif[27] considered whether a persuader should take a position very far from that of the listener—or only slightly different. Again, the most effective strategy hinged on involvement. With low-involvement they claimed that a major discrepancy in positions is likely to persuade the audience, whereas with high involvement such a discrepancy will not be effective.

It has also been suggested that involvement level determines whether a communicator should forewarn an audience that an attempt is about to be made to change its mind. Several studies support the idea that forewarning *inhibits* persuasion of highly involved audiences, but has precisely the opposite effect on uninvolved audiences. In an illustrative study, Apsler and Sears used a message advocating that college classes be taught by teaching assistants rather than professors. To create high involvement one group was told that the policy was slated for one year hence; to create low involvement another group was told that the policy was to be introduced in twelve years. The two groups were then separated into people who were forewarned and people who were not forewarned. Forewarning had the opposite effects on the two groups. The low-involvement subjects accepted the policy more when forewarned than when not. The high-involvement subjects were more resistant to the policy when forewarned than when not.[28]

forewarning

Finally, involvement seems to have a bearing on the level of attitude change due to **source effects,** that is, attitude change brought about by the perceived characteristics of the communicator—independent of the message. The general view is that source effects, resulting, for example, from the charisma, credibility, or attractiveness of the communicator, apply mainly under low-involvement conditions. In contrast, the message content is more influential under high-involvement conditions.[29] This suggests that endorsers will be more important for low-involvement than high-involvement products.

Repetition

Krugman has predicted that the uninvolved consumer needs more **repetition** of a message to be persuaded than the more highly involved consumer. Although the resistance of an uninvolved consumer to discrepant messages is low (given the wide latitude of acceptance), interest is also low, so that multiple exposures are required to have influence. The implied converse is that highly involved consumers can be persuaded with fewer messages.

The value of repetition was researched in a study of high- versus low-involvement elections. A senatorial race was chosen as the high-involvement condition and a county-treasurer race as the low-involvement condition. The result was that repetition had its major effect on voting in the low-involvement race. The disturbing conclusion reached by the researchers is that ". . . within limits in the low-level races, but not the high, the candidate with the greater advertising budget can win the election."[30]

Recently, the work of Zajonc on the effects of repetition has received growing attention. Although he does not explicitly limit his conceptualization to conditions of low involvement, all of his experimental work employs uninvolving kinds of stimuli. Zajonc's early work demonstrated the **mere exposure effect,** namely, that *mere exposure to an object is sufficient to produce liking* *of the object.* He exposed subjects to unfamiliar objects, such as Chinese ideographs, nonsense syllables, and faces. Those objects with high frequency of exposure were later rated more positively on attitude scales than objects with lower exposure.[31]

Zajonc's later research has made the controversial claim that this liking is not a result of familiarity, but is in some sense "pre-cognitive," that is, *without* a thought process. He has evidence to suggest that exposure can increase liking even when it is insufficient to create recognition.[32] The implication apparently is that communication may influence an audience's liking for an object, product, or brand without necessarily engaging its cognition. This claim, backed by research, may offer contemporary support for Krugman's idea that low-involvement communications bypass perceptual defenses.

Brand Preference

Brand preferences may exist for both high- and low-involvement product categories. However, the motivational bases for these preferences may be different. Under high-involvement conditions, brand preferences may represent the development of a fairly complex attitude structure and a loyalty to that brand. In extreme cases of high involvement—such as BMW ownership for a certain set of consumers—the attitude may be backed by a fairly extensive technical knowledge or an experience base to justify the brand preference.

In a low-involvement product category, brand preferences are also common. However, the attitude structure may be fairly simple and tenuous. Routinization of brand selection is generally the preferred mode of purchase because it involves less energy and fewer decisions. The act of decision-making, which is often frustrating, can logically be handled by repetitive buying behavior. Brand loyalty may reflect, therefore, only the convenience inherent in repetitive behavior rather than much commitment to the brand purchased. This argument is consistent with the mass brand switching which often occurs because of the entry of new products into the market, innovative advertising appeals, or consumer price deals. Consumers may simply get bored with habitual purchases, even under conditions of low involvement, or may have a need for variety or "stimulus variation."[33] The consumer may, in fact, be interested in maintaining some intermediate level of stimulus variation between habitual purchase and constant switching.[34]

Cognitive Dissonance

In the study of consumer behavior, **cognitive dissonance** refers to the psychological discomfort that people often experience after buying something. (This concept is developed more fully in Chapter 11, "Consumer Attitudes".) Dissonance occurs because the consumer is committed to a brand decision, yet may have doubts about how good the decision is. The other brands also had desirable features or might have been cheaper or might be more popular.

Almost by definition, cognitive dissonance is a function of the level of involvement. For high-involvement purchases, dissonance is a common phenomenon, and consumers will seek to overcome it—for example, by seeking information consistent with their decision. The most likely person to read brand advertisements for a new car is the person who has just bought that brand. For low-involvement purchases, however, there is by definition very little commitment to the brand purchased, and the consumer should experience only minimal cognitive dissonance. If you buy a new facial tissue and don't like it, you will simply reject it. You don't have to seek ways of confirming that you bought the right brand.

Some postpurchase rationalization may still occur, however, for low-involvement purchases. This may help account for the development of brand preferences despite the overwhelming similarities among brands in many low-involvement product categories. **Attribution theory,** which suggests that people attribute motives to their actions *after* the fact,[35] helps to account for such rationalization. The logic seems to be, "If I buy it, then it must be good." This is often the case even when consumers cannot tell one brand from another in a blind taste test.

Personal Influence

Finally, the high- and low-involvement views are distinguished by the levels of **personal influence** which operate. For high-involvement products, like clothes and other "social" products, consumers may use other people as sources of information or may imitate other people. For low-involvement products, however, personal influence may be low, just as all information sources are less influential under low involvement.

Personal influence (see Chapter 16) is operative mainly when a product is on social display or when the purchase is important and ego-involving. By its very nature, therefore, personal influence applies to high-involvement information seeking and is not very likely to operate under low-involvement conditions.

MARKETING STRATEGIES UNDER LOW-INVOLVEMENT CONDITIONS

Under low-involvement conditions, the marketing manager's objective is to find ways to build involvement toward his or her brand. The alternative, a brand perceived to be interchangeable with other brands in the product category, is likely to result in highly price-sensitive sales and low profits (unless the brand has significant cost advantages).

The following are strategies for building involvement:

1. achieving innovation or product differentiation,
2. achieving perceived differentiation based on advertising, and
3. reaching high-involvement market segments.

If these strategies are infeasible, then the challenge is to build sales and profitability under conditions of low involvement. Some strategies are as follows:

1. using advertising weight to generate sales,
2. designing advertising content appropriate to low-involvement conditions,
3. designing distribution support programs, and
4. "dealing" the brand to increase sales.

A further strategy is to achieve cost advantage over competitors, but we shall not cover this option since it would carry us beyond the boundaries of this discussion.

Building Involvement: Product Differentiation

innovation

Perhaps the most logical means of achieving product differentiation in order to build involvement is *innovation*. When Sony's Walkman portable stereo system was introduced, for example, it stood alone in the marketplace, where it achieved high involvement and it commanded a high price. Over time, as competition has duplicated the Sony feat, the question is then whether further innovation can occur (Walkman 2 and Walkman 3), which will again build involvement for that brand over others in the market.

salient attribute

A related means of achieving differentiation in order to build involvement is through a **salient attribute.** The challenge here is to find a way of setting the brand apart from others in the product category. Two examples of differ-

EXHIBIT 6–5
MARKETING STRATEGIES FOR BUILDING BRAND INVOLVEMENT

I. Build involvement by achieving product differentiation.
   A. Seek product innovation.
   B. Find a salient attribute to achieve differentiation.
II. Build involvement by advertising.
   A. Achieve symbolic differentiation via advertising.
   B. Use high-credibility endorsers in advertising.
   C. Link the brand advertised to a high-involvement situation.
   D. Link the brand advertised to another high-involvement brand.
III. Build involvement by segmenting the market by involvement level.
   A. Place primary emphasis on the high-involvement segment.
   B. Reach the high-involvement (opinion leader) segment to influence the low-involvement segments.
IV. Alternatively, accept low involvement.
   A. Generate sales based on advertising weight.
   B. Design advertising content appropriate to low-involvement conditions.
   C. Focus on distribution programs for retailer support to generate sales.
   D. Generate sales based on dealing.

entiation based on a salient attribute are the Harvard Business School (the "case method") and 7-Up ("no caffeine"). These "products" have achieved high levels of differentiation *relative to competition.* Indeed, the involvement level achieved still depends on the product category and will obviously not be as high for the selection of a soft drink as for the choice of a business school to attend. However, the objective is to achieve involvement *sufficiently* high relative to other brands in the product category to gain some measure of competitive advantage.

7-Up is an interesting example of a brand which was in the doldrums until it focused on its lack of caffeine: "Never had it. Never will." It was not the only brand of soft drink without caffeine, but it was the first to focus aggressively on this attribute, which had become salient as the American public was exposed to the scientific controversy surrounding caffeine's possible harmful effects. Other brands then followed with no-caffeine products, but 7-Up had by then built momentum and increased involvement.

Building Involvement: Advertising

Advertising may be used to build involvement (1) by achieving *symbolic differences,* (2) by utilizing *source effects,* (3) by linking the brand to a *high-involvement situation,* or (4) by linking the brand to another *high-involvement brand.*

A considerable amount of the perceived differentiation among products is actually **symbolic,** rather than any actual difference that the consumer might detect when products are unlabeled, for example, or presented in a blind taste test. A prime example of creating symbolic differentiation is provided by Miller beer. When Phillip Morris acquired Miller in the early 1970s, Miller, with its "High Life" and "Champagne of Bottled Beer" campaigns, was an also-ran, number five in beer sales. Phillip Morris changed the advertising symbolism, creating a working-class aura and "Quitting Time is Miller Time." Miller is now number two in beer sales, an achievement made without any actual change in the product—only a change in the advertising symbolism.

Advertising may also build brand involvement by the use of *source effects.* Consumers not involved in a product category may be reached by extraneous cues, such as endorsers. Research by Petty and Cacioppo, for example, finds some tentative evidence that under low-involvement conditions, ". . . non-content factors such as the credibility or attractiveness of the message source are more important."[36] Examples of endorsers to build brand involvement in low-involvement product categories are Bill Cosby for Coca-Cola, Don Meredith for Lipton tea, and Bruce Jenner for Tropicana orange juice.

Advertising may also build brand involvement for a low-involvement product by linking the brand to a *high-involvement situation.* Eveready, for example, has advertised its batteries—surely a low-involvement product—using high-involvement situations; in one a car is shown broken down on a deserted road late at night, with the driver dependent on his or her flashlight batteries to signal for help. Goodyear tires has advertised similarly, linking its brand to

symbolic differences

source effects

high-involvement situation

a high-involvement situation by focusing on family safety: a mother and children are shown driving in the rain at night.

Finally, advertising may seek to build involvement by linking the brand to another *high-involvement brand* in the same product category. In fact, much comparative advertising explicitly links a low-involvement brand to a high-involvement brand—in effect to borrow from the positive attributes of the high-involvement brand. Thus, comparative advertisements may refer to Coca-Cola (but not to Royal Crown Cola) or to Perrier (but not to Poland Springs water).

Building Involvement: Segmentation

Different market segments may have varying levels of product involvement. A general marketing assumption is that the high-involvement segment is the more profitable one, since it will generally include the heavy users and will generally be less price sensitive. However, it is necessary for marketers to determine just how large the high-involvement segment is; it may or may not be large enough to warrant an exclusive marketing focus. Some stereo and camera manufacturers, for example, go after only the high-involvement market segment.

A related strategy suggested by Tyebjee is to try to reach the *entire market by marketing initially to the high-involvement segment.*[37] The hypothesis for testing here is that the high-involvement segment has higher opinion leadership; that is, the people in this segment are sought for advice and influence by their peers. If the high-involvement segment (for example, camera buffs) can be identified, and if they have disproportionate influence on their peers, then succeeding with high-involvement consumers may be the key to reaching the entire market.

Accepting Low Involvement

If building involvement is considered infeasible, then what strategies are available for low-involvement products—products like salt, paper towels, or aluminum foil? Under low-involvement conditions, there are at least four means of generating sales: (1) through advertising weight or scheduling, (2) through advertising content, (3) through distribution programs, and (4) through price dealing.

In low-involvement product categories, *advertising weight* may be the key to sales since the message content is essentially the same for all competitors. Given the minimal learning requirements under low involvement, the sheer repetition of the message may "get through" to consumers—even if there is limited encoding of the message. As we saw earlier in this chapter, the effects of repetition seem to be more pronounced for low-involvement products than for high-involvement products, for which the message *content* is of much more importance.[38]

Appropriate *advertising content* also can be effective under low-involvement conditions. Rothschild and Tyebjee, for example, indicate that the amount of information in an advertising message should be limited to one or two key points since consumers have little interest in processing information.[39] Tyebjee also suggests heavy repetition of the brand name for low-involvement products. Other authors have suggested that elements of argument in advertising communications are much more important for high-involvement products.[40] Finally, it has been suggested that advertising for low-involvement products should be oriented to inducing trial.[41]

Focusing on *distribution programs* to support retailers is another means of generating sales under low involvement. This is part of the classic *push* (generate demand via the retailer) *versus pull* (generate demand via the consumer) distinction in marketing. If high involvement cannot be built with the consumer, then perhaps it can be built with the retailer. This retailer-support strategy as a means of generating sales is prevalent, for example, in home furnishings (such as matresses) and clothes. Retailer support can be based on margins or on in-store promotional programs for helping the retailer to sell the product—displays, brochures, videotapes, or even training for the retailer's sales personnel.

distribution programs

A final means for generating low-involvement sales is *dealing the brand,* that is, offering various price incentives (such as coupons and "cents-off") to the consumer or to the retailer (case deals). The assumption here is that low involvement is highly correlated with price sensitivity. Of course, excessive dealing may simply reduce profits—especially if competitors retaliate, as they are quite likely to do in a commodity market. Dealing may also lower involvement with consumers further, causing them to buy the brand only when it is on sale.

dealing

SUMMARY

Consumer involvement with the purchase-decision process varies by product category and by brand. Level of involvement increases with (1) the cost of the product, (2) the consumer's interest in the product category, (3) the degree of perceived risk in buying the product, (4) certain types of situation in which the product will be used, and (5) the social visibility of the product.

Behavioral research indicates distinctions between high- and low-involvement behavior. As contrasted to high-involvement behavior (such as the purchase of a stereo), low-involvement behavior (such as the purchase of facial tissue) has most of the following characteristics.

- less information seeking
- fewer cognitive defenses
- less information processing
- transient attitude change
- exposure may be equivalent to persuasion
- brand preference based on routinized behavior
- lack of cognitive dissonance
- lack of personal influence

In general, marketing managers wish to build involvement for their brand. Strategies for doing so include (1) achieving product differentiation, (2) achieving advertising advantage, and (3) marketing through high-involvement market segments. Exhibit 6–5 provides a summary of marketing strategies to be used in building involvement. If building high involvement is not feasible, then low-involvement strategy can attempt to increase sales through advertising weight, advertising content, retailer support, or price incentives.

KEY CONCEPTS

involvement	information-seeking	salient attribute
perceived risk	cognitive response	symbolic
incidental learning	information-processing	differentiation
latitude of acceptance	attitude change	source effect
social judgment theory	repetition	mere exposure effect
Krugman's low-	cognitive dissonance	attribution
involvement	personal influence	
learning theory		

DISCUSSION QUESTIONS

1. Describe some of the basic distinctions between high- and low-involvement consumer decision processes.
2. What are the basic strategies for building brand involvement? For each strategy provide some examples of brands that have built involvement using that strategy.
3. What is Krugman's theory of low-involvement learning and what are its implications for advertising?
4. Determine where a camera would fit on the product-involvement continuum by evaluating the product category on its characteristics of cost, interest, perceived risk, situation, and social visibility. Discuss how the involvement level might vary by brand.
5. Is brand loyalty indicative of high- or low-involvement? Explain.
6. Can a product category have both high- and low-involvement brands? Explain.
7. What is the essence of social-judgment theory? How might it affect advertising for high- versus low-involvement products?
8. Some analysts of the grocery industry have suggested that trade deals (for example, $5 off per case) and consumer deals (for example, 5¢ off per pound) lead to a decline in the "brand franchise" or the brand-involvement level. Do you agree? It is better to spend promotional funds in advertising instead of trade and consumer deals?

NOTES

1. John L. Lastovicka and David M. Gardner (1979), "Components of Involvement," in *Attitude Research Plays for High Stakes*, ed. John C. Maloney and Bernard Silverman (Chicago: American Marketing Assn.), p. 65.
2. Mark B. Traylor (1981), "Product Involvement and Brand Commitment," *Journal of Advertising Research*, 21 (Dec.,), pp. 51–56.
3. Mark B. Traylor (1981).
4. Herbert E. Krugman (1965), "The Impact of Television Advertising: Learning Without Involvement," *Public Opinion Quarterly*, 29 (Fall), pp. 349–56.
5. Herbert E. Krugman (1979), "Low Involvement Theory in the Light of New Brain Research," in *Attitude Research Plays for High Stakes*, ed. John C. Maloney and Bernard Silverman (Chicago: American Marketing Assn.), pp. 16–22.
6. Csikszentmihalyi Mihaly and Robert Kubey (1981), "Television and the Rest of Life: A Systematic Comparison of Subjective Experience," *Public Opinion Quarterly*, 45 (Fall), p. 317.
7. See L. Postman, "Verbal Learning and Memory," in *Annual Review of Psychology*, vol. 26, pp. 291–335 or D. A. Walsh and J. J. Jenkins (1973), "Effects of Orienting Tasks on Free Recall in Incidental Learning," *Journal of Verbal Learning and Verbal Behavior*, 12, pp. 481–88.
8. Michael L. Ray (1973), "Marketing Communication and the Hierarchy-of-Effects," in *New Models for Mass Communication Research*, ed. Peter Clarke, vol. 2 (Beverly Hills, Cal.: Sage), pp. 147–76.
9. Michael L. Ray and Alan G. Sawyer (1971), "Repetition in Media Models: A Laboratory Technique," *Journal of Marketing Research*, 8 (Feb.), pp. 20–29.
10. Alvin J. Silk and Terry G. Vavra (1974), "The Influence of Advertising's Affective Qualities on Consumer Response," in *Buyer/Consumer Information Processing*, ed. David Hughes and Michael L. Ray (Chapel Hill: Univ. of North Carolina Press).
11. Kapferer, as cited by Alan G. Sawyer (1981), "Repetition, Cognitive Responses, and Persuasion," in *Cognitive Responses in Persuasion*, ed. R. E. Petty, T. M. Ostrom, and T. C. Brock (Hillsdale: Erlbaum).
12. Muzafer Sherif and Hadley Cantril (1947), *The Psychology of Ego Involvement* (New York: Wiley).
13. Muzafer Sherif and Carl E. Hovland (1961), *Social Judgment* (New Haven, Conn.: Yale Univ. Press).
14. Richard W. Olshavsky and Donald H. Granbois (1975), "Consumer Decision Making—Fact or Fiction," *Journal of Consumer Research*, 6 (Sept.), p. 98.
15. Richard W. Olshavsky and Donald H. Granbois (1975), p. 99.
16. Donald H. Granbois (1977), "Shopping Behavior and Preferences," in *Selected Aspects of Consumer Behavior*, ed. Robert Ferber (Washington, D.C.: GPO), p. 264.
17. Louis P. Bucklin (1965), "The Informative Role of Advertising," *Journal of Advertising Research*, 5 (Sept.), pp. 11–15.
18. George Katona and Eva Mueller (1954), "A Study of Purchase Decisions," in *Consumer Behavior*, ed. Lincoln H. Clark (New York: New York Univ. Press), p. 53.
19. Robert A. Westbrook and Claes Fornell (1979), "Patterns of Information Source Usage Among Durable Goods Buyers," *Journal of Marketing Research*, 16 (Aug.), pp. 303–12.
20. Peter Wright and Barton Weitz (1977), "Time Horizon Effects on Product Evaluation Strategies," *Journal of Marketing Research*, 14 (Nov.), pp. 429–43.
21. Michael L. Ray (1973).
22. Gary A. Steiner (1966), "The People Look at Commercials: A Study of Audience Behavior," *Journal of Business* (Apr.), pp. 272–304.
23. Scott Ward, Thomas S. Robertson, and Daniel Wackman (1971), "Children's Attention to Television Advertising," in *Proceedings, Association for Consumer Research*, ed. David M. Gardner (Assn. for Consumer Research), pp. 143–56.
24. Herbert E. Krugman (1965).

25. Michael L. Ray (1973).

26. Carl J. Hovland, Irving L. Janis, and Harold H. Kelley (1953), *Communication and Persuasion,* (New Haven: Yale Univ. Press).

27. Muzafer Sherif and C. W. Sherif (1967), "Attitude as the Individual's Own Categories: The Social Judgment-Involvement Approach to Attitude and Attitude Change," in their *Attitude, Ego Involvement, and Change* (Westport, Conn.: Greenwood Press).

28. R. Apsler and D. O. Sears (1968), "Warning, Personal Involvement and Attitude Change," *Journal of Personality and Social Psychology,* 9, pp. 162–68.

29. See, for example, Richard E. Petty and John T. Cacioppo (1980), "Issue Involvement as a Moderator of the Effects on Attitude of Advertising Content and Context," in *Advances in Consumer Research,* ed. Kent B. Monroe, vol. 8 (Assn. for Consumer Research), pp. 20–24.

30. William R. Swinyard and Kenneth A. Coney (1978), "Promotional Effects on a High Versus Low Involvement Electorate," *Journal of Consumer Research,* 5 (June), p. 47.

31. Robert B. Zajonc (1968), "The Attitudinal Effects of Mere Exposure," *Journal of Personality and Social Psychology Monograph,* 9 (2, pt. 2).

32. See Robert B. Zajonc (1980), "Feeling and Thinking: Preferences Need No Inferences," *American Psychologist,* 35, pp. 151–75 and Robert B. Zajonc and Hazel Markus (1982), "Affective and Cognitive Factors in Preferences," *Journal of Consumer Research,* 9 (Sept.), pp. 123–31.

33. Leigh McAlister and Edgar Pessemier (1982), "Variety Seeking Behavior: An Inter-Disciplinary Review," *Journal of Consumer Research,* 9 (Dec.), pp. 311–22.

34. M. Venkatesan (1973), "Cognitive Consistency and Novelty Seeking," in *Consumer Behavior: Theoretical Sources,* ed. Scott Ward and Thomas S. Robertson (Englewood Cliffs, N.J.: Prentice-Hall), pp. 354–84.

35. Edward E. Jones, et al., eds. (1971), *Attribution: Perceiving The Causes of Behavior* (Morristown, N.J.: General Learning Press).

36. Richard E. Petty and John T. Cacioppo (1980).

37. Tyzoon T. Tyebjee (1979), "Refinement of the Low Involvement Concept: An Advertising Planning Point of View," in *Attitude Research Plays for High Stakes,* ed. John Maloney and Bernard Silverman (Chicago: American Marketing Assn.), pp. 94–111.

38. The low involvement-advertising repetition relationship is discussed in Clark Leavitt, Anthony G. Greenwald, and Carl Obermiller (1980), "What is Low Involvement Low In?" in *Advances in Consumer Research,* ed. Kent B. Monroe, vol. 8 (Assn. for Consumer Research), pp. 15–19 and in Michael L. Rothschild (1979), "Advertising Strategies for High and Low Involvement Situations," in *Attitude Research Plays for High Stakes,* ed. John C. Maloney and Bernard Silverman (Chicago: American Marketing Assn.), pp. 74–93.

39. Michael L. Rothschild (1979), "Advertising Strategies for High and Low Involvement Situations," pp. 74–93 and Tyzoon T. Tyebjee (1979), "Refinement of the Low Involvement Concept: An Advertising Planning Point of View," pp. 94–111, both in *Attitude Research Plays for High Stakes,* ed. John C. Maloney and Bernard Silverman (Chicago: American Marketing Assn.).

40. Richard E. Petty, John T. Cacioppo, and Rachel Goldman (1981), "Personal Involvement as a Determinant of Argument-Based Persuasion," *Journal of Personality and Social Psychology,* 41, 5, pp. 847–55.

41. Robert E. Smith and William R. Swinyard (1982), "Information Response Models: An Integrated Approach," *Journal of Marketing,* 46 (Winter), pp. 81–93.

Low-Involvement Advertising Effects

An interview with Dr. Herbert E. Krugman, former director of public affairs at the General Electric Company. Krugman now heads his own firm specializing in advertising and public affairs consulting.

Q *How did you derive the low-involvement concept?*

A When I started in academic psychology, I came with a background in psychoanalysis and a long-standing interest in Freudian theory. Yet, introspection and the Freudian and neo-Freudian streams of theoretical analysis were not accorded much respect at that time. The question of what was happening inside people's heads was rarely treated in the theory and research of the day.

Then I moved into advertising research and was faced with enormous amounts of data that tracked advertising campaigns. It seemed to me that a lot of the learning of advertising was meaningless. In fact, the learning of advertising copy was like the learning of nonsense syllables.

There was a very pronounced U-curve effect: people recalled the first and last advertising messages but not those in the middle. This was similar in character to Ebbinghaus's work on the learning of meaningless rote material. [see Chapter 9].

Basically, advertising tries to communicate trivia to the public—for example, the name of the brand or a simple product benefit. Of course, if such advertising is successful in doing so, it can have enormous marketing implications. Sizable advertising budgets are spent in the hope that small effects occur.

Some advertising, we have found, was more relevant and resisted the U-curve. If the advertising was relevant and meaningful to the consumer, its effects were more pronounced. Now here is where I got back to my earlier psychoanalytic training. The critical factor in an advertisement's effectiveness was whether in the individual's thought processes at the time there was something in the advertisement that *connected* to the individual's personal life. Most advertisements had zero connections. Some involving advertisements had one connection. Very few advertisements had two or more personal connections for the consumer.

Q *What is a "connection"?*

A A *connection* is a thought that relates something about the stimulus (the advertisement) to something in the individual's personal experience. For a long time, as I mentioned, psychology focused more on behavior than on thoughts. But the key to me was whether a connecting thought occurred.

A The main point is that most advertisements generate very low involvement. Most often there are no connections between the advertisement and the consumer's personal life.

When advertisements do "get through" to the consumer, they involve only slight changes in perception. There is very low attention and almost no recall of the advertisement. However, if it were played back, there could be some recognition.

Even when we might conclude that there is "no attention," there are still levels of no attention. We can use physiological data to measure flickers of attentive activity. These data might reveal some minor levels of advertising effects.

A The advertiser should try to communicate only one good idea per advertisement. There is very limited ability to communicate effectively in a thirty-second commercial.

For low-involvement products, high advertising frequency is necessary. Pulsing or flighting advertisements in groups (rather than spreading them out over some number of months) will work for high involvement but not low involvement, where you need the constant drip-drip-drip of advertising over time.

For low-involvement products it will be important to have point-of-sale aids to reinforce the low-involvement advertisements. Such point-of-sale promotional materials may help to trigger response.

Future technologies may change some of these involvement relationships. For example, if consumers view a twenty-minute commercial delivered via videotext, the advertiser will be guaranteed high involvement. New shapes and sizes and resolution levels for television receivers may also change sensory responses in some ways. For example, new wider, higher-definition television screens encourage more eye movement. This should lead to greater involvement and more thinking. If so, television may be able to raise its involvement level.

7 Consumer Socialization and Cognitive Development

The field of consumer behavior is most concerned with adults, since they do the vast majority of buying and consuming goods and services. But adults do not suddenly become consumers. Rather, they develop patterns of consumer behavior over the years as they are exposed to marketplace stimuli, and as they earn and spend money in order to satisfy changing needs over their life cycles. Thus, consumer behavior is a learned process. Some of that learning process begins in childhood as children observe their parents buying things, as they see advertising (some of it directed to them) and begin to form perceptions of and attitudes toward products and brands, and as they begin to acquire and spend money.

We refer to these aspects of children's development as consumer socialization. *This term is defined as the broad set of processes by which children and adolescents acquire skills, knowledge, and attitudes regarding consumption behavior.*

In recent years, consumer researchers and marketers have devoted considerably more attention than in the past to the consumer behavior of children, for several reasons. First, competition among marketers of products consumed primarily, or heavily, by children has increased. For example, the number of presweetened breakfast cereals has increased, and competition in the toy and game industry has intensified as marketing oriented companies such as Quaker Oats and General Mills have acquired toy companies, and as new competitors have established a new toy product category: electronic games.

Greater attention to children's consumption is also due to recognition of the role of children in family decision-making. While most research in the area has focused on husband-wife decision-making, it is clear that children are often directly or indirectly involved in consumption decisions. Conceptual frameworks for the study of children's consumer socialization have emerged, since general theories of child development and family processes have received increased recognition and acceptance among marketers and consumer researchers.[1]

Finally, the most important reason for increased attention to children's consumer behavior is the dramatic surge of concern among consumer activist groups and federal and state regulators over advertising's influences on children.

In this chapter, we examine children's consumer socialization in terms of a general model of the process, beginning with the influence of major inputs, such as advertising, parents, and peers, and continuing through children's information processing and consumer behaviors. Finally, we discuss the impact of childhood consumer behavior on later patterns of adult behavior. Throughout the chapter, we examine the concerns of consumer activists and regulators—the effects of marketing practices on children.

THE NATURE OF CHILDREN'S PURCHASING BEHAVIOR

It is important to understand that children's consumer behavior varies markedly from adults'. Obviously, children's needs for products and services are considerably more focused than those of adults. Children also process information about products and brands in qualitatively different ways from adults, as we shall see. Finally, children must normally ask their parents to buy things for them, since they do not have the independence and the disposable income to do much buying on their own. As children grow older, of course, more independent buying occurs.

Children influence many purchases, both for their own consumption (candies and presweetened breakfast cereals, for example) and for consumption that may be shared with family members (eating out at fast-food restaurants)

EXHIBIT 7–1
PERCENTAGE OF REQUESTS FOR TYPES OF PRODUCTS BY AGE OF CHILD[a]

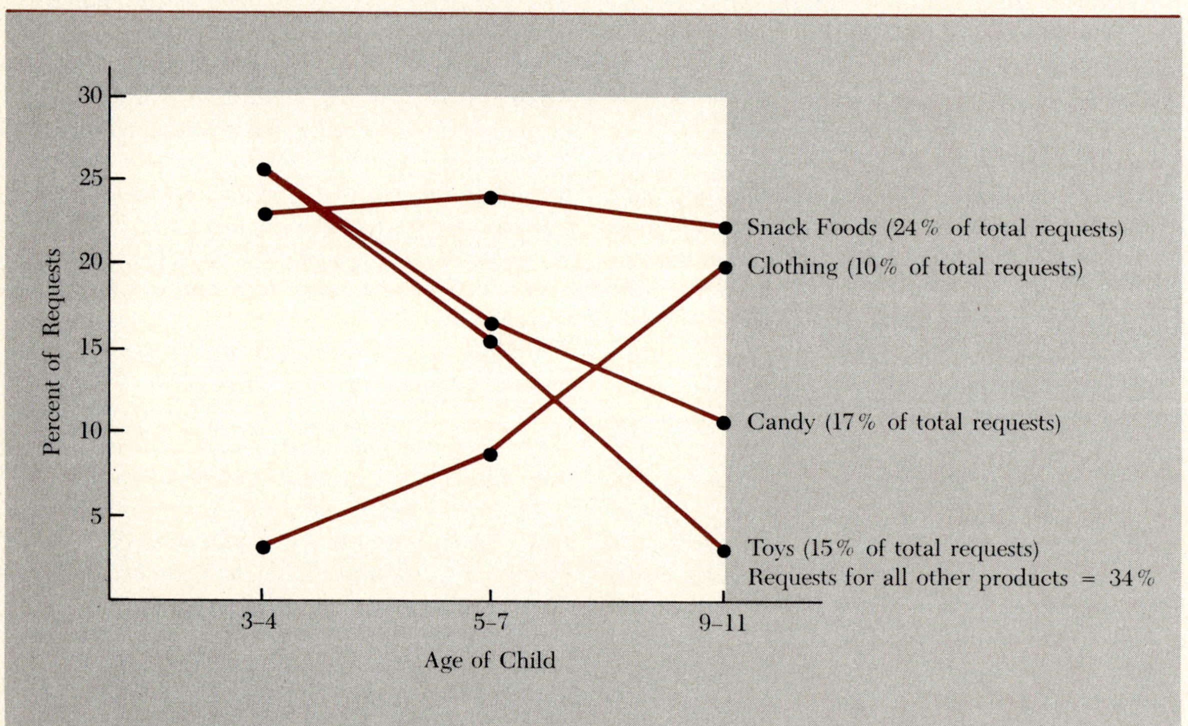

[a] Data are percentages of total requests for products in four categories made by children over a 28-day period, as recorded by their mothers in a diary study. Total number of requests = 3374 by 250 children (average number of requests per child = 13.5).

SOURCE: Leslie Esler, Edward Popper, and Scott Ward (1979), "Children's Purchase Requests and Parental Responses: Results from a Diary Study," working paper (Cambridge, Mass.: Marketing Science Inst.).

or with peers (a game played with friendship groups). Young children's exposure to advertising is likely to be concentrated on Saturday mornings and late weekday afternoons. As they grow older and diversify their media behavior, they are likely to be exposed to a greater diversity of advertising, paralleling their expanding interests in different kinds of products and services.

Such age-related changes in children's viewing behavior and product interests are also reflected in the kinds of things they request their parents to buy for them. Exhibit 7–1 shows results from a diary study in which mothers recorded every explicit request for a purchase made by one of their children over a twenty-eight day period in the spring. While snack foods were the purchase most requested by children regardless of age, older children were much less likely to ask for candy (they may be more likely to buy it themselves) or for toys (they are generally less interested than younger children). However, predictably, older children were more likely to request clothes.

A MODEL OF CONSUMER SOCIALIZATION

Consumer socialization is a lifelong process, in that we continually develop the knowledge, skills, and attitudes we employ in our day-to-day lives as consumers. The model in Exhibit 7–2 portrays the overall process of consumer socialization and suggests major variables affecting the process during childhood. This model will organize our discussion of consumer socialization.

Like many models of consumer behavior, it is basically an elaboration of the psychologist's *S-O-R* framework *(Stimulus-Organism-Response)*. Here, the *stimuli* are "Major Inputs"—advertising and other forms of marketer-controlled influences (such as in-store displays), and parents and peers (nonmarketer-controlled influences).

The *organism* in the model is the developing child, and the most important aspect of development is how children *process* information provided by the major inputs. As shown in the model, these inputs may be expected first to affect the child's attention (such as making the child aware of a product) and to stimulate his or her interests. (Of course, parents sometimes try to discourage children's interests in some products or brands.)

Information Processing in the model refers to both cognitive and affective processes—that is, what the child comes to know and feel concerning products, brands, and services. These aspects of information processing are greatly affected by the extent to which children "filter" incoming information. Obviously, for example, young children have less experience and less-developed abilities to process consumer-related information than adults have. Such abilities develop over time, with maturation and experience, and serve to "filter" (or provide a basis for evaluation of) consumption-related information. The inclusion of the concept of *cognitive filters* is a major difference between models for adult information processing and models for children.

As *responses,* or outcomes of consumer socialization, the model portrays two kinds of behaviors children exhibit in order to obtain things they want: they can buy themselves *(independent buying)* or they can ask their parents

EXHIBIT 7–2
A PICTORIAL MODEL OF CONSUMER SOCIALIZATION[a]

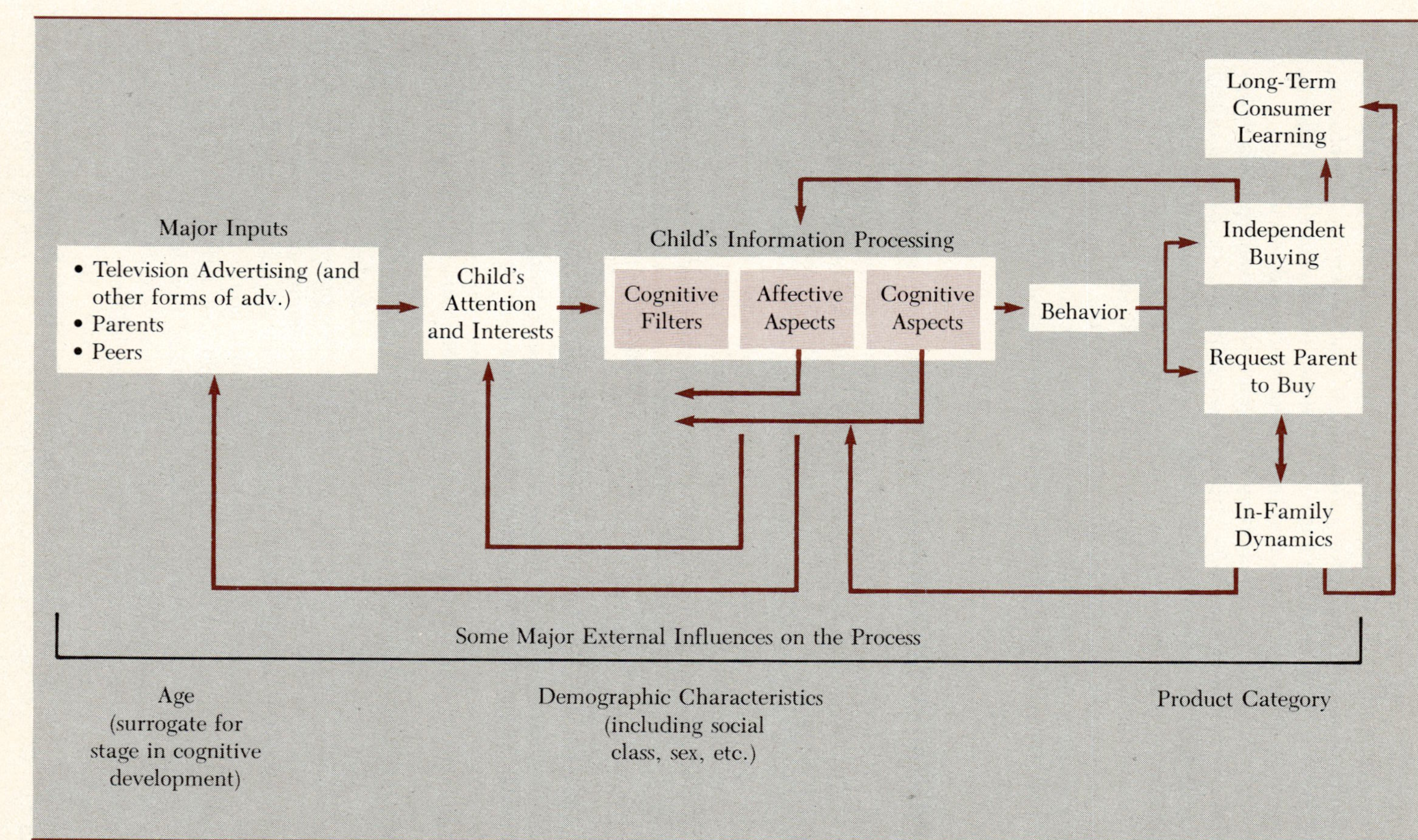

[a] Feedback loops indicate learning—for example, loops backward from *Information Processing* to *Child's Attention* and to *Major Inputs* suggest that as children age and their information-processing abilities develop, they are likely to change their patterns of attention to various major inputs.

to buy for them *(request parent to buy)*. Both of these behavioral modes have long-term consequences. For example, children's purchase requests in the family can affect (and be affected by) the norms and interrelationships among family members. As a case in point, parents sometimes object to children's requesting certain things, or they object to the manner or frequency of requests; on the other hand, in very strict families, the child learns not to request things. In most families, children are expected to learn various strategies for achieving their goals, such as those discussed in Chapter 18.

Independent buying among children increases with age. The experience children gain from buying and consumption may be expected to influence longer-term patterns of consumer learning. These longer-term patterns are undoubtedly affected by family processes as well. For example, children may adopt patterns of saving, product evaluation, and perhaps even brand preferences from their parents.

Finally, the model portrays some major external influences on consumer socialization processes. The most important of these is the child's age. This variable is a surrogate for a more important concept—the child's **stage in cognitive development.** The notion of cognitive development refers to various capabilities of children to select, evaluate, and use stimuli in processing information. We will deal with the concept in detail later in this chapter.

Other external influences include demographic characteristics of the child's environment and the product categories. As we have seen, children's interest in product categories varies according to age.

Major Inputs to Consumer Socialization

Parents are normally the most pervasive and important influence on all aspects of children's lives. Since parents usually control monies available to children, and since they are "gatekeepers" for purchases of products and services children desire, they are also critically important in consumer-socialization processes. The other major influences on general socialization processes are societal institutions such as schools and the church, which aid in the process of acculturating children, providing them with the requisite skills for later functioning as adults. In this century, many feel that another socializing institution has emerged: the mass-communication media—especially television. Since television is an advertising medium and since it appeals to children, commercials are an important influence on consumer-socialization processes.

Advertising Influences   Children watch television far more than they use any other form of mass communication. It is clearly the dominant source of information for them about products and services. In the late 1970s, the average American child aged 2–5 watched about twenty-five hours of television per week (just under three and two-thirds hours per day).[2] Older children, aged 6–11, watched slightly more, although children's viewing peaks by about third grade, and then decreases during the teenage years. The time that children under 12 spend watching television has increased by a full hour per day over the last two decades.

As children watch commercial television, they are exposed to commercial messages. One report estimates that children aged 2 through 5 view an average of 10,476 commercials per year and that children 6 through 11 view an average of 19,236.[3] These estimates are slightly lower than estimates made by FTC Chairman Lewis Engman, who put the figure at 21,875 per year from early childhood through high school[4] and by Robert Choate, who put the figure at about 22,000 per year for "the average child."[5] This amounts to about 3 hours of television advertising per week.

The range of products that advertisers promote directly to children over television is fairly limited. About 25 percent of this advertising is for "candy/sweets"—e.g., cakes, cookies, fruit drinks; another 25 percent is for "cereals"; and another 10 percent is for "eating places," principally fast-food restaurants. The remaining major category is toys, whose commercials are concentrated most heavily just prior to Christmas.[6] Of course, these kinds of products and services reflect children's interests.

Much of the television advertising addressed to children is broadcast during weekend daytime hours—especially during the Saturday morning animated-cartoon programs. This is not to say that children do most of their viewing during those hours; that is far from being the case. But the Saturday and Sunday morning audiences do include a high concentration of preteenage children.

The importance of television as a source of information about products and services for children is reflected in various studies. For example, Atkin's review of the literature notes that when black elementary-school children were asked to name their favorite toy and tell where they first found out about it, *TV watching* was most frequently mentioned, followed by *seeing it in-store* and *friends' having it*.[7] Caron and Ward asked children to list their Christmas gift wishes in a letter to Santa and to indicate where they got the idea for each item. The four most important sources were TV, friends, stores, and catalogs.[8] When asked where they would find out about toys and snack foods, about one-third of kindergartners and more than half of the third- and sixth-graders cited TV.[9]

According to mothers of young children interviewed by Barry and Sheikh, TV ranked first as the learning source for products in general, followed by friends and catalogs.[10] Both mothers and children studied by Howard, Hulbert, and Lehmann cited TV as the most important information source for cereal and toy products.[11]

The implications of these studies of advertising's influences on children for marketing strategy are fairly obvious. Television is by far the most cost-efficient medium for reaching child audiences, since children do not spend nearly as much time reading or attending to other advertising media as they do watching television. Buying advertising time at children's "prime viewing times," such as Saturday mornings and after-school hours, represents the lowest cost-per-thousand *children* reached. Larger numbers of children may be watching at, say, 8 P.M. on weekday evenings, but the cost is higher, since the audience is more heterogeneous in early evening hours.

While television is the dominant advertising medium for reaching children, other forms of advertising and promotion are used to appeal to children. For example, McDonald's is associated with Ronald McDonald, a clown, via advertising, personal appearances, and in-store promotions. If children are an important influence in product purchases, marketers may design in-store displays with children as well as adults in mind. For example, the Fisher-Price toy company generally stocks its items together in one part of toy stores, and uses red, white, and blue, colors which have become strongly associated with the brand. Such tactics encourage recognition and familiarity among both children and their parents, who often shop together for toys.

other forms of advertising

Finally, premium offers represent an important form of promotion to children. These are referred to as "pack-ins" or "pack-ons," meaning respectively, "prizes" that are inside the product container or "prizes" that must be obtained by mailing in a coupon or redeeming it at a store.

Parent and Peer Influences   Parents clearly are an important input to consumer socialization, exerting influence in various explicit and implicit ways. For example, parents may *explicitly* influence their children's behavior through specific discussions about buying things, television advertising, allowances, and so forth. However, they may *implicitly* influence their children's developing consumer skills as their offspring observe their day-to-day consumption behavior, as they discuss (or fail to discuss) major purchases, and as they generally act as "models" (wittingly or unwittingly) that children may learn to imitate. In a large-scale study, Ward, Wackman, and Wartella found that direct communication (specific discussions) between parents and children were most effective in fostering consumer skills among younger children, while "setting examples" (providing opportunities for modeling) were most effective for older children.[12]

Of course, the major inputs portrayed in Exhibit 7–2 interact with each other and with other variables—such as intelligence, social class, and so on— but the interaction patterns are not fully understood. Some research findings indicate that the *amount* of television advertising may not be as important as the *motivations* that children and adolescents have for watching. Ward and Wackman found, for example, that learning advertising slogans is more a function of intelligence than amount of television watching; however, attitudes toward advertising and "materialistic" attitudes are influenced primarily by the *reasons* for watching commercials. Particularly important were "social utility" reasons (operationally defined as a *motivation to watch commercials as a means of gathering information about lifestyles and behaviors associated with uses of specific consumer products*). The study found that younger adolescents talked more with parents about specific consumption practices and acts, and that such intra-family communication appeared to mediate advertising's impact on purchasing.[13]

Another study examined the relative influences of parents and peers on brand preferences and brand loyalty among high-school aged boys from predominantly working-class families.[14] The results showed that peer influences on brand preferences increase with age, but parental influences decrease. Interestingly, brand loyalty was found to increase with age, but decrease with intelligence and media exposure. It may be that youths who spend more time with mass media are exposed to advertising for a greater variety of brands, reducing their brand loyalty. While these results would probably be different for preteenage children—parents are probably more important in shaping brand preferences—it seems clear that one way children become more independent as they grow older is to rely more on peers and less on parents for their brand preferences.

Children's Attention

In the consumer socialization model shown in Exhibit 7–2, children's *attention* to marketing stimuli precedes information processing. Attention is a necessary, but not a sufficient, condition for information processing of advertising and other marketing cues.

Children's attention to television advertising has been examined in studies using observers (usually parents) to unobtrusively watch children watching television in the natural, in-home environment. These studies build on earlier research involving adults. For example, one study found that, among adults, no audience was present or the audience was "inattentive" during 48 percent of recorded commercial minutes during one week (the total number of commercial minutes was 224).[15] In general, studies of children's attention to television show a decrease in attention from programming to commercials. For example, commercials were ranked last of eleven types of television content in percentage of time watched while the material was aired.[16] Children watched commercials 55 percent of the time they were on, compared to 76 percent of the time for movies, the most watched type of broadcast material.

Another study used mothers to unobtrusively code *changes* in their children's attention to programs and commercials.[17] Interestingly, very young children (about age 5–6) did not show much change in attention at the onset of commercials, while older children did (see Exhibit 7–3). This finding is consistent with results of other kinds of research among children, in which they respond to direct questions about the nature of differences between programs and commercials. It appears that younger children do not fully distinguish between programs and commercials—reflected both in their attention behavior and in their responses to direct questions about the differences. These findings—and considerable regulatory pressure—led the networks to utilize various audiovisual techniques to more clearly separate programming and commercials on Saturday morning television (for example, "Now we'll take time out for these commercial messages").

The attention study also reinforces a point made earlier in this chapter— that children's preferences and their interests in different products change. Note, for example, the changes in attention to advertising for different product types in Exhibit 7–4. As children's cognitive levels increase (over ages 5– 12 in the study), their attention patterns vary markedly, depending on the product advertised.

Children's Processing of Information

Just as there are very important age-related differences in children's product interests and their attention to advertising, there are also crucial differences in their abilities to process information concerning matters relating to consumption. Very young children, for example, are likely to believe a nickel is more valuable than a dime because it is larger! They are considerably less sophisticated than older children in their abilities to understand advertising—that it is intended to *persuade*, that it is *biased* information, even that it is somehow *different from programming*. These kinds of age-related differences in understanding advertising have been at the heart of consumer activists' concerns about advertising directed toward children.

Merely describing age-related differences in children's cognition does not tell us *why* different-aged children process information differently. Without such understanding, we cannot design marketing programs—or propose regulations on marketing activities—on the basis of much more than subjective impressions of how children think and behave. Explanation of age-related differences in children's cognitive processing is required. The most useful concepts and theories have come from developmental psychologists.

EXHIBIT 7–3
**FULL ATTENTION TO PROGRAM AND FIRST COMMERCIAL
BY COGNITIVE LEVEL**

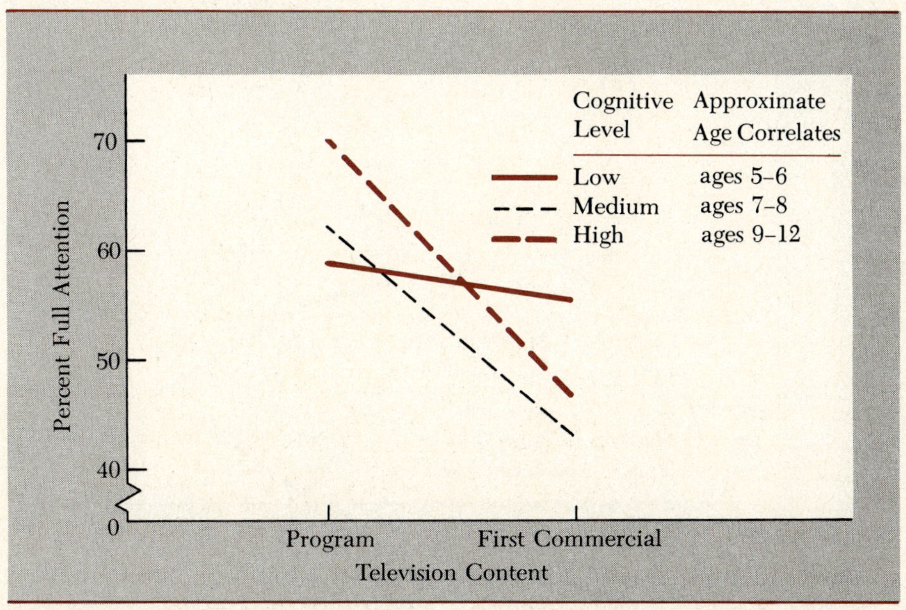

SOURCE: Scott Ward and Daniel Wackman, p. 137, *New Models for Mass Communication Research*, ed. Peter Clarke. Copyright © 1973 by Sage Publications, Inc. Reprinted by permission.

Cognitive-Development Theory

The eminent Swiss psychologist Jean Piaget was the first to articulate theories of cognitive development, which stress the evolving nature of children's abilities to process information about the world around them.[18] *Cognitive-development theory* refers to Piaget's general theory and to extensions and modifications of it others have proposed. Its essential notion is that children are not simply "less developed" than adults in their cognitive processing, but rather that the ways in which they select, evaluate, and use information is qualitatively different from adults. And the rate and nature of qualitative changes in cognitive processing is a result of the interaction of personal and environmental factors. Cognitive-development theories are quite different from *learning* theories, which characteristically view behavior simply as a function of forces applied to the child, and from *psychoanalytic* theories, which focus primarily on affective dimensions of parent-child relationships.

In Piaget's theory, the process of cognitive development is characterized by four cognitive stages: the *sensorimotor stage* (up to about age 2), the *preoperational stage* (from 2 to about 7), the *concrete operational stage* (7 to about

EXHIBIT 7–4

FULL ATTENTION TO COMMERCIALS FOR DIFFERENT PRODUCT TYPES BY COGNITIVE LEVEL

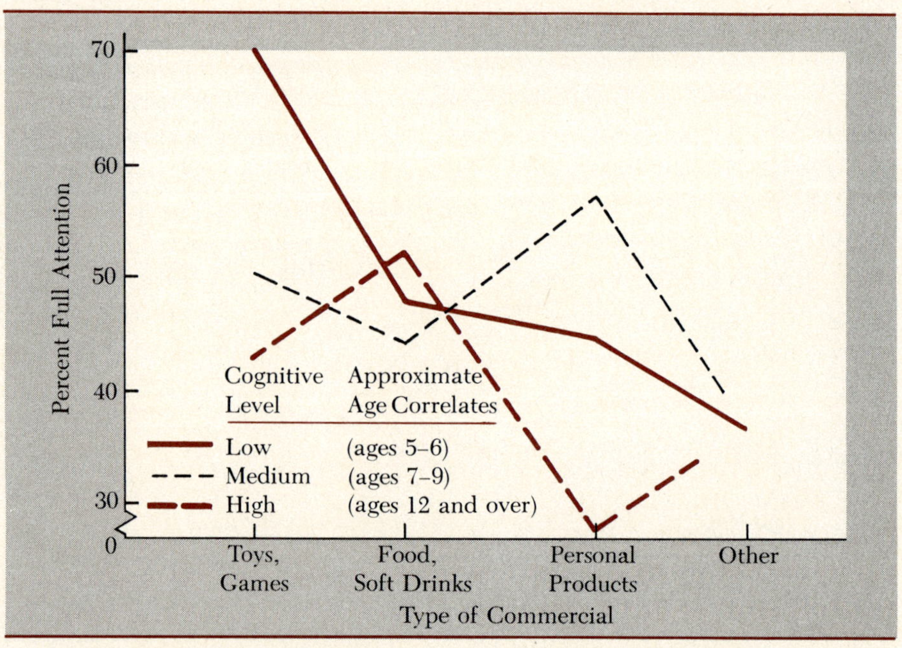

SOURCE: Scott Ward and Daniel Wackman, p. 139, *New Models for Mass Communication Research*, ed. Peter Clarke. Copyright © 1973 by Sage Publications, Inc. Reprinted by permission.

11) and the *formal operations stage* (11 through adulthood). These four developmental stages are defined in terms of the **cognitive structures** characterizing each. These refer to different ways children perceive and understand their environment, and formulate plans of action based on these perceptions and cognitions. For example, preoperational children are likely to exhibit **perceptual boundedness,** a tendency to focus on and respond primarily to aspects of their immediate perceived environment. This concept may be related to the difficulty very young children have in discriminating between television programming and advertising, discussed earlier.

Another concept distinguishing children at different developmental stages is **centration,** the tendency to focus on a limited amount of information available. Preoperational children tend to focus on one dimension of a situation, failing to make use of other dimensions that may be of equal relevance.

As an example of these two cognitive structures, consider the following scenario, based on one of Piaget's early experiments. If you fill two tall, thin glasses halfway with water and ask either a preoperational child or a concrete-operational child "Which has more water?" either will be likely to say that the glasses have "the same amount of water." Now take a smaller, wider glass, and pour the water from one of the original glasses into the third glass. The water will fill the glass to the top. If you then ask both children "Which has more water?" the preoperational child is likely to point to the smaller glass (which is now filled) while the concrete-operational child is likely to realize that nothing has really changed—that both glasses contain the same amounts of water.

Aspects of Children's Information Processing

Because of the interest of consumer activist groups and regulators in the area of advertising to children, much research has been devoted to extending the Piagetian, cognitive-development notions to examining age-related differences in children's abilities to evaluate advertising. In general, studies show not only age-related differences in children's abilities to discriminate between programs and commercials, but also increasing awareness with age of "what commercials are," understanding commercials' purposes, complexity of recall, and skepticism about perceived truthfulness in commercials (see Exhibit 7–5).*

---

*To some extent findings about children's cognitive understanding of advertising may depend on the measures used and on what is being measured. Atkin notes that about 25 percent of under-8-year-olds and about 75 percent of over-10-year-olds exhibit generalized distrust of advertising when they respond to dichotomous forced-choice questions asking whether ads are true or untrue.[19] However, rejection of specific advertising claims might not be as prevalent as the generalized measures would indicate. His laboratory studies indicate that children "readily accept" technical claims of a medical or nutritional nature, even though they are skeptical about assertions in commercials for familiar toys.

Macklin argues that children may "know more" than they can verbalize at different stages.[20] Her research and other studies[21] suggest that children can recall and recognize various elements in commercials when prompted, although they might not be able to verbalize their recall or recognition when asked specific questions.

Piaget's four stages of cognitive development

Besides the kinds of developmental differences we have discussed, children's ability to store information in memory also varies. Exhibit 7–6 shows that kindergarten-aged children recall far fewer brands of products, regardless of whether they are highly relevant to children's interests (chewing gum and soft drinks) or less relevant (cameras and gasoline), or whether they are relatively frequently advertised (gasoline and soft drinks) or less advertised (cameras and chewing gum). By sixth grade, on the other hand, children's levels

EXHIBIT 7–5

FOUR ASPECTS OF CHILDREN'S PROCESSING OF TELEVISION ADVERTISING BY AGE AND BY STAGE OF DEVELOPMENT

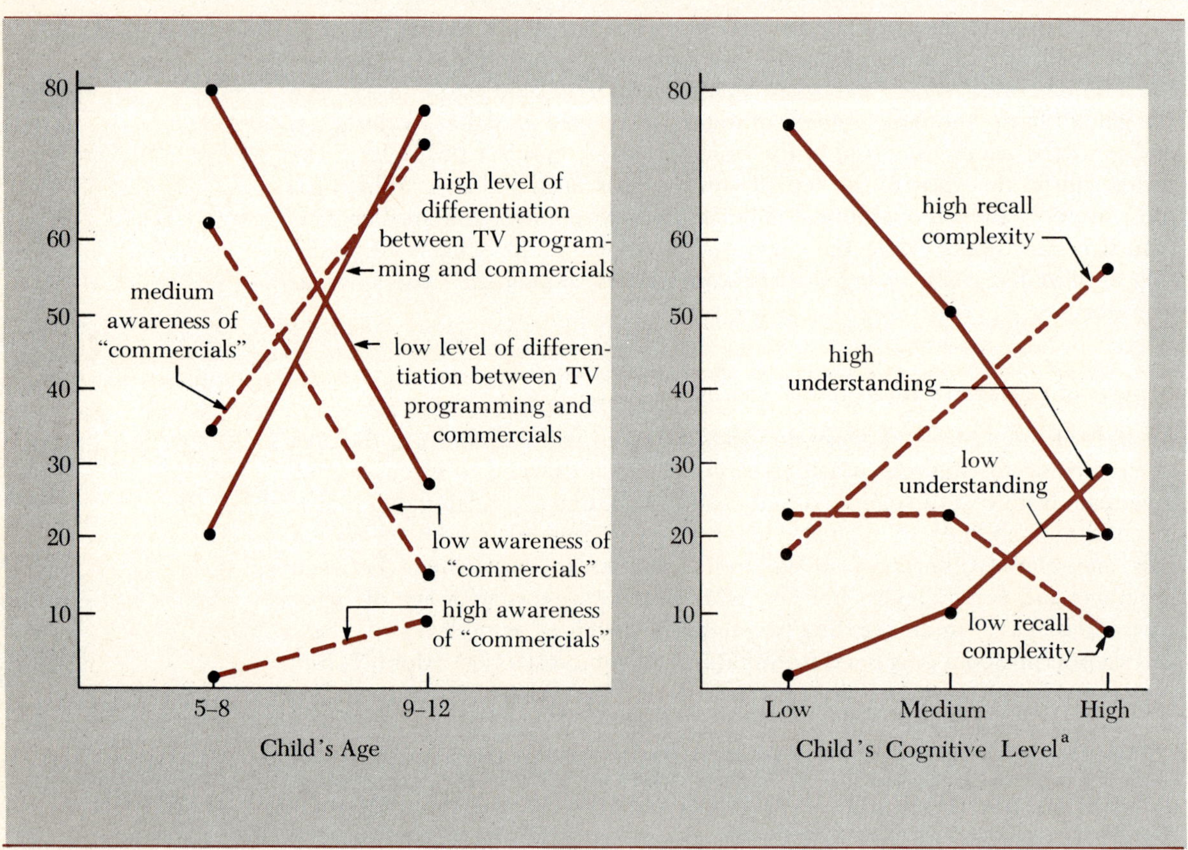

[a]Approximate age correlates: low = 5–6 years; medium = 7–8 years; high = 9–12 years.

SOURCE: Scott Ward, David Levinson, and Daniel Wackman (1972), "Children's Attention to Television Advertising," in *Television and Social Behavior*, ed. Eli Rubinstein et al., Vol. 4 (Washington, D.C.: GPO), pp. 491–511.

of brand recall are high for all but cameras—which are generally less relevant to children, and less advertised than the other products.

Further evidence concerning children's information processing is seen in Exhibit 7–7, which shows the percentage of children at three grade levels (kindergarten, third, and sixth grades) who mentioned different types of attributes (at least once) that they would use in response to the following hypothetical question:

Suppose you wanted a new television set. What would you want to know about it?

Responses were coded as referring to physical attributes (such as color versus black and white, size of the set, etc.); performance attributes (such as how easy the set is to operate); price attributes, and functional attributes (such as how well the set works). A large majority of children mentioned physical attributes, but younger children were particularly likely to refer to physical attributes, reflecting perceptual boundedness. Note that interest in all types of information (other than physical attributes) increases with age, indicating the interest and willingness of older children to use multiple dimensions in evaluating products.

Data from these studies show that children process information quite differently depending on their stage of cognitive development. They differ in the kinds of attributes they use to evaluate products, in their abilities to make inferences and use multiple dimensions in brand evaluations, and in their

EXHIBIT 7–6

MEAN NUMBER OF BRANDS IDENTIFIED FOR DIFFERENT TYPES OF PRODUCTS AT EACH GRADE LEVEL

Product Typology		Child Relevance	
		Low	*High*
Amount of Advertising	*Low*	Camera	Gum
	High	Gasoline	Soft Drinks

	Camera	Gum	Gasoline	Soft Drinks
K (N = 205)	.1	.6	.6	1.2
3 (N = 202)	.8	2.3	2.6	2.4
6 (N = 208)	1.4	3.2	3.3	3.3

SOURCE: Scott Ward, Daniel B. Wackman, and Ellen Wartella, p. 68, *How Children Learn to Buy: The Development of Consumer Information Processing Skills.* Copyright © 1977 by Sage Publications, Inc. Reprinted by permission.

abilities to store and retrieve information. Some research also suggests that black children exhibit less comprehension of advertising than white children, perhaps reflecting different family values.[22]

Affective aspects of children's information processing are most clearly seen in their attitudes toward advertising. These attitudes mirror the kinds of advertising to which they are exposed. That is, their like or dislike of advertising for food and for toys reflects the high incidence of advertising for these products on television. Reasons for liking and disliking commercials are shown in Exhibit 7–8. More than half of the answers indicate that commercials are liked because they are entertaining. Among younger children, however, a substantial number of answers indicate that a commercial is liked because the product is liked. On the other hand, children also dislike commercials primarily for entertainment reasons—they dislike commercials which are seen as boring and dull. Note that one third of the reasons for disliking commercials are in the "other" category, indicating that reasons for disliking commercials are more heterogeneous than reasons for liking commercials.

Strategic Implications

The patterns of children's attention and information processing we have discussed suggest rather strongly that marketing efforts, and the efforts of those who wish to regulate marketing efforts aimed at children, must be geared to the child's stage in cognitive development. For example, many toy manufacturers have abandoned the phrase "some assembly required" and replaced it with "you have to put it together," in commercials for toys. The latter terminology is much more likely to be understood by a broad range of children. Still other advertisers have institutionalized pretesting procedures for adver-

EXHIBIT 7–7

CHILDREN'S INFORMATION SELECTION ABOUT A TELEVISION SET BY GRADE LEVEL[a]

	K (percent)	3 (percent)	6 (percent)	Total (percent)
Physical Attributes	84	87	71	80
Performance Attributes	36	49	57	48
Price Attributes	15	31	41	30
Functional Attributes	13	26	43	28
N =	(137)	(199)	(202)	(558)

[a]Because of multiple responses, columns total more than 100 percent.

SOURCE: Scott Ward, Daniel B. Wackman, and Ellen Wartella, p. 69, *How Children Learn to Buy: The Development of Consumer Information Processing Skills.* Copyright © 1977 by Sage Publications, Inc. Reprinted by permission.

tisements which will be aired during children's viewing times, in order to detect any audio or visual aspects of the commercial which might mislead children. These procedures might also usefully monitor children's attitudes toward commercials, since the kinds of things they like or dislike about advertising may be quite different from what adult copywriters suppose.

In an effort at industry self-regulation, the Children's Advertising Review Unit of the National Council of Better Business Bureaus has convened a group of behavioral scientists who have studied children in order to propose guidelines for advertisers and to review potentially troublesome advertisements that might appear in print or broadcast media. The television networks also screen commercials to be aired during children's prime viewing times.

Children can learn positive, "pro-social" values that have been incorporated into televised messages, according to a study conducted by Eli Rubinstein, a member of the advisory panel to the Better Business Bureau's Children's Review Unit.[23] The study suggested several specific ways these values could be geared to age-related abilities so that children could comprehend them in the context of commercials.

Behavioral Outcomes

As shown in Exhibit 7–2, consumption outcomes for children most often mean asking parents to buy things for them, or, as they get older, buying independently. As suggested in the model, parents both provide *input* to children's consumer socialization processes and *respond* to children's purchase requests. It is quite possible that the patterns of parental responses affect children's asking behavior. That is, if parents continually "give in" to children's purchase requests, then the behavior is reinforced, and children may be more likely to ask for things in the future. Conversely, if parents continually refuse to purchase things their children request, then the children may learn not to ask for things with much frequency.

Marketers of child-relevant products have long been interested in the dynamics of children's asking their parents to buy things for them. From a totally different perspective, consumer activists have suggested that one negative effect of television advertising is that it encourages children to want things and to nag their parents to buy,[24] although explicit appeals to "ask your parents to buy" are prohibited in codes for advertising directed to children. As we have seen, television advertising is a major source of information about products and services for children, but it does not necessarily follow that family interrelationships suffer because of children's purchase requests. This subject has been addressed by empirical research, and important findings are summarized in the following paragraphs.

Purchase Requests to Parents

Among younger children, purchase requests are made to parents—most often the mother. Studies assessing these child-mother request patterns have employed a variety of research approaches. One method is to employ diaries to record specific requests made in a given period of time. Another method is to ask mothers and/or children themselves for self-report data. For example, Atkin asked 3–12 year-olds the following question.[25]

> *Many of the TV commercials are for toys—things like games and dolls and racing cars. After you see these toys on TV, how much do you ask your mother to buy them for you?*

His results show that 28 percent said "a lot" and 55 percent said "sometimes." The patterns for breakfast cereals were 33 percent and 45 percent. Other self-report data were obtained in a survey of 109 mothers of 5–12-year-old children, in which mothers indicated on four-point scales the frequency with which they felt their children requested products and the frequency of their "yielding" to these purchase requests.[26] The basic finding is that children's purchase-influence attempts decrease with age, but parental yielding increases with age; it seems that younger children ask for more, but get less, while older children ask for less but get more! It may be that older children

EXHIBIT 7–8

REASONS FOR LIKING AND FOR DISLIKING COMMERCIALS[a]

Reasons for Liking Recalled Commercials by Age[b]
(total mentions, n = 81)

	Age			
	5–7	8–10	11–12	Total
Entertainment	40%	60%	69%	55%
Aesthetics	6	10	8	7
Product	43	20	8	26
Other	11	10	15	12
	100%	100%	100%	100%

Reasons for Disliking Recalled Commercials by Age[c]
(total mentions, n = 67)

	Age			
	5–7	8–10	11–12	Total
Entertainment	14%	62%	41%	37%
Aesthetics	32	5	18	20
Effect	4	5	18	10
Other	50	28	23	33
	100%	100%	100%	100%

[a]Data in both tables were responses to an open-ended question about why children like (or dislike) specific commercials.

[b]Reasons include:
Entertainment—*funny, interesting*
Aesthetics—*liked the pictures, people are nice*
Product—*good product*
Other—*just like it, like the program*

[c]Reasons include:
Entertainment—*dull, boring*
Aesthetics—*scary, people are rude to each other, brags*
Effects—*repetition irritating, aimed at opposite sex*
Other—*just don't like it, product no good, etc.*

SOURCE: Scott Ward, Greg Reale, and David Levinson (1972), "Children's Perceptions, Explanations and Judgments of Television Advertising: A Further Exploration" (Cambridge, Mass.: Marketing Science Inst.).

learn to become more selective in what they request, and, therefore, ask for less, with a greater probability of success. Of course, it is also true that they do more independent buying, so have to ask their parents less frequently, and it is also likely that **passive dictation** occurs. This is what William Wells labels the process by which parents eventually learn their child's favorite products and brands, as a result of their continued requests; as children grow older, therefore, their requests are no longer necessary. You might say that the child has "trained" the parent!

These patterns of asking and yielding do not themselves indicate whether there was any conflict between children and mothers that might be dysfunctional within the family. One study did find a modest correlation between mothers' reports of children's asking and level of family conflict, but another study examined the existence and nature of parent-child conflict through unobtrusive observation of parent-child interaction. Galst and White unobtrusively observed mother-child pairs shopping in supermarkets.[27] They report that children made an average of fifteen purchase-influence attempts during a shopping trip. Sixty-four percent of the requests took place in front of the item, and children were successful in obtaining 45 percent of the items requested. However, Galst and White's data reveal that children ask for products all over the store, although the authors focus on cereal requests only, and their results may be inflated since the shopping trips took place immediately after children were exposed to advertising in a laboratory part of the study. Moreover, the study does not examine "conflict" *per se*.

Parent-child conflict while shopping has been studied by Atkin.[28] He observed 516 mother-child pairs during grocery shopping, and found 62 percent of parents acceded to the child's "request" or "demand." "Conflict" occurred in 65 percent of cases in which children's cereal requests were denied and "unhappiness" in 48 percent. Atkin notes that conflict and unhappiness are greatest among 6–8-year-olds, but that these negative responses are "seldom intense or persistent." In his other research, Atkin found that one sixth of children report arguing with their mothers "a lot" and one third "sometimes," after denial of requests for toys.[29]

In a laboratory experiment, Goldberg and Gorn showed children a commercial for a fictitious toy, and then presented them with pictures and verbal scenarios which portrayed a boy either receiving or not receiving the advertised toy from his father.[30] Children who viewed the commercials showed more negative feelings toward the hypothetical father who did not give the toy to his son and more disappointment than children in a control group.

The nature of in-family dynamics is more fully described in the pictorial model in Exhibit 7–9. This model omits the part of the consumer-socialization process focusing on children's information processing, but it elaborates on the kinds of asking and response patterns characterizing children's purchase requests in the family. Based on group interviews with mothers of 3–12-year-olds, the kinds of processes described in Exhibit 7–10 were tested by a larger-scale diary study.[31] Data reported earlier in this chapter (see Exhibit 7–1) show the kinds of products requested by children in different age groups. Results from the diary study show that, over a 28-day period, 250 children made 3374 explicit purchase requests, or an average of 13.5 requests per child (the range of requests was from 3 to 125). The average number of requests varied markedly by age, from 24.9 among an exploratory sample of 3–4-year-olds, to 13.3 for 5–7-year-olds, decreasing to 10.4 for 9–11-year-olds.

The diary study also reveals the ways in which children ask for things, and how their mothers respond. Most often, children "just ask" (81 percent of requests); pleading or bargaining is much less frequent (13 percent of requests), as was basing the request on an argument like "I saw it on TV" (6 percent of requests). Mothers agreed to buy in response to two thirds of requests and refused in response to one third. There were some age-related differences in mothers' responses, but the most important determinant of mother's response was the product requested (see Exhibit 7–10). In general,

EXHIBIT 7–9

PICTORIAL MODEL OF IN-FAMILY DYNAMICS: CHILDREN'S PURCHASE REQUESTS AND PARENTAL RESPONSES

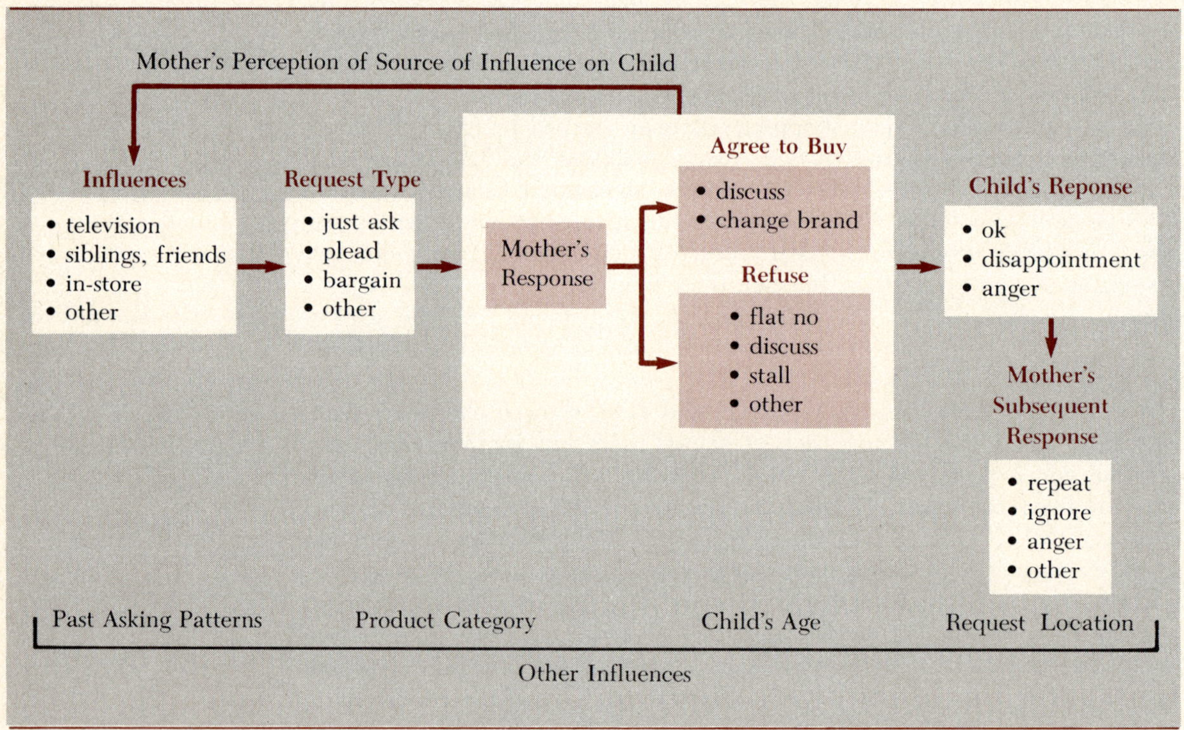

SOURCE: Leslie Isler, Edward Popper, and Scott Ward (1979), "Children's Purchase Requests and Parental Responses: Results from a Diary Study," working paper (Cambridge, Mass.: Marketing Science Inst.).

mothers are most agreeable to buying less expensive items children request and most reluctant to purchase more expensive ones.

On the issue worrying consumerists and regulators—whether purchase requests lead to disappointment and perhaps to dysfunctional parent-child conflict—the diary study indicates that the modal response is for children to take a refusal to buy "OK," as reported by parents, although disappointment is reported to 26 percent of the requests mothers deny (see Exhibit 7–11). Mothers report children arguing in response to about 20 percent of denied requests.

To summarize, children's purchase requests have been studied from a number of perspectives, and a number of research methodologies have been employed. The findings indicate that children do indeed ask their parents to buy products which interest them, but it does not appear that frequent dysfunctional conflict occurs between parents and children over these requests.

Long-Term Socialization Results

A final aspect of our consumer-socialization model is the question of the endurance of early learning—what things learned about consumption early in life endure into adulthood?

In addressing this question, it is first useful to distinguish between skills, knowledge, and attitudes necessary for consumption behavior—that is, consumer-role enactment of spending money, reacting to advertising, using planning in making purchases, careful price comparisons, and so forth—and the acquisition of more general attitudes, knowledge, and skills that are *relevant to* such consumer-role enactment. As Ward observes,

EXHIBIT 7–10

MOTHER'S INITIAL RESPONSES TO CHILD'S REQUESTS, BY PRODUCT/SERVICE REQUESTED

	Cereal	Candy	Toys	Snacks, etc.	Total Requests
Yes, didn't mind buying	65.7%	55.0%	20.0%	63.7%	50.7%
Yes, but discuss with child	10.0%	14.8%	13.8%	12.6%	14.3%
No	2.9%	10.5%	10.7%	4.4%	6.2%
No, but discuss with child	9.6%	11.5%	22.3%	11.5%	13.0%
Stall or substitute	11.7%	8.2%	33.2%	7.9%	15.8%
Percent of Total	6.9%	16.9%	15.1%	23.9%	100.0%
N =	(239)	(582)	(521)	(826)	(3374)

SOURCE: Leslie Isler, Edward Popper, and Scott Ward (1979), "Children's Purchase Requests and Parental Responses: Results from a Diary Study" (Cambridge, Mass.: Marketing Science Inst.).

A child's earliest experience with consumption may consist of learning how he should behave in order to receive material goods as a reward and to avoid having them withheld as punishment. Children also acquire skills in influencing parental purchases of products which they will use but which they do not consider a "reward."

At some point, it would seem that material goods acquire "social meaning"—more accurately, that children begin to see goods as being instrumental in achieving social goals, rather than as simply fulfilling a functional need or as being the consequence of social behavior. That is, a child can obtain a candy bar as a reward for good behavior, or he can ask his

EXHIBIT 7–11
CHILDREN'S REACTIONS TO MOTHER'S REFUSAL TO BUY REQUESTED ITEMS[a]

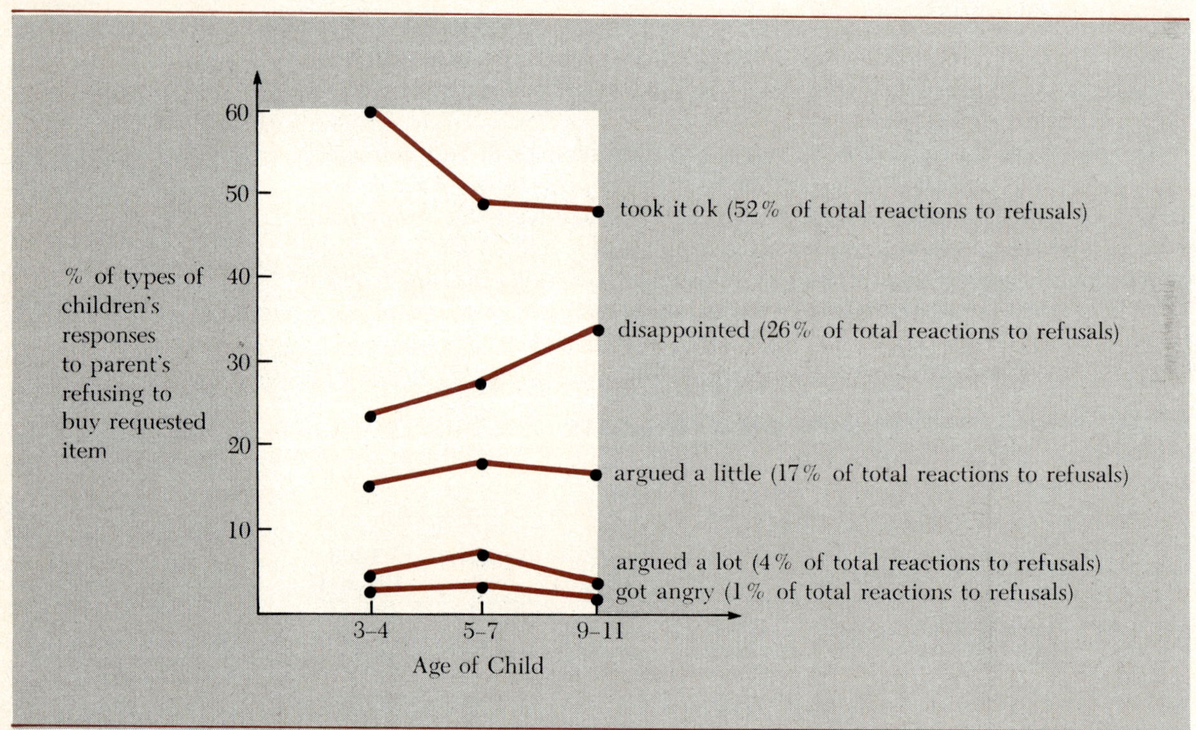

[a]Data are based on total number of refusals to requests made by children in a diary study covering a twenty-eight-day period. Should be read: "Of those instances in which children's purchase requests were denied, 61% were characterized by mothers of 3–4 year olds as "child took it ok," while 50% were characterized by mothers of 5–7 year olds as "child took it ok," etc.

SOURCE: Leslie Isler, Edward Popper, and Scott Ward (1979), "Children's Purchase Requests and Parental Responses: Results from a Diary Study," working paper (Cambridge, Mass.: Marketing Science Inst.).

mother to buy it simply because he is hungry and wants something sweet, or because he feels it will (temporarily, at least) place him a "cut above" his friends. These motivations are different, are acquired by different processes, and involve quite different kinds of skills, attitudes, and knowledge. Moreover, consumption as "reward" and consumption as "status symbol" are both social in nature; functional consumption is asocial. [32]

Little is known about the development and permanence of these direct and indirect aspects of consumer socialization. In fact, **longitudinal studies** that trace the attitudes, skills, and behaviors of the same individuals for many years are exceptional in behavioral research. This lack of extensive longitudinal data forces Brim to observe,

> *The potential and durability of . . . [early childhood learning] are assumed on the basis of the frequency of learning situations, their primacy in the career of the organism, and the intensity of the rewards and punishments administered. Moreover, what is learned in childhood is difficult to change because much of it was learned under conditions of partial reinforcement.* [33]

Results of longitudinal investigations have supported the socialization hypothesis, as have earlier findings concerning relationships between childhood learning and adult behavior in such fields as clinical psychiatry and criminology. [34] In perhaps the best-known research, Kagan and Moss, in a 25-year longitudinal study, found consistency of a variety of social behaviors over the period of the study. [35] Similarly, Lefkowitz et al., having followed children from third to thirteenth grade, concluded that aggressive behavior in early and late adolescence is predictable from aggressive behavior in childhood. [36]

A crucial question for consumer-socialization research is the extent to which early learning experiences influence later patterns of consumer behavior. One might assume that changes in the context of consumption from childhood to adulthood, and changes in the role requirements encountered in various stages of the life cycle, would "wash out" early learning. Two studies are relevant to this issue.

In one of the few longitudinal studies in consumer research, Guest interviewed a group of subjects regarding brand loyalty twelve years after he had first interviewed them. [37] At the time of the original interviews, the subjects were children in grades 3–12 in the Washington, D.C., area who had indicated "favorite brands." Guest suggests that his data indicate a strong degree of "brand loyalty," since about one third of the subjects preferred the earlier-named brands.

Another study, by Arndt, examines long-term parental influence on offspring's consumer behavior. [38] Arndt found significant relationships between college freshmen and sophomores and their parents regarding favorite types of stores, brand loyalty, opinion leadership, and innovativeness. Arndt reported that college students and their parents differ concerning "perceptual variables" (perceived product importance and perceived brand differences), but it is not clear whether this difference is simply a function of the different kinds of items or the different patterns of use of the items that are purchased by both college students and their parents. He also reported parent-offspring similarity in "behavioral variables" (favorite store-type pattern, opinion leadership, innovativeness), but these findings may correlate with other variables, since the students lived at home. Moreover, the small sample size (n = 55) does not permit generalizations to the large population of college-aged students who do not live with parents.

More longitudinal research is needed to address the issues of the extent to which early learning affects later consumer behavior. One extreme view would hold that role changes which occur with age would render early learning meaningless. (Even if this were literally true, studying consumer socialization would still be necessary in order to characterize adequately children's consumer behavior and the influence of children on purchases by others in the family.) On the other hand, early learning may be an important determinant of later patterns of cognitions and behavior. Virtually all behavioral research assumes that people are in some way influenced by earlier learning. The question may not be "how much" early learning experiences influence later consumer patterns, but "what aspects" of consumer socialization are important in influencing patterns of adult consumer behavior.

SUMMARY

Human beings are a product of their upbringing. The kinds of experiences we undergo as children exert a powerful influence on our patterns of behavior in later life. Since consumption behavior is an aspect of human behavior, and since patterns of consumer behavior are learned over time, it follows that childhood consumption experiences comprise the foundations of adult consumer behavior to some extent.

We have examined these "consumer-socialization" processes in this chapter, noting that the study of children's consumer behavior is useful in its own right, as well as useful in understanding later patterns of consumption behavior. Children directly buy and consume many products, as well as indirectly influence purchases by parents. Understanding consumer-socialization processes is important not only in marketing strategies which target children or families, but also in formulating programs which modify or regulate marketing practices affecting children. Such modifications are necessary since children are indeed a "special audience" for marketers. Their lack of experience and developing abilities to process information require marketers to proceed carefully to insure that children comprehend marketing efforts. Many consumer activists maintain that marketers do not go far enough and have long called for more stringent controls on marketing efforts directed to children.

We have used a pictorial model of the consumer-socialization process in order to highlight important variables. Marketing stimuli—especially television advertising—as well as parents and peers provide the major inputs to consumer-socialization processes. Piaget's cognitive developmental framework provides a basis for exploring children's information processing. Piaget's theory provides explanatory concepts to help us understand age-related abilities of children to process information.

The outcomes of consumer socialization include children's independent buying behavior, which increases with age, and asking their parents to buy for them. Since children most often ask their parents to buy, marketing strategies should not only assess children's stage-related abilities to process information, but should also take into account the "gatekeeper" role of parents in children's consumption. For example, major amusement parks, such as Disney World, advertise *both* to parents and to children. Some toy companies, such as Fisher-Price, market toys primarily for preschool-aged children. Consequently, the company directs the majority of its marketing activities to mothers. Companies that market toys for somewhat older children advertise directly to them, since they have more focused interests in specific toys, and are more likely to ask their parents to buy specific toys for them.

Finally, we have addressed the question of whether and how early consumer-socialization experiences affect later adult consumer behavior. The little longitudinal research that has been done suggests some long-term effects of early learning, but more complete and comprehensive studies must be done before we fully understand what aspects of adults' consumer behavior are affected by consumer-socialization processes in childhood.

KEY CONCEPTS

cognitive level (or stage)	centration	cognitive filters
cognitive structure	perceptual boundedness	long-term socialization
	passive dictation	longitudinal studies

DISCUSSION QUESTIONS

1. What are the major reasons for increasing interest in consumer socialization? What groups are most interested?
2. What are the important differences between children's and adults' consumer behavior? What are the key differences between young children's consumer behavior and that of older children?
3. A major criticism of television advertising is that it causes children to nag their parents for things they see advertised. Comment.
4. What are the most important concepts that cognitive-development theory implies for consumer-socialization issues? What are the strengths of cognitive-development theories versus other theories in their implications for consumer socialization?
5. What are the major influences on children's consumer-socialization processes? Compare their effectiveness in terms of various dimensions you feel are important. That is, discuss *how* they influence children.
6. Why might young children's attention to television *not* vary much, compared to older children's attention?

7. Discuss the most important aspects of children's information processing of consumption-related stimuli.

8. How do children's attitudes toward television commercials change with age? Why do these changes occur?

9. What are the various ways children obtain things they want from their parents?

10. What are some possible long-term consequences of early consumer-socialization experiences?

NOTES

1. See the following books by Jean Piaget: (1928), *The Child's Conception of the World* (New York: Harcourt, Brace; (1950), *The Psychology of Intelligence* (London: Routledge and Kegan Paul); (1952), *The Origins of Intelligence in Children* (New York: International Univs. Press); and (1954), *The Construction of Reality in the Child* (New York: Basic Books). An excellent overview of family processes and socialization theories is Edward Zigler and I. L. Child (1969), "Socialization," in *The Individual in a Social Context,* vol. 3 of *The Handbook of Social Psychology,* 2nd ed., ed. Gardner Lindzey and Elliot Aronson (Reading, Mass.: Addison-Wesley), pp. 450–90.

2. A. C. Nielsen Co. (1979), *The Television Audience* (Chicago: A. C. Nielsen).

3. Richard P. Adler, ed. (1980), *The Effects of Television Advertising on Children* (Lexington, Mass.: Lexington Books).

4. Federal Trade Commission (1978), *Staff Report on Television Advertising to Children,* Feb. (Washington, D.C.: GPO).

5. Federal Trade Commission (1978).

6. Richard P. Adler (1980). See also Earle F. Barcus (1975), "Weekend Commercial Children's Television" (Newton, Mass.: Action for Children's Television) and (1978), "Commercial Children's Television on Weekends and Weekday Afternoons: A Content Analysis of Children's Programming and Advertising Broadcast in October, 1977" (Newton, Mass.: Action for Children's Television).

7. Charles Atkin (1975), "Effects of Television Advertising on Children," Rpt. Nos. 1 and 2 (East Lansing, Mich.: Michigan State Univ.).

8. Andre Caron and Scott Ward (1975),"Gift Decisions by Kids and Parents," *Journal of Advertising Research,* 15 (Aug.), pp. 12–20.

9. Scott Ward, Daniel B. Wackman, and Ellen Wartella (1979), *How Children Learn to Buy: The Development of Consumer Information-Processing Skills* (Beverly Hills, Cal.: Sage).

10. Thomas E. Barry and Anees A. Sheikh (1977), "Race as a Dimension in Children's TV Advertising: The Need for More Research," *Journal of Advertising,* 6 (3), pp. 5–10.

11. John Howard, James Hulbert, and Donald R. Lehmann (n.d.), "An Exploratory Analysis of the Effect of Television Advertising on Children" (New York: Columbia Univ. Sch. of Business).

12. Scott Ward, Daniel B. Wackman, and Ellen Wartella (1979).

13. Scott Ward and Daniel B. Wackman (1971), "Family and Media Influences on Adolescent Consumer Learning," *American Behavioral Scientist,* 14 (3), pp. 415–27. See also Lowndes F. Stephens and Roy L. Moore (1973), "Consumer Socialization: A Communication Perspective," paper presented to International Communication Assn. Student Summer Conference, Athens, Ohio and Roy L. Moore and L. F. Stephens (1975), "Some Communication and Demographic Determinants of Consumer Learning," *Journal of Consumer Research,* 2, pp. 80–92.

14. Bruce C. Fauman (1966), "Determinants of Adolescents' Brand Preferences," unpublished thesis, Sloan School of Management, MIT, Cambridge, Mass.

15. C. L. Allen (1965), "Photographing the TV Audience," *Journal of Advertising Research,* pp. 2–8.

16. Robert B. Bechtel, Clark Achelpohl, and Roger Akers (1972), "Correlates Between Observed Behavior and Questionnaire Responses on Television Viewing," in *Television and Social Behavior, vol. 4,* ed. Eli Rubinstein et al. (Washington, D.C.: GPO), pp. 274–344.

17. Scott Ward, D. Levinson, and D. Wackman (1972), "Children's Attention to Television Advertising," in *Television and Social Behavior, vol. 4*, ed. Eli Rubinstein et al. (Washington, D.C.: GPO), pp. 491–516.

18. Jean Piaget (1928, 1950, 1952, 1954).

19. Charles Atkin (1982), "Television and Consumer Role Socialization," in *Television and Behavior: Ten Years of Scientific Progress and Implications for the Eighties*, Appendix B, State of Knowledge Paper (Washington, D.C.: National Inst. of Mental Health).

20. Carole M. Macklin (1983), "Do Children Understand TV Ads?" *Journal of Advertising Research*, 23 (1), pp. 63–70.

21. Lawrence J. Gianinno and Paul A. Zuckerman (1977), "Measuring Children's Responses to Television Advertising," in *Proceedings: American Psychological Assn. Div. 23*, ed. Clark Leavitt, 85th Annual Convention, San Francisco, Cal.

22. Thomas R. Donohue, Timothy P. Meyer, and Lucy L. Henke (1978), "Black and White Children: Perceptions of TV Commercials," *Journal of Marketing* (Oct.), pp. 34–40.

23. E. A. Rubinstein, R. M. Liebert, J. M. Neale, and R. W. Poulos (1974), "Assessing Television's Influence on Children's Prosocial Behavior" (New York: Brookdale International Inst.). See also Eli Rubinstein (1975), "Remarks on Pro-Social Research in Children's Television," remarks to the Children's Advertising Review Unit Seminar (National Council of Better Business Bureaus), New York City (June).

24. See, for example, Action for Children's Television (1971), *The First National Symposium on the Effect on Children of Television Programming and Advertising*, text prepared by Evelyn Sarson (New York: Avon Books). See also Action for Children's Television (1971), "General Comments on Television Advertising to Children," testimony before the FTC (Newton, Mass.: Action for Children's Television).

25. Charles Atkin (1975), "Effects of Television Advertising on Children–Survey of Children's and Mothers' Responses to Television Commercials," Rpt. No. 8 (East Lansing, Mich.: Michigan State Univ.).

26. Scott Ward and Daniel B. Wackman (1972), "Children's Purchase Influence Attempts and Parental Yielding," *Journal of Marketing Research*, 9 (Aug.), pp. 316–19.

27. JoAnn Paley Galst and Mary Alice White (1976), "The Unhealthy Persuader: The Reinforcing Value of Television and Children's Purchase Influence Attempts at the Supermarket," *Child Development*, 47 (Dec.), pp. 1089–96.

28. Charles Atkin (1975), "Effects of Television Advertising on Children–Parent-Child Communication in Supermarket Breakfast Cereal Selection," Rpt. No. 7 (East Lansing, Mich.: Michigan State Univ.).

29. Charles Atkin (1975), "Effects of Television," Rpt. No. 8.

30. Marvin Goldberg and Gerald R. Gorn (1978), "Some Unintended Consequences of TV Advertising to Children," *Journal of Consumer Research*, 5, pp. 22–29.

31. Leslie Isler, E. Popper, and S. Ward (1979), "Children's Purchase Requests and Parental Responses: Results from a Diary Study," working paper (Cambridge, Mass.: Marketing Science Inst.).

32. Scott Ward (1974), "Consumer Socialization," *Journal of Consumer Research*, 1 (Sept.), pp. 1–13.

33. Orville G. Brim, Jr. (1968), "Adult Socialization," in *Socialization and Society*, ed. J. Clausen (Boston: Little, Brown).

34. E. Zigler and I. L. Child (1969).

35. Jerome Kagan and H. A. Moss (1962), *Birth to Maturity: A Study in Psychological Development* (New York: Wiley).

36. M. M. Lefkowitz, L. D. Eron, L. O. Walder, and L. R. Huesmann (1972), "Television Violence and Child Aggression: A Follow-Up Study," in *Television and Social Behavior*, vol. 3, ed. G. Comstock and E. Rubinstein (Washington, D.C.: U.S. Dept. of Health, Education, and Welfare), pp. 35–135.

37. Lester Guest (1955), "Brand Loyalty—Twelve Years Later," *Journal of Applied Psychology*, 39, pp. 405–8.

38. Johan Arndt (1971), "A Research Note on Intergenerational Overlap of Selected Consumer Variables," *Markeds Kommunikasjon*, 3, pp. 1–8.

8 Consumer Perceptions and Product Positioning

This chapter deals with perception, a key concept in psychological theory and in the practice of marketing. Ultimately, it is how the consumer perceives products and services that guides purchase decisions in the marketplace. Perception is also the cornerstone of marketing managers' efforts to "position" brands.

Product positioning locates a product or brand relative to other products or brands in the consumer's mind.[1] The usual marketing objective is to seek brand differentiation relative to competitors. In this chapter we use the term product positioning to refer not only to products but also brands and even companies; IBM, for example, seeks to achieve a company positioning distinct from those of other information-processing manufacturers.

Perception can be thought of as the individual's set of mental impressions within a stimulus field. It depends on what there is to be seen, the stimulus factors, as well as the individual's own beliefs and experience, the personal factors. People see selectively some proportion of what is available to be seen, and see in an organized manner, whereby they attach meanings and interpretations to the stimuli.

The critical nature of consumer perception in product positioning is repeatedly demonstrated in marketing practice. In fact, what ultimately matters is only what consumers perceive—even if these perceptions are not in line with "objective reality." As Philip Zimbardo explains it, ". . . perception of reality is 'mediated.' That is to say, perception is not always a direct reflection of the external world, but appears to be constructed out of information from the world outside. For one thing, we know that many of our everyday perceptions can be grossly incorrect. . . ."[2] To illustrate:

- *Maxim coffee, by most standards, has not met its manufacturer's (General Foods) expectations. Yet when it was introduced, the product was different from other products on the market mainly because of its production process, in which the coffee was freeze-dried rather than spray-dried, like instant coffees. In blind taste tests, 47 percent of instant-coffee drinkers preferred Maxim to the company's other brand, Instant Maxwell House, 39 percent preferred Instant Maxwell House, and 14 percent had no preference.[3] Yet, consumers did not perceive Maxim to be better than other coffees in a real market situation, when the product actually appeared on supermarket shelves, and were not willing to pay more for this premium product, which cost General Foods some 35 percent more to produce than Instant Maxwell House. Thus, the product never achieved its sales expectations as a higer-priced premium coffee.*

- *Listerine's market share advanced considerably when it was advertised as tasting bad. The prevailing consumer perception seemed to be that "medicines" should taste bad if they are going to be effective. Listerine's advertising succeeded in creating an impression of efficacy on that basis.*

PERCEPTION THEORY

The study of **perception** can be based on six principles.

1. Perception is *selective*. An individual cannot possibly perceive all stimulus objects within a perceptual field; therefore, only certain objects are selected.
2. Perception is *organized*. Perceptions have meaning for the individual: they do not appear to be a "buzzing, blooming confusion."
3. Perception depends upon *stimulus factors*. The nature of the stimuli presented have a strong bearing on whether something is perceived and how it is perceived.
4. Perception depends upon *personal factors*. The individual's physiological, emotional, and experiential characteristics have a powerful impact on perception.
5. *Sensory threshold levels* operate in perception. Human beings have upper and lower limits in responding to sensory stimulation and have differential thresholds in noticing minimal differences in stimuli.
6. Perception is subject to a *halo effect*. This is a tendency for the person to apply general impressions, frequently based on limited information, to specific attributes. For example, a consumer's favorite airline may be rather indiscriminately judged to be best in all respects.

Perceptual Selectivity

Each day the consumer is confronted with a mass of stimuli in the total environment. But it is beyond the individual's capabilities and interests to "see" everything. Instead, we selectively perceive some percentage of what is available to be perceived.

This **selectivity** leads to some very real marketing problems. For example, advertisers obviously want consumers to perceive their commercials. Yet, consumers screen out most commercials and are most likely to perceive advertisements for products that they already use. This may reach an extreme for new-car buyers, who are likely to read large numbers of advertisements for the cars that they just bought in order to justify their decisions and to overcome any "cognitive dissonance" (or post-purchase doubts).[4]

In one study of advertising effects, Bauer and Greyser referred to "advertising's folklore" that the consumer is potentially *exposed* to 1500 advertisements per day. In their study, however, consumers were found to *perceive* only 76 advertisements per day, and perhaps as few as 12 of these advertisements were remembered.[5] Similarly, a recent study using eye-tracking cameras recorded what consumers actually saw when exposed to commercials. One result was that in some 43 percent of the commercials, the sponsor's name was overlooked.[6]

The selectivity of perception is also demonstrated in today's mass-merchandising environment. The typical supermarket, for example, exposes the shopper to some 7500 items. Given this "clutter" and the consumer's propensity to perceive selectively, the challenge for the manufacturer is to "break through" to achieve consumer perception. This breakthrough could be achieved, for example, through package design or in-store merchandising programs, such as point-of-purchase displays, which increase the probability of consumer *attention*, the basic prerequisite for perception.

Perceptual Organization

Perceptual **organization,** or the meaning attached to stimuli by the perceiver, involves a compromise between the stimuli that are present and the individual's personal interpretation of these stimuli. Furthermore, the more ambiguity in the stimulus field (as, for example, in an advertisement), the more the opportunity for personal factors to govern organization. Psychologists use this principle of stimulus ambiguity to gain insight into the individual's self-concept. The person reveals more about himself or herself by organizing an unstructured Rorschach inkblot test, for example, than by describing a sharply focused photograph.

The individual's personalized organization of perceptual stimuli is well described in a classic work by Krech, Crutchfield, and Ballachey.

> *The cognitive map of the individual is not, then, a photographic representation of the physical world; it is, rather, a partial, personal construction in which certain objects, selected out by the individual for a major role, are perceived in an individual manner. Every perceiver is, as it were, to some degree a nonrepresentational artist, painting a picture of the world that expresses his individual view of reality.*[7]

Exhibit 8–1 presents a number of principles of perceptual organization. For example, the individual tends to perceive incomplete figures, such as the incomplete circle shown, as though they were complete. The individual may feel the need to complete incomplete stimuli—the need for closure. Kellogg's, for example, has sometimes run magazine advertisements with large letters running off the page, missing the *K* in its name. Perhaps the reasoning is that consumers will be motivated to complete the name and that this leads to better recall of the advertisement.

Stimulus Factors

The likelihood of attention and perception occurring depends on the **stimulus factors** presented. The challenge for the marketing communicator is to present stimuli that are most likely to capture attention, most frequently via the senses of sound and sight—although taste and smell are also relevant senses in determining perception.

Advertising strategy is particularly concerned with qualities of the stimulus itself.[8] *Size* affects the likelihood of attention: large advertisements are more likely to be seen than small advertisements. Advertisements in *color* are more likely to gain attention than are ones in black and white—except when a black

EXHIBIT 8–1
PRINCIPLES OF PERCEPTUAL ORGANIZATION

1. Similarity
Similar elements are seen as belonging to each other more than to other elements equally close but less similar. In this figure, do you see columns of Xs and Os or rows of alternating letters?

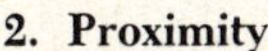

2. Proximity
Elements that are physically close are seen as belonging to each other more than to similar elements that are farther away. Below you see pairs of XOs, not OXs

XO XO XO XO

Proximity can also make things look more alike than they really are. The same figure that looks like an antelope when seen among antelopes looks like a bird in the company of other birds.

3. Closure
We tend to perceive incomplete figures as if they were complete. We see the line as a circle with a break in it and the irregular fragments as an animal.

4. Continuation
Elements are seen as belonging to each other if they appear to be a continuation of the direction of previous elements. The curving line is seen as one figure, the line with the right angles as another figure.

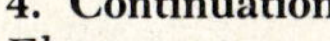

5. Common fate
Elements that move in the same direction are seen as belonging to each other. When alternate dancers in a ballet line step forward and make the same motion, we see them as a unit.

6. Reversible figure and ground
Occasionally a stimulus pattern is so organized that more than one figure-ground relationship may be perceived. When these conflict, they alternate in consciousness. In the example shown here, when the vase becomes "figure," the black ground seems to extend behind it; the reverse occurs when the two faces are seen as figures.

7. Good figure
The nervous system seems to prefer regular, simple forms. We see two overlapping squares here instead of a triangle and two irregular forms, equally possible from the sensory input.

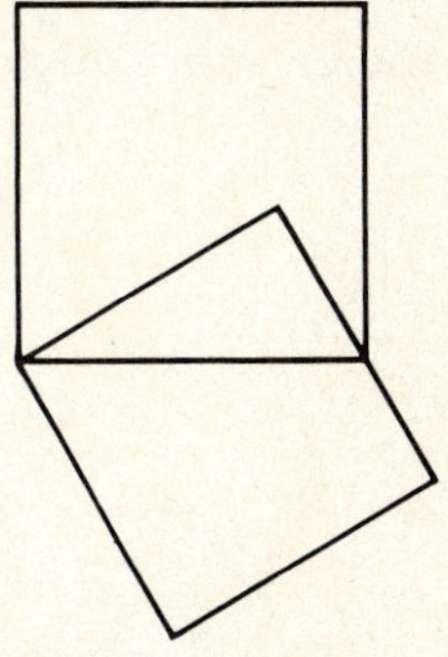

SOURCE: Philip G. Zimbardo (1979), *Psychology and Life*, 10th ed. (Glenview, Ill.: Scott, Foresman), p. 355.

and white ad is alone with many ads in color: black and white may then command attention because of *contrast*. Similarly, a soft commercial on a rock station may gain attention. *Position* of an advertisement affects attention; the cover advertisements on a magazine are more likely to be seen than the inside advertisements, and the first and last commercials in a sequence of commercials are more likely to be seen than the commercials in the middle. Commercials louder than the program context in which they appear operate on the principle of *intensity* and *contrast*. Frequency of the message has long been recognized by advertisers as a key factor in gaining message perception. *Movement* may also encourage perception, as in the flashing of a neon sign.

Personal Factors

Numerous studies, primarily from psychology but also in consumer behavior, clearly indicate that perception is, in part, determined by **personal factors**—the motivations and need-value systems of the observer—as well as the context in which the stimulus appears. Reality is personal and is somewhat different for each individual. It is formed by individuals' needs, drives, and past experiences; by what they have learned; by their motives and personalities; and by their cultural environments. Each of these factors influences whether a stimulus is perceived and how it is perceived. For example, the man who views himself as a playboy is more likely to perceive an ad for a sports car than for a sedan.

The person's needs at a particular moment are also determinants of perceptual selectivity. The thirsty person is more likely to perceive a beer ad. Span of attention limits perception; for example, we expect that the consumer's attention level declines as a sales speech gets longer. Mental set is reflected in positive or negative moods which may influence susceptibility to messages. And, of course, because of past experiences, the individual has formed brand preferences, making perception more likely for favored brands and less likely for unfavored brands.

In experiments with children, it has been found that the greater the child's valuation of or need for an object, the more important it is in his or her perceptual organization. In one classic study, when children were asked to match the size of coins to a variable light circle, poorer children "saw" the coins as much larger than did richer children.[9] In another such study, four-year-olds matched the size of a disk to a variable circle of light. They were then told that the disk was a candy wafer they would be allowed to eat. When they matched sizes again, their estimates increased by 35 percent.[10]

Of course, personal factors and stimulus factors do not work independently, as some classic experiments have demonstrated. In one study a tachistoscope was used to flash a variety of words on a screen for progressively longer periods of time. The researchers wanted to know which words the individual would discriminate first, that is, in the shortest exposure time. The subjects were found to favor or perceive those objects (words) which were personally valued or needed and to exclude or not perceive objects which were threatening or irrelevant.[11] In another set of experiments, subjects were shown ambiguous pictures after being deprived of food. As their hunger increased, they perceived more and more food objects in the ambiguous perceptual field. Beyond a certain point, however (about nine hours), they began to see fewer food objects, as perceptual defense or repression took hold.[12]

An interesting issue, and one constantly faced by marketing management, is whether marketer and consumer perceptions are, in any sense, consistent. Do consumers see the brand the same way as marketers, advertisers, and package designers see it? This question of consumer versus marketer perceptual consistency was directly assessed in a study of reactions to a new package design. The product involved was intended for use by men, but would normally be bought by women as a gift item. Male and female consumers, as well as the firm's managers and designers, gave their reactions to eighteen proposed package designs. The males and females in the consumer group were similar in their evaluations, and the members of management and the designers in the other group agreed for the most part, but fairly substantial disagreement existed between the two groups. According to the researchers, they "were apparently using conflicting criteria in evaluating the designs." The researchers stressed the marketing implication that if the package-design decision had been made by management and designers, "the net effect would have been to select designs which would have had the least appeal so far as the consumers sampled were concerned."[13]

The interplay of stimulus and personal factors is also illustrated in Exhibit 8–2, which relates the story of Anheuser-Busch's entry into the soft-drink market. The stimulus offered, an adult soft drink called *Chelsea*, was designed and packaged to appeal to adult tastes, in competition with such products as Perrier water. However, some consumer groups viewed the new product as a "baby beer" because it contained traces of alcohol (less than one half of one percent) and was packaged in a unique way for a soft drink. (The photographs on p. 331 show Chelsea's packaging compared with that of some other products.) Again, the perception of the stimulus varied from management to consumers and among different consumer groups.

The Chelsea case illustrates the concept of *stimulus generalization*, whereby some consumers respond in the same manner to a new stimulus (Chelsea soft drink) as to an unintended stimulus (beer). In general, the marketing manager's objective is to achieve stimulus discrimination for a particular brand and to avoid confusion with other brands. Occasionally, however, a manufacturer will attempt to be associated with a successful brand and to "borrow" some of the positive attributes of that brand. For example, a number of car manufacturers compare themselves to BMW, hoping that consumers will then consider their brand in the same, desirable way.

stimulus generalization

Such deliberate attempts at stimulus generalization may also have the goal of increasing the probability that a brand will fall within the *evoked set* of brands considered for purchase. For example, if Saab says that it is better than BMW, the hope is that when a consumer contemplates purchase, Saab will be one of the brands considered. The evoked set may actually be limited to a group of cars with somewhat similar attributes—for example, BMW, Volvo, Saab, and Peugeot. Frequently, consumers have a limited evoked set of brands within a product category. Howard reports that for coffee, although consumers know 10.2 brands, the evoked set of brands considered is 4.2; for toothpaste the evoked set is 3.1 from 10.4 brands known.[14]

Threshold Levels

Human senses have upper and lower limits of response to sensory stimulation, known as **threshold levels.** The lower threshold is the point below which

EXHIBIT 8–2
THE INTERPLAY OF STIMULUS AND PERSONAL FACTORS

CHELSEA SOFT DRINK

In 1978 Anheuser-Busch, the nation's largest beer producer, entered the soft-drink market with a new product called *Chelsea*. Anheuser-Busch was attracted by the high sales and growth of soft drinks and sought to offer an adult soft drink in competition with Perrier. Chelsea was an all-natural product of amber color made of ginger, apple, lemon, and malt. It was foamy when poured and was positioned as a less sweet, premium-priced soft drink for adults. Only adults appeared in its commercials.

Soon after introduction to test market, however, problems began. The new soft drink contained traces of alcohol (less than one-half percent), as did a number of other soft drinks. It was advertised as the "not-so-soft" drink, and it utilized nontraditional soft-drink packaging to help establish an adult image, give it uniqueness, and justify its premium price. However, some people felt it resembled a beer bottle. You can judge for yourself from the pictures on page 331 whether this new product could have been confused with beer.

A public protest began from nurses, clergy, and educators, who believed that Anheuser-Busch was attempting to "precondition" children to beer; they dubbed the new product a *baby beer*. Despite Anheuser-Busch's adult targeting and advertising, and despite the fact that the alcohol traces were so small in quantity, the Anheuser-Busch name on the bottle was a "stimulus" that suggested that this was an alcoholic beverage and not a soft drink.

Anheuser-Busch responded to the public criticism by eliminating all traces of alcohol, taking out the foam, modifying the bottle, changing the advertising campaign from "not-so-soft" to "the natural alternative," and moving the name *Anheuser-Busch* from the front of the label. However, this "new" Chelsea never caught on, and the product was withdrawn from the market. The question is whether the product could have succeeded if it had been positioned slightly differently initially in order to avoid the perception of *baby beer* and to achieve recognition as an adult-only soft drink.

SOURCE: Based on the following newspaper reports: *Washington Post*, Oct. 17, 1978, p. 1, 6; *Advertising Age*, Oct. 23, 1978; and *New York Times*, Dec. 13, 1978, p. D5.

a stimulus cannot be perceived. The upper threshold is the point above which any increase in the intensity of the stimulus will not be noticed. Related to the lower threshold is the notion of *subliminal perception* (discussed later in this chapter), whereby a stimulus may be perceived "subconsciously" by the individual. A concern here is that people may be persuaded by advertising messages of which they are not conscious.

Of particular interest in marketing is the *differential threshold level,* that is, the minimum difference *in* a stimulus that will be noticed by the individual or the minimum difference *between* stimuli that will be noticed. We sometimes refer to this as the "just-noticeable difference"—j.n.d. The formalization of this concept is reflected in **Weber's Law,** which relates initial stimulus intensity level and change in intensity as follows.

differential threshold level

$$K = \frac{\Delta I}{I}$$

where

ΔI = the smallest increase in stimulus insensity that will be just noticeable to the person,

I = the intensity of the stimulus before the increase, and

K = the constant increase or decrease necessary for the stimulus to be noticed.

Basically, Weber's law states that the amount of the just-noticeable difference will depend upon the initial stimulus intensity: the higher the initial intensity, then the greater the increase in intensity for the individual to notice the change.

The differential threshold-level concept has some interesting implications for several aspects of consumer behavior.

Pricing   When is a price change *meaningful* (noticeable) to the consumer? In line with Weber's law, this depends on the initial price. A price increase of $100 for a $400 television set will be more noticeable to the consumer than a price increase of $100 for an $8000 car. In seeking to create a "discount" image a store will have to cope with this phenomenon in reverse. Consumers may not perceive significant change because most changes will be of limited dollar value. This suggests the approach followed by many discounters of severely discounting a limited set of popular items in order to cross the differential threshold and to gain consumer attention.

Monroe, in a review of price-perception research, confirms the value of Weber's law and its reformulation as the Weber-Fechner law, which adds the thesis that buyers have upper and lower price thresholds. Research confirms that there is a range of prices consumers are willing to pay and that consumers may refrain from buying a product not only when the price is too high, but also when it is too low. Research also shows that people are more sensitive to price increases than to price decreases.[15]

Product or Service Design   Small improvements in a product or service may follow the same principle of failing to cross the differential threshold. This may be desirable in some cases. For example, a coffee may be produced using different combinations of beans depending on commodity prices by country, and yet the consumer may not be aware of any change in the product. Similarly, as a manufacturer updates a package or a symbol, care must be taken to avoid losing identity. Exhibit 8–3, for example, shows the changes in Betty Crocker over the years as the corporate symbol for General Mills. These changes would seem to fall below the level of the just-noticeable difference.

However, a manufacturer may sometimes have the opposite objective—breaking through, and having consumers notice a change. For example, if a brand was being improved, it might be better to improve just one or two attributes dramatically than all attributes a limited amount.

Advertising   The probability of an advertisement's being seen depends on many factors, especially the personal factors a consumer brings to the situation. Weber's law again applies, however, in breaking through the consumer's differential threshold level. Whether an advertisement will be seen depends on its stimulus intensity relative to the stimulus intensity of other ads. In today's advertising environment advertisers sometimes have to go to extremes to achieve a just-noticeable difference: multiple-page ads in magazines, color ads in newspapers, and so forth. But whether the additional awareness of the advertisements justifies the additional cost is always a question.

Halo Effect

A major advantage of a well-known brand or company name is its **halo effect**—the tendency of the consumer to form a generally positive impression across items in the product line. IBM products, for example, are frequently judged to be superior, whether or not they actually are.

Psychologists interested in measurement have observed the halo-effect phenomenon for over a half century. As early as 1920, Edward L. Thorndike, an experimental psychologist, wrote that when employees in large industrial corporations were rated by their supervisors, there was a high correlation among ratings for such traits as intelligence, industriousness, technical skills, and reliability.[16] He believed that the ratings on specific traits were affected by a marked tendency for the supervisors to judge the employees in global terms as good or inferior, and for that global assessment to bias specific judgments on specific traits. Those judged *good* were then perceived as being good in everything, and those judged *bad* were perceived as being poor in everything. Thorndike termed this "constant error" the *halo effect*.

Since then many studies in psychology[17] and consumer behavior[18] have documented the tendency for the individual to form consistent impressions. Contradictory information is often ignored, and the perceiver distorts or rearranges information to eliminate inconsistencies.[19]

An interesting example involving the halo effect was a case brought by the Federal Trade Commission against ITT Continental Baking Company and its advertising agency, Ted Bates Company. It was alleged that Wonder Bread was falsely represented to be "an extraordinary food for producing dramatic growth in children."[20] In testimony introduced at the hearings, some percentage of consumers did think that Wonder Bread was superior in nutritional value to other breads—about 5 percent of consumers in one study and 17 percent in another. The Wonder Bread defense was that consumers were not influenced by the specific content of the advertisements but rather by the halo effect that Wonder Bread had achieved as the best-selling brand. The student may judge for himself or herself whether the perceived nutritional advantage over other breads was due to "the general aura of superiority ascribed by consumers" to the widely used brand, or due to Wonder Bread's advertising campaign showing children in commercials and claiming that "Wonder Bread builds strong bodies twelve ways."

1968

1972

1980

PRODUCT POSITIONING

The general objective of **product positioning** is to achieve brand differentiation relative to competitors in the consumer's mind. In simple terms, the goal is to move consumers from perceiving the company's offering as a **commodity** to perceiving it as a **specialty** (as shown below) that is identifiable and differentiated from other manufacturers' offerings within the product category.

Commodity ───────────────▶	**Specialty**
Company's market offering is perceived by consumers to lack attributes distinguishing it from other companies' market offerings. For example, it is "just another coffee."	Company's market offering is perceived by consumers to have attributes distinguishable from other companies' market offerings. For example, *Maxwell House* or *Folger's* coffee.

The logic and value of brand differentiation is in the market "leverage" it provides. Brand differentiation yields the following kinds of leverage.

- *Pricing Leverage.* Achieving brand differentiation gives the brand some degree of pricing leverage. In general, this means that the brand can command a higher price. Sometimes brand differentiation is based on lower price, however, as with Suave shampoo.

  The ability to command a higher price is shown in such cases as that of Bayer aspirin, which sells far above the price of a private-label (store brand) aspirin, despite the identical chemical composition of all aspirin. Similarly, Smirnoff vodka commands a premium price over Popov, which sells for more than Relska; yet all three brands of vodka are produced by Heublein. Furthermore, U.S. government controls are such that all brands are essentially the same. American-made vodka must be "neutral spirits . . . so treated . . . as to be without distinctive character, aroma, or taste." By this edict vodka is really nothing but pure, colorless, odorless, tasteless alcohol.

- *Advertising Leverage.* A company must have brand differentiation in order to advertise, or must create that differentiation through advertising. Otherwise, the advertising may benefit competitors as much as the company doing the advertising. For example, some time ago McDonald's modified its "You deserve a break today" campaign by adding a more promotional orientation (free posters, free glasses, contests, and so forth) and some specific commercials which are more uniquely McDonald's ("Big Mac attack," "Egg McMuffin"). The logic was to have the advertising benefit *only* McDonald's in a way that "You deserve a break today" does not uniquely do, since you could also get a break at Burger King, Wendy's, or any other restaurant. Executives at Yamaha once suggested to the authors that Honda advertising benefited Yamaha as well as Honda, since the stress was on the "escape and freedom" of riding a motorbike—benefits which can be achieved with any bike (except, perhaps, Harley-Davidson, which appeals to the "macho" segments of the market!).

- *Distribution Leverage.* Strong brand differentiation makes it easier to gain distribution. A supermarket *must* carry Tide, Heinz Ketchup, Kleenex, and other well-known brands. Other factors (such as profit margins) operate, but a retail store wants to sell brands that people are looking for to build volume and satisfaction with the store. Lacking strong differentiation places a brand at a considerable disadvantage.

- *Salesforce Leverage.* Strong brand (or company) differentiation makes it easier for the salespeople to gain entry to the buyer. Buyers would rather talk to representatives of companies that they know and in which they have confidence.

METHODS FOR PRODUCT POSITIONING

In recent years some sophisticated techniques have become available for measuring consumer perceptions concerning product positioning. The two most widely used of these techniques are *perceptual mapping* and *conjoint analysis*. We shall first discuss these techniques and then relate them to the strategic issues of positioning new products and of whether to reposition established products.

Perceptual Mapping

Much as a road map "positions" cities relative to one another in a two-dimensional space, a **perceptual map** is designed to position objects or brands relative to one another. The distinction is that the basis for the positioning is consumer perceptions of how similar or dissimilar brands are.

Perceptual mapping is based on multidimensional scaling techniques developed by mathematical psychologists. Data are gathered by asking consumers to rate brands as *similar* or *dissimilar*. The perceptual map is derived by mathematically combining all of the individual judgments and finding a geometric representation (map) in which brands judged to be similar are plotted near each other and brands judged to be dissimilar are plotted away from each other.

multidimensional scaling

For example, consumers might be asked to rate the following brands from *most similar* to *least similar*: Special K, Wheaties, Frosted Flakes, and Life. The data from a single respondent might be as follows.

Special K and Life	Most similar
Wheaties and Life	
Special K and Wheaties	
Wheaties and Frosted Flakes	
Frosted Flakes and Life	
Special K and Frosted Flakes	Least similar

Using a multidimensional scaling algorithm for all consumers' judgments, the perceptual map in Exhibit 8–4 might be obtained. The algorithm provides the map and positionings, but the researcher must label the axes. In this case, the researcher might label the horizontal dimension *high sugar–low sugar* and the vertical dimension *high nutrition–low nutrition.*

The value of such a perceptual map is in showing the positioning of your brand relative to competition. In Exhibit 8–4 Special K is perceived to be highest on nutrition and lowest on sugar; Life is also quite high on nutrition and near the midpoint on sugar; Wheaties is near the midpoint on nutrition and reasonably low on sugar; and Frosted Flakes is low on nutrition and high on sugar. A number of diagnostic questions can be asked based on this map, such as the following:

- Are these perceptions in line with reality? For example, is Frosted Flakes really low on nutrition?
- What is the ideal point for a particular market segment? For example, Special K may be near the ideal preference point for a major segment of adults.
- Should a brand consider repositioning? For example, should Frosted Flakes seek to build its nutritional image among adults, who are likely to do the actual buying for their children?
- Are new product opportunities suggested? For example, what would be the market reaction to a new high sugar/high nutrition cereal?

An actual perceptual map for Flying Tiger Line, a nonpassenger airline, is shown in Exhibit 8–5. The map shows Flying Tiger's positioning on the key dimensions of *small package–large package* (vertical axis) and *low service/low*

EXHIBIT 8–4
HYPOTHETICAL PERCEPTUAL MAP FOR CEREALS

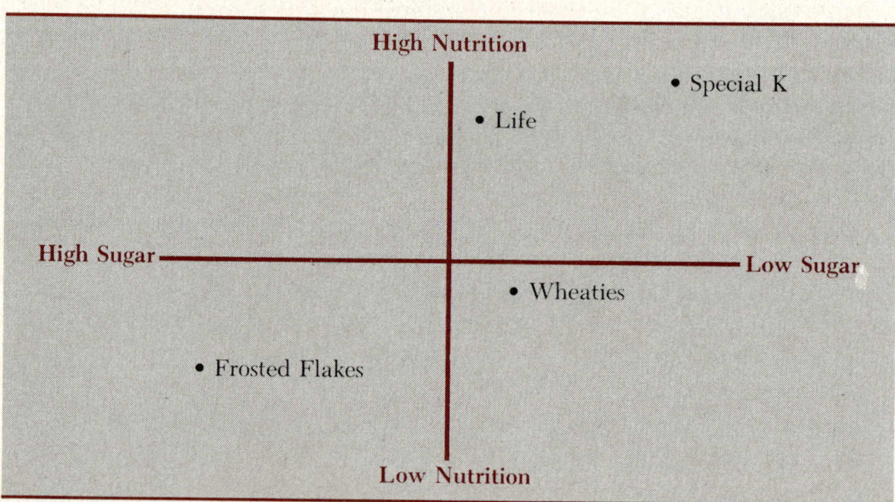

rates–high service/high rates (horizontal axis). The map also shows the positioning of Flying Tiger's major competitors. As can be seen, some of these competitors, such as UPS, Federal Express, and Emery, are perceived very differently from Flying Tiger.

The marketing-strategy questions raised by this map are whether Flying Tiger is perceived in a way that is compatible with management's objectives and whether any repositioning should be attempted or new products introduced in other positions within the market. The latter depends on the demand levels in the various quadrants, the level of competition, and the profitability of the various quadrants. For example, Flying Tiger has implemented plans to broaden its portfolio and to compete not only in the large-package (freight) part of the market but in the small-package part of the market as well, since this part of the market is more profitable.

Conjoint Analysis

As with perceptual mapping, **conjoint analysis** is an approach developed by mathematical psychologists.[21] It is concerned with measuring the impact of specific product or service attributes (such as punctuality of an airline or type of aircraft) on consumer preference or utility. Consumers are asked to make trade-offs among various attributes and to give an evaluation of the relative utility of various combinations of alternatives.

As an example of the conjoint approach, Green and Wind have studied the decision concerning choice of a flight to Paris for a business meeting. Two alternatives (among many others) might give some sense of the approach.

EXHIBIT 8–5
A PERCEPTUAL MAP OF AIR FREIGHT AND AIR EXPRESS COMPETITORS

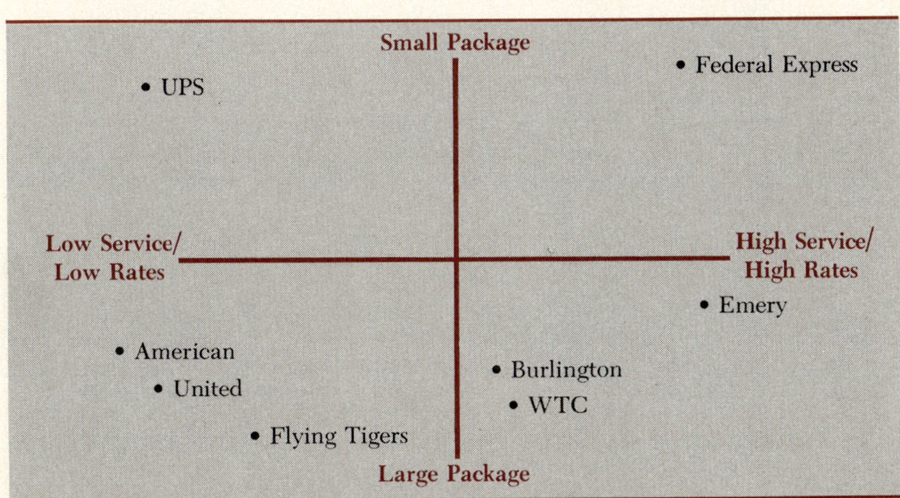

SOURCE: Flying Tiger Line Marketing Research, 1978. Used with permission.

EXHIBIT 8–6
UTILITY FUNCTIONS FOR AIR TRAVELERS TO PARIS

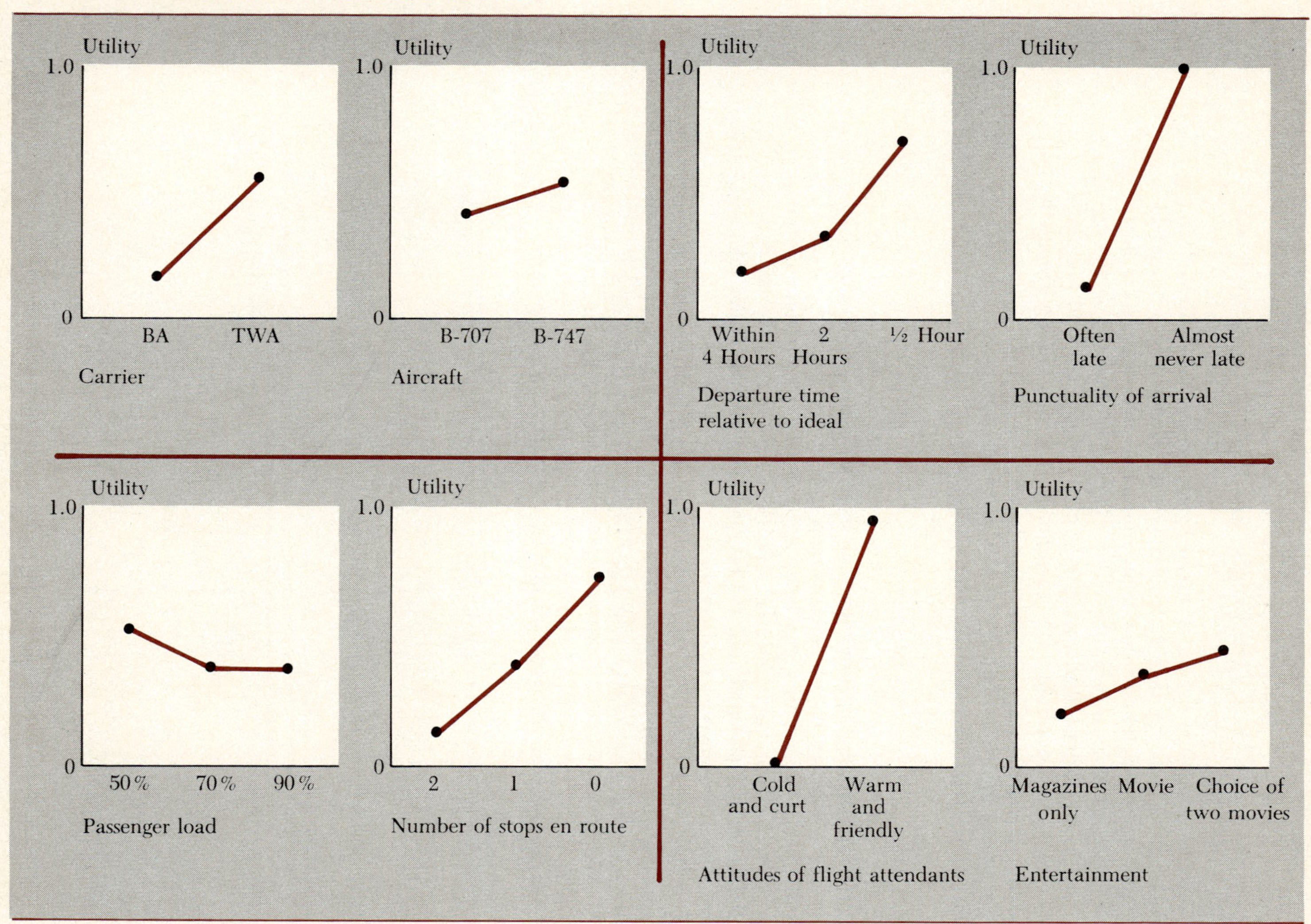

SOURCE: Paul E. Green and Yoram Wind (1975), "New Ways to Measure Consumers' Judgments," *Harvard Business Review*, 53 (July-Aug.), p. 112.

A B-707 flown by British Airways that will depart within two hours of the time you would like to leave and that is often late in arriving in Paris. The plane will make two intermediate stops, and it is anticipated that it will be 50% full. Flight attendants are "warm and friendly," and you would have a choice of two movies for entertainment.

A B-747 flown by TWA that will depart within four hours of the time you would like to leave and that is almost never late in arriving in Paris. The flight is nonstop, and it is anticipated that the plane will be 90% full. Flight attendants are "cold and curt" and only magazines are provided for entertainment.[22]

The attributes being considered include carrier (British Airways vs. TWA), type of aircraft, punctuality of arrival, and so forth. Consumers are asked to make trade-offs among the various alternatives—as can be seen from the two examples—since the ideal can rarely be achieved. These evaluations then lead to a set of utilities for each attribute, again based on a mathematical algorithm. For the airline study, the utilities are shown in Exhibit 8–6. It can be seen that:

- The name TWA has a considerably higher utility than British Airways.
- A Boeing 747 is preferred to a Boeing 707, but not by much.
- Departure time close to the ideal is very important.
- Punctuality of arrival is critical.
- Lower passenger load (50%) has some value over higher passenger load (70% or above).
- Number of stops is highly important.
- Attitude of flight attendants is critical.
- Level of entertainment is of some value.

Such results are of considerable value in product design. From Exhibit 8–6 we gain direction as to how to design an airline service with the highest possible utility—subject, of course, to the economic feasibility of providing such a service. We see, for example, that type of aircraft is not nearly as important as punctuality and that in-cabin entertainment is not nearly as important as the attitudes of flight attendants. Again, we have gained insight and direction for positioning our product or service relative to competition.

THE SYMBOLIC NATURE OF POSITIONING

Product positioning, as perceived by consumers, is a function not only of objective product attributes (such as punctuality or type of aircraft), but also of more symbolic dimensions (such as status or popularity). The term **brand image** is often used to refer to the consumer's overall impression of a brand.

    The symbolic nature of positioning and the consumer's reliance on brand images is shown, for example, in the automobile market. Fairly consistent

brand image

brand images of cars exist within market segments. For example, when students were asked to match cars with occupations, very definite profiles emerged; senior executives were expected to drive Mercedes or Cadillacs, grandmothers to drive Buick Skylarks, and so on (see Exhibit 8–7).

The consumer's behavior in the market is in many ways a response to such brand images, which provide a shorthand means of coping with the array of product stimuli offered. Sidney J. Levy, who has had a major impact on the development of consumer-behavior theory, concludes that people buy things not only for what they can do but also for what they mean.[23] Often we buy a product or service because we invest it with a symbolic meaning above and beyond its actual physical characteristics. For example, many clothing styles are purchased because they imply chic, sexuality, or a flouting of the values of an older generation, rather than because they provide warmth or protection. In most cases, consumers who buy a new car trade in a car that runs; they are not buying transportation but rather style, status, luxury, and the like.

impression formation

The realization that consumers will use consumption as a means of saying something about themselves—*impression formation*—has been recognized for generations. Thorstein Veblen, in *The Theory of the Leisure Class*, was an early proponent (at least among economists) of the principle of consumer self-enhancement or **conspicuous consumption**. Veblen viewed consumer motivation as "a race for reputability on the basis of an invidious comparison." He summarized his leisure-class theory as follows.

conspicuous consumption

> *In order to gain and hold the esteem of men it is not sufficient merely to possess wealth or power. The wealth or power must be put in evidence, for esteem is awarded only on evidence.*[24]

EXHIBIT 8–7
BRAND IMAGES OF CARS

When 300 students at the University of Pennsylvania were asked which car was most appropriate for the following people, they made the following choices from a list of 30 cars.

Young Executive	BMW
Grandmother	Dodge Dart or Buick Skylark
College Male	Mustang
Senior Executive	Mercedes or Cadillac
Playboy	Corvette
Nurse	Toyota
College Professor	Volvo
Teacher	VW Rabbit
Doctor	Mercedes
College Female	Toyota or Datsun

More recently, Belk has summarized the value of conspicuous consumption and its role in impression formation in the following terms:

> *The belief that a person's possessions and expenditures reveal something about the person may be one of the strongest cultural universals affecting consumer behavior. In virtually all cultures, visible products and services are the bases for inferences about the status, personality, and disposition of the owner or consumer of these goods. Relevant cues may be noted not only in the number and type of goods consumed, but also in such features as their style, color, uniqueness, condition, and brand name.*[25]

The importance of the symbolic meaning, or image, of a product in an affluent society probably cannot be overestimated. A created image, combined with our ability to perceive what we want to perceive, is an important factor in brand selection for many products. Research has shown, for example, that subjects are not able to discern the taste differences among various brands of beer when labels are removed, despite clear brand preferences. That is, the associations the labels evoke in the minds of the subjects influence their evaluations of such attributes as taste, aroma, and carbonation.[26] The repositioning of Miller beer from "the champagne of bottled beer" to "quitting time is Miller time" was essentially an image change, not a product change.

Studies of consumers' abilities to discriminate among brands have been carried out dozens of times, with similar results, on products ranging from cigarettes, to bread, to cola beverages, to turkey meat. However, as is typical in the social sciences, not all studies support the same conclusion (in this case, that consumers cannot discriminate among brands in a blind test). For example, some researchers believe that some of these experimental results may have been due to methodological shortcomings rather than to people's inherent inability to discriminate.[27] In a follow-up to the original study on beer, for example, the conclusion that beer drinkers cannot distinguish among brands was challenged.[28] Nevertheless, across considerable amounts of research the basic principle of selective perception holds. It would seem that consumers are simply not highly skilled in discriminating among brands unless the label or other symbolic identification is provided. When these cues are present, consumers generally prefer Bayer aspirin over a private-label brand, Coors beer over Schlitz, and Revlon over Walgreen.[29]

A question logically may be raised as to why consumers hold brand images and why they don't know that they cannot discriminate among brands. In fact, consumers *may* know that they cannot discriminate—as with beers—and still hold brand images and preferences. This may be due to social reasons (drinking what friends drink) or just because it is easier to hold brand preferences. This *routinizes* behavior. If we had to decide which brands to buy each time we visited a store, all of our cognitive energies would be devoted to shopping. Instead, we settle on brand preferences in order to simplify decision-making.

PERCEIVED RISK

A further concept based on perception and relevant to consumer behavior is the amount of risk that consumers perceive when considering a purchase. **Perceived risk** has been a topic of interest in the consumer-behavior literature since about 1960. Taken from psychology, the concept was first introduced in marketing by Raymond Bauer, another leading scholar in the development of consumer behavior as a field of study, who claimed that much of consumer behavior involved risk "in the sense that any action of a consumer will produce consequences which he cannot anticipate with anything approximating certainty, and some of which at least are likely to be unpleasant."[30]

The thesis behind the perceived-risk concept is that consumers will tend to make risk-minimizing decisions based on their perception of purchase risk. Of course, if no risk is perceived, then there will be no effect on consumer behavior. The level of perceived risk is considered to be a function of the possible *consequences* of a purchase and the *uncertainty* involved. *Consequences* can be thought of as the costs if a given event occurs and may range from simple monetary loss and disappointment if a new food item does not live up to expectations to food poisoning. The *uncertainty* element can be phrased in terms of probabilities that given consequences will occur.

Types of Risk

The types of risk that a consumer might perceive are as follows.

- *Functional risk.* The product may not perform as expected. This may be a particular concern with new products.
- *Financial risk.* The product may not be worth its cost. Consumers may perceive financial risk, for example, in buying a new technology for which prices are expected to come down, as with home computers.
- *Physical risk.* The product may be harmful, as in the case of Rely Tampons.
- *Psychological risk.* The product may not fulfill self-concept needs. Psychological risk would seem to be particularly important for products that are high in psychological benefits, such as fashion and cosmetics.
- *Social risk.* The product may not be socially accepted, as with a new clothing style.[31]

Products may be high or low on each dimension. Some products, such as cars, may have high perceived-risk profiles when there can be concern about functional risk, financial risk, psychological risk, and social risk. Other products, such as dry spaghetti, may have low risk profiles.[32] Research on leisure activities has shown very different perceived-risk profiles for activities ranging from snowmobiling (high on almost all risk dimensions) to reading (low on almost all risk dimensions).[33] Risk may also be perceived differently by shopping situation. High-income consumers, for example, are less likely to patronize discount stores for high social-risk products (such as fashion or style items) than for low social-risk products (such as toys or cookware).[34]

Consumer Risk Handling

The amount of risk perceived varies by consumer. Some consumers seem to
have a high tolerance for discrepant information, ambiguity, and perceived
risk, whereas others have a low tolerance.[35] High-risk perceivers have sometimes been referred to as *narrow categorizers* who find security by limiting
their choice considerations; low-risk perceivers are *broad categorizers*, willing
to expand their search and choice considerations.[36] Alternatively, we may
think of high-risk perceivers as *simplifiers,* who limit search and avoid discrepant information.[37]

    Ultimately, if it is perceived, consumers will seek to reduce risk to some
"tolerable" level, which, as we have seen, will vary by individual. We discuss
the major ways consumers handle risk below, and then list marketing actions
that might be taken to help reduce consumer perception of risk.

narrow and broad categorizers

Consumer Risk-Reduction Strategies   An initial consumer strategy for reducing risk could be to reduce the amount at stake, by buying in smaller
quantities, for example. Alternatively, the consumer could secure more information in order to make a more informed decision. For high social-risk products, the consumer might seek increased "social" information from other people; for high functional-risk products, he or she might seek more "objective"
information from such sources as *Consumer Reports.*

    The shopping experience may also help reduce risk. The consumer may
examine the product, learn how to use it, seek in-store help and expertise,
and engage in comparison shopping for the best price in order to reduce
financial risk.

    Further risk-reduction strategies are brand loyalty, buying the brand with
the highest price (on the assumption of a price-quality relationship), buying
the brand with the lowest price (on the assumption of least financial risk), and
buying the brand with the best warranty.[38] Different strategies, and even
conflicting strategies, may be used depending on the individual consumer and
the risk dimension at issue. If the consumer is seeking to reduce functional
risk, for example, a different method may be used (such as reliance on *Consumer Reports*) from that for reducing social risk (reliance on friends).

    Some of the variety of methods of risk handling are illustrated in the com-
ments of two consumers in interviews. One consumer tended to rely on quality brands and past experience, and was particularly susceptible to the perception of social risk. Her comments reflect her handling of risk:

> *I always stick with the tried and true because if something has been on the
> market a long time you can be sure it is good. . . . I think it always pays
> to buy the more expensive of two things. . . . If I'm having guests I'll buy
> the best quality food.*

The other consumer tended to rely on information gathering and analysis and
was more susceptible to the perception of financial risk: ". . . when I am
buying something, I will try to get the best buy." She was therefore likely to

compare prices at more than one store and to compute price per ounce when faced with more than one size of an item.[39]

Marketing Strategies for Risk Reduction   The challenge for marketers of products with a high-risk profile is to help consumers reduce perceived risk, by actions such as the following.

- providing extensive information in advertising and packaging
- providing seals of approval (for example, the *Good Housekeeping* seal)
- providing endorsements from influential people (for example, Arnold Palmer endorsing golf clubs)
- providing free trial of the product and small (lower risk) sized packages
- providing extensive usage instructions (for example, as Clairol does for haircoloring)
- providing access to further information (for example, Whirlpool Appliance's "Cool Line" 800-number that a buyer can call for help)
- providing warranties and guarantees
- providing high personal service (for example, IBM's sales approach for many of its business products)

These strategies, alone or in combination, may help reduce consumer risk perception and encourage product purchase.[40]

SUBLIMINAL PERCEPTION

A final topic of particular interest is **subliminal perception,** a phenomenon that supposedly can enable advertisers to broadcast or present messages that are "invisible" but that can cause consumers to buy products without being aware that they have been influenced. Public concern over the topic emerged some years ago with the announcement that a mysterious new technique had been used to induce unsuspecting moviegoers in New Jersey to eat popcorn and drink Coca-Cola. It was reported that the technique (repeatedly flashing popcorn and Coca-Cola ads on the screen so quickly that the audience was unaware of them) made use of something called *subliminal perception*. Nearly 50,000 people were exposed in New Jersey, and the sales of popcorn and Coca-Cola increased 18 to 58 percent (according to the proponents of this "new" technique).[41]

A segment of the population responded with alarm and anxiety. The technique seemed ominous, and official government agencies began to hold hearings. Here was an exciting—or frightening—idea: People could be influenced without being aware of it. Mass hypnotism, brainwashing, and loss of free will were all conjured up in the surrounding hysteria.

But in the scientific community the question that arose immediately was, Does the technique work? Was this a scientifically controlled study? Unanswered questions abounded. How hot was it in New Jersey on those critical days? Was the theater air-conditioned? In the film shown, *Picnic*, people ate and drank just such products. Did that have an effect? Is it conceivable that showing a "commercial" for 1/50 or 1/100 or even a reported 1/3000 of a second works? Interestingly, psychologists had studied the phenomenon for years with negative results. The conclusion among psychologists and serious consumer researchers was that subliminal perception was simply another gimmick to which little attention need be paid.

Interest in subliminal perception has rekindled recently, however, perhaps to a large extent because of the writings of Wilson Bryan Key, who "finds" subliminal cues embedded in advertising. The author alleges that erotic cues have been hidden in advertisements which will appeal to subconscious sex drives.[42] However, the proof for this allegation is most debatable, and no evidence is provided that such hidden cues do indeed lead to advertising effectiveness.

In short, the value of subliminal perception has been largely discredited. In an exhaustive review of the topic and its relevance for advertising, Moore concludes that the effects of subliminal advertising simply do not match the power ascribed by certain advocates.

In general, the literature on subliminal perception shows that the most clearly documented effects are obtained only in highly contrived and artificial situations. These effects, when present, are brief and of small magnitude. The result is perhaps best construed as an epiphenomenon—a subtle and fleeting by-product of the complexities of human cognitive activity. These processes have no apparent relevance to the goals of advertising.[43]

SUMMARY

A great deal of consumer behavior depends on consumer perception—the individual's impression of the stimulus. Whether the consumer becomes aware of a brand and the meaning attached to it depends on a number of principles of perception theory.

1. Perception is selective in that a person perceives only a small part of the total perceptual field.
2. Perception is organized and possesses meaning.
3. What the individual sees (selection) and how it is seen (organization) are dependent upon the stimulus itself and the personal characteristics of the individual.

Ultimately, the marketing challenge is to build a desired perception, or "positioning," relative to other brands, but consumers have an amazing ability not to notice advertisements, to misinterpret them, or to fail to attach the meanings desired by marketing communicators. Marketers aim to have the consumer think of a brand as part of the "evoked set" of brands considered, and to discriminate and differentiate the brand from other brands.

For many product categories, brand differentiation must be based on symbolic attributes and, indeed, consumers often buy on a symbolic basis, depending on the product category. Clothes are purchased less for warmth than for style, for example, and many brand decisions by consumers are in response to the brands' images.

The concept of perceived risk recognizes that consumers experience a sense of risk in purchase, and that consumer behavior can profitably be studied as risk-reducing behavior. Various types of risk may be perceived—functional, financial, physical, psychological, and social—and consumers perceive varying amounts of risk and have varying tolerance levels for risk. Consumer risk-reduction strategies include a range of alternatives depending on the type of risk.

Subliminal perception, perception of stimuli presented just below the individual's perceptual threshold level, has been viewed with great interest and with alarm. Despite the sensationalism of the topic, there is no evidence to suggest the value of subliminal approaches.

KEY CONCEPTS

product positioning	stimulus factors	Weber's law
brand differentiation	personal factors	perceived risk
commodity	selectivity	subliminal perception
specialty	organization	conspicuous
brand image	threshold level	consumption
perception	halo effect	perceptual mapping
		conjoint analysis

DISCUSSION QUESTIONS

1. What stimulus factors should you be concerned with in developing an advertising strategy?
2. What is the halo effect? How might this affect a consumer's purchasing behavior?
3. Why do consumers hold brand preferences if they often cannot distinguish among brands in blind taste tests?
4. Discuss the impact of Weber's law on decisions involving pricing, product design, and advertising.
5. Describe risk-reduction strategies that a consumer might use for each of the five types of perceived risk. Discuss how a marketing organization could help consumers reduce each type of risk.
6. What is subliminal perception? Does it pose a threat to unaware consumers?
7. Discuss the kinds of leverage that brand differentiation provides.
8. Refer to the discussion of Chelsea brand soft drink in Exhibit 8–2. How would an understanding of perception theory have helped Anheuser-Busch avoid its problems?

NOTES

1. The concept of *positioning* seems to have been proposed by advertising executives Al Ries and Jack Trout in a 1972 article in *Advertising Age.* For an elaboration of their view, see Al Ries and Jack Trout (1981), *Positioning: The Battle for Your Mind* (New York: McGraw-Hill).

2. Philip G. Zimbardo (1979), *Psychology and Life,* 10th ed. (Glenview, Ill.: Scott, Foresman), p. 342.

3. George S. Day (1973), "General Foods Corporation—Maxim," in *Cases in Computer and Model Assisted Marketing: Planning,* ed. George S. Day et al. (Cupertino, Cal.: Hewlett Packard), pp. 65–92.

4. D. Ehrlich, I. Guttman, P. Schonbach, and J. Mill (1957), "Post-Decision Exposure to Relevant Information," *Journal of Abnormal and Social Psychology,* 54 (Jan.), pp. 98–102.

5. Raymond A. Bauer and Stephen A. Greyser (1968), *Advertising in America: The Consumer View* (Boston: Harvard Business School).

6. Bill Abrams (1983), "Sponsor Recall," *Wall Street Journal* (March 24), p. 35.

7. David Krech, Richard S. Crutchfield, and Egerton L. Ballachey (1962), *Individual in Society* (New York: McGraw-Hill), p. 20.

8. For a discussion of stimulus factors in advertising, see David A. Aaker and John G. Myers (1982), *Advertising Management* (Englewood Cliffs, N.J.: Prentice-Hall), Ch. 11.

9. Jerome Bruner and Cecil C. Goodman (1947), "Value and Need as Organizing Factors in Perception," *Journal of Abnormal and Social Psychology,* 42, pp. 33–44.

10. Jerome Bruner and Leo Postman (1951), "An Approach to Social Perception," in *Current Trends in Social Psychology,* ed. Wayne Dennis (Pittsburgh: Univ. of Pittsburgh Press).

11. Jerome Bruner and Leo Postman (1951).

12. R. Levine, I. Chein, and G. Murphy (1954), "The Relation of the Intensity of a Need to the Amount of Perceptual Distortion, A Preliminary Report," *Journal of Psychology,* 49, pp. 129–34.

13. Milton Blum and Valentine Appel (1961), "Consumer Versus Management Reaction in New Package Development," *Journal of Applied Psychology,* 45 (Aug.), pp. 222-24.

14. John A. Howard (1977), *Consumer Behavior: Application of Theory* (New York: McGraw-Hill), p. 32.

15. For a detailed discussion of Weber's law and price perception theory, see Kent Monroe (1979), *Pricing* (New York: McGraw-Hill), Ch. 3.

16. Edward L. Thorndike (1920), "A Constant Error in Psychological Ratings," *Journal of Applied Psychology,* 4 (March), pp. 25–29.

17. Richard E. Nisbett and Timothy DeCamp Wilson (1977), "The Halo Effect: Evidence for Unconscious Alterations of Judgments," *Journal of Personality and Social Psychology,* 35 (Apr.), pp. 250–56.

18. Neil E. Beckwith, Harold H. Kassarjian, and Donald R. Lehmann (1978), "Halo Effects in Marketing Research: Review and Prognosis," in *Advances in Consumer Research,* ed. H. Keith Hunt, Vol. 5 (Assn. for Consumer Research).

19. Jonathan L. Freedman, David O. Sears, and J. Merrill Carlsmith (1981), *Social Psychology* (Englewood Cliffs, N.J.: Prentice-Hall), p. 89.

20. Federal Trade Commission (1973), Final Order, Docket No. 8860 (Oct. 19).

21. For further reading on perceptual mapping and conjoint analysis, see Paul E. Green and Donald S. Tull (1978), *Research for Marketing Decisions* (Englewood Cliffs, N.J.: Prentice-Hall), Ch. 14 or Yoram J. Wind (1982), *Product Policy* (Reading, Mass.: Addison-Wesley), Ch. 4.

22. Paul E. Green (1975), "New Ways to Measure Consumers' Judgments," *Harvard Business Review,* 53 (July-Aug.), p. 107.

23. Sidney J. Levy (1959), "Symbols for Sale," *Harvard Business Review,* 37 (July-Aug.), pp. 117–24.

24. Thorstein Veblen (1899), *The Theory of the Leisure Class* (New York: Macmillan), p. 32.

25. Russell W. Belk (1977), "Assessing the Effects of Visible Consumption on Impression Formation," in *Advances in Consumer Research,* ed. H. Keith Hunt, Vol. 5 (Assn. for Consumer Research), p. 39.
26. Ralph I. Allison and Kenneth P. Uhl (1964), "Brand Identification and Perception," *Journal of Marketing Research,* 1 (Aug.), pp. 80–85.
27. Jacob Jacoby, Jerry C. Olson, and Rafael A. Haddock (1971), "Price, Brand Name and Product Composition Characteristics as Determinants of Perceived Quality," *Journal of Applied Psychology,* 55 (Dec.), pp. 570–79.
28. Gary A. Mauser (1979), "Allison and Uhl Revisited: The Effect of Taste and Brand Name on Perceptions and Preferences," in *Advances in Consumer Research,* ed. William L. Wilkie, Vol. 6 (Assn. for Consumer Research), pp. 161–65.
29. Bobby J. Calder and Robert E. Burnkrant (1977), "Interpersonal Influence on Consumer Behavior: An Attribution Theory Approach," *Journal of Consumer Research,* 4 (June), pp. 29–38.
30. Raymond A. Bauer (1960), "Consumer Behavior as Risk Taking," *Proceedings of the American Marketing Association,* ed. Robert S. Hancock (Chicago: American Marketing Assn.), p. 389.
31. Jacob Jacoby and Leon B. Kaplan (1972), "The Components of Perceived Risk," in *Proceedings of the Third Annual Conference of the Association for Consumer Research,* pp. 382-93.
32. Scott Cunningham (1967), "Major Dimensions of Perceived Risk," in *Risk Taking and Information Handling in Consumer Behavior,* ed. Donald F. Cox (Boston: Harvard Business School), p. 87.
33. Emmanuel J. Cheron and J. R. Brent Ritchie (1982), "Leisure Activities and Perceived Risk," *Journal of Leisure Research,* 14 (Spring), pp. 139–54.
34. V. Kanti Prasad (1975), "Socioeconomic Product Risk and Patronage Preferences of Retail Shoppers," *Journal of Marketing,* 39 (July), pp. 42–47.
35. Charles M. Schaninger (1976), "Perceived Risk and Personality," *Journal of Consumer Research,* 3 (Sept.), pp. 95–100.
36. B. T. Popielarz (1967), "An Explanation of Perceived Risk and Willingness to Try a New Product," *Journal of Marketing Research,* 4, pp. 368–73.
37. James R. Bettman (1971), "The Structure of Consumer Choice Processes," *Journal of Marketing Research,* 8, pp. 465–71.
38. Ted Roselius (1971), "Consumer Rankings of Risk Reduction Methods," *Journal of Marketing,* 35 (Jan.), pp. 56–61.
39. Donald F. Cox (1967), *Risk Taking and Information Handling in Consumer Behavior* (Boston: Harvard Business School), pp. 43, 55, 62, 65.
40. For a critical review of the perceived-risk concept, see Ivan Ross (1975), "Perceived Risk and Consumer Behavior: A Critical Review," in *Advances in Consumer Research,* ed. Mary Jane Schlinger, Vol. 2 (Assn. for Consumer Research), pp. 1–19.
41. This section is based on Harold H. Kassarjian and Thomas S. Robertson (1981), *Perspectives in Consumer Behavior* (Glenview, Ill.: Scott, Foresman), pp. 8–9.
42. See, for example, Wilson Bryan Key (1980), *The Clam-Plate Orgy: And Other Subliminal Techniques for Manipulating Your Behavior* (Englewood Cliffs, N.J.: Prentice-Hall).
43. Timothy E. Moore (1982), "Subliminal Advertising: What You See Is What You Get," *Journal of Marketing,* 46 (Spring), pp. 38–47.

9 Learning Theory: Advertising and Brand Loyalty Effects

A product manager for a nationally distributed brand of shampoo is developing an annual advertising and promotion plan and must make a number of difficult decisions. While the brand's market share grew rapidly after its introduction, it has declined slightly over the last year. The manager is wondering if the drop in share is partially a result of advertising "wear-out"—that is, since the same campaign has been used over the years, it may no longer be effective in generating and holding consumer interest. Perhaps a new campaign could revitalize the brand's image. On the other hand, moving to a new campaign would entail the lengthy process of generating consumer awareness and building knowledge, and there is a risk that a new campaign may be less memorable than the current advertisements.

Besides deciding on the overall campaign, the manager must also decide how to allocate the budget. Should funds be spent at a constant rate throughout the year, or should advertising be "pulsed," with periods of intense spending occurring, say, only three or four times a year?

Finally, the manager is considering using promotional coupons to encourage sales. Short-term sales of consumer goods tend to increase when cents-off coupons are offered to the consumer. However, the question of whether or not such coupons are effective in building long-term brand loyalty remains. Would it perhaps be wiser to allocate additional funds to advertising rather than to promotional coupons?

Decisions relating to advertising wear-out, continuous versus pulsed advertising schedules, and building brand loyalty, may benefit from an understanding of learning theory, which is derived from studies of the processes whereby individuals gain and retain knowledge about various stimuli. Psychologists have long examined the ways in which learning occurs, and much of this information is directly applicable to the field of consumer behavior.

This chapter treats consumer behavior as learned behavior. We examine the various categories of learning theory, beginning with the stimulus-response theories. Then we move to a discussion of the relationship between concepts from learning theory and consumer behavior. The chapter concludes with a consideration of stochastic models of buyer behavior, which offer a probabilistic approach to the study of brand loyalty and consumer learning.

CONSUMER BEHAVIOR IS LEARNED BEHAVIOR

Much of the behavior we exhibit as consumers is learned. As young children, we learn from our parents and society not only what we should eat, but also how we should eat. We learn that chicken constitutes "good food," but that many other birds, such as pigeons, do not. We learn to appreciate the taste of clams, mussels, and scallops, while shunning periwinkles and barnacles. Interestingly, all of these seemingly "natural" tastes are arbitrary, and they are not shared by all societies and cultures. While we prepare our chicken by discarding all but the meat, the Chinese consider chicken feet an appropriate food. And in France pigeon is a delicacy. In Spain, a relative of the periwinkle is a popular food.

These examples come from the very basic realm of food. But culture has an impact on many other types of consumption as well. Americans were once taught that goods made in Japan were of inferior quality. Today, we learn the reverse. We also learn that automobiles manufactured in Germany are highly reliable, that Marlboro is a "masculine" cigarette, and that McDonald's serves "fast" food.

Learning can be defined as any relatively permanent change in behavior that results from previous experience.[1] This definition taps two major provisos about learning. First, since experience is the key, we exclude from learning any behavioral changes that are the result of physiological change alone (like growth or changes from disease). Second, also excluded from the definition of learning are behavioral changes that are induced in response to temporary conditions (like conditions induced by drugs). It is important to note that not all learning is beneficial to the individual. Harmful habits can be learned as readily and as thoroughly as beneficial ones.

Important questions for psychologists are how—exactly—does learning occur? And what types of factors help or hinder learning? Two of the major families of psychological learning theories are *stimulus-response* theories and *cognitive* theories.

STIMULUS-RESPONSE THEORIES

The stimulus-response theorists believe that for learning to occur, all that is necessary is a temporal proximity between a stimulus and a response. Learning, then, is the establishment of a connection between a stimulus and a response. This approach is typified by the process of teaching an animal to do tricks, in which the trainer rewards the animal every time a correct response is emitted and withholds the reward for incorrect responses. Two stimulus-response theorists who have made major contributions to our knowledge of learning are Pavlov, known for salivation experiments with dogs, and Skinner, who developed the theoretical basis for behavior modification and programmed learning.

Pavlov: Classical Conditioning

Ivan Pavlov, known as the "Father of Learning Theory," was the first to make the relationship between stimulus and response explicit. Pavlov noticed that at feeding times, his dogs would salivate at the sight of food. The connection between food and salivation is not taught, but is an innate reflex reaction of the dog. Thus, Pavlov spoke of an **unconditioned stimulus** (food) eliciting an **unconditioned response** (salivation).

stimulus-response

Pavlov wondered if salivation could become the conditioned response to another, neutral stimulus. He paired the ringing of a bell with the presentation of food, and, after a number of trials, the dogs learned to salivate at the sound of the bell alone. The bell is a **conditioned stimulus,** and the salivation a **conditioned response.**

Classical conditioning utilizes an innate response; in Pavlov's case, this was the dog's salivation. Learners are essentially passive, since they do not consciously control the emission of the response.

Reinforcement is also important in classical conditioning. While the subject is learning to give the conditioned response, a reinforcement is presented. Pavlov used food—a positive reinforcement (reward). Reinforcement can also be negative (punishment).

reinforcement

Another concept treated by Pavlov was **stimulus generalization,** which refers to the process whereby the subject emits the same conditioned response not only to the original conditioned stimulus, but also to other stimuli. For example, once they were conditioned, Pavlov's dogs salivated for bells of various tones and intensities.

stimulus generation

When he began to experiment with dogs, Pavlov noticed that the learning process seemed to follow a definite pattern. During the initial few trials, the dogs did not salivate at the sound of the bell, indicating that no learning had yet occurred. Then there followed a series of trials in which the amount of salivation steadily increased, finally reaching a plateau when the dogs had established a firm connection between conditioned stimulus and conditioned response. When Pavlov plotted the number of trials against the amount of saliva, the graph presented in Exhibit 9–1 occurred: this is known as the **learning curve.** This S-shaped learning curve depicts the general process of learning for people as well as for animals; exposure to only a few stimuli elicits little learning, followed by a rapid increase with continuing exposure until a plateau is reached.

learning curve

Two other concepts discussed by Pavlov are **extinction** and **spontaneous recovery.** If, after the dog had learned to associate the salivation and the stimulus bell, the reinforcment (food) was withdrawn, the dog eventually forgot the connection between conditioned stimulus and conditioned response— the response was extinguished. However, when the stimulus-response association was conditioned, then extinguished, and then conditioned all over again, the dog relearned the bell-salivation association. This time, the slope of the learning curve was steeper, indicating that the dog relearned more quickly. The relearning process is termed *spontaneous recovery*.

extinction

spontaneous recovery

Human Learning

distributed versus massed practice

One of the first researchers to investigate human learning was Ebbinghaus,[2] who, in the late nineteenth century, tracked his own ability to learn nonsense syllables by repeating them aloud. Ebbinghaus found that *distributed* practice (that is, incorporating breaks into the learning process) was superior to *massed* practice (concentrating all learning into a limited time, with no breaks). Another conclusion drawn by Ebbinghaus was that learning progresses very rapidly with early repetitions, but then tapers off, finally reaching a plateau.

Interestingly, these two findings have been borne out over time. Today researchers generally agree that human learning—be it learning in the academic sense or gaining new information about a product—begins slowly, then increases rapidly, then finally reaches a plateau where it seemingly slows down. After a pause (distributed practice), more practice will initiate additional learning, up to a higher plateau. To accommodate these conditions, the generalized learning curve in Exhibit 9–1 can be modified as shown in Exhibit 9–2, which incorporates plateaus.

Researchers agree that during human learning, the plateaus represent pe-

EXHIBIT 9–1
S-SHAPED LEARNING CURVE

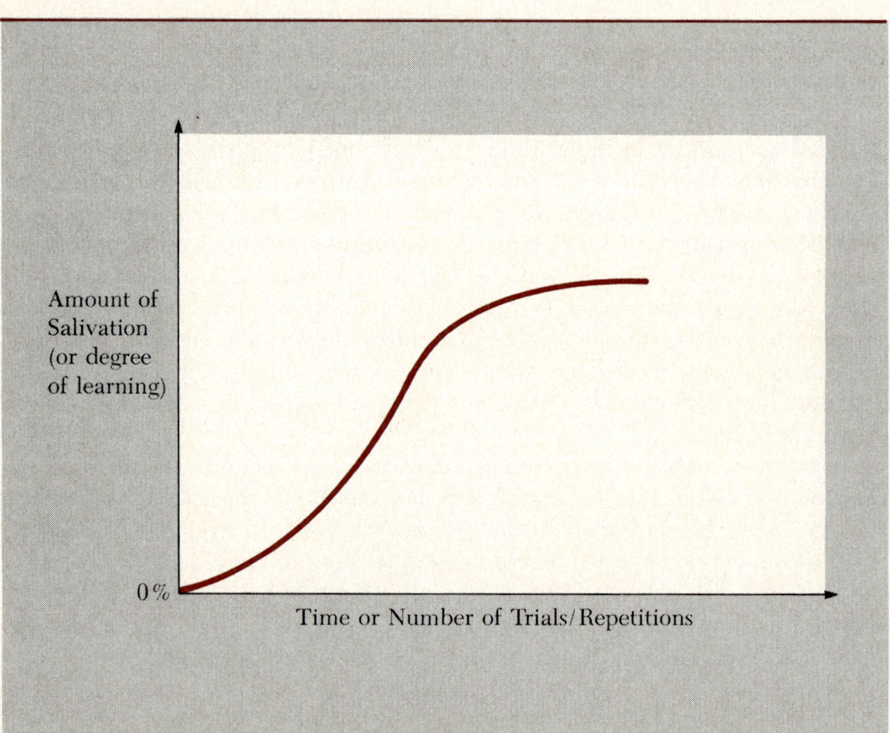

riods where *consolidation* occurs. *Consolidation* is basically the process whereby material is integrated into an individual's long-term memory and is thus retained permanently.

consolidation

Classical Conditioning and Consumer Learning

A study by Gorn investigated consumer learning from the perspective of classical conditioning.[3] Gorn asked whether unconditioned stimuli such as attractive colors, enjoyable music, and humor in a commercial can lead consumers to evaluate advertised products favorably. More generally, the question is which positive advertising elements (unconditioned stimuli) can lead to positive product evaluations (conditioned stimuli)?

Gorn asked samples of students to assist a hypothetical advertising agency in choosing the music to use in an advertisement for a 49¢ pen (neutral stimulus). While viewing a slide of the pen the agency was presumably about to advertise, students were exposed to one of two unconditioned stimuli—liked music (from *Grease*) and disliked music (Indian music). The pen "advertised"

EXHIBIT 9–2
S-SHAPED LEARNING CURVE

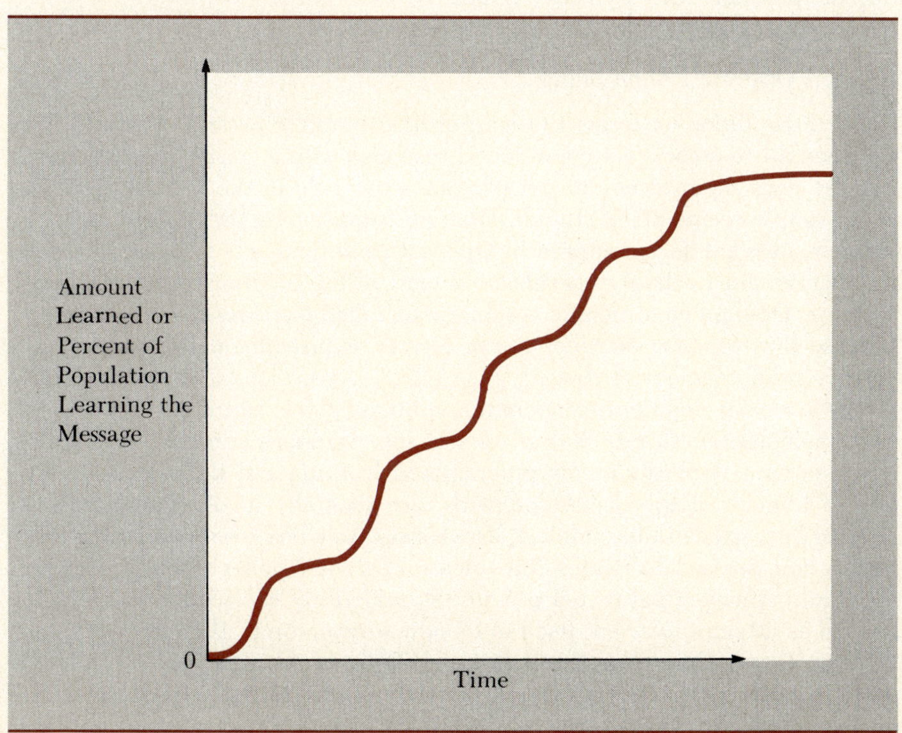

in the slide was either blue or beige. Four groups of students were exposed to one each of four experimental treatments:

1. liked music paired with a picture "advertisement" for the blue pen,
2. liked music paired with a picture "advertisement" for the beige pen,
3. disliked music paired with a picture "advertisement" for the blue pen, and
4. disliked music paired with a picture "advertisement" for the beige pen.

After evaluating the music they heard, the respondents were told they would receive a pen donated by the advertiser in appreciation for their assistance. They could choose either a blue pen or a beige pen. Gorn found that the "advertised" pen (regardless of its color) was chosen when it was presented against the background of the liked music and that the "nonadvertised" pen was selected when the disliked music was played.

Gorn concluded that the simple association between the music (unconditioned stimulus) and product (conditioned stimulus) does indeed affect product choice. In general, then, commercials can be extremely important in that "the positive emotions they generate become associated with the advertised product through classical conditioning."[4] Nord and Peter provide other examples of this type of pairing of stimuli such as a previously neutral product stimulus repeatedly advertised during an exciting sports event or advertisements for an unknown contender for political office with patriotic music.[5] The use of positively perceived celebrities to advertise products can similarly imbue the products with a positive image.

Skinner: Operant Conditioning

Classical conditioning treats the learner as essentially passive. Pavlov's dogs were taught to associate a conditioned response with a conditioned stimulus. But the dogs themselves did not play an active role in the learning process, being simply recipients of stimuli. Operant conditioning, developed by B. F. Skinner, uses a different approach. **Operant conditioning** is so named because the learner must actively *operate* some part of the environment for learning to occur. Operant conditioning is sometimes called *instrumental conditioning*, because the response emitted by the learner is instrumental in procuring a positive reinforcement or reward.

instrumental conditioning

The core development of operant conditioning was accomplished through experimentation with rats, but as we will see, Skinner's approach to learning has important implications for programmed learning and behavior modification of humans. Experimentation with rats generally involves the use of a Skinner box, which in its simplest form consists of a box equipped with a lever that, when pressed, activates the release of a food pellet from an attached dispenser. A naive (that is, not previously trained) rat is placed in the Skinner box. In an attempt to orient itself to its new surroundings, the rat will explore the box. Part of the exploratory behavior will bring the rat to press the lever, thereby releasing a pellet of food. At later times, the rat will repeat the lever-pushing (known as the *operant*) and ultimately make the association between the operant and the reinforcement (*food*).

Skinner box

the operant

Principles of operant conditioning have been applied directly to human learning. Two particularly strong examples are the Schick smoking control centers, which punish (negative reinforcement) the smoker each time he or she approaches smoking behavior, and the behavior modification of inmates in mental hospitals, who are punished for emitting antisocial behaviors. When applied to humans, operant conditioning is generally referred to as *programmed learning*.

programmed learning

Two differences between operant and classical conditioning are that (1) operant conditioning reinforces responses that are presumed to be under the conscious control of the individual, while classical conditioning reinforces involuntary responses, and (2) classical responses occur as a result of stimuli that occur *prior* to the response, whereas operant responses are reinforced by consequences that occur *after* the behavior.[6]

Schedules of Reinforcement   In learning theory, a major distinction is drawn between a **continuous** reinforcement schedule, which rewards a correct response each and every time it is emitted, and a **partial** or **intermittent** reinforcement schedule, which rewards only some of the correct responses.

There are two types of partial schedules. The first is a **ratio** reinforcement schedule, in which only every *n*th response is rewarded. If one of every two responses is reinforced, we have a 50 percent ratio reinforcement schedule; one of every four is a 25 percent ratio reinforcement schedule; and so on. The second is the **interval** reinforcement schedule, in which only responses occurring, say, at each successive ten-minute or twenty-minute period are rewarded; those responses emitted between reward times are not reinforced. An interesting phenomenon that has occurred with rats under this schedule is that they emit many responses at the time of reward, and very few during the interval when rewards are not provided. Rats, then, appear to be able to differentiate time periods; and, like their human counterparts, they generally choose not to work when they are aware that no rewards will be forthcoming.

Use of the various schedules of reinforcement produces different effects in the learning process. Learning occurs fastest with a continuous (100 percent) reinforcement schedule. However, learning that occurs with a partial reinforcement schedule is deeper and more resistant to extinction. And learning utilizing a variable partial-reinforcement schedule, that is, one that changes from 25 percent to 20 percent to 30 percent, is the most strongly absorbed and least subject to forgetting. This effect is probably due to the fact that the learner does not expect a reward for each response, nor for responses at some regular interval; he or she continues emitting responses for a longer time in the absence of reinforcement and even after reinforcement ceases altogether.

Operant Conditioning and Consumer Behavior   Exhibit 9–3 lists examples of four types of applications of operant-conditioning principles to consumer behavior. First, using a continuous schedule of reinforcement, the desired behavior (product purchase) is rewarded by receipt of trading stamps, bonuses, and so forth.

Second, product purchase can also be reinforced using a partial schedule.

Gambling devices such as slot machines provide partial reinforcement. Partial reinforcement can also be geared toward rewarding every *n*th individual, as with lotteries, contests, and door prizes.

shaping

The third application of operant conditioning is *shaping*, in which the desired behavior is gradually reinforced in stages, each of which approximates the desired responses more closely.

Fourth are cases in which the simple presence or absence of a stimulus can evoke behavior. A consumer who sees a sign promoting a "50 percent off sale" (a discriminative stimulus) may then emit the desired behavior of entering the store. As Nord and Peter state, "previous experiences have perhaps taught the customer that purchase behavior will be rewarded when the distinctive symbol is present and not rewarded when the symbol is absent."[7]

EXHIBIT 9–3
SOME APPLICATIONS OF OPERANT CONDITIONING PRINCIPLES

1. Rewards for desired behavior (continuous schedule)

Desired Behavior	Reward Given Following Behavior
Product purchase	Trading stamps, cash bonus or rebate, prizes, coupons

2. Rewards for desired behavior (partial schedules)

Desired Behavior	Reward Given (sometimes)
Product purchase	Prize for every second, or third, etc., purchase
	Prize to some fraction of people who purchase

3. Shaping

Approximation of Desired Response	Consequence Following Approximation	Final Response Desired
Opening a charge account	Prizes, etc., for opening account	Expenditure of funds
Trip to point-of-purchase location	Loss leaders, entertainment, or event at the shopping center	Purchase of products
Entry into store	Door prize	Purchase of products
Product trial	Free product and/or some bonus for using	Purchase of products

4. Discriminative Stimuli

Desired Behavior	Reward Signal	Examples
Entry into store	Store signs	50% off sale
	Store logos	K-mart's big red "K"
Brand purchase	Distinctive brandmarks	Levi tag

SOURCE: Walter R. Nord and J. Paul Peter (1980), "A Behavior Modification Perspective on Marketing," *Journal of Marketing*, 44 (Spring), p. 42.

The general applicability of operant conditioning to consumer behavior has been debated. Both Kassarjian[8] and Rothschild and Gaidis[9] have argued that operant conditioning is a relevant perspective from which to explain low-involvement consumer behavior. However, Peter and Nord contend that operant-conditioning principles are also applicable to high-involvement situations.[10] They provide the example of an automobile dealer who offers free coffee and doughnuts to anyone who visits the showroom, five dollars for licensed drivers who test drive a car, and a $500 rebate for all buyers. This example shapes high-involvement purchase behavior by breaking it down into components, applying operant principles to each substage in the decision-making process.

COGNITIVE THEORIES

Cognitive theories constitute the second major approach to the study of the learning process. Unlike stimulus-response theories, these theories do not view learning as the establishment of a connection between a stimulus and a response. Instead, they argue that learning is a more complex process that utilizes problem-solving and insightful thinking in addition to repetition of a stimulus-response chain.

Cognitive learning theory has roots in the classical work of Kohler,[11] who experimented with a caged monkey. Bananas were placed outside of the cage, out of the monkey's reach, and a stick was placed inside the cage. The monkey had to solve the problem of reaching the bananas by using the stick as a tool. In this case learning did not occur as a result of merely associating a stimulus and a response. Rather, *insight* intervened between goal recognition (procurement of food) and goal achievement.

The cognitive approach is exemplified by the Gestalt school of psychology, which maintains that learning goes beyond acquiring new habits and developing connections between various stimuli and associated responses. Rather, Gestaltists view learning as **cognitive reorganization;** and the learning process is seen as encompassing insight, thinking, and problem-solving, which lead to changes in an individual's cognitive structures. **Gestalt**

Gestalt psychology is predicated upon the familiar phrase that "the whole is equal to more than the sum of the parts." This means that in order to understand the function of any particular component of a whole, we must not view that component alone, but in respect of its role and relationships with all other parts. Also, changing any one part will affect the structure of the whole by causing reorganization of all components to accommodate the change.

The work of Kurt Lewin, a prominent Gestalt psychologist, has had considerable impact in both psychology and social psychology and, hence, indirectly on consumer behavior. Lewin developed *field theory*, the basic premise of which is that the human mind is a "psychological field" consisting of a pattern of cognitions or beliefs operating in a psychological environment.[12] The environment includes beliefs, attitudes, goals, and psychological barriers. **field theory**

Recall our original definition of learning, as *change resulting from experience*. In Lewin's view, experience would act as new input into an individual's psychological field. Learning entails a cognitive reorganization that enables the new material to be incorporated into the field. In this view, learning goes beyond the establishment of a stimulus-response association. And to understand learning, we must consider all of the various stimuli affecting the individual in light of his or her psychological field.[13]

BRAIN HEMISPHERE LATERALIZATION

Cognitive learning theories emphasize the structure of cognitive patterns and ways in which this structure changes in response to new environmental stimuli. This cognitive approach underlies one of the dominant streams of consumer-behavior research today—information-processing and cognitive response, which were discussed in Chapter 5. Information-processing is fundamentally concerned with exploring the structure of knowledge, the impact of new information, and cognitive reorganization. A related topic that did not receive explicit attention in Chapter 5 is *brain hemisphere lateralization*.

left and right hemispheres

A recent trend in consumer-behavior research involves differentiating between the activities of the left and the right hemispheres (sides) of the brain. Although much of the basic research on the functions of the brain has been conducted by psychologists, consumer researchers have noted the applicability of many of the findings to consumers' responses to stimuli and to subsequent learning.

The two hemispheres of the brain have specialized functions. The left hemisphere controls analytical thinking, reading, language, and logic, while the right hemisphere is involved in perceiving mental and spatial images and in artistic endeavors. Applying these specializations, Krugman states that print media relate to the left brain, while television relates to the right brain.[14] He further suggests that high-involvement consumer behavior, which emphasizes evaluation of information about brands, is a left-brain activity. Low-involvement, in which an overall nonanalytical image of a brand is formed, is a right-brain activity.

Lending support to Krugman's contention, a study by Weinstein, Appel, and Weinstein found that magazine advertising produced higher levels of brain-wave activity (measured by an electroencephalograph) than television advertising, indicating higher involvement.[15] They also found that compared with television, magazine ads produced more brain-wave activity in the analytical, left hemisphere than in the pictorial, right hemisphere. From a managerial perspective, these findings reaffirm the notion that magazine advertising is more effective for high-involvement products, while television is the preferred medium for low-involvement products.

Krugman also suggests that the image-receptive right hemisphere of the brain scans and screens stimuli in the environment and selects material for the left brain to attend to in more detail. Interestingly, the right brain can operate over long periods of time without fatigue, while the left brain does suffer fatigue over time—requiring that breaks be incorporated to facilitate learning.[16] This suggests that the learning-theory concepts of the *learning curve* and *consolidation* may be more relevant to high-involvement situations.

Electroencephalograph measures have also been used to evaluate the relative effectiveness of television advertisements. Advertisements that produce the most brain-wave activity (regardless of the hemisphere in which the activity occurs) have higher recall levels than other ads,[17] a finding that can have considerable impact on advertising pre-testing. If a manager is unsure about which of a number of possible ads to use, the decision can be facilitated by measuring subjects' brain-wave activity for each contending ad.

Another study has indicated that the differences in the functions of the hemispheres go beyond those of verbal skills. Evidence suggests that the right brain is largely responsible for the communication and understanding of emotions.[18] This raises an interesting issue related to advertising copy: Should advertising for an "emotional" product (such as perfume or cologne) consist primarily of pictorial imagery, or should it incorporate some verbal or analytical elements through the use of written copy? Using only imagery suggests that the right brain will be the main information processor, while incorporating verbal elements may involve both hemispheres.

Lutz and Lutz maintain that since the right hemisphere is responsible for picture-viewing and forming mental images, and the left hemisphere for reading and verbal skills, advertising effectiveness should be maximized when an advertisement simultaneously stimulates both halves of the brain.[19]

A stimulus that integrates these two components is called an *interactive image*. In a study of the recall of advertisements selected from the Yellow Pages, Lutz and Lutz hold that promoting new or unfamiliar products is a learning task, since consumers must learn to associate a new brand name with a particular product or service.[20] To test the efficacy of various ads in aiding learning, they use two types of images: interactive images (that integrate the brand name and the product) and noninteractive images (that depict brand name and type of product separately). Exhibit 9–4 provides examples of the two types of images. The Dixon Crane Company merges a pictorial representation of the product with the actual brand name (interactive). In contrast, the O'Bear ad visually presents the brand name, but does not integrate information about the type of product offered (saws).

interactive images

In their study, Lutz and Lutz found that individuals had a significantly high level of brand recall for ads using interactive imagery. They conclude:

*Merely presenting a picture in an ad will not necessarily be an improvement over a purely verbal presentation. A distinction must be made between the types of external imagery and their differential effectiveness. An interactive image facilitates recall better than a non-interactive image, presumably by increasing the concreteness of the material to be learned, that is, the association of the two items. The more concrete the association becomes, the more memorable it is."[21]

Extending Lutz and Lutz's finding, it appears that advertising campaigns that activate both brain hemispheres maximize learning. Brain-wave activity is increased, and synergy results from simultaneous information-processing operations of the brain halves.

LEARNING AND CONSUMER BEHAVIOR

Some of the basic concepts of learning theory long studied by psychologists have direct relevance to the field of consumer behavior. The concept of the learning curve, for instance, is a helpful tool in gaining an understanding of how advertising works. Similarly, forgetting and extinction serve as the basis for the discussion of the "decay" of advertising messages. We now turn to an examination of the value of specific concepts from learning theory to consumer behavior.

Learning

Psychologists' work on the learning process is directly relevant to the study of advertising impact. Advertising impact is viewed in two ways. We may focus on the individual level, measuring the degree of recall (aided or unaided) a consumer has of a particular advertisement. Alternatively, we may focus on the aggregate level, determining the proportion of a specified population that recalls the message. In either case, the generalized learning curve applies. The first time an advertisement appears, it produces only a minimum effect. In fact, it has been proposed that it takes three exposures to an ad before any real impact is generated.[22]

EXHIBIT 9–4
PICTORIAL IMAGERY

Interactive Imagery	Noninteractive Imagery

Dixon Crane Co.	O'Bear Abrasive Saws

SOURCE: Kathy A. Lutz and Richard J. Lutz (1977), "Effects of Interactive Imagery on Learning: Application to Advertising," *Journal of Applied Psychology*, 62, pp. 493–98.

In a frequently quoted study, Zielske compared the effectiveness of massed advertising (also known as *pulsing* or *flighting*) and advertising evenly spread over a longer period.[23] Zielske's study used two groups of women randomly selected from a telephone book. Each group was mailed thirteen advertisements. The first group received these advertisements once every four weeks over a total of fifty-two weeks (**spaced schedule**). The second group received the same ads, but once a week for a total of thirteen weeks (**pulsed schedule**). In both cases, recall increased as the number of exposures increased. Interestingly, for the first group, 48 percent of the women were able to recall the advertisement after the thirteen exposures, compared with 63 percent recall for the second, pulsed group. Zielske, however, does not draw a definite conclusion about the relative efficacy of spaced and pulsed advertising, although later research suggests that a pulsed schedule can be more effective.[24]

pulsed versus spaced schedules

A recent reanalysis of Zielske's original data, however, reaches a different conclusion. Rather than simply measuring the percentage of respondents who recall the advertisement, Simon calculates the number of "recall-weeks," defined as the number of weeks multiplied by the appropriate recall rate. Using recall-weeks as the indicator of advertising impact he concludes that the spaced schedule is more effective than the pulsed schedule. He concludes,

> *The implication is clear: a given advertising budget is most efficient if it is spread out over the maximum period rather than concentrated in a single burst. Several bursts will be better than one burst but worse than an even spread. . . ."[25]*

Simon's conclusion parallels Ebbinghaus' contention that distributed practice is superior to massed practice.[26] However, as Simon points out, his conclusion applies to an established product. The best advertising approach for a new product might well be different. In fact, Levy and Simon suggest that new products benefit from intensive advertising at the time of introduction (to push consumers up the initial, steep portion of the learning curve), followed by reduced levels.[27] Katz also recommends using a "sliding schedule," with heavy advertising in the introductory stage of a campaign, and reductions in advertising frequency as consumers learn and internalize the material.[28]

Other factors may also temper the superiority of a spaced schedule. If a product is highly seasonal (like sun-tan lotion), then obviously advertising should be concentrated in the sales period. Zielske and Henry have shown that concentrated schedules produce the highest *recall peaks*—a factor which can be important for one-time promotions or short-term offers as well as for seasonal goods.[29]

recall peaks

Speed of Learning   The speed at which learning occurs (that is, the speed at which an individual moves up the learning curve) is influenced by a number of factors. One of these is the *motivation* of the learner: The more highly motivated the learner, the more quickly learning occurs. This fact has relevance for advertising practice, since more motivated market segments will be more willing to learn information transmitted in advertising messages than

motivation

less motivated ones. For example, one study demonstrated that individuals in a "decision-making context" (that is, about to select a product) were more affected by the information presented in a commercial than were individuals who saw the same ad, but who were not considering selecting a product.[30]

amount of material

The *amount of material* to be learned also affects the speed of learning. Too much information crammed into a single message can lead to information overload, decreasing the amount and speed of learning. Most effective television advertisements, for example, limit the number of important points stressed. The common use of short slogans illustrates this. Millions of consumers have "learned" that "Coke is it," "Gentlemen prefer Hanes," and that "No salt salts like Morton's salt salts."

familiarity and meaningfulness

Finally, the *familiarity* and *meaningfulness* of the material influence the speed of learning. Material that is familiar and/or meaningful to the subject is more readily learned than material that is not. When "gel" toothpastes were introduced, many major manufacturers chose to use product-line extensions (such as Colgate Gel and Crest Gel) rather than to introduce totally new products. This managerial decision capitalizes on the notion that consumer learning occurs more quickly given familiar material.

Forgetting

Related to the topic of learning is the notion of *forgetting*. In advertising practice, the **decay of advertising messages** is part of forgetting.

decay

The theoretical basis of the process of forgetting information rests in Pavlov's notion of *extinction*. Recall that when Pavlov ceased rewarding his dogs as they salivated at the sound of the bell, they eventually appeared to "unlearn" the association. When rewarding was reinstituted, however, spontaneous recovery occurred, and the resulting learning curve was much steeper than the initial one.

The situation is similar for consumer learning of advertising messages. If advertising for a product is withdrawn, consumers gradually forget the information. However, renewed advertising works very quickly to reestablish the previously learned associations, implying that extinction is rarely complete. Material may be latent or suppressed, but it is not totally forgotten.

There are other factors that can inhibit the rate of decay of learned material. One of these is the amount of *repetition* that is involved in the learning process. The more repetition, the greater the depth of the learning and the slower the rate of decay. This implies that knowledge of old, established brands is less subject to extinction than knowledge of newer brands. Hence, a cutback in advertising for a younger brand would be more detrimental to sales performance. The decay rate can also be reduced by high meaningfulness of the material and high motivation of the consumer.

In discussing the relevance of extinction to marketing, Rothschild and Gaidis suggest two applications of the concept of extinction that go beyond advertising.[31] First, if a product ceases providing positive reinforcement through poor performance, then purchase behavior will be rapidly extinguished. The second, more subtle, application concerns purchase incentives. Sometimes consumers repeat purchase a product not because of their preference for the product, but only because of incentives, such as price-off coupons. If consumers have not built up a loyalty to the product, then discontinuation of the incentive may lead to extinction of the purchase behavior. In this case, the underlying loyalty is to the incentive rather than to the product—a situation that can arise when marketers place too much emphasis on incentives.

Corrective Advertising

The Federal Trade Commission has the power to regulate advertising and is responsible for investigating advertising claims that are thought to be misleading or deceptive. If an advertisement is found to be deceptive, the FTC has a number of options available. One is to order the advertiser to use **corrective advertising,** that is, advertising that corrects the earlier, false claims. Although the FTC will be discussed more fully in Chapter 23, the topic of corrective advertising is integrally related to learning theory, and thus warrants attention here.

We have discussed the difficulty of extinguishing a learned response. A question of interest here, then, is how can corrective advertising contribute to changing material previously learned by consumers? In fact, learning theory suggests that change will be affected in two stages. First, consumers must "unlearn" the false or misleading information imparted by the initial advertisement or series of advertisements. Second, new, corrective information must be provided to replace the original message.

The case of Listerine provides an example of this two-stage process. For many years, Listerine had been advertised as capable of curing colds—which, in fact, it could not do. In order to end consumer deception, the FTC had two choices. It could have ordered Listerine merely to cease and desist advertising this claim. Or, it could, and did, not only order cessation, but also corrective advertising, requiring that all advertising for Listerine had to state that Listerine does *not* cure colds. In the view of the FTC, mere cessation would not necessarily have led to an alteration of consumers' beliefs about the cold-remedying characteristics of Listerine.

The reading in Exhibit 9–5 provides another example of an FTC ruling on deceptive advertising, this time concerning Hawaiian Punch. While reading the case history, notice the explicit relevance of learning theory to the issue of consumers' responses to deceptive and corrective advertising.

STOCHASTIC LEARNING MODELS

Psychologists have attempted to describe the learning process using what are known as **stochastic** or **probabilistic** models. These mathematical models are called *stochastic* because they rely on statements of probability to model behavior, rather than on *deterministic* or behavioral elements. An underlying

EXHIBIT 9–5
CORRECTIVE ADVERTISING

HAWAIIAN PUNCH: A CASE

The research evidence on the difficulties of forgetting has led the Federal Trade Commission to the concepts of corrective advertising and affirmative disclosure. In the belief that advertising effects do not decay only with the passage of time, but that the consumer response must be "unlearned," the staff of the Federal Trade Commission has asked for corrective advertising in cases of national scope including *Firestone Tires, Hi-C Fruit Drink, Listerine, Profile Bread, Domino Sugar, Wonder Bread,* and *Chevron F-310.* Some of these cases have lost on appeal. However, a signed consent order for *Hawaiian Punch* illustrates the goal of the Commission staff.

The complaint alleged that, by featuring fresh fruit and fruit trees prominently in television commercials and by using the phrase "seven natural fruit juices," advertisements had represented Hawaiian Punch beverages as consisting predominantly of natural fruit juices. In fact, the complaint said, the predominant ingredients were water and sweetening agents, which were added to fruit juices and other ingredients.

In addition to banning misrepresentations of natural fruit content, the order prohibited any advertisement or label which depicted fruit or juice unless the total percentage of single-strength fruit juice concentrate contained in a serving was clearly and conspicuously disclosed. This provision in the order will remain in effect until the firm submits to the Commission a survey on consumers' perception of Hawaiian Punch fruit-juice content. The form of the survey is included in the order. The affirmative disclosures will not be required after the one-year period if 67% of current purchasers of fruit-flavored beverages, 80% of current or prospective purchasers of Hawaiian Punch products, or 95% of current purchasers of these products think that Hawaiian Punch products contain no more than 20% natural fruit juice.

In this order the R. J. Reynolds Foods Company is not only asked to cease and desist alleged misrepresentations, but also to disclose the true facts until such time as a substantial proportion of consumers is no longer misled into thinking that Hawaiian Punch contains major amounts of "seven natural fruit juices," that is, until a true process of "unlearning" and relearning occurs.

It is the FTC's intention that corrective advertising impart to the consumer a short, readily comprehensible message like the original ad, but with accurate information to correct the impression left by the challenged advertising. The regulators feel consumers must be carefully exposed to the fact that what they learned earlier was in error, lest they continue to suffer from the misleading effects of that earlier "learning."

SOURCE: Harold H. Kassarjian and Thomas S. Robertson (1981), *Perspectives in Consumer Behavior*, 3rd ed. (Glenview, Ill.: Scott, Foresman), pp. 63–64.

assumption of many of these models is that an individual's behavior is influenced by his or her earlier behavior. The consumer receives either positive reinforcement (satisfaction with a brand) or negative reinforcement (dissatisfaction), and this outcome has an impact on brand selection in the future.

Stochastic learning models have been increasingly useful in marketing, especially in regard to *brand loyalty*. According to such models, the best predictors of a person's future purchase patterns are the sequence, rhythm, and frequency of his or her past purchase patterns, especially the most recent of these.[32]

Two classes of stochastic models that are frequently discussed in the consumer-behavior literature are *linear learning models* and *Markov models*.

brand loyalty

Linear Learning Models

Linear learning models are derived from psychological learning theory and are so named because they treat learning as a linear process. Psychologists Bush and Mosteller applied concepts such as *reinforcement* in their mathematical treatment of learning.[33] Kuehn later applied Bush and Mosteller's work to purchase data for frozen orange juice obtained from the *Chicago Tribune* consumer panel.[34]

Kuehn proposed that the probability that a consumer will buy a particular brand is influenced by his or her past sequence of purchases. For example, if a consumer had bought, say, Minute Maid the last four times he or she had purchased orange juice, the probability of buying it again the next time would be high. The probability of another consumer's buying Minute Maid—when none of his or her last four purchases had been Minute Maid—would be much lower. Underlying Kuehn's model are the notions that brand loyalty results from positive reinforcement and that the effects of positive reinforcement are cumulative: Each successive reinforcement cements loyalty further.

Exhibit 9–6 summarizes Kuehn's model, which is defined by the *purchase operator* and the *rejection operator*. To interpret the model, assume that the probability of purchasing brand A on trial t is 0.45. If A is bought, then draw a line perpendicular to the x-axis, from 0.45, to intersect the purchase operator. Then draw a line parallel to the x-axis from the intersection point, I, of 0.45 and the purchase operator, to the y-axis. The point 0.60 at which this second line intersects the y-axis gives the probability of purchasing brand A at $t+1$.

purchase and rejection operators

Conversely, if brand A is not purchased at t, draw a line from 0.45 at t to the rejection operator point I'. Then read across horizontally to obtain 0.30, the probability of purchasing brand A at $t+1$, given that A was not bought at t.

Using the linear learning model, the probability of purchasing brand A is revised after each purchase.

There are two important characteristics of the linear learning model. First, individuals are neither completely loyal nor completely disloyal to a particular brand; that is, $0 < P_A < 1.0$. This condition admits the possibility that future learning may affect purchase behavior. Second, each purchase of brand A at t increases the probability of buying A at $t+1$. The more A is bought, the greater the brand loyalty. The *rate* of increase, however, decreases with additional consecutive purchases.

The linear learning model has been used to describe the purchase of a nondurable drug and some grocery products[35] and dental products,[36] and to depict store choice.[37] Massey, Montgomery, and Morrison applied the LLM to twenty-one different sets of data and concluded that it "can be used with confidence as a tool for analyzing brand switching data."[38]

EXHIBIT 9–6
KUEHN'S LINEAR LEARNING MODEL

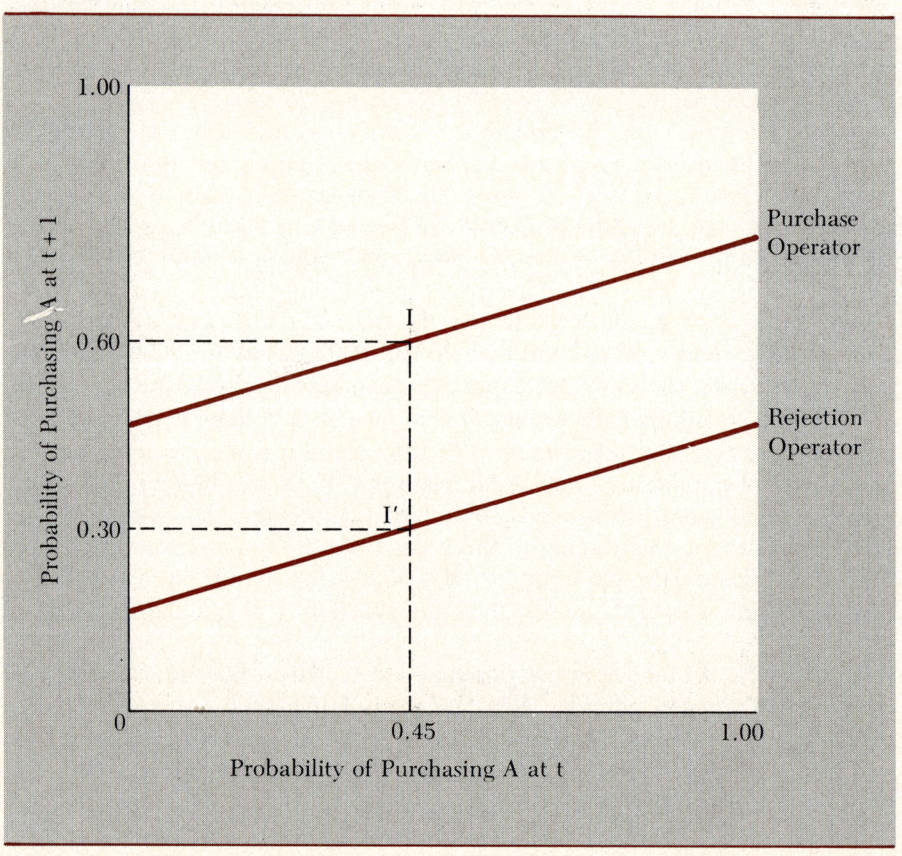

However, there are limitations to the model. Perhaps the major criticism is that in its original form, all buyers are assumed to have the same probability for buying brand A. Obviously, personal preferences vary across consumers. More recent work with the LLM has broadened its scope, so that individuals' probabilities (hence, preferences) are allowed to vary.[39]

model limitations

Markov Models

The second major type of stochastic learning model is the **Markov model.** Markov models also assume that the current brand purchased is affected by the brands selected on previous occasions. Markov models are defined by their "order," where *order* refers to the number of previous purchases that are said to influence the current purchase. In other words, a first-order Markov process includes the influence of only the last purchase an individual has made, while a second-order Markov process depends on the last two purchases.

The simplest type of Markov model is a first-order, homogeneous model, in which the present purchase is influenced only by the brand last bought (first order), and each consumer is assumed to have the same probability of purchasing a particular brand as all other consumers (homogeneity).

A Markov model uses a *transition matrix* to describe the probability of buying one brand at time t and the same or another brand at time $t+1$. Exhibit 9–7 shows an example of a Markov transition matrix for a three-brand market. This "From-To" matrix gives the probabilities of switching from a brand bought at time t, to the brand bought at $t+1$. P_{11}, for example, is the probability of buying brand 1 at t and $t+1$. P_{12} is the probability of switching from brand 1 at t to brand 2 at $t+1$. The column totals represent the market shares of each brand at $t+1$.

transition matrix

EXHIBIT 9–7
MARKOV TRANSITION MATRIX

		To Brand			
		1 · · ·	2 · · ·	3	Σ
	1	P_{11}	P_{12}	P_{13}	1.0
From Brand	2	P_{21}	P_{22}	P_{23}	1.0
	3	P_{31}	P_{32}	P_{33}	1.0
	Σ	$MS_{1,\,t+1}$	$MS_{i,\,t+1}$	$MS_{n,\,t+1}$	

As with the linear learning model, the concepts of positive reinforcement (inducing repeat buying) and negative reinforcement (leading to brand switching) underlie the Markov matrix. And like the linear learning model, the Markov matrix has been criticized for assuming that all consumers have the same probabilities of purchasing each of the brands (assumption of homogeneity).

Nonetheless, a Markov analysis can provide managers with a better understanding of the structure of the market. For example, in a multi-brand market, buyers of one brand (brand A) may switch primarily to one other brand (brand B), indicating that brand B is the major competitor for brand A. Alternatively, switching may occur equally among all brands in the market. In the first situation, advertising and promotional efforts could be geared specifically to convince consumers that brand A is superior to brand B, and advertising media would target users of both brands. On the other hand, if competition occurs across all brands, advertising and promotional efforts would be aimed at users of the entire product category, and brand A's superiority in the product category could be stressed.

Other Stochastic Models

There are other, more sophisticated, stochastic models. While they are relevant to the analysis of brand loyalty and brand switching, for the most part they are not built on consumer-behavior theory. Rather, they are based on relatively complex mathematical approaches and probability theory.

Two popular models, stochastic preference theory[40] and Hendrodynamics,[41] use primarily aggregate empirical market shares of various brands as input data. Using relatively complex mathematics and probability theory they then generate theoretical estimates of brand-switching and repeat buying patterns or draw conclusions about the structure of the market.

Although these approaches have value for forecasting purposes, they do not explain consumer behavior. Neither the psychological nor the sociological aspect of buyer behavior is relevant to these approaches. A full consideration of these models is beyond the scope of this book.

SUMMARY

Stimulus-response theories are among the major psychological approaches to the investigation of learning. The basic premise of stimulus-response theories is that learning is the establishment of an association between a stimulus and a response.

The two major stimulus-response approaches are classical conditioning and operant conditioning. In classical conditioning, an unconditioned stimulus which, in the absence of learning, elicits an unconditioned response, is paired with a neutral stimulus. In time, the previously neutral stimulus becomes conditioned and is able to elicit a conditioned response. Operant conditioning approaches also recognize learning as the establishment of a stimulus-response connection, but require the learner to assume a more active role. The response that is reinforced is under the control of the learner, whereas classical conditioning reinforces involuntary responses. The response is called an *operant*, because the learner must operate on the environment in order to obtain the reinforcement.

Various schedules of reinforcement can be used with stimulus-response learning. A continuous reinforcement schedule rewards every correct response, while a partial schedule rewards every *n*th response (ratio schedule) or rewards on a time schedule of, say, every ten or twenty minutes (interval schedule).

The cognitive approach to learning theory focuses on the structure of existing cognitive patterns and the ways in which that structure adapts to new knowledge and new stimuli. Studies of brain-hemisphere lateralization suggest that cognitive patterns differ for the right and left sides of the brain. The right hemisphere perceives images and is the seat of emotions, while the left hemisphere is analytical and controls language, logic, and verbal activities. Advertising research can benefit from knowledge of these specialized functions. Consumers have better recall of advertisements that generate more overall brain activity and that stimulate both hemispheres.

The concept of the learning curve is a fundamental one in learning theory and has direct relevance to consumer behavior. The learning curve underlies discussion of the relative effectiveness of massed (or pulsed) and distributed (or spaced) advertising schedules. Whereas a pulsed schedule generates the highest peak level of recall, a spaced schedule results in greater total recall, measured in recall-weeks. But a managerial decision about which schedule to use must go beyond this basic finding. While established products benefit from spaced advertising, evidence suggests that new products and new campaigns benefit from more concentrated advertising at the beginning, followed by gradual decreases in advertising frequency as consumers learn the new information.

The speed of learning varies across consumers and across advertising campaigns. In general, learning occurs more quickly if the learner is highly motivated, if the amount of material to learn is small, and if the material is familiar and meaningful.

The learning-theory concept of forgetting is related to the advertising-decay rate, which is slower if the material was thoroughly learned and is still meaningful to the learner. Extinction can occur if a product ceases rewarding consumers through poor performance.

Corrective advertising involves both learning and forgetting. Before corrective advertising can succeed, consumers must "unlearn" previously accepted knowledge and then relearn new, correct information.

Stochastic models of buyer behavior have approached learning theory from a probabilistic point of view. These models attempt to quantify the impact of previous learning (resulting from the consumer's history of purchases) on current choice behavior.

KEY CONCEPTS

classical conditioning
unconditioned stimulus
unconditioned
  response
conditioned stimulus
conditioned response
operant conditioning
reinforcement
reinforcement
  schedules
   continuous
   partial (or
    intermittent)
    ratio
    interval
stimulus generalization

learning curve
extinction
spontaneous recovery
cognitive theory
cognitive
  reorganization
brain hemisphere
  functions
pulsed advertising
  schedule
advertising-decay rate
corrective advertising
stochastic learning
  models
linear learning model
Markov matrix

DISCUSSION QUESTIONS

1. Does more consumer learning parallel classical conditioning or operant conditioning? Defend your position.
2. Which are more influential on consumer behavior: continuous reinforcement schedules or partial reinforcement schedules?
3. Locate an advertisement that stimulates only the left hemisphere of the brain, another that stimulates only the right hemisphere, and a third that stimulates both hemispheres. Discuss the relative merits and drawbacks of the ads, and suggest ways of improving them.
4. "The growing emphasis on brain-wave activity and brain-hemisphere lateralization is unethical, since soon consumers will be unwillingly influenced by manipulative advertisements." Do you agree with this statement?
5. When would a pulsed advertising schedule be preferable to a spaced schedule?
6. How can the advertising-decay rate be impeded?
7. If an advertiser is ordered to undertake corrective advertising, is there a chance that sales will increase, since consumers may perceive the advertiser as particularly honest?
8. What is the managerial relevance of stochastic models of consumer behavior?

NOTES

1. Ernest R. Hilgard, Richard C. Atkinson, and Rita L. Atkinson (1979), *Introduction to Psychology*, 7th ed. (New York: Harcourt Brace Jovanovich).
2. Herman Ebbinghaus (1885), *Über das Gedächtnis;* trans. (1964), *Memory* (New York: Dover).
3. Gerald J. Gorn (1982), "The Effects of Music in Advertising or Choice: A Classical Conditioning Approach," *Journal of Marketing*, 46 (Winter), pp. 94–101.
4. Gorn (1982), p. 100.
5. Walter R. Nord and J. Paul Peter (1980), "A Behavior Modification Perspective on Marketing," *Journal of Marketing*, 44 (Spring), pp. 36–47.
6. Nord and Peter (1980), p. 38.
7. Nord and Peter (1980), p. 40.
8. Harold H. Kassarjian (1978), "Presidential Address, 1977: Anthropomorphism and Parsimony," in *Advances in Consumer Research*, ed. H. K. Hunt, vol. 5 (Assn. for Consumer Research), pp. xii–xiv.
9. Michael L. Rothschild and William C. Gaidis (1981), "Behavioral Learning Theory: Its Relevance to Marketing and Promotions," *Journal of Marketing*, 45 (Spring), pp. 70–78.
10. J. Paul Peter and Walter R. Nord (1982), "A Clarification and Extension of Operant Conditioning Principles in Marketing," *Journal of Marketing*, 46 (Summer), pp. 102–7.
11. Wolfgang Kohler (1925), *The Mentality of Apes* (New York: Harcourt, Brace, & World).
12. Kurt Lewin (1951), "Field Theory and Learning," in *Field Theory and Social Science* (New York: Harper & Row).
13. For an explicit consideration of the role of field theory in consumer behavior, see Harold H. Kassarjian (1973), "Field Theory in Consumer Behavior," in *Consumer Behavior: Theoretical Sources*, ed. Scott Ward and Thomas S. Robertson (Englewood Cliffs, N.J.: Prentice-Hall), pp. 118–40.
14. Herbert E. Krugman (1977), "Memory Without Recall, Exposure Without Perception," *Journal of Advertising Research*, 17 (Aug.), pp. 7–12.
15. Sidney Weinstein, Valentine Appel, and Curt Weinstein (1980), "Brain Activity Responses to Magazine and Television Advertising," *Journal of Advertising Research,* 20 (June), pp. 57–63.
16. Herbert E. Krugman (1980), "Point of View: Sustained Viewing of Television," *Journal of Advertising Research*, 20 (June), pp. 65–68.
17. Valentine Appel, Sidney Weinstein, and Curt Weinstein (1979), "Brain Activity and Recall of TV Advertising," *Journal of Advertising Research*, 19 (Aug.), pp. 7–15.
18. Sidney Weinstein (1982), "A Review of Brain Hemisphere Research," *Journal of Advertising Research*, 22 (June/July), pp. 56–63.
19. Kathy A. Lutz and Richard J. Lutz (1977), "Imagery—Eliciting Strategies: Review and Implications of Research," working paper no. 59, Working Paper Series, Center for Marketing Studies (Los Angeles: Univ. of California).
20. Kathy A. Lutz and Richard J. Lutz (1977), "Effects of Interactive Imagery on Learning: Application to Advertising," *Journal of Applied Psychology*, 62 (Aug.), pp. 493–98.
21. Lutz and Lutz (1977), "Effects," p. 497.
22. Herbert E. Krugman (1972), "Why Three Exposures May Be Enough," *Journal of Advertising Research*, 12 (Dec.), pp. 11–14.
23. Hubert A. Zielske (1959), "The Remembering and Forgetting of Advertising," *Journal of Marketing*, 23 (Jan.), pp. 229-43.
24. See, for example, Russell Ackoff and James R. Emshoff (1975), "Advertising Research at Anheuser-Busch, Inc. (1963-1968)," *Sloan Management Review*, 16 (Winter), pp. 1–15.
25. Julian L. Simon (1979), "What Do Zielske's Real Data Really Show About Pulsing?" *Journal of Marketing Research*, 16 (Aug.), pp. 415–20.
26. Ebbinghaus (1885).
27. Haim Levy and Julian L. Simon (1979), "Choosing the Best Advertising Appropriation When Appropriations Interact Over Time," in *Research in Marketing*, ed. Jagdish Sheth, Vol. 1 (Greenwich: JAI Press), pp. 149–67.

28. William A. Katz (1980), "A Sliding Schedule of Advertising Weight," *Journal of Advertising Research*, 4 (Aug.), pp. 39–44.

29. Hubert A. Zielske and Walter A. Henry (1980), "Remembering and Forgetting Television Ads," *Journal of Advertising Research*, 20 (Apr.), pp. 7–13.

30. Gerald J. Gorn (1982).

31. Michael R. Rothschild and William C. Gaidis (1981).

32. Not all stochastic models incorporate this learning assumption. Bernoulli models specifically assume that successive purchases are independent. This is termed the "zero-order assumption," in which past purchases are taken not to affect present purchases. The interested reader can consult W. F. Massey, D. B. Montgomery, and D. G. Morrison (1970), *Stochastic Models of Buying Behavior* (Cambridge, Mass.: The M.I.T. Press).

33. Robert Bush and Frank Mosteller (1955), *Stochastic Models for Learning* (New York: Wiley).

34. Alfred A. Kuehn (1962), "Consumer Brand Choice As a Learning Process" *Journal of Advertising Research*, 2 (Dec.), pp. 10–17.

35. Alfred A. Kuehn and R. L. Day (1964), "A Probabilistic Approach to Consumer Behavior," in *Theory in Marketing*, ed. R. Cox, W. Alderson, and S. Shapiro (Homewood, Ill.: Irwin), pp. 380–90.

36. J. M. Carman (1966), "Brand Switching and Linear Learning Models," *Journal of Advertising Research*, 6 (June), pp. 23–31.

37. D. A. Aaker and J. M. Jones (1971), "Modelling Store Choice Behavior," *Journal of Marketing Research*, 8 (Feb.), pp. 38–42.

38. Massey, Montgomery, and Morrison (1970), pp. 179–89.

39. F. S. Zufryden (1977), "Composite Heterogeneous Models of Brand Choice and Purchase Timing Behavior," *Management Science*, 24, pp. 121–36; J. M. Jones (1973), "A Composite Heterogeneous Model for Brand Choice Behavior," *Management Science*, 19, pp. 499–509; and M. Givon and D. Horsky (1978), "Market Share Models as Approximators of Aggregated Heterogeneous Brand Choice Behavior," *Management Science*, 24 (Sept.), pp. 1404–16.

40. The original statement of stochastic preference theory can be found in Frank M. Bass (1974), "The Theory of Stochastic Preference and Brand Switching," *Journal of Marketing Research*, 11, pp. 1–20. Note that Professor Bass' initial formulation has been both extended (e.g., Bass, A. Jeuland, and G. P. Wright [1976], "Equilibrium Stochastic Choice and Market Penetration Theories: Derivations and Comparisons," *Management Science*, 22, pp. 1051–63), and criticized (e.g., J. Zielinski [1980]), "Stochastic Preference Theory: Some Unresolved Questions," *Journal of Marketing Research*, 17 (Aug.), pp. 379–82.

41. The Hendry Corporation (1970), *Hendro Dynamics: Fundamental Laws of Consumer Dynamics*, Ch. 1, and (1971), *Hendro Dynamics: Fundamental Laws of Consumer Dynamics*, Ch. 2. An alternative statement of the Hendry model is suggested in M. U. Kalwani and D. G. Morrison (1977), "A Parsimonious Description of the Hendry System," *Management Science*, 23 (Jan.), pp. 467–77.

10 Communication Theory

Communications form a crucial link between marketing strategy and consumer behavior. Consider the following:

- Mass-media advertising is a major element of marketing strategies, particularly for consumer package goods. For example, Procter & Gamble spent $671 million on mass-media advertising in 1981 and $103 million on personal selling.[1]

- For industrial marketers, the interpersonal communication effort—the sales force—is often more important than media advertising. The average cost of a salesperson's call is $175, and salespeople often earn considerably more than technical support staffs and engineers, for example, reflecting their critical importance to the implementation and the articulation of a firm's marketing strategy.[2]

- Although advertising is a highly visible form of communication, virtually all elements of the marketing mix communicate something to consumers. For example, price connotes value for some goods to some consumers (consider perfume); the store in which a good is sold also can connote value; and, of course, product style, shape, and status symbols (like the "preppie" alligator on clothing) also are forms of communication.

- It is often said that word-of-mouth communication can help or hurt a marketer more than any amount of paid advertising in mass media. The success of movies and plays, for example, is highly contingent upon interpersonal communication among consumers.

In this chapter, we assess marketers' use of mass communications—advertising—as an element of marketing strategy. We examine first how theories of mass communications have developed over this century, from simplistic models that portrayed the media as all-powerful influences on human behavior, to more complex models that recognize how consumers mediate the impact of mass communications through such factors as perceptions, cognitive defenses, prior experience, and selective processes.

Next, we examine the nature of communications decisions in marketing strategy, focusing on issues involved in deciding when and how to use mass communications to achieve strategic goals. We also discuss issues involved in determining advertising's effects on individual consumer behavior.

Finally, we review findings from research on mass communications, focusing on (1) effects of different message structures (for example, the effects of comparative advertising), (2) effects of different media and different media vehicles (for example, print versus broadcast media), and (3) effects of communication campaign timing on consumer behavior.

CONCEPTUAL MODELS OF MASS COMMUNICATIONS: AN HISTORICAL PERSPECTIVE

Our views of the effect of mass communications on consumer behavior have changed markedly in this century with the emergence of radio and television, complementing the earlier mass media: newspapers, catalogues, and billboards. Early theories of mass communications assumed that the mass media were quite powerful and that audiences of mass media were simply passive recipients of media content. In more recent years, empirical research has resulted in a considerable shift in our models of effective mass communications. Although there is considerable debate about the impact of mass media in particular areas—notably, their possible role in stimulating violent behavior, in shaping cultural values, and in affecting "special" audiences, such as children—the contemporary view is that an individual's predispositions, cognitive processes, and experiences significantly mediate the impact of mass communications. The media are clearly an important source of information about the world, including products and services. The impact of mass-media content on the attitudes and behaviors of audience members, however, is not nearly as direct or powerful as had once been thought.

Early Views of Mass Communications Processes and Effects

Earlier in this century, the notion that mass media such as posters and radio directly influenced people's behavior was called the **one-way flow** or *hypodermic-needle* model of mass-communications effects.[3] It is graphically represented in Exhibit 10–1.

In this model, *source* refers to the perceived originator of a message. For a news story, this might be a government official. In advertising, the source

EXHIBIT 10–1

***ONE-WAY FLOW* OR *HYPODERMIC NEEDLE* MODEL OF MASS COMMUNICATIONS EFFECTS**

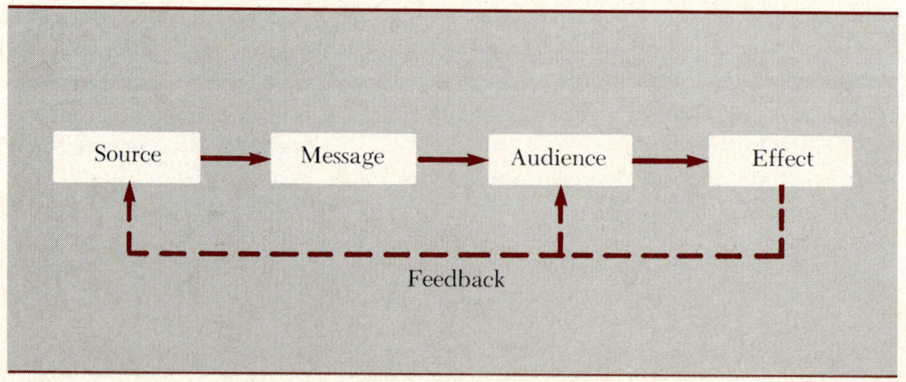

is the message sponsor. The *message* is the particular content—of a news story or an advertisement—communicated via some medium, such as a newspaper or radio. The *audience* is any and all individuals exposed to the message. Effects include changes in attitudes as well as behavior; whatever effects occur provide some kind of *feedback* to the message source and to the member of the audience. For advertising, product sales provide the most important type of feedback to the message source, and degree of satisfaction with the product provides feedback to the member of the audience.

The one-way arrows in the model imply that messages "get through" to audiences. That is, people are reached and affected by messages communicated via mass media. Consequently, early advertising often included long messages, as in the advertisement from 1927 in Exhibit 10–2. The assump-

"rational man"

tion that people would actually read all the copy was reinforced by economic theories prevalent in the early part of this century, especially the classic economic notion of "rational man." Advertisers apparently felt that consumers would read any and all messages, and read them thoroughly, as they sought to maximize the utility of their expenditures.

Recent Views of Mass Communications Processes and Effects

Several events challenged the one-way flow model of mass communication. First, advertisers discovered that simply placing an advertisement in a mass medium did not insure sales results: consumers do not respond in the stimulus-response fashion the model portrays. Second, traditional microeconomic theories, with their notions of "rational man," were being displaced by Freudian notions that emphasized unconscious drives and motivations—quite different from economic theories. Finally, television developed in the post World-War II years, and rapid developments in graphic arts made it possible for advertisers to use vivid illustrations as well as copy in their advertisements.

Researchers began to show that audience members are not passive recipients of persuasive mass-media content. Rather, they are active information-processors, who selectively attend to the mass media, selectively perceive media content, and evaluate media information in terms of their beliefs, attitudes, and experiences. Raymond Bauer put it this way:

> *The time may well be at hand to revise the traditional communications formula, "who does what, with which, and to whom." The suggested revision is that we view communications as a transactional process in which both audience and communicator take important initiative. A successful communication is usually a good "deal" in which each party gives and takes in some pattern that is acceptable to him.*[4]

This *two-way* or **transactional** model, portrayed in Exhibit 10–3, provides a number of conceptual improvements over the one-way model. It more completely indicates the elements in the structure of mass communications, and it suggests how mass communications work. The model's representation of "Advertiser-Message-Source" more accurately reflects what consumers actually perceive when they view advertising. For example, Frank Sinatra, who promoted Chrysler automobiles, is a highly recognized message *source*, delivering a *message* on behalf of the *advertiser*.

The model also portrays such factors as "noise," or extraneous influences, and other influences, such as price, product quality, and competitor's advertising, that may affect particular audience segments (in contrast with the undifferentiated, mass audience implied in the one-way model).

The two-way arrows binding audience segments and the advertising stimuli transmitted via some *medium* suggest that audience members *bring some-*

thing to the mass communication situation that mediates message impact. A consumer's prior experience with a brand, for example, shapes his or her reactions to advertisements for the brand.

Finally, the two-way model of mass communications suggests that individuals will first form cognitions about the advertised object—become aware and knowledgeable, and possibly change attitudes—and, ultimately, some will purchase the product. This step-wise process underlies the hierarchy-of-effects notions discussed in Chapters 4 and 5. However, if these processes always occurred, prepurchase measures of cognitions resulting from exposure to mass communications should predict ultimate consumer behavior. Yet, as we have seen, cognitions such as attitudes do not always predict ultimate behavior, leading some researchers to suggest that the two-way flow model of mass communications may not always be valid, and that a low-involvement model may be more appropriate (see Chapter 6).

Advertising's effects are complex, as are the cognitive processes underlying those effects. The effectiveness of advertising in creating awareness and recall and the relationship of those cognitive effects to sales illustrate this complexity. As the story in Exhibit 10–4 indicates, some advertising can achieve high memorability at a very low cost, but such cognitive effects are not necessarily correlated with buying behavior. Moreover, the low-involvement notion would seem to be supported by the finding that users of some products (such as soft drinks) confuse brands in advertising they recall.

EXHIBIT 10–3
TWO-WAY OR TRANSACTIONAL MODEL OF MASS COMMUNICATION EFFECTS

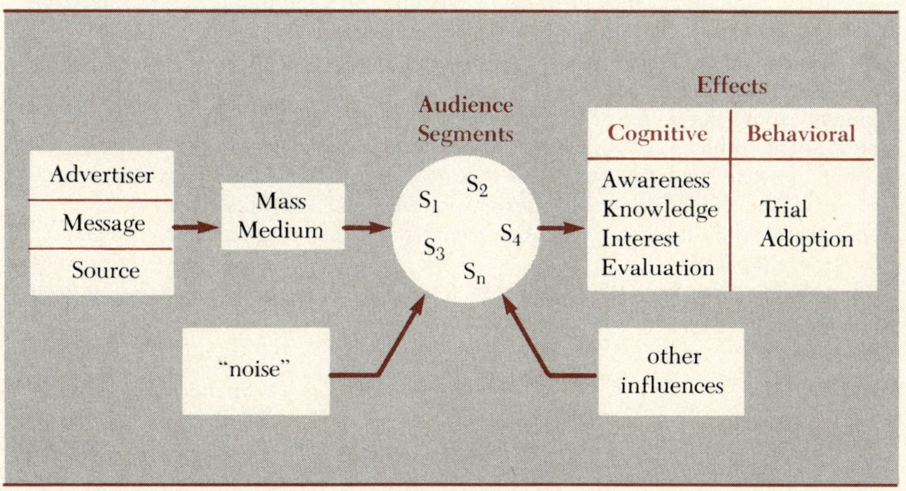

An Information-Processing Model of Advertising Communication

The model in Exhibit 10–5 elaborates the two-way model and specifies many of the variables determining consumer responses to advertising. Advertising's impact is a function of message, media, and timing variables. Ultimately, ad-

EXHIBIT 10–4
COGNITIVE EFFECTS NEED NOT BE CORRELATED WITH BUYING BEHAVIOR

MILLER LITE'S ADS BEST LIKED, BUT AREN'T THE MOST EFFICIENT

The most popular advertising on television in 1982, for the second consecutive year, was the campaign for Miller Lite beer. When it came to being remembered by potential customers, though, no well-liked brand did it more economically than Oscar Mayer. To make a lasting impression on meat buyers, it spent only one-fifth the amount Miller shelled out.

Those are the conclusions of Video Storyboard Tests Inc., a New York ad-testing company. In telephone surveys last year, it asked 22,000 adults to name the "most outstanding" TV commercial they had seen. Listed below are the 25 most often noticed, remembered and liked.

But recognition often can be bought with big ad budgets alone. To further determine how effective campaigns were, Video Storyboard also compared their popularity with their TV spending.

The first step was a separate survey of 4,000 adults in which regular users of a product were asked to cite a commercial they had seen in the previous week. Soda drinkers, for example, were asked what soft-drink commercials they recalled.

The number of mentions for each brand then was divided by its TV budget to develop a measure of cost efficiency that Video Storyboard calls the "cost per 1,000 retained impressions." Thus, Kodak's 1982 TV budget of $69.1 million reached camera owners at a cost of $22.22 per thousand. Rival Polaroid's smaller budget of $31.8 million was more efficient, though, catching the same number of prospects for $13.89 per thousand.

By that standard, Coca-Cola Co. spent far less to reach prospects for Coke than for its Tab diet drink. Among sellers of long-distance telephone services, MCI Communications got by for $11.77 per 1,000 viewers, two-thirds the amount the Bell System spent. Miller Lite advertising was more efficient than Budweiser Light's, probably because the latter was a new product and needed more advertising.

Here are the Video Storyboard rankings for 1982 and 1981; asterisks indicate brands that weren't listed in 1981. Also included are the ad agencies that helped create the campaigns. . . .

The column at the far right indicates the cost of reaching 1,000 prospects for each campaign.

1982 Rank	1981 Rank	Brand (Agency)	1982 TV Spending (Millions)	1982 Cost Efficiency
1	1	Miller Lite (Backer & Spielvogel)	$44.4	$29.86
2	2	Coca-Cola (McCann-Erickson)	38.6	8.96
3	16	Federal Express (Ally & Gargano)	19.9	22.01
4	5	McDonald's (Leo Burnett)	59.9	11.50

vertising can affect cognitive structures and purchase behavior, but its impact is mediated by situational factors and consumer information-processing. The events and processes portrayed in the model occur in some environment or context, such as the family and the general economic situation.

Many of the personal factors and message-processing variables that influence consumers' processing of advertising messages were discussed in Chap-

5	3	Pepsi-Cola (BBDO)	42.0	10.35
6	*	Burger King (J. Walter Thompson)	35.4	9.08
7	*	Budweiser Light (Needham, Harper & Steers)	31.2	41.67
8	4	Dr Pepper (Young & Rubicam)	13.3	7.83
9	*	Atari Video Games (Doyle Dane Bernbach)	46.9	NA
10	6	Bell System (N. W. Ayer)	66.7	18.33
11	7	Polaroid (Doyle Dane Bernbach)	31.8	13.89
12	10	Oscar Mayer (J. Walter Thompson)	11.7	6.37
13	*	Shasta (Needham, Harper & Steers)	5.3	11.33
14	*	Velveeta (J. Walter Thompson)	13.8	NA
15	14	Tab (McCann-Erickson)	18.0	19.33
16	11	Life Cereal (BBDO)	7.2	13.40
17	9	Seven-Up (N. W. Ayer)	24.5	10.00
18	8	French's Mustard (J. Walter Thompson)	3.4	10.16
19	*	Toyota (Dancer Fitzgerald Sample)	66.0	29.44
20	12	Kibbles 'n Bits (J. Walter Thompson)	5.5	16.56
21	*	Levi's (Foote, Cone & Belding)	12.1	6.81
22	25	Kodak (J. Walter Thompson)	69.1	22.22
23	21	Ford (J. Walter Thompson)	107.7	32.56
24	*	MCI Communications (Ally & Gargano)	21.1	11.77
25	*	Wonder Bread (Ted Bates)	9.4	NA

. . . . .

Kids played important roles in eight of the 25 campaigns on the Video Storyboard list, more than ever before. David Vadehra, president of the ad-research concern, says children attract attention more easily and often enhance credibility. As one consumer told Video Storyboard, "Kids make commercials seem more honest."

A high ranking doesn't guarantee, though, that a campaign will make cash registers ring. Advertising executives contend that advertising sometimes works subconsciously, so that effective ads aren't necessarily the ones shoppers think of when polled.

There's also the problem of faulty memories. Some people told Video Storyboard surveyers they liked Coke commercials and then went on to describe a Pepsi ad, for example. A viewer recently said his favorite TV spot was the one with the Marlboro cowboy; cigarettes ads, however, have been banned from television since 1971.

SOURCE: From Bill Abrams (1983), *Wall Street Journal* (March 3), p. 27.

ters 4 and 5. In this chapter, we focus on the communication variables *per se:* message structure, media, and timing variables. First, however, we shall examine advertising's role in marketing strategy.

THE ROLE OF ADVERTISING IN MARKETING STRATEGY

Advertising, personal selling (the sales force), and sales promotion tools, such as trade shows, coupons, and the like, are forms of communication marketers use to reach segments of consumers. Collectively, they are referred to as the

EXHIBIT 10–5
AN INFORMATION-PROCESSING MODEL OF ADVERTISING'S IMPACT ON CONSUMER COGNITIONS AND BEHAVIOR

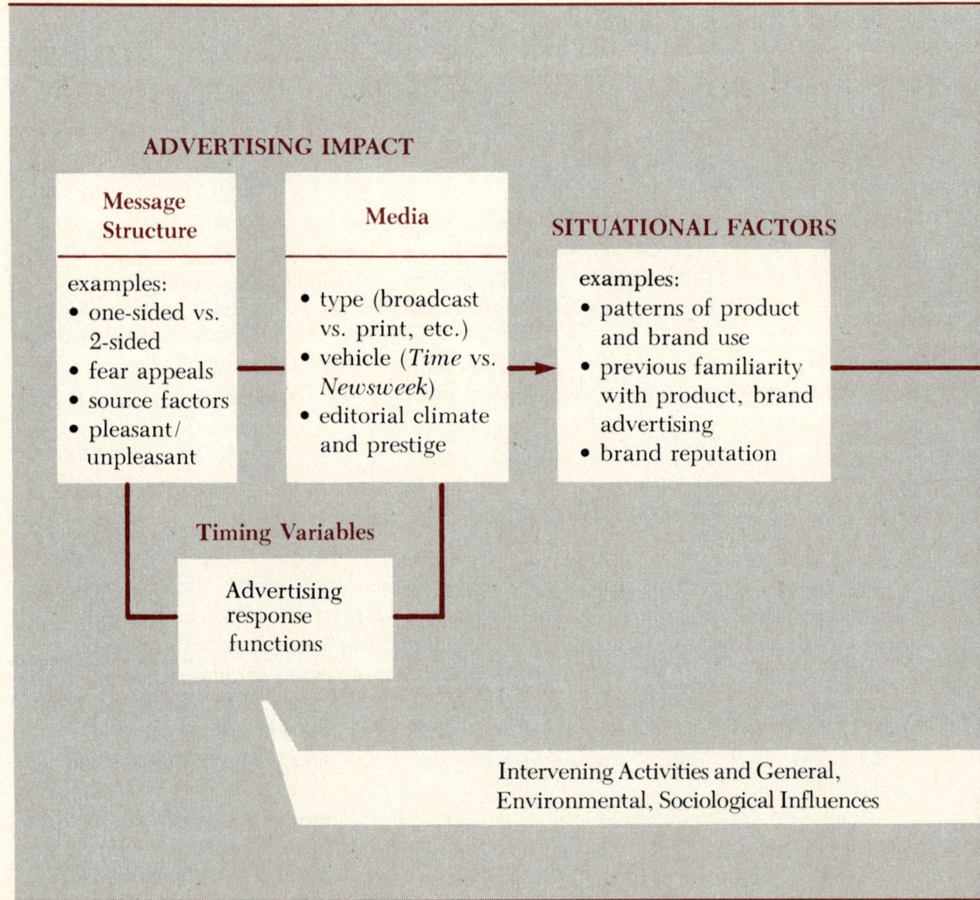

SOURCE: Based on Alan Sawyer and Scott Ward (1977), "Carry-over Effects in Advertising Communication: Evidence and Hypotheses from Behavioral Science," in *Cumulative Advertising Ef-*

promotion mix. In general, advertising is used to promote consumer goods and services for large markets that can be reached efficiently via the mass media, and when product information and brand imagery can be communicated via those media. Conversely, personal selling is usually a more important element of the promotion mix in industrial marketing, since the customer base is smaller, and information must be targeted to the needs of particular companies.

The importance of advertising in marketing strategy is largely determined by the consumer-behavior patterns that advertising attempts to influence. The importance of advertising—reflected in amounts budgeted for it—vary by in-

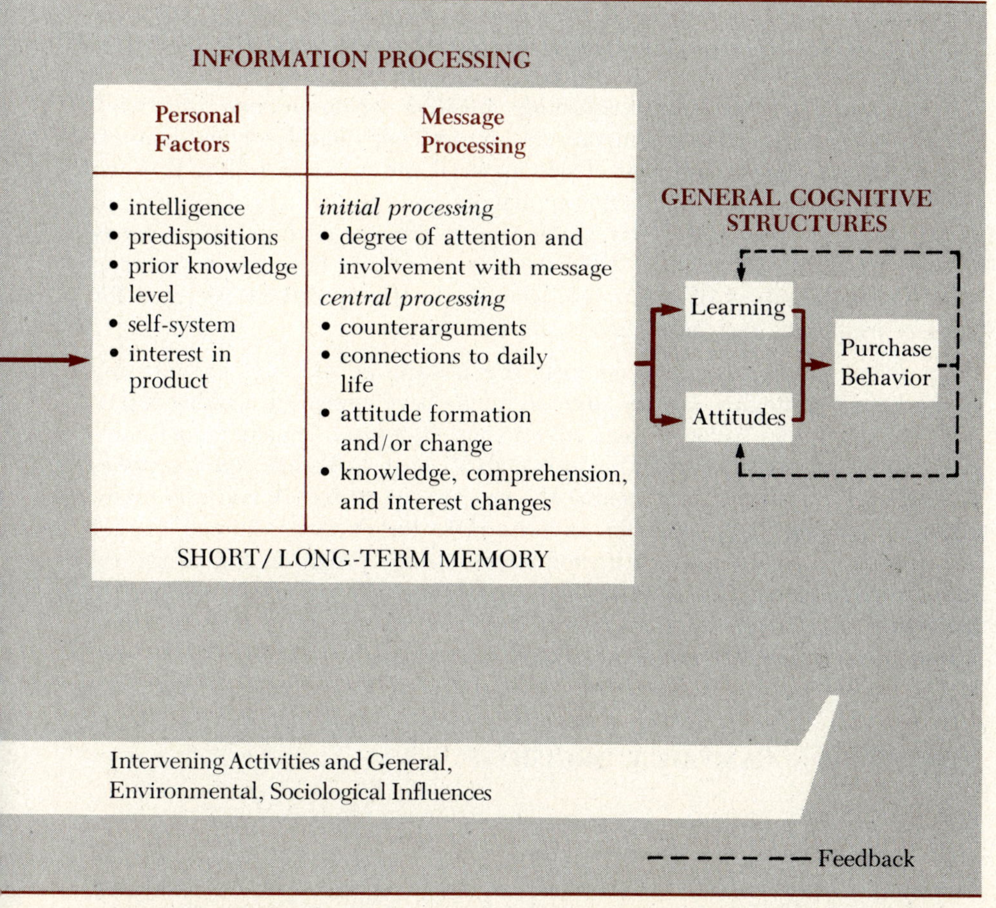

fects: Sources and Implications, ed. Darral Clarke, Report 77–111 (Cambridge, Mass.: Marketing Science Inst.).

dustry, product type, and brand. In turn, these variables reflect differences in underlying consumer factors. For example, greater relative amounts of advertising have been found with the following conditions:[5]

1. There is a *basis for differentiating* products and brands within product groups. For example, detergents are quite similar in their chemical composition and prices, but advertising differentiates among brands by communicating that some brands are better for stains, others work best in cold water, and so forth.
2. There are *hidden qualities*. For example, the introduction of caffeine-free and sugar-free drinks has necessitated advertising to communicate the different attributes of these types of sodas.
3. There are *emotional buying motives*. Advertising is particularly useful in creating and maintaining brand images for products such as perfume and clothing, since "emotional" motives are important determinants of purchasing behavior.
4. Products are in the *early and growth stages* of the product life cycle, reflecting consumer needs for information when new products are introduced.
5. Goods are *low-priced and nondurable*. Because consumers need relatively extensive and specific information on high-priced, durable goods, marketers will spend more on point-of-sale material and personal selling for such products (automobiles and major appliances, for example). Furthermore, at any one time there are fewer consumers in the market for durable goods than for nondurable goods. Advertising is more cost effective in reaching the larger numbers of consumers who are in the market at any time for more frequently purchased goods and services.

In recent years, a trend has emerged that has altered the role of advertising in marketing strategies. Highly targeted media have appeared, making it possible for marketers to focus their advertising strategies. Consider, for example, the homogeneous readership of magazines such as *Tennis, Photography,* and *Seventeen.* In electronic media, the emergence of pay TV and cable television may make it possible for advertisers to target more defined market segments than are currently attracted to prime-time programming on the established networks. It is now possible for advertisers to go beyond generating awareness in a large, undifferentiated audience to providing more detailed information to narrowly-defined audience segments.

ADVERTISING CAMPAIGN DECISIONS

In implementing marketing strategies through advertising campaigns, advertisers must make decisions about message structure, media, and campaign timing (see Exhibit 10–5). These variables comprise important aspects of advertising campaign decisions. Before such tactical decisions can be made, however, strategic decisions are necessary about overall promotional objectives and about how they fit with more general corporate objectives. For example, if an advertiser's objective is to dominate a market, then large advertising budgets will be required, and products must be designed to appeal to the diverse needs of segments within the overall market. As a case in point, it would appear that Procter & Gamble dominates the washing-detergent market. The company sells the overall market leader (Tide, with nearly 30 percent of the U.S. market) and a number of other brands that are tailored to specific segment needs—for example, Cheer, designed for cold-water use; Gain, useful for pre-soaking and stains; and Duz and Bonus, lower-priced brands, featuring premiums that are packed in each box.

Other strategic and tactical decisions require additional information about consumer behavior. For example, should an advertiser make comparisons with another brand? This decision requires information about consumer perceptions of the two brands, as well as information about what particular attributes should be compared.

Message-Structure Decisions

Advertising messages are constructed in line with the **creative objectives** a marketer and the advertising agency set for a given advertising campaign. These creative objectives follow from advertising objectives and from overall marketing-strategy objectives. For example, a marketer introducing a new, high-priced, bottled mineral water might state the following marketing, advertising, and creative objectives.

- *marketing objective:* Achieve X level of sales in first three months.
- *advertising objective:* Copy—create awareness that Product X is a high-status, refreshing drink. Media—reach X percent of the target market at least four times in six months.
- *creative objective:* Show obviously well-to-do people enjoying the beverage after engaging in "upscale" sports such as tennis and skiing.

Advertising messages are extremely complex stimuli—each is a "Gestalt" or overall impression (as the two-way model suggests) of source, message, and advertiser, as well as of many other variables, such as tone and connotations evoked by pictures, words, and format of advertising. Making things even more complex, different consumers may have widely varying reactions to the same ad: one person may find it quite attention-getting and perhaps humorous, while another person might find it boring or offensive. Little wonder, then, that advertising copywriters have often been guided by intuitive assessments of effective advertising techniques, rather than by systematic empirical research. For example, David Ogilvy, former head of one of the world's largest advertising agencies, makes the following suggestions, based on his years of experience in advertising:[6]

1. What you say is more important than how you say it.
2. Unless your campaign is built around a great idea, it will flop.
3. Give the facts.
4. You cannot bore people into buying.
5. Be well-mannered, but don't clown.
6. Make your advertising contemporary.
7. Committees can criticize advertisements, but they cannot write them.
8. If you are lucky enough to write a good advertisement, repeat it until it stops pulling.
9. Never write an advertisement which you wouldn't want your own family to read.
10. [Assess the] image and the brand.
11. Don't be a copy-cat.

Empirical research on message-structure variables adds a perspective to experience-based suggestions such as Ogilvy's. For example, research findings provide some guidance on the extent to which advertisers should try to refute possible negative points about the product being advertised. These are called **refutational appeals,** in contrast with more usual "supportive" appeals that simply give positive reasons for buying the product. For example, consider the response of one insurance company to the consumer trend toward investing more in stocks and money-market funds than in insurance: an ad for Mutual of New York portrays a stockbroker saying, "I'm in stocks and bonds; I'll take them over life insurance, but a MONY man gave me a new look at life insurance. As an investment cornerstone, it would protect my family . . . and build cash too."

Or, to take another example, consider the problem facing Tylenol when they reintroduced the product following the poisonings that occurred in late 1982. The company had little choice but to refute the beliefs shared by many consumers about the product's safety (see page 322). Interestingly, Tylenol did not extend the kind of advertising shown beyond a reintroductory campaign. After that, they returned to general appeals about the product's effectiveness. Tylenol's competitors did little to feature their similar packaging modifications, perhaps fearing that the problem might be magnified.

Advertisers have been quite reluctant to employ refutational appeals. They fear that consumers might become confused, and remember only the negative points or limitations brought up in the advertising. They also fear that such advertising might set off a "war" of refutational appeals among competitors, harming all advertising for the products, as well as brand reputations. The matter is particularly vexing since research suggests that refutational appeals can be more effective than appeals that merely offer supportive statements about the advertised brand.[7] The idea is that refutational appeals **inoculate** consumers against later advertising appeals they might encounter from competitors. It appears that supportive appeals are initially superior (measured by attitude change) but that later, after consumers are exposed to advertising that attacks the initial, supportive appeals, refutational appeals are superior.

More recently, advertisers have increasingly used a variation of refutational appeals with **comparison advertising,** which refers to the practice of making specific and explicit comparisons with competitors whose products are identified. The Federal Trade Commission officially encourages such advertising, instead of vague comparisons (like "better than brand X").[8] An example of a comparative ad is shown on p. 329.

The following are some hypotheses growing out of consumer-behavior research about the effectiveness of comparative advertising.[9]

- Comparative advertising may lead to information overload (discussed in Chapter 6), so consumers do not closely attend to it.

- Comparative ads may lead to counterarguing, thereby producing a boomerang effect, especially if users of the competing brand experience cognitive dissonance, and, therefore, become more likely to purchase the "attacked" brand in order to reduce dissonance.

- Consumers may fail to recall advertising points that are discrepant with their beliefs, so that the net effect may be misidentification of the sponsoring brand or even a net gain for the competition.

- Comparative advertising may be seen as more believable, since consumers may feel that an advertiser is officially permitted to compare the advertised brand with named competitors; on the other hand, there is some evidence that consumers do not believe comparative ads, since all advertisers are seen as making essentially the same claim.

- Some advertisers may benefit more from making a comparative claim than other advertisers. It is hypothesized that an underdog effect may occur, meaning that lesser known brands have little to lose in comparing themselves to the market leader (for example, Avis' "We try harder" campaign).

Research that has examined the effects of comparative advertising shows that it is a multidimensional phenomenon that must be very carefully assessed by advertisers. For example, Prasad examined the relative effects of a comparative ad and a "brand X" ad for a movie camera.[10] He found that consumers who saw the comparative ad had somewhat greater recall of the message and the advertising claim, but that there were no differences in brand recall. He also found that individuals who preferred the competitor named in the comparative advertisement rated the advertised brand lower than did another group of consumers who saw the noncomparative ad.

Another exploratory study showed that comparative and noncomparative ads are not significantly different in effects on purchase intentions, believability of claims, or advertisement credibility. Curiously, however, comparison advertising was found to have the potential to improve purchase intentions.[11] The use of comparative advertising in marketing strategy is illustrated in Burger King's aggressive comparative advertising campaign, which has stressed that Burger King broils its hamburgers, while Wendy's and McDonald's do not (see pp. 243–44).

The Message Source   Another important decision about message structure is the choice of a source to deliver the actual message. For example, should an advertiser choose a highly attractive fashion model (who is likely to get high attention), an expert on the product or service, or a "typical" consumer of the product or service?

Some guidance for such decisions comes from research on the credibility of message sources. **Source credibility** involves the following dimensions.[12]

- *expertise*—the extent to which a source is perceived as being capable of providing correct information
- *trustworthiness*—the degree to which a source is perceived as providing information that reflects the source's actual feelings or opinions
- *attraction*—the extent to which a source elicits positive feelings from audience members, such as a desire to emulate the source in some way
- *referent other*—the degree to which a source is similar to the target audience members, or is depicted as having similar problems or other characteristics relating to use of a particular product or brand

testimonial advertising

Testimonial advertising involves direct assertions about a product or service by a message source. The underlying process is related to balance theories, or to "congruity theories," of attitude change (see Chapter 11). If a consumer has a neutral or negative attitude toward brand X, but a highly positive attitude toward spokesperson Y, and that spokesperson makes a positive assertion (endorsement) about brand X, then the attitude should change toward the positive for the product (see p. 334).[13] For example, if football star-turned-actor Joe Namath endorses a men's cologne, positive attitudes might result among target-audience members to the extent that Namath is seen as attractive and knowledgeable about men's cologne.

Of course, a basic problem with testimonial advertising is that the source might be seen as untrustworthy, since he or she is believed to be highly paid by the advertiser for making the endorsements. As psychologist Roger Brown notes, in reviewing testimonial advertising over the years, ". . . word got around among consumers that money was changing hands."[14] Perhaps because of this fact, there appears to be increasing use of "hidden camera" commercials employing *referent-other* spokespeople. These people are meant to be seen by audiences as (1) "just like me," (2) having problems "just as I do," and (3) apparently giving unpaid and (therefore) genuine attitudes (the commercials appear to be recording spontaneous attitudes given in product-research settings, in stores, and so on).

referent-other

The use of testimonial advertising raises many issues, which may be carefully evaluated by using consumer research. For example, an advertiser might choose a highly attractive fashion model to endorse a product in order to gain high levels of initial attention. In fact, McGuire has posited a "compensation principle," which suggests that high levels of response in one part of the hierarchy of effects (see Chapters 4 and 5) might actually lead to lower levels of response in other parts of the hierarchy. In the extreme case, some consumers might pay so much attention to the model that they do not even remember the brand name!

Other problems involve the interaction of various dimensions of source credibility. For example, Jack Nicklaus is a logical person to use in a testimonial ad for a brand of golf clubs. However, as attractive and expert as he may be to target-audience members, some might feel that his level of play is so superior that the brand of clubs he endorses would be inappropriate for weekend golfers. On the other hand, the late J. Paul Getty was an effective spokesman for the financial services provided by E. F. Hutton because he was considered to be an expert on financial matters and a person for investors to emulate. In addition, Getty's personal wealth probably increased his trustworthiness, since few consumers would feel his primary motive for doing the commercial was to collect a fee. A problem might have been an "incredulity" response, since some may have felt Getty's extraordinary wealth was not attributable to the services of any brokerage house.

Message Tone and Intensity Another message-variable decision involves message *tone* and the kind of affective responses advertisements may stimulate among target-market audience members. Of course, a key factor in shaping such responses to advertising communication is *repetition*—our affective reactions to the first ad in a campaign may be very different after we have seen it several times. We will discuss repetition effects in the next section.

repetition

An important dimension of advertising tone or intensity is the degree to which messages are "hard sell" or "soft sell," or irritating or pleasant. While advertisers do not attempt to irritate consumers, we have all seen instances of hard-sell advertising that irritate us. One famous example is the "ring around the collar" campaign for Lever Brothers' Wisk detergent. The fifteen-year-old campaign has achieved high levels of recall and sales, despite the fact that many people cite it as highly irritating. Defenders of the advertising suggest that different types of responses to the advertising may be due to market segmentation. Detractors are generally not those who have a "ring around the collar" problem (see Exhibit 10–6).

hard sell or soft sell

There are two directly conflicting theories about the superiority of message tone dimensions such as *hard sell/irritating* and *soft sell/pleasant:* the **law of extremes** and the **superiority of the pleasant** hypothesis. Briefly, the law of extremes states that whether consumers like or dislike an advertisement is less important than the intensity with which they perceive it. Some studies have found a curvilinear (U-shaped) relationship between an advertisement's effect (measured by recall) and liking of the ad: ads that are strongly liked *or* disliked are more likely to be remembered than ads that do not evoke strong feelings one way or the other.

The superiority-of-the-pleasant hypothesis suggests, obviously, that pleasant stimuli are more effective than unpleasant stimuli. The behavioral foundations of this notion are found in Freudian literature and in learning theory. Freud stressed that we repress unpleasant experiences, and the learning theorist Thorndike posited in his "law of effect" that connections between a stimulus and a response are strengthened or "stamped in" by satisfying experiences and weakened or "stamped out" by unpleasant or annoying ones.

Silk and Vavra compared the pleasant hypothesis and the law-of-extremes hypothesis by constructing soft-sell and hard-sell test ads.[15] They found that brand awareness, recall of the commercial, and brand preference were significantly greater for the hard-sell than for the soft-sell commercial. However, among consumers who were exposed to the commercials twice and who were interviewed two days later, the levels of effects were raised sharply, but the magnitude of increase was greater for the soft-sell than for the hard-sell commercial. After a second exposure, the hard-sell ad continued to be more effective, but its margin of superiority had been reduced. Repetition (two exposures) produced no statistically significant effects for either commercial, but the incremental effect of the second exposure was positive for the soft-sell and negative for the hard-sell commercial.

EXHIBIT 10–6
A DIMENSION OF ADVERTISING TONE

'RING AROUND THE COLLAR' ADS IRRITATE MANY YET GET RESULTS

The most obnoxious ad on television, in the view of some Madison Avenue professionals, is the "ring around the collar" commercial for Wisk detergent. Critics say it is irritating, insults women—especially the housewives who are Wisk's most important customers—and even damages the credibility of advertising in general.

"Ring around the collar," it also can be argued, is one of the greatest advertising campaigns ever. It reversed the fortunes of a troubled brand and has kept it growing ever since. Ranking third in U.S. detergent sales, Wisk accounts for about 8% of the market and brings Lever Brothers Co., its manufacturer, revenue of more than $200 million a year.

The campaign has lasted 15 years—far longer than most—and has outscored dozens of alternatives tested by Lever and its agency, Batten, Barton, Durstine & Osborn. Procter & Gamble Co. and Colgate-Palmolive Co. have brought out their own liquid detergents to compete with Wisk but never have come close to its success.

"It would be fair to call that commercial a screeching commercial, an abrasive commercial, an intrusive commercial," says James Jordan, author of the slogan and now chairman of his own agency. "But the one thing you can't call it is a bad commercial because the purpose of a commercial is to do a commercial job."

Marschalk Co., a New York ad agency, says its surveys show that a disliked commercial may prompt 33% of its viewers to consider buying a competing brand. Notes Rena Bartos, a J. Walter Thompson senior vice president, "Many people buy a product in spite of its advertising, not because of it." Her studies of irritating commercials show that they generate negative attitudes toward the entire advertising industry.

Defenders of "ring" say that critics are the sort of folks who, unlike most consumers, rarely are troubled by dirty collars. "The people who are critical work in air-conditioned offices and send their shirts to the laundry," says Sam Thurm, an official

---

Media Factors

Advertisers must make significant decisions about what *types* of media to use (for example, print or broadcast) and what specific media *vehicles* to use (for example, within print media, *Time* or *Business Week*, and within television, news shows or prime-time entertainment shows).

In practice, decisions about advertising media are based on quantitative and qualitative assessments of consumer behavior, analysis of the structure of audiences for given media types and vehicles, and analysis of the consumer-behavior processes involved in using various media and their ultimate effects.

Advertisers are first interested in determining which media reach intended audience segments, and at what costs. If messages are targeted to highly specialized audiences, then advertisers will choose media vehicles that focus on those audiences. For example, Schweppe's might advertise in "highbrow" publications, such as *Gourmet* magazine, while Canada Dry might seek to appeal to much broader audiences through prime-time television. Such deci-

---

of the Association of National Advertisers and Lever's advertising chief when "ring" was born in 1967.

Embarrassment is critical to the commercial's effectiveness. A typical 30-second "ring" ad of the early 1970s shows a couple arriving for a Hawaiian vacation. As a grass-skirted native places a lei around the husband's neck, she loudly discovers his dirty collar. He looks at his wife as if she'd just murdered their firstborn. She is horrified and ashamed.

"Those dirty stains," intones an off-camera voice, which explains why she should use Wisk. She does, and the commercial closes with the husband placing a lei around her neck as they smile together. The problem is gone, the tension resolved. The tension was gone at Lever, too; Wisk sales tripled between 1967 and 1974.

Still, Lever and B.B.D.O. decided the campaign wasn't quite right. In 1979, blame for dirty collars was shifted to competitors' detergents; the wife's moment of shame was cut. "We wanted to tone down the pain a little bit," explains Kenneth Rogers of B.B.D.O.

Little else has changed. Not every version uses husband and wife, and new spots scheduled for next year will feature new scenarios but the same format. When Lever recently experimented with a "hidden camera" ad in which ordinary consumers talked about ring-around-the-collar ("I got crazy and ran out of the room," a wife confesses after her husband's collar became a topic of conversation at a party), Wisk sales fell in test cities.

Lever says the "ring" campaign's work isn't finished. There are new liquid detergents to fight and powdered-detergent buyers to convert. And even after 15 years and more than $100 million worth of "ring" on TV, some people haven't gotten the message. Although the slogan is almost universally known, Lever research shows that one of every three viewers still doesn't associate it with Wisk.

SOURCE: Bill Abrams (1982), *Wall Street Journal* (Nov.), p. 33.

sions are based on quantitative assessments of the size and composition of media audiences. For example, the Nielsen television-rating service provides information about the size and demographic composition of audiences for television programs; other research services, such as Target Group Index and Simmons, provide information about the demographic and psychographic composition of media audiences.

Advertisers must also confront more qualitative factors in reaching media decisions. Exhibit 10–7 summarizes many of these, as well as quantitative, factors.

The characteristics we ascribe to the various advertising media involve differences in the ways we react to messages. We can take our time in reading a magazine ad, but a television commercial is in front of us for just thirty seconds. We may be very involved in reading a magazine such as *Business Week*, and less involved in watching a situation comedy on television. Of course, our level of involvement may vary depending on the advertising content or our level of interest in the product, as well as our level of involvement with the medium itself.

In an important experiment, Peter Wright examined the responses of consumers who were exposed to identical messages transmitted via print and via broadcast media.[16] He also manipulated the level of involvement with the content of the message by telling half of the subjects that they would be asked to evaluate the product in the advertisement, while the other half received no such information. Respondents were instructed to list all thoughts relevant to the product or message that occurred to them during exposure; other measures were taken of recall and attitudinal acceptance of the message.

Wright's results are interesting. He found that there were no differences in recall, but that respondents exposed to print media generated far more counterarguments, source derogation (that is, thoughts attacking the message source), and support arguments (that is, thoughts supporting the arguments in the ads) than did consumers exposed to the broadcast media. Moreover, the number of counterarguments generated by those exposed to the broadcast message did not vary with level of involvement. But among those exposed to the print message, highly involved consumers generated far more counterarguments than did those with little involvement.

One variable that Wright did not investigate was the effect of repetition or the "timing" of consumer exposures to advertising. Yet campaign timing (see Exhibit 10–5) may interact in important ways with the message and media variables we have just discussed.

Timing Variables

In advertising campaigns, decisions must be made about scheduling over set periods of time and about amounts of repetition of a message. Both decisions depend on understanding underlying patterns of consumer behavior. In particular, advertising planners must address issues such as the duration of advertising effects. What are the effects of **pulsing** advertising (that is, concentrating messages in short blocks of time) versus *spacing* out advertising (over a longer period of time)? What kinds of effects of an advertisement **carry over** to the next exposure? Does each exposure to an advertisement have an equal impact on consumers, or do successive exposures increase or decrease in their effectiveness?

EXHIBIT 10–7
GROSS MEDIA COMPARISONS

	TV	Radio	Magazines	Newspapers
Total population reach (adults & children)	very strong	good	fair	good
Selective upscale adult reach	fair	good	very strong	good
Upscale adult selectivity (per ad exposure)	poor	fair	very strong	good
Young adult selectivity (per ad exposure)	fair	very strong	very strong	fair
Local market selectivity	good	good	poor	very strong
Ability to control frequency	fair	good	good	very strong
Ability to pile frequency upon reach base	very strong	very strong	good	fair
Seasonal audience stability	poor	very strong	good	good
Predictability of audience levels	fair-poor	good	good	very good
Depth of demographics in audience surveys	poor	poor	very strong	fair-good
Opportunity to exploit editorial "compatibility"	poor	fair	very strong	good
Selective ad positioning	poor	fair	good	very strong
Advertising exposure	good	good	good	good
Advertising intrusiveness	very strong	good	fair	poor
Audience concern over ad "clutter"	very high	high	almost none	almost none
Emotional stimulation	very strong	fair	fair	poor
Sensory stimulation	fair-good	fair	very strong	fair
Brand name registration	very strong	good	fair	fair
Product or efficacy demonstrations	very strong	poor	fair	fair
Ability to exploit attention-getting devices	very strong	poor	very strong	good
Ability to use humor	very strong	good	poor	poor
Ability to use slice-of-life approach	very strong	good	poor	poor
Ability to convey detail and information	fair	fair	very strong	very strong
Ability to stimulate imagination	fair-good	very strong	fair	poor
Package identification	good	poor	very strong	good
Prestige & respectability of medium	fair	fair	very strong	strong
Ability to talk person-to-person with audience	fair-good	very strong	poor	poor

SOURCE: *The Media Book, 1978* (1978), (New York: Min-Mid Publishing), pp. 433, 436.

The Duration of Advertising Effects   A first step in planning advertising-campaign timing is to analyze how long advertising effects on consumers last. That is, how long do consumers remember the advertising or some elements of advertising messages? Also, how long do different kinds of effects last—effects such as recall, recognition, and attitude change?

These questions are all related to human learning processes, which we discussed in Chapter 9. Basic memory processes are related to the duration of advertising recognition and recall. The classic findings of Ebbinghaus in this area have been replicated many times, with various kinds of stimuli. He identified three basic memory processes.[17]

1. *The negatively accelerated forgetting curve.* After 20 minutes, Ebbinghaus observed that subjects forgot one third of what was learned; after six days, about one fourth; and a full month later, about one fifth.
2. *Serial position effects.* Items at the beginning or the end of a series were most easily learned; items in the middle were learned most slowly and forgotten most rapidly.
3. *Overlearning.* Overlearning or repetition beyond the point of retention made very long conscious memory possible (for example, "Things go better with ______").

The length of time an advertisement can be recalled depends on a host of factors, such as prior experiences, the meaningfulness of the stimuli, the size of the advertisement and so forth. However, it appears that the degree of original learning is the most important determinant of retention. Therefore, the processes that occur during and immediately following the time of exposure and attention to a communication are likely to be extremely important in determining any persistence of learning effects. For example, such processes as *connections* and *counterarguments,* discussed in Wright's experiment and in Chapters 5 and 6, occur during exposure, and have been found to affect retention. It seems that greater cognitive activity encourages processes by which advertisements are placed in long- or short-term memory. Similarly, it may be that commercials carried on "high quality" television programs are more effective than commercials carried with lower quality programs, a finding that would be consistent with a study that showed that "high interest" magazine articles were retained in memory considerably longer than "low interest" articles.[18]

Advertisers often seek to change existing cognitions about products and brands, as well as to encourage recall and recognition. Research on the duration of attitude change is therefore relevant to decisions about how long advertising campaigns should run and when they should be reinstated. In an extensive literature review, McGuire found studies in which induced opinion change persists for up to ten months, while other studies showed very little persistence.[19] He concluded that a rough estimate of the average duration of attitude change is about six months. Unlike learning, yielding (behavior change) and attitude change have no typical retention curves.

A common communication phenomenon with implications for advertising schedules is the **sleeper effect,** which refers to attitude change that actually increases over time. In a classic experiment, Hovland, Lumsdaine, and Sheffield showed soldiers *The Battle of Britain,* a World War II propaganda film; opinion change was measured either five days or nine weeks afterward.[20] For some opinion-change items the difference between the experimental group and a control group (that did not see the film) was larger after nine weeks than after five days.

This delay in impact would seem to be due to initial discounting of the film's message. That is, the army, which sponsored the film, may have been viewed as a biased source of information. This discredited source led to the initial discounting of the message and a reduction of the initial impact. Over time, the bias of the source was either forgotten, or, as later research showed, dissociated from the message. While other explanations have been advanced to explain sleeper effects, this **discounting-cue hypothesis** is probably the most widely accepted. But all explanations postulate similar cognitive activities following exposure to account for later increases in attitude change.

Since advertisers are often seen as biased sources of information, sleeper-effect studies may suggest that advertising changes attitudes in similar ways. However, advertising messages are quite different from the types of persuasive messages used in such studies, and, more importantly, consumers normally are repeatedly exposed to advertising messages. These repeated exposures may continually remind consumers of the biased nature of advertising, preventing increases in attitude change because the source remains associated with the message. Or consumers may see all advertising as biased, reducing this factor's importance in determining advertising's effects.

In any case, advertising effects on attitudes may persist for several weeks or even months, depending on such factors as the message source and the degree of initial discrepancy between the position advocated in the advertisement and consumer attitudes.

Moreover, as we have seen, the more an advertisement stimulates cognitive responses, the more likely it is to be retained and to influence attitudes and behavior. It appears that the amount of cognitive response sparked by an advertisement strengthens the relationship between degree of initial message processing and later impact. For example, one study found that one television antidrug-abuse commercial, that had induced more initial counterarguing than another commercial on the same topic, seemed to produce more reports of subsequent drug discussions ten to fourteen days later. Viewers of another ad, that had produced more personal connections, were more likely to report that they had read an antidrug booklet sent to them by mail and that they had found it helpful.[21]

Many other studies have shown that repetition is effective in inducing persistence primarily through slowing the process of memory decay.[22] But how much repetition is necessary to maximize effectiveness and inhibit forgetting among consumers—that is, to get the maximum impact from a given advertisement or advertising campaign? Since so many factors are involved—message-structure variables, audience variables, the type of product, competition, and so forth—there is no easy answer to this question. However, at a conceptual level, Krugman suggests that three exposures may achieve maximum impact in many cases. For example, three sequential exposures to advertising for a new product might elicit the following kinds of reactions:[23]

1. What is it? (the typical response of a consumer to the first perceived exposure to the advertisement)
2. What of it? (the typical response when recognition of the advertisement allows the consumer to consider the relationship of the product to himself or herself)
3. Oh, yes. . . . (the consumer has recognized and related the product to himself or herself and further exposure to the advertisement is a reminder of previously formed intentions—either to purchase or to ignore)

Heavy repetition results in **overlearning,** which refers to very long conscious memories—one can think of several advertising slogans as examples. However, heavy repetition over a short period of time can result in a "boomerang" effect because of the irritation of excessive exposure to messages.

Another perspective on the duration of advertising's effects is represented by *econometric* studies of advertising's impact on sales. While such studies simply relate amounts of advertising to sales, and do not examine intervening consumer-behavior processes, it appears that 90 percent of the cumulated effects of advertising on sales of mature, frequently purchased, low-priced products occurs within three to nine months of the advertising.[24]

Scheduling Advertising Campaigns   Other aspects of advertising planning are the scheduling of media exposures—the spacing of exposures and the degree of isolation of a brand's advertising from that of competitors.

Again, consumer-behavior processes are important to these decisions. Basic research shows that massed practice (short intervals between exposures to stimuli) is more effective than distributed practice in producing initial learning.[25] Using advertising stimuli, Strong found that greater advertising recognition occurred when consumers were exposed to weekly intervals of magazine advertising than to monthly or daily intervals.[26] Other studies of advertising scheduling have used direct-mail advertising. The results of one study, shown in Exhibit 10–8, show that repetition was very effective in increasing advertising recall, in both conditions. Shortly after the thirteenth exposure, 63 percent of the people who had been mailed ads weekly recalled some of the content, as did 48 percent of those receiving monthly ads. After the monthly ads stopped, that group exhibited decay of recall, similar to the negatively accelerating forgetting curve observed by Ebbinghaus.

Notice that the rate of forgetting decreases as the number of exposures increases. Over the entire year, the monthly schedule was superior, with an average weekly recollection of 29 percent, compared with 21 percent for the weekly schedule.

Also significant in timing repeated exposures in an advertising campaign is the *sequencing* of exposures relative to competitors' advertisements. Research shows that, in presenting stimuli designed to influence attitudes and behavior, there is an advantage to being last in a series of arguments.[27] This is called the *recency effect*. But in some cases, it may be wise for a marketer to be first—rather than most recent—with advertising. As we have seen, such ad-

sequencing

recency effect

EXHIBIT 10–8
RECALL AS A FUNCTION OF THE TIMING AND NUMBER OF EXPOSURES

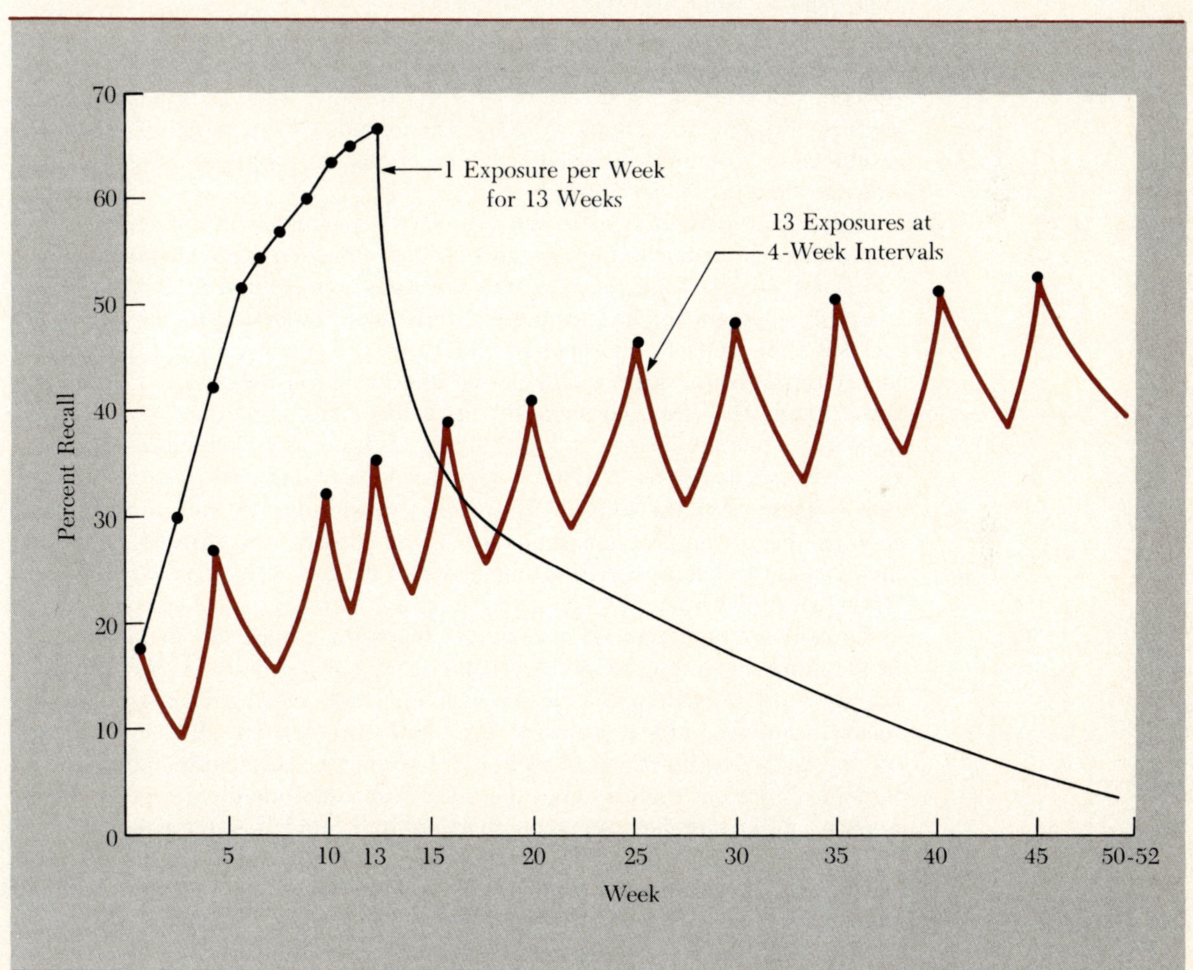

SOURCE: H. A. Zielske (1959), "The Remembering and Forgetting of Advertising," *Journal of Marketing*, 23, pp. 239–43.

vertising may "inoculate" consumers against claims made in competitors' advertising they may see later. Scheduling for recency may also be attractive if a marketer has a very strong argument or the ability to purchase a lot of exposures, or if the goal is to affect consumers' attitudes and behavior over the long term.

The problem of these **order effects** is difficult, since individual consumers are continually in the market for many goods. It is not always possible to control the order of exposure to consumers, since competitors are continually advertising as well. In any case, it is safe to conclude that advertisers should purchase media and exposure schedules that reflect positioning distinct from competitors', while still reaching the target audience.

Response Functions   Ultimately, advertisers want to influence **response functions** of consumers to advertisements, whether they seek to move consumers through an extensive "hierarchy of effects" (for high-involvement products) or to influence consumer perceptions and behavior in more subtle ways (for low-involvement products).

Response functions refer to the cumulative magnitude of impact of a communication campaign and the pattern of that impact on individual consumers. Consider, for example, the response functions represented in Exhibit 10–9. A *linear* response function for a given individual indicates that each message has the same impact—an effect we don't expect, since we probably have different responses to advertisements we've never seen before, compared with those to ads that are "old hat." On the other hand, sometimes commercials have an immediate impact, followed by rapid decay as we see more of them—the *decreasing returns* of Exhibit 10–9. The *learning curve* response function suggests that the impact of messages takes some time to develop, but then increases rapidly, and then decreases. Finally, the *threshold* (or low-involvement) response function suggests that it takes many exposures to messages before we respond.

Of course, the variations of response functions a marketer might consider in planning the timing of an advertising campaign are infinite. But timing is not the only consideration. The media in which messages appear, the intended audience, and the message appeals themselves may all have an impact on the response function. Consider, for example, an advertising campaign targeted at serious dieters about the ingredients of a brand of prepared foods. Such a highly targeted campaign suggests that highly targeted media types and vehicles should be used—for example, exercise shows on television. If the message is complex, as it might be in this case, then a large number of exposures per individual might be needed to achieve some impact. Thus, an advertiser might buy media time in order to maximize frequency of exposures to a market segment (repetition), rather than attempt to reach larger numbers of consumers with less repetition. Such scheduling reflects either the learning curve or threshold response function. That is, the media planner attempts to maximize repetition among consumers within the serious-dieter market segment.

The most appropriate response function to seek depends greatly on the degree of involvement among members of the target audience. For example, Krugman contrasts two views of communication effects on consumer cognitions—specifically, effects on attention, perception, and retention of communications.[28] Some evidence suggests what he calls a **hard in/easy out** model, in which attention requires effort, perception mediates selection for short-term or long-term memory, and rapid forgetting means advertisers must spend relatively more money to "get into perceptions or to get back in." This model is the prevalent one in advertising circles, but Krugman suggests that evidence exists for some opposing views—like the **easy in/hard out** model. In this case, there is selective perception and much input to, and easy retrieval from, memory. Later associated stimuli can trigger stimuli stored much earlier, which means that advertisers can spend fewer dollars to "get into" (memory) or "remind." The learning curve or threshold response functions reflect the hard in/easy out model, while the decreasing returns response function reflects the easy in/hard out model.

EXHIBIT 10–9
EXAMPLES OF ADVERTISING RESPONSE FUNCTIONS

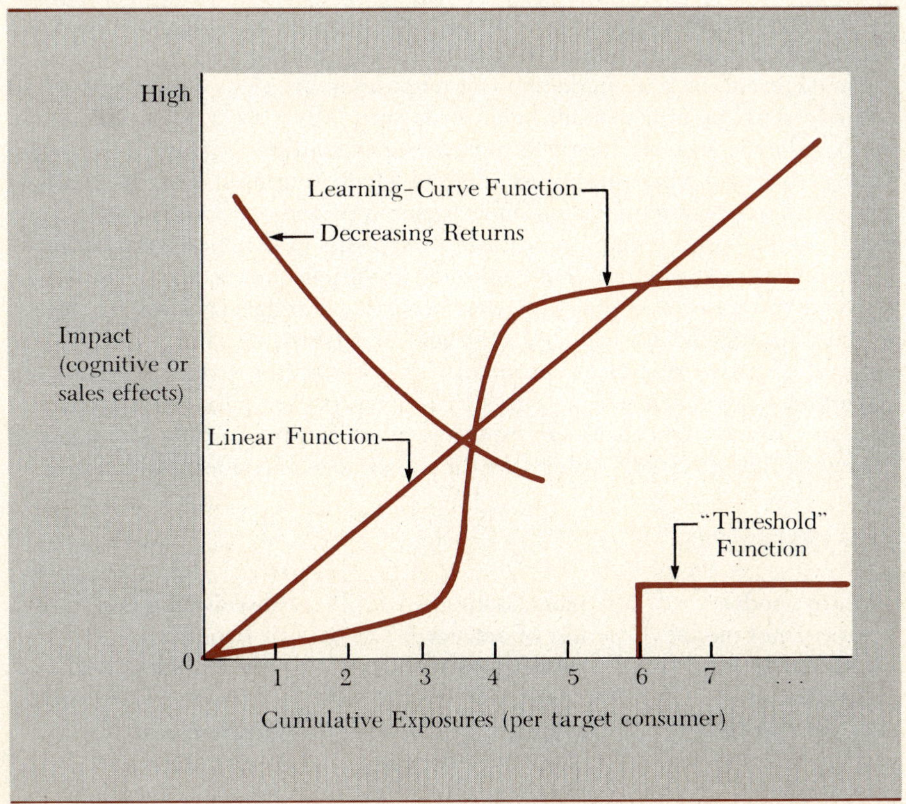

SUMMARY

We have examined the cognitive and behavioral processes involved when consumers are exposed to marketing communication, focusing on mass-media advertising. An understanding of patterns of consumer behavior is critical to making advertising decisions—like the initial decision about how much money to budget for advertising, both absolutely and relative to other elements of the *promotion mix* (the sales force and sales promotion). Sales of some products are more sensitive to advertising than sales of others. Sales are particularly sensitive when emotional buying motives are involved and when advertising can effectively be used to communicate attributes that are not obvious. In contrast, personal selling is more effective in most industrial marketing situations.

Advertising's impact on consumers is largely determined by three factors: message structure, media, and timing. *Message structure decisions* refer to types of appeals to employ, types of commercial spokespeople to use, message tone and intensity, and so forth. *Media decisions* must be made about the type of medium in which to communicate an advertiser's message (such as print or broadcast) and the particular vehicle—a television show or a publication—within each type. Advertisers must consider the degree of involvement consumers are likely to experience with different media, as well as audience coverage and economic factors. Finally, *timing decisions* must be made about such matters as advertising repetition and scheduling.

Strategic and tactical marketing-communication decisions must be based on an understanding of consumer behavior factors. Advertisers must understand not only how consumers respond to factors they control—appeals, media, and timing—but also what consumers bring to advertising messages. The earliest models of mass-communication effects portrayed audience members as relatively passive—and highly persuasible—recipients of communication stimuli. More recent models stress that consumer predispositions mediate the impact of communication, and that processes occurring during exposure are crucial in determining the ultimate effectiveness of advertising. For example, the kinds of cognitive responses consumers have when they view advertising are important determinants of its effects. These responses have been found not only to characterize consumer responses to advertising in different types of media, but also to largely determine the persistence of communication effects.

KEY CONCEPTS

one-way model	inoculation	discounting-cue
transactional model	law of extremes	hypothesis
source credibility	superiority of the	"easy in/hard out" and
promotion mix	pleasant	"hard in/easy out"
creative objectives	pulsing	overlearning
refutational appeals	carry-over/duration	order effects
comparison	effects	response functions
advertising	sleeper effect	

DISCUSSION QUESTIONS

1. Under what circumstances is mass-media advertising likely to be a particularly important element of the promotion mix? Under what circumstances is personal selling likely to be more important?
2. Describe some kinds of advertising which might be characterized by the following types of response functions: learning curve, decreasing returns, threshold, linear.
3. What is the evidence for the *easy in/hard out* model? What is the evidence for the *hard in/easy out* model?
4. Under what circumstances should an advertiser aim for *recency?* For *primacy?*
5. What is the *sleeper effect,* and what are the explanations for it? Does it apply to advertising? Why?
6. Under what circumstances should an advertiser consider comparative advertising? Refutational appeals? "Hard sell" advertising?

NOTES

1. *Advertising Age* (1982), Sept. 9, p. 2.
2. Laboratory of Advertising Performance (1981), Research Report 8013.6 (New York: McGraw-Hill).
3. For an excellent review of early models of mass communications, see Raymond A. Bauer and Alice H. Bauer (1960), "America, Mass Society, and Mass Media," *Journal of Social Issues,* 16, p. 3.
4. Raymond A. Bauer (1963), "The Initiative of the Audience," *Journal of Advertising Research,* 3, 2, pp. 2–7.
5. See Paul W. Farris (1977), "Determinants of Advertising Intensity: A Review of the Marketing Literature," Report 77–109 (Cambridge, Mass.: Marketing Science Inst.) and Paul W. Farris (1978), "Advertising Intensity in Consumer Goods Businesses: An Empirical Analysis," Report 78–118 (Cambridge, Mass.: Marketing Science Inst.).
6. David Ogilvy (1964), *Confessions of an Advertising Man* (New York: Atheneum).
7. See W. J. McGuire (1964), "Inducing Resistance to Persuasion: Some Contemporary Approaches," in *Advances in Experimental Social Psychology,* ed. L. Berkowitz, 1 (New York: Academic Press), pp. 191–229 and A. G. Sawyer (1973), "The Effects of Repetition of Refutational and Supportive Advertising Appeals," *Journal of Marketing Research,* 10, pp. 23–33.
8. A review of various regulatory postures on comparative advertising is in Stanley M. Ulanoff (1975), "Comparison Advertising: An Historical Perspective" (Cambridge, Mass.: Marketing Science Inst.).
9. William Wilkie and Paul W. Farris (1975), "Comparison Advertising: Problems and Potential," *Journal of Marketing,* 39 (Oct.), pp. 7–15.
10. V. Kanti Prasad (1976), "Communications Effectiveness of Comparative Advertising: A Laboratory Analysis," *Journal of Marketing Research,* 13 (May), pp. 128–37.
11. Linda L. Golden (1979), "Consumer Reactions to Explicit Brand Comparisons in Advertisements," *Journal of Marketing Research,* 16 (Nov.), pp. 517–32.
12. The original conceptualization is based on research in small-group behavior. See John R. P. French, Jr., and Bertram Raven (1959), *Studies in Social Power,* ed. D. Cartwright (Ann Arbor, Mich.: Inst. for Social Research).
13. A review of the congruity notion and related theories is H. Abelson, et al. (1968), *Theories of Cognitive Consistency: A Sourcebook* (Chicago: Rand McNally).
14. See Roger Brown (1962), "Models of Attitude Change," in *New Directions in Psychology,* ed. Theodore M. Newcomb (New York: Holt, Rinehart, & Winston).
15. Alvin J. Silk and Terry G. Vavra (1974), "The Influence of Advertising's Affective Qualities on Consumer Response," in *Buyer/Consumer Information Processing,* ed. G. David Hughes and Michael L. Ray (Chapel Hill, N.C.: Univ. of North Carolina Press), pp. 157–87.

16. Peter L. Wright (1974), "Analyzing Media Effects on Advertising Responses," *Public Opinion Quarterly*, 38 (Summer), pp. 192–205.

17. Herman Ebbinghaus (1885), *Über das Gedächtnis;* trans. (1964), *Memory* (New York: Dover).

18. Herbert E. Krugman (1983), "Television Program Interest and Commercial Interruption," *Journal of Advertising Research*, 23 (Feb./March), pp. 21–25.

19. W. J. McGuire (1962), "Persistence of the Resistance to Persuasion Induced by Various Types of Prior Belief Defenses," *Journal of Abnormal and Social Psychology*, 64, pp. 241–48.

20. C. I. Hovland, A. A. Lumsdaine, and F. D. Sheffield (1949), *Experiments on Mass Communication* (Princeton: Princeton Univ. Press). A later summary of the early, World War II mass-communications research is C. I. Hovland, I. L. Janis, and H. H. Kelley (1953), *Communication and Persuasion* (New Haven: Yale Univ. Press).

21. Michael L. Ray, Scott Ward, and Jerome B. Reed (1976), "Pretesting of Anti-Drug Abuse Education and Information Campaigns," in *Communication Research and Drug Education*, ed. Ronald E. Ostman (Beverly Hills, Cal.: Sage), pp. 193–221.

22. For an excellent review, see A. G. Sawyer (1974), "The Effects of Repetition: Conclusions and Suggestions About Laboratory Research," in *Buyer/Consumer Information Processing*, ed. G. D. Hughes and M. L. Ray (Chapel Hill, N.C.: Univ. of North Carolina Press), pp. 190–219.

23. Herbert E. Krugman (1972), "Why Three Exposures May Be Enough," *Journal of Advertising Research*, 12 (Dec.), pp. 11–14.

24. Darral G. Clarke (1977), "Cumulative Advertising Effects: A Synthesis," in *Cumulative Advertising Effects: Sources and Implications*, ed. D. G. Clarke, Report 77–111 (Cambridge, Mass.: Marketing Science Inst.).

25. J. W. McCrary and W. S. Hunter (1953), "Serial Position Curves in Verbal Learning," *Science*, 117, pp. 131–34.

26. Edward C. Strong (1972), "The Effects of Repetition on Advertising: A Field Study," unpublished Ph.D. diss., Stanford Univ.

27. C. A. Insko (1964), "Primacy vs. Recency in Persuasion as a Function of the Timing of Arguments and Measures," *Journal of Personality and Social Psychology*, 69, pp. 381–91.

28. Herbert E. Krugman (1975), "What Makes Advertising Effective?" *Harvard Business Review*, 53 (March/Apr.), pp. 96–103.

Burger King Versus McDonald's

An Interview with Nancy Levy, J. Walter Thompson

Q *Why did you decide on a head-on comparative strategy?*

A A combination of factors. The market itself is saturated, and it's a market in which distribution is fixed. We only have as much distribution as we have stores open. McDonald's has two to one in terms of stores and outspends Burger King by three to one in advertising dollars. Prior to this strategy, we had switched to a strategy which emphasized food quality. From this we learned that the consumers perceived that our burgers actually tasted better. The more research we did, the more confirmation we got that it was not just an opinion but a quantifiable number. The management at Burger King said, "Look, let's get aggressive with this." The strategy chosen made sense in terms of the prior one to extend the quality position and the support of it with our consumer taste tests.

Q *What risks were considered? Was one a law suit?*

A Oh, the first thing was a law suit, that goes without saying. But, it also goes without saying that if you anticipate that, you do your homework very carefully. Much research was done to substantiate.

Q *Was the challenge worth it?*

A Yes, not only in terms of greater consumer interest, but it generated 6 to 7 million dollars of free publicity via news coverage. As far as I know, it's the first time that an advertising campaign made national news. That type of publicity probably doubled the effect of the campaign at the time.

Q *After the legal proceedings, how was the settlement?*

A There was a settlement in which we had to cease comparative advertising *at that point in time*. There was no agreement not to do it in the future, hence the second wave of our campaign.

Q *Was the strategy effective in generating sales?*

A Of the three major chains, we were the only one to post real sales growth—in double digits. The industry sales are measured in "comp-sales," sales comparable to the same period last year. Frankly, it benefited all three chains because of the interest it generated. [The third chain is Wendy's.]

A No. I think it has enabled them to articulate
better what it is that makes them like Burger
King. You may know that the burgers taste
good, but you may have never really paid a lot
of attention to the fact that they broil and that
Wendy's and McDonald's fry. Suddenly you've
got a reason to believe that your initial impressions are in fact true.

A Only in the short term; long term, the campaign has done more for our sales.

A At the time, yes. Clearly, there is a risk in
how many times you can do it. Avis started
something like that years ago, and they are
firmly solidified in their position now as #2.
Burger King's goal is eventually to be #1, and
at some point you have to stop taking pot shots
at #1. People will assume that you are always
going to be an underdog and will treat you like
one.

11 Consumer Attitudes

The concept of attitude has been studied intensively by social psychologists, and has received increasing attention from marketers in recent years. The manager's interest in attitudes stems from the desire to predict and/or influence purchase behavior. If consumers are favorably oriented toward a product or service, that is, if they hold a favorable attitude, the marketer may wish to institute communications designed to confirm this favorable attitude. On the other hand, if consumers view the product unfavorably, the marketer will wish to change the unfavorable attitudes. And for new products, the goal is to create a favorable attitude. The marketer, then, may wish to influence attitudes in any of three ways: (1) by confirming existing attitudes, (2) by changing existing attitudes, or (3) by creating new attitudes.

The purpose of this chapter is to investigate the relationship between attitude theory and consumer behavior. We begin with a discussion of the various social psychological approaches to attitudes. Next, we consider the different approaches to attitude measurement. We conclude with a discussion of the marketer's use of attitude theory and measurement in the confirmation, change, and creation of attitudes toward products and services.

THE CONCEPT OF ATTITUDE[1]

learned

predisposition to respond

consistent and stable

beliefs

Perhaps the most popular definition of attitudes is that proposed by Gordon Allport: "Attitudes are learned predispositions to respond to an object or class of objects in a consistently favorable or unfavorable way."[2] This definition taps three important dimensions of attitudes. First of all, they are *learned*, not innate. They are learned through socialization and through experience. Second, attitudes represent a *predisposition to respond*. When we say that an individual has an attitude toward some object (a product), then we are making an implicit prediction about that individual's behavior (purchase). Finally, Allport's definition points to the fact that attitudes are *consistent and quite stable* over time. Thus, attempting to change attitudes can be a difficult task.

When we discuss attitudes, it is important to differentiate between attitudes and beliefs. **Beliefs** are the organized patterns of cognitions, the knowledge the individual holds to be true about some aspect of his or her world. It is what a person "knows" about some object. We hold our beliefs to be true because we "know" they are right. There need not be a close relationship, or any relationship, however, between a belief and facts. An important aspect of beliefs is that they are neutral in affect, that is, they are not accompanied by positive or negative feelings. Beliefs tend to be stable and do not change rapidly. Most readers believe the world to be nearly spherical rather than flat. It is a belief not to be changed easily or quickly. This is not to suggest that beliefs cannot be changed, for even such established scientific beliefs, such as gravitational theory, change from time to time. And it may be that some day evidence will prove the world to be a perfect cube. But for any given moment in time, a belief is the stable totality of neutral cognitions and perceptions an individual holds about a given object.

An **attitude,** however, is by definition not neutral, but rather has a strong affective component. Attitudes have an enduring, emotionally charged character about them that is reflected in such statements as "I hate it," "I love it," and "I am vehemently opposed." Attitudes often act as a triggering mechanism to behavior. Although it is quite possible to hold a belief without an accompanying attitude, an attitude naturally includes and incorporates relevant beliefs. Beliefs, then, are a component of attitudes.

hypothetical construct

When social psychologists discuss attitudes, they emphasize that *attitudes are hypothetical constructs*, that is, internal psychological orientations. An *attitude* is a hypothetical intervening variable that acts to organize environmental stimuli. A consumer perceives a stimulus (product), uses an attitude (learned predisposition) to categorize that stimulus favorably or unfavorably, and then behaves toward that stimulus (purchase or no purchase) on the basis of the evaluation. *Attitudes*, then, are orientations which exist within the consumer's mind.

THE STUDY OF ATTITUDES

As for almost every aspect of consumer behavior, a number of schools of thought exists on attitudes and attitude change.

The Structural Approach

The **structural approach**[3] to the study of attitudes, also termed the *triparite view*, believes that attitudes can be conceptualized as consisting of three separate components. First is the **cognitive component,** which refers to the beliefs an individual holds about an object. Included in the cognitive component are evaluative beliefs and knowledge that give an object a positive or negative valence, and that provide the information upon which the consumer makes judgments. Second is the **affective component,** which deals with the person's overall feelings of liking or disliking toward an object. This is the emotional, stirred-up aspect of attitude. Finally, there is the **conative component,** which refers to the tendency *to act,* the readiness of an individual to behave *overtly* toward an attitude object. For example, a consumer may be very, somewhat, or not at all likely to buy a refrigerator, take a vacation on the Galapagos Islands, or boycott certain television programs.

    cognitive component

    affective component

    conative component

Each attitude component can be described in terms of its **valence** and degree of **multiplexity.**[4] *Valence* is a measure of positiveness or negativeness, or how much an individual's beliefs, feelings, and action tendencies are for or against an object. For example, an individual may have only a slightly positive or negative affective valence for certain low-involvement products, such as paper goods or canned vegetables. On the other hand, high-involvement products, such as automobiles or clothing styles, may elicit much stronger emotional reactions—that carry strongly positive or negative valences. *Multiplexity* is a measure of the number and variety of elements forming an attitude component. Thus, the feeling component may be composed of a simple like/dislike emotion or of a complicated set of emotions such as love, passion, anger, and regret. In general, we view low-involvement, non-ego-related products as characterized by a lower degree of multiplexity than those products which function to enhance or involve the consumer's ego.

    valence

    multiplexity

The structural approach maintains that an attitude generally does not exist in isolation from other attitudes. The individual's cognitions about music, for example, may tend to relate to cognitions about entertainment or relaxation. Or a woman's cognitions about cleaning products relate to her cognitions about her role as a housewife. Thus attitudes as a whole tend to form **clusters** with other attitudes within the person's attitudinal system.

This structural or consonance theory of attitudes maintains the following.

1. The beliefs making up the cognitive component of an attitude will be fairly consistent. For example, an individual is not likely to accept the findings

of the Surgeon General's report on smoking *and* believe that cigarette smoking is harmless.[5]

2. The attitude components (cognitive, feeling, and action tendency) tend to be consonant with one another. Thus, an individual who believes in and likes new products is unlikely to be loyal to established products.
3. Attitudes within a particular cluster tend to be consonant with one another. A staunch Democrat would not have been expected to vote for Ronald Reagan in 1980.

Although the structural approach has received much attention from a theoretical point of view, there has been little empirical research on its three proposed components. As Lutz points out, most studies of attitudes fail to measure all three of the suggested components, concentrating instead on measurement of affect.[6] The measure of the affective element is then taken as a summary measure of the overall attitude.

Multiattribute Models

Somewhat similar to the structural approach is the expectancy-value approach, a multiattribute model that assumes that an attitude toward a particular object is composed of a combination of beliefs about and evaluations of various attributes of that object. Perhaps the best known expectancy-value model is that developed by Martin Fishbein, whose ideas created a flurry of research in consumer behavior. Fishbein considers only the affective nature of attitudes, claiming that an individual's attitudes toward any object can be predicted from a knowledge of his or her beliefs about what attributes an object possesses and evaluations of those attributes.

Fishbein's attitude model may be expressed algebraically as

$$A_o = \sum_{i=1}^{n} B_i a_i,$$

where

A_o = the overall attitude toward an object "o";

B_i = the belief of whether or not object "o" has some particular attribute or achieves some particular goal;

a_i = the evaluative aspect, that is, the importance, to the consumer, that "o" has the attribute or achieves the goal; and

n = the number of beliefs.[7]

For example, if we are concerned with toothpaste, we may specify, say, three attributes for consideration—decay prevention, ability to whiten teeth, and taste. B_i refers to a consumer's belief about whether or not a particular brand actually prevents decay, whitens teeth, or has a pleasant taste. B_i is typically measured using a scale that ranges from "very likely" to "very unlikely." The a_i component allows for different standards of evaluation for different consumers. One individual may choose a toothpaste solely on the basis of its ability to prevent decay, while another consumer may be interested only in taste. Thus, various consumers can differentially evaluate the importance of the specified attribute. a_i may be measured by having the consumer distribute, say, ten points among the various attributes to indicate the relative importance of each; that is, very important attributes would be assigned a large proportion of the ten points, whereas unimportant attributes would be assigned few (if any) points.

Exhibit 11–1 shows a hypothetical consumer's evaluation of three toothpaste brands. The a_i component, which remains stable across all brands, indicates that this consumer views decay prevention as the most important attribute of toothpaste (5 out of 10 points allocated to *prevents decay*) and views taste as least important (2 out of 10 points). Each of the three brands is then evaluated according to the degree of the three attributes it possesses. In this case, the consumer used a five-point Likert scale, where the score 5 indicates that the brand is very likely to achieve attribute i, and *1* indicates very unlikely. In this example, Brand 1, which receives the most favorable overall evaluation ($\Sigma B_i a_i = 34$), is the most preferred brand.

After stating his model in its original form, Fishbein realized that the model was limited in two major ways.[8] The **extended Fishbein model** was then postulated to remedy these limitations. First, Fishbein stated that the attitude a consumer has toward a product (A_o) does not necessarily *predict* that consumer's behavior. Fishbein postulated that the **attitude toward the act** (that is, toward engaging in a certain type of behavior—in this case, brushing teeth) was more important than the attitude toward the object involved in the act (the toothpaste itself). Thus, Fishbein's extended model incorporates

extended Fishbein model

attitude toward the act

EXHIBIT 11–1
A CONSUMER'S MULTIATTRIBUTE EVALUATION OF TOOTHPASTES

Attribute	Brand 1			Brand 2			Brand 3		
	a	·	B_1	a	·	B_2	a	·	B_3
prevents decay	5	·	4 = 20	5	·	3 = 15	5	·	2 = 10
whitens teeth	3	·	2 = 6	3	·	2 = 6	3	·	2 = 6
pleasant taste	2	·	4 = 8	2	·	4 = 8	2	·	5 = 10
$\Sigma B_i a_i$			34			29			26

where Beliefs (B_i) are measured as

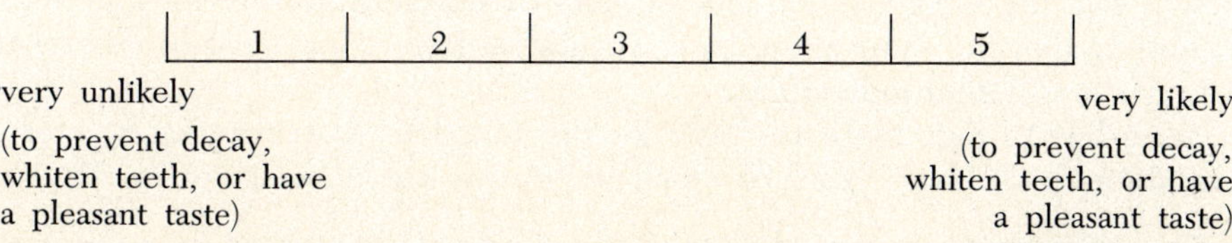

| 1 | 2 | 3 | 4 | 5 |

very unlikely   very likely

(to prevent decay,   (to prevent decay,
whiten teeth, or have   whiten teeth, or have
a pleasant taste)   a pleasant taste)

the attitude toward the act (A_{act}) rather than A_o. Second, Fishbein also took note of the vital importance of reference groups and group norms to an individual's behavior.[9] Since individuals are generally under pressure to comply with group norms, this normative component is also incorporated into the extended model. To return to our example of toothpaste, consider that much toothpaste advertising equates group acceptance and popularity with the use of a specific brand.

The extended Fishbein model is formally stated as

$$OB \approx IB \approx (A_{act})w_0 + (NB)(MC)w_1,$$

where

$$
\begin{aligned}
OB &= \text{overt behavior;} \\
IB &= \text{intended behavior;} \\
A_{act} &= \text{the attitude toward taking a certain action,} \\
&\quad \text{given a certain situation;} \\
NB &= \text{normative beliefs, i.e., the norms which operate} \\
&\quad \text{for the situation;} \\
MC &= \text{the consumer's motivation to comply with the} \\
&\quad \text{situational norms; and} \\
w_0 \text{ and } w_1 &= \text{statistically determined regression weights.}
\end{aligned}
$$

Note that the extended Fishbein model measures behavioral intentions rather than actual behavior. This is extremely important in the discussion of the empirical validity of the model. Validation of the model entails comparing model predictions against a different, independently obtained, prediction of behavioral intention. In fact, a number of researchers have provided reasonable empirical support for the extended Fishbein model.[10] However, research has suggested that the normative control component is less influential in determining behaviors than is the attitudinal component of the model.[11] Nonetheless, results are promising, and this form of the model continues to provide a framework for future research.

The Functional Approach

Functional theorists look upon attitudes in the same manner as they look upon perception, thinking, reasoning, and other aspects of our cognitive organization.[12] They want to know what functions an attitude serves for the individual. If it serves no function at all, it ceases to exist. The crux of this view is that the same attitude may be held by different persons for different reasons or that the same stimuli and situational factors may lead to different attitudes in different individuals.

According to Katz there are basically four functions that attitudes can perform for an individual,[13] each of which advertisers are known to utilize.[14]

1. **The utilitarian function** of an attitude can be instrumental in achieving desirable goals and in avoiding undesirable alternatives. Thus, utilitarian

attitudes act to attain those objects which provide a reward and to avoid those objects which provide punishment. For example, consumers may hold a utilitarian attitude when they purchase automobiles, being attracted to and considering only those brands which have especially strong mechanical reputations. A recent advertising campaign for Polaroid cameras and film uses the bold headline, "**GET THE 10 GOOD SHOTS YOU PAID FOR,**" stressing that Polaroid provides a foolproof system for taking good photographs every time, thereby appealing to the utilitarian function of attitudes.

2. The **value-expressive** function of an attitude gives *positive* expression to the individual's central values and self-concept. Value-expressive attitudes en-

able individuals to enhance their images. For instance, the lifestyle advertising campaigns used by both Pepsi-Cola and Coca-Cola stress the belongingness and positive attributes of product users. Revlon's campaign for Charlie perfume depicts a confident and stylish young woman, who serves as a positive image with whom potential Charlie buyers can identify. Exhibit 11–2 shows one of the series of advertisements for *Fortune* magazine, in which reading *Fortune* is depicted as a means of attaining success. Each of these campaigns attempts to capitalize on the value-expressive function of attitudes by suggesting that use of the product will enhance or bolster a consumer's self-image.

3. The **ego-defensive function** helps the individual deal with inner conflicts. Such attitudes build up defense mechanisms, rationalize problems, and generally help to protect the self from what is perceived to be a hostile environment. As opposed to value-expressive attitudes, which act to enhance a positive self-image, these are attitudes that protect the individual from negative consequences. An ego-defensive attitude may operate when an individual is exposed to fear campaigns, in which marketers attempt to promote a product as the solution to a personal problem. Advertising for mouth washes, dandruff shampoos, and deodorants often is aimed at the ego-defensive attitudes.

4. The **knowledge function** of attitudes helps an individual to cope with a complex world, and to give order and meaning to the environment. Attitudes serving a knowledge function have become increasingly important in today's world, characterized by the increasing speed and complexity of technological developments. With the introduction of its personal computer, IBM wanted to develop an advertising campaign that would convey the message that the computer was useful, nonthreatening, and enjoyable for the average person. The result, as shown in Exhibit 11–3, was to use a Charlie Chaplin tramp as the spokesperson. Presumably, if Charlie Chaplin can use the product, so can the average consumer. Another IBM print campaign also eschews the Einstein image, depicting a teenager asking his father, "Dad, can I borrow the IBM personal computer tonight?" This appeal, using the knowledge function, tries to impose order and understanding on a complex innovation.

Like the structural approach to attitudes, the functional approach has not been widely subjected to empirical research. There is no proof that the four suggested attitudinal functions are the only ones, or even that they are the most commonly evidenced ones.

Cognitive Consistency Theory

A different approach to the study of attitudes is represented by **cognitive consistency theory.** In fact, consistency theory is a label given to a group of theories including Heider's *balance theory*[15] and Osgood and Tannenbaum's *con-*

EXHIBIT 11–3
ADVERTISEMENTS CAPITALIZING ON THE KNOWLEDGE FUNCTION OF ATTITUDES

gruity theory.[16] Festinger's cognitive dissonance theory[17] is sometimes grouped with the consistency theories. We will, however, treat it separately for reasons to be discussed below. In this section we concentrate on Heider's balance theory, since it embodies the major concepts of each of the consistency theories.

Balance Theory   The basic premise of **balance theory** is that an individual seeks to have a balanced relationship between the affective (emotional) and cognitive (knowledge) elements of an attitude. A balanced relationship between these elements produces a stable attitude. But an unbalanced state leads to psychological tension or disequilibrium, unstable attitudes, and ultimately to attitude change.

There are three elements in Heider's balance theory: (1) an individual person in the role of "perceiver" P, (2) another person O, and (3) some attitude object X. The attitude object may be another person, a product, a political party, or anything else about which an attitude can be formed and held. Additionally, Heider proposes that relationships are either positive ($+$) or negative($-$). Depending upon the structure of the positive or negative relationships among P, O, and X, the resulting cognitive structure is either *balanced* or *unbalanced.*

Exhibit 11–4 depicts the eight possible relationships for P, O, and X. A balanced state exists when P likes O, and when both P and O share a common positive *(a)* or negative *(b)* evaluation of X. Balance also exists when P dislikes O, and when P and O have differing evaluations of X *(c and d).*

The structures of unbalanced states are also shown in Exhibit 11–4. In *e,* for instance, although P likes O, their evaluations of X differ, giving rise to tension in the relationship between P and O. Heider maintains that individuals in an unbalanced state strive to regain balance, and that this is affected by changing the direction of *one* of the relationships. For example, in *e* P could come either to dislike O or to like X. This attitude change, then, is motivated by the original unbalanced state.

Balance theory has applications for consumer purchase situations.[18] A manager might, for instance, attempt to create an unbalanced state, and suggest that some action or purchase would remedy this state. The Prune Advisory Board's advertising campaign, which features adorable children munching prunes, can be interpreted as an attempt to create the structural relationship shown in *e,* in which P (consumer) likes O (child), O (child) likes X (prunes), but P does not currently purchase prunes. Balance can be restored to this relationship if the consumer purchases prunes, yielding structure *a.*

A number of problems are inherent in balance theory. First, the degree of affect (liking or disliking) is not permitted to vary. If attitude object X or person O is only mildly disliked, then it seems less than logical to suggest that great attitudinal transformations will be induced. Another problem is that Heider's formulation of balance theory incorporates only one attitude object X and one other person O. Yet most relationships exist in clusters, including a multiplicity of objects and actors. But like the functional approach, balance theory does provide a basic orientation that the marketer can use to categorize consumer attitudes.

Congruity Theory **Congruity theory,** proposed by Osgood and Tannenbaum,[19] builds on balance theory. Congruity theory adapts balance theory to take on a specific mass-communications perspective, with the other person O becoming the source of a communicated message. Thus, positive or negative relationships exist among the perceiver, message source, and attitude object.

Congruity theory also overcomes one of the problems of balance theory, in that the degree of affect (positive or negative feeling) is allowed to vary from strong to weak. Also, very strongly held attitudes, positive or negative, are presumed to be less readily altered or shifted than weakly held attitudes.

Cognitive Dissonance Theory

Cognitive consistency theory is based on the premise that people strive for consistency. But inconsistencies in behavior do exist. A person who knows that smoking cigarettes is clearly and unequivocally a health hazard may con-

EXHIBIT 11–4
RELATIONSHIPS ACCORDING TO BALANCE THEORY

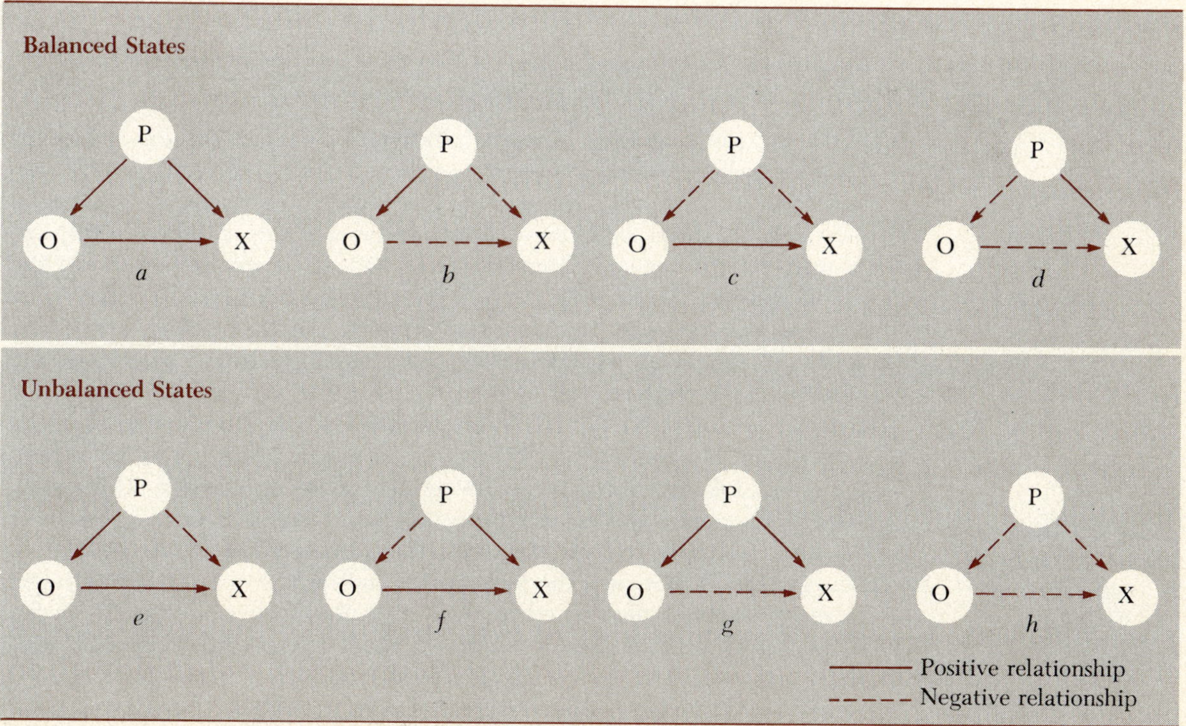

tinue to smoke them. When inconsistencies are discovered, they are of interest primarily because of their dramatic contrast with consistency. We pay little attention to the World War II refugee who refuses to buy a Volkswagen because it is a German product. The person of interest is the one who purchases a VW in spite of negative attitudes toward Germany.

Such inconsistencies in cognitive systems are termed *cognitive dissonance*. Dissonance theory was developed by Leon Festinger, who proposed that dissonance exists when cognitions or beliefs held by an individual logically contradict one another.[20] Festinger maintained that dissonance creates a state of psychological tension, which motivates the individual to attempt to reduce that tension and return to a state of psychological equilibrium or balance.

Dissonance theory may sound very similar to cognitive consistency theory. In fact, dissonance theory is sometimes treated as a special case of consistency theory. But we have chosen to present it separately because of its special applicability to consumer behavior. A major difference between dissonance and consistency theories is that dissonance theory places great emphasis on *post-decisional dynamics*. Given commitment to a decision, a person experiences dissonance because he or she will then probably recall the positive attributes of the rejected alternatives (products), and ask the question, "Did I make the right choice?" Dissonance is aroused. The consumer wonders if the chosen alternative is indeed the best alternative. This state, maintains Festinger, is one of *disequilibrium*. The consumer will be motivated to regain a state of psychological balance.

Dissonance-Reduction Strategies   Although there are many **dissonance-reduction** strategies, a few can be readily categorized.

- *Changing the Cognitive Elements.* Individuals can reduce dissonance by eliminating or revaluing either one of their cognitive elements or their responsibility or control over the act or decision. To reduce dissonance, a man who has purchased a new car can sell it, but this is quite unlikely. So instead, he can persuade himself that he had no choice: he had to buy the car he did because his wife insisted on it. Or he can begin to believe that the product he owns is a superior product, clearly better than others. Brehm designed an experiment to test this alternative.[21] Subjects were asked to rate products, all of them small electrical appliances, from extremely desirable to definitely undesirable. Each subject was then informed that he or she would be given a gift for participating in the experiment and was offered a choice between two of the items rated. The chosen item was wrapped and handed to the subject. Next each subject was given research reports to read on the products, and then asked to rate each product once again. Between the first and second ratings, the selected product increased and the unselected product decreased in desirability. Similarly, a study by Knox and Inkster compared the levels of confidence that racetrack bettors had in their selections before and after they actually placed their bets.[22] Confidence levels after placing bets (making an actual com-

post-decisional
dynamics

mitment) were significantly higher than before. Similarly, Ginter found that consumers had more positive attitudes toward brands after actually selecting them.[23] It would seem that "asking the man who owns one" is not really a good way of gathering unbiased information about a product.

- *Denying Information.* Information can be denied, distorted, or forgotten in the efforts to reduce dissonance. Kassarjian and Cohen asked a sample of subjects whether or not they felt the linkage between cigarette smoking and lung cancer and various other medical problems had been proven.[24] Forty-one percent of the heavy smokers, twenty-one percent of light smokers, and eleven percent of nonsmokers felt the linkage had not been proven.

- *Minimizing the Issue.* Dissonance can be effectively reduced by minimizing the importance of the issue or decision that led to the dissonant state. Although a buyer may have spent several hours deciding among several brands of a product, he later claims that he merely grabbed the first one on the shelf. Dissonance is reduced by the claimed lack of interest in an "unimportant" issue.

- *Adding New Elements.* New cognitive elements can be added to support the decision. Once a new car is purchased, the buyer begins to read technical information, brochures, and ads to buttress the decision. The buyer may begin to believe that a person of his or her station in life deserves such a car. Smokers often assert that many doctors smoke and that some scientists claim that smoking is not detrimental to health.

Festinger has noted a number of conditions which give rise to post-purchase dissonance. Importantly, during the evaluation stage of product decision-making, a consumer may assess various product alternatives on the basis of attributes not associated with the stimuli themselves. For example, a product which is accompanied by a severe threat (perhaps a very high price or great deal of social risk) is often perceived as being more desirable than a nearly identical product accompanied by only a mild threat (more moderate price and so forth).

Thus, by the time a consumer has evaluated, chosen, and purchased a product, the purchase decision-making process has been colored by numerous external and psychological factors. And when the consumer begins using the product on a regular basis, he or she may find that the chosen alternative does not live up to all expectations. At this point, the various dissonance-reduction strategies are invoked.

Consumer Dissonance   Holloway has proposed a typology of factors that lead to dissonance arousal in consumer decision-making situations.[25] Exhibit 11–5 provides a brief description of each of these factors. The Holloway typology was developed specifically to apply to consumer behavior, whereas Festinger's original approach was intended to apply to decision-making in general.

One factor suggested by Holloway—importance of cognitions involved—relates to the concept of product involvement, which has become increasingly

EXHIBIT 11–5
DISSONANCE AND BUYING SITUATIONS

Factors Affecting Dissonance	Buying Situation	Conditions with High Dissonance Expectation	Conditions with Low Dissonance Expectation
1. Attractiveness of rejected alternative	A high-school graduate decides which of several pictures to order	Three of the proofs have both attractive and desirable features.	One of the proofs clearly is superior to the rest.
2. Negative factors in chosen alternative	A man chooses between two suits of clothing	The chosen suit has the color the man wanted but not the style.	The chosen suit has both the color and style the man wanted.
3. Number of alternatives	A teacher shops for a tape-recorder.	There are eight recorders from which to choose.	There are only two recorders from which to choose.
4. Cognitive overlap	A housewife shops for a vacuum sweeper.	A salesman offers two similarly priced tank types.	A salesman offers a tank type and an upright cleaner.
5. Importance of cognitions involved	A child buys a present for her sister.	The sister has definite preferences for certain kinds of music.	The sister has no strong tastes for certain records.
6. Positive inducement	Parents decide to buy a photo-enlarger for their son.	The son already has hobby equipment and does not need the enlarger.	The son never has had a true hobby and needs something to keep him occupied.
7. Discrepant or negative action	A man purchases an expensive watch.	The man had never before paid more than $35 for a watch.	Fairly expensive watches had been important gift items in the man's family.
8. Information available	Housewife buys a detergent.	The housewife has no experience with the brand purchased—it is a new variety.	The housewife has read and heard a good deal about the product, and has confidence in the manufacturer.
9. Anticipated dissonance	A small boy buys a model airplane.	The boy anticipates trouble at home because of the cost of the model.	The boy expects no trouble at home relative to the purchase.
10. Familiarity and knowledge	A family buys a floor polisher.	The item was purchased without much thought.	The item was purchased after a careful selection process.

SOURCE: Robert J. Holloway (1967), "An Experiment on Consumer Dissonance," *Journal of Marketing*, 31 (Jan.), p. 40.

important to researchers studying dissonance. In fact, recent studies have explicitly related dissonance to involvement. Crosby and Taylor point out that commitment/involvement is a precondition for dissonance arousal.[26] And in a study which varies the level of product involvement, Korgaonkar and Moschis conclude that cognitive dissonance plays a significantly more important role in the post-purchase evaluation process for high-involvement products than for low-involvement products.[27]

The applicability of dissonance theory to consumer behavior has sometimes been challenged. But a thorough review of the marketing literature concludes that "the evidence in favor of the applicability of dissonance theory is more voluminous and somewhat more substantial than the evidence against."[28]

In summary, attitudes, values, and cognitions tend to be consistent with each other and with behavior. Inconsistencies which do exist are uncomfortable states which individuals attempt to change either by adding new cognitions, changing their behavior, distorting dissonant information, or changing their attitudes and beliefs.

ATTITUDES AND BEHAVIOR

So far our discussion has made the tacit assumption that there is a relationship between attitudes and behavior. Fishbein's extended model, for example, postulates that overt behavior is approximately equal to intended behavior (that is, stated attitude).

However, many early studies did not find strong correlations between attitude and behavior. In fact, one review article concluded that, in general, "attitudes will be unrelated or only slightly related to overt behavior."[29] But other evidence contradicted this conclusion. As shown in Exhibit 11–6, Achenbaum found a direct relationship between the following attitudes and product usage:

1. The more favorable the attitude, the higher the incidence of product usage.
2. The less favorable the attitude, the lower the incidence of usage.
3. The more unfavorable people's attitudes are toward a product, the more likely they are to stop using it.
4. The attitudes of people who have never tried a product tend to be distributed around the mean in the shape of a normal distribution.[30]

In a continuing effort to resolve these apparent contradictions, current-day thinking has shifted its emphasis. In a comprehensive review of the topic, Cialdini, Petty, and Cacioppo point out that "no longer are researchers questioning *if* attitudes predict behaviors, they are investigating *when* attitudes predict behaviors."[31] They suggest that the attitude-behavior relationship is tempered by a number of factors, some of which we discuss below.

EXHIBIT 11–6
RELATIONSHIP BETWEEN ATTITUDES AND USAGE FOR SELECTED CATEGORIES OF CONSUMER PRODUCTS

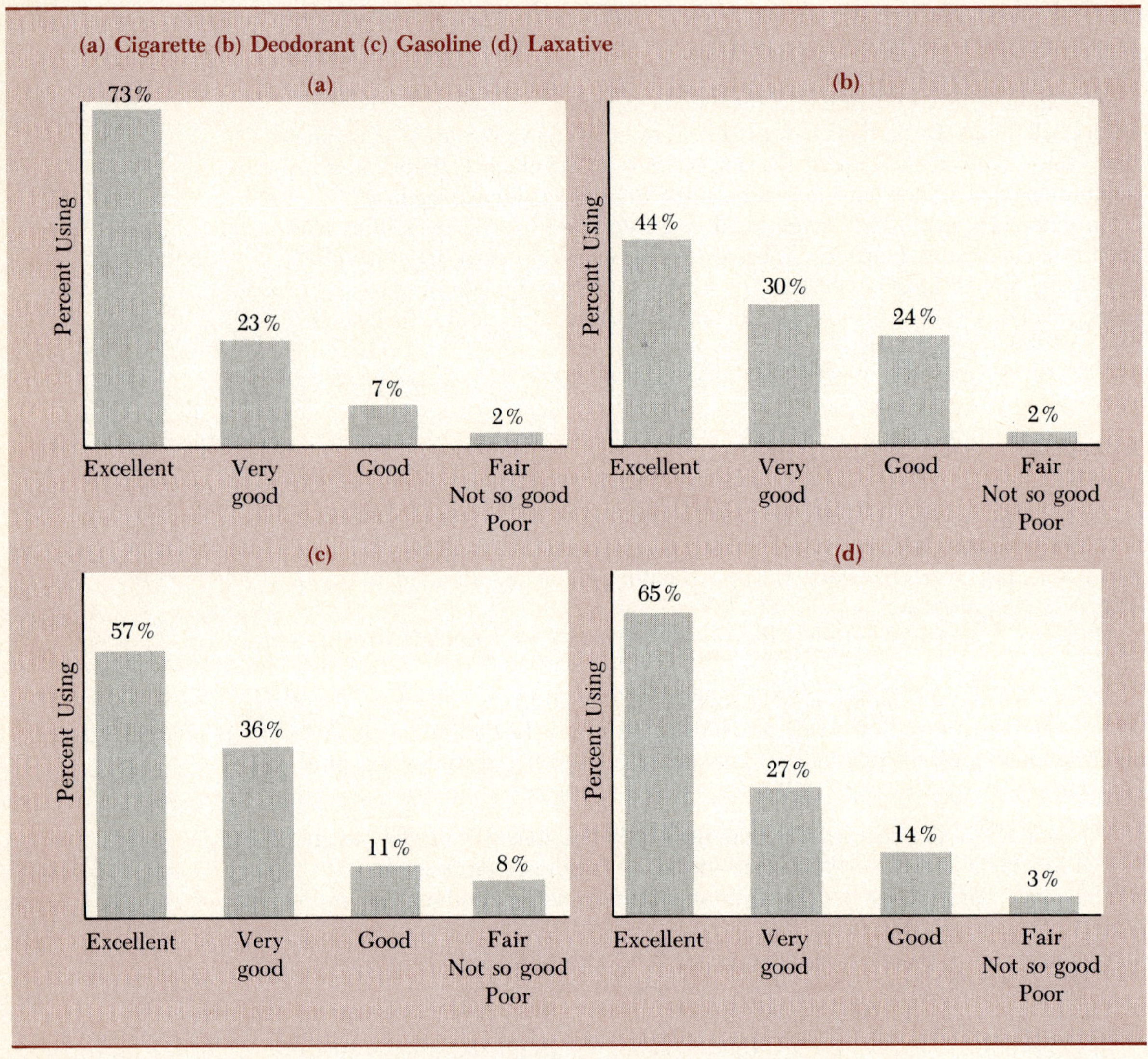

SOURCE: Alvin A. Achenbaum (1966), "Knowledge Is a Thing Called Measurement," in *Attitude Research at Sea,* ed. Lee Adler and Irving Crespi (New York: American Marketing Assn.), p. 113.

Measurement Issues

Measures of attitudes can be used to predict behavior only when the attitudinal and behavioral *measures* are closely interrelated.[32] Measuring a very general negative attitude toward, say, convenience foods will not predict whether or not a specific consumer will occasionally serve frozen TV dinners after a long day at work. However, the more specific the correspondence between the measure of attitude and the measure of behavior, the higher the correlation between the two.[33]

Normative Influences

As we noted in our discussion of the extended Fishbein model, an individual's degree of motivation to comply with norms can be an important factor influencing the relationship between attitudes and behavior. But as Cialdini et al. state, researchers have not yet agreed on the manner in which motivation to comply should be measured.[34] Differences in approaches to measurement can lead to contradictory research findings.

Effects of Habit

Future behavior may be conditioned by habit or past behaviors. For example, if a consumer has a long history of loyalty to a particular brand, then it may be easier to continue using that brand (thereby forgoing the necessity of engaging in search and evaluation), despite a stated willingness to try a new alternative.

Direct Experience with the Attitude Object

Attitudes that are formed after individuals have actual experience with the attitude object (product or brand) are more closely correlated with behavior than attitudes formed in the absence of such experience (on the basis of only advertising, for instance).[35] This finding supports the consumer-behavior contention that buyers' attitudes solidify after trial.

Situational Factors

Situational factors—that is, the environmental characteristics affecting a consumer at a particular time—can influence attitudinal-behavioral consistency.[36] Belk has suggested that physical surroundings (for example, the store in which a purchase occurs), social surroundings (presence of other people), temporal factors (time of day, time since last purchase), task definition (the way in which a buyer personally defines the purchase task), and antecedent states (temporary states such as mood) can all have an impact on the act of purchase.[37] Measured attitudes do not account for such situational factors, thereby introducing a possible source of attitudinal-behavioral inconsistency.

Level of Involvement

The correlation between attitudes and behavior can differ between high- and low-involvement products (see Chapter 6). For example, Calder found that for low-involvement goods, behavior change preceded attitude change.[38] In another study, Day and Deutscher found that attitudes formed in low-involvement situations were very susceptible to change prior to an actual purchase decision.[39] Both of these studies illustrate the point that attitude measurements obtained prior to measurements of overt behavior may fail to correlate.

In summary, the relationship between measured attitudes and overt behavior is complex and subject to the influence of a wide variety of factors. Understanding these factors helps provide the student with a more comprehensive grasp of consumers, their attitudes, and their behavior.

MARKETING APPLICATIONS OF ATTITUDE THEORY

With respect to attitudes the marketer's task is one or more of the following: (1) maintaining existing attitudes toward a given product, brand, service, corporation; (2) changing consumer attitudes toward a product, brand, and so on; and (3) creating attitudes toward a novel product, brand, or service.

Maintaining Attitudes

Maintaining existing attitudes is perhaps the least difficult task for the marketer of consumer products. Even though a favorable attitude may be established with consumers, a manager must reinforce the acceptance of various beliefs about a product. If such reinforcement is not provided, then beliefs about products are subject to the effect of extinction (see Chapter 9 on learning theory).

Numerous products have used the same promotional appeal, stressing one product attribute, over a long period of time, in an attempt to maintain consumer attitudes. For nearly thirty years, Marlboro cigarettes has used the Marlboro Man/Marlboro Country approach. This successful "masculine" image was developed in 1954 by the Leo Burnett Advertising Agency. Interestingly, prior to this campaign, Marlboro had been perceived as a woman's cigarette, but had never achieved a substantial share of the market. The successful repositioning has been reinforced over time.

Another product that has used a long-term advertising campaign is Pepsi-Cola, with its "Pepsi Generation" theme and its variations. This advertising, which was first broadcast in the mid-1960s, consistently emphasizes how Pepsi-Cola is part of today's lifestyles. This strategy has been very successful for Pepsi-Cola, and prolonged use of the campaign has reinforced an existing attitude among a large segment of consumers.

Changing Attitudes

Change in attitudes toward existing products can be induced in two major ways: (1) through product repositioning and (2) through the influence of changes in broad societal values.

Product Repositioning Strategies   Consumer perception was discussed in Chapter 8, where we pointed out that the goal of some marketing strategies may be to *shift* a product's positioning. Shifts in positioning may be undertaken by any number of means, including stressing a previously unadvertised benefit of a product, appealing to an untapped market segment that seeks a particular product attribute, or attempting to attack competitive brands in a more novel or aggressive manner. Each of these means shares a fundamental similarity with the others—namely, that the marketer is trying to modify existing attitudes toward an established brand.

If we think of a consumer's existing attitude toward a brand in the terms proposed by the Fishbein model, then that attitude consists of beliefs about a number of attributes, each of which is characterized by a specific weight. Products can be repositioned by adding a new attribute to the consumer's perceived set of attributes, eliminating an attribute commonly associated with the product, or substituting a new for an old attribute.

An example of a product which succeeded in adding a new attribute is Crest toothpaste, which in 1960 was the first toothpaste to be endorsed by the American Dental Association.[40] Crest continued to present itself as an effective dental aid, but added the ADA endorsement.

The second approach to product repositioning through attitude change involves eliminating a product attribute. For instance, a commonly held belief about prepackaged cookies is that they appeal primarily to children, who do not discern quality in sweets as readily as adults. But Peek Frean's cookies are advertised as "serious cookies" that are much too good to "waste on children." Or, to take another example, after the social concern of the late 1970s, many marketers of aerosol sprays stressed that their brands did not contain the fluorocarbons which were environmentally detrimental.

The third approach to product repositioning substitutes a new for an existing attribute. This type of attitude change is the most difficult to achieve of those we have discussed, because consumers must first "unlearn" one belief and then learn a contradictory belief. Stouffer Corporation has undertaken this approach with regard to its hotels, which were originally positioned as "suburban motels." The image change is to one of hotels with an upwardly mobile business clientele, with an emphasis on luxuriousness of decor.[41]

Changes in Broad Societal Values   Changes in consumer attitudes can also be induced by changes in the corresponding broad social values. Changes in the value orientation of society can precipitate shifts in consumer attitudes, needs, and behavior (see Chapter 14). The increased participation of women in the workforce, for example, and the changing roles of men and women have had especially strong impact on consumer behavior.

Other shifts in values that have had impact on consumer attitudes and behavior include an increased awareness of and concern with health, based at least in part on advances in medical research. For example, caffeine has come to be regarded as a potentially harmful substance. In response, the Seven-Up Company introduced the caffeine-free cola-drink Like in 1982, using the theme, "You don't need caffeine, and neither does your Cola." Like's thirty-second television ads showed children engaged in sports or playing the piano, and stressed to parents that children, especially, don't need caffeine. Noting the trend, Pepsi-Cola and Coca-Cola have introduced their own caffeine-free entries.

There are numerous other examples. The growing concern with weight and physical fitness has led to both the growing incidence of "how to diet" books on the best-seller lists and the emergence of exercise and weight control centers, clubs, and classes.

Creating New Attitudes

Creating new attitudes is relevant primarily for the marketing of new products, brands, or services. There are two circumstances under which marketers may wish to create new attitudes: (1) the introduction of new products and (2) the extension of product lines.

New Product Introductions   Innovations are classified as continuous, dynamically continuous, or discontinuous. The more discontinuous the innovation, the more radical the required alteration in behavior. For discontinuous innovations, then, the marketer is faced with more than the task of creating new, favorable attitudes toward a product; the challenge is to create new, favorable attitudes toward the innovative *behavior* itself.

An example from the realm of consumer goods, introduced in Chapter 5, is Nescafé Instant Coffee, which was first marketed in the late 1940s. Recall that the use of a projective research technique revealed that housewives reacted negatively to the concept of instant coffee.[42] Traditionally, the preparation of ground coffee, with the resulting sounds and pleasant aroma, constituted a domestic ritual. Nescafé was faced not simply with the task of creating a favorable attitude toward its new product; it also had to change the attitude that the *act* of making percolated coffee was tantamount to being a "good wife."

Product-Line Extensions   In 1982, Colgate-Palmolive launched an $40+ million annual advertising campaign for its new gel toothpaste, Colgate Winterfresh. Not to be left behind, competitor Procter & Gamble has budgeted close to $40 million to herald the arrival of Crest Gel.[43] Interestingly, both companies chose to use their existing brand names, rather than to launch an entirely new toothpaste.

New-product introductions tend to be substantially riskier, and more costly, than product-line extensions. With a product-line extension, leading marketers can capitalize not only upon existing favorable consumer attitudes, but also upon favorable retailer relationships in getting increased shelf space.

ATTITUDE MEASUREMENT

Because of the importance and centrality of attitudes in consumer-behavior research, it is important to consider some of the techniques that have been used to measure attitudes. A basic problem is that since they are hypothetical constructs, attitudes cannot be measured directly, as can body temperature or blood pressure. Attitudes are intricately interwoven with affective feelings, motivations, and personality characteristics, as well as with experiences that often cannot be verbally expressed. Additionally, some attitudes are held on an unconscious level. Therefore, attitudes are typically *inferred* from opinions and responses expressed by individuals when they are exposed to the stimuli of measuring instruments.

Most commonly, researchers try to tap attitudes through the use of attitude and opinion *scales*. Although they differ in type and method of construction, the various scales have similar objectives—to assign the respondent's attitude a numerical score along a continuum or scale from *highly favorable* at one end to *highly unfavorable* at the other.

attitude scales

Three major types of scales are used in consumer research: simple dichotomous scales, Likert scales, and the semantic differential. The simpler types of scales ask **dichotomous questions** such as: "In your opinion, are Sony radios well constructed or poorly constructed?" Perhaps a dozen such questions are asked, the responses are totaled, and each individual is assigned a score from which can be inferred each consumer's attitude toward Sony radios. Two problems are associated with totaling up the responses to several items in this manner. First, there is the issue of whether the responses are of equal weights. If one of the items (that is, questions) is more important to the structure of the overall attitude, then treating all items equally risks incorrect conclusions. Second is the question of whether or not the scale is unidimensional. That is, is each scale item tapping the same attitudinal dimension? If more than one dimension underlies the attitude, then adding all items is comparable to adding apples and oranges.

dichotomous questions

A slightly more complex type of scale, that attempts to measure the intensity of opinion as well as favor or disfavor, was originally developed by Rensis Likert and is today called a **Likert scale.**[44] The subject is asked to indicate his or her response on a scale with five or seven or more equal-appearing intervals, such as *strongly agree, agree, neutral, disagree*, and *strongly disagree*.

Likert scales

Likert scales are commonly used in marketing research. Exhibit 11–7 shows two examples from empirical studies utilizing Likert scales. In the first, a study examining the behavior attitudes of adult buyers of toys, a four-point Likert (that is, giving four possible intensities of response) scale is used. The

EXHIBIT 11–7
EXAMPLES OF LIKERT-SCALE ITEMS FROM TWO EMPIRICAL STUDIES

The Adult Toy Buyer:
An Exploration of How Parents and Nonparents Buy Toys
Responses based on a four-point scale: Very True, Somewhat True, Somewhat False, Very False.

	Very True	Somewhat True	Somewhat False	Very False
Good toys are very important in molding a child.	______	______	______	______
People spend too much money on toys.	______	______	______	______
Toys are poorly made and don't last.	______	______	______	______
Toys keep children occupied and quiet.	______	______	______	______
When buying toys, I think about those I would have liked when I was a child.	______	______	______	______
In shopping for toys, I often play with them myself before I buy.	______	______	______	______
I get confused when choosing from the great variety of toys.	______	______	______	______

Ocean Spray Cranberries, Inc.:
"Description of Personalities and Lifestyles Data"
Responses based on a five-point scale: ranging from "Describes Me Completely" to "Describes Me Not at All."

	Describes Me Completely				Describes me Not at All
I like to have friends over for dinner.	├	┼	┼	┼	┼ ┤
I prefer fresh vegetables to canned or frozen products.	├	┼	┼	┼	┼ ┤
I watch my calories carefully.	├	┼	┼	┼	┼ ┤
I like to rough it and live simply.	├	┼	┼	┼	┼ ┤
I'm not a good cook.	├	┼	┼	┼	┼ ┤

SOURCES: Data from "The Adult Toy Buyer" by Bureau of Advertising, A.N.P.A. (1967). Reprinted by permission of Newspaper Advertising Bureau, Inc. Cited in F. S. DeBruicker and S. Ward (1980), *Cases in Consumer Behavior* (Englewood Cliffs, N.J.: Prentice-Hall), p. 53. Data collection for "Ocean Spray" sponsored by Ocean Spray Cranberries, Inc. As reproduced in DeBruicker and Ward (1980), p. 158.

second, the Ocean Spray study, attempted to generate a lifestyle portrait of cranberry-sauce users, using a five-point Likert scale.

The five-point Likert scale illustrates an additional problem associated with many scales—the *neutral-point* or *no-opinion* category. In most scales, it is not clear what "no opinion" means. To some individuals it apparently implies that he or she has considered the issue (for example, the construction of radios or the applicability of a statement to his or her lifestyle), weighed the alternatives, and still has not formed an opinion. To others, it means, "Go away, I don't want to think about it." To still others, it means a nonopinion or nonattitude. The individual has not heard of the brand and does not particularly care what it is. Nonetheless, a response is still given.

In recent years another technique that has become quite popular, almost to the point of a fad, is the **semantic differential,** developed by Osgood, Suci, and Tannenbaum.[45] Pairs of words or statements of opposite meaning which might describe a concept, product, or corporation (such as *good-bad, reliable-unreliable, clean-dirty, strong-weak, active-passive*) are presented to the respondent. He or she is asked to rate each concept on each dimension on a seven-point scale reflecting intensity of feeling—*very reliable, moderately reliable, slightly reliable, neutral, slightly unreliable, moderately unreliable, very unreliable.* The results are summed across respondents, producing a profile of the concept that reflects its image—the meaning or the attitudes held toward it.

semantic differential

Besides using scales, marketing researchers sometimes employ a *rank-order* technique to generate a comparison of brands or products. In this case, the individual is presented with a list of brands (say, of beer—Budweiser, Schlitz, Miller's, Coors, and perhaps two or three others). He or she is asked to rank them into *best liked, second-best liked,* and so on, to *least liked.* The scores are summed across individuals in the attempt to rank order the public's opinions, images, or attitudes toward the various brands.

rank-order techniques

SUMMARY

Managerial interest in attitude theory stems from the attempts of numerous institutions (from business to government to churches) to *confirm* existing positive attitudes, to *change* negative attitudes, or to *create* new attitudes.

Attitudes are defined as learned predispositions to respond to objects in consistently favorable or unfavorable ways. Attitudes differ from beliefs in that attitudes are accompanied by positive or negative feelings. Beliefs, on the other hand, are neutral, and concern knowledge we have about our world.

There are five approaches to the study of attitudes: the structural approach, multi-attribute models, the functional approach, cognitive-consistency theory, and cognitive-dissonance theory. Although these approaches differ in their particular orientations, they all subscribe to the basic definition of attitudes as learned predispositions to respond, and they all at least implicitly incorporate the notion that clusters of related attitudes exist.

An important issue underlying attitudes and attitude measurement is the nature of the relationship between measured attitudes and overt behavior. Some studies have indicated that stated attitudes do not correlate highly with observed behavior. This discrepancy can be explained by reference to measurement issues, normative influences, the effects of habit, the amount of direct experience with an attitude object, situational factors, and the level of involvement characterizing the purchase situation.

Among the methods of attitude measurement are dichotomous questions, Likert scales, and the semantic differential scale.

Marketers can benefit from a knowledge of attitude theory. They are faced with marketing situations in which they may wish to maintain, change, or create attitudes.

KEY CONCEPTS

attitudes
beliefs
structural approach
  cognitive component
  affective component
  conative component
  valence
  multiplexity
attitude clusters

multiattribute models
  Fishbein model
  extended Fishbein
    model
functional approach
  utilitarian function
  value-expressive
    function
  ego-defensive
    function
  knowledge function

cognitive consistency
  theory
  balance theory
  congruity theory
cognitive dissonance
  post-decision
    dissonance
  dissonance reduction
attitude measurement
  Likert scales
  semantic differential

DISCUSSION QUESTIONS

1. What are the basic similarities and differences among the structural approach to the study of attitudes, multiattribute models, the functional approach, and cognitive-consistency theory?
2. Discuss the applicability of the Fishbein model for measuring consumer attitudes toward (a) frequently purchased, nondurable goods, such as paper products and canned food, (b) "image" types of goods, such as designer clothing, and (c) durable household goods, such as major appliances.
3. Are the four types of attitude functions appropriate for different types of products (durables versus nondurables, ego-involving versus non-ego-involving, for example)? Explain.
4. Under what conditions is cognitive dissonance most likely to arise?
5. What are the major problems involved in attitude measurement?
6. The relationship between attitudes and behavior has been discussed at length by attitude researchers. Under what conditions do measured attitudes best correlate with observed behavior?
7. What are the major components of attitude theory that managers should consider when attempting to change consumer attitudes toward a product or brand?

8. Identify three current advertising campaigns that are attempting to create new consumer attitudes. Evaluate and compare these campaigns in light of your knowledge of attitude theory.

NOTES

1. Some of the material in this section of the chapter borrows from Harold H. Kassarjian and Thomas S. Robertson, eds. (1981), *Perspectives in Consumer Behavior* (Glenview, Ill.: Scott, Foresman), pp. 221–27.
2. Gordon W. Allport (1935), "Attitudes," in *Handbook of Social Psychology*, ed. C. W. Murchison (Clark Univ. Press). Reprinted in *Readings in Attitude Theory and Measurement* (1967), ed. Martin Fishbein (New York: Wiley), p. 3.
3. The structural approach has been discussed extensively by D. Krech, R. S. Crutchfield, and E. Ballachey (1962), *Individual in Society* (New York: McGraw-Hill).
4. D. Krech et al. (1962).
5. Harold H. Kassarjian and Joel B. Cohen (1965), "Cognitive Dissonance and Consumer Behavior," *California Management Review*, 8 (Fall), pp. 55–64.
6. Richard J. Lutz (1981).
7. Martin Fishbein (1972), "The Search for Attitudinal-Behavioral Consistency," in *Behavioral Science Foundations of Consumer Behavior*, ed. Joel S. Cohen (New York: Free Press).
8. Martin Fishbein (1975), "A Theoretical Overview," in *Attitude Research Bridges the Atlantic*, ed. Philip Levine (Chicago: American Marketing Assn.).
9. Martin Fishbein and Icek Ajzen (1975), *Belief, Attitude, Intention and Behavior: An Introduction to Theory and Research* (Reading, Mass.: Addison-Wesley).
10. See, for instance, David T. Wilson, H. Lee Matthews, and James W. Harvey (1975), "An Empirical Test of the Fishbein Behavioral Intentions Model," *Journal of Consumer Research*, 1 (March), pp. 39–48; R. J. Lutz (1977), "An Experimental Investigation of Causal Relations Among Cognition, Affect, and Behavioral Intentions," *Journal of Consumer Research*, 3 (March), pp. 197–207; and M. J. Ryan and E. H. Bonfield (1980), "Fishbein's Intentions Model: A Test of External and Pragmatic Validity," *Journal of Marketing*, 44 (Spring), pp. 82–95.
11. M. J. Ryan and E. H. Bonfield (1975), "The Fishbein Extended Model and Consumer Behavior," *Journal of Consumer Research*, 2 (Sept.), pp. 118–36.
12. Perhaps the leading proponent of the functional approach is D. Katz (1960), "The Functional Approach to the Study of Attitudes," *Public Opinion Quarterly*, 24 (Summer), pp. 163–204. See also M. B. Smith, J. S. Bruner, and R. W. White (1956), *Opinions and Personality* (New York: Wiley).
13. D. Katz (1960).
14. Richard J. Lutz (1979), "A Functional Theory Framework for Designing and Pretesting Advertising Themes," in *Attitude Research for High Stakes*, ed. John C. Maloney and Bernard Silverman (Chicago: American Marketing Assn.), pp. 37–39.
15. Fritz Heider (1958), *The Psychology of Interpersonal Relations* (New York: Wiley).
16. Charles E. Osgood and Percy H. Tannenbaum (1955), "The Principle of Congruity in the Prediction of Attitude Change," *Psychological Review*, 62, pp. 42–55.
17. Leon Festinger (1957), *A Theory of Cognitive Dissonance* (Stanford, Cal.: Stanford Univ. Press).
18. For a more complete treatment of this topic, see Bobby J. Calder (1981), "Cognitive Consistency and Consumer Behavior," in *Perspectives in Consumer Behavior*, ed. H. H. Kassarjian and T. S. Robertson, 3rd ed. (Glenview, Ill.: Scott, Foresman), pp. 258–69.
19. Charles E. Osgood and Percy H. Tannenbaum (1955).
20. Leon Festinger (1957).
21. J. W. Brehm (1956), "Post-Decision Changes in the Desirability of Alternatives," *Journal of Abnormal and Social Psychology*, 52 (July), pp. 384–89.

22. Robert E. Knox and James A. Inkster (1968), "Post-Decision Dissonance at Post-Time," *Journal of Personality and Social Psychology*, 8, pp. 319–23.

23. James L. Ginter (1974), "An Experimental Investigation of Attitude Change and Choice of a New Brand," *Journal of Marketing Research*, 11 (Feb.), pp. 30–40.

24. H. H. Kassarjian and J. B. Cohen (1965), "Cognitive Dissonance and Consumer Behavior: Reactions to the Surgeon General's Report on Smoking and Health," *California Management Review*, 8 (Fall), pp. 55–64.

25. Robert J. Holloway (1967), "An Experiment on Consumer Dissonance," *Journal of Marketing*, 31 (Jan.), pp. 39–44.

26. Lawrence A. Crosby and James R. Taylor (1983), "Psychological Commitment and Its Effects on Post-Decision Evaluation and Preference Stability Among Voters," *Journal of Consumer Research*, 9 (March), pp. 413–30.

27. Pradeep K. Korgaonkar and George P. Moschis (1982), "An Experimental Study of Cognitive Dissonance, Product Involvement, Expectations, Performance and Consumer Judgement of Product Performance," *Journal of Advertising*, 11, pp. 32–43.

28. William H. Cummings and M. Venkatesan (1976), "Cognitive Dissonance and Consumer Behavior: A Review of the Evidence," *Journal of Marketing Research*, 13 (Aug.), p. 303–8.

29. Allan W. Wicker (1969), "Attitudes Versus Actions: The Relationship of Verbal and Overt Behavioral Responses to Attitude Objects," *Journal of Social Issues*, 25 (Autumn), p. 65.

30. Alvin A. Achenbaum (1966), "Knowledge Is a Thing Called Measurement," in *Attitude Research at Sea*, ed. Lee Adler and Irving Crespi (New York: American Marketing Assn.), pp. 111–26.

31. Robert B. Cialdini, Richard E. Perry, and John Cacioppo (1981), "Attitude and Attitude Change," *Annual Review of Psychology*, 32, p. 366.

32. Icek Ajzen and Martin Fishbein (1977), "Attitude-Behavior Relations: A Theoretical Analysis and Review of Empirical Research," *Psychological Bulletin*, 84, pp. 888–918.

33. J. Jaccard, G. W. King, and R. Pomasal (1977), "Attitudes and Behavior: An Analysis of Specificity of Attitudinal Predictors," *Human Relations*, 30, pp. 817–24.

34. Robert B. Cialdini et al. (1981).

35. D. T. Regan and R. H. Fazio (1977), "On the Consistency Between Attitudes and Behavior: Look to the Method of Attitude Formation," *Journal of Experimental Social Psychology*, 13, pp. 28–45.

36. Gordon Foxall (1981), "The Treatment of 'Attitudes' in Consumer Research," discussion paper (series B, no. 77), prepared for the Marketing Theory Seminar on Buyer Behavior organized by the Dept. of Marketing, Univ. of Strathclyde.

37. Russell W. Belk (1975), "Situational Variables and Consumer Behavior," *Journal of Consumer Research*, 2 (Dec.), pp. 157–64.

38. Bobby J. Calder (1979), "When Attitudes Follow Behavior—A Self Perception/Dissonance Interpretation of Low Involvement," in *Attitude Research Plays for High Stakes*, ed. John C. Maloney and Bernard Silverman (Chicago: American Marketing Assn.), pp. 25–49.

39. George S. Day and Terry Deutscher (1982), "Attitudinal Predictions of Choices of Major Appliance Brands," *Journal of Marketing Research*, 19 (May), pp. 192–98.

40. Peter C. Riesz and Abe Schuchman (1974), "Responses to the ADA Crest Endorsement," *Journal of Advertising Research*, 14 (Feb.), pp. 21–25.

41. Margaret G. Maples (1982), "4.5MM Stouffer Hotel Drive Aims to Shed Suburban Motel Syndrome," *Adweek* (Jan. 18), p. 19.

42. Mason Haire (1950), "Projective Techniques in Marketing Research," *Journal of Marketing*, 24 (Apr.), pp. 649–56.

43. Bill Meyers (1981), "An American Dilemma: Paste or Gel?" *Adweek* (Nov. 16), p. 1 and "Brushing Aside Reluctance, P&G and Colgate Ready Gels," p. 21.

44. R. A. Likert (1932), "A Technique for the Measurement of Attitudes," *Archives of Psychology*, no. 140 (June).

45. C. E. Osgood, C. J. Suci, and P. H. Tannenbaum (1957), *The Measurement of Meaning* (Urbana, Ill.: Univ. of Illinois Press).

Advertising and Attitudes

An Interview with Tom Hall, Senior Vice President and Group
Creative Director, J. Walter Thompson

Q *How does advertising benefit the consumer?*

A In the broadest sense, advertising is the news of the marketplace. People are born consumers. I think we discovered thousands of years ago, when we started painting animals on the cave wall, there's more to life than just food and clothing. So when you think about it, biologically we are curious, sociologically we are possessive, psychologically we like to be in control of our lives: We are really born consumers. As a species, we think the human animal is just a natural born consumer. As a result, the news of the marketplace is a very important part of your life.

You want to know about new products. Think about a nation coming out of World War II and a depression in the late 40s and early 50s; we were *starved* for new products, and new products came along at a fantastic rate. People wanted to know about them. "What is this thing called a vacuum cleaner?" "What is this thing called a frozen food?" All of these products come with the hope of filling a need in the marketplace; advertising is the news vehicle. As I said, in its broadest sense it brings you news, information, that you need to make informed decisions. We think the more informed a consumer is the more effective or better a consumer is. So our role in advertising is to bring you the news of the marketplace and tell you about products and services.

Q *Does advertising make people want things they don't need?*

A *Impossible.* That's sheer nonsense. I don't have the statistics, but the rate of new-product failures is frightening—it's awesome. The consumer ultimately judges whether you should have that product out there or not. The notion that we, through advertising, can force products upon people is just fantasy. We might be able to induce you to *try* something, because that is our primary objective in introductory advertising—to generate a level of awareness, to induce trial. But the advertising cannot bring you back for a second time. If the product does not fulfill your expectations, if the product does not do the job, you are not going to come back and buy it again. As a result, advertising can kill a product more effectively than anything else, in that it can bring people to an awareness about it very quickly. So the answer is "no"—we cannot force people to use products they don't need or want.

Q *Does advertising manipulate people?*

A No. "Manipulate" certainly brings along some editorial implications. But what we *will* say, and I do think this is reasonable, is that we hope to modify behavior in some cases, certainly to influence people to prefer a certain brand to another. We try to dramatize the benefits of products, to make them more important than competitive products. The ultimate result of all this, though, is improvement in virtually all product categories. And again, information that is brought to you by advertising only tends to make that process work more effectively. But the thought of advertising manipulating people in some sort of an Orwellian or hypnotic fashion is preposterous. All you have to do is go to the marketplace and see the millions of dollars that are spent to develop products, to design them, to develop packaging, to get them into distribution, to advertise them—and then see the efforts fail—to know that the most powerful advertisers in the world cannot force people or manipulate them.

Q *But don't you think that certain ads—for example, ads portraying the "beautiful people" selling designer clothes or expensive perfumes— try to make people emulate other people, telling them this is how you* should *be, and this is what you* must *buy to be this way, and therefore make them buy products that they don't really need?*

A Let me go along with you, just for the sake of discussion. What's wrong with that? What's wrong with people who have disposable income and who feel better when they put on some designer jeans; who feel better about themselves when they change their hair color; or who feel better when they lose weight, or buy something special? What would be wrong with that?

Q *Possibly that you don't have the disposable income and you're always wanting things you can't have?*

A That's life! Nobody goes into business to develop products to give them away. We have certain realities in life, among them are the amount of disposable income we have and how fortunate we are. I don't see anybody anywhere saying that you *have* to buy designer jeans. If you're an informed consumer and you know that you can get a comparable product from a mass merchandiser for one third—or one tenth—the cost, you should probably go do that. You should also know that the designer jeans carry along with them a pretty high premium just to put a designer's name on your bottom. And if you are informed, that is either meaningful to you or not. We are not saying

you have to wear them. We are only setting up a product category or an extension of a product category that allows you to gain some value. The added value of the designer's name is also sorted out in the marketplace. If those designer jeans get to a price where they are not effectively delivering value, they don't stay there. And you will notice, by the way, there are a lot fewer advertisers in that category right now than there were twelve months ago.

Q *How does an advertiser use consumer-behavior theory and ideas in the design of an advertising campaign?*

A We use it a lot. There are essentially two kinds of research that are used in the development of advertising. Let me come back to the category that you are asking about after I mention briefly that we have ongoing research tracking or testing the effectiveness of advertising before it goes on air all the time. These days virtually all clients pretest commercials, sometimes even before producing them in animated or photomatic form. There are ongoing tracking studies not only to measure sales results, obviously, but to measure attitudinal shifts, awareness levels. All of this kind of research is conducted in an effort to see how our advertising is doing. We are held accountable for our advertising—that's why we need to know how it's performing. But the kind of research you asked about in your question is more allied to human behavior: How do people think and feel about products? We know that for any given product category, the demographic input about the target audience might be misleading. Demographics really cut a broad swathe through the marketplace and identify large groups of people, but, unfortunately, tell us nothing about how they feel, how they think, how they act, what their attitudes and opinions are. These things are very important in developing advertising because we feel that what we're trying to do is to generate a specific response—a target or desired response. It's not what I say, it's what you hear. If I were to tell you that the Cadillac Fleetwood is an economy car and delivers seventy miles to the gallon, I could say that all I want, and your response would probably be "nonsense!" If I were to tell you that the Toyota Tercel two-door coupé for $3685 is a luxury car with fine luxury appointments, your response would be "nonsense!" Therefore we can't claim things, state things in advertising that will elicit the improper response. This is a long way of getting to the point, which is: We must know how people feel and can act with our products. I just called for some focus groups recently. As a creative director, I want to know how people use a product—what they think about it. Is it part of their lives? Is it a casual thing they come across everyday? Are they involved in the product? Do they care about it? Do they have a feeling of loyalty toward a given product? They may say, "it depends"—and it does depend on the product categories. But there often are great surprises for us. We assumed for many years that Seven-up was a soft drink. We did some outstanding soft-drink advertising until some research told us that it was not consumed in soft drink patterns: It wasn't consumed in social situations; it wasn't consumed when you wanted to take a break; it wasn't consumed when you were thirsty. It was mixed with Canadian whiskey; it was consumed at parties in punch; you might have some if you didn't feel well. The insight from talking to consumers told us that this product had to be positioned as an alternative to colas, and we embarked on "The Un-Cola." Again, we dig and probe and talk to people; we conduct focus groups and we conduct individual interviews. Creative people sit and watch these televised interviews; we can pass questions right in. On occasion I go into the room myself and talk directly to consumers: "How do you use this? How do you like it? Why *don't* you like it?" We get incredible insights. We even

go and live with them if necessary. We go to stores; we go into the marketplace. We have to be as intimately aware of a product and how it's used and how the consumer feels about it as we can. We use this kind of research extensively, and it's very important to us.

Q *Can you give an example of a successful advertising campaign based on an understanding of consumer behavior?*

A We developed a campaign for Allegheny Airlines that was part of a total repositioning of the airline. It involved a new name, USAir. The campaign took the point of view and theme line, "It takes a big airline." In the airline business, people equate safety with bigness. Allegheny Airlines was perceived as a smaller, regional carrier and, as such, was not receiving the highest impressions of safety. The new name and telling people how big the airline was dramatized the change. It went from a name that implied "regional-local" to a name that said more. By pointing out to people how many cities USAir flew to, how many more flights it had than Pan-Am, how many more passengers it carried than other airlines, we saw dramatic results. People's attitudes and impressions changed quite quickly about the product, and people started traveling on USAir much more frequently; passenger levels went up quite a bit.

Our results came from *understanding*. In research, people do not necessarily articulate their feelings. In some categories it is hard to get people to say what they actually think or feel. They may tell you, "I'm not influenced by advertising," or they may *not* say, "I'm afraid to fly on this airline." Because they will not always *say*, we have to probe and dig to better understand our consumer—to find out what the real answer is. If I say "this is a safe airline," you are probably going to respond, "why is he saying that?" But if I say "it's a big airline," you say "safe." I think that is a good example of *un-*

derstanding—that consumers wanted the reassurance, the comfort of a big airline, because that is the stimulus for feeling safe. It was indeed what Allegheny was: The airline had an incredible safety record, and still does. But the perception was not there to match the reality. In this case, advertising was able to do that very effectively.

Q *Can you give an example of an unsuccessful campaign based on a misunderstanding of consumer behavior?*

A I was responsible for developing a campaign once for Oscar Mayer [that failed because of] misunderstanding the consumer's feelings about Oscar Mayer. Oscar Mayer is a remarkable company: outstanding products, higher standards than the government requires—probably the highest standards in the industry. They are well liked by consumers. Mothers feel very confident with Oscar Mayer products since they are the highest quality processed meats. At any rate, we'd done advertising for Oscar Mayer over the years that associated Oscar Mayer products with fun and good times. We had used children in the advertising; we had done light-hearted advertising. People feel good about Oscar Mayer advertising. I developed some advertising that extended that thinking, because of a misunderstanding, and did some advertising that was very funny or humorous. But it was making fun of itself in a way that was not consistent with the Oscar Mayer image. I understood that anything that was humorous would be representative of fun and good times—like the fun of a family picnic or a birthday party. Imagine, if you will, a commercial where a guy falls asleep, and in his dream he dreams he's an Oscar Mayer weiner, and he wakes up in red pajamas with a mattress wrapped around himself. This wasn't the commercial, but a commercial like this was produced. It was a funny commercial. But there is a difference between *funny* and *fun and good times* in the wholesome, family sense. That misunderstanding led to a commercial or two that I developed that were just dead, flat, wrong. They never ran. They were pretested, and the pretesting told us loud and clear that we had exceeded the boundaries; we had gone too far. This wasn't fun and good times; this didn't look and act like Oscar Mayer. Consumers told us it was just a genuine bomb.

12 Motivation Theory, Personality Theory, and Psychographics

This chapter develops two streams of research, based on motivation theory and personality theory. The motivational stream concerns why people behave as they do, and the personality stream attempts to identify stable underlying traits that might characterize a person's behavior. This research is important to the development of psychographics by consumer researchers. A detail of the two streams is shown in Exhibit 12–1.

By psychographics *is meant a set of dimensions that measures the psychological attributes of consumers. The goal is to assess whether different psychological profiles of consumers are related to particular consumption patterns. Here are some sample psychographic items:*

- *I believe that most of the events in a person's life are beyond his or her control.*
- *A woman's place is in the home.*
- *Being liked by other people is very important to me.*
- *A major problem in the world today is disrespect for authority.*

Before the introduction of psychographics into marketing research in the late 1960s, marketers relied heavily on whatever product-usage and demographic data they could gather from consumers. However, the problem was that demographic characteristics of consumers explain only part of the variance in consumer-behavior patterns and for some products have almost no significant explanatory ability.[1] Here are two examples of cases in which marketers of a product could benefit from psychographic information about their mar-kets. In the first example, about Mercedes automobiles, demographics are good predictors of who will purchase, whereas in the second example, about coffee, demographics are of limited predictive value.

- *Mercedes. The demographic profile of Mercedes buyers is quite distinct—high education and income, professional and managerial occupations, concentrated in a few metropolitan markets. But not everyone with this profile buys a Mercedes. A question for the manufacturer, then, is why some such people buy a Mercedes and some do not. Could a certain "personality type" buy a Mercedes—perhaps someone with high needs for security or social respect or self indulgence?*
- *Coffee. The demographic profile for coffee drinkers is not very distinct; coffee is drunk by consumers in many income, educational, and age levels. A question for the manufacturer, then, is whether there is any way to characterize heavy coffee drinkers. Might they have a certain "personality profile"—perhaps excessively driven, compulsive, and active?*

As these examples suggest, marketers can benefit from knowing something about the personality and motivational characteristics of consumers of their products. Are they motivated by status considerations, or are security motives a stronger element in their purchase decisions? Do they tend to be people with sociable personalities, or do they tend to be more individualistic? Such questions are the questions addressed by psychographic research.

THE MOTIVATIONAL STREAM

Motivation theory and personality theory are quite interconnected. Whether a given theory belongs in the motivation field or in the personality field is often debatable, and many psychologists disagree about the distinction between motivation and personality. One broad distinction that is useful as a rule of thumb is that most motivation theories focus on what people have *in common* (i.e., a finite set of motivations), whereas most personality theories focus more on *individual differences* among people.

Freudian Psychoanalytic Theory

Sigmund Freud, often referred to as the "father of psychoanalysis," is the twentieth century's most influential psychological theoretician. His major creation, the body of psychological theories known as *psychoanalysis*, deals with a wide variety of topics—motivation, learning, culture, and personality. Because the focus of this chapter is on describing the origins of psychographic research, we will focus on the motivational aspects of Freud's theories.

instincts

Freud believed that a few **instincts** were the bases for all human motivation. The instincts can be divided into two basic categories. The *life instincts*, which serve either the survival of the individual or the survival of the species, include hunger, thirst, and sexual drive. The *death instincts* include the wish to harm others (aggression) and the wish to die (self-destructiveness).

According to Freud, instincts are inherited and therefore fixed, but the object of an instinct changes over the course of a lifetime. A well-known example is the case of sexual instincts. Freud believed that during childhood the object of a boy's sexual instincts was his mother, but that as the boy matured, other persons in his life replaced the mother as the object of his sexual instincts.

id, ego, and superego

How can all the complexities of human behavior and motivation be accounted for by reference to a handful of instincts like hunger, thirst, sex, and aggression? The answer to this lies in Freud's division of the *psyche* into three functional entities: the **id, ego,** and **superego.** The *id* is the location of the

EXHIBIT 12–1

THE TWO MAJOR STREAMS INFLUENCING THE DEVELOPMENT OF PSYCHOGRAPHIC RESEARCH

Theories and Research in Motivation	Theories and Research in Personality
Freudian Theory	Murray's Theory of Personology
Neo-Freudian Theory	Allport's Trait Theory
Projective Techniques	Cattell's Factor-Trait Theory
Motivation Research in Marketing	Standardized Personality Tests

instincts and is completely unconscious. The function of the id is to seek immediate satisfaction of the instincts. The id functions according to the **pleasure principle** in the sense that its sole concern is the gratification of instincts.

The immediate unbridled satisfaction of sex and aggressive instincts would result in the individual's being in constant conflict with the rest of society. Fortunately, the *ego* helps to mediate between the raging impulses of the id and the demands of reality. While the hunger instinct presses the id for immediate gratification, the ego guides the individual to seek, find, prepare, and eat food. Unlike the id, which operates on the pleasure principle, the ego operates on the **reality principle.** The reality principle helps the id delay gratification until the appropriate object for the instinct is available.

The third component, the *superego*, is the internal representation of society's values, prohibitions, and moral standards within the individual. Freud envisioned a process where the parents consistently communicate to the child the values and prohibitions of the culture through the daily "do's and don'ts" of parenting. Eventually, the voice of the parents is internalized and becomes the superego, or conscience.

Given the existence of the basic instincts (hunger, sex, aggression), and the existence of the id-ego-superego structure of the psyche, we can begin to see how a few instincts can account for a wide range of human behavior. Consider the case of the simple hunger instinct. This instinct presses the id toward immediate gratification. But the ego must conceive and execute some realistic plan for the fulfillment of this need. This plan may be as direct as walking to the refrigerator and removing and eating a snack; or it may involve extended deliberations concerning how the individual will obtain education, job training, and employment in order to gain money to pay for food. The role of the superego should not be overlooked in this example. When the hunger instinct presses the id, the id's sole function is to seek immediate gratification. Presumably, were it not for the superego, pressures from the id would lead the individual to satisfy a hunger impulse by smashing the window of the nearest bakery and helping himself or herself. Thus, one simple instinct, when translated through the complex functioning of the ego and superego, can lead to a very wide range of behaviors and choices.

A further insight into how a few instincts can underlie all human motivation is provided by an understanding of the **defense mechanisms.** According to Freud, the pleasure-seeking id, the realistic ego, and the moralistic superego are in constant conflict, which the individual experiences as frustration and anxiety. In addition, if people were conscious of the existence of their undesirable instincts, they would experience even more anxiety. To protect the individual from these feelings, the *ego* employs a variety of *defense mechanisms.* Among these are identification, projection, displacement, and rationalization.

defense mechanisms

Identification is a common and powerful mechanism whereby people tend to imitate others whom they admire. It can be accomplished through consumption behavior, as when the individual imitates a manner of dress. The presence or creation of "trend-setters" and "opinion leaders" with whom consumers identify sometimes plays a significant role in marketing strategy.

Projection, the reverse of identification, consists of attributing to other people those motives and forms of behavior the individual unconsciously recognizes as undesirable in himself or herself. Advertisers sometimes exploit this mechanism by featuring unattractive models, whose undesirable attributes are implied to be a consequence of their failure to use the product advertised, such as mouthwashes and complexion products.

Displacement rechannels energy from one object to another. The poor white person, for example, may blame his or her misfortunes on blacks rather than on personal inadequacies. The purchase of a sports car has been claimed by some motivation researchers to be a substitute for sex. Dogs, as we shall see later in the chapter, are sometimes "baby substitutes."

Rationalization serves all of the defense mechanisms by providing the individual with acceptable reasons for actions. Offering consumers a rationalization for purchasing is a basic sales principle. Even advertising with apparent id-emphases contains rationalization copy to neutralize the superego, as when, for example, a luxury-car manufacturer refers to "investment" value.

Although today the critics of Freudian psychoanalytic theory seem to outweigh the adherents, Freud contributed much to our understanding of human behavior and to advances in marketing theory. Freud's views have been major influences on all subsequent theories of motivation. In particular, his emphasis on the unconscious and his theory that all of human behavior can be traced back to a small number of physiological instincts (especially sex and aggression) are central to any discussion of human motivation.

Neo-Freudian Theory

Several of Freud's colleagues and successors—the so-called "neo-Freudians"—were unhappy with his emphasis on physiological instincts, especially sex and aggression, as the basis of personality. They believed that an understanding of human motivation must take into account *social influences* and *social interactions*. Three of these "neo-Freudians," Alfred Adler, Erich Fromm, and Karen Horney, developed their own theories.

Rather than emphasizing the importance of sexual and aggressive instincts, Adler focused on the individual's striving for superiority. Adler believed that in the course of growing up, children are instilled with feelings of inferiority, and that the primary goal in adulthood is to overcome this *inferiority complex* by striving for superiority. Thus, a person's selection of a large luxurious automobile or a husband's purchase of a conspicuously expensive fur coat for his wife may be motivated by the desire to overcome feelings of inferiority.

In Fromm's view, life in our complex industrialized society gives rise to deep-seated feelings of isolation, loneliness, and alienation. Therefore, the basic human motivation is to "escape from loneliness." The search for love, interpersonal security, and human connectedness are basic human preoccupations. Many advertisements today feature elements of belonging and conviviality, such as Lowenbrau's "Here's To Good Friends" campaign.

Horney believed that the basic component of personality was the anxiety that developed in the child as a result of parent-child relationships. According to Horney, the individual could choose one of three ways of coping with this anxiety, with all three strategies based in interpersonal relationships. A person could either move toward others (*compliant* type), against others (*aggressive* type), or away from others (*detached* type). The choice of interpersonal strategy then becomes the basis of the individual's personality.

In general, the work of these neo-Freudians has had limited impact on research in consumer behavior. An exception is a study by Cohen[2] which investigates the relationship among Horney's personality types and purchases. Cohen found that (1) *compliant* types prefer brand names, use more mouthwash, use more toilet soap; (2) *aggressive* types use razors rather than electric shavers, use more cologne, use more after-shave lotion; and (3) *detached* types seem to be least aware of brands. Although Cohen's work is highly exploratory and does not tell us *why* these findings occur, it does suggest that Horney's theory may have some relevance to marketing. Some other researchers have also utilized Cohen's instrument to measure these personality types but the implications for marketing are limited so far.[3]

Although the neo-Freudians differed from Freud in various ways, they continued the tradition of placing emphases on the importance of powerful unconscious motivations, wishes, and fears. It was this emphasis that provided the rationale for the development of *projective techniques*.

Projective Techniques

You will recall from Chapter 3 that **projective techniques** are an important component of behavioral methodology. The essential idea of these techniques—including the Rorschach inkblot and the Thematic Apperception Test—is that because the stimuli are ambiguous, the person will have to *project* his or her own needs and motives onto the response. Freudian theory then would predict that a large percentage of an individual's responses to projective techniques would contain sexual or aggressive content, even though the inkblot itself is totally formless.

According to Henry Murray, the developer of the TAT, the individual's response is psychologically meaningful for the following reasons.

> *The test is based on the well-recognized fact that when a person interprets an ambiguous social situation he is apt to expose his own personality as much as the phenomenon to which he is attending. Absorbed in his attempt to explain the objective occurrence, he becomes naively unconscious of himself and of the scrutiny of others, and, therefore, defensively less vigilant. To one with double hearing, however, he is disclosing certain inner tendencies and cathexes: wishes, fears, and traces of past experiences.*[4]

Thus, the individual's responses are analyzed and scored according to the motives, needs, and wishes assumed to have been projected onto the story's characters.

Maslow's Hierarchy of Needs

An important conceptualization of motivation is Maslow's **hierarchy of needs.** Maslow proposed the following order.

1. *Physiological needs:* food and water
2. *Safety needs:* security and protection
3. *Love needs:* affection and belonging (family and friends)
4. *Esteem needs:* self-respect, prestige, success, and achievement
5. *Self-actualization need:* desire for self-fulfillment

According to Maslow, the lower-level needs must be met before the higher-level needs become relevant.[5] Only after the individual has satisfied the need for immediate survival is he or she concerned with the need for safety, and only after safety has been provided do love needs emerge, and so on.

A casual examination of current advertising messages suggests that advertisers believe that most individuals in American society operate at the love or esteem levels. You will not see a message claiming that "Crispy crackers are more filling than other brands"; more typically the message might say, "Your guests will enjoy your parties more when you serve Crispy crackers."

Lewin's Field Theory

life space

The **field-theory** approach to motivation is best represented by Kurt Lewin,[6] for whom the most fundamental of the field-theory concepts is the **life space** or **psychological field.** Behavior, including consumption,[7] is a function of forces in the individual's life space, which is the totality of the person's world as he or she perceives it; it is the individual's "reality" and the aggregate of all simultaneously existing facts. In order to understand behavior, the researcher must understand all of the forces within this life space—the goals, the positive and negative aspects, the forces pushing and pulling the individual in various directions, and the barriers that block efforts to reach goals.

tension

There are several further Lewinian concepts; one is the concept of **tension.** An individual is in a state of tension when a need is unfulfilled, whether a physiological need, such as hunger, or a psychosocial need, such as the desire to own a new car. As the goal is reached, tension is released and the individual achieves equilibrium. Also important is the concept of **valence**—the at-

valence

tractiveness or unattractiveness of some region of the individual's psychological field. Objects in general have positive or negative valence, but valence is also coordinated with needs, and whether an object and region of the psychological field has positive or negative valence depends upon the individual's state of tension. As the individual seeks to reduce tension, *energy* is exerted which, combined with valence, creates a *force* acting upon the person, and leads to *behavior.* The strength and direction of a force can be thought of as a *vector,* and more than one vector is likely to act upon a person. Purchase alternatives may place the person in the position of choosing between two products that both possess positive valences. Or, both positive and negative valences may attach to a purchase consideration. The outcome, or purchase behavior, in these cases is a function of relative vector strengths. Thus, given a state of tension, purchase depends upon whether the positive valences outbalance the negative. If a purchase decision is made, the brand selected will depend upon the valences attached to the alternative brands.

Motivation Research in Marketing

Motivation researchers in marketing believe that products frequently hold "hidden meanings" for consumers and that knowledge of such "hidden meanings" can provide a crucial competitive advantage. Research based on these ideas, known as *motivation research,* emerged in the late 1950s. The goal of motivation research was, by a lengthy psychoanalytically oriented interview, to probe the consumer psyche for unconscious psychological responses to products. Its leading proponents, most particularly Ernest Dichter, tended to be Freudian in orientation. What distinguished motivation research from marketing research was its emphasis on the "why" of individual consumer behavior and its use of indirect or nonstructured research techniques. Depth interviews and projective techniques were part of the standard repertoire.

In time, motivation research became integrated with traditional marketing research, influencing and expanding the inventory of marketing research techniques. In the process, however, motivation research was subjected to severe criticism from academicians, researchers, and businesspeople who found fault on a number of grounds—including small sample sizes, questionable research procedures, inconsistent findings, and difficulties in using the findings in the design of marketing programs.

Many motivation research studies, because of the intensive method used, required interviews of several hours. Sample sizes, as a result, were most often small—frequently fewer than 100 people—and statistical analysis could not be conducted with any confidence. Another particular difficulty of motivation research was that results could be analyzed only by trained psychologists, and these psychologists did not always agree on their interpretations.

Here are some representative motivation research "findings."

Soup is a profoundly emotion-charged food. It has become identified with the positive symbols of abundance, security, warmth, comfort, and friendliness. Moods of nostalgic reverie characterize the way respondents recall the soups of their childhood. Highly emotional associations with soup center around family ties, especially mother's love.[8]

The ceremonial nature of smoking is usually explained as a continuation of, or regression to, infantile forms of autoeroticism (such as thumbsucking).[9]

Other motivation researchers have suggested that men prefer odoriferous cigars as a sign of masculinity; that a convertible can serve its owner psychologically as a substitute "mistress"; that baking a cake is for a woman unconsciously the symbolic act of giving birth; and that prunes are disliked because they are a symbol of parental authority.

From a historical perspective, motivation research made certain positive impressions on the field of marketing. In particular, it encouraged marketers to move away from demographic analyses only—to go beyond income, occupation, and education. The question of why consumers behave as they do, once raised, was not to be dismissed. Motivation research, and motivation theory in general, was to become an important theoretical stream in the development of psychographics.

THE PERSONALITY STREAM

The second major theoretical stream in the development of psychographics is *personality*. Following the schema presented in Exhibit 12–1, we will focus on those theories of personality that led to the development of psychographic research as used in marketing today.

Murray's Theory of Personology

Henry A. Murray developed a theory of personality known as *personology*. Personology was influenced by Freud in that Murray accepted Freud's concept of the id. However, although Freud saw the id as consisting primarily of sexual and aggressive impulses, Murray claimed that the id also contains socially constructive impulses, such as the need to empathize with others and the need to master the environment. Unlike Freud, Murray asserted that there were *individual differences* among individuals in regard to the intensity of their id impulses. He pointed out, for example, that some people seem to have more "intense appetites" than others.

Another major difference between Freud and Murray is that while Freud based his theory on discussions with disturbed patients, Murray based his theory on an intensive study of college students. Murray headed a team of twenty-eight psychiatrists, psychologists, and social workers who studied fifty-one male Harvard undergraduates for six months. The team used a wide array of research techniques—tests, questionnaires, behavior ratings, analysis of autobiographical sketches—in order to probe topics such as sexual practices, family interaction, childhood memories, and social interaction. After analyzing this vast amount of data, Murray concluded that the most important concept in understanding human personality was the concept of *need*.

According to Murray's analysis, human personality is guided by twelve **physiological needs** and twenty-eight **psychogenic needs.**[10] The physiological needs are related to survival and include needs for air, water, and food. The *psychogenic needs* do not have physiological origins but develop after the primary needs. Exhibit 12–2 shows a list of some of the psychogenic needs.

One important aspect of Murray's theory is that it accounts for *individual differences* among people. In respect to needs, individuals can differ in two basic ways. First, not everyone has all needs; for example, there are probably people who do not have the need for Deference (the need to admire or honor a superior). Second, one person might have a high level of a need (like Affiliation), whereas another might have a moderate or low level.

Murray's taxonomy of needs has had a major impact on the development of psychological testing. The Edwards Personal Preference Schedule, an extremely well-known personality test in the consumer-behavior field, is based on fifteen of Murray's needs.

Allport's Theory of Traits

Vernon Allport was an American psychologist who is credited with two important "firsts" in the area of personality. Allport's Ph.D. dissertation was the

EXHIBIT 12–2
MURRAY'S PSYCHOGENIC NEEDS: A PARTIAL LIST

Psychogenic Need	Brief Definition
Achievement	To accomplish something difficult. To master, manipulate, or organize physical objects, human beings, or ideas. To rival and surpass others.
Affiliation	To draw near and enjoyably co-operate or reciprocate with an allied other (an other who resembles the subject or who likes the subject). To please and win affection.
Aggression	To overcome opposition forcefully. To fight. To revenge an injury. To oppose forcefully or punish another.
Autonomy	To get free, shake off restraint, break out of confinement. To resist coercion and restriction. To be independent and free to act according to impulse. To defy convention.
Deference	To admire and support a superior. To praise, honor, or eulogize. To emulate an exemplar. To conform to custom.
Dominance	To control one's human environment. To influence or direct the behavior of others by suggestion, seduction, persuasion, or command. To dissuade, restrain, or prohibit.
Exhibition	To make an impression. To be seen and heard. To excite, amaze, fascinate, entertain, shock, intrigue, amuse or entice others.
Nurturance	To give sympathy and gratify the needs of a helpless object; an infant or any object that is weak, disabled, tired, inexperienced, defeated, lonely, sick or mentally confused.
Play	To act for "fun" without further purpose. To like to laugh and make jokes. To seek enjoyable relaxation from stress. To participate in games and sports.
Understanding	To ask or answer general questions. To be interested in theory. To speculate, formulate, analyze, and generalize.

SOURCE: Henry A. Murray (1938), *Explorations in Personality* (New York: Oxford Univ. Press), pp. 80–83.

first study of **traits** in the United States, and Allport was the first personality theorist to challenge the fundamental assertions of Freudian psychoanalysis.

Allport's conception of *traits* was extremely simple. He asserted that if you observe a person over time, you will observe consistencies and regularities in the person's behavior in a variety of different stimulus situations. Allport called these consistencies/regularities *traits*. To assist psychologists in naming traits, he compiled a list of 18,000 trait labels. Included in his list were such everyday trait labels as conformity, dominance, authoritarianism, neuroticism, and masculinity.

According to Allport, particular traits have more or less influence on an individual's behavior depending on whether they are *cardinal, central,* or *secondary traits.* A *cardinal trait* is one that has a major influence in guiding behavior, affecting every aspect of the individual's life. Examples of such traits are religiosity and chauvinism. A *central trait* is less influential in the individual's overall behavior pattern than a cardinal trait. Allport believed that each individual possesses five to ten central traits that constitute the "theme" that describes an individual's behavior. Examples of central traits are aggressiveness, sentimentality, and self-pity. A *secondary trait* is the least influential trait on overall behavior patterns. Secondary traits are those that the individual may exhibit only in privacy or with intimate friends. Examples of secondary traits are cattiness and miserliness.[11]

But Allport's contribution to the study of personality goes beyond his formulation of trait theory. Allport was also the first personality theorist to challenge the fundamental assertions of Freudian psychoanalytic theory. Allport pointed out that Freud's concepts and theories were based exclusively on the observation of neurotic and other emotionally disturbed people. Allport asserted that the study of personality functioning must be based on observations of normal, healthy, functional human beings. While conceding that the role of unconscious processes may be significant in neurotic functioning, Allport insisted that the healthy adult is rational, conscious, and aware.[12]

Another major disagreement with Freudian theory was over the generalizability of findings. Whereas Freud believed that his observations of personality resulted in general, *universal* laws that applied to everyone, Allport believed that each individual has a *unique,* specific personality. Thus, while Freud asserted that all individuals are primarily driven by sexual and aggressive impulses, Allport countered that one individual might be primarily motivated by acquisitiveness (a cardinal trait), while another might be primarily motivated by religiosity (a cardinal trait).

Cattell's Factor-Trait Theory

While Allport contributed the concept of traits to personality theory, Raymond B. Cattell provided an analysis and classification of traits. Cattell's approach focused on collecting massive amounts of data from healthy adults. He administered questionnaires, gave objective tests, and obtained ratings of behavior in naturalistic settings. After obtaining many test and rating scores on individuals, Cattell then analyzed the scores to find subsets of scores with a high degree of interrelationships. For example, take a group of individuals' scores on two separate personality tests—the Authoritarianism scale and the Dependency scale—for which we note a high correlation between the scales (that is, people who scored high on one also scored high on the other; people who scored low on one also scored low on the other). At this point, we might conclude that these two tests are actually measuring one personality factor. Actually, Cattell used a more sophisticated tool to perform this search—a statistical methodology called **factor analysis.**[13] The purpose of factor analysis is to begin with a large number of scores, to search for any possible underlying relationships among the scores, and then to reduce the number of scores to a smaller number of underlying dimensions or *factors*.

factor analysis

In Cattell's terminology, each of the underlying dimensions that result from factor analysis is a *trait*. To Cattell, an individual's personality consists of the sum of these traits. In order to understand an individual's personality, we must have a knowledge of the person's trait structure. Cattell ultimately published a personality test called the *16 P.F. Test*[14] that included the sixteen basic traits he considered the "building blocks" of personality.

traits

Standardized Personality Tests and Consumer Behavior Research

One major development in the study of personality has been the emergence of standardized personality tests based on a wide range of personality theories. We have already seen that Cattell devised a sixteen-factor test based on his trait-factor theory of personality. In addition, hundreds of other standardized tests, or *inventories*, exist today, which attempt to measure personality variables such as authoritarianism,[15] dogmatism,[16] introversion/extroversion,[17] locus of control,[18] and sensation-seeking.[19]

Many of these personality tests have been used in the study of consumer behavior. Researchers have attempted to link various personality variables with purchase behavior, media choice, innovativeness, opinion leadership, and information acquisition. Following is a brief review of the extensive literature on this subject. The student interested in a more extensive review should refer to Kassarjian and Sheffet.[20]

Brand Choice The most famous study assessing the value of personality in explaining buyer behavior was conducted in 1959 by Franklin B. Evans.[21] Evans used a standardized personality test, the Edwards Personal Preference Schedule, which is based on Henry Murray's psychoanalytic theory of needs. Evans' objective was to relate fifteen traits to the prediction of Ford versus Chevrolet ownership.

The results indicated that there were no significant differences between Ford and Chevrolet owners on the Edwards scales. Publication of Evans' study resulted in a swirl of controversy among consumer-behavior researchers, many of whom suggested improvements in Evans' research procedure. Evans did replicate his study and found a slight relationship between Edwards' scales and Ford vs. Chevrolet owners, but this relationship was too small to be of any theoretical or practical value.

Product Category Usage   Research relating personality to type of automobile owned was conducted by Westfall.[22] He administered the Thurstone Temperament Schedule to a sample of full-sized, convertible, and compact car owners and found that the convertible owner is more active, impulsive, and sociable, but somewhat less stable and reflective than the full-sized or compact owner.

Research by Tucker and Painter[23] using the Gordon Personal Profile test found certain distinguishable relationships between personality traits and use or nonuse of a range of products. In a predominantly male sample, the acceptance of new fashions was positively related to ascendency and sociability; the use of headache remedies was negatively related to ascendency and emotional stability. Some products (such as vitamins) were found to be related to all four personality traits measured; other products (such as cigarettes) were exclusively nonrelated.

Koponen used the Edwards Personal Preference Test in a study relating personality to cigarette smoking.[24] He found that the male smoker scored significantly higher than the general male average in expressed needs for sex, aggression, achievement, and dominance, but significantly lower in compliance, order, self-depreciation, and association. Koponen further found that filter-cigarette smokers differed in personality from nonfilter smokers.

Alpert also used the Edwards test to examine the role of personality in choosing a residence. He found some significant exploratory relationships.[25]

Cohen, as we discussed earlier in this chapter, administered a test based on Horney's paradigm of compliant (*moving toward*), aggressive (*moving against*), and detached (*moving away from*) individuals. His results, across a wide range of products, were suggestive of differences in interpersonal orientation for product use and brand choice.[26]

Innovativeness   Robertson investigated the personality characteristics of innovators (first buyers) for a small-appliance consumer innovation. Using the Thurstone Temperament Schedule, he found that such innovators were significantly more impulsive, active, and dominant.[27] In another study, Robertson and Myers assessed the relation of personality to innovativeness across a number of product categories, using the California Personality Inventory. Their general conclusion was that personality and innovativeness are statistically only slightly related.[28]

Jacoby studied the relationship between individuals' scores on the dogmatism scale and their tendency to be innovators. He found that individuals who scored low on dogmatism (that is, they are more open-minded) tend to be more willing to buy new products than those who scored higher, although the statistical relationship was reasonably low.[29]

Opinion Leadership   In the Robertson and Myers study mentioned above, the researchers also examined the relationship between opinion leadership and the personality variables of the California Personality Inventory. They concluded that personality is not associated with opinion leadership. Research by other consumer-behavior researchers has also found little or no relationship between personality and opinion leadership.[30]

Susceptibility to Persuasion Moderate relationships of personality and susceptibility to persuasion have been reported.[31] In general, two conclusions are well established. The first is that males low in self-esteem or *generalized* self-confidence are more readily persuaded than males of high self-esteem. This finding has typically not held for females. The second conclusion is that individuals of low *specific* self-confidence—with regard, for example, to a specific purchase situation— are more readily persuaded than individuals of high specific self-confidence. This typically holds for both females and males.

Self Concept Research has also tested the notion that people reflect their self concept in the products they own.[32] A number of researchers, for example, have found that the type of car owned is congruent with the consumer's view of self.[33] Grubb and Hupp also have found that owners of one brand of car perceive themselves as similar to others who owned that car but different from owners of another brand.[34] Dolich has found that there is more similarity between a person's self concept and most preferred brand than least preferred brand.[35]

Information Acquisition In recent experimental research on the amount of information used for decision-making, Schaninger and Sciglimpaglia have found a personality relationship.[36] Their results show that the people most likely to examine many cues and alternatives are more tolerant of ambiguity and have higher self-esteem. They are also what might be called "clarifiers"; that is, they use new information for clarification rather than avoiding or rejecting such information (avoiders are referred to as "simplifiers").

Other Research Other studies in consumer behavior have related personality to the selection of industrial salespeople,[37] retail-store selection,[38] blood donorship,[39] and the use of time.[40] These studies have generally been exploratory, sometimes showing a positive relationship with personality and often not.

Conclusion Following is the most accurate summary of the usefulness of personality tests in the study of consumer behavior.

> *By 1980, some 200 studies were available in the marketing literature relating personality variables to consumer behavior. A review of these studies can be summarized by the single word "equivocal."*[41]

Personality as a predictive variable for consumer actions would appear to be unsatisfactory. The available evidence, using a variety of standard personality instruments, is quite discouraging—reporting a good number of negative and some contradictory findings. Of course, some of the variability in data may be due to the use of different personality tests and to measurement error. This is not to say that personality is unrelated to consumer actions, but that the relationships are limited and not of much practical value.

The weak relationships between personality and purchase behavior may be due to the lack of an adequate "theoretical framework," and it is necessary to

EXHIBIT 12–3
A PSYCHOGRAPHIC INVENTORY

Price Conscious	I shop a lot for "specials."
	I find myself checking the prices in the grocery store even for small items.
	I usually watch the advertisements for announcements of sales.
	A person can save a lot of money by shopping around for bargains.
Fashion Conscious	I usually have one or more outfits that are of the very latest style.
	When I must choose between the two I usually dress for fashion, not for comfort.
	An important part of my life and activities is dressing smartly.
	I often try the latest hairdo styles when they change.
Child Oriented	When my children are ill in bed I drop most everything else in order to see to their comfort.
	My children are the most important thing in my life.
	I try to arrange my home for my children's convenience.
	I take a lot of time and effort to teach my children good habits.
Compulsive Housekeeper	I don't like to see children's toys lying about.
	I usually keep my house very neat and clean.
	I am uncomfortable when my house is not completely clean.
	Our days seem to follow a definite routine such as eating meals at a regular time, etc.
Homebody	I would rather spend a quiet evening at home than go out to a party.
	I like parties where there is lots of music and talk. (Reverse scored)
	I would rather go to a sporting event than a dance.
	I am a homebody.

posit the conditions under which personality should and should not be a relevant explanatory variable. Indeed personality may be important only for high-involvement products and situations. It may also be that the use of standardized personality tests is inappropriate for studying consumer behavior. These tests were generally developed for measuring social or antisocial behavioral tendencies and were not meant to predict brand ownership.

Community Minded	I am an active member of more than one service organization.
	I do volunteer work for a hospital or service organization on a fairly regular basis.
	I like to work on community projects.
	I have personally worked in a political campaign or for a candidate or an issue.
Credit User	I buy many things with a credit card or a charge card.
	I like to pay cash for everything I buy. (Reverse scored)
	It is good to have charge accounts.
	To buy anything, other than a house or a car, on credit is unwise. (Reverse scored)
Cook	I love to cook.
	I am a good cook.
	I love to bake and frequently do.
	I am interested in spices and seasonings.
Self-Designated Opinion Leader	My friends or neighbors often come to me for advice.
	I sometimes influence what my friends buy.
	People come to me more often than I go to them for information about brands.
Information Seeker	I often seek out the advice of my friends regarding which brand to buy.
	I spend a lot of time talking with my friends about products and brands.
	My neighbors or friends usually give me good advice on what brands to buy in the grocery store.
New Brand Tryer	When I see a new brand on the shelf I often buy it just to see what it's like.
	I often try new brands before my friends and neighbors do.
	I like to try new and different things.

SOURCE: William D. Wells and Douglas J. Tigert (1971), "Activities, Interests, and Opinions," *Journal of Advertising Research*, 11 (Aug.), pp. 27–35.

PSYCHOGRAPHICS

The concept of psychographics emerged in the study of consumer behavior in the late 1960s.[42] Its roots are in the attempt to relate personality to consumer behavior and the frustration with the limited explanatory power of standardized personality tests. Much of the problem may be that these standardized personality tests were not designed for purposes of understanding consumer behavior but rather for such diagnostic purposes as career counseling or assessing abnormal behavior.

Psychographics, in its broadest sense, has been defined by Wells[43] as a quantitative research tool intended to place consumers on psychological, as distinguished from demographic, dimensions. This all-encompassing definition accurately reflects the current use of psychographic research, which includes such diverse categories of variables as Activities, Interests, and Opinions (often called *AIO*s), personality traits, lifestyle measures, and attitude measures.

Although the purposes of psychographics research are broad, the basic premise is to relate personality-type variables (relatively stable personal characteristics) to consumer behavior. Wells sees this new "blend" of research combining "the objectivity of the personality inventory with the rich, consumer-oriented, descriptive detail of the qualitative motivation research investigation."[44] Thus, psychographics is an outgrowth and combination of earlier work on personality and motivation.

A portion of a psychographic inventory is shown in Exhibit 12–3. The respondent taking the inventory would answer by checking the level of agreement or disagreement with each item using a six-point scale that runs from 1 (*definitely agree*) to 6 (*definitely disagree*). The individual would then be "profiled" by adding the scores for each factor—how child-oriented, how fashion conscious, and so on.

The basic difference between this "psychographic" inventory and the "personality" inventories discussed earlier is that the factors measured are much more relevant to consumer behavior: "fashion conscious" instead of such factors in the Edwards test as "dependency," "compliance," or "exhibitionism." The factors selected for study actually vary considerably depending on the product category. The range of factors is suggested by Plummer's nonexhaustive list in Exhibit 12–4.

Psychographic Segmentation

Psychographics have been used chiefly as a means of segmenting markets. Psychographic analysis has been conducted as an adjunct to demographic analysis in order to better profile users vs. nonusers or heavy users vs. light users of a product. Some examples of psychographic segmentation follow.

Soft Drink Segmentation: Canada Dry   The strength of the Canada Dry franchise is in the "mixer" (with hard liquor) positioning in the beverage market, although its products, particularly ginger ale, also are drunk as soft drinks. Some time ago, in order to better understand its segmentation, Canada Dry and its agency, Grey Advertising, conducted psychographic research that identified five segments in the soft-drink market: (1) Adult—Morally Concerned, (2) Adult—Socially Concerned, (3) Adult—Pleasure Oriented, (4) Adult & Teen—Low Calorie Concerned, and (5) Other Teens. These segments had varying demographic profiles coinciding with the distinct psychographic profiles. The value of the research, however, is in the analysis of the soft-drink and mixer usage patterns.

- Although soft-drink consumption in general is roughly proportional to each segment's share of the total population, there are major differences in mixer consumption.

- Usage of mixers is extremely low for the Adult—Morally Concerned segment (35 percent of population but only 7 percent of mixer consumption) but correspondingly very high for the Adult—Socially Concerned segment (19 percent of population but 39 percent of mixers) and the Adult—Pleasure Oriented segment (24 percent of population but 44 percent of mixers).

- Ginger ale, in particular, is very heavily used as a mixer by the Adult—Socially Concerned segment.

The marketing implications for Canada Dry are reasonably straightforward. As a brand it is not competing so much in the soft-drink category as in the mixer category. Two segments (Adult—Socially Concerned and Adult—Pleasure Oriented) account for 83 percent of its sales as a mixer. Its advertising, therefore, should be geared to these segments, with appeals relevant to the motivations of these segments. Canada Dry, of course, could consider repositioning its products more as soft drinks than mixers, but this would probably be a difficult task.

EXHIBIT 12–4
VARIATION IN FACTORS FOR PSYCHOGRAPHIC STUDY

Activities	Interests	Opinions
Work	Family	Themselves
Hobbies	Home	Social Issues
Social Events	Job	Politics
Vacation	Community	Business
Entertainment	Recreation	Economics
Club Membership	Fashion	Education
Community	Food	Products
Shopping	Media	Future
Sports	Achievements	Culture

SOURCE: Joseph T. Plummer (1974), "The Concept and Application of Life Style Segmentation," *Journal of Marketing*, 38 (Jan.), pp. 33–37.

Television Viewer Segmentation   Psychographics have also been used to segment the television-viewer market.[45] By so doing it may then be possible to develop and offer different kinds of programs for different audience segments.

Exhibit 12–5 presents research results indicating the major psychographic segments among adult females. As can be seen, the "family-oriented" seg-

EXHIBIT 12–5
SOME PSYCHOGRAPHIC SEGMENTS OF ADULT FEMALE TELEVISION VIEWERS[a]

Segment	Segment Descriptors	Television Viewing Profile
Family Oriented	Highest proportion of adult women with young children. Average age of 35. Interested in a broad range of home and family activities. High on need for maintaining family ties.	High on viewing of children's programs, drama and movies.
Home and Community Oriented	Married homemakers with an average age of 44. Interested in home and community affairs. Oriented to maintaining family ties and social stimulation.	High on viewing of soap operas and religious programming.
Art and Cultural Activity Oriented	Highly educated and either pursuing a professional or managerial career or married to a manager or professional. Average age is 44. Interested in a broad range of intellectually upscale activities, especially the classic arts.	High viewing for theatrical performances, musicals, documentaries, news, and specials. Low on viewing of adventure programs, science fiction and soap operas.
Elderly Concerns	Oldest age segment (average of 61 years). Relatively few interests but need for social integration and belonging in the absence of direct interpersonal contact.	Highest levels of viewing of all segments for dramas, soap operas, game shows and religious programming. Higher than average viewing for news, talk and variety shows. Low on viewing of sports, movies and specials.
Cosmopolitan Self Enrichment	Extremely high socioeconomic profile. Average age of 36. Diverse patterns of intellectual and cultural interests; physically active; high need for intellectual stimulation.	Low on overall television viewing and selective. Oriented toward theatrical performances, news, documentaries and talk shows.
Detached	Low socioeconomic profile. Average age of 46. Extremely few interests and activities. Low need for intellectual stimulation or interpersonal contact.	Low on overall television viewing. Relatively non-discriminating by type of program. Viewing oriented toward crime drama, movies, science fiction and soap operas.

[a]These groups represent about 90% of adult females.

SOURCE: Ronald E. Frank and Marshall G. Greenberg (1980), *The Public's Use of Television* (Beverly Hills, Cal.: Sage).

ment has quite a different profile from the "cosmopolitan self enrichment" segment, although they are approximately the same age. The interest patterns are distinct and the types of television shows watched are divergent.

Psychographics and Advertising

Psychographics may be of value in the selection of advertising media and the design of advertising appeals. For example, in the Canada Dry psychographic segmentation, it would seem that quite different appeals would be appropriate for the "Morally-Conscious" and the "Pleasure Concerned" segments. Because these segments have different demographic profiles, different media should be used to reach them.

The reasons for using different advertising appeals and different media for various psychographic segments are especially apparent from the contrasts in Exhibit 12–6, which show the profiles of heavy users of eye makeup and of shortening. These groups of women have quite distinct demographic profiles and psychographic profiles, as you might expect. The heavy user of eye makeup is younger and better educated, as well as fashion conscious, social, with wide horizons and a dislike of housekeeping. The heavy user of shortening by contrast, is middle-aged, child oriented, and a homebody, with a liking for cooking and housekeeping.

The implications for media selection are clear—fashion magazines and TV shows like the *Tonight Show* and adventure programs should be selected for eye makeup advertising, and home magazines and TV shows like soap operas and sit-coms for shortening advertising. The advertisements themselves should depict the eye-makeup consumer in a cosmopolitan, social environment, whereas the shortening consumer should be depicted in the kitchen with her children eagerly gathered around.

Psychographics and Product Positioning

Research on psychographics may also be of value in positioning products within an overall product category or in finding new product ideas. In research on males in the beer market for Anheuser-Busch, for example, Ackoff and Emshoff report four dominant psychographic profiles of beer drinkers.[46]

- *The reparative drinker*. A middle-aged person who has not achieved all of his aspirations and has sacrificed some of them in the interests of others, particularly spouse and children. For this person, most drinking occurs at the end of the work day (rather than weekends) and is seen as a self reward. This person is a controlled drinker who seldom becomes drunk.

- *The social drinker*. A younger adult who believes that achieving his aspirations requires the approval and support of others. Most drinking is on weekends, holidays, and vacations in larger groups and is associated with friendliness and acceptance of and by others. Also generally a controlled drinker but less so than the reparative drinker.

- *The indulgent drinker*. Of any age and considers himself an irretrievable

EXHIBIT 12–6
PSYCHOGRAPHIC PROFILES OF HEAVY USERS OF EYE MAKEUP VERSUS SHORTENING

Heavy User of Eye Makeup	Heavy User of Shortening
DEMOGRAPHICS	**DEMOGRAPHICS**
Young, well-educated, lives in metropolitan areas	Middle-aged, medium to large family, lives outside metropolitan areas
PRODUCT USE	**PRODUCT USE**
Also a heavy user of liquid face makeup, lipstick, hair spray, perfume, cigarettes, gasoline	Also a heavy user of flour, sugar, canned lunch meat, cooked pudding, catsup
MEDIA PREFERENCES	**MEDIA PREFERENCES**
Fashion magazines, *Tonight Show*, adventure programs	*Reader's Digest*, daytime TV serials, family situation TV comedies
PSYCHOGRAPHICS	**PSYCHOGRAPHICS**
Fashion Conscious	*Cook*
I often try the latest hairdo styles when they change	I love to bake and frequently do
I usually have one or more outfits that are of the very latest style	I save recipes from newspaper and magazines
An important part of my life and activities is dressing smartly	The kitchen is my favorite room
I enjoy looking through fashion magazines	
	Like Housekeeping
Wide Horizons	I enjoy most forms of housework
I would like to take a trip around the world	Usually I have regular days for washing, cleaning, etc. around the house
I would like to spend a year in London or Paris	I am uncomfortable when my house is not completely clean
Social	*Child Oriented*
I like parties where there is lots of music and talk	I try to arrange my home for my children's convenience
I do more things socially than do most of my friends	Our family is a close-knit group
	I spend a lot of time with my children talking about their activities, friends, and problems
Dislikes Housekeeping	*Homebody*
I would like to have a maid to do the housework	I would rather spend a quiet evening at home than go out to a party

SOURCE: Based on William D. Wells and Arthur D. Beard (1973), "Personality and Consumer Behavior," in *Consumer Behavior: Theoretical Sources*, ed. Scott Ward and Thomas S. Robertson (Englewood Cliffs, N.J.: Prentice-Hall), p. 195.

failure; life is viewed as tragic. Drinking is associated with escape and is often done alone. This drinker is the least controlled and is most likely to become drunk or an alcoholic.

- *The oceanic drinker*. Similar to the indulgent drinker but is more likely to blame himself for failure rather than others. Also a heavy and noncontrolled drinker but more likely to drink with others than alone.

This segmentation was of value to Anheuser-Busch in that further surveys, according to Ackoff and Emshoff, revealed that the company's brands—Michelob, Budweiser, and Busch—appealed to different personality segments, despite some overlap. This allowed Anheuser-Busch to specify further the target markets by each existing brand or by new brands. The company was able, therefore, to keep its brands positioned relatively separately in the market and to avoid cannibalization (stealing sales from your own brands).

Psychographic research has also been used by General Foods in the dog-food market (in order to characterize owners rather than dogs) and to study which segments use which types of dog food.[47] Two of the more interesting segments are the "family mutt" and "baby substitute." Let us briefly characterize each segment and the implications for consumer behavior.

- *Family Mutt*. This segment, about 25 percent of dog owners, is composed of people of lower income who own one average-sized dog, often the children's dog. There is little adult interest in the dog, and it is perceived as playful and no bother. This segment is heavy in its usage of dry dog food and low-priced canned dog food. There is little interest in nutrition.
- *Baby Substitute*. This segment, about 10 percent of dog owners, is composed of people of higher income who own one very small, older dog, often an adult's dog (frequently a woman's). There is high attachment to the dog, and it is viewed as fragile, a finicky eater, and an indoor animal. This segment is heavy on usage of premium dog foods—high-priced canned, semi-moist, and biscuits.

The implications for a dog-food manufacturer are interesting. Different types of dog food may be bought by different segments of people. The "family mutt" segment may be a dominant market for twenty-five-pound bags of Purina Dog Chow but not for Alpo or Gainesburgers (semi-moist). By contrast, the "baby substitute" segment may be a dominant market for premium items and new products. In fact, it is suggested that General Foods' introduction of Cycle dog food was, in part, based on this research. The Cycle concept of four types of dog food based on the age of the dog was geared to the baby substitutes as one of the segments. Results have seemingly been positive.[48]

Limitations of Psychographics

As with all theoretical perspectives, psychographics may lead to an incremental gain in our understanding of consumer behavior, but it is by no means a sufficient explanatory theory by itself. In fact, although motivation and personality approaches have many adherents, they also have critics. It is therefore important to point out some limitations.[49]

First, psychographics may sometimes have predictive value in explaining consumer behavior and sometimes not. In general, the closer the degree to which the psychographic items relate to the behavior being studied, the better the explanatory power. By the same token, however, the level of insight

EXHIBIT 12–7
HOW TO CONDUCT A PSYCHOGRAPHICS STUDY

The typical psychographics study is conducted in the following sequence of stages:

1. Develop a questionnaire containing relevant psychographic dimensions, such as those in Exhibit 12–4. The dimensions selected will be those which are relevant to the product category and behavior under study. These may have been determined based on a pilot research project. Each dimension is measured by a number of questions to which respondents indicate agreement or disagreement, usually on a six-point scale. For example, if *fashion consciousness* is a relevant dimension, then it is measured by consumers agreeing or disagreeing with such statements as, "I usually have one or more outfits that are of the very latest style." Include also demographic and product usage questions to be related to the psychographic segments eventually derived.

2. After surveying consumers the results of the questionnaire are analyzed. The researcher may conduct a *factor analysis*[a] at this point—a procedure whose purpose is to reduce the set of questions to a summary set of factors or dimensions. This might be done to check that the questions used actually related to the dimensions expected (e.g., fashion consciousness). Or if the researcher did not have dimensions in mind originally but simply used a set of relevant questions, then a factor analysis after the fact would reveal the underlying dimensions.

3. Each respondent's scores on the factors are then computed. Within each factor the researcher could also examine how each question "loads" (or is correlated with) the factor for each respondent.

4. Next respondents are "clustered" into segments that are relatively homogeneous using a *cluster analysis*[b] program. This procedure splits the sample into psychographic segments (clusters) such that all members of a given cluster are relatively similar in terms of their factor scores and such that each successive group is relatively dissimilar when compared to all other groups.

5. These clusters are then labeled based on the factors which most typify each cluster. Labels such as "baby substitute" or "family mutt" to characterize segments are ultimately selected by the researcher.

6. Finally, the segments are cross-tabulated with demographic and usage variables so as to examine their usage behavior and to help characterize who these psychographic segments are.

---

[a]For details on factor analysis, refer to Paul E. Green and Donald S. Tull (1978), *Research for Marketing Decisions*, 4th ed. (Englewood Cliffs, N.J.: Prentice-Hall), Ch. 13.
[b]Green and Tull, Ch. 13.

goes down. For example, it is hardly surprising to find that the innovators for new clothing styles are also those who score high on the psychographic dimension of fashion consciousness.

Second are questions of validity and reliability—especially if a new psychographic questionnaire is developed for each product category. It may be that the psychographic dimensions do not measure what we think they are measuring and are therefore not valid.[50] Or the items may be unreliable in not uniformly measuring a single dimension, or people may answer differently at different times. These issues of reliability and validity are common in all research but more severe if the same test is not being replicated and refined over time.

A final limitation is that the analyses used (as detailed in Exhibit 12–7) lead researchers to interpret and label the psychographic segments or clusters that are identified. This is appropriate, but different researchers have sometimes interpreted the same results quite differently. Yet the labels used, such as "baby substitute," tend to dominate thinking about the segments, even if the segments are fairly complex in their composition.

SUMMARY

In this chapter we have reviewed the parallel theoretical streams of *motivation* and *personality* and the development of *psychographics* as a convergence of these theories applied to consumer behavior.

We have seen that the theoretical work of Freud provided the basis for many developments in the field of motivation. Freud's emphasis was on the unconscious nature of much of human motivation, together with his belief that behavior can be traced back to a small number of physiological instincts (especially sex and aggression). Other motivation theorists included the neo-Freudians, such as Adler, Fromm, and Horney, who suggested important modifications of Freudian theory, as well as Maslow, who developed the "hierarchy of needs" and Lewin, who developed "field theory." Motivation research in marketing has relied heavily on Freudian theory and projective techniques which attempt to discover the "hidden meanings" of products.

The concept of *personality*, as used by psychologists, is meant to denote a consistent pattern of responses by the individual. Personality assessment is usually based on traits: how the individual compares with other people on such traits as sociability, dominance, or exhibitionism. Standardized personality inventories have generally revealed limited relationships to consumer behavior.

Psychographics refers to the development of psychological measures for assessing consumer behavior. Psychographics is an outgrowth of motivation theory and of personality theory. Psychographic tests have been developed and found to be of value for market segmentation, advertising, and product positioning purposes. The key to a psychographics test is that the variables selected are related fairly closely to consumer behavior. This contrasts with the variables or traits used in personality inventories, which are meant to assess more basic and consequential patterns of behavior, such as choice of a marriage partner or a career. Psychographics today represent an important explanatory perspective for understanding consumer behavior.

KEY CONCEPTS

psychographics	ego	pleasure principle
instincts	superego	reality principle
defense mechanisms	displacement	identification
projection	life space	rationalization
projective techniques	psychological field	tension
physiological needs	traits	valence
psychogenic needs	hierarchy of needs	factor analysis
motivation	field theory	cluster analysis
id	personality	

DISCUSSION QUESTIONS

1. In what ways can psychographic research be of value in product positioning?
2. Describe the process normally followed in conducting psychographic research.
3. What value do psychographic inventories have over personality inventories?
4. What are the marketing implications of the Canada Dry psychographic segmentation?
5. What are the implications and limitations of Freudian theory for marketing?
6. Discuss the major neo-Freudian theories and hypothesize some marketing implications.
7. Create a psychographic inventory to assess the following factors: pleasure in shopping, orientation to physical exercise, novelty-seeking, and relaxation needs. Prepare a set of hypotheses about the relationships of these factors to consumer behavior in the following product categories: clothes, furniture, and video systems.
8. What is the theory of personality traits? Why might this theory fail to predict consumer behavior? Even if this theory did predict consumer behavior, why might it not be useful for market segmentation?

NOTES

1. For a discussion of the explanatory value of demographics, see Ronald E. Frank (1968), "Market Segmentation Research: Findings and Implications," in *Applications of the Sciences in Marketing Management*, ed. Frank M. Bass, Charles W. King, and Edgar A. Pessemier (New York: Wiley), pp. 39–68.
2. Joel B. Cohen (1967), "An Interpersonal Orientation to the Study of Consumer Behavior," *Journal of Marketing Research*, 4 (Aug.), pp. 270–78.

3. See Jerome Kernan (1971), "The CAD Instrument in Behavioral Diagnosis," in *Proceedings, Association for Consumer Research*, ed. David M. Gardner (Assn. for Consumer Research), pp. 307–12; Jon P. Noerager (1979), "An Assessment of CAD—A Personality Instrument Developed Specifically for Marketing Research," *Journal of Marketing Research*, 16 (Feb.), pp. 53–59; and Joel B. Cohen and Ellen Golden (1972), "Informational Social Influence and Product Evaluation," *Journal of Applied Psychology*, 50 (Feb.), pp. 54–59.

4. Henry A. Murray (1938), *Explorations in Personality* (New York: Oxford Univ. Press), pp. 530–31.

5. Abraham H. Maslow (1943), "A Theory of Human Motivation," *Psychological Review*, 50, pp. 370–96.

6. Kurt Lewin (1935), *A Dynamic Theory of Personality* (New York: McGraw-Hill).

7. For a discussion of field theory and its application to consumer behavior, see Harold H. Kassarjian (1973), "Field Theory in Consumer Behavior," in *Consumer Behavior: Theoretical Sources*, ed. Scott Ward and Thomas S. Robertson (Englewood Cliffs, N.J.: Prentice-Hall), pp. 118–40.

8. Ernest Dichter (1964), *Handbook of Consumer Motivations* (New York: McGraw-Hill), p. 67.

9. Harry Henry (1958), *Motivational Research* (New York: Ungar), p. 27.

10. Henry A. Murray (1938).

11. Gordon Allport (1955), *Becoming: Basic Considerations for a Psychology of Personality* (New Haven, Conn.: Yale Univ. Press).

12. Gordon Allport (1961), *Pattern and Growth in Personality* (New York: Holt, Rinehart & Winston).

13. For details on factor analysis, refer to Paul E. Green and Donald S. Tull (1978), *Research for Marketing Decisions*, 4th ed. (Englewood Cliffs, N.J.: Prentice-Hall), Ch. 13.

14. R. B. Cattell, D. R. Saunders, and G. F. Stice (1950), *The 16 Personality Factor Questionnaire* (Champaign, Ill.: Inst. for Personality and Ability Testing).

15. T. W. Adorno, E. Frenkel-Brunswik, D. Levinson, and N. Sanford (1950), *The Authoritarian Personality* (New York: Harper).

16. Milton Rokeach (1960), *The Open and Closed Mind* (New York: Basic Books).

17. H. J. Eysenck and S. B. G. Eysenck (1964), *Manual of the Eysenck Personality Inventory* (London: Univ. of London Press).

18. J. B. Rotter (1966), "Generalized Expectancies for Internal Versus External Control of Reinforcement," *Psychological Monographs*, 80 (no. 609).

19. M. Zuckerman (1971), "Dimensions of Sensation Seeking," *Journal of Consulting and Clinical Psychology*, 36, pp. 45–52.

20. Harold H. Kassarjian and M. J. Sheffet (1981), "Personality and Consumer Behavior: An Update," in *Perspectives in Consumer Behavior*, 3rd ed. (Glenview, Ill.: Scott, Foresman), pp. 160–80.

21. Franklin B. Evans (1959), "Psychological and Objective Factors in the Prediction of Brand Choice," *Journal of Business*, 32, pp. 340–69.

22. Ralph Westfall (1962), "Psychological Factors in Predicting Product Choice," *Journal of Marketing*, 26 (Apr.), pp. 34–40.

23. William T. Tucker and John J. Painter (1961), "Personality and Product Use," *Journal of Applied Psychology*, 45 (Oct.), pp. 325–39.

24. Arthur Koponen (1960), "Personality Characteristics of Purchasers," *Journal of Advertising Research*, 1 (Sept.), pp. 6–12.

25. Mark I. Alpert (1972), "Personality and the Determinants of Product Choice," *Journal of Marketing Research*, 9 (Feb.), pp. 89–92.

26. Joel B. Cohen (1967).

27. Thomas S. Robertson (1967), "Determinants of Innovative Behavior," in *Proceedings of the American Marketing Association*, ed. Reed Moyer (American Marketing Assn.), pp. 328–32.

28. Thomas S. Robertson and James H. Myers (1969), "Personality Correlates of Opinion Leadership and Innovative Buying Behavior," *Journal of Marketing Research*, 6 (May), pp. 164–68.

29. Jacob Jacoby (1971), "Personality and Innovation Proneness," *Journal of Marketing Research*, 8, pp. 244–47.

30. See, for example, Johan Arndt (1967), "Role of Product-Related Conversations in the Diffusion of a New Product," *Journal of Marketing Research*, 4 (Aug.), pp. 291–95. See also William R. Darden and Fred D. Reynolds (1972), "Predicting Opinion Leadership for Men's Apparel Fashions," *Journal of Marketing Research*, 9 (Aug.), pp. 324–28.

31. See, for example, Jeffrey A. Barach (1967), "Self-Confidence and Reactions to Television Commercials," in *Risk Taking and Information Handling in Consumer Decisions*, ed. Donald F. Cox (Boston: Harvard Business School), pp. 428–41. See also M. Venkatesan (1968), "Personality and Persuasibility in Consumer Decision Making," *Journal of Advertising Research*, 8 (March), pp. 39–45.

32. E. Laird Landon, Jr. (1974), "Self Concept, Ideal Self Concept, and Consumer Purchase Intentions," *Journal of Consumer Research*, 1 (Sept.), pp. 44–51. For a recent critical review, see M. Joseph Sirgy (1982), "Self-Concept in Consumer Behavior: A Critical Review," *Journal of Consumer Research*, 9 (Dec.), pp. 287–300.

33. See, for example, A. E. Birdwell (1968), "A Study of the Influence of Image Congruence on Consumer Choice," *Journal of Business*, 41 (Jan.), pp. 76–88.

34. Edward L. Grubb and Gregg Hupp (1968), "Perception of Self, Generalized Stereotypes, and Brand Selection," *Journal of Marketing Research*, 5 (Feb.), pp. 58–63.

35. Ira J. Dolich (1969), "Congruence Relationships Between Self Images and Product Brands," *Journal of Marketing Research*, 6 (Feb.), pp. 80–84.

36. Charles M. Schaninger and Donald Sciglimpaglia (1981), "The Influence of Cognitive Personality Traits and Demographics on Consumer Information Acquisition," *Journal of Consumer Research*, 8 (Sept.), pp. 208–16.

37. Lawrence M. Lamont and William J. Lundstrom (1977), "Identifying Successful Industrial Salesmen by Personality and Personal Characteristics," *Journal of Marketing Research*, 14 (Nov.), pp. 517–29.

38. Stewart W. Bither and Ira J. Dolich (1972), "Personality as a Determinant Factor in Store Choice," in *Proceedings of the Third Annual Conference*, ed. M. Venkatesan (Assn. for Consumer Research), pp. 9–19.

39. John J. Burnett (1981), "Psychographic and Demographic Characteristics of Blood Donors," *Journal of Consumer Research*, 8 (June), pp. 62–66.

40. Robert B. Settle, Pamela L. Alreck, and John W. Glasheen (1977), "Individual Time Orientation and Consumer Life Style," in *Advances in Consumer Research*, ed. H. Keith Hunt, Vol. 5 (Assn. for Consumer Research), pp. 315–19.

41. Harold H. Kassarjian and M. J. Sheffet (1981).

42. For an historical account of the development of psychographics, see William D. Wells, ed. (1974), *Life Style and Psychographics* (Chicago: American Marketing Assn.), pp. 11–30.

43. William D. Wells (1975), "Psychographics: A Critical Review," *Journal of Marketing Research*, 12 (May), pp. 196–213.

44. William D. Wells (1975), p. 196.

45. Ronald E. Frank and Marshall G. Greenberg (1980), *The Public's Use of Television* (Beverly Hills, Cal.: Sage).

46. Russell L. Ackoff and James R. Emshoff (1975), "Advertising Research at Anheuser-Busch, Inc. (1968–74)," *Sloan Management Review*, 16 (Winter), pp. 1–15.

47. Harvard Business School, "General Foods: Opportunities in the Dog Food Market" (Boston: Harvard Business School), revised 1978.

48. Peter W. Bernstein (1978), "Psychographics Is Still an Issue on Madison Avenue," *Fortune* (Jan. 16), p. 80.

49. For an evaluation of psychographics, see William D. Wells (1975).

50. For a recent critical review, see John L. Lastovicka (1982), "On the Validation of Lifestyle Traits: A Review and Illustration," *Journal of Marketing Research*, 19 (Feb.), pp. 126–38.

13 Psychological Economics

In this chapter we survey the contributions of psychological economics to the study of consumer behavior. First, we examine the rise of the affluent consumer and modern forms of consumer wealth as the motivating forces behind the field of study. Next, we review important theories of demand to establish a perspective on the contributions of economics to consumer behavior. Third, we describe and illustrate the addition of consumer-sentiment variables to economic models of demand. Finally, we summarize recent findings of consumer experiments on the assumptions of economic models.

Two dimensions identify the major differences between economics and psychology and serve to highlight the topics of interest in psychological economics. These are the unit of analysis *and the* method of measurement. *The unit of analysis divides roughly into studies of the individual or of large populations. The two major methods of measurement are observation of behavior and self reports about behavior. Exhibit 13–1 identifies the topics of psychological economics as well as the principal domains of its sister disciplines—psychology and economics.*

Psychologists usually begin their study with self-report measures at the individual unit of analysis. Psychoanalysis is the extreme case of this point of view. Economists, on the other hand, prefer observable measures of large populations.

These philosophical preferences represent points of departure for the two professions. Kenneth Boulding has stated the economist's position clearly: "It is the behavior of commodities not the behavior of people which is the prime focus of interest in economic studies."[1] George Katona summarized the psychologist's point of view: "It is the individual who represents the starting point of psychology. . . . it is the individual who thinks, feels, and learns."[2]

Psychological economics *takes over the middle ground left open by these competing philosophies. It adds the useful concepts of* **consumer sentiments** *to the classic observations of aggregate economic analysis. It studies individual consumer behavior in the laboratory to validate the assumptions of economics and to enrich its theory with concepts from psychology. George Katona was the founding father of the field, and his Survey Research Center at the University of Michigan was responsible for the development of systematic studies of consumer sentiment. The development of consumer experiments is a newer direction for psychological economics. Beginning with studies of Vernon Smith in the late 1950s, many of the fundamental assumptions made by economists concerning the behavior of individuals in free markets have been subjected to rigorous laboratory testing. The results provide finer insights into the working of these markets.*

THE AFFLUENT CONSUMER

Before the nineteenth century consumers had little discretionary spending power. What little income was available to the average consumer went to securing the basic necessities of life. Food was quite simply the most important component of a consumer's budget, as it remains today in many undeveloped countries. Having little or no discretionary income, consumers were not a source of direct investment in the wealth of a country. Human resources were not considered a source of the wealth of a nation.

Since consumers did not have the means to make investments, their willingness to invest was of no concern to economists. It should be no surprise that the study of psychological economics, first expressed in Katona's work with consumer sentiments, grew with the rise of the affluent consumer and the creation of wealth by the average family.

Katona argued "the sine qua non of a mass consumption economy is a substantial increase in the average family's income together with a great change in the distribution of income."[3] In the twentieth century the *income revolution* has produced a fundamental change in both the distribution of wealth and its forms in developed countries like the United States, Japan, and Western Europe. The extent of this income revolution in the U.S. is portrayed in Exhibit 13–2.

The distribution of effective buying income among four groups called the *Wealthy*, the *Affluent*, the *Strugglers*, and the *Poor* reflects their importance in the economy. The exhibit shows the percent of households in the United

EXHIBIT 13–1
THE TOPICS OF PSYCHOLOGICAL ECONOMICS

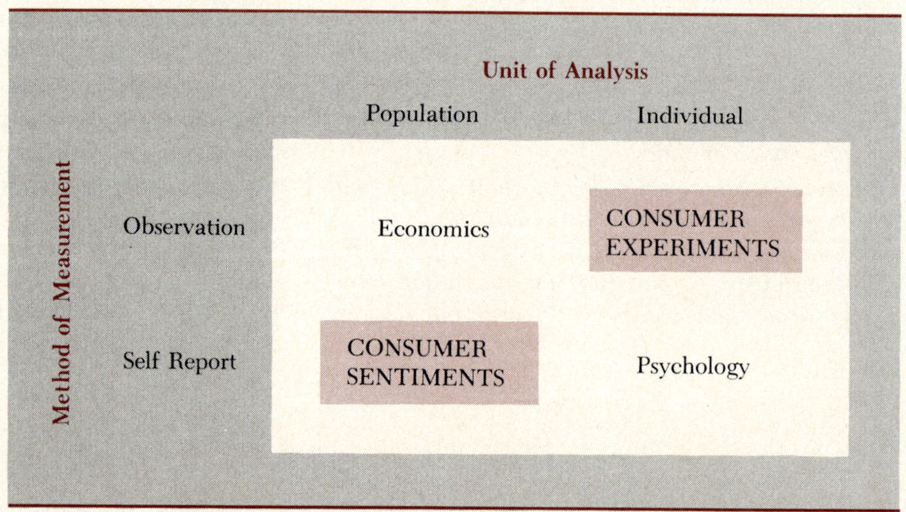

States that fit each of these classifications and the percent of total effective buying income for which each group accounts, according to an analysis of the 1980 census conducted by Market Statistics, Inc. The point of real interest is neither that the top 8 percent—wealthy households—account for 22 percent of effective buying income nor that the bottom 15 percent—poor households—earn barely 3 percent of the buying income. It is rather that well over one half of U.S. households are affluent and account for over two thirds of the nation's buying power. It is this majority of consumers with an effective buying income between $15,000 and $50,000 that has significant discretionary spending power. It is this majority of consumers that has become a new moving force in the pattern of modern economic development.

In the nineteenth century, economists considered business investment the only source of wealth. Later, the government was added to the list of major sources of wealth. The rise of the affluent consumer brought the average household boldly into the creation of wealth through its investments in durable goods. Since World War II consumers have come to have an impact on the nation's wealth nearly equal to the investments of business or government. Consumer investments in transportation, housing, education, and securities are even more volatile than business investments, as recent history has reaffirmed. The size and the volatility of consumer investments have focused attention on the factors governing the willingness of consumers to make such investments.

THEORIES OF DEMAND

Until recently economists have only theorized about how the individual consumer makes choices that provide satisfaction among goods. This theorizing quite naturally required some heroic assumptions about consumer behavior.

EXHIBIT 13–2
U.S. INCOME DISTRIBUTION: THE ROLE OF THE AFFLUENT CONSUMER

Groups	Boundaries	Households	Income
The Wealthy	$50,000 plus	8.0%	21.9%
The Affluent	$15,000–49,999	59.1	67.3
The Strugglers	$8,000–14,999	17.5	8.0
The Poor	$7,999 or less	15.4	2.8

SOURCE : The percent distribution of households and of effective buying income is based on 1980 census data, provided as a special service by Market Statistics, Inc., New York, July, 1983.

Assumptions

First, economists assumed individuals **behave rationally.** Consumers make only those choices that are best suited to their goals, recognizing their budget constraints and earning power. Second, economists assumed that the individual weighs all available alternatives and chooses the one that **maximizes his or her utility.** This assumption presupposes that the consumer has specific **preferences** for goods and services that are **consistent** among the alternatives. Next, economists assumed the consumer has complete knowledge of all the means available to satisfy wants—the assumption of **perfect information.** Finally, they assumed material **wants to be insatiable.** The consumer always prefers more of a desirable product or service to less.

Classical Utility Theory

Given the assumptions, the classical *theory of utility* followed naturally. Total utility, or satisfaction derived from the expenditure of income, increases as additional units of goods and services are consumed, but at a diminishing rate. Marshall theorized that it is this marginal or additional utility that an individual derives from a product that determines the price he or she will pay for it.[4] **Marginal utility** is the subjective value to the consumer of the next or incremental unit of a good.

A complete modern statement of classical utility theory is found in Theil.[5] Designating **n** the number of commodities and **q** the quantities bought during a certain time, the consumer behaves in such a way as to maximize a utility function:

$$u(\mathbf{q}) = u(\mathbf{q}_1, \ldots, \mathbf{q}_n),$$

subject to a budget constraint:

$$\sum_{i=1}^{n} \mathbf{p}_i\mathbf{q}_i = \mathbf{m},$$

where

    $\mathbf{p}_1, \ldots, \mathbf{p}_n$ are the prices of the n commodities,
    $\mathbf{q}_1, \ldots, \mathbf{q}_n$ are the quantities consumed, and
    m is the budget (or income).

Consequently, the economist arrives at an equilibrium where the theoretical behavior of the individual consumer is a function of the quantity of a good that could be purchased at a given price, his or her utility schedule, and the budget constraint. A market demand curve is derived by aggregating over individual utility schedules. Typically, the total market demand for a good **Q** is plotted as a function of its price **P** with the understanding that all other prices and consumer incomes are held constant. The resulting "law" of the negatively sloping consumer-demand function is one of the fundamental postulates of economics. This theorizing about individual behavior gave rise to countless studies of the relationship between aggregate quantities consumed as a function of the observed market prices of the goods.

The key to the successful application of the classical economic theory of utility to real world problems is the use of aggregate quantities. Summed over a consumer population the classical demand schedule can be estimated for any class of products or services. It is usually well behaved for aggregates of goods and consumers. The classical demand schedule thus applies to *total market demand.* It is useful in determining the change in market quantities that will accompany a change in average price. It is of little use in estimating which brand will be selected from among a group of substitutable goods offered at different retail prices. For example, classical demand theory helps explain the share of consumer income spent on toothpaste, but gives little clue as to why some consumers always buy Crest, while others prefer Ultrabrite.

The concept of **price elasticity** was developed to explain changes in total demand due to changes in price. The elasticity of demand with respect to price is simply a ratio of the percent change in quantity expected from a given percent change in average price. If this ratio is greater than 1.0 it suggests a change in price will yield a more than proportional change in demand. This expectation is important to suppliers of products and services alike. If airlines *decrease* their average price between city-pairs by 20 percent, management expects demand to *increase* proportionately more, so that total revenues will increase despite the drop in average ticket prices. Similarily, when price elasticity is greater than 1.0, an *increase* in price will produce a greater than proportional *decrease* in total demand. Elasticities are usually reported as absolute values disregarding their implicit negative sign.

price elasticity

Take the sale of new passenger cars as a detailed example. The effect of price on total market demand for new automobiles is illustrated in Exhibit 13–3. The quantity of new car demand (**Q**) appears on the lower axis, while the average price of new cars (**P**) is on the vertical axis. Demand levels at two points in time are compared. The model year 1975 is represented by Q_1 when 8.716 million new cars were sold. The (median) price of a new car in 1975 was $3907, identified at P_1.

The negatively sloping demand schedule is plotted with a price elasticity of 1.3 at a particular point, suggesting that a 10 percent increase in price will produce a 13 percent decrease in total demand *if the prices of all other goods and consumer incomes remain unchanged.*[6]

The (real) price of new passenger cars in the U.S. market rose approximately 10 percent between 1975 and 1981. If all other things were in fact equal and if the estimated price elasticity is correct, we should expect a decline in total market demand of 1.133 million units in this six-year period. The observed price increase of 10 percent appears as P_2 and the predicted decrease in market demand due to this price increase appears as Q_2 in Exhibit 13–3. If the assumptions were correct and the theory worked, a total of 7.583 million new cars would have been sold in the U.S. market in the 1981 model year. In fact, demand for new cars in 1981 was 8.533 million units. Fortunately for the economy, the prediction was off by more than a million units! Apparently, something is missing from the theory. To the economist, the "something" is *consumer income.*

income elasticity

Income elasticity is another concept from classical demand theory useful in the study of consumer behavior. It measures the percentage change in demand, given constant prices, expected from a percentage change in real income. Since real (deflated) income rose in the 1975–81 period, this has a moderating effect on the fall in demand predicted from a price increase.

The estimate by Lanzillotti of the income elasticity of demand for new cars was about + 3.0.[7] A 4-percent improvement in real income would have neutralized the observed price increase. In fact, real income increased by more

EXHIBIT 13–3
A MARKET DEMAND SCHEDULE FOR AUTOMOBILES

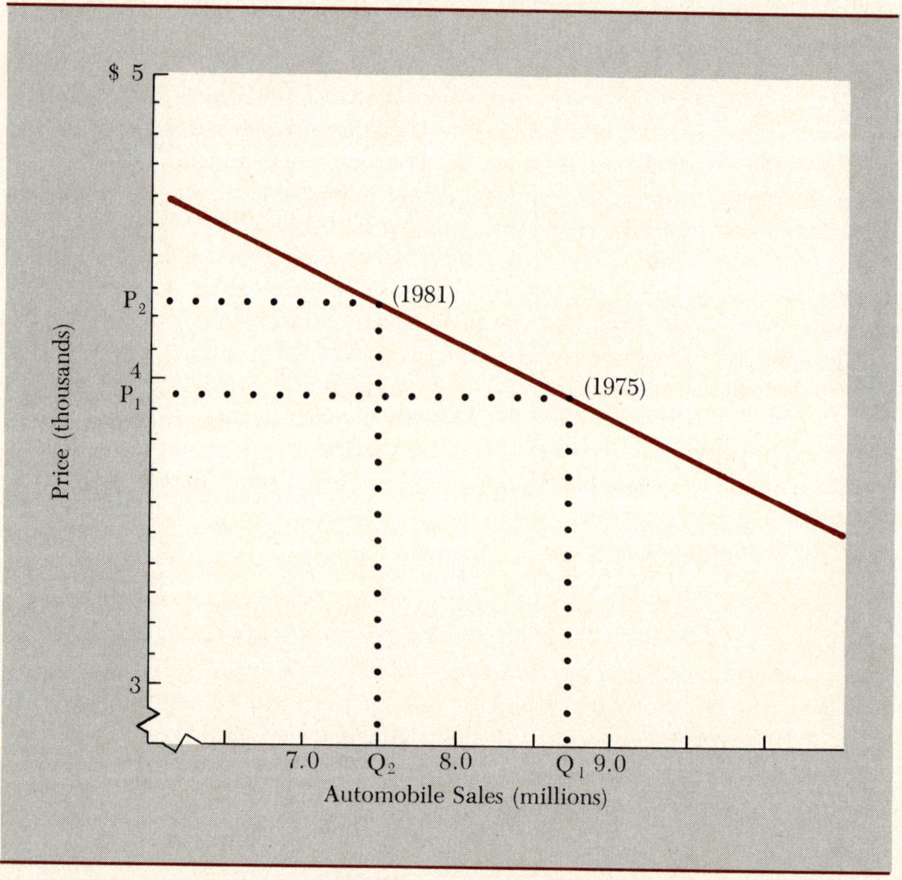

SOURCE : Based on Robert F. Lanzillotti (1961), "The Automobile Industry," in *The Structure of American Industry*, ed. Walter Adams, 3rd ed. (New York: Macmillan), p. 337 and (1980) *Ward's Automotive Yearbook* (Detroit), various pages. A more comprehensive analysis of the demand for automobiles is available in James Wetzel and George Hoffer (1982), "Consumer Demand for Automobiles: A Disaggregated Market Approach," *Journal of Consumer Research*, 9 (Sept.), pp. 195–99.

than 4 percent, yet new-car sales fell more than 2 percent. Indeed, the demand for new automobiles is a complex phenomenon! The psychological economist would agree and suggest the addition of measures of consumer sentiment to the model. Before making this change, it is important to examine the larger picture, the effect of national income on aggregate demand.

The Consumption Function

As income began steadily to rise for the average consumer in the first third of the twentieth century, the effect of this march toward affluence was incorporated into economic theory by John Maynard Keynes. He captured the relationship between steadily rising incomes and consumption at the aggregate level, as well as the imagination of free-world political leaders, with his **consumption function.**

It was Keynes who first proposed in his *The General Theory of Employment, Interest, and Money* that we "are disposed, as a rule and on the average, to increase our consumption as our income increases, but not by as much as the increase in our income."[8] A graphic representation of Keynes' consumption function appears in Exhibit 13–4. As current income increases from Y_1 to Y_2, consumption increases from C_1 to C_2.

This leads, "as a rule, to a greater *proportion* of income being saved as real income increases," or to what Keynes termed the **marginal propensity to consume.** This propensity is the amount of each extra dollar of income a community will spend on consumer goods.

marginal propensity to consume

The concept of the consumption function is given operational form with the expression:

$$C(t) = a + bY(t),$$

where

$C(t)$ is consumption expense in the current period (t),

a is the intercept, or minimum level of consumption,

b is the increase in consumption for each added dollar, and

$Y(t)$ is dollar income in the current period (t).

The slope term b is equivalent to the marginal propensity to consume. Keynes thought this value to be less than 1.0 and argued: "the stability of the economic system essentially depends on this rule prevailing in practice."[9] After publication of *The General Theory*, many empirical studies confirmed the existence of the consumption function and of a marginal propensity to consume less than 1.0.

Further exploration of Keynes' consumption function led to the search for variables other than current income that might explain the observed volatility of the marginal propensity to consume and the (apparent) stability of the average propensity to consume over the very long run. Researchers found, for example, quite different consumption functions for rural, village, and urban dwellers.[10] The former tended to consume less and save more than the latter, apparently in response to their different *relative* levels of current income compared on a cross-sectional basis. Duesenberry[11] and Modigliani[12] found further support for this **relative-income hypothesis** from time-series observations on consumption and income. Both found that consumption tends to be "sticky" over time. Once accustomed to a given level of consumption, in the face of either falling or rising income, consumers tend to maintain this customary standard of living. The relative-income hypothesis was thus tested in two ways. First, incomes relative to different community standards (rural vs. urban) were compared. Second, incomes relative to historical standards were compared, such as highest previous income.

The existence of a **permanent-income effect** was implied by the positive intercept (the *a* term in Keynes' consumption function) in Exhibit 13–4, which means people will spend (dissave) at a positive level even in the absence of current income. The permanent-income effect is best illustrated by the **life-cycle hypotheses.** Young families are more likely to dissave and bor-

EXHIBIT 13–4
THE CONSUMPTION FUNCTION

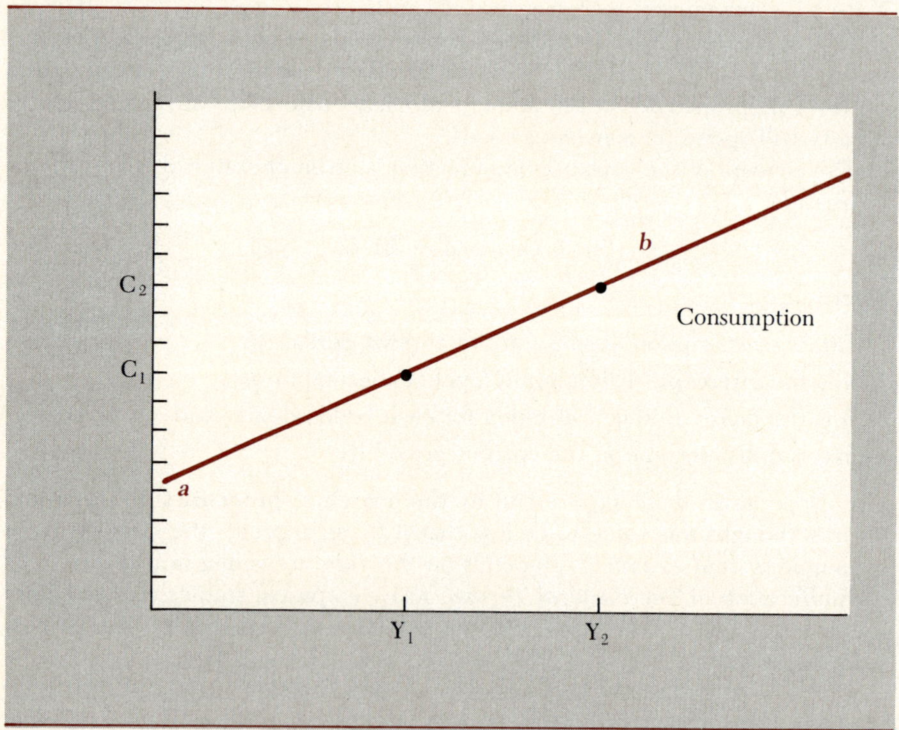

SOURCE : Based on John Maynard Keynes (1936), *The General Theory of Employment, Interest, and Money* (New York: Harcourt, Brace).

row against their future earnings, while older families will rely heavily on past accumulations. Both draw on an implicit permanent, or lifetime, income. These hypotheses were successfully tested by Friedman[13] and Modigliani,[14] who found permanent income a better predictor of consumption than current income.

Finally, several **stock-adjustment theories** have been advanced that suggest consumption is a dynamic process of adjusting current purchases to the stock of goods consumers have on hand. Consumers are influenced by their physical stocks or inventories of goods, by their psychological inventory of tastes and habits, and by their own human capital accumulations (education). Households are, after all, producers of utility as well as consumers of goods and services.[15]

The New Theory of Consumer Demand

Classical demand theory postulated simply that utility is a function of the *quantity* of a good consumed. The French Legionnaire stranded in the desert placed a high value on his first glass of water and derived enormous satisfaction from it because he had had none for days. Given a second glass of water, he derived perhaps somewhat less utility from it, and was willing to pay slightly less for it. With access to an increasing number of glasses of water his satisfaction from each additional quantity would continue to decline along with its marginal value. At some point, our Legionnaire would place no higher utility on water than you or I do and would be willing to buy it only to place in inventory for future needs.

Classical demand theory never bothered to consider the characteristics of water that provided the Legionnaire with satisfaction. In effect, the *quality* of the water was taken for granted! It was only the *quantity* that mattered. Classical demand viewed most consumer products in the same light. A glass of water is a glass of water. A tube of toothpaste is a tube of toothpaste. Since the benefit characteristics of goods and services were taken as given and homogeneous, little attention need be paid to the qualities of a good that provide utility.

The newer **multiattribute theory of consumer demand** follows from discoveries in the study of consumer behavior. It proposes that goods are also valued for the attributes they possess and that different products are different packages of these attributes. In his interpretative essay on the new theory, Ratchford[16] identified three scholars primarily responsible for this multiattribute theory of consumer demand. These are Lancaster,[17] Ironmonger,[18] and Baumol.[19]

The theory proposes that utility is a function not just of the quantity ($\mathbf{q}$) of goods consumed but also of the characteristics they possess ($\mathbf{z}$):

$$u(\mathbf{z}) = u(\mathbf{Bx}),$$

where $\mathbf{B}$ is an r $\times$ n matrix that transforms the n goods into r characteristics, subject to the traditional budget constraint. The characteristics $\mathbf{z}_1, \ldots, \mathbf{z}_r$

are the want-satisfying qualities, or attributes, of different brands of consumer goods. The transformation matrix **B** represents the current state of **consumption technology,** which may have either objective (miles per gallon) or subjective (style) dimensions. A consumption technology is a common set of characteristics that consumers can find in a given group of goods or are able themselves to produce through a combination of different goods. Goods with a common set of characteristics are **substitutes.** Different goods combined by the consumer to produce a consumption technology are **complements.**

Unlike classical demand theory, which provides little insight into why consumers choose purposefully among different brands within a substitute consumption technology, the new theory offers a direct and useful explanation of this behavior. Price continues to play an explicit role in choice, but it is modified by the consumer's perception of the *benefit characteristics* of brands that best meet his or her wants.

Ratchford illustrated this new theory using two attributes, or want-satisfying characteristics, of different brands of toothpaste. His example, with simplified hypothetical relationships among three brands of toothpaste popular in the U.S., is used here. Ratchford set up a consumption technology $z = Bx$ in such a way that three brands provided the following different levels of "whiteness" (z_1) and "decay prevention" (z_2).

	Brands of Toothpaste		
	x_1	x_2	x_3
Benefit Characteristic			
Whiteness (z_1)	4	3	1
Decay Prevention (z_2)	1	3	5
Cost Characteristic			
Price	$0.40	0.40	0.50
Units/Dollar	2.5	2.5	2.0

For illustration, think of x_1 as Ultrabrite, x_2 as Colgate, and x_3 as Crest. Each *unit* of Ultrabrite provides the consumer with 4 whiteness and 1 decay-prevention benefit characteristics. Each unit of Colgate, on the other hand, provides a balance of 3 whiteness and 3 decay-prevention characteristics, while Crest offers 1 and 5 of the benefit characteristics, respectively.

Suppose the prices per unit of each brand are respectively $0.40, $0.40, and $0.50. The amount of each benefit characteristic a consumer may obtain per dollar is determined by the units per dollar of each brand multiplied by the number of benefits it offers on each characteristic. At $0.40 per unit of Ultrabrite, a consumer may buy 2.5 units of that brand. Ultrabrite offers 4 whiteness benefits per unit, so the consumer acquires 10 of these (2.5 units × 4 benefits) per dollar. At the same time, Ultrabrite offers 1 decay-prevention benefit per unit. Thus, at 2.5 units per dollar, the consumer acquires 2.5 decay-prevention benefits per dollar. In the same fashion, benefits per dollar (z/$) on each characteristic may be computed for the other two brands. These are plotted in Exhibit 13–5.

The lines connecting the three brands form what Lancaster called an **efficiency frontier,** because these lines define the maximum combinations of benefits the consumer can obtain from a given expenditure. If these benefit characteristics are taken to be linear among the different brands, the shape of this frontier is independent of the total amount spent on the product. In addition, only the group of brands which offer these characteristics are substitutes for each other. The consumption technology thus defines a group of goods which are in competition for consumer preferences.

Which brand will a consumer prefer? That depends on his or her preference for combinations of whiteness and decay-prevention benefits and the *relative* prices of each brand. All other things equal, a brand must be positioned on the efficiency frontier if it is to find a place in the market. Brands below the frontier offer too little of either benefit characteristic per dollar to compete successfully.

EXHIBIT 13–5
THE MULTIATTRIBUTE THEORY OF CONSUMER DEMAND

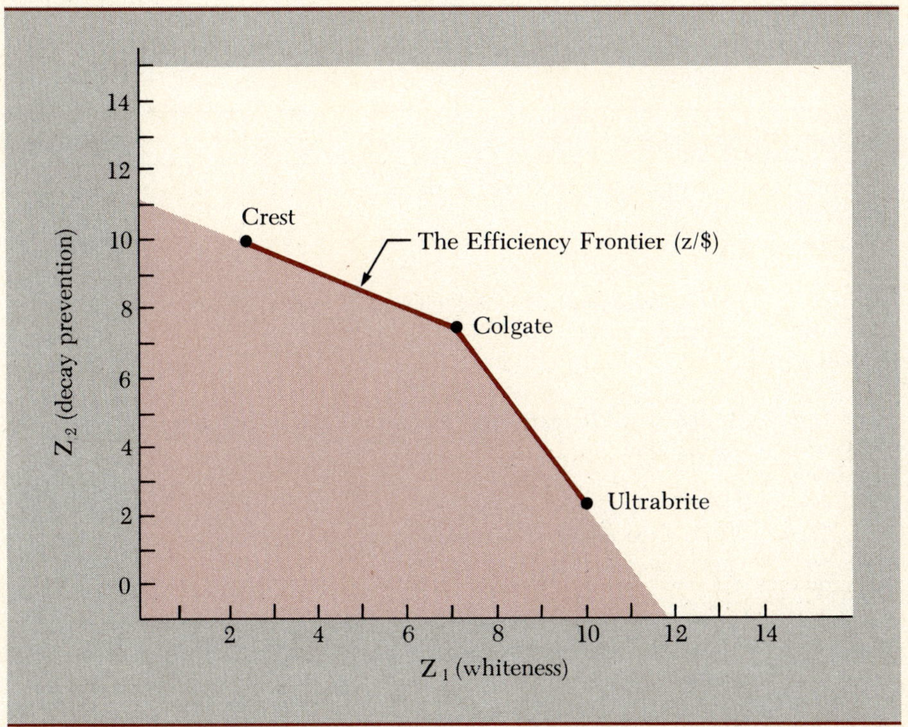

SOURCE: Hypothetical relationships among popular brands of toothpaste based on Brian T. Ratchford (1975), "The New Economic Theory of Consumer Behavior: An Interpretive Essay," *Journal of Consumer Research,* 2 (Sept.), pp. 65–75.

The new theory of demand adds the psychological dimension of consumer perception to our understanding. A consumer who has a strong preference for decay-prevention benefits will find that Crest offers more of that per dollar than any other brand in this hypothetical example. A consumer who prefers more whitening to decay-prevention benefits will properly see Ultrabrite as the best. Consumers in search of a balance between these two characteristics will prefer Colgate.

The theory has powerful implications for product positioning and advertising strategy. It also ties economic theory directly to the considerable developments in perceptual mapping pioneered by Paul Green, Yoram Wind, and other marketing scholars, and discussed briefly in Chapter 8.

CONSUMER SENTIMENT AND DEMAND[20]

If George Katona was the father of psychological economics, Keynes must be considered its godfather: "The amount that the community spends on consumption obviously depends partly on the amount of its income . . . and

EXHIBIT 13–6
THE INDEX OF CONSUMER SENTIMENT

Concept	Question	Response	
Current Financial Situation	Are you better off or worse off than you were a year ago?	Better	+
		Same	0
		Worse	−
Future Financial Situation	A year from now will you be better off, worse off, or about the same?	Better	+
		Same	0
		Worse	−
Near-Term Business Conditions	In the next 12 months will the country have good times or bad times?	Good	+
		Bad	−
Long-Term Business Outlook	During the next five years would you say we will have good times or bad times?	Good	+
		Bad	−
Buying Conditions	Generally speaking, is it a good or a bad time to buy big things for your home?	Good	+
		Bad	−

SOURCE : Based on George Katona (1975), *Psychological Economics* (New York: Elsevier), p. 78 and Richard T. Curtin (1982), "Indicators of Consumer Behavior: The University of Michigan Surveys of Consumers," *Public Opinion Quarterly*, 46, pp. 351–52.

partly on the subjective needs and other psychological propensities and habits of the individuals composing it."[21] These subjective needs and other psychological propensities led Katona to frame the first postulate of psychological economics: Consumption is a function of both the ability (income) and the willingness (sentiments) to buy. It is in the empirical measurement of the *willingness* to buy that Katona had an enduring impact on psychological economics.

The *Index of Consumer Sentiment* was first constructed in 1952 as a part of the continuing studies of the Survey Research Center at the University of Michigan. It began appearing at regular intervals in 1955. Since that year the *Index* has been made up of the same five questions designed to measure consumer sentiments on a similar number of concepts. These are summarized in Exhibit 13–6.

Index of Consumer Sentiment

The basic concepts measured by the *Index of Consumer Sentiment* (ICS) are how individuals feel about their present and future personal financial situation, their short- and long-term expectations for business conditions in the country, and their perceptions about the buying climate for major durable goods. The answers given to these questions by a large probability sample of consumers are grouped according to their responses. There are three categories of responses. The first reflects positive sentiments (*better off* or *good times*). The second category is essentially neutral (*same as before* or *no change*). The third category contains negative sentiments (*worse off* or *bad times*). The *Index* is constructed by subtracting the percentage of consumers holding negative opinions (those in category three) from the percentage holding positive opinions (category one) and adding 100 as a scaling constant.

Katona believed consumer confidence must precede major spending decisions. When people in large numbers foresee a bright outlook and are confident in the future they will undertake commitments not considered under the opposite conditions. The *Index of Consumer Sentiment* should be a leading indicator of economic activity and add to our understanding of changes in spending on major durable goods like housing and automobiles. This brings us back to the problem of new-car sales in 1981. The influence of price and income in the previous section of this chapter led to incomplete results. New car sales in 1981 were higher than price changes would suggest, and lower than the combined effects of price and income would lead us to expect.

The addition of the ICS to the picture should improve our understanding of consumer demand for new cars if Katona's basic hypothesis is valid, that is, if demand for new cars is a function of both the *ability* and *willingness* to buy. Some recent evidence is presented in Exhibit 13–7. The heavy line is the ICS (left-hand scale) for periods from 1966 through 1981. The light line is the unit sales of new cars (in millions on the right-hand scale) for the same period. Notice how the ICS tends to foreshadow or lead new-car sales over much of the sixteen-year period. The ICS is a leading indicator of new-car sales in eleven of these years beginning with 1971. It appears to be coincident in the first five years of the series.

Richard T. Curtin,[22] director of consumer surveys for the Survey Research

Center, performed a multiple regression analysis of these data, combined with real personal, disposable income per household for the same period. A summary of the results appears in Exhibit 13–8.

Using income alone, the model is able to explain only 30 percent of the variation in new-car sales from 1966 through 1981. The addition of consumer sentiments (ICS) improves the model's performance more than two-fold, explaining 73 percent of the variation in new-car sales. The amount of variation explained by the ICS alone was relatively small, compared with income, but the *combination of the two variables* yields a significant improvement in our understanding. While price and income effects would have left the demand for new cars unchanged or up slightly, falling consumer sentiments, reflecting uncertainty about the future and the expectation of bad times, decreased consumer willingness to undertake automobile purchases. As Katona hypothesized, consumer sentiments do indeed play an important role in decisions to make major investments in durable goods.

EXHIBIT 13–7
THE INDEX OF CONSUMER SENTIMENT AND NEW CAR SALES 1966–81

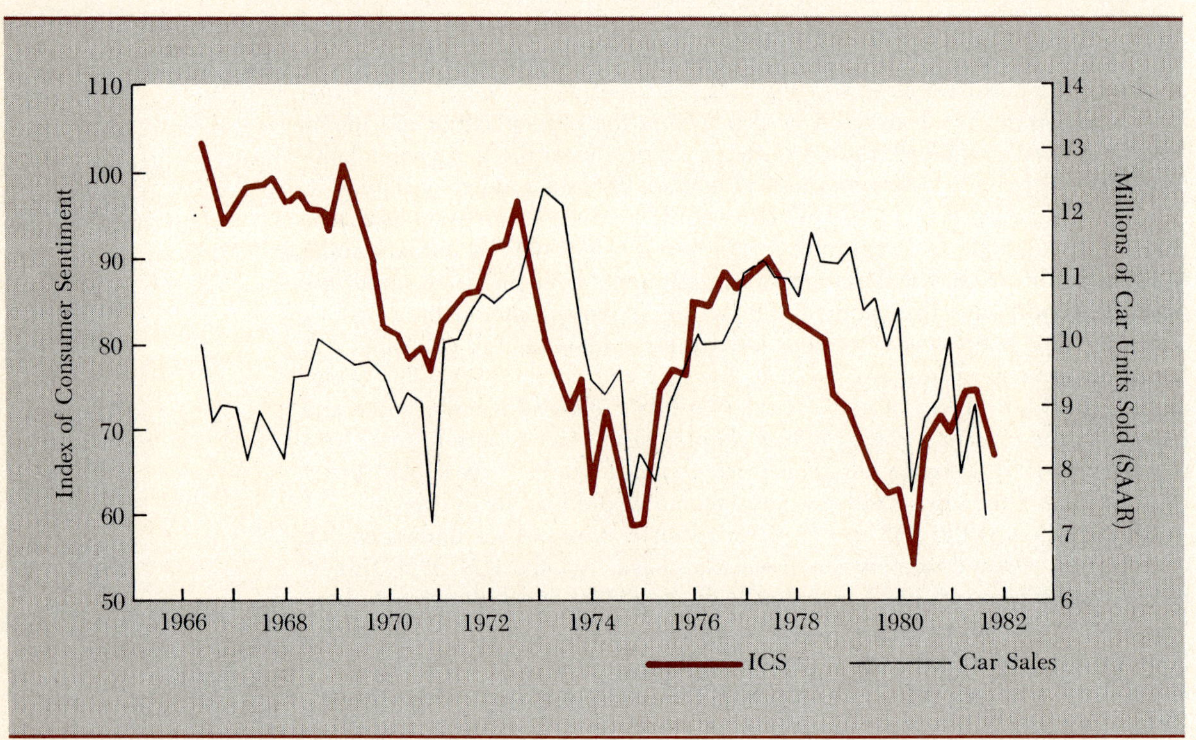

SOURCE : Richard T. Curtin (1982), "Indicators of Consumer Behavior: The University of Michigan Surveys of Consumers," *Public Opinion Quarterly*, 46, p. 349.

PSYCHOLOGICAL ECONOMIC EXPERIMENTS

For nearly two hundred years the assumptions economists routinely made about the behavior of individuals remained untested. Principal among these assumptions was the notion that free markets tend toward a **competitive equilibrium.** This assumption means buyers and sellers in a competitive market will come to a price acceptable to all through a process of bid-and-take, and this price will be stable if technology and preferences do not change. It is the basis for our belief that free competitive markets are the most efficient way of providing the highest level of consumer satisfaction. Equally important was the assumption that people are *rational*, or have comparable and consistent preferences when choosing among available alternatives. The assumption of *perfect information* was, of course, known to be unrealistic, but was permitted on grounds of analytical tractability. The study of consumer behavior has done much in recent years to fill the gap left by the assumption of perfect information.

EXHIBIT 13–8
EXPLAINING CAR SALES WITH INCOME AND CONSUMER SENTIMENTS 1966–81

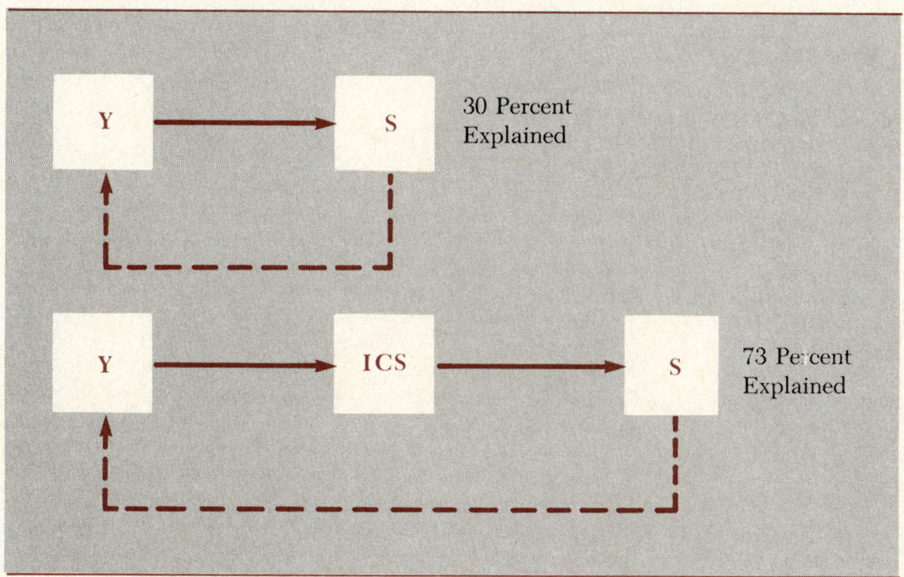

[a]Percent of variation in new car sales (S) explained by income (Y) alone and by income plus the index of consumer sentiment (ICS) using generalized least squares to correct for autocorrelated errors.

SOURCE : Based on Richard T. Curtin (1982), "Indicators of Consumer Behavior: The University of Michigan Surveys of Consumers," *Public Opinion Quarterly*, 46, p. 349.

Individual observation of behavior in a laboratory is a meaningful method by which to test the assumptions of economic theory. It was psychological economists who were to lead the way. The results of a series of experimental tests of economic assumptions have produced both good and bad news for the science.

The Assumption of a Competitive Equilibrium.

The good news is markets do indeed converge on a competitive equilibrium, and the process takes fewer transactions and far fewer numbers of buyers and sellers than traditionally thought by economists.

The first results were published by Vernon Smith, who has since replicated and refined them: "The literature reporting the results of a large number of experimental studies . . . documents what appears to be a remarkably rapid convergence to a competitive equilibrium."[23] These studies created laboratory markets with the following characteristics. Each buyer (seller) knew the value

EXHIBIT 13–9
TESTING THE ASSUMPTION OF COMPETITIVE EQUILIBRIUM

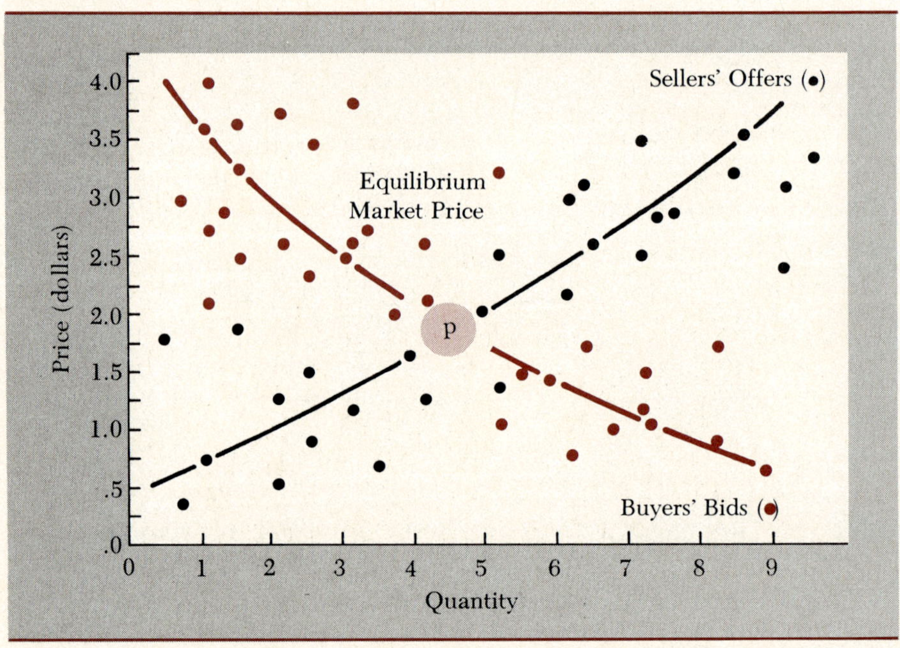

SOURCE : Based on Vernon Smith, Arlington W. Williams, W. Kenneth Bratton, and Michael G. Vannoni (1982), "Competitive Market Institutions: Double Auctions vs. Sealed Bid-Offer Auctions," *American Economic Review*, 72 (March), p. 62.

(cost) of the alternatives when each transaction was made. This is the important assumption of perfect information, a luxury which many real-world buyers and sellers do not share. Exchange followed the rules of a double auction where buyers and sellers freely make bids and accept offers. Market demand per trading period was held constant, and there were at least four buyers and as many sellers in each market.

Various trading conditions were imposed on these laboratory markets by the experimenters. Some of these conditions replicate real-world markets like the New York Stock Exchange, while others are based on conditions not found in the real world. One set of conditions used by Smith, called the *PQ process*, is illustrated in Exhibit 13–9. The name derives from conditions that require buyers and sellers to submit sealed bid *prices* along with the maximum *quantity* they are prepared to trade in each period. The functions describing seller's offers (prices and quantities) and buyer's bids begin quickly to emerge from the swarm of points and x's to reveal classical demand and supply curves. Their intersection is the market clearing equilibrium price assumed in classical economic theory.

The Assumption of Consumer Rationality

The bad news, from experimental testing of the assumption of consumer rationality, is that preferences are too often inconsistent! Grether and Plott, in the best scientific tradition, designed a series of experiments in choice-making behavior intended to discredit "a body of data and theory . . . developed within psychology [that] are simply inconsistent with preference theory."[24] The evidence to which these writers refer suggested that "no optimization principles of any sort lie behind even the simplest of human choices."

Suppose individuals under laboratory conditions are asked which of the two lotteries, A and B (shown at the side), they prefer. This is exactly like asking consumers which of two brands they prefer, based on their apparent characteristics. Their answers should be consistent, if the rationality assumption of economic theory is correct. The minimum requirement is that their judgments be transitive among alternatives, that is, if an individual *prefers* A to B, he or she should place *less value* on B than on A.

In this experiment, the characteristics of the two lotteries are the payoffs and the probabilities of winning. Individuals are told a random dart is to be thrown at target A. If it hits the line, they lose (win nothing). If the dart misses the line in target A, they win $4.00. Since there is a *very high probability* the dart will not hit the line in target A, leading to a win, this is called the probability bet. On the other hand, if the individual prefers lottery B, a random dart will be thrown at target B, and if it hits in the $0.00 region they win nothing. If it hits the region bounding $16.00 they win that amount. Lottery B is called a money bet, because there is a high money reward. After indicating their preference for one of these lotteries, the individual is asked to place a money value on each one.

Psychologists observed a large proportion of people will express a prefer-

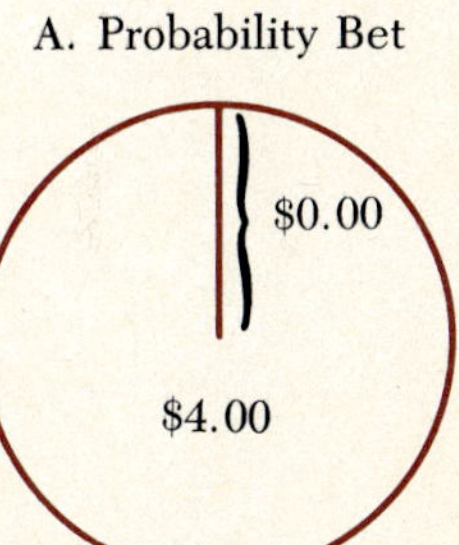

ence for lottery A, but place a higher monetary value on lottery B! It was this result—preference reversal or irrationality—that Grether and Plott set out to discredit. Their objective was not to be attained. After building in experimental controls for all possible economic and psychological explanations, the null hypothesis that people are irrational was not rejected. Attempts by other psychological economists to reject the same hypothesis in replications of the Grether and Plott experiments also failed.[25]

Grether and Plott concluded, "the fact that preference theory and related theories of optimization are subject to exception does not mean they should be discarded. . . . it stands as a challenge to theorists."[26]

SUMMARY

Consumer behavior is an integrative field of study drawing on psychology, economics, sociology, statistics, and other disciplines as well. Psychological economics helps the student of consumer behavior sharpen this integrative perspective by filling in the gaps between the first two sister disciplines. This often requires different *units of analysis* and *methods of measurement*. The topics of psychological economics have grown in their importance with the rise of the *affluent consumer* and the *income revolution* of the last several decades. One measure of its growing importance is the introduction of an international scholarly journal dedicated to the topics of psychological economics.[27]

Economics has made valuable contributions to the study of consumer behavior, though its usefulness is often obscure. Psychological economics as a field of study is sympathetic to the theoretical rigor of economics as well as the need for realism in consumer behavior and marketing. Recognizing the usefulness of the concept of *marginal utility*, the psychological economist will add the realism of *multiattribute choice* behavior to the classical viewpoint. Utility is not a simple function of the quantity of a good or service consumed; it is a complex function of the *consumption technology* sought by a consumer, which is in turn a composite of *benefit characteristics* that provide both subjective and objective values to the user. The maximum benefit levels offered by a group of goods define an *efficiency frontier* for market competition.

While demonstrating the importance of *price* and *income elasticity*, the psychological economist points to the limitations of these concepts. Price elasticity applies only to large aggregates of products and services, or *total market demand*. In addition, there are many useful definitions of *price* and *income*. The economist may be content to look at price as a single valued concept. The student of consumer behavior knows better. The measurement of average price masks variation that is important to consumers' perceptions of price.

The impact of *current income* on consumption overlooks other equally useful concepts. Income is affected by the *family life cycle*, by the consumer's *cultural setting*, and existing *stocks* of goods and services in ways classical consumption theory fails to consider. Finally, the concepts of price and income elasticity alone come up short. The need exists to add *consumer senti-*

ments to develop a more complete understanding of consumer behavior. The psychological economist would suggest the willingness to spend as reflected in the *Index of Consumer Sentiment* is just as important as price and income.

Psychological economics is more recently concerned with testing the basic *assumptions* of classical economics. Some of these, like *competitive equilibrium,* hold up remarkably well in the laboratory. Others, like the bedrock assumption of *consumer rationality,* have been found wanting.

The importance of psychological economics is thus in filling in the corners of consumer behavior. Interest in the study of consumer sentiments appears in every chapter of this book. The effects of consumer experiments are seen everywhere in efforts to validate consumer-behavior theories.

KEY CONCEPTS

consumer sentiments
psychological
  economics
classical demand
  theory assumptions
  rational behavior
  utility maximization
  perfect information
  consistent
    preferences
  insatiable material
    wants

marginal utility
price elasticity
income elasticity
consumption function
marginal propensity to
  consume
relative income
  hypothesis
permanent income
  effect
life cycle hypothesis
stock adjustment
  theories

multiattribute theory
  of consumer
  demand
consumption
  technology
substitute/complement
efficiency frontier
competitive
  equilibrium
*Index of Consumer
  Sentiments*

DISCUSSION QUESTIONS

1. Give a brief definition of psychological economics, distinguishing it from psychology and from economics. What are its concerns?
2. What are the basic tenets of classical demand theory? What is its value to the study of consumer behavior?
3. Explain the concept of price elasticity and the assumptions behind it. What implications does it have for pricing policy by the firm?
4. Briefly describe the following theories: Keynes' consumption function, relative-income hypothesis, permanent-income hypothesis, life-cycle hypothesis, and stock-adjustment theories.
5. How does the *Index of Consumer Sentiment* contribute to a greater understanding of consumers' decisions to purchase major durable goods?
6. How has classical demand theory been revised to incorporate consumer perception of differences among goods of the same product category?
7. How does the new theory of consumer demand relate to product positioning and advertising strategy?
8. Are consumers "rational"? What is rationality? From whose perspective should rationality be defined?

NOTES

1. Kenneth E. Boulding (1956), *The Image* (Ann Arbor: Univ. of Michigan Press), p. 82.

2. George Katona (1975), *Psychological Economics* (New York: Elsevier), p. 41.

3. George Katona (1975), p. 21.

4. Alfred Marshall (1920), *Principles of Economics*, 8th ed. (London: Macmillan), Bk. III, Chs. 5 & 6.

5. Henri Theil (1975), *The Theory and Measurement of Consumer Demand,* Vol. 1 (Amsterdam: North-Holland), p. 1.

6. Robert F. Lanzillotti (1961), "The Automobile Industry," in *The Structure of American Industry*, ed. Walter Adams, 3rd ed. (New York: Macmillan).

7. Robert F. Lanzillotti (1961).

8. John Maynard Keynes (1936), *The General Theory of Employment, Interest, and Money* (New York: Harcourt, Brace), p. 96.

9. John Maynard Keynes (1936), p. 97.

10. Dorothy S. Brady and Rose Friedman (1947), "Savings and the Income Distribution," *Studies in Income and Wealth,* Vol. 10 (New York: Natl. Bureau of Economic Research).

11. J. Duesenberry (1949), *Income, Saving, and the Theory of Consumer Behavior* (Boston: Harvard Univ. Press).

12. Franco Modigliani (1949), "Fluctuations in the Saving-Income Relation: A Problem in Economic Forecasting," *Studies in Income and Wealth,* Vol. 11 (New York: Natl. Bureau of Economic Research).

13. Milton Friedman (1957), *A Theory of the Consumption Function* (Princeton: Natl. Bureau of Economic Research).

14. Franco Modigliani (1966), "The Life-Cycle Hypothesis, the Demand for Wealth, and the Supply of Capital," *Social Research*, 33, pp. 160–217.

15. Gary S. Becker (1965), "A Theory of the Allocation of Time," *Economics Journal*, 75, pp. 493–517 and Henri Theil (1975).

16. Brian T. Ratchford (1975), "The New Economic Theory of Consumer Behavior: An Interpretative Essay," *Journal of Consumer Research*, 2 (Sept.), pp. 66–75.

17. Kevin Lancaster (1966), "A New Approach to Consumer Theory," *Journal of Political Economy*, 74, pp. 132–57 and (1971), *Consumer Demand: A New Approach* (New York: Columbia Univ. Press).

18. D. S. Ironmonger (1972), *New Commodities and Consumer Behavior* (Cambridge: Cambridge Univ. Press).

19. William J. Baumol (1967), "Calculation of Optimal Product and Retailer Characteristics: The Abstract Product Approach," *Journal of Political Economy*, 75 (Oct.), pp. 674–85.

20. This section draws from Victor J. Cook (1984), "A New Role for Psychological Economics in Consumer Research," in *Advances in Consumer Research*, Vol. 11, ed. Thomas C. Kinnear (Assn. for Consumer Research).

21. John Maynard Keynes (1936), p. 90.

22. Richard T. Curtin (1982), "Indicators of Consumer Behavior: The University of Michigan Surveys of Consumer," *Public Opinion Quarterly*, 46, pp. 340–52.

23. Vernon Smith, Arlington W. Williams, W. Kenneth Bratton, and Michael G. Vannoni (1982), "Competitive Market Institutions: Double Auctions vs. Bid-Offer Auctions," *American Economic Review*, 72 (March), pp. 58–77.

24. David M. Grether and Charles R. Plott (1979), "Economic Theory of Choice and the Preference Reversal Phenomenon," *American Economic Review*, 69 (Sept.), pp. 623–38.

25. Werner W. Pommerehne, Friedrich Schneider, and Peter Zweifel (1982), "Economic Theory of Choice and the Preference Reversal Phenomenon: A Reexamination," *American Economic Review*, 72 (June), pp. 569–74.

26. David M. Grether and Charles R. Plott (1979), p. 634.

27. W. Fred van Raaij (1981), "Economic Psychology," *Journal of Economic Psychology*, 1 (March), pp. 1–24.

Its shape is understated and classic. It is quick and responsive in motion. Its interior is designed with quiet elegance. The car is Jaguar's XJ6 and it is the best Jaguar ever built.

The engine purrs. It is the latest version of Jaguar's double overhead cam six. Electronically fuel injected, it is a remarkable combination of strength and smoothness. The car's reflexes are sure and precise. Power rack and pinion steering, surefooted four wheel independent suspension and the unwavering authority of four wheel power disc brakes all combine to give this notably comfortable sedan athletic abilities you might expect of a sports car.

Inside the XJ6 there is a level of elegance as uncommon as the car itself. Supple leather faces the seats. Hand finished mirror-matched walnut veneers enrich the dashboard and driver's console. Electronic conveniences await your command: power sunroof; power windows, door locks and antenna; a trip computer; stereo AM/FM radio and cassette player; cruise control and a heating and air conditioning system that regulates itself are all standard equipment. Uncommon? Not for the best Jaguar ever built.

The quality inherent in the Jaguar XJ6 is backed by the best warranty Jaguar has ever offered. For two years or 36,000 miles, whichever comes first, Jaguar will repair or replace any part of the car which proves defective. The Pirelli P5 tires come with their own warranty. Ask your dealer for full details of the Jaguar limited warranty. And ask for a test drive in the best Jaguar ever built. It will be an uncommonly pleasing experience. For the name of the dealer nearest you, call toll-free: (800) 447-4700.

JAGUAR CARS INC., Leonia, N.J. 07605.

JAGUAR: HIGH INFORMATION CONTENT

High information is provided to help the buyer "rationalize" the purchase. (See Chapters 4 and 5.)

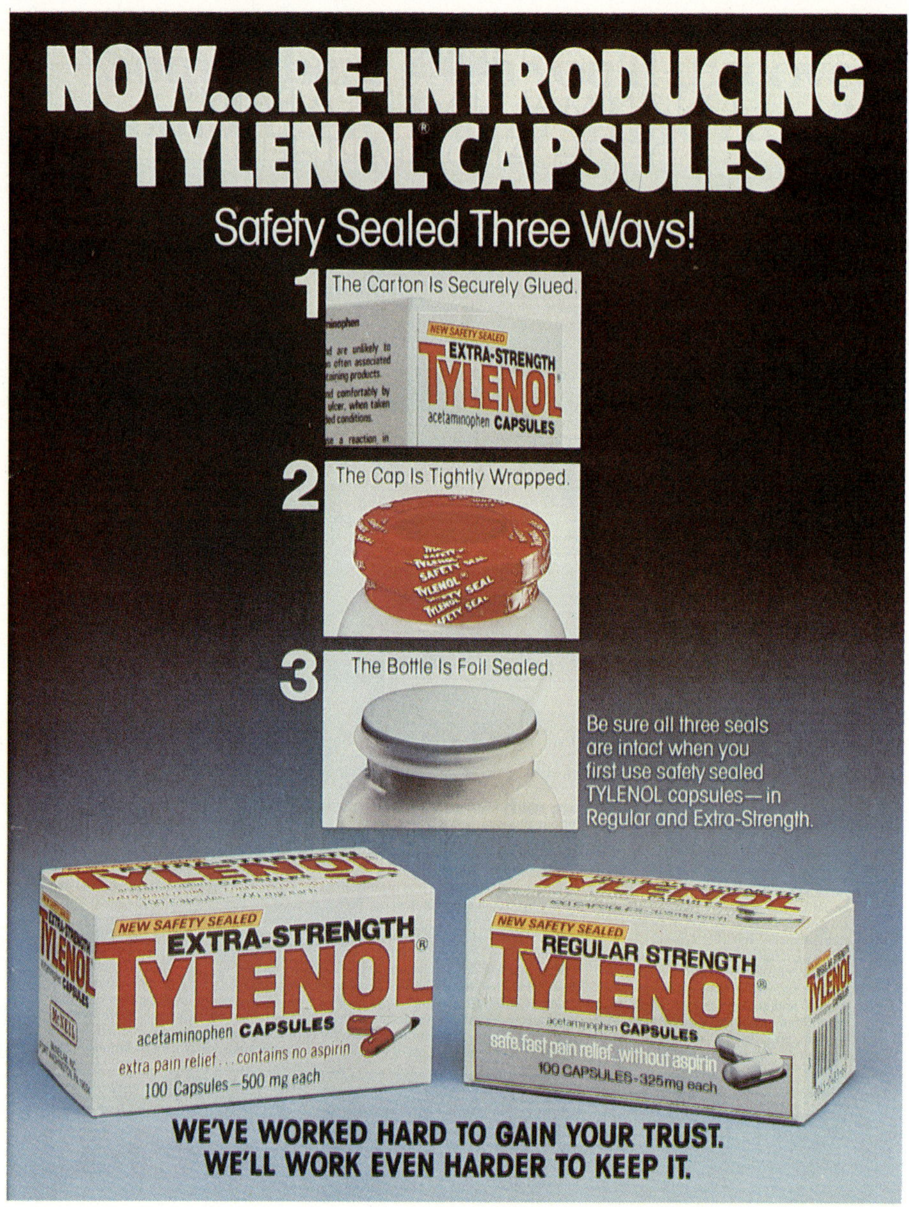

TYLENOL: REGAINING CONSUMER CONFIDENCE

An advertisement stressing the safety of Tylenol's packaging in response to the poisonings associated with the product. (See Chapters 5 and 10.)

PERDUE CHICKEN: CREATING PRODUCT DIFFERENTIATION

A commercial storyboard that is part of an ongoing, highly successful campaign to build product differentiation for the advertiser and to gain greater brand involvement. (See Chapters 6 and 8.)

CLIENT: PERDUE
PRODUCT: FRESH CORNISH GAME HEN

30 SECONDS

TITLE: "TENDER TEST"
COMM'L NO.: TV-PD-30-94

FRANK PERDUE: I thought my Perdue Fresh Cornish Game Hen

was tender like no rock cornish game hen.

So I decided to see if I was right.

I had my Fresh Cornish Game Hens tested against all the frozen competition.

And found my Cornish, is at least 40% more tender than any of them.

If you thought a frozen rock cornish game hen made good eating,

wait'll you taste the one

that doesn't come frozen like a rock.

(SILENT)

ANACIN: ENDORSEMENT

Endorsers are often quite effective for low-involvement products, particularly if they are perceived as credible—which Patricia Neal may be for this product, given that she has battled poor health. (See Chapters 6 and 10.)

LIP-SMACKERS: ADVERTISING TO CHILDREN

This advertisement, directed to children, may encourage a form of "anticipatory socialization"—consumption that emulates an adult pattern. (See Chapter 7.)

GRAND MARNIER: STIMULUS GENERALIZATION

The objective in this advertisement is to "borrow" from the positive Grand Marnier name and image and to encourage the consumer to generalize the benefits to a second Grand Marnier product. (See Chapters 8, 9, and 11.)

SANKA: ATTITUDE CHANGE

This advertisement is part of a campaign that seeks to change Sanka's positioning from that of an "imitation" coffee for "old people" to a "real" coffee for the "mass market." This particular advertisement complicates the attitude-change task even further by asking people to drink Sanka on ice rather than hot. (See Chapters 8 and 11.)

FERRARI: A PLAY ON EMOTIONS

This advertisement is notable for its lack of product information and its exclusive play on the emotions. (See Chapters 8 and 12.)

ALPHA MICRO: COMPARATIVE ADVERTISING

A comparative advertisement aimed directly at a competitor. (See Chapter 10.)

CHARLIE: ADVERTISING BASED ON SOCIAL VALUES

Revlon's television commercial for Charlie perfume takes into account America's shifting value structure. (See Chapters 2 and 14.)

CHELSEA: PERCEPTUAL CONFUSION

Chelsea, as discussed in Chapter 8, was an adult soft drink marketed by Anheuser-Busch. From these pictures would you say that the bottle was more like a soft drink's or a beer's? (See Chapters 7, 8, and 23.)

POLO: ADVERTISING BASED ON VALUE-EXPRESSIVE INFLUENCE

This advertisement encourages consumers to bolster their egos by identifying with a reference group. (See Chapters 8, 17, and 20.)

CHIVAS REGAL: HEIGHTENING AWARENESS

This advertisement not only does not provide information about the product, it does not fully show the product's brand name. The advertiser may assume that this heightens awareness, since the consumer has a need for "closure" and will fill in the missing details, thus becoming more actively involved in processing the advertisement. (See Chapters 9 and 20.)

EF HUTTON: ENDORSEMENT

Another example of the often used endorser approach to advertising. This endorser, however, has no obvious connection with the service being advertised. (See Chapters 10 and 16.)

PHILLIPS PETROLEUM: PUBLIC SERVICE

An advertisement from a campaign that promotes a positive image for the advertiser. (See Chapters 9 and 23.)

MARLBORO: A CROSS-CULTURAL CAMPAIGN

This advertisement from Japan shows the comparability of Marlboro advertising worldwide. Very few symbols, however, have the universal appeal and communicability of the cowboy. (See Chapter 22.)

SEAGRAM: SOCIAL RESPONSIBILITY

This advertisement shows awareness of a problem associated with a product and the advertiser's encouragement of social responsibility. (See Chapter 23.)

PART
III

Sociological Theories and Applications

14 Consumer Demographics and Values

Demographics *are indicators of society's characteristics—age, sex, income, geographic location, and so on. Relatively easy to measure, they provide a quantitative profile of markets. In contrast, an understanding of* **society's values** *provides a qualitative profile. In order to have practical utility, market segments must be identified on the basis of both their demographic characteristics and their values. Segments identified by only one type of information do not provide the strongest basis for the development of marketing strategy. For example, although the purchase of foods for low-salt, low-calorie diets is related to increasing age, age alone does not best define the buyer profile. Because of medical problems and health needs, elderly consumers often follow low-salt, low-calorie diets. Yet to define the market for these foods solely on the basis of age would not take account of the significance of physical fitness, an important value for some members of all age segments. Sound marketing strategy for low-salt, lower-calorie foods would rely on an understanding of the role of age and other demographic variables and of consumers' values as they relate to health and fitness issues.*

Monitoring shifts in society's demographic structure and values can assist marketers in three major ways.

1. *Demographic data and information about consumer values are instrumental in the identification and selection of target market segments for both introducing new products and repositioning existing products.*
2. *Demographics and consumer values influence advertisers' media selections.*
3. *Demographic trends provide forecasts for product category sales.*

In this chapter we discuss changes in society that can lead to corresponding changes or adaptations in marketing strategy. We will consider both shifts in the demographic structure *of society and shifts in the* values *held by society. Analysis of these two spheres helps managers to identify patterns of consumer needs and to position products to meet changing consumer needs.*

USING DEMOGRAPHICS AND VALUES

Market Segmentation

One of the most important uses of demographics is in the development of segmentation strategy—that is, the selection of the "best" potential segments, or sets of consumers, for a product. The potential of a segment depends on the level of need for the product or service and the likelihood of purchase. The market for magazines, for instance, is made up of numerous segments defined by such characteristics as age, interest, and lifestyle. A population breakdown by age, income, education, and so forth provides a starting point for determining the most feasible and potentially profitable target market. After demographic targeting of the segment, a consideration of values held by that segment adds to knowledge about consumer needs and tastes. For example, readers of magazines such as *Ms., Cosmopolitan,* and *Ladies Home Journal* all have some demographic similarities but considerable differences in values.

Introducing New Products or Services   An accurate demographic and value profile of the target market helps managers discover new product ideas. For example, Stouffer's has aimed its new line of single-serving frozen dinners at the single-person household. Demographics have shown such households to be on the increase because of the rising divorce rate and the increase in the age for first marriages. These households place great importance on the value of convenience. For another example, Winchester has responded to the demographic trend of a growing number of elderly consumers by introducing a lightweight, hunting firearm especially targeted for the senior-citizen market.

Repositioning Products or Services   A knowledge of demographic trends and values also help in repositioning products. For example, the $25-billion-dollar, fast-food industry first emerged as restaurants for the children of the baby boom. But with the aging of those consumers, McDonald's, for example, is changing its brightly colored, child-oriented decor to more subtle shades of gold and brown. McDonald's is also providing breakfast for early morning workers and introducing a new evening meal to serve patrons who place more value on a "slow food" evening meal with a greater choice of food.

A second example of a creative product repositioning involves M&M/Mars Snickers candy bar. Snickers is the largest selling candy bar in the United States. But with the aging of the population, M&M/Mars began advertising the bars to a heterogeneous adult market. One commercial depicts a man wearing a hard hat saying, "I can eat a Snickers, go back to work, and not worry about being hungry until it's time for lunch." A contrasting commercial shows a businessman clad in suit and tie. In other ads, a truckdriver and housewife appear, as do some older teenagers. The commercials are notable for the virtual absence of young children. Similarly, former Mouseketeer Annette Funicello, now nearing 40, advertises Skippy peanut butter. As the baby boom continues to age, consumer purchasing power will continue to shift to a more mature segment.

Media Strategy

Some television programs and magazines appeal to a very large cross-section of the population. Evening news programs on the national networks and *People* magazine, for example, cut across demographic boundaries. But in general, consumers with different demographic profiles tend to expose themselves to different print and television media vehicles. Magazines such as *Town and Country* and *Architectural Digest* have great appeal to high-income consumers, while *Boxing World, True,* and *Argosy* appeal to lower-income consumers. Specialized magazines such as *Hot Rod, Gay Life, Boston,* and *Southwest Life* reach audiences defined according to interest, sexual preference, or geographic locale.

The proliferation of women's magazines targeted to working or professional women is a response to the recent demographic trend of more women entering the workforce and the changing value patterns of women. Such magazines provide marketers the opportunity to reach a market segment that traditionally watches little TV with an advertisement surrounded by editorial matter of high interest.

Since demographics influence the media patterns of consumers, they correspondingly affect advertisers' selection of media. They also affect the allocation of budgets for advertising. For example, Yamaha motorcycles are marketed throughout the United States, but the highest penetration is in California, because of its favorable climate. As a result, the firm's media budget is skewed in the direction of California and similar climatic areas, which have higher sales and sales potential.

Long-Range Planning

Monitoring changes in society can assist managers in long-term planning. The growing number of older consumers, together with higher interest rates and energy costs, and the corresponding inability of young couples to purchase large houses point to a booming future demand for smaller individual houses and condominiums. Migration of urban dwellers from the Northeast to Sunbelt States points to a similar long-term demand for housing in Sunbelt areas.

The growing number of women in the workforce and their entry into the professional ranks have led to dramatic growth in the demand for women's business suits. This demand, which reflects movement away from traditional values, can be expected to continue.

Keeping abreast of long-range demographic shifts gives management a headstart in responding to ever-changing consumer wants and needs.

DEMOGRAPHIC TRENDS IN THE UNITED STATES

The demographic structure of the United States is currently undergoing some dramatic changes. First, the **age distribution** is changing. The median age is increasing, which means the proportion of senior citizens is growing. Second, **household composition** is radically different from that of the 1950s and 1960s. The delay in the average age of first marriages and a rising divorce rate have led to an increasing proportion of single-person households. Third, the number of **women in the workforce** is growing. Correspondingly, the roles of men and women are changing. Fourth, our **population is being redistributed,** with heavy movement to the Sunbelt states. Finally, **black and Hispanic populations** in the United States are growing as a proportion of the total.

The Changing Age Structure

The American population is aging. The median age in 1970 was 28.0 years. It had increased to 30.2 years by 1980, and is projected to increase to 32.8 years by 1990. Exhibit 14–1 shows that during the decade of the 1970s, the 25–34-year-old segment grew from 12.3 percent to 16.3 percent of the population and is expected to grow to 17.1 percent by 1990. The 35–44-year-old group is expected to grow from its 1980 level of 11.5 percent to 15.1 percent in 1990.[1]

The Baby-Boom Market   The *baby boom* refers to the rise in the birthrate which occurred following World War II. It began in 1946, peaked in 1957,

EXHIBIT 14–1

AGE DISTRIBUTION OF THE POPULATION 1960–1990

Age	1960 %	1970 %	1980 %	(projected) 1990 %
Under 5	11.1	8.3	7.1	7.5
5–14	19.8	19.9	15.2	14.3
15–24	13.6	17.8	18.7	14.4
25–34	12.8	12.3	16.3	17.1
35–44	13.4	11.7	11.5	15.1
45–54	11.4	11.4	10.2	10.5
55–64	8.6	9.1	9.6	8.7
65 years and over	9.2	9.8	11.3	12.4
	100.0	100.0	100.0	100.0

SOURCE: Based on Predicasts Composite Forecasts (1981), April, pp. A4-5.

and continued into the early 1960s. Approximately 76 million people, who now comprise almost one third of the American population, were born during that time period. Interestingly, on either side of the baby boom were baby "bust" periods (the Depression and the 1970s), when the birthrate was very low. Demographers often refer to the mass of baby-boom individuals as the "pig in the python," because on demographic charts they resemble a very large morsel recently swallowed, but not yet digested, by a long snake.

The **baby-boom generation** is of particular interest to managers, because it represents the largest demographic segment in society. The advertising for Pepsi Cola, for example, has been responsive to the aging of the baby-boom consumers. In the 1960s, the "Pepsi Generation" of young people was featured in ads. But today's campaigns focus on a more mature group.

Levi Strauss and Company, which experienced dramatic growth from the early 1960s through the mid 1970s, has also responded to the pressure exerted by aging baby-boom consumers. When the earliest baby boomers were just about to become teenagers, James Dean donned jeans in *Rebel Without a Cause,* and, shortly thereafter, Marlon Brando followed suit in *The Wild One*. The young baby boomers adopted jeans, not only as an article of cloth-

EXHIBIT 14–2
THE POTENTIAL OF THE MATURE MARKET

MEASURING MATURE MARKETS

Forty-six million Americans—one out of every five—are 55 or over, a number nearly twice Canada's total population. Over one-third of all consumer households in the United States—28 million of them—are headed by a person aged 55 or over. Between today and the year 2000, the median age of Americans will rise from 30 to 35, a phenomenal rise in so short a time.

Despite such statistics, many marketers still do not believe in the older market. . . .

Mistaken perceptions abound: some marketers still believe that older persons have limited needs, little money, and scant inclination to spend it. They think large numbers of older persons live in institutions—in fact, less than 1 in 20 persons aged 65 or over lives in an institution—23 million do not.

They believe that most older persons do not head their own households—in fact, the vast majority maintain their own households and make their own consumer decisions. . . .

By any standard, the economics of the older population are impressive: households headed by a person 55 or over account for a remarkable $400 billion of annual personal income in the U.S. in 1978—approximately 30 percent of total aggregated income. These households account for nearly 80 percent of all money in savings and loan institutions in the country. They spend an estimated 28 percent of all discretionary money in the marketplace—nearly double that available to households headed by persons 34 or under. In contrast, the much sought-after youth market—households headed by a person aged 25 or under—hold a mere 1 percent of all discretionary money. . . .

ing, but as a symbol of being anti-adult and anti-establishment. Outfitting the largest population segment, Levi Strauss became the world's largest clothing manufacturer by 1977. But as the baby boomers began to age, their bodies changed, widening in places critical for jeans. Levi's response was to introduce their Levi's for Men line, targeted at the 25–35-year-old market. Levi's for Men, cut somewhat fuller in the thighs and seat, accommodated both the changing consumer physique and the unchanging consumer demand for blue jeans.

Cosmetic companies, too, have responded. The early 1970s saw the introduction of numerous brands of makeup appealing to the teenage market. The product lines of, say, Yardley of London and Love consisted primarily of makeup: eyeshadow, lipstick, and blusher. But today's older consumer is more concerned with skin care, with cleansing and moisturizing the skin. Most major cosmetic manufacturers have introduced full lines of skin-care products. Max Factor, for instance, has entered the market with both Living Proof—an expensive line targeted to upper-income consumers—and Skin Principle, which is more moderately priced.

Numerous products have been *repositioned* as a direct consequence of the

It is time for marketers to change their traditional views of the elderly. The process of aging is a continuum—there is no set chronological age at which one suddenly becomes old, loses interest in lifetime pursuits, or stops being open to new ideas. The major difference between interests at various stages of the life cycle is often in how ends are achieved. A person's interest in participatory sports during younger years is likely to continue throughout a lifetime, but the games may change. Retirees constitute a large segment of participants in such sports and recreational activities as hunting, fishing, golf, and camping. With age, however, natural changes occur in physical strength and flexibility, which affect how one plays the game and the equipment one needs.

Similarly, interest in appearance remains strong throughout life, but few cosmetics are promoted as assisting the older woman's expressed desire to "look her best"—regardless of age. Advertisers rarely use older models, even though research reveals that the older women desire not so much new makeup products as role models their own age to provide guidance in selecting the products adapted to the aging process.

Marketers should be directing their attention to many heretofore underdeveloped areas, from fashion design and cosmetics to furniture and housing design. An expansion of catalog and home delivery services could pay off because the energy crisis will pose particular problems for many in the older age groups, who will need in-home services more than before. Many new personal care products and services are possible; opportunities abound, and the challenge is to respond.

SOURCE: Adapted from Carole B. Allan (1981), "Measuring Mature Markets," *American Demographics* (March), pp. 13–17.

aging of the baby-boom consumers. i.e., For example, Johnson and Johnson, the manufacturer of baby oil, baby powder, and baby shampoo, realized that there was no longer a sufficient number of babies to maintain sales levels of its products. Research showed, however, that these "baby" products were sometimes used by most members of a household. Johnson and Johnson mounted a respositioning effort that involved not only promoting its products to an older target market, but also using well-known male sports figures in product advertisements. Yankee pitcher "Goose" Gossage, using Johnson's Baby Powder, advises others to "take a powder." And former quarterback Fran Tarkenton tells the virtues of Johnson's Baby Shampoo.

Of course, as the original baby boomers start their families, their children will become another population surge in society. But because of cultural changes, including the trends toward delayed marriage, smaller families, and the older age at which women have their first child, demographers expect the surge to be only a baby "boomlet."

Manufacturers of such products as toys, children's clothing and furniture, disposable diapers, and even cameras (parents enjoy photographing babies) should benefit from the boomlet. Thus firms that produce child-oriented products should gear up for a resurgence of interest in their goods.

The Mature Market   In 1980, approximately 20 percent of the American population was aged 55 or older.[2] Exhibit 14–1 shows that this age group will continue to represent one fifth of the population through 1990.

In the past the **mature market** was relegated to an unimportant position in marketing planning. Only marketers of health-care products and dentures seem to have paid any attention to older consumers. But because of its size and its purchasing power, this group has become a powerful consumer segment. An excerpt from an article on the demographics of the mature market, in Exhibit 14–2, makes some interesting observations about the potential of that market. The appearance of magazines such as *Modern Maturity* and *Prime Time* is also indicative of the increasing attention being directed toward the mature market. The attention afforded the mature market will continue to grow and will peak as the baby-boom generation approaches old age.

Changing Household Composition

A second major demographic trend in the United States today is a change in the structure of households. The traditional notion of the American household is that of a **nuclear family** consisting of a breadwinner father, a mother who is not employed outside the home, and their children. This profile no longer describes the average American home, however. Exhibit 14–3, which provides a synopsis of the composition of American households in 1970 and 1979, shows that in 1979 only 15 percent of households conformed to the stereotype of a working father, homemaker mother, and at least one child under 18 at home! An additional 16 percent of households consist of the nuclear family, but with the mother employed outside the home.

nuclear family

The decline of the nuclear family is due to a number of factors, including a **delay in the age of first marriage** for both men and women and the high **divorce rate,** although that rate may be stabilizing. The divorce rate in 1980 was the same as in 1979; in contrast, the 1980 rate was three times as large as the 1960 rate.

marriage and divorce rates

Additionally, more married women are choosing to remain childless or to defer childbearing.[3] A possible explanation of the former is that **childlessness** is becoming acceptable. Deferred childbearing can indicate a desire for smaller families or a desire on the part of women to become established in their careers before having children. In any case, increased childlessness will lead to increases in discretionary purchasing power for these individuals. And,

childlessness

EXHIBIT 14–3
HOUSEHOLD COMPOSITION DATA

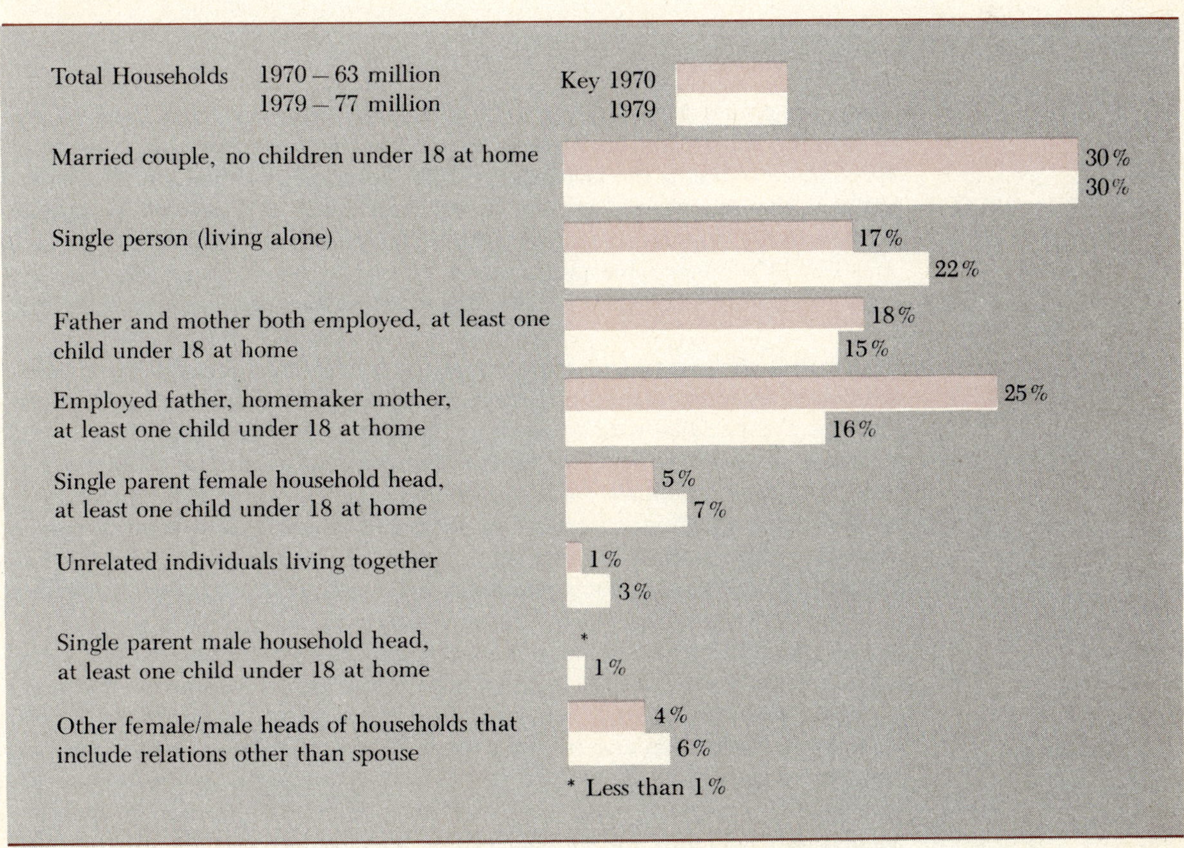

SOURCE: U.S. Department of Commerce, Bureau of Census, *Current Population Reports,* Series P-20, no. 352, March 1979, p. 1; and Bureau of Labor Statistics.

when these relatively older couples do have children, disposable income for child-oriented purchases will be substantially larger than in previous decades.

Corresponding to the decreased incidence of the nuclear family is a growth in the number of *nonfamily households*. The U.S. Census defines a nonfamily household as a man or woman either living alone or living with nonrelatives. In 1979, approximately one quarter of all households were nonfamilies, and this figure is expected to rise to approximately 30 percent by 1990.[4]

Smaller families and more nonfamilies create a long-term demand for smaller housing units and for condominiums. Already the owners of condominiums do not fit the expected profile of elderly, former homeowners. Many are young professionals and managers earning over $20,000 per year. And 57 percent of condominiums are occupied by one person only.[5]

Single people and childless couples also account for a disproportionate amount of nonbusiness air travel. Club Med has long targeted the singles travel segment, and more travel packages geared toward this affluent segment are being marketed.

Participation of Women in the Work Force

Over the period from 1970 to 1978 the percentage of women aged 16 and over in the American work force increased from 43.4 percent to 50.1 percent.[6] Even more telling is the fact that the labor-force participation rate of married women, that is, married women in the work force as a percent of married women in the population increased from 30.5 percent in 1960 to 49.4 percent in 1979.[7] The labor-force participation rate of women with children has increased steadily since 1960 for all women, *regardless of the age of their children*.

The fact that more and more women are entering the work force is extremely relevant to managers. The implications for media selection for advertising are especially strong. Daytime television, which has long been the province of advertisements for frequently purchased foods and other nondurable household products, is less and less able to reach large numbers of women. This situation is further complicated by the fact that working women tend to watch fewer hours of television overall (including prime time) than their housewife counterparts. On the other hand, both magazine readership and radio listening (especially during early-morning and after-work "drive time" hours) are more common among employed women. In the long term, then, we can expect a shift in dollar allocations for the various media in accordance with these trends.

Buyer behavior can also be expected to change in response to the growing number of women in the work force. Whereas women were once the exclusive purchasing agents for grocery and household-cleaning products, men are increasingly assuming the shopper's role—making decisions about both products and brands.

Another implication of the growing number of women in the work force involves *time:* Less time is available for shopping and for household chores.

Correspondingly, consumer demand for longer, more flexible shopping hours is increasing. This growing consumer need affects not only traditional retail shopping outlets, but also providers of services. The entry of more women into the work force and the ensuing decreasing availability of time can be expected to sustain high demand for convenience goods and time-saving devices.

Corresponding to the increasing incidence of women in the work force is growth in the incidence of dual-career families—whose incomes are expected to rise. Although incomes will also rise for households headed by women and for nonfamilies, the greatest proportional rise will be for the dual-career couple. Increases in demand for top-of-the-line goods and in conspicuous consumption should follow.

dual-career families

Regional Growth

Another important demographic trend occurring in the United States today is the population shift from the North and East to the West and South. Although the actual population is increasing in all States (except New York, Rhode Island, and the District of Columbia), migration is influencing the rate of growth of various states. From 1970 to 80, the five fastest growing states were Nevada, Arizona, Florida, Wyoming, and Utah. It is projected that the West and South will continue to grow faster than the North and East during the 1980s.[8]

These shifts in the population can affect marketing practices in three ways. First, sales of products geared toward warmer climates can be expected to grow, affecting obvious product categories such as outdoor furniture and lighter clothing. But more subtle changes will occur as well. The consumption of "white" liquors such as gin and vodka increases with warmer climates. Warmer climates also induce more casual lifestyles. Sales of microwave ovens and plastic microwave cookware, both of which are associated with casual living, are strongest in the South and West.

A second way the population shift will influence marketing efforts is in the allocation of corporate resources. Advertising and promotional expenditures are frequently broken down by region, and advertising and promotional dollars are allocated in proportion to regional product-purchasing patterns.

Finally, managers must be responsive to the variation in acceptability of different channels of distribution by geographic region. For example, Avon experiences a resistance to door-to-door selling in the industrial Northeast and on the West coast, stemming from fly-by-night encyclopedia sellers and bogus magazine-subscription salespeople. But in the Midwest and South, Avon's friendly neighborhood representative is a welcome caller.

A fascinating analysis of nine regions of North America has been proposed by Joel Garreau.[9] He suggests that it is wiser to look at the whole of North America, rather than just the United States, to develop an understanding of the attitudes and orientations that characterize various segments of the continent. He proposes that each region holds a distinctive set of norms and values and, hence, of consumer attitudes and consumer behaviors. His analysis incorporates demographics, interviews, and his own observations. Although his *Nine Nations of North America* is not based on scientifically rigorous empirical research, it provides an interesting qualitative appraisal of regional differences. A synopsis of Garreau's *Nine Nations* appears in Exhibit 14–4.

Ethnic and Racial Trends

A final major demographic trend is the growth of the black and Hispanic populations in the United States. According to the census, the black population accounts for 11.7 percent and the Hispanic population for 6.4 percent of the total population.[10] Both segments are expected to grow, with blacks reaching 12.2 percent and Hispanics 7.0 percent of the total population by 1990.[11] Hispanic women from ages eighteen through thirty-four expect to have an

EXHIBIT 14–4
CAPSULE SUMMARIES OF GARREAU'S NINE NATIONS

The Foundry

Nation: Foundry
Capital: Detroit
Geography: Ohio, Pennsylvania, New Jersey, northeastern Illinois, northern Indiana, Michigan (excluding northwest region), New York (excluding Manhattan), southwest Connecticut, Northern Virginia, northern Maryland, eastern Wisconsin, northern Delaware, northern West Virginia, and southeast Ontario.
Description: The industrialized northeast that is losing population, jobs, and investment to other "nations" is marked by gritty "urban prison camps," decaying infrastructures, heavy trade unionism, obsolete technologies, and racial friction. "The whole point of living in the Foundry is work. No one ever lived in Buffalo for its climate or Gary for its scenic vistas. . . ."
Outlook: This is the only "nation" on the decline, due to soft demand for autos, steel, rubber, and its other major products. It no longer represents "America" in a business or social sense, even though it is home to 90 million people. . . .

Mexamerica

Nation: MexAmerica
Capital: Los Angeles
Geography: Southwest and south central California, southern Arizona, western New Mexico, southern Texas, southern Colorado, and Mexico.
Description: The southwest "nation" of North America has as its capital the second largest Mexican city in the world. Its language, culture, economics, food, politics, and lifestyle are under heavy Hispanic influence. . . . Houston, which is starting to strongly resemble Los Angeles, is the world's new energy capital . . . . Phoenix is now the 11th largest city in the U.S. MexAmerica is a watershed of the future but its No. 1 problem is water, most of which is "imported."
Outlook: It is rapidly becoming the most influential of all nations. If a circle were

average of 2.4 children, and black women in the same age group plan to have 2.2 children. White women, however, expect to have only 2 children.[12]

As blacks and Hispanics continue growing as a proportion of the American population, their influence in the marketplace will also increase. See Chapter 21 for a treatment of subcultural differences in buyer behavior.

CHANGES IN VALUE ORIENTATION

At the beginning of this chapter we pointed out that an understanding of demographics can assist managers in developing segmentation schemes, selecting media, and forecasting long-term industry trends. Demographics provide a quantitative profile of the market. We now turn our attention to social values, which can enrich demographic profiles by providing a qualitative perspective on the needs and wants of consumers.

---

drawn around Southern California, it would be the 14th wealthiest country in the world. A strong entrepreneurial spirit and "unlimited growth" perspective attract hard-working Anglos and Hispanics. . . .

The Islands

Nation: The Islands
Capital: Miami
Geography: Florida south of the Jupiter Inlet, northern Venezuela, northern Columbia, Cuba, Jamaica, Puerto Rico, Bahamas, Virgin Islands, Dominican Republic, Haiti, and dozens of other Caribbean islands.
Description: This "nation" consists of southern Florida, which looks south for its future, and the Caribbean, which sees Miami as its capital. The major industries are (1) the $55 billion illegal drug trade, (2) the trade with the "Latin American Rim," and (3) non-Anglo tourism. The Latin American influence is strong and pervasive. The *Miami Herald* circulates editions in Central America. JC Penney stores in Miami stock fur coats in the summer—for tourists south of the equator who arrive during their own winter.
Outlook: The hardest to track civilization in North America. . . . Miami has become a world-class capital with a Caribbean influence. . . . Southern Florida has very little in common with the rest of the state. . . .

Quebec

Nation: Quebec
Capital: Quebec City
Geography: Province of Quebec
Description: The French-speaking area of Canada, steeped in history, tradition, ethnic pride, and a homogeneous culture. It is blessed with plentiful hydroelectric

power, prosperous transportation industries, a diversified economy, and a perspective conducive to the acceptance of high technology.

Outlook: Because they've had to struggle to maintain their identity since the first French settlers arrived, the Quebecois feel they've withstood the test of time. . . . Fiercely independent, the Quebecois make a habit of saying they want to be "mais tres chez nous," or "masters of our own house." While Quebec may never separate from the rest of Canada, . . . the people feel they can, and would, succeed on their own.

Dixie

Nation: Dixie
Capital: Atlanta
Geography: Georgia, Alabama, Mississippi, Louisiana, Arkansas, Kentucky, Tennessee, North Carolina, South Carolina, southern Virginia, southern Maryland, southern Illinois, southern Indiana, southern Missouri, north and central Florida, eastern Texas, southeastern Oklahoma, southern West Virginia, and southern Delaware.
Description: . . . Dixie is an emotion, an idea, a way of life in small towns and cities, calling oneself a "Southerner," the Confederate flag, and waving to strangers. . . .
Outlook: No longer predominantly backward, rural, poor, and racist, Dixie is undergoing the most rapid social and economic change on the continent. However, Dixie's growth is all "catch up," since most of its "impressive" growth statistics (per-capita income, for example) are still below the national average. Southern cities tend to annex surrounding towns with industries, thus creating "artificial" population growth. . . .

New England

Nation: New England
Capital: Boston
Geography: Massachusetts, Maine, New Hampshire, Vermont, Rhode Island, eastern Connecticut, Nova Scotia, Prince Edward Island, Labrador, Newfoundland, and New Brunswick.
Description: With virtually no energy or raw materials, little agriculture, few basic industries, high taxes, and expensive home fuel and auto gas, New England is the poorest of the nine "nations." . . . The oldest and most civilized Anglo "nation" on the continent has people who are environmentally aware, tolerant, intelligent, political, fair, but somewhat elitist. . . .
Outlook: New England was the first "nation" to enter economic decline and a post-industrial society. It is rebounding thanks to an influx of high-tech industries, the proprietors and employees of which like New England's charm and quality of life. . . .

Empty Quarter

Nation: Empty Quarter
Capital: Denver
Geography: Wyoming, Nevada, Montana, Utah, Idaho, western Colorado, eastern California, northern Arizona, western Oregon, western Washington, northwestern

New Mexico, northern Alaska, Yukon, Northwest Territories, eastern British Columbia, Alberta, northern Manitoba, north and southwest Saskatchewan, and northern Ontario.

Description: The Intermountain West boasts wide-open spaces, energy . . . and minerals. . . . While it is the largest "nation" in terms of land area, it has the smallest population, which makes it politically weak-voiced. With its pristine environment, it is the true "west.". . .

Outlook: The future of the Empty Quarter will largely be determined by outsiders; for example, environmentalists who want to preserve its beauty. . . . The people still believe in the "frontier ethic," but this "nation" will undergo radical change over the next 20 years. It's estimated that development of the Overthrust Belt alone could result in one million jobs and eight million additional population.

Ecotopia

Nation: Ecotopia
Capital: San Francisco
Geography: Northwest California, western Oregon, western Washington, western British Columbia, and southeastern coastal Alaska.
Description: The only part of the west blessed with adequate water and renewable resources (and volcanoes). The home of "Silicon Valley," computer chips, aluminum, timber, hydroelectric power, fisheries, bioengineering, environmentalism, outdoor nature lovers, energy conservation, and recycling. "Quality of Life" is a religion in the great Pacific Northwest. . . .
Outlook: Ecotopia's economy is interest-rate-based, so it won't explode with opportunity until interest rates fall. . . . Still, the residents will only want clean, high-tech industries, and will cling to the "small-is-beautiful" ideology. Ecotopia is best positioned to exploit the growing Pacific Rim nations. . . .

Breadbasket

Nation: Breadbasket
Capital: Kansas City
Geography: Minnesota, Iowa, Kansas, North Dakota, South Dakota, Nebraska, northern Missouri, western Wisconsin, northwest Michigan, western and central Oklahoma, eastern New Mexico, eastern Colorado, western and central Illinois, north and central Texas, southeastern Saskatchewan, southern Manitoba, and southwest Ontario.
Description: The Breadbasket is marked by agriculture and agriculture-related industries and economies. If there is a mainstream American, this is it—conservative, hard-working, religious residents. . . .
Outlook: This nation works best. It is stable and at peace with itself by virtue of its enviable, prosperous, renewable economy. The Great Plains also have acquired great political power because of the strategic world importance of food. But farmers are being hurt financially by their own productivity: they are 3% of the population yet feed North Americans and millions of others around the world.

SOURCE: Bernie Whalen (1983), "The Nine Nations of North America," *Marketing News* (Jan. 21), p. 18. Based on Joel Garreau (1981), *The Nine Nations of North America* (Boston: Hougton Mifflin).

social values

A *social value* can be defined as an enduring set of beliefs or attitudes pertaining to a broad concept or a class of objects. According to Milton Rokeach, who believes that values are culturally derived and that they give meaning, stability, and cohesion to the world of the individual, "To say that a person has a value is to say that he has an enduring belief that a specific mode of conduct or end-state of existence is personally and socially preferable to alternate modes of conduct or end-states of existence."[13]

social roles

A concept related to values is *role structure*. A *social role* is an expected pattern of behavior associated with a particular social position. For example, we have beliefs about what constitutes appropriate behavior for a student, teacher, doctor, and man or woman. Social roles are derived from values; values set forth general expectations, and roles define acceptable behavior in light of those values for particular individuals. Since values and social roles are related, a shift in social values leads to a corresponding shift in a society's role structure.

lifestyles

Although values have been extensively discussed in the disciplines of sociology,[14] psychology,[15] and anthropology,[16] they have received little formal attention in the study of consumer behavior.[17] In consumer research, values have sometimes been interpreted as equivalent to *lifestyles*. In fact, the values subscribed to by a society do underlie lifestyles. In other words, lifestyles are predicated upon and emerge from the value structure of a society.

Just as knowledge of demographics helps managers to acquire a quantitative understanding of the market, knowledge of values—the qualitative aspects of the consumer environment—can also prove valuable to managers. Revlon, Inc., for example, has made use of a return to the traditional social value of long-term relationships, marriage, and the family in its advertising campaign for its Charlie fragrance.[18] When the product was introduced a series of advertisements showed "Charlie" as independent and successful, with men assuming only a background role in her life. But the end of 1982 saw the introduction of a new campaign, with a television advertisement in which a very clean-cut man is proposing marriage (see p. 330) and a print advertisement prominently featuring a man (Exhibit 14–5). Revlon's intent is to continue to develop this campaign in light of knowledge of shifts in social values. Whereas demographic data such as users' ages and incomes can help define the market for Charlie, an awareness of shifting values can lead to a more accurate and more comprehensive qualitative profile of the target market.

Changing Social Values

The notion of monitoring broad social changes is relatively recent in consumer research. Two widely known analyses of changing social values are provided by the Yankelovich *Monitor*, an annual publication of Yankelovich, Skelly, and White, Inc. and the Stanford Research Institute. Both organizations view the social climate of the United States as the basis for understanding consumer behavior.

Yankelovich Monitor[19]   The Yankelovich organization began tracking social change in 1970. Since that year, the firm has enlarged the scope of the *Monitor* to provide an ongoing study of American consumers, their lifestyles and their values, and the implications of changes in the social climate as they induce corresponding changes in consumer behavior.

Before we discuss current findings of the *Monitor*, and the ways in which its subscribers—primarily business firms and advertising agencies—utilize the material, it may be helpful to examine the *Monitor's* view of broad patterns of social change as they have emerged since World War II. The *Monitor* believes that that war marks a turning point in the value system of the United States. Before the war, the great majority of Americans aimed to attain a traditional middle-class lifestyle through adherence to the Protestant Ethic. The Protestant Ethic maintains that success results from hard work coupled with self-denial.

At the war's end, booming economic conditions, fueled by generous government programs, resulted in conditions which precipitated movement away from the **old values.** The *Monitor* believes that America's new affluence had two effects. First, for a large part of society, it reinforced the Protestant Ethic by demonstrating that success was now achievable more quickly than in the past. But, for another relatively affluent and well-educated segment of the population, the new, seemingly limitless prosperity caused a change of values. The *Monitor* maintains that this segment questioned the need for self-denial. Because the country was so prosperous, struggling for a share of that affluence seemed unnecessary. This group raised its children to believe that the economic struggle which had once dominated life need not continue. As a result, these children, when they came of age in the 1960s, openly challenged not only the Protestant Ethic, but also most other traditional values, with attacks on materialism, big business, and the treatment of minorities and women. The "rebels" were interested in living fulfilling, meaningful lives, with emphasis on personal relationships and self-development.

Although society remained stable overall, this revised view of America, and the purported need for a better personal life, had an impact on a large portion of the population. When the *Monitor* began its tracking studies in 1970, these attitudes were labeled the **new values,** and over 50 percent of the American population subscribed to them to some degree.

In addition to identifying major social values, the *Monitor* specifies population segments, termed *social-values groups*, which subscribe to the new values to a greater or lesser degree. In 1981, the *Monitor* identified five groups.

- *Classic Values* (26 percent). This group is the oldest (median age 55) and is characterized by a low educational level and a relative lack of affluence. The Classic-Values segment continues to subscribe to the old values and the Protestant Ethic, and also incorporates a resistance to new lifestyles and an active opposition to new values.
- *Balanced New Values* (21 percent). This is a young, financially well-off group, whose focus is on the self. The Balanced segment combines work achievement and fulfilling personal experiences as valuable goals: they seek self-fulfillment through work and personal effort.
- *Detoured New Values* (18 percent). This young (median age 35) segment is more downscale than the Balanced segment. They remain committed to the new values, but they are finding the road to personal experience blocked by economic realities. An angry group, they are financially limited by larger families, less education, limited job mobility, and so on.

old values

new values

- *Idealized New Values* (18 percent). This middle-aged (median age 39), largely female segment is still basically following the Protestant Ethic, as in the Classic-Values segment. But unlike the Classic segment, this group is also committed to the achievement of personal fulfillment—a new-values goal.
- *Aimless New Values* (17 percent). This young (median age 29) segment is characterized by a lack of purpose and goals and a highly hedonistic lifestyle.

The differentiation between old and new values also precipitates a distinction between what the *Monitor* has termed "me" products and "we" products. *Me products* are ego-involving and are related to meaningful personal experience and fulfillment. Such "me" products as perfume, clothing, travel, and other image-creating products are used by consumers to make statements about themselves. As the degree of importance placed on fulfilling personal experience grows, sensitivity to the price of these products declines. Quite the reverse holds for *we products,* such as paper goods, which are not ego-involving. Price sensitivity to these products continues to be high.

But, as indicated in the *Monitor,* not all consumers accept or are able to achieve the goal of fulfilling personal experience. The Detoured New-Values group is financially unable to avail itself of many of the new products or services aimed at consumers who have this goal. And the Classic-Values group, as we have seen, actively opposes the new values.

Stanford Research Institute   A different typology of American value segments is suggested by the **Stanford Research Institute**.[20] SRI proposes three major groups based on a nationally representative survey: (1) **need-driven** or money-restricted, (2) **outer-directed,** and (3) **inner-directed.**[21]

Need-Driven   This segment, which consists of approximately 11 percent of the adult American population, is characterized by low income and the corresponding lack of discretionary purchasing power. These money-restricted individuals tend to be older and to have little education. Their dominant values are survival and security. Because of their financial situation, the need-driven confine the majority of their purchases to necessities, and they do not represent a large market for innovative new products.

Outer-directed   This segment, which represents 68 percent of the population, is composed of "middle America." These consumers are concerned with the image they present to others: their purchases comply with set group norms. There are three distinct subgroups.

- *The Belongers* (35 percent of the population) are basically the mass market. This is an older group (mean age 51), with middle-to-low education, income, and social status. The Belongers are conforming consumers who adhere to group norms and who hold traditional values. They are not innovative in their buying behavior.
- *The Achievers* (23 percent) are competitive, successful, and confident individuals who want the best and are willing to work for it. These well-educated and affluent consumers comprise the best market for top-of-the-

line luxury goods as well as for innovative products. Although they are status conscious and want their products to reflect their status, they are moving away from traditional success symbols (such as club memberships, the yearly new car, and being in *Who's Who*). SRI believes that their future status symbols will be more subtle, such as having free time anytime, being viewed as creative individuals, and having a broad range of interests. Achievers are interested in innovation and are among the first to try new products. Since they do not resist change, they are the creators of new social norms rather than adherents to old ones.

- *The Emulators* (10 percent) are ostentatious consumers who engage in a great deal of conspicuous consumption. They attempt to imitate the behavior and purchasing patterns of people they believe to be rich and successful. Although on the surface the Emulators may appear to be similar to the Achievers, on further analysis, they seem to be unhappy and insecure. They have a strong need to appear fashionable, which they satisfy through imitation rather than innovation.

Inner-Directed   The third SRI segment, consisting of 21 percent of the population, is concerned primarily with its own wants and needs. Unlike the Outer-Directed, they do not purchase products to impress other people or to satisfy group norms. There are three subgroups.

- *The I-Am-Me Consumers* (5 percent) are young, highly individualistic people who purchase products primarily to show their independence and autonomy. SRI believes that this may be a transitional group for consumers moving from outer-directedness to inner-directedness. Interestingly, group members tend to be either younger, adolescent-phase consumers or recently divorced—both of whom have a great need to establish themselves as individuals.

- *The Experiential Consumers* (7 percent) are highly active socially, participating in politics, volunteer work, and so forth, and will "try anything once." They seek varied experiences, and this attitude affects their buying behavior. They buy numerous products on a trial basis—but they become committed buyers only if a product offers definite benefits.

- *The Societally Conscious Consumers* (9 percent) are highly aware of social issues. They are interested in and knowledgeable about world affairs, ecological issues, and spiritual concerns. They seek out products which offer value for money, and although they are willing to pay a high price for goods, they will do so only if they believe the goods are of very high quality. They differ from the Experiential in that they are not particularly interested in having a great variety of experiences; rather, they focus on developing a lifestyle that is characterized by social responsibility.

While both the *Monitor* and SRI present interesting typologies, it should be noted that the major segments are identified using cluster analysis, a data-analysis procedure that cannot evaluate statistical significance. Also, the subgroups are not necessarily "clean," that is, there is a degree of overlap among segments. Finally, we must ask if these typologies are in fact truly relevant to consumption behavior, since there is no rigorous empirical research that shows significant differences in the actual purchase patterns of the behavior groups. Nonetheless, the two approaches provide an interesting appraisal of various consumer orientations.

Consumer Implications

Although the details of the SRI typology differ from those of the *Monitor,* the approaches agree on the basic forces at work in the consumer environment. Traditional conservative values coexist with innovative values; consumers span a continuum of willingness to adopt new products, from avid innovativeness to complete lack of interest. Some consumers are limited only by their whims, while others are restricted by lack of economic means.

One of the keys to marketing success is an appreciation of the values of society, which enriches the quantitative profile provided by demographics. One company that has undertaken a comprehensive analysis of long-range trends is General Mills, historically a consumer packaged-goods company.[22] In 1966, General Mills decided to embark on a diversification program, acquiring over forty companies from 1967 to 1979. Acquisitions were focused to correspond with high-growth, consumer market segments, identified on the basis of both changing demographics and changing value structures.

General Mills noted the aging of the population, the baby boomlet, and the trend to delaying childbearing. The high divorce rate and the increasing incidence of deferred first marriage were seen as contributing to the increase in the proportion of nontraditional, nonfamily households. The increasing number of women in the work force was seen as a major social trend. General Mills also identified a number of changes in value orientation occurring in American society, such as greater emphasis on the quality of life, the search for personal fulfillment, and rising interest in interpersonal relationships. Women were shifting their focus from home to career, signaling increased value placed on convenience. More emphasis was placed on "naturalness" and physical fitness. And there was more interest in "investment spending," that is, spending on high-quality goods.

These consumer trends formed the basis of a number of managerial decisions. Demographics and values indicated that food-consumption patterns were changing: consumers were eating in restaurants more frequently, pointing to a long-term decrease in the proportion of food dollars spent in supermarkets. This trend was crucially important for General Mills, whose mainstay had been packaged foods. As a result of this analysis, General Mills decided to acquire Red Lobster Inns and York Steak Houses and to develop the Good Earth Restaurants. Recognizing increased consumer concern with physical fitness, nutrition, and diet, they introduced a range of granola-based products and high-fiber cereals. They took account of emerging values in formulating advertising communication strategies for traditional cereals like Cheerios and Wheaties. They identified new distribution channels: mail-order, for example, represents a convenient and time-saving mode of shopping. They acquired both The Talbots (known for classic clothing styles and high quality) and Eddie Bauer (high-quality outdoor products). After generating strong mail-order sales, they established new retail outlets for the products of these companies.

Their knowledge of demographics and values enabled General Mills to develop an understanding of general patterns of consumer behavior and to utilize that understanding in managerial analysis and decision-making.

Changing Role Structures

As demographics and values shift, social roles also change. We have seen that one of the major demographic changes in the United States is the growth in the number of women in the work force. As their work-force participation has increased, women's attitudes toward themselves and their roles have changed. This signals a shift in the value orientation of society toward a more egalitarian view of women and men.

Rena Bartos, writing in the *Harvard Business Review*, questions whether marketing and advertising specialists have truly responded to the attitudinal changes that have occurred among women.[23] She points out that many products and advertising appeals are targeted to "any housewife, 18–49." Bartos' discussion identifies four segments which comprise the 18–49 female market. These segments are based on (a) whether or not the woman works outside the home and (b) attitude toward working outside the home. They are

1. housewives who intend to continue to stay at home;
2. housewives who plan to work in the future;
3. working women who view their work-force participation as "just a job" and who would prefer not to work; and
4. career women who value professional achievement for its own sake.

Exhibit 14–6 shows some interesting demographic and behavioral similarities and differences among the four groups. First of all, the rank ordering of educational level indicates that career women have the most education, followed by the plan-to-work housewives, who are better educated than just-a-job women. Next, the plan-to-work women are the youngest (and thus the most likely to have young children at home). The career and just-a-job segments are similar in age, while the stay-at-home segment is the oldest. Media behavior, too, varies across the segments. As might be expected, both groups 238 of working women are more likely to listen to the radio and less likely to view television.

Bartos discusses the impact of these segments on traditional assumptions about women's buying behavior. For example, whereas marketers frequently assume that "the traditional housewife is house proud; the working woman wants convenience," data indicate that the stay-at-home housewife is *below* the norm in usage of floor wax and rug shampoo, and only slightly above the norm in usage of furniture polish. But the plan-to-work housewife and the career woman are both above the norm in usage of all three products.

Another long held marketing belief is that "women may pick the color of the upholstery, but men choose the car." But, as Bartos indicates, women currently account for approximately 40 percent of all decisions about car purchases. Among all married women, the career woman is most likely to live in a two-car household. If there are no children present, then the household of the plan-to-work woman is more likely to have two cars than that of the just-a-job working woman, while the stay-at-home housewife is least likely to have two cars. Also contrary to popular belief, it is the career woman (rather than the stereotyped harried mother driving children to school and Dad to the train) who is the heaviest driver.

The effects of increased participation of women in the work force and the influence of the women's movement have not been limited to attitudinal changes among women. Men, too, are undergoing role and behavioral changes.

A study by Benton and Bowles, Inc., a New York-based advertising agency, sampled 617 married men (73 percent response rate), and found that

- 32% shop for food,
- 74% take out the garbage,
- 47% cook for the family,
- 53% wash the dishes,
- 29% do the laundry,
- 28% clean the bathroom,
- 39% vacuum the house, and
- 80% take care of the children (in households with children under age 12).[24]

Four segments of men, varying in their attitudes and behavior, were identified.

EXHIBIT 14–6
DEMOGRAPHIC AND BEHAVIORAL CHARACTERISTICS OF FOUR GROUPS

Segment	% of Sample[a]	Educational Level[b]	Age	Radio Listening	TV Viewing
"Career Women"	19	1	middle	1	less
"Just a Job"	36	3	middle	2	less
"Plan to Work Housewives"	15	2	youngest	3	more
"Stay at Home Housewives"	30	4	oldest	4	more

[a]1976 figure

[b]1 indicates highest educational level/ most radio listening

SOURCE: Reprinted by permission of the *Harvard Business Review*. Excerpt from "What Every Marketer Should Know About Women," by Rena Bartos (May, June 1978). Copyright © 1978 by the President and Fellows of Harvard College; all rights reserved.

1. *The Progressives*. Although they comprise only 13 percent of the population, these young, affluent, well-educated husbands not only are comfortable with a new, "liberated" role structure, but about 80 percent also freely perform a variety of household chores, from vacuuming to shopping for groceries.
2. *The Traditionalists*. This older, less well-educated group (only 10 percent have college educations) represent 39 percent of the married male population. They hold traditional values, believing that a woman's place is indeed in the home, and they are traditional in their behavior, rarely performing any household duties.
3. *The Ambivalents*. This segment, comprising 15 percent of the population, tends to average in its demographic profile, conforming closely to national norms. But the Ambivalents seem to be in a state of conflict over old and new values. For instance, while they believe that a woman's place is in the home, they simultaneously believe that it is good that more women are currently employed outside the home. And interestingly, 60 percent of them do household chores. They are second only to Progressives in their performance of household chores.
4. *All Talk, No Action*. This segment represents 33 percent of the population. These men are young, but are about average in other demographic respects. Members of this group "talk like Progressives, but act like Traditionalists." That is, while they support the idea that men and women should share household responsibilities, only one third of this group actually performs household chores.

The Benton and Bowles study concludes that men will increasingly accept new societal roles:

> *Increased male use of traditional female household products will have a significant impact on packaging, new product development, line extensions, and product modifications.*
>
> *Therefore, product needs of male users will be considered in categories where men play an important role in selection and use. This will mean more product testing among men as well as research to identify unfilled needs of men.*[25]

As women's roles change, men's roles also shift. Exhibit 14–7 shows two examples of advertisements of national brands in which men are depicted in loving relationships with children—a dramatic movement away from stereotypical advertising practices.

As women become more influential in decision-making for durable goods, and as men purchase more nondurables, traditional approaches to advertising are changing. Even more basically, definition of the target market is changing. Accurate identification of present and potential buyers is a prerequisite for marketing success: As male and female roles overlap more and more, traditional assumptions about sex roles and buying behavior will become less accurate.

SUMMARY

Societal structure is dynamic. In order to keep abreast of changing consumer needs, managers must be aware of shifts in the demographic structure and the values of society.

An appreciation of demographic and value patterns can assist managers in three major ways. First, it facilitates identification of market segments. Decisions about new-product introductions and product repositioning require the identification of the "best" consumer segment to target. These segments are qualitatively depicted by an understanding of their value orientation. Second, demographic and value patterns help managers develop sound communication strategies: media selection, budget allocation, and copy strategy all benefit. Third, knowledge of societal trends assists managers in developing long-range strategic plans, making marketing decisions more responsive to shifts in the consumer climate.

EXHIBIT 14–7
CHANGING MEN'S ROLES

We have discussed the demographic shifts characterizing American society. The baby-boom generation—our largest age group—is aging, increasing the median age of society. Household consumption is also changing. No longer is the traditional nuclear family representative of the average household's structure. In fact, only 15 percent of households today consist of a breadwinner father, homemaker mother, and children. A high divorce rate, increased childlessness, and delay in the age of first marriage all contribute to the decreasing incidence of the traditional family.

We have examined several other demographic shifts, including the influx of women into the paid work force and the corresponding increase in the number of dual-career couples; population shifts, especially from the North and East to the West and South; and the increase in the proportion of both blacks and Hispanics in the population, an increase that is expected to continue.

The values of American society are also changing. Organizations such as Yankelovich, Skelly and White, Inc., and the Stanford Research Institute identify the main components of the *social climate* in an attempt to understand the structure of the consumer environment. The Yankelovich *Monitor* suggests that the market is composed of five value-segments differentiated by their commitment to new values (such as self-fulfillment) versus traditional values (belief in the Protestant Ethic). The SRI analysis identifies three groups of consumers: the need-driven, the outer-directed, and the inner-directed.

As demographics and social values shift, so do social needs. Stereotypical male and female roles are no longer the norm. Separate studies of women and of men indicate that the attitudes and behaviors of each sex span a range from highly traditional to very liberated. As men's and women's roles continue to blur (at least for selected population segments), buyer behavior will change. Managers will be unable to define target markets, media patterns, and consumers' preference solely on the basis of sex-role stereotypes.

One key to successful marketing lies in understanding the consumer. Knowledge of demographic patterns coupled with an understanding of the value orientation of the marketplace provide the ideal starting point for the development of marketing strategy.

KEY CONCEPTS

demographics	changing value	Stanford Research
social values	orientation	Institute
baby-boom consumers	role structures	need-driven
the mature market	social climate	consumers
household composition	Yankelovich *Monitor*	outer-directed
nuclear family	new values	consumers
black and Hispanic	old values	inner-directed
population growth		consumers

DISCUSSION QUESTIONS

1. Why is it important that managers study demographic trends and value changes?
2. Of the major demographic trends occurring in the United States, which *one* do you think is having the greatest impact on short-term marketing decisions (within the next two to three years)? Why? Which *one* is having the greatest impact on long-term marketing decisions? Why?
3. What long-term effects can be expected as a result of (a) the aging of the baby-boom consumers and (b) changing composition of households?
4. What types of products will be most affected by the regional population redistribution?
5. What marketing actions might a manager take to appeal to dual-career couples?
6. What are the five value segments identified by the Yankelovich *Monitor*? How do these segments affect marketing strategy for (a) luxury goods, (b) frequently purchased food products, and (c) household furnishings?
7. How would the key elements of marketing strategy differ for the affluent segment versus the financially underprivileged segment for (a) a major household appliance such as a refrigerator or washing machine and (b) children's clothing. In what ways would the elements of the marketing approaches be similar for each of these goods?
8. How will the changing roles of men and women affect the consumer purchasing-process for (a) frequently purchased nondurable goods and (b) durable household goods?

NOTES

1. "Forecast Abstracts" (1982), *Predicasts Forecasts,* (Apr.), Sec. E120, p. B–5.
2. David L. Kaplan and Cheryl Russell (1980), "What the 1980 Census Will Show," *American Demographics,* (Apr.), p. 15.
3. "Openers" (1981), *American Demographics* (May), p. 9.
4. U.S. Department of Commerce, Bureau of the Census (1979), Current Population Reports, Series P-20, no. 345 (March), p. 1 and Population Projections, Series P-25, no. 805, p. 3.
5. Cheryl Russell (1981), "The Condo Craze," *American Demographics* (March), pp. 42–44.
6. U.S. Department of Commerce, Bureau of the Census, Current Population Reports, Series P-23, no. 100.
7. U.S. Department of Commerce, Bureau of the Census, Current Population Reports, Series P-23, no. 100.
8. "Demographic Forecasts" (1981), *American Demographics* (March), pp. 46–47.
9. Joel Garreau (1981), *The Nine Nations of North America* (Boston: Houghton Mifflin).
10. U.S. Bureau of the Census (1981), "Age, Sex, Race, and Spanish Origin of the Population by Regions, Divisions, and States: 1980," *1980 Census of Population, Supplementary Reports,* PC 80-S1-1 (Washington, D.C.: GPO), p. 3.
11. Reid T. Reynolds, Bryant Robey, and Cheryl Russell (1980), "Demographics of the 1980s," *American Demographics,* 2 (Jan.), pp. 16–17.
12. "Openers" (1980), *American Demographics* (May), p. 9.
13. Milton Rokeach (1968), *Attitudes and Values* (San Francisco: Jossey-Bass), pp. 159–60.
14. See, for example, Howard Becker (1941), "Supreme Values and the Sociologist," *American Sociologist Review,* 6, pp. 155–72; Peter Blau (1964), *Exchange and Power in Social Life* (New York: Wiley); and Talcott Parsons (1960), "Pattern Variables Revisited," *American Sociological Review,* 25, pp. 467–83.

15. See, for example, Gordon W. Allport and Philip E. Vernon (1931), *The Study of Values* (Boston: Houghton Mifflin) and Milton Rokeach (1968).

16. See, for example, Clyde Kluckhohn (1951), "Values and Value Orientations in the Theory of Action: An Explanation in Definition and Classification," in *Toward a General Theory of Action,* ed. P. Talcott and E. Shills (Cambridge, Mass.: Harvard Univ. Press).

17. Notable exceptions include C. Joseph Clawson and Donald E. Vinson (1978), "Human Values: A Historical and Interdisciplinary Analysis," in *Advances in Consumer Research,* ed. H. Keith Hunt (Assn. for Consumer Research), pp. 396–402; Donald E. Vinson, Jerome E. Scott, and Lawrence M. Lamont (1977), "The Role of Personal Values in Marketing and Consumer Behavior," *Journal of Marketing,* 41, pp. 44–50; and Walter A. Henry (1976), "Culture Values Do Correlate with Consumer Behavior," *Journal of Marketing Research,* 13, pp. 121–27.

18. Bill Abrams (1982), "Why Revlon's Charlie Seems to Be Ready to Settle Down," *Wall Street Journal* (Dec. 23), p. 11.

19. *Monitor* (1981) (New York: Yankelovich, Shelley, and White).

20. Marie Spengler, "The Consumer of the Eighties—Changing Values and Lifestyles," paper presented at the ANA New Product Marketing Workshop, New York (1980) and Los Angeles (1981).

21. The distinction between inner- and outer-directed is similar to the difference between inner-directed and other-directed behavior proposed by Riesman et al. in David Riesman, Nathan Glazer, and Reuel Denney (1961), *The Lonely Crowd,* abridged ed. (New Haven, Conn.: Yale Univ. Press).

22. Sandra Kresch (1983), "The Impact of Consumer Trends on Corporate Strategy," *Journal of Business Strategy,* 3, pp. 58–63.

23. Rena Bartos (1978), "What Every Marketer Should Know About Women," *Harvard Business Review* (May-June), pp. 73–85.

24. *Marketing News* (1980), Oct. 3.

25. Despite the increasing participation of men, a consistent finding is that women still do most of the household chores. For an excellent review of this literature, see Joanne Miller and Howard H. Garrison (1982), "Sex Roles: The Division of Labor at Home and in the Workplace," *Annual Review of Sociology,* 8, pp. 237–62.

15 New Product Diffusion and Consumer Innovators

Diffusion *is the process by which something spreads. Anthropologists have studied the diffusion of language, religion, and ideas across tribes and societies. Sociologists have studied the diffusion of new ideas and new practices—such as farming and medical innovations—within societies. Consumer-behavior researchers have studied the diffusion of new products and services within market segments.*

The diffusion literature, as developed across a number of disciplines, offers a well-developed theoretical framework which applies to the flow of information, ideas, and products. It is the integration of this framework with the traditional marketing framework that may advance our understanding of how new products disseminate and gain consumer acceptance and that may suggest means of improving new-product marketing strategies.

Here are the five key concepts underlying diffusion theory, together with some important questions regarding each.

1. *The concept of* innovation. *What constitutes a new product or service? What attributes of an innovation are most likely to speed or slow the diffusion process?*
2. *The concept of the* diffusion process. *This is probably most familiar as the "product life cycle" within the marketing literature. Can marketing activities affect the takeoff point in diffusion (when sales begin to rise rapidly), the speed of diffusion (the acceleration of sales), and the shape of the diffusion curve? To what extent must marketing strategy be modified in response to the diffusion curve?*
3. *The concept of the consumer* innovator. *What are the characteristics of those who buy a new product first—the "innovators"? How can they be reached?*
4. *The concept of the* adoption process. *We have discussed adoption previously, when we examined consumer information processing and decision processes (Chapter 4). How does the consumer reach a decision as to whether to buy a new product? How does the adoption process differ for innovators compared with later adopters?*
5. *The concept of* personal influence, *or the flow of information which is transmitted among consumers about products and services. Particularly important in this process are the opinion leaders—those with high influence on their peers. How can marketing managers affect the flow of personal influence? How can opinion leaders be reached? Personal influence is developed fully in the next chapter.*

THE INNOVATION

Product and service innovations are a major source of corporate sales growth. In high-technology industries particularly, innovations may be essential to survival. But in many other industries, from clothing fashion to toys to packaged goods, innovations, even if minor, may provide competitive advantage for a firm.

What is an *innovation*? At least three definitional criteria have frequently been used:

1. *Newness in contrast with existing products and services.* Those who propose this definition suggest that a "new" product must be very different from established products. But it is difficult to make such a criterion operational. Ultimately, all products and services are modifications or recombinations of existing items. Innovation results as the outcome of an evolutionary sequence. Even an innovation such as the computer can be considered to be a recombination of existing elements coupled with a measure of creative insight.
2. *Newness in time.* Length of time on the market is a second possible criterion in defining an innovation. But firms have tended to promote a product as new for as long as two or three years after introduction, under the assumption that the word "new" in advertising, or on the package, is a positive sales appeal. The Federal Trade Commission once proposed, in an advisory opinion, to arbitrarily limit the use of the word "new" to the six months after the product entered regular distribution after test marketing.[1]
3. *Consumer perception of newness.* Another proposed criterion for defining an innovation is that consumers must perceive the product to be new. This consumer view is, of course, the ultimate test in the marketplace.

For our purposes, we will rely on this last definition—a product or service is an *innovation* if consumers perceive it as such. The most essential factor in defining an innovation will be its perceived effect on established patterns of consumption. We recognize, however, that there is actually a continuum of innovations, not a simple dichotomy of products that are either innovations or not innovations.

The Innovation Continuum

All new products or services introduced to the market have some level of impact on established consumption patterns. At one extreme consumers may judge products to have limited effect on their consumption patterns. Such products are referred to as **continuous innovations** and include line extensions (like Crest spearmint toothpaste or Michelob light beer) as well as minor product modifications (like annual new-model automobiles). Alternatively, the product may be judged by consumers to involve fundamental changes in their consumption patterns, or the creation of new patterns. Such products are referred to as **discontinuous innovations** and include the products of new technologies at the time of introduction (like the computer, the electric light bulb, or the jet aircraft). There is also a considerable range of innovation between these extremes. Exhibit 15–1 shows an innovation continuum with representative products.

Most innovation is of a continuous nature and, especially in the consumer sector, the result of attempts to differentiate products to increase market share. Few and far between are innovations of a discontinuous nature that significantly alter or create new consumption patterns. The stereotype of the inspired genius creating innovations does not match the typical process leading to innovation. Even discontinuous innovations are increasingly the result of team research. Most innovation today results from programmed, systematic research efforts combined with insight and occasional luck. Exhibit 15–2 details the process of new product design and introduction to the market.

In the long run, the successful company must manage the total innovation continuum, although in some industries (high technology) the stress is more toward the discontinuous end, and in other industries (low technology) the stress is more toward the continuous end. A firm must also be sensitive to external innovation that takes place beyond the boundaries of the industry, but that may have the potential to change the industry. Much innovation comes not from the established companies in an industry but from new competitors. Du Pont (a chemical company) is an example of an external company which has dramatically helped change the clothing industry with the invention of such new fabrics as nylon, dacron, and rayon.

EXHIBIT 15–1
THE INNOVATION CONTINUUM

Continuous Innovations			Discontinuous Innovations
Line Extensions (For example, new flavors, sizes, packages)	Minor Product Modifications (For example, annual new models in cars or new fashions)	Major Product Modifications (For example, compact cars when first introduced or color television vs. black & white)	New Technologies (For example, the invention of the computer or jet aircraft)

Here are some examples which demonstrate the need for companies to manage the total innovation continuum.

- *Boeing*. The 757 and 767 aircraft are fairly continuous innovations. They were planned and programmed after assessing airline needs in terms of such variables as range, seating capacity, cost of operation, and number of flight personnel in the cockpit. The 757 and 767 are designed to fill gaps

EXHIBIT 15–2
THE NEW-PRODUCT DEVELOPMENT SEQUENCE[a]

Most new products are derivatives of existing technology and fundamentally new technologies are rare. Furthermore, while new technologies may be the desired goal, R&D efforts are frequently nonpredictable. The discussion to follow on new-product development, therefore, applies more to continuous than discontinuous innovations—especially the new-product design component of the sequence.

New-Product Design	**Market Introduction**
1. New Product Strategy	
2. Idea Generation	
3. Concept Testing	
4. Prototype Testing	
5. Business Case Analysis	
6. Test Marketing	
7. Regional Rollout	
8. National Marketing	

1. *New-Product Strategy*. The logical starting point in new product development is the company's new-product objectives. A line-extension objective (e.g., develop a new flavor) leads to a very different process from a new-technology objective to match a competitor's superior technology (e.g., if Zenith were to try to match Japanese technology for in-home video systems, rather than licensing the technology as it presently does).

2. *Idea Generation*. Ideas for new products come from within the company (salesforce, designers, and managers) and from customers (for example, focus-group sessions). Perceptual maps may be used to find "gaps" in markets where there is consumer preference but limited competition. Conjoint analysis may be used to find the combination of product attributes that is most desired by consumers and can be feasibly offered. Two ideas that have been studied are "nutritional coffee" and "vegetable yogurt."

3. *Concept Testing*. At this stage ideas are phrased as concepts and tested with consumers.

- "Would you like a new coffee with the taste of Maxwell House but nutritionally enriched to give you the value of two eggs and bacon?"

- "Would you like a new vegetable yogurt that can be served as an appetizer in summer or as a nutritious between-meals snack?"

in the market and represent only minor variations of the existing technology. Boeing expects its line of 737, 747, 757, and 767 to be competitive through at least the 1980s. Yet, it must concurrently work on the development of more innovative, discontinuous, aircraft, such as the SST, VTOL (vertical takeoff and landing), and STOL (short takeoff and landing), or it may be caught and surpassed technologically by competitors.

- *Monroe, Marchant, and Frieden.* During the decade of the 1960s these companies competed with each other in the rotary-calculator market. Each

---

Most ideas fail concept testing and are not pursued, but the concepts that pass go to the next stage in the new-product development sequence.

4. *Prototype Testing.* Here the new concept is turned into a product and tested with consumers. The nutritious coffee and vegetable yogurt might, for example, be subjected to in-home usage tests. Consumers will try these new products for a week or so with their families and then will be asked, "Did you like the product?" "What did you like most or least about it?" "Which member of the family liked it most?" "Would you be willing to pay [a certain amount of] money for it?"

5. *Business Case Analysis.* If the product passes concept testing, it is time to conduct a rigorous case analysis in order to decide whether to proceed further. What are the anticipated costs of producing and marketing the product relative to the projected size of the market and the price that can be charged? Does this appear to be a sound business proposition relative to other investment alternatives that the company has?

6. *Test Marketing.* At this stage the product is introduced to the market in a very limited way, but under "real" conditions. The product may be sold only in two or three locations (favorite test markets are Omaha, Syracuse, and Bakersfield, California). The key question is whether the product will achieve its sales objectives when actually offered for sale to consumers at a certain price and with a particular advertising program supporting it. It is also possible that somewhat different marketing programs could be used in different test markets. For example, we could vary the price of our nutritional coffee and track test market results.

7. *Regional Rollout.* If the new product succeeds in test market, then we move toward national marketing. We may, however, engage in a rollout region by region as we build production capacity or if we have limited resources for nationwide advertising and sales. Generally the product will be marketed first in the high potential regions, which will vary with the type of product.

8. *National Marketing.* The final stage in a successful new-product development sequence is national (or eventually multinational) marketing. Unfortunately, the vegetable-yogurt idea failed in test market, and nutritional coffee never got beyond concept testing. Tastes do change, however, and there may be some hope at some point in the future for both products.

---

[a]For greater detail on the new-product development sequence see Yoram Wind (1982), *Product Policy* (Reading, Mass.: Addison-Wesley), Ch. 8–14.

year they introduced new models of a highly continuous nature—with new colors, minor new functions, and so on. Then electronic calculators appeared from Texas Instruments, Sony, and Hewlett-Packard, that were discontinuous innovations—smaller, quieter, cheaper, faster, and with memory units. Monroe, Marchant, and Frieden were out of business almost overnight in the calculator market because they could not match the new technology.

* *Smith-Kline-Beckman.* Perhaps the most significant drug innovation in the decade of the 1970s was Tagamet—an ulcer drug that eliminates the need for surgery on bleeding ulcers. This discontinuous innovation contributes hundreds of millions of dollars in sales to Smith-Kline-Beckman and about one half of the company's profits. Yet, this drug took years to develop and was the payoff of hundreds of millions of dollars in research and development.[2] In order to invest such sums in R&D and to sustain the business while waiting for a breakthrough, Smith-Kline-Beckman introduced such continuous innovations as Contac—essentially a cold tablet with a time-release feature. It was necessary to manage both the long run (discontinuous innovation) and the short run (continuous innovation) in order to survive in the drug market.

The innovation continuum represents increasing risk. As we move from continuous to discontinuous innovations, the financial risk increases considerably. Line extensions involve minimal investment in either R&D, production capacity, or marketing resources, whereas new technologies may involve huge long-run commitments to R&D and new production capabilities, together with major marketing expenditures in consumer education and in building a distribution system.

It is difficult to estimate the rate of new-product success by stage of the innovation continuum. Estimates of new-product success rates run from as high as two out of three to as low as two out of ten.[3] The discrepancy in estimates is due, at least in part, to different definitions of what a new product is and different definitions of what failure means—while one study may include only products which are withdrawn from the market, another may include all unprofitable products, even if they remain on the market.

For our purposes a reasonable estimate is that somewhat less than one half of new products succeed. However, success rates may be higher in the following cases.

* Large companies in sophisticated industries tend to market fewer failures than small companies in less sophisticated industries. Thus, research by the Conference Board[4] and Booz Allen & Hamilton[5] with major (generally sophisticated) clients finds that almost two thirds of new products succeed. This is probably because these more sophisticated companies are more likely to conduct research on the consumer need for new products.
* It may be the case—although evidence is very limited—that discontinuous innovations have a better success rate than continuous innovations. This might be expected since discontinuous innovations offer significant alter-

natives to existing patterns of consumption. Thus, research on new grocery products by the A. C. Nielsen Company reports significantly lower success levels of from only 35 percent to 49 percent for these relatively continuous innovations[6] versus the 67 percent success reported in the Conference Board study.

- The new product's probability of success is also greater if the company has conducted an assessment of the market attractiveness and the company's capabilities. Exhibit 15–3 suggests such a framework for finding products that are likely to fit the company's strengths.

Factors Determining New Product Success

The general reasons for new product failure are not technical inadequacies of the product but rather a failure to meet consumer needs. Most new products work; when failure occurs it is because consumers either don't want the product or competitors are already making a similar product and consumers have no reason to change behavior.[7]

From a more positive perspective, the logical question is, what factors affect the likelihood that a new product will succeed? The most common framework for assessing the likely acceptance of an innovation is that of Rogers, who is the foremost scholar on diffusion theory. Rogers suggests five factors affecting rate of diffusion.[8]

1. **Relative advantage,** which refers to consumer evaluation of the new product's benefits relative to other products on the market. The greater the perceived relative advantage, the faster the rate of diffusion. A product that lacks obvious advantage (even if it is a good product) may have a slow rate of diffusion. For example, health-care innovations focused on prevention (such as screening procedures) diffuse slowly because the benefits are somewhat remote.[9]
2. **Compatibility** of an innovation with the social system's values and norms. High compatibility will speed diffusion. Graham, for example, in studying the early diffusion of television, found that it diffused more quickly at lower social-class levels where, he argued, it was more consistent with the lower-class value system and more passive way of life.[10] Light beer seems to have met with a lack of compatibility with the Mexican beer market, probably because the social system places so little emphasis on controlling weight.
3. **Complexity,** which refers to the degree of difficulty in understanding and using the new product. In general, the more complex the item, the slower its rate of diffusion and the narrower its potential market. For example, IR-8 "miracle rice," which can achieve more than four times the yields of ordinary rice varieties, was hampered in its introduction in the Philippines by its complexity. In order to plant this hybrid rice and to harvest these additional yields, it was necessary to use certain fertilizers and fungicides which were unfamiliar to the farmer. More equipment such as tractors was needed. A means of storage was required, as well as some mechanism for getting the surplus yields to the cities. Because this was all too complex for

a subsistence-level farmer (and lacked compatibility with existing farming methods), the "miracle rice" initially failed.

4. **Trialability**, which refers to the extent to which a new product may be tried on a limited scale. For consumer goods, marketing tactics which take this factor into account include free sampling programs, taste tests, and small package sizes. For industrial products, manufacturers have moved toward more display centers and trade shows to enable customers to see the actual product and to try it.

EXHIBIT 15–3
ASSESSING NEW-PRODUCT OPPORTUNITIES

In assessing new-product opportunities, a particularly useful analysis is a framework developed by General Electric and McKinsey Management Consultants. This framework combines an examination of the company's strengths and capabilities with the attractiveness of the market under consideration. This matrix can also be used for deciding which products to delete from the product line.

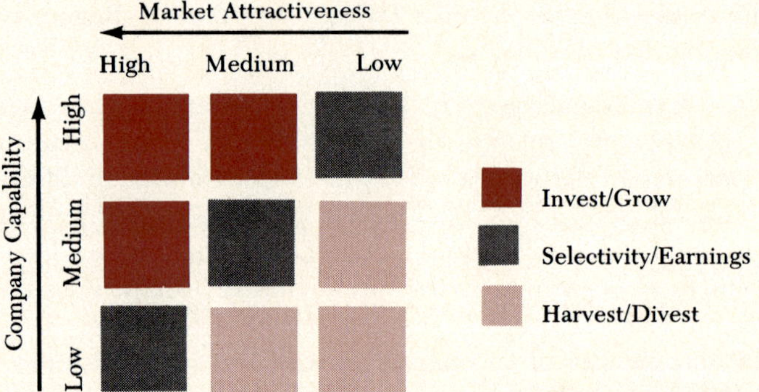

The *company capabilities* dimension (vertical axis) is a composite factor assessing the company's competitive strengths in a particular market. The following are some of the key factors:

- *Marketing strength.* Does the company have a unique or differentiated product that meets customer needs? What is the company's market share relative to competitors? Is the company known and recognized among the relevant market segments? Does the company have capabilities in marketing program execution for this market—e.g., mass media advertising experience?

- *Financial and economic strength.* Does the company have the financial resources to compete? Can equivalent economies of scale or experience curve effects (declining costs because of cumulative production experience) be achieved relative to major competitors?

- *Technological strength.* Can the company surpass (or at least meet) competitors'

5. **Observability,** which refers to the degree to which an innovation is visible to others. Socially conspicuous products generally follow a more rapid diffusion process than products which are not observable. Pharmaceutical companies must hold seminars and encourage dissemination of research results in order to build sales for new drug products. Medical-equipment manufacturers, however, benefit from the built-in observability of their products, which sit in physicians' offices.

In the consumer-behavior literature, a sixth factor has frequently been added to account for new-product acceptance—perceived risk.

---

technology? Can R&D be expected to keep abreast of emerging technology? Does the company have any key patents or copyrights?

Based on examining these and other factors we can classify opportunities as high, medium, or low on company capabilities.

The *market attractiveness* dimension (horizontal axis) is a second composite factor whereby new product opportunities are classified as high, medium or low. The following are relevant factors to consider:

- *Market factors.* How large is the market-demand level? Is the market growing? Is it profitable? Is it subject to seasonal or cyclical swings? Is the consumer need for this product likely to continue?

- *Competitive factors.* Who are the major competitors and how would we assess their capabilities? How concentrated is the market (how many competitors)?

- *Sociopolitical factors.* Is the market highly regulated? How unionized is the industry?

Based on conducting these analyses, opportunities will be positioned on the matrix, and three overall strategies emerge:

Strategy 1: Invest/Grow. If the analysis suggests high company capabilities and an attractive market, this is an obvious strategy for investment and growth. Seagram's entry into the wine market fell in the high/high position.

Strategy 2: Selectivity/Earnings. Opportunities on the diagonal are much less obvious. Occasionally, a company may enter a relatively unattractive industry because it feels that it has such high competitive capabilities in this market. Procter and Gamble's entry into paper products (a mature industry) may have been based on the assumption of superior company capabilities relative to Scott Paper and Kimberly Clark. A company may also occasionally enter a high-growth market where it lacks competitive capabilities (e.g., Honeywell in computers) but where it intends to invest in order to achieve competitive parity on its capabilities.

Strategy 3: Harvest/Divest. This part of the matrix—with low company capabilities and a market low on attractiveness—is an obvious place not to design new products. It may also be the case that if the company is presently competing in this market, it should consider divesting the product or harvesting the product, that is, raising price and keeping it in the product line only while it remains profitable.

6. **Perceived risk,** a function of the possible consequences in buying a new product (such as product failure or social embarrassment, as in the adoption of a new fashion) and the probabilities of these consequences. Products perceived as risky will tend to diffuse slowly unless their manufacturers can find ways to reduce risk, such as guarantees, warranties, and so on.

The importance of these six factors in accounting for new-product acceptance has been confirmed in research by Ostlund.[11] These factors were strong predictors of new-product acceptance, particularly the perceptions of relative advantage and compatibility. Measuring consumer perceptions in advance of new-product introductions would seem to have the potential to avoid many new product failures.

THE DIFFUSION PROCESS

The diffusion process can be meaningfully related to the more familiar concept of the product life cycle.[12] The essential difference is that *diffusion* usually refers to the *percentage of potential adopters* within a market segment who adopt the product over time, whereas the *product life cycle* is based on *absolute sales levels* over time.

The diffusion curve for successful products frequently resembles an S-shaped pattern (see Exhibit 15–4). This S-shaped, or logistic, pattern of the diffusion curve suggests that at least the following stages can be distinguished.

- *Introduction.* The product is placed on the market, and sales increase slowly.
- *Growth.* The product enters a period of rapid growth.
- *Maturity.* Sales growth continues, but at a declining rate. Sales eventually reach a plateau.
- *Decline.* Sales begin to decrease.

The idea of an S-shaped diffusion process seems to have originated with the sociologist Gabriel Tarde in his studies of fashion diffusion.[13] Evidence for such a generalized pattern has been found in a number of contexts, including the diffusion of a new drug among physicians,[14] of new agricultural technology among farmers,[15] of new food products among consumers,[16] and of new medical technology among hospitals.[17]

Reasons for an S-Shaped Pattern

The overall factors which frequently underlie a generalized S-shaped diffusion pattern are (1) the social interaction effect, (2) the marketing program effect, and (3) the competitive effect.

social interaction effect

The **social interaction effect** refers to a process of influence and imitation among consumers by which adopters of a new product lead others to purchase. The interaction effect is often posited to account for the rapid-growth stage in the diffusion process. It is reasoned that if every consumer considered adopting on an individual basis, without social influence, then the probability of adopting in any given time period would be the same (no account is taken of the impact of marketing activities over time). If, however, consumer adoption decisions are based on social influence, then a "snowball," or rapid-growth, process will occur, since the probability of a consumer's adoption in any one time period is a function of the number of consumers who have already adopted.

It has been documented extensively that consumers go beyond promotional information sources and that other people often may be the most important source in the purchase process—varying, of course, by product type. (The occurrence and functioning of such "personal influence" is explored in the next chapter). Suffice it for the present to generalize that personal influence gains in importance with higher price, greater product conspicuousness, greater product complexity, and a lack of objective standards by which to evaluate the product. Under such conditions we would expect the interaction effect to be most pronounced.

Evidence for the effect of social interaction upon the diffusion process is offered by Coleman, Katz, and Menzel in their study of the diffusion of a new drug among physicians. They were able to compare the diffusion processes for socially integrated and isolated doctors using information on the number

EXHIBIT 15–4
THE DIFFUSION PROCESS

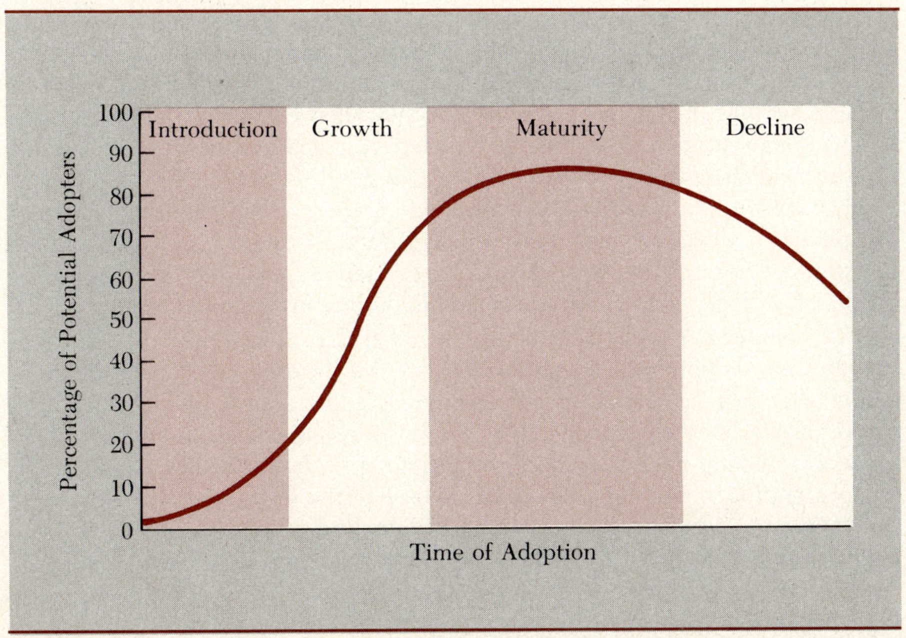

of friendship choices received. They found that the more socially integrated doctors introduced the new drug sooner than more isolated doctors. Since the socially integrated doctor's "receptivity" to adoption was not found to be particularly different from his more isolated colleague's receptivity, the authors attributed the difference in diffusion rate to greater interaction and resulting influence. Indeed, the diffusion curve of the socially integrated doctors approximated a "chain reaction," or snowball process, whereas the diffusion curve of the isolated doctors approximated a curve based on "individual" adoption decisions.[18]

The effect of social integration was further studied by Arndt—this time on the adoption of a new coffee product. His results, shown in Exhibit 15–5, are similar to the physician diffusion patterns for the adoption of the new drug. More socially integrated individuals are likely to adopt sooner and in greater concentrations, attesting to the powerful effect of social interaction.

marketing program effect

The **marketing program effect** also tends to suggest a somewhat slow take-off in diffusion, followed by a more rapid growth phase. Since consumers engage in a learning and decision-making process before purchasing, it follows that an immediate rush to purchase should not be expected. Some advertising repetition may be necessary before the consumer becomes aware of the new product, gains sufficient knowledge about it, and exhibits some interest in it. The cumulative effectiveness of promotional efforts over time can help account for the rapid growth stages in the product life-cycle model. Advertising coupled with sales efforts, in-store displays, and other promotional efforts can provide the consumer with several kinds of information necessary to make a purchase decision. These sources may be mutually reinforcing, but it may take some time before complete promotional exposure occurs.

Similarly, the time necessary to build in-store distribution for a new product is a limiting factor on initial sales. Nielsen data for grocery products, for example, suggest that new food items achieve a build-up in distribution levels from an average of 9 percent of total food-store distribution after two months, to 41 percent after four months, to 81 percent at the end of the year.[19] Lack of in-store distribution obviously hinders sales.

Prices also tend to decline over the range of the product life cycle (adjusted for inflation), which suggests that sales will increase over time if demand for the product is price sensitive. How aggressively a new product is priced at introduction may, in fact, have a considerable bearing on initial sales.

competitive effect

The **competitive effect** is the third major factor affecting the diffusion curve. One variable which may operate at the growth stage is the entry of competition which helps educate consumers and expands total primary demand (especially for products with high consumer-information needs). In turn, the stage of decline in the product life cycle is due either to saturation (consumers may need only one videotape) or to the development by competitors of new products possessing superior attributes, superior either technologically or simply stylistically. In some product categories, such as shampoos, decline may be due to consumer boredom, rather than to new, functionally superior alternatives.

At this point it may be concluded that the effects of social-interaction, marketing program, and competition all contribute to a diffusion pattern which is an S-shaped curve (logistic). But, because this is generally not the diffusion curve that a firm wants to achieve, several questions arise:

- How can marketing efforts shape the diffusion pattern in line with company objectives?
- What other patterns are found in addition to the S-shaped curve?
- Can the diffusion pattern be predicted?

EXHIBIT 15–5
THE SOCIAL INTERACTION EFFECT IN THE DIFFUSION OF A NEW COFFEE

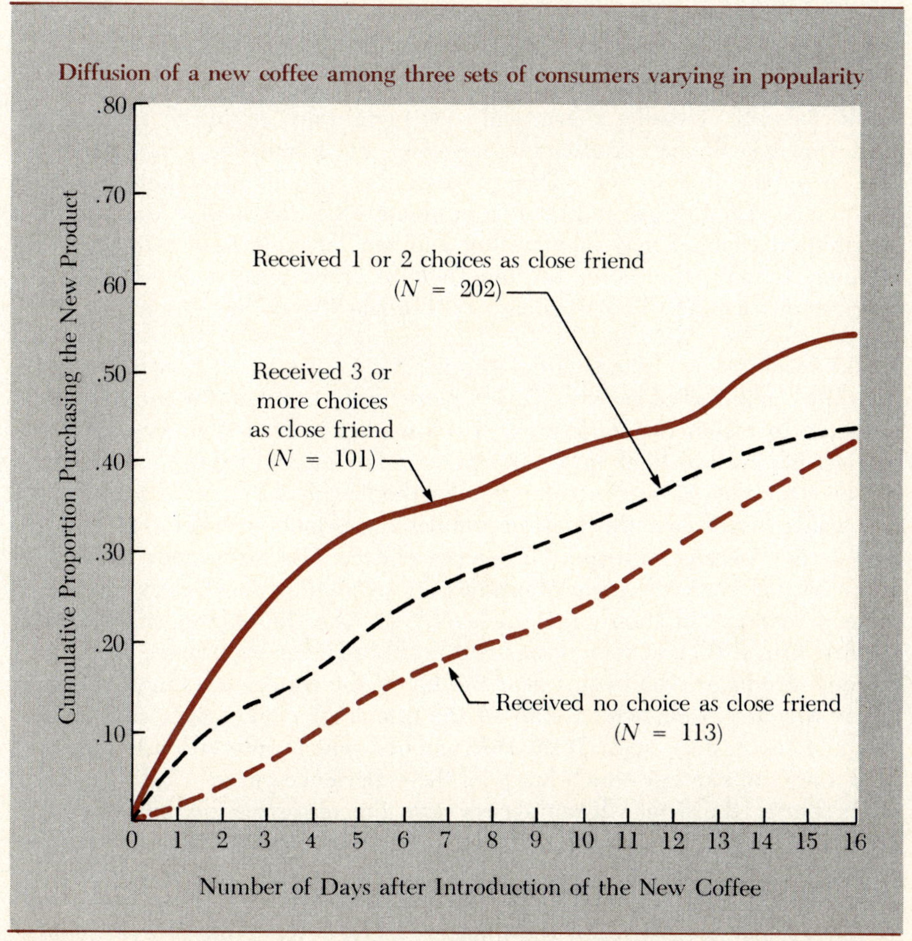

SOURCE: Johan Arndt (1967), "The Role of Product-Related Conversation in the Diffusion of a New Product," *Journal of Marketing Research*, 4 (Aug.), p. 293.

Shaping the Diffusion Pattern

The particular diffusion pattern that the firm wishes to achieve may vary. For example, if the firm has patent protection or is a monopoly, it may wish to avoid rapid sales growth if this would lead to shortages and higher production costs. For most firms in a competitive market and without strong patent protection, however, the objective is to manage the diffusion process (see Exhibit 15–6) in such a way as to

- achieve **rapid takeoff,** that is, to secure initial sales as quickly as possible;
- achieve **rapid acceleration,** that is, to secure cumulative sales in a steep diffusion curve;
- achieve **maximum penetration,** that is, to secure the highest possible potential within the market segments selected; and
- achieve a **long-run franchise,** that is, to keep the product alive as long as possible.

Rapid Takeoff   Usually, a firm will seek initial sales as quickly as possible. Achieving takeoff may be difficult, however, since consumers may be reluctant to be the first to buy. This suggests the wisdom of initially targeting consumers with a desire to buy new products—the innovators. Similarly, the distribution channel may take a "wait and see" attitude before stocking the product. It may, therefore, be important to reach retail innovators in the distribution channel (Bloomingdale's or Neiman-Marcus, for example).

Rapid Acceleration   The firm in a competitive environment generally prefers to achieve rapid sales growth. This is particularly important if competition is expected to match the innovation, if the market is limited in size, or if the product life cycle is likely to be short—as in fashion and fads.

The advantage of rapid acceleration for the first firm to market a new product is that it will gain the most accumulated production experience and the lowest costs because of experience-curve effects. The **experience curve** suggests that for every doubling of production, average per-unit costs will fall to some percentage of their previous level.[20] By the time competition enters, the first firm will be at some lower cost position on the experience curve than the new producer who begins near the top of the experience curve. Perhaps this is why Rockwell, which entered the calculator market late, could never compete successfully with Texas Instruments, which entered early and pursued a pricing strategy which followed the experience curve.

Of course, the firm will not always have the resources for rapid acceleration, since this calls for bringing major production capacity online at the beginning of the product life cycle. Or, if the sales potential for the new product is tenuous (as with the video-disc), the firms entering the new industry may be reluctant to commit major resources.

Maximum Penetration   Usually a firm will seek maximum penetration, that is, the highest possible level of sales for a new product within a particular market. This depends, however, on whether competition exists as well as the cost structure and consumer price sensitivity. If competition is limited because of patent protection or a significant technological advantage, the firm may charge a high price and penetrate the market more slowly. If the consumer is price sensitive and costs are high, it will be difficult to bring the price down enough to achieve maximum penetration.

Long-Run Franchise   Finally, firms frequently seek to keep products alive as long as possible. But it is probably more accurate to say that a firm will seek to participate in a particular market as long as possible.

There are really two primary strategies for achieving a long-run consumer franchise. The first is **product enhancement,** that is, augmenting the basic product over time to give it competitive differentiation; the second is **product migration,** that is, deliberately killing your own product by introducing a better product.

product enhancement

product migration

Product enhancement is most commonly used for packaged goods and product migration for high technology industries. For example, Procter and

EXHIBIT 15–6
"DESIRED" AND "NATURAL" DIFFUSION PATTERNS

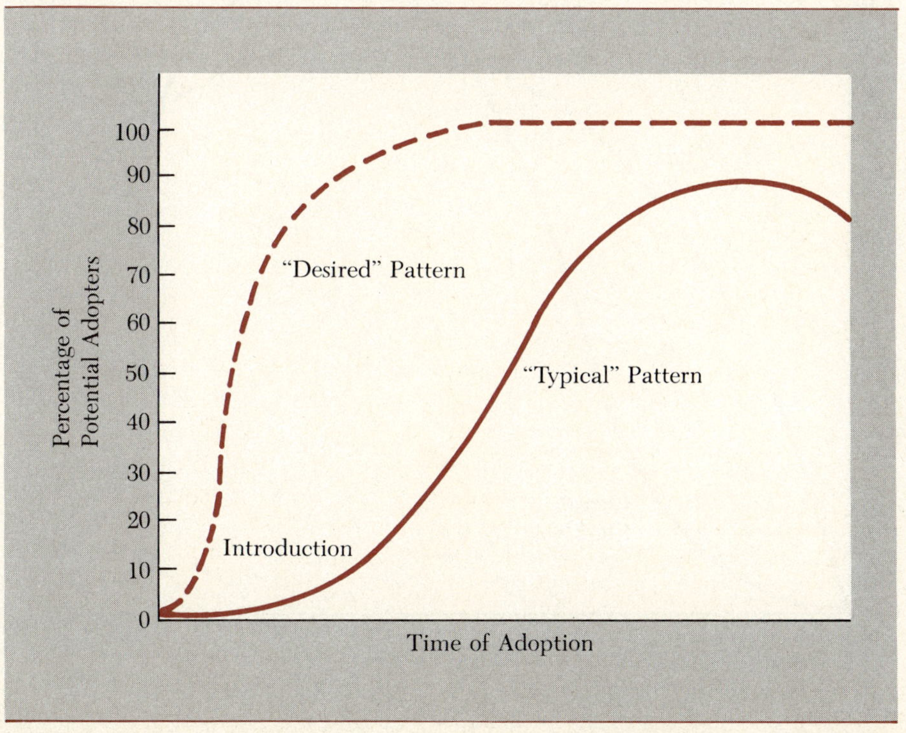

Gamble has augmented Tide detergent over many years to sustain leadership in its market. So too has Mattel augmented its Barbie doll over many years, through new clothes, new friends, and a voice box; and now she kisses. IBM's computers provide a classic example of pursuing a product migration strategy—the 1401 computer is replaced by the 360, which in turn is replaced by the 370, 4300, and so on.

Ultimately, the diffusion pattern achieved is a function of both the firm's actions and factors beyond its control, including actions of competitors and changing patterns of consumer behavior. Therefore, the firm must both attempt to *manage* the diffusion process to its advantage and to *respond* to the developing pattern. This suggests that it is necessary to adjust the marketing program (pricing and levels of advertising, for example) by stage of the product life cycle.

EXHBIT 15–7
LOGISTIC AND EXPONENTIAL LIFE CYCLE PATTERNS

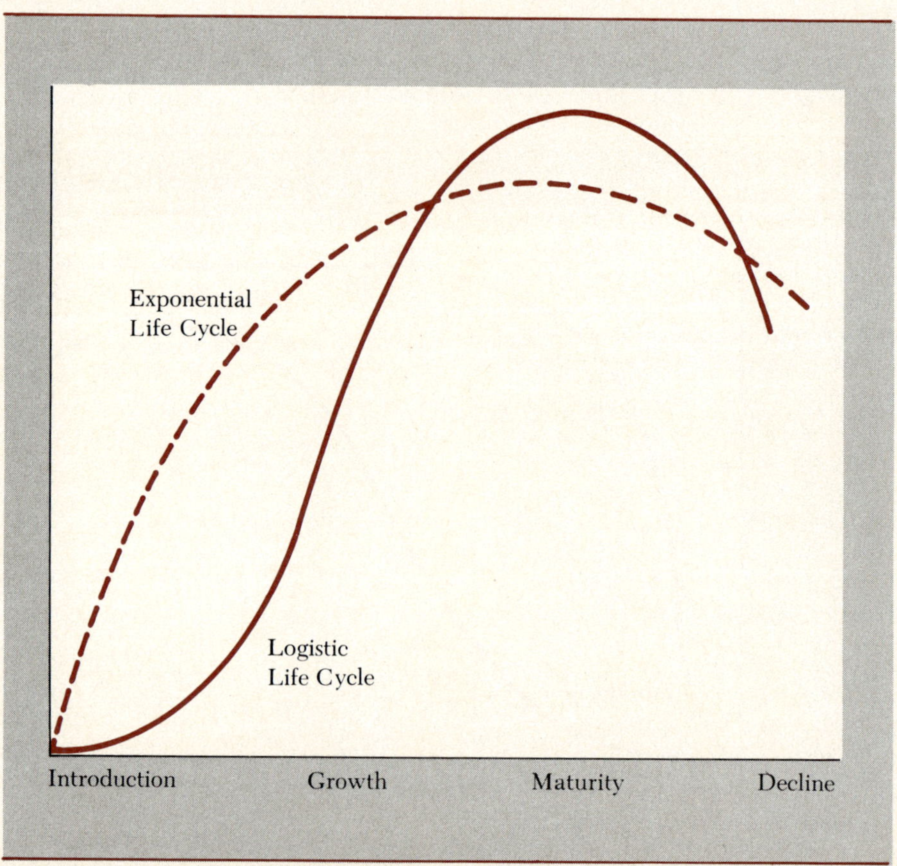

Alternative Diffusion Patterns

The S-shaped diffusion pattern, although the most common, is by no means the only possible diffusion curve.[21] An alternative to this logistic curve is the exponential curve (see Exhibit 15–7), which eliminates the initial period of slowly growing sales during introduction.

For many packaged goods for which consumer-information needs are low, sales may build quickly and actually achieve a maximum level within a short period of time. For example, in introducing a new cereal backed by heavy advertising and free samples, Quaker found that sales were near maximum levels within three months.

Similarly, fads and fashions tend to follow quite different diffusion patterns. Perhaps the most essential feature distinguishing fads and fashions from other new products is that their adoption is related largely to the *perception of newness* rather than to relative advantage or better functional performance. Simmel, in his classic treatise on fashion, emphasizes that as fashion spreads, it goes to its doom.[22] This can be seen now in designer labels, which may be

EXHIBIT 15–8
GENERALIZED DIFFUSION PATTERNS FOR A NEW PRODUCT, A FASHION, AND A FAD

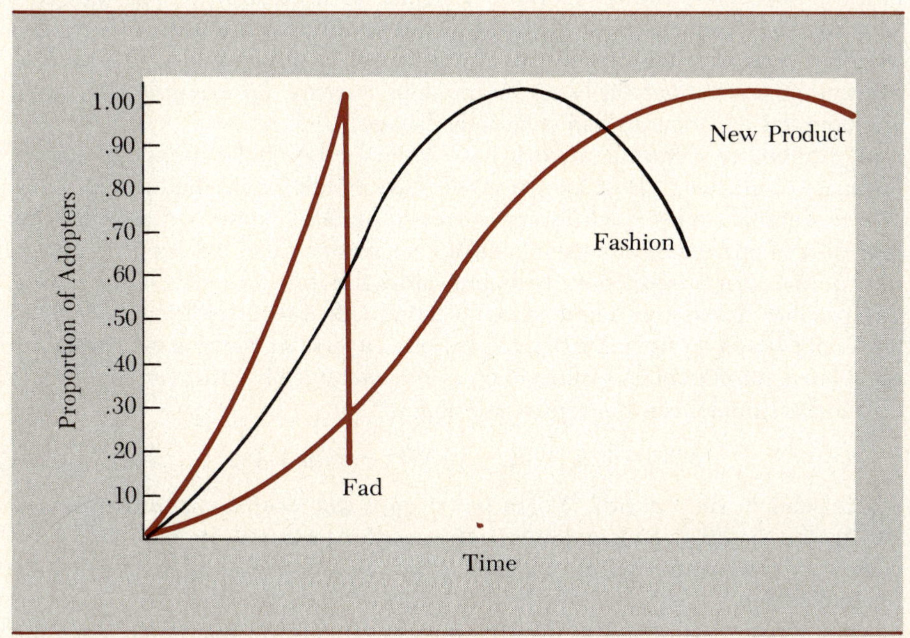

SOURCE: Thomas S. Robertson (1971), *Innovative Behavior and Communication* (New York: Holt, Rinehart & Winston), p. 50.

losing their appeal. Status stores, such as Saks Fifth Avenue, Bloomingdale's, and Neiman-Marcus, are becoming reluctant to carry designer labels that have broad distribution. "These stores are beginning to snub designer merchandise, calling it too commonplace. . . . The 'name game' could be about to end."[23]

Can fads be distinguished from fashion? Fashions are of a cyclical nature and typically exhibit a diffusion process resembling an S-shaped pattern, although more pronounced and more condensed in time. Fads, in contrast, tend not to repeat themselves and to exhibit much more rapid growth generally followed by complete collapse, although adoption can sometimes stabilize at a low level. Exhibit 15–8 shows generalized diffusion patterns for a new consumer product (such as instant coffee), a fashion item (such as clothing of a new style), and a fad (such as the hula hoop or Pet Rocks).

Can the Diffusion Pattern Be Predicted?

Ability to predict the diffusion pattern would be a major asset to a corporation in preempting competition and controlling costs by avoiding premature production capacity. However, prediction of the diffusion pattern is difficult, since the diffusion process is a function of many factors beyond the control of the firm, including consumer behavior and competitive actions.

The newer the technology, the more difficult it is to project the diffusion process since consumers will have difficulty in accurately telling the firm whether they want the new technology. For continuous innovations (new flavors, for example), consumers can definitively provide opinions, but for discontinuous innovations (in-home information systems, for example), consumers' opinions are tenuous and subject to change.

A number of diffusion models have been proposed for projecting new-product acceptance.[24] Best known is the Bass model for predicting the diffusion of durable goods (such as appliances). The Bass model is based on the modeling of epidemics as a useful analogy for new-product diffusion. For each time period after introduction, both innovators and imitators will be buying the new product. Innovators adopt based on an individual-level decision, but imitators adopt based on the influence of previous buyers. As the process continues the relative number of innovators decreases monotonically with time.

The Bass model can be written as follows:[25]

$$S(T) = pm + (q - p)\,Y(T) - q/m[Y(T)]^2$$

where sales in time period (T) are based on p (the coefficient of innovation) and q (the coefficient of imitation). The market potential for first-time purchasers is represented by m, and Y(T) is the cumulative number of previous buyers at time T.

Bass applied his model to predict the sales for eleven major-appliance innovations. Based on least-squares regression, the model generated reasonably good forecasts for most of these innovations, including room air-conditioners, as shown in Exhibit 15–9.

EXHIBIT 15–9
SALES PREDICTION USING THE BASS MODEL

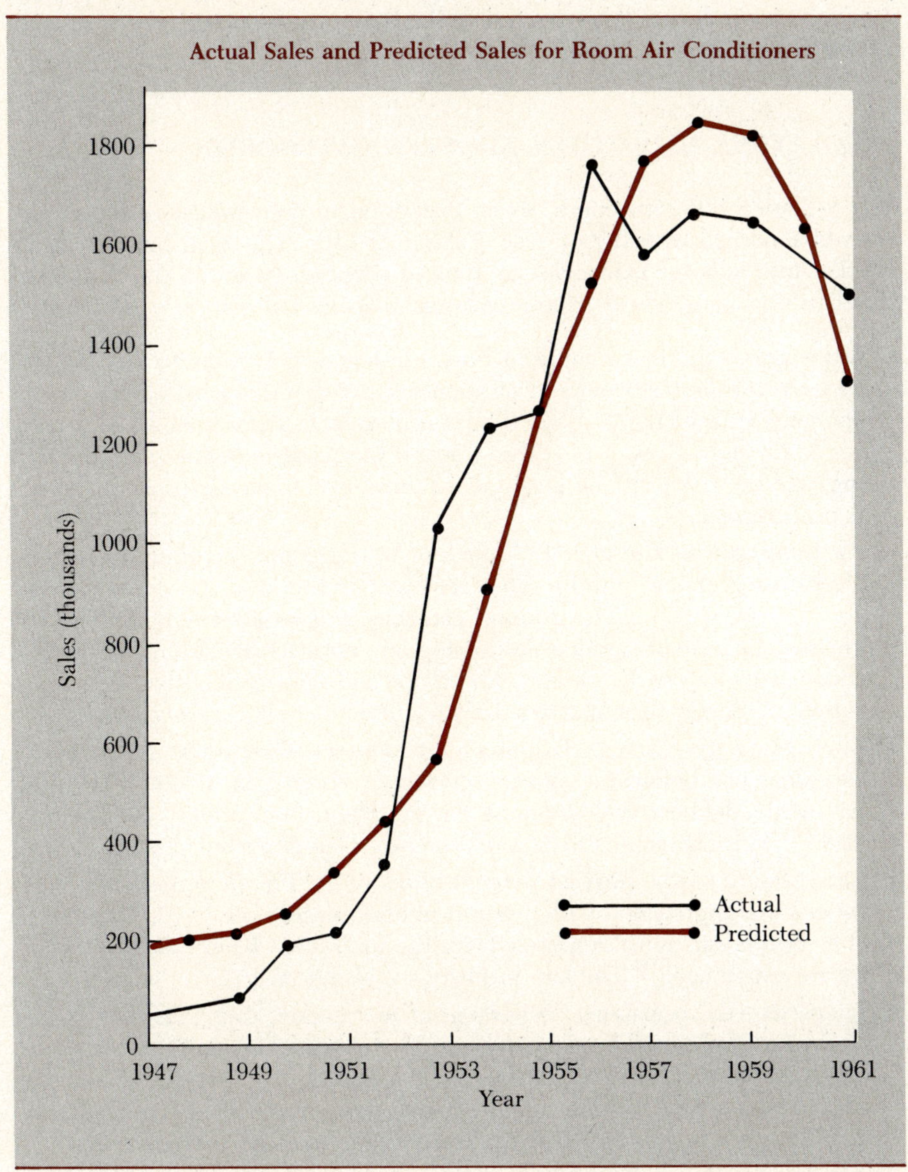

SOURCE: Frank M. Bass (1969), "A New Product Growth Model for Consumer Durables," *Management Science*, 15 (Jan.), p. 219.

The Bass model has since been applied to high technology products with good success.[26] Alternative estimation procedures for the Bass model, such as a maximum-likelihood approach, have also been demonstrated.[27] Finally, there are a number of other models in the literature for predicting new-product diffusion that have also shown good results.[28]

INNOVATORS AND OTHER ADOPTER CATEGORIES

The S-shaped diffusion curve, when expressed in noncumulative form, represents a normal distribution (see Exhibit 15–10). This distribution can be divided into **adopter categories** by time of adoption based on the use of the standard deviation. These adopter categories are as follows.

- **Innovators**—the first people to buy. As shown in Exhibit 15–10, innovators are the first 2.5 percent of adopters. As described by Rogers, in his summary of the adoption and diffusion literature, innovators are ". . . eager to try new ideas. . . . [They] desire the hazardous, the rash, the daring, and the risky."[29] The most salient term used to characterize innovators is *venturesome*.

- **Early Adopters**—the next 13.5 percent of adopters. According to Rogers, "Early adopters are a more integrated part of the local social system than are innovators. . . . This adopter category, more than any other, has the greatest degree of opinion leadership in most social systems. Potential adopters look to early adopters for advice and information about the innovation."[30] Rogers characterizes early adopters overall as *respectable*.

- **Early Majority**—the next 34 percent of adopters. They adopt new products and ideas just before the average person. According to Rogers, "They follow with deliberate willingness in adopting innovations, but seldom lead."[31] This characteristic of *deliberateness* best describes them.

- **Late Majority**—the next 34 percent of adopters. For these people, "innovations are approached with a skeptical and cautious air. . . . The weight of system norms must definitely favor the innovation before the late majority are convinced."[32] The late majority are *skeptical*.

- **Laggards**—the remaining 16 percent of the market. Laggards may be described as *traditional* because they use the past as their point of reference. They are suspicious of innovators, and according to Rogers, "When laggards finally adopt an innovation, it may already have been superseded by another more recent idea that is already being used by the innovators."[33]

This classification of adopter categories is used in much of the diffusion literature. Other definitions of innovators are quite common, however, and in many marketing studies, innovators are defined as the first 5 or 10 percent of consumers in the market to buy.

EXHIBIT 15–10
GENERALIZED CUMULATIVE DIFFUSION PATTERN

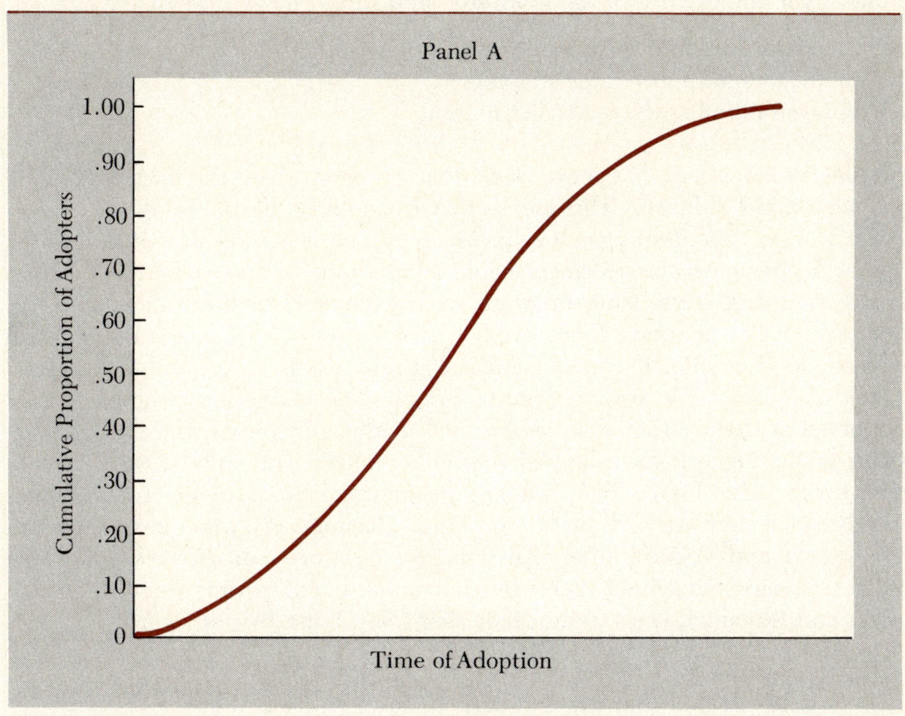

GENERALIZED NONCUMULATIVE DIFFUSION PATTERN

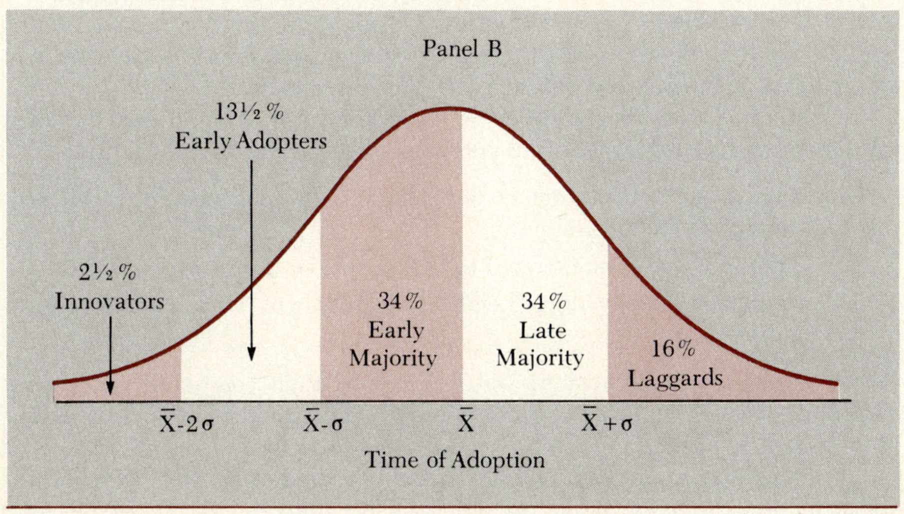

The Innovator

Of particular concern in most new-product marketing programs is the innovator. The importance of the innovator stems from three reasons:

1. Innovators account for initial levels of penetration.
2. Innovators influence later adopters.
3. Innovators influence retail distribution.

Initial Penetration   We have seen that in most cases the firm wishes to achieve rapid diffusion. This means that it would be desirable to reach innovators in an expeditious manner in order to mount initial sales. If innovators possess characteristics distinguishable from those of later adopters, then a marketing and advertising program can be tailored to these characteristics until innovator adoption is achieved. If a new women's fashion is being introduced, for example, the manufacturer logically wants to know the characteristics of those at the leading edge of fashion. The marketing program is then directed at them rather than at the total market of women who buy clothes. This might suggest, for example, reaching younger women who work outside the home, have higher than average income, and live in major metropolitan areas, since they are high on fashion innovativeness. Print media such as *Mademoiselle* and *Vogue* (rather than *Family Circle* or *Good Housekeeping*) are logical means of reaching such women. Similarly, compatible retail stores are Saks and Bloomingdale's (rather than Sears and Lane Bryant).

Innovator Influence over Later Adopters   It has been documented fairly extensively that innovators influence later adopters. Such influence may be direct, as when innovators evaluate or recommend products to potential adopters. Such influence may also be indirect, as when innovators display the product, as in fashion. If innovators do not display a product, other consumers are less likely to be aware of the item's existence and, even if aware, are less likely to feel that adopting the item is socially acceptable.

In a study of the diffusion of home computers, it was found that the level of communication from owners to potential adopters was quite extensive.

- The average home-computer owner talked to thirteen people in the previous month about the computer.
- The computer was demonstrated to five people in the previous month.
- The average owner encouraged eight other people to buy a home computer since purchase.[34]

These results are for innovators who had owned their computers for a short period of time. The level of interpersonal influence declines considerably from month to month.

Thus, innovators are influential, through *social display* and *legitimation*, for many new products. While the innovator is willing to risk purchasing new products and may even achieve satisfaction from such avant-garde behavior, later adopters want to minimize risk. Later adopters often take a wait-and-see attitude, hoping to gain from the experience of innovators and to have the innovators legitimize the benefits of the product.

Innovator Influence over Retail Distribution   An interesting "Catch 22" is that the retailer may be reluctant to handle the new product until it begins to sell, but that, of course, it can't begin to sell unless the retailer handles it. This problem is particularly acute for small manufacturers who don't have the power and resources to introduce new products with large advertising budgets and large sales forces.

Again, reaching innovators quickly may be the solution. If initial sales can be demonstrated, a snowball effect often occurs, with retailers quickly becoming interested. They may then see the new product as a traffic builder or a source of higher profit margins. In the fashion area, for example, early-season sales have a major bearing on how much retailers order and whether they push particular styles.

Characterizing the Consumer Innovator

Before marketing a new product, it is necessary to establish the profile of the most likely consumer innovators. Exhibit 15–11 suggests a profile of the consumer innovator across a number of product categories and a profile of the "industrial" innovator based on research in farming, medicine, and industrial companies. This might be a logical starting point. However, most research suggests that there are *separate innovators by product category*, rather than innovators across all product categories.

The idea of separate innovators by product category seems reasonable. It would not be expected that the innovator for new food products would be the *same person* as the innovator for cars or stereos. However, innovators may have some overlapping characteristics, as suggested by Exhibit 15–11.

Research on the profiles of innovators suggests the following characteristics.

* *Demographics.* The consumer innovator has higher education, income, and occupational status than the average adopter, as well as higher social mobility (upward movement in social class). This is particularly true of innovators for new appliance and clothing products but not for a number of other categories, such as new food products, where cost is not a factor.[35]

  The industrial innovator profile confirms that innovators have higher education and higher income and social status relative to their peers as well as higher social mobility. No consistent relationship has been found between age and innovativeness.[36]

* *Personality Variables.* The consumer innovator has consistently been found to be more venturesome and (not unexpectedly) to have a more positive attitude toward innovations. Innovators also tend to perceive less risk in buying new products, tend to have distinguishable traits on standardized personality inventories, and are sometimes less dogmatic.[37] It has also been suggested, but not documented, that innovators are more creative.[38]

EXHIBIT 15–11
PROFILING THE INNOVATOR

The Consumer Innovator		The Industrial Innovator	
Generalizations	% of Studies Supporting Generalization	Generalization	% of Studies Supporting Generalization
Demographics		*Demographics*	
Higher education	70	Higher education	74
Higher income	69	Higher income &	
Higher occupational		social status	68
status	55	Younger	19
Younger	36	Higher social mobility	100
Higher social			
mobility	100		
Personality Variables		*Personality Variables*	
More venturesome	100	More able to cope with	
Less perceived risk	44	uncertainty	73
More favorable		More favorable attitude	
attitude toward		toward education	
innovations	100	and science	78
Distinguishable traits		More favorable attitude	
on personality		toward change	75
inventories	40	Less fatalistic	82
Less dogmatic	50	Higher aspiration	
		levels	74
		Less dogmatic	47
Communication Behavior		*Communication Behavior*	
Greater exposure to		Greater exposure to	
print media	78	print media	69
More social		More social	
participation	53	participation	73
Greater opinion		Greater opinion	
leadership	77	leadership	76
More cosmopolitan	25	More cosmopolitan	76
		More change-agent	
		contact	87
		Greater knowledge of	
		innovations	76
Usage Behavior		*Usage Behavior*	
Greater product-		Larger-sized units,	
category usage		e.g., farms	67
rate	88	More specialized	
Less brand loyalty	75	operations	60

SOURCES: Based on Thomas S. Robertson (1971), *Innovative Behavior and Communication* (New York: Holt, Rinehart & Winston), pp. 100–101 and on Everett M. Rogers (1983), *Diffusion of Innovations*, 3rd ed. (New York: Free Press), pp. 260–61. These studies include farming, medical, and industrial innovations.

The industrial innovator profile concludes that innovators are more able to cope with uncertainty, have more favorable attitudes toward education and science and toward change, are less fatalistic, have higher aspiration levels, and are less dogmatic.

- *Communication Behavior.* The consumer innovator is more likely to gain information via print media and informal communications. Innovators have higher social participation than later adopters and higher opinion leadership, that is, more influence over their peers. But they tend not to be more cosmopolitan, that is, oriented beyond their local community.

  The industrial innovator is more cosmopolitan and has more change-agent (such as agricultural scientists) contact. Change-agent contact may be necessary except for those consumer products for which information is so likely to come to consumers (via advertising, for example) that they don't have to seek it. Industrial innovators also have greater knowledge of innovation—a finding that has not been researched much in consumer-behavior studies.

- *Usage Behavior.* Finally, the consumer innovator is already a heavier user of the product category and is less brand loyal. This suggests that the most likely innovator is someone who is already a heavy user of the product category and that the marketing program should be oriented initially to these heavy users.[39]

  The industrial innovator has a larger-sized unit (for example, a larger factory) and a more specialized operation. In a certain sense this is similar to the "heavy user" finding in consumer research.

Two Cases of Marketing to Innovators

Coleman, Katz, and Menzel conducted a classic study on innovation.[40] They traced the spread of a new drug among physicians in some midwestern cities. Their results showed that the doctor who prescribed the new drug first—the innovator—had the following characteristics.

- unlikely to be old, although likely to be either middle-aged or young
- more likely to be an internist than a general practitioner
- more socially integrated (that is, more accepted by peers in the medical community)
- more oriented toward professional goals than toward patients
- much more likely to be a heavy prescriber for other, similar drugs
- more likely to have attended an east-coast medical school
- receives more medical journals
- more likely to share an office with another physician
- more cosmopolitan—more in touch with out-of-town medical institutions and more likely to attend medical conferences

Now if we place ourselves in the position of a pharmaceutical company about to launch a new drug, what are the implications? Basically, our advertising and "detailing" (sales) program can draw on the findings above. It can do the following, for example.

- Identify the most likely innovators based on their heavy prescriptions for other, similar drugs or based on the other characteristics listed.
- Have the sales force detail (sell) to those identified as the most likely innovators.
- Advertise in the specialty medical journals instead of those journals directed to general practitioners.
- If seminars are offered on the new drug and how to use it, invite physicians with the identified innovator characteristics.
- Reach these innovators at medical-association meetings since they are likely to attend.

A second study with implications for the design of marketing programs is Zenith's analysis of the potential innovators for videodisc machines. Their assumptions were that innovators would have the following characteristics.

- greater than $15,000 annual household income (as of 1977)
- color television in the household
- medium to heavy viewing of television
- nonplanning—that is, not prone to lengthy pre-purchase deliberation[41]

Using the innovator profile for video-discs, it is possible to specify implications for advertising and distribution, such as the following.

- Advertise in magazines that reach consumers with this profile.
- Choose distribution channels to reach these consumers.
- Use advertising and sales appeals toward which consumers with this profile will be receptive.

SUMMARY

Diffusion is the process by which something spreads. Diffusion theory has been studied by researchers across a number of disciplines, including anthropology, sociology, education, and marketing. Marketing's interest in diffusion relates to the flow of goods and services from producer to consumer. The general objective is to speed the diffusion process, that is, to gain rapid new product dissemination.

Innovations may be classified on a scale from continuous to discontinuous, depending on their effects on established consumption patterns. A *continuous innovation* (for example, line extensions such as new flavors) has limited impact on existing consumption patterns, whereas a *discontinuous innovation* (for example, the computer) may radically alter consumption patterns. The speed with which an innovation diffuses depends on the innovation's characteristics. In general, diffusion will be faster if the product has high relative advantage, is compatible with values, is not very complex, can be tried on a limited basis, is observable, and has low perceived risk.

The concept of diffusion is related to the *product life cycle*, which traces adoption over time. This pattern often follows an S-shaped curve as the product moves from *introduction* to *growth* to *maturity* and into *decline*. The diffusion curve tracks the cumulative percentage of adopters for a product within a social system or market segment over time. The S-shaped pattern of diffusion depends on the *social interaction effect*, whereby adopters of a new product influence others to purchase. This is often posited to account for the rapid-growth stage (the bend in the S-curve). *Marketing strategies*—pricing, distribution, and promotion decisions—also influence the pattern of the diffusion process. Diffusion is further influenced by *competitive effects*—the presence or absence of competition has a major influence on the shape of the diffusion curve.

A key issue is the extent to which the diffusion process can be managed to the firm's advantage. Can marketing strategy achieve a desired diffusion curve—fast takeoff and rapid acceleration? What diffusion curves are usually achieved? Can the diffusion curve be predicted?

Innovators are the first consumers to buy. They account for initial levels of penetration and have the potential to speed the diffusion of new products. Innovators may also exercise personal influence on peers by recommending the product or by providing social display, which can stimulate awareness among other consumers and serve to legitimatize purchase of the product by later adopters.

Innovators tend to possess characteristics that distinguish them from later adopters. Innovators, however, are not innovative across all product categories; innovativeness tends to be bound to one product category or to closely related product categories. Thus, if a marketing program is to be precisely targeted toward innovator characteristics, it should be based on the characteristics relevant to that product category. Nevertheless, an innovator profile derived from many studies shows a profile distinct from that of later adopters on demographic, personality, communication, and usage factors.

KEY CONCEPTS

diffusion process	relative advantage	competitive effect
innovation	compatibility	rapid takeoff
adopter categories	complexity	rapid acceleration
innovators	trialability	maximum penetration
early adopters	observability	experience curve
early majority	perceived risk	product enhancement
late majority	S-shaped logistic	product migration
laggards	diffusion pattern	exponential life-cycle
adoption process	social interaction	pattern
innovation continuum	effect	personal influence
continuous innovation	marketing program	
discontinuous	effect	
innovation		

DISCUSSION QUESTIONS

1. What is the typical shape of the diffusion curve? What factors account for this?
2. What is the shape of the diffusion process that the firm generally desires? To what extent can the firm manage the diffusion process? To what extent is it subject to factors beyond the firm's control? Discuss.
3. Distinguish a new product from a fashion and those two from a fad. Why is it important to know which you are dealing with?
4. What is an innovation? Why would consumer perception be the ultimate test of newness?
5. What is the *innovation continuum*? Consider a product category such as in-home entertainment. How might various products fit the continuum at the time of their introduction to the market?
6. What factors affect the rate of acceptance of a new product? For each factor discuss how marketing actions might be designed to affect that factor (for example, how to reduce product complexity).
7. Why is the innovator important in the new-product diffusion process? How can the marketing program take the innovator concept into account?
8. Consider the introduction of a new clothing fashion. Propose a set of hypotheses about the characteristics of college students most likely to adopt that fashion first; in other words, who will be the innovators?

NOTES

1. Federal Trade Commission (1967), "Permissible Period of Time During Which New Product May Be Described as 'New'," *Advisory Opinion Digest*, 120 (Apr. 15).
2. Arthur M. Louis (1980), "Smith Kline Finds Rich Is Better," *Fortune* (June 30), pp. 63–66.
3. C. Merle Crawford (1979), "New Product Failure Rates—Facts and Fallacies," *Research Management* (Sept.), p. 12.
4. David S. Hopkins (1980), *New-Product Winners and Losers* (New York: The Conference Board).
5. Booz Allen & Hamilton, Inc. (1981), *New Product Management for the 1980's: Phase 1* (Chicago: Booz Allen & Hamilton).
6. A. C. Nielsen (1980), *The Nielsen Researcher*, 2 (Chicago: A. C. Nielsen), p. 17.
7. See, for example, Robert G. Cooper (1979), "The Dimensions of Industrial New Product Success and Failure," *Journal of Marketing*, 43 (Summer), pp. 93–103.
8. Everett M. Rogers (1983), *Diffusion of Innovations*, 3rd ed. (New York: The Free Press), Ch. 6.
9. Thomas S. Robertson and Lawrence H. Wortzel (1977), "Consumer Behavior and Health Care Change: The Role of Mass Media," in *Advances in Consumer Research*, Vol. 5, ed. H. Keith Hunt (Assn. for Consumer Research), pp. 525–27.
10. Saxon Graham (1956), "Class and Conservatism in the Adoption of Innovations," *Human Relations*, 9, pp. 91–100.
11. Lyman E. Ostlund (1974), "Perceived Innovation Attributes as Predictors of Innovativeness," *Journal of Consumer Research*, 1 (Sept.), pp. 23–29.
12. For a review on product life-cycle theory, see the special issue of *Journal of Marketing* (1981), ed. George S. Day, 45 (Fall).
13. Gabriel Tarde (1968), *The Laws of Imitation* (New York: Holt, Rinehart & Winston).
14. James S. Coleman, Elihu Katz, and Herbert Menzel (1966), *Medical Innovation: A Diffusion Study* (Indianapolis: Bobbs-Merrill).
15. Everett M. Rogers (1983).

16. Johan Arndt (1967), "Role of Product-Related Conversations in the Diffusion of a New Product," *Journal of Marketing Research*, 4 (Aug.), pp. 291–5.

17. Yoram Wind, Thomas S. Robertson, and Cynthia Fraser (1982), "Industrial Product Diffusion by Market Segment," *Industrial Marketing Management*, 11, 1, pp. 1–8.

18. James S. Coleman et al. (1966).

19. A. C. Nielsen (1979), "New Product Distribution," in *The Nielsen Researcher*, 4 (Chicago: A. C. Nielsen), p. 3.

20. For coverage of the logic of experience curves, see Derek F. Abell and John S. Hammond (1979), *Strategic Market Planning* (Englewood Cliffs, N.J.: Prentice-Hall), Ch. 3.

21. William E. Cox, Jr. (1967), "Product Life Cycles as Marketing Models," *Journal of Business*, 40 (Oct.), pp. 375–84.

22. Georg Simmel (1957), "Fashion," *American Journal of Sociology*, 62 (May), p. 547.

23. "Why Designer Labels Are Fading" (1983), *Business Week* (Feb. 21), p. 70.

24. See, for example, Vijay Mahajan and Eitan Muller (1979), "Innovation Diffusion and New Product Growth Models in Marketing," *Journal of Marketing*, 43 (Fall), pp. 55–68.

25. Frank M. Bass (1969), "A New Product Growth Model for Consumer Durables," *Management Science*, 15 (Jan.), p. 217.

26. Douglas Tigert and Behrooz Farivar (1981), "The Bass New Product Growth Model: A Sensitivity Analysis for a High Technology Product," *Journal of Marketing*, 45 (Fall), pp. 81–90.

27. David C. Schmittlein and Vijay Mahajan (1982), "Maximum Likelihood Estimation for an Innovation Diffusion Model of New Product Acceptance," *Marketing Science*, 1 (Winter), pp. 57–78.

28. See, for example, Lewis G. Pringle, R. Dale Wilson, and Edward I. Brody (1982), "NEWS: A Decision-Oriented Model for New Product Analysis and Forecasting," *Marketing Science*, 1 (Winter), pp. 1–29; Peter C. Wilton and Edgar A. Pessemier (1981), "Forecasting the Ultimate Acceptance of an Innovation: The Effects of Information," *Journal of Consumer Research*, 8 (Sept.), pp. 162–71; and David F. Midgley (1976), "A Simple Mathematical Theory of Innovative Behavior," *Journal of Consumer Research*, 3 (June), pp. 31–41.

29. Everett M. Rogers (1983), p. 248.

30. Everett M. Rogers (1983), p. 249.

31. Everett M. Rogers (1983), p. 249.

32. Everett M. Rogers (1983), p. 249–50.

33. Everett M. Rogers (1983), p. 250.

34. Everett M. Rogers, Hugh M. Daley, and Thomas D. Wu (1982), *The Diffusion of Home Computers: An Exploratory Study* (Inst. for Communication Research, Stanford Univ.), pp. 56–58.

35. Thomas S. Robertson (1971), *Innovative Behavior and Communication* (New York: Holt, Rinehart & Winston), p. 102.

36. Everett M. Rogers (1983), p. 260.

37. The conclusion that innovators are less dogmatic is confirmed by Jacob Jacoby (1971), "Personality and Innovation Processes," *Journal of Marketing Research*, 8 (May), pp. 244–47 and replicated by Kenneth A. Coney (1972), "Dogmatism and Innovation: A Replication," *Journal of Marketing Research*, 9 (Nov.), pp. 453–55. Other research, however, has found that the dogmatism-innovation relationship is situational. See Kenneth A. Coney and Rogert R. Harmon (1978), "Dogmatism and Innovation: A Situational Perspective," in *Advances in Consumer Research*, ed. William L. Wilkie, 6 (Assn. for Consumer Research), pp. 118–22 and Brian Blake, Robert Perloff, and Richard Heslin (1970), "Dogmatism and Acceptance of New Products," *Journal of Marketing Research*, 7 (Nov.), pp. 483–86.

38. Elizabeth C. Hirschman (1980), "Innovativeness, Novelty Seeking, and Consumer Creativity," *Journal of Consumer Research*, 7 (Dec.), pp. 283–95.

39. James W. Taylor (1977), "A Striking Characteristic of Innovators," *Journal of Marketing Research*, 14 (Feb.), pp. 104–7.

40. James S. Coleman et al. (1966).

41. Scott Ward (1978), "Zenith Radio Corporation: Videodisc," Harvard Business School Case No. 9-576-092, p. 26.

16 Personal Influence

The subject of this chapter, and a number of the chapters to follow, is social influence—the process by which people influence other people. Here we focus on personal influence, informal social influence transmitted among peers. This is frequently referred to as "word-of-mouth advertising."

The social influence we study in subsequent chapters occurs in a more structured manner within the context of a group or family or organization. In the next chapter, "Group Behavior," for example, social influence may be quite deliberate in order to achieve conformity to group norms. In "Family Behavior," social influence is subject to the role relationships among mother, father, and children. And in "Organizational Buying Behavior," social influence is often tied to formal relationships, specified in the organizational chart of the company.

In this chapter we shall review the nature of personal influence as a source of information in consumer purchase decisions, and we shall consider when personal influence is likely to occur. We then turn to behavioral science theories for an understanding of why personal influence can be so persuasive. Next, we explore how personal influence is transmitted and the role of opinion leaders. Finally, we suggest marketing strategies for affecting the personal-influence process.

Personal influence plays a key role in the pattern of diffusion. The typical S-shaped diffusion or product life-cycle curve can be attributed to the process of personal influence. Diffusion begins slowly until a few innovators adopt and then enters a rapid growth phase as people influence one another. This pattern can be seen in the diffusion of fashion, or new movies and television shows, for which personal influence significantly affects diffusion. In the absence of personal influence, we expect a linear pattern of diffusion, rather than slow takeoff followed by rapid acceleration of sales.

THE ROLE OF PERSONAL INFLUENCE

Consumers often find it desirable to turn to other people as sources of information. They may do so because they recognize the bias and incomplete nature of advertising and in-store sales presentations. They may do so because they have difficulty evaluating the competing and contradictory claims of advertising and sales presentations. Or, they may do so because other people are simply an easier and more available source of information on many occasions. Whatever the reason, other people are generally perceived to be more credible than marketer-initiated communications and are, therefore, frequently quite influential communication sources.

The importance of personal influence to the marketing of a product or service stems from its pervasiveness and impact. The difficulty, of course, is in finding a way to gain some leverage or control over personal influence, that is, to have consumers say the "right things" about the product. At the other extreme, the marketer certainly doesn't want consumers to say the "wrong things." Exhibit 16–1 provides an extreme example of negative personal influence and transmission of rumor with which K-mart had to deal.

Negativity Bias

A consistent finding in behavioral-science research is the **negativity bias**—that negative information is given greater weight in decision-making than positive information. This finding has been documented in studies of *impression formation*—how a person forms an impression of another person—and it is particularly applicable to the employment interview as well as to the personal sales situation.[1] A negativity bias has also been found in risk taking, namely, that the deterrence value of possible failure often exceeds the attraction value of possible gains.[2] A negativity bias may also operate in mass media. Negative information about a company from such sources as *Consumer Reports* has particularly serious effects on sales.[3]

The importance of the negativity bias has recently been explored in studies of negative word-of-mouth transmission by dissatisfied consumers. Whether negative personal influence occurs has to do with the severity of the problem as perceived by the consumer and the responsiveness of manufacturers or retailers in dealing with the problem.[4]

The detrimental impact of negative personal influence was shown in a study for Coca-Cola in which consumers who had complained to the company were interviewed. It was found that consumers who were satisfied with the company's handling of their complaints told four or five people about the positive experience. On the other hand, consumers who were dissatisfied with the handling of their complaints told nine or ten people about the negative experience.[5] In research involving a new coffee product, however, Holmes and Lett found that only 20 percent of consumers with unfavorable attitudes engaged in word-of-mouth versus 38 percent of consumers with favorable attitudes.[6]

Negative personal influence is more persuasive, however, than positive personal influence. In another research study on a new coffee product, it was found that, "Of the persons who reported exposure to favorable word of mouth, 54 percent purchased the product. . . . Only 18 percent of those receiving unfavorable word-of-mouth purchased the product."[7] Similarly, in a

EXHIBIT 16–1
A PERSONAL INFLUENCE RUMOR DETRIMENTAL TO THE COMPANY

K MART HAS A LITTLE TROUBLE KILLING THOSE PHANTOM SNAKES FROM ASIA

DETROIT—Not long ago, the story goes, a woman shopper at a K mart store tried on a coat. As she put an arm through a sleeve she felt a pricking sting. Thinking nothing of it, she went home. Then her arm began to swell, so badly that she had to be rushed to a hospital, where her arm was amputated.

Just what happened? Practically everybody in Detroit can tell you:

Somehow, a poisonous Asian snake had laid its eggs in a carton of Taiwan-made coats; they hatched inside the coat the woman tried on, and one of the baby snakes bit her.

The only trouble with the story—like the one about spider eggs in a well-known bubble gum and ground worms in a well-known hamburger—is that not a word of it is true. That hasn't stopped it from becoming the talk of the town in Detroit's beauty parlors, offices and lunchrooms. It has become "a traditional urban legend," says Philip LaRange, an assistant in the folklore archives at Wayne State University. Such legends, he says, "are hard to kill."

K mart's Troy, Mich., headquarters, north of Detroit, has received about 20 calls from people, mainly newsmen, who actually bothered to try to track the story down. Susan McKelvey, the chain's publicity director, says she doesn't know how the story started. "Nobody has produced a victim," she observes. "Nobody has come forward and said, 'I was bitten by a snake.' " Miss McKelvey called a herpetologist to learn whether venomous snakes live on Taiwan. They do, but she said she was told it was highly unlikely one could survive the long trip to Detroit.

Tom McIntyre, a reporter for WWJ radio, spent a day digging through hospital and police records in search of a victim. "I got to play detective," he says, but found no victim.

Tales of spider eggs in gum, worms in hamburgers and exotic snakes in women's coats tell "more about what people are thinking than the objects of the story," says Alan L. Wilkins, a professor at Brigham Young University's graduate school of management. He studies corporations as subcultures with their own lore and legends. He thinks the K mart tale could have an origin in Detroit's worries about Asian automobile imports and their blow to the area's economy. The story also could reflect residents' "concern about the quality of products from Taiwan and the ruthlessness in the world," Prof. Wilkins says.

SOURCE : Charles W. Stevens (1981), *Wall Street Journal* (Oct. 20), p. 29.

recent experiment it was found that unfavorable word-of-mouth had a stronger impact on beliefs and affect than favorable word of mouth had.[8] Personal influence, then, can be positive or negative. If it is negative, it can exert powerful pressure not to buy a company's products or services.

When Personal Influence Operates

The importance of personal influence varies with the product's characteristics. Personal influence increases for high-involvement products, for highly visible products, for products for which trial is difficult, for complex products, and for products that are high on perceived risk.

Personal influence is greater for *high-involvement* products than for low-involvement products. For low-involvement products, the incentive to seek personal influence is minimal, whereas for high-involvement products, such as cars, clothing, and appliances, personal influence may be the primary source of information for many buyers.

high involvement

Visibility of the product stimulates personal influence. Thus, clothing is more susceptible to personal influence than is laundry detergent. Highly visible items such as swimming pools, color television sets, and room air conditioners have been observed to diffuse in clusters rather than randomly—presumably because of the functioning of personal influence. This pattern was noted initially in a classic study of how window air conditioners spread within a neighborhood in the 1950s[9] and reconfirmed recently after subjecting the original data to more rigorous analysis.[10] The conclusion is that these window units diffused in a clustered rather than random pattern.

visibility

Another product characteristic related to personal influence is its *testability*, that is, can it be tried and tested against some objective criteria? The merits of certain products, notably food items, can be physically tested in a convenient manner. Other products, such as appliances, cannot readily be judged by observation or physical testing, except in use over some period of time. When the individual can rely on physical reality in the purchase decision, personal influence is not important. On the other hand, when it is not possible to rely on physical reality, reliance upon social reality is correspondingly high. Similarly, the more the product can be used on a *trial* basis, the less the consumer relies on other people.

testability

Personal influence also seems to be related to *complexity*. The influence of other people increases as products become more complex. We should expect high personal influence, therefore, for stereos and personal computers—particularly if a learning process is necessary in order to be able to use them effectively.

complexity

Finally, personal influence depends upon the amount of *perceived risk* which consumers associate with a product, not only as a function of cost but also of the consequences of an error. The use of illicit drugs is high on perceived risk and high on personal influence. So too are social products for which it is important to have group approval—for example, clothing or wine.

perceived risk

THEORIES OF PERSONAL INFLUENCE

The acceptance of personal influence by the individual is tied directly to satisfying a need; that is, there must be some incentive for seeking personal influence, such as the need for impartial evaluation of competing brands. This is true for communication situations in which the individual deliberately engages in information-seeking, as well as those in which communication is directed to the individual even though it was not sought.

The following are descriptions of two important theories accounting for personal influence.

Bauer's Scheme

Bauer suggests that social processes need not lead to "influence" or "conformity" in the traditional sense. He proposes that people engage in two different kinds of social "games," which he calls the **psychosocial game** and the **problem-solving game.** In the psychosocial game, the individual attempts to gain social status or acceptance and reward (by wearing group-sanctioned clothing styles, for example). In the problem-solving game, the individual uses information gained from other people as a reference point in defining the environment and in decision-making (in choosing among insurance companies, for example). Both games involve influence, but the problem-solving game does not denote behavior in order to gain social rewards from others.[11]

Undoubtedly most consumer influence is a mix of problem-solving and psychosocial influence. Much of what has been labeled "conformity" is actually an attempt by the individual to establish a meaningful and valid frame of reference for decision-making. Other people serve as standard makers, and the individual willingly participates in the process of establishing and adhering to group standards. Personal influence has perhaps too often been considered from a negative point of view. "Conspicuous consumption," "keeping up with the Joneses," and "status seeking" have been viewed as essentially negative aspects of American society. Yet following other people's consumption experiences may be the logical procedure in an ambiguous environment or if the costs of information search are high. Problem-solving influence may be just as pervasive as psychosocial influence.

Festinger's Scheme

An especially encompassing and meaningful theory of social influence is that provided by Leon Festinger.[12] He elaborates a theory of **social comparison processes** which implicitly recognizes the psychosocial and problem-solving aspects of group influence. Festinger's basic assumption is that individuals seek to evaluate their opinions and abilities. He further postulates that, to the extent that objective, nonsocial means of evaluating opinions are available, individuals will use them. However, to the extent that nonsocial means are not available, individuals will turn to other people for advice and information. The latter is typically the case in the marketing situation in which nonsocial means, basically advertising, are designed to be persuasive and one-sided.

The importance of the Festinger scheme is that it provides a rationale for personal influence. Throughout the Festinger model run the notions of psychosocial and problem-solving behavior. The motivation for social comparison at times lies in the desire to gain social acceptance—but social acceptance is not always at stake. In many cases the individual who must make a decision without an objective test depends on other people to help make or validate it.

THE TRANSMISSION OF PERSONAL INFLUENCE

The conceptualization of the transmission of personal influence has changed over time. At the turn of the century, the dominant view was the "trickle-down" theory. This gave way to the "two-step flow" from the 1940s to the 1960s, which, in turn, has been replaced by the "multiflow theory" in the 1970s and 1980s.

Trickle-Down Theory

The historic view of the transmission of personal influence is the **trickle-down theory.** This theory has its roots in the works of Veblen and Simmel. Veblen's *Theory of the Leisure Class* introduced the concept of "conspicuous consumption" and the notion that the wealthy seek reputability by the display of products symbolizing wealth. Such visual display is then emulated by the lower classes.[13] Simmel, who did the classic work on fashion, offers the following view of the trickle-down theory.

> *Social forms, apparel, aesthetic judgment, the whole style of human expression are constantly transformed by fashion, in such a way, however, that fashion—in all these things—affects only the upper classes. Just as soon as the lower classes begin to copy their style, thereby crossing the line of demarcation the upper classes have drawn and destroying the uniformity of their coherence, the upper classes turn away from this style and adopt a new one, which in its own turn differentiates them from the masses; and thus the game goes merrily on. Naturally, the lower classes look and strive toward the upper, and they encounter least resistance in those fields which are subject to the whims of fashion; for it is here that mere external imitation is most readily applied. The same process is at work as between the sets within the upper classes, although it is not always as visible here.* . . .[14]

The trickle-down theory undoubtedly has some validity but the actual degree to which influence is transmitted "vertically" by social class may be limited. In a recent review of fashion diffusion, Sproles observes that:

> *Nearly all books of fashion history and museum collections chronicle exclusive and aristocratic fashions. Based on such historical precedents it is easy to conclude that fashion has traditionally been the province of the wealthy, upper class, celebrated few. But the degree to which fashions trickled to the lower classes is difficult to document, for there is little record of lower class fashions either in historical collections or art from most periods of history.*[15]

Indeed, the trickle-down theory would seem to be less valid today than in the past because of the advent of mass production, mass distribution, and mass media. Today the latest "haute couture" styles from the leading designers in Paris and Milan are shown in newspapers worldwide the next day, and copies may be in the stores in a matter of weeks.

The Two-Step Flow

The thesis adhered to by many communication researchers until recently is that personal influence occurs in a **two-step flow.** This model was originally derived in research during the course of the 1940 presidential election campaign, in which the influence of *people* was documented as the main factor in voting decisions. Radio and print media were found to have "only negligible effects on actual vote decisions and particularly minute effects on *changes* in vote decisions."[16] Further analysis revealed that those individuals more influential than others in affecting voting decisions were more often in contact with and more influenced by mass media than those who were less influential. This is the basis of the two-step flow of communication model as shown in Exhibit 16–2. It implies that the mass media (1) influence "opinion leaders," who in turn (2) influence a set of followers.

The importance of the two-step flow is its stress on the informal peer group as the transmitter of most influence, rather than on a high-status source. People look to their peers (people of their own status) and not to higher social-class referents. The two-step theory therefore posits a *horizontal* flow of influence rather than a *vertical* flow, as in the trickle-down theory.

Further research, however, has not conclusively demonstrated the occurrence of such a two-step process. The model has been criticized on a number of grounds, particularly that it assumes a "passive" set of followers who are completely uninfluential in their own right. The most basic criticism of the model, however, is that it is overly simplistic.

Multiflow Theory

The most recent theory of personal influence, **multiflow theory,** builds on the two-step flow by recognizing that most influence is transmitted horizontally at the peer-group level. However, it goes beyond the two-step flow in that it is not bound by a single pattern but instead proposes multiple patterns of personal influence.

The multiflow view suggests that personal influence can occur in a number of ways.

1. Influence may be transmitted among *peers* ("strong ties") or *nonpeers* ("weak ties").
2. Influence may be initiated by the *source* (person influencing) or the *recipient* (person being influenced).
3. Influence can be *one-way* or *two-way*. The individual can influence while being influenced.
4. Influence may occur as a result of *verbal* or of *visual* communication.

Strength of Ties Most influence occurs among peers. This is referred to as **homophilous** influence, that is, influence among people who are similar to each other on such variables as age, education, and social status.[17] The probability of homophilous influence is high simply because most interaction among people is with similar others. People seem to be more comfortable interacting with other people like themselves and more willing to accept their

EXHIBIT 16–2
THE TWO-STEP FLOW OF PERSONAL INFLUENCE

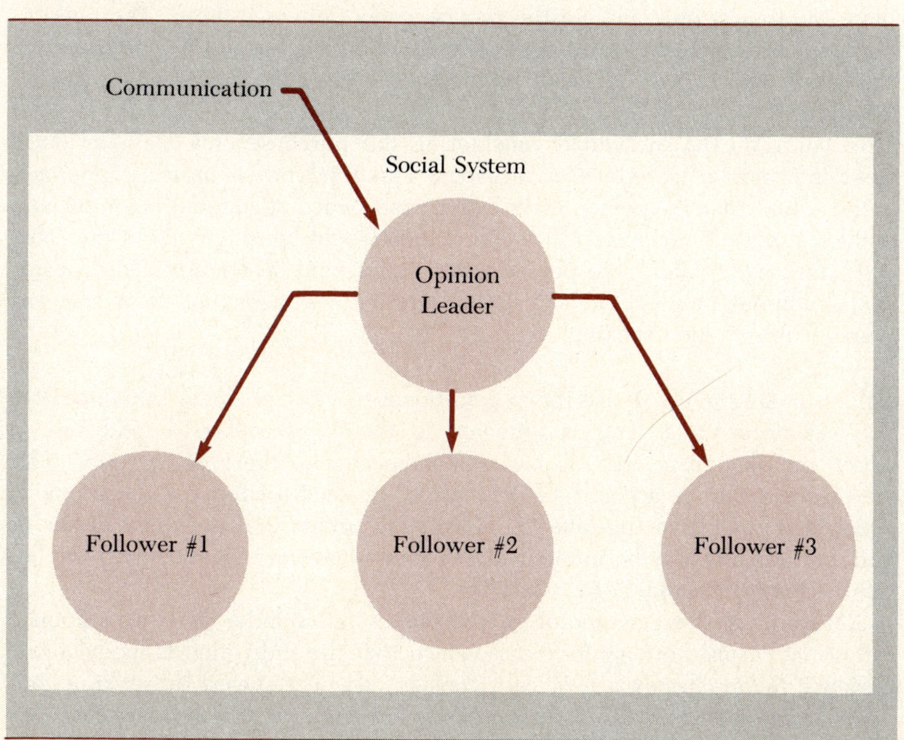

opinions. We could also refer to homophilous influence as based on "strong ties" among people.

Some significant level of influence, however, is **heterophilous,** that is, influence transmitted among people who are dissimilar. Rogers notes that "heterophilous communication has a special informational potential, even though it may be realized only rarely."[18] The value of heterophilous influence is tied to research by Granovetter on the **strength of weak ties.**[19] In an analysis of how people found new jobs, it was discovered that they heard about their new positions from heterophilous social contacts. These "weak ties" were important probably because the homophilous ties did not know anything more than the individual. In some sense this is similar to the concept of the "marginal" in the anthropology literature—a person who transcends cultures and is, therefore, critical to the dissemination of new ideas.

Thus, influence may occur on a homophilous (strong ties) or heterophilous (weak ties) basis. Most influence is homophilous but heterophilous influence, when it does occur, may be quite important, especially to the diffusion of new ideas and new products.

Influence Initiation   At times it may be rewarding for the individual to communicate information to another person, and at other times it may be rewarding to seek information from another person. For example, the person who has just purchased a new car may experience a need to talk about the purchase to other people and, in the process, may influence them. The need to communicate could result from a desire to "show off," as in the purchase of a first Mercedes, or it could result from a need to seek social support for buying the right car.

In contrast, the individual considering the purchase of a new car often seeks information to reduce uncertainty. This tendency is more pronounced to the extent that the person lacks experience. Since an automobile is socially visible, it might be expected that information would be sought about the "correct" purchase relative to a person's age, status, and occupation. The considerable number of potentially desirable alternatives in buying a car also encourages information seeking.

Influence Direction   It has been traditional to view personal influence as a one-way occurrence. This is reflected in the two-step flow hypothesis, in which the change in attitude or behavior occurs in the receiver only. This view seems not to account for the many product-related conversations in which a mutual give-and-take of information occurs and in which either or both participants may be influenced. An individual can influence (one-way) or influence *and* be influenced (two-way).

Returning to our example of purchasing an automobile, two-way influence can occur because of cognitive dissonance that the individual is likely to experience in purchasing a new car. Tension can be reduced by seeking confirming evidence that the right decision was made. Social support provides such confirmation, so the new-car buyer may talk about the car to others, thus rationalizing his or her behavior. In so doing, the individual may influence others while also being influenced.

Influence Mode   It is not necessary to talk to another person to be influenced. Seeing a neighbor wear clothes of a certain fashion may influence a consumer to do likewise. Such visual communication may, in fact, be as persuasive as verbal communication, particularly for goods high in visibility. Visual cues can be just as meaningful as verbal cues—a raised eyebrow or the failure of friends to mention, say, a new clothing fashion could cause a person to doubt its acceptability.

OPINION LEADERSHIP

Consistent with the concept of personal influence is the recognition that not all consumers wield equal influence. Those who are most influential are designated **opinion leaders,** that is, those to whom others turn for information and advice. The term *leader* is unfortunate, however, because it suggests an absolute leader whom others seek to follow. Yet opinion leadership is a relative concept, and the opinion leader may not be much more influential than the "followers."

Marketers have long attempted to reach "influentials," but have generally defined these influentials in terms of high occupational status or community position. A major value of the *two-step flow* was in its noting that people are most often influenced by others with whom they are in everyday contact— people just like themselves. The individual is not going to look to a senator or a doctor for advice on appliances, but rather to the nearest friend or neighbor who has some expertise or opinions on the matter. There are opinion leaders, therefore, at every status level and in every informal group.

Opinion-Leader Characteristics

The first formulation of characteristics of the opinion leader is in Katz and Lazarsfeld's classic study among women analyzing the flow of influence in four areas of interest: food shopping, fashion, public affairs, and movies. Differing opinion-leader profiles were obtained. The *food opinion leader* tended to be a married woman with a comparatively large family who was gregarious or outgoing. She could be located on all status levels, and her influence was limited to the status level on which she was found. The *fashion leader* tended to be young and highly gregarious. She was also somewhat more likely to be of higher status. The *public-affairs leader* was a high-status woman of considerable gregariousness. Public-affairs influence crossed status boundaries, moving from high to low status. Finally, the *movie-going leader* was most often a young woman, often unmarried. Social status and gregariousness were not of significance.[20]

In another classic study, Coleman, Katz, and Menzel traced the flow of influence among physicians in the adoption of a new drug. They found that "social networks affected the [drug] adoptions of only those doctors who were well integrated into them; . . . the relatively isolated doctors tended to innovate by a more individualistic process."[21] The flow of personal influence functioned best, therefore, for doctors who were gregarious or socially integrated; and social integration was a primary determinant of the amount of opinion leadership exerted and received. Exhibit 16-3 is a **sociogram** showing the flow of information and advice among the doctors in this community. Sociograms and network analyses that plot information flow among members of a community are useful ways of assessing personal influence.

The physician opinion leader for the new drug was profiled as follows:

- attended a quality medical school;
- had more experience with out-of-town medical institutions;
- had a longer tenure of practice;
- was more often a specialist than a general practitioner;
- was more likely to be a native of the town in which the practice was located;
- was more likely to hold a senior staff position at a local hospital;
- was more likely to share an office with other physicians;
- attended more medical meetings;
- read more professional journals;
- was somewhat conservative in attitudes toward therapy; and
- was more profession-oriented than patient-oriented.[22]

(Compare and contrast this *opinion-leader profile* with the *innovator profile* for physicians discussed in the last chapter.)

More generally, Rogers has summarized opinion-leader characteristics across hundreds of research studies in a number of fields—rural sociology, education, medicine, and marketing. Four key generalizations are offered.

1. Opinion leaders have greater exposure to external communication. This suggests more exposure to *relevant* mass media (for example, fashion opinion leaders are more exposed to fashion magazines) and a more cosmopolitan (worldly) orientation than for followers.
2. Opinion leaders have greater social participation than followers. This seems to increase the opportunities for personal influence.
3. Opinion leaders have "somewhat" higher social status than followers. Influence is still transmitted at the peer-group level, however.
4. Opinion leaders are "more innovative" than their followers, but they are not the "innovators"; that is, they adopt new products early but not first.[23]

To these generalizations we could add two others.

5. Opinion leaders have more expertise than their followers.
6. There are separate opinion leaders by product category.

EXHIBIT 16–3

A SOCIOGRAM SHOWING THE FLOW OF ADVICE AMONG PHYSICIANS IN A COMMUNITY[a]

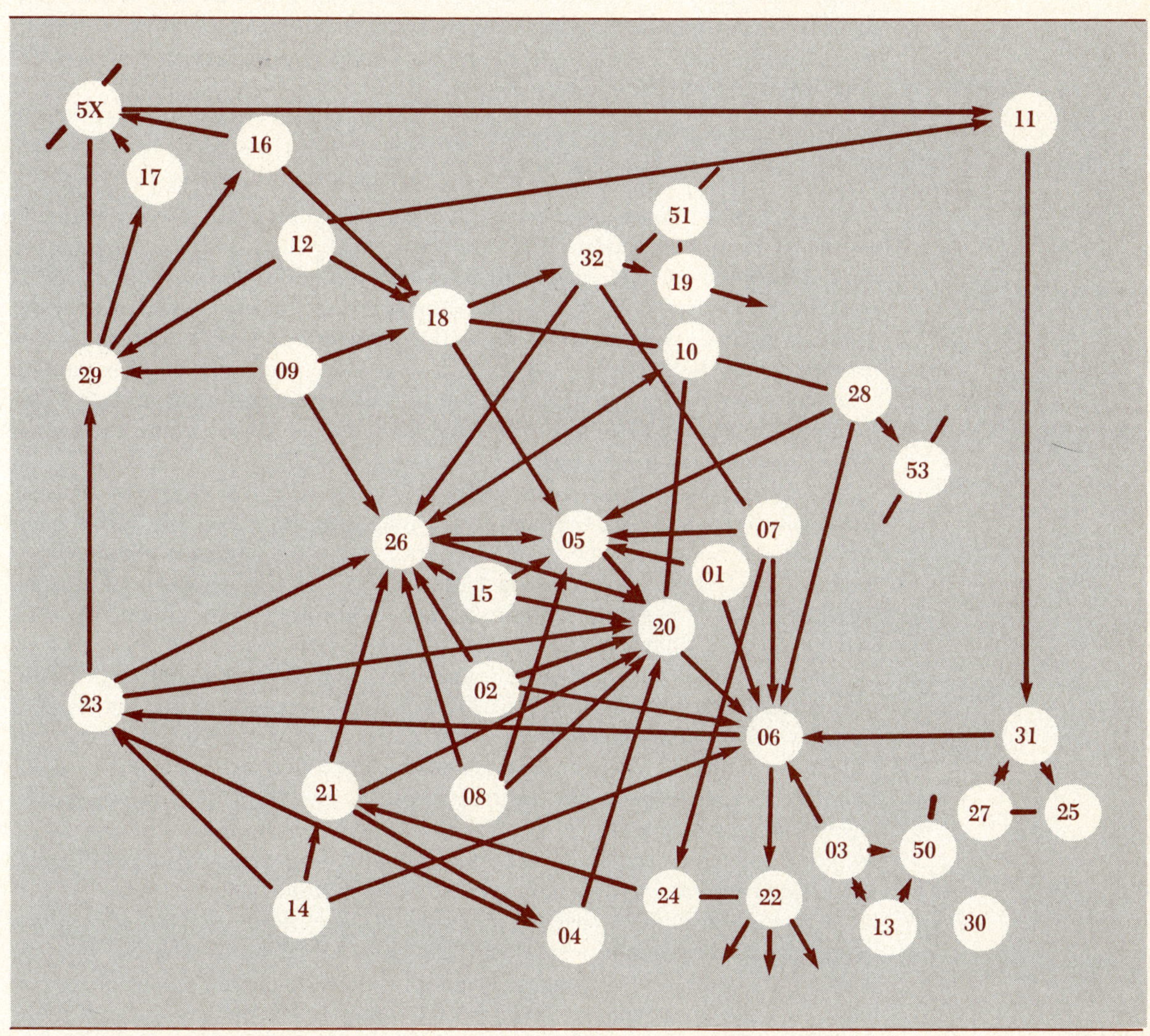

[a]The physicians mentioned most frequently in responses to the question "Who do you turn to for advice and information about new drugs?" are No. 26, No. 5, and No. 6. They would seem to be at the center of the advice-and-information network.

SOURCE : James S. Coleman, Elihu Katz, and Herbert Menzel (1966), *Medical Innovation: A Diffusion Study* (Indianapolis: Bobbs-Merrill), p. 75.

The generalization about the overlap of opinion leadership and innovativeness bears comment. Research seems to suggest somewhat different roles for the innovator and the opinion leader. In research on fashion, for example, King described the distinction in roles as follows: "The innovator is the earliest visual communicator of the season's styles for the mass of fashion consumers. The influential appears to define and endorse appropriate standards."[24] The roles can be characterized as follows:

- The innovator is an *adventurer*.
- The opinion leader is an *editor*.

The amount of overlap between the two roles also seems to vary with the *norms* of the social system. The innovator and opinion leader roles coincide to a greater extent in the medical social system than in the agricultural social system, for example. Medical norms appear to be progressive and, therefore, more receptive to innovations than the agricultural norms. For consumer products, the innovator and opinion-leader roles may overlap more among younger people, among whom the norms favor change, than among older people. The two roles may also overlap more in California, where the norms favor change, than in Nebraska.

A further distinction is made by Baumgarten, who has suggested that occasionally innovator and opinion-leader roles coincide. The *innovative communicator* is someone who is high on both innovativeness and opinion leadership.[25] In research on male fashion innovations, Hirschman and Adcock conclude that innovative communicators, innovators, and opinion leaders have somewhat different characteristics, however.[26]

Another notion that has been proposed is that of the **gatekeeper.** Within the group there may be a person who influences whether or not information *reaches* other members, but who may not actually *transmit* information or *influence* people as does an opinion leader. For example, secretaries often function as gatekeepers who control access to managers, just as purchasing agents are gatekeepers who control access to the actual users of a product within a company. The *shopper* within the family is an important gatekeeper, often determining whether new products will be tried.

It may seem obvious that opinion leaders have more expertise than other people, but occasionally a question has been raised as to whether opinion leaders are more knowledgeable or simply more dominant. Research by Jacoby and Hoyer seems to confirm that opinion leaders are indeed more knowledgeable—at least about stereos.[27] A related question is how knowledgeable or expert a source is preferred when people seek information from someone else. The conclusion seems to be that consumers prefer a source who is knowledgeable, but not very much more knowledgeable than themselves. A major gap in expertise can actually make communication difficult.[28]

Finally, a recurring question concerning opinion leadership is whether a "general" opinion leader exists—someone who has leadership across many product categories. There has been a considerable amount of research on this question, beginning with the classic Katz and Lazarsfeld study in which they concluded that there was very little overlap of opinion leadership across different product categories. In more technical terms, opinion leadership was found to be **monomorphic** (related to a single topic) rather than **polymorphic** (extending across topics).[29] Other researchers have found either limited overlap of opinion leadership or no overlap at all.[30]

Although overall the conclusion is that there is no such thing as a general opinion leader, some overlap of opinion leadership may occur across *related*

EXHIBIT 16–4
MEASURING OPINION LEADERSHIP

There are four methods of measuring opinion leadership—the sociometric, key-informant, self-designating, and observation methods.[a]

The **sociometric method** asks questions such as, "Who do you turn to for advice and information about new drugs?" By asking a set of people, it is possible to locate the opinion leaders, defined as those who receive the greatest number of sociometric choices as information-givers. This method would seem to be the most valid measure since it relies on the followers to designate the leaders. Its use is particularly applicable in industrial selling, in which there are a limited number of consumers within a defined social system. However, the sociometric method is unwieldy with large numbers of consumers. (Exhibit 16–3 shows a sociogram constructed from results of a sociometric study.)

The **key-informant method** asks a set of judges to identify the opinion leaders. Again this would seem to work best within a circumscribed social system but not with large numbers of consumers. In a recent study of new air freight distribution systems, for example, the key-informant method was used. The editors of the trade journals in air freight identified the opinion leader firms for interviewing and assessing the new distribution system ideas. The rationale was simply that it made more sense to talk to a few opinion leaders than to a large sample of followers.

The **self-designating method** asks consumers to assess whether they themselves are opinion leaders. A set of questions may be asked, such as, "Are you likely to be asked your advice on new clothing fashions?" or "Are you more influential or less influential than your friends regarding new clothing fashions?" This method allows the measurement of opinion leadership in the population as a whole and not just within a defined social system. The validity of self-designation may be questioned however, since there may be a tendency to overstate one's influence. Nevertheless, this method measures the individual's self-perception, which, after all, is what generally determines behavior.

Finally, the **observation method** tracks opinion leadership based on recording communications and influence as it occurs. This usually requires that the observer be a participant in the social network and, of course, a disadvantage of this method might be its obtrusiveness. This method is sometimes used in assessing leadership within group meetings.

---

[a]For more detail, see Everett M. Rogers (1983), *Diffusion of Innovations*, 3rd ed. (New York: The Free Press), p. 278.

product categories. Furthermore, some people in a social system may be "somewhat" higher in general opinion leadership simply because of their leadership and exposure positions. But the overall absence of strong overlap should not be surprising since the abilities and knowledge that make a person an opinion leader in one situation, such as food purchasing, are apparently quite different from those required in another situation, such as automobile purchasing.

A summary profile of the characteristics of the opinion leader is provided in Exhibit 16–5. This summary is rather tentative, however, because of the absence of a general opinion leader. The marketing manager will derive a much clearer profile of opinion-leader traits on a product category basis. Exhibit 16–6, for example, shows who the people are who influence others on motor-bike selection. This study, conducted for Yamaha, also shows the marketing implications.

MARKETING STRATEGIES TO AFFECT PERSONAL INFLUENCE

Before considering strategies to affect the process of personal influence, the marketing manager must determine if personal influence is important for the product being marketed. Because personal-influence strategies are difficult to design, marketing efforts should be concentrated elsewhere unless personal influence is deemed highly relevant for the product.

Many advertising executives and product managers feel that attempting to affect or control personal influence involves more expense than simply advertising to the total potential market. Mass media can stimulate personal influ-

EXHIBIT 16–5
A SUMMARY PROFILE OF OPINION LEADER CHARACTERISTICS

Variable	Results
• Demographics (age, income, education, etc.)	• Vary by product category
• Social status	• The same as followers or only slightly higher
• Social participation	• More than followers
• External communication exposure	• Higher than followers (for example, more exposure to relevant mass media)
• Innovativeness	• Adopt new products earlier than followers
• Expertise	• More knowledgeable about the product category than followers
• Opinion leadership overlap	• Limited to related product categories

ence, however, providing the marketer with a measure of control over the personal-influence process. In this section we review a number of other strategies for taking advantage of personal influence.

EXHIBIT 16–6
YAMAHA MOTOR CORPORATION: PERSONAL INFLUENCE IN MOTORCYCLE BRAND DECISIONS

Findings	Marketing Implications
Importance of Personal Influence	
1. Personal influence the dominant information source for new buyers	Strategies should build on personal influence processes.
2. Dealers the second most important source of information for most new buyers	Dealers should be provided with maximum support and educated as to their vital role as information givers.
Characteristics of Influentials	
3. Likely to be someone who can work skillfully on his motorcycle	Most influence is transmitted by people who are good at working on their bikes but not by "experts." The person is much like the person being influenced, but has product experience.
Information Sought	
4. New buyers most interested in information on reliability and dependability	Personal influence provides a reality test to a potential buyer through the experience of a previous buyer.
Ownership Characteristics of High Information Seekers	
5. Most likely to be first-time buyers and reported to know less about motorcycling	This is consistent with generally high information needs of new product buyers in any product category.
Topics Discussed by High Information Seekers	
6. More likely to seek brand advice and less likely to seek advice on features or characteristics	New buyers are unsure of their ability to evaluate product features and are likely to rely on a strong brand name.
Personal Characteristics of High Information Seekers	
7. Likely to be younger and to be students	Younger people have less experience and are more in contact with a relevant peer group.
Influence Behavior of New Buyers	
8. New Yamaha buyers highly influential in inducing further purchases of Yamaha	65% talked to other people about their motorcycle. 35% felt they may have influenced one or more persons to buy a Yamaha. 25% are sure they influenced at least one person to buy a Yamaha.

Identifying Opinion Leaders

To affect personal influence, the most logical strategy is to reach opinion leaders and to allow them to influence their followers. The key to this strategy is in whether it is actually possible to *identify* opinion leaders. It may be possible if the potential market represents a small number of consumers and if the unit price of the product is high. This is frequently the case in industrial selling, in which it may be found that as company X goes, so goes the industry. For example, what IBM does, other computer companies may also do. When this kind of relationship exists, the earliest and strongest promotional efforts should be directed toward the key company, and later sales appeals should emphasize that this company has already adopted the product. For the consumer-goods marketer, locating and identifying opinion leaders very seldom is worth the cost, since this is indeed a difficult and expensive undertaking.

The logic of identifying opinion leaders and selling through them can be appreciated if you refer back to the sociogram in Exhibit 16–3, which shows the influence network for new drugs among physicians in a certain city. If you were a pharmaceutical sales manager, you would want your detail force (sales personnel) to call on the influential physicians who are looked to for advice by others. If you can persuade the opinion-leader physicians to prescribe your new drug you have made real progress in your sales effort, since these physicians are the source of advice to their peers.

Creating Opinion Leaders

Sometimes it is possible to *create* opinion leaders. For example, a swimming-pool company may go into a new neighborhood and try to locate a pool near the center of each block. The central homeowner is offered the pool "at cost" if neighbors are allowed to examine it. The company then canvasses the area, informing people that neighbors are buying the pool and that it can be seen at a designated address. In effect, the chosen homeowner is being established by the company as an opinion leader for its product. Of course, it is desirable to choose a person whose natural attributes are effective in influencing others. Similarly, in party-plan selling, the neighbor who holds the party, although often a paid sales agent of the company, may not be perceived as such. Because of the nature of the role, the person may be more effective if he or she is seen as possessing the attributes of an opinion leader.

Characterizing Opinion Leaders

The most basic approach toward affecting the personal influence process does not focus on specific people, but rather studies the *characteristics* of opinion leaders, including their media behavior. Then the promotional program is aimed at the general product opinion leader, who, because of selective perception, should be more likely to receive and process the message.

Although, as we have noted, we do not have a very clear-cut profile of a general opinion leader, we often have a very well-delineated profile of opinion leaders for particular product categories. If, for example, we can derive a profile of the movie opinion leader (age, sex, social class, social contact, and so forth), we can advertise to reach people with this profile in advance of a mass campaign. In the Yamaha example considered earlier (Exhibit 16–6), advertising can be directed to the opinion leader designated for motor-bikes.

Simulating Personal Influence

For many products, advertising can perform the function of *simulating* personal influence, replacing or reducing the need for actual personal influence. By portraying the idea that the consumer's fellow group members buy the product and that buying it is an appropriate behavior, advertising reduces the need for the individual to turn to other people for purchase validation. Another very common example of personal influence simulation is the use of testimonial advertising by a famous person or by "the person on the street"; the marketer simulates opinion leadership through setting up these people as "opinion leaders."

As with the actual occurrence of personal influence, testimonials are believable mainly to the extent that the product is subject to personal influence. But it is also important that the media "opinion leader" be viewed as a valid source of information. Dean Martin's popular image makes him a likely endorser for liquor, but it is doubtful that his influence would be felt across a range of product categories. Much testimonial advertising probably goes astray because the endorser is not seen as a credible source of information.

The sales agent may also be capable of simulating the personal influence process, especially if he or she is perceived as credible and trustworthy. Indeed, in many industrial and consumer purchasing situations, the salesperson is a major information source. The salesperson's ability to simulate personal influence will be enhanced if he or she sells multiple brands and if the seller/consumer relationship is long-term enough to have built trust.

Stimulating Personal Influence

Some advertising campaigns are much more successful than others in *stimulating* personal influence, that is, in getting consumers to talk about the product. Few advertising agencies pretest advertising for its conversational impact. This is not commonly recognized as an advertising objective. Yet, advertising should encourage dissemination of positive information about the product.

A number of advertising techniques can be used to stimulate personal influence. One well-known technique is the "teaser" campaign, which may be run in advance of a new product's introduction. Before entering business, for example, Southwest Airlines ran teaser advertisements with provocative headlines such as "The 48-minute love affair" or "At last a $20 ticket you won't mind getting." These ads did not identify the sponsor but gave a telephone number for people to call in order to find out that the sponsor was Southwest

Airlines.[31] Other advertising techniques, such as slogans and music, may also be used to heighten the conversational value of advertisements.

On a more fundamental level, personal influence can be stimulated by encouraging information-giving and information-seeking. The most likely information givers are people who have just bought the product. Such people can be advertised to specifically, if purchase records are available (as for cars, appliances, and furniture), using direct mail. Since they may be in a state of cognitive dissonance, these recent purchasers are likely to be quite receptive to product information justifying their purchase. The information provided may then place them in a better position to communicate with friends about the product and may encourage them to do so. The most likely information seeker is a person who is considering the purchase of a product. Mass media advertising directed at these people can use an "Ask the person who owns one" approach.

Monitoring Personal Influence

It is possible to *monitor* personal influence, that is, to find out what people are saying about the product. Monitoring may provide valuable information for marketing decision-making. For new products, monitoring personal influence may be especially valuable in discovering what product attributes are discussed, what product uses are emphasized, what disadvantages or problems are discussed, and what the overall attitude toward the product is. As often happens, the features being emphasized in advertising may not be perceived as the most relevant ones by consumers. Consumers also find new uses for products. On the other hand, very minor disadvantages of the product may create a negative overall feeling about the product.

Advertising can be used in reacting to what is taking place in the interpersonal communication channels. Thus, if positive things are being said about the product, advertising can emphasize these positive aspects to reinforce and encourage such word of mouth. For example, if consumers are talking about the quietness of a vacuum cleaner while advertisements are stressing its efficiency, the advertising appeal can be adjusted to emphasize the quietness. If unpleasant things are being said about the product, advertising may be able to combat such misunderstandings—if they are misunderstandings—by providing more detailed usage information or emphasizing positive aspects of the product.

Retarding Personal Influence

Companies may find it desirable to *retard* personal influence under some circumstances. This situation is most common when the product is inferior. It is unlikely that personal influence can be retarded for an inferior product, except on a very short-run basis.

Motion pictures provide an interesting case of how to manage personal influence. If a movie is bad, its distributors adopt a mass-penetration strategy—multiple showings and mass advertising, aiming to get in and out of town before people can start telling other people about how poor the movie is. Conversely, if a movie is good, a strategy of limited distribution is used, aiming to capitalize on favorable word-of-mouth. Of course, it is not always clear whether a movie is good or bad. For example, Mel Brooks' *History of The World, Part I*, which was eagerly awaited because of his previous hits (such as *Blazing Saddles* and *Young Frankenstein*), opened with limited distribution and had a good first week. Then, however, "ticket sales shriveled because of poor word-of-mouth."[32] Similarly, *Endless Love*, starring Brooke Shields, was supposed to be the summer hit of 1981, opened well because of her name, but quickly died as personal influence took hold.

The fact that personal influence can be dysfunctional, especially for radically new or complicated products, suggests the need for extensive dissemination of factual material and product demonstrations for some products. Thus, if physicians rely on other physicians for information, adoption may actually be slowed if the people forming the interpersonal channels lack product knowledge. But, if physicians can readily turn to company information sources for advice and demonstrations, adoption may be encouraged. Pharmaceutical firms, therefore, may provide 800-numbers that physicians may call for information, sometimes from a physician within the company. Negative personal influence can conceivably be retarded, therefore, by the ready availability of other information sources.

Personal influence is not always desirable. Opinion leaders communicate negative as well as positive information and can recommend against adoption of the product. In such cases, it is desirable to neutralize such negative opinion leaders. Unfortunately, the concept of negative opinion leadership has barely been researched.

Group Sanctioning

A final strategy for affecting personal influence is through *group sanctioning* or *referral*. Union or school endorsement are examples of group sanctions that sales agents often seek.

The more it is possible to sell within the boundaries of specific social systems, the more the flow of personal influence will benefit the seller. For example, some companies establish student campus representatives. Because the college social system is well defined, the presence of such a representative who stands ready to help fellow students can be made known rather quickly. If he or she provides good service, knowledge of this reputation disseminates quickly among social-system members. (Of course, poor service can also be made known quickly.) It is also possible to focus on specific *groups* within the social system. This approach tends to maximize any benefits to be obtained from personal influence. The campus representative, for example, could choose to sell the product by approaching each living unit in turn.

In order to make full use of personal channels, sales agents should request *referrals* within the social system whenever possible. This is a particularly effective way of taking advantage of personal influence. The insurance sales agent, for example, often relies heavily on referrals to gain entry and a higher level of perceived trustworthiness than might otherwise be the case. Even if the sales agent does not use the informant's name in selling, referrals are still useful as leads to prospects who are considering purchase.

Implicit referral also may be used as a selling technique. In calling upon succeeding group members, for example, the sales agent may indicate that purchases already have been made by other group members, especially those high on opinion leadership. Or a product or service may be sold on the basis of a special price for group members, as with insurance for senior citizens or veterans only.

SUMMARY

Personal influence is a major factor in the transmission of information about products. The importance of personal influence varies with the product's characteristics, increasing for high-involvement products, visible products, products for which trial is difficult, complex products, and products which are high on perceived risk. The marketing executive for products subject to a high degree of personal influence logically seeks to affect the flow of personal influence.

The consumer's acceptance of personal influence may be due to conformity behavior or to information-seeking behavior. In other words, consumers may accept personal influence in order to gain social approval or as an alternative to seeking information through other communication sources, such as advertising and in-store shopping.

The earliest views of personal influence suggested that it was transmitted vertically from high to low status levels in a society. This *trickle-down theory* was replaced by the *two-step flow,* which recognized that most influence was transmitted horizontally among peers. More recently, the *multiflow* theory has pointed to a number of different patterns that personal influence can follow.

Central to the theory of personal influence is the concept of the *opinion leader.* Within the peer group, opinion leaders, by product category, influence other consumers. An important marketing task is to discover these opinion leaders and what their characteristics are. The marketing program can then be disproportionately directed to them, preparing them to influence their followers. Opinion leaders have the same social status as (or slightly higher than) their followers. They have greater social participation, have more contact with communication sources, are more innovative, and have greater expertise than their followers. Opinion leadership is for the most part *monomorphic,* that is, limited to a given product category. Thus, the opinion-leader profile is clearer for a specific product category.

A number of strategies can be useful in affecting personal influence: identifying opinion leaders, creating opinion leaders, characterizing opinion leaders, simulating personal influence, stimulating personal influence, monitoring personal influence, retarding personal influence, and group sanctioning.

KEY CONCEPTS

negativity bias
psychosocial game
problem-solving game
social comparison
   processes
trickle-down theory
two-step flow theory

multiflow theory
homophilous-
   heterophilous
key-informant method
self-designating
   method
observation method

sociometric method
strength of weak ties
opinion leaders
sociogram
gatekeeper
polymorphic-
   monomorphic

DISCUSSION QUESTIONS

1. Distinguish between the concept of the "innovator" and the concept of the "opinion leader." What do these concepts have in common?

2. A number of ideas for affecting the personal-influence process for products have been discussed. Which of these might be most appropriate for a new perfume? Which for a new medical technology for hospitals?

3. Provide some examples of personal influence based on the "psychosocial game" and some examples based on the "problem-solving game."

4. Why would a consumer seek personal influence? Why would a consumer give personal influence?

5. Design a specific marketing approach to help Yamaha take advantage of personal influence in selling motorcycles (see Exhibit 16–6).

6. Under what conditions should a marketing manager be concerned with personal influence and seek to affect the personal influence process?

7. Evaluate the "two-step" and "trickle-down" theories of communication. What are their values and limitations?

8. How would you measure opinion leadership for the following products: a new ethical drug sold to physicians, a new personal computer for the home, a camera with a new design, a new fashion, a new soft drink?

NOTES

1. Susan T. Fiske (1980), "Attention and Weight in Person Perception: The Impact of Negative and Extreme Behavior," *Journal of Personality and Social Psychology*, 38, 6, pp. 889–906 and S. W. Constantin (1976), "An Investigation of Information Favorability in the Employment Interview," *Journal of Applied Psychology*, 61, 6, pp. 743–49.

2. David E. Kanouse and L. Reid Hanson, Jr. (1972), "Negativity in Evaluations," in *Attribution: Perceiving the Causes*, ed. E. E. Jones, et al. (Morristown, N.J.: General Learning Press), pp. 47–62.

3. Marc G. Weinberger, Chris T. Allen, and William R. Dillon (1981), "The Impact of Negative Marketing Communications: The Consumers Union/Chrysler Controversy," *Journal of Advertising*, 10, 4, pp. 20–28.

4. Marsha L. Richins (1983), "Negative Word-of-Mouth by Dissatisfied Consumers: A Pilot Study," *Journal of Marketing*, 47 (Winter), pp. 68–78.

5. *Wall Street Journal* (1981), "Coke Drinkers Talk a Lot . . . 'Lite' Is Hot . . . So Is WATS," (Oct. 22), p. 29.

6. John H. Holmes and John D. Lett, Jr. (1977), "Product Sampling and Word of Mouth," *Journal of Advertising Research*, 17 (Oct.), p. 35–40.

7. Johan Arndt (1967), "Role of Product-Related Conversations in the Diffusion of a New Product," *Journal of Marketing Research*, 4 (Aug.), p. 292.

8. Richard W. Mizerski (1982), "An Attribution Explanation of the Disproportionate Influence of Unfavorable Information," *Journal of Consumer Research*, 9 (Dec.), pp. 301–10.

9. William H. Whyte (1954), "The Web of Word-of-Mouth," *Fortune,* 50 (Nov.), p. 104 ff.

10. Sanford L. Grossbart, Robert A. Mittelstaedt, and Gene W. Murdock (1977), "Nearest Neighbor Analysis: Inferring Behavioral Processes from Spatial Patterns," in *Advances in Consumer Research,* ed. H. Keith Hunt, Vol. 5 (Assn. for Consumer Research), pp. 114–18.

11. Raymond A. Bauer (1967), "Source Effect and Persuasibility: A New Look," in *Risk Taking and Information Handling in Consumer Behavior,* ed. Donald F. Cox, Boston: Harvard Business School, pp. 559–78.

12. Leon Festinger (1954), "A Theory of Social Comparison Processes," *Human Relations,* 7 (May), pp. 117–40.

13. Thorstein Veblen (1899), *The Theory of the Leisure Class* (New York: Macmillan).

14. Georg Simmel (1904), "Fashion," *International Quarterly,* 10, pp. 130–55.

15. George B. Sproles (1981), "Analyzing Fashion Life Cycles—Principles and Perspectives," *Journal of Marketing,* 45 (Fall), p. 119.

16. Elihu Katz and Paul F. Lazarsfeld (1955), *Personal Influence* (Glencoe, Ill.: The Free Press), p. 31.

17. Paul F. Lazarsfeld and Robert K. Merton (1964), "Friendship as Social Process: A Substantive and Methodological Analysis," in *Freedom and Control in Modern Society,* ed. Monroe Berger, et al. (New York: Octagon).

18. Everett M. Rogers (1983), *Diffusion of Innovations,* 3rd ed. (New York: The Free Press), p. 275.

19. Mark S. Granovetter (1973), "The Strength of Weak Ties," *American Journal of Sociology,* 78, pp. 1360–80.

20. Elihu Katz and Paul F. Lazarsfeld (1955), p. 324.

21. James S. Coleman, Elihu Katz, and Herbert Menzel (1966), *Medical Innovation: A Diffusion Study* (Indianapolis: Bobbs-Merrill), p. 124.

22. James S. Coleman, Elihu Katz, and Herbert Menzel (1966), p. 148.

23. Everett M. Rogers (1983), pp. 281–84.

24. Charles W. King (1963), "Fashion Adoption: A Rebuttal to the 'Trickle-Down' Theory," in *Proceedings of the American Marketing Association,* ed. Stephen A. Greyser (Chicago: American Marketing Assn.), p. 124.

25. Steven A. Baumgarten (1975), "The Innovative Communicator in the Diffusion Process," *Journal of Marketing Research,* 12 (Feb.), pp. 12–18.

26. Elizabeth C. Hirschman and William O. Adcock (1977), "An Examination of Innovative Communicators, Opinion Leaders and Innovators for Men's Fashion Apparel," in *Advances in Consumer Research,* ed. H. Keith Hunt, Vol. 5 (Assn. for Consumer Research), pp. 308–13.

27. Jacob Jacoby and Wayne D. Hoyer (1980), "What If Opinion Leaders Didn't Know More? A Question of Nomological Validity," in *Advances in Consumer Research,* ed. Kent B. Monroe, Vol. 8 (Assn. for Consumer Research), pp. 299–303.

28. See, for example, research by Stewart W. Bither and Peter Wright (1977), "Preferences Between Product Consultants: Choices vs. Preference Functions," *Journal of Consumer Research,* 4 (June), pp. 39–47.

29. Elihu Katz and Paul F. Lazarsfeld (1955), p. 334.

30. See, for example, Alvin J. Silk (1966), "Overlap Among Self-Designated Opinion Leaders," *Journal of Marketing Research,* 3 (Aug.), pp. 255–59; James H. Myers and Thomas S. Robertson (1972), "Dimensions of Opinion Leadership," *Journal of Marketing Research,* 9 (Feb.), pp. 41–46; Charles W. King, Jr., and John O. Summers (1970), "Overlap of Opinion Leadership Across Consumer Product Categories," *Journal of Marketing Research,* 7 (Feb.), pp. 43–50; and E. Langeard, M. Crousillat, and R. Weisz (1977), "Exposure to Cultural Activities and Opinion Leadership," in *Advances in Consumer Research,* ed. H. Keith Hunt, Vol. 5 (Assn. for Consumer Research), pp. 606–10.

31. Christopher H. Lovelock (1975), "Southwest Airlines (A)" (Boston: Harvard Business School Case Series).

32. Aljean Harmetz (1981), "Hollywood Is Joyous over Its Record-Grossing Summer," *New York Times* (Sept. 9), p. C25.

17 Group Behavior

Each of us belongs to many groups. Some of these groups exert a great deal of influence upon us; others have virtually no real effect on our behavior. Those groups that do have an impact on our beliefs, attitudes, and behavior exert only a selective influence. Our groups pressure us to select certain products and brands, but apply little or no pressure for other products and brands.

Understanding the impact of group influence on various types of products can greatly assist managers in the development of marketing strategy. Knowing whether or not the purchase of a particular good is subject to group influence gives managers direction in defining a product's image and in developing advertising and promotional programs. For example, during the 1950s, Pepsi Cola introduced an advertising campaign featuring the "Pepsi generation." Prospective buyers were urged to "come along." Presumably, selecting Pepsi Cola would symbolize membership in the "Pepsi generation." This campaign and those that followed have proven very successful: Pepsi Cola's market share has steadily grown over the years.

The type of influence exerted by groups is another aspect of group behavior of interest to marketers. Groups do not all have the same type of influence on consumers. Although a consumer may look to the American Medical Association as an authoritative source of information, the influence of that group is restricted to relatively few consumer goods and is vastly different in character from the influence of his or her bowling league. Thus, after managers gain an understanding of the kinds of goods that are subject to influence by groups, they should then differentiate among the types of influence that groups can have.

In the last chapter, we examined the effect of personal influence on the individual. The individual was treated primarily as a psychological or social psychological entity, making independent buying decisions after processing information from personal sources. In this chapter, we adopt a sociological perspective, that is, we examine the group itself. We discuss various types of groups, the process of group formation, and the differential impact of various groups on their members, and we examine the implications of group behavior for marketing strategy.

The general principles expounded here will also serve to set the stage for a later consideration of family buying behavior (Chapter 18), and organizational buying behavior (Chapter 19).

THE GROUP CONCEPT

What distinguishes a group from a random collection of individuals? For instance, the people riding a public bus do not constitute a group. However, if that busload of people were to become stranded in a snowstorm, they might rapidly become a group. There are three definitive features of a group. First, the individuals involved must have *common needs and goals*. Our snowbound riders, for example, have a need and a goal in common, and they would probably begin to interact to secure their freedom. This *interaction* is the second definitive characteristic of a group: group members share an interlocking set of social relationships in which members are interdependent, with each member perceiving every other member as part of the group. The third distinguishing feature of a group is that group members interact *over a period of time*. The sociologist Michael Olmsted provides a classic definition of a group, which takes these three characteristics into account. He says that a group is ". . . a plurality of individuals who are in contact with one another, who take one another into account, and who are aware of some significant commonality."[1]

In contemporary society the individual belongs to a great variety of groups, including family, school, work, neighborhood, and friendship groups. Each group, to a greater or lesser extent, has certain beliefs, values, and norms, to which it expects its members to conform by behaving in appropriate ways. Some groups, particularly religious groups, may have very demanding standards of conformity concerning diet, stimulants, codes of dress, and so on. Other groups may have limited or fairly subtle standards of conformity; for example, friendship groups may have an implicit dress code about what is "appropriate" to wear for a party.

Formal and Informal Groups

Sociologists commonly distinguish between formal and informal groups. A **formal group** is one in which the organizational structure and functions for which it exists are specified. Universities, corporations, and labor unions are examples. The structure is often explicitly defined by organizational charts, and the interaction patterns are formalized. Conformity is encouraged by an organizational manual that establishes rules and a system of sanctions for inappropriate behavior. Within a formal group, many informal groups may also exist.

The structure of an **informal group** is less evident than that of a formal group, and its functions may be less explicit, although still very real and important. A circle of neighborhood friends, a group of work associates, a tennis group, or a teenage clique are typical informal groups. An implicit organizational structure may exist in that a particular group member usually organizes activities or is most central to the communication network. An informal group may have rules, although they, too, are less obvious. Rules may be inferred from behavior of members, such as giggling at other members, pointing, ig-

common needs and goals

interaction

time

noring, or even expelling individuals who fail or refuse to do what is expected. The functions of the informal group are often social, because these groups are primarily intended to fulfill the social and emotional needs of the members.

Both formal and informal groups affect consumer choice decisions. The buyer behavior of many formal organizations is explicitly defined. Purchasing departments have overt responsibility for acquiring products, and the selection criteria are often explicitly stated. Of course, not all purchases of an organization are made solely by the purchasing department or on the basis of explicit rational criteria. In the purchase of a corporate jet, for example, the chief executive officer may initiate the idea, the chief pilot may help select the aircraft, the company financial officer must approve the purchase, and other influencers, including perhaps the CEO's spouse, may lend support or advice.

Informal groups are more influential than formal ones in consumer decision-making. As individuals interact with each other in informal groups, they transmit information and attitudes. A group member considering a purchase may seek new ideas or more objective information than is available through marketer-controlled information channels, such as advertising, point-of-purchase displays, or sales talks. He or she often turns to members of informal groups for advice and information. Through group interaction and participation, major as well as minor purchasing decisions are affected.

Primary Groups

Interpersonal communication is a key element in the discussion of the ways in which groups influence purchase decision-making. In discussing interpersonal relationships, sociologist Charles Cooley coined the term **primary group** to refer to a group characterized by *face-to-face interaction*.[2] Examples of primary groups are the family and friendship groups. Members of the primary group have *primary relations*, which have three major features, with one another.

face-to-face interaction

First, primary relations are characterized by *responses to whole persons* rather than responses to particular facets of people. This means that group members react to all aspects of one anothers' personalities, and that responses are spontaneous, free, and sometimes emotional. Because interactions both occur between whole persons and are spontaneous, responses are said to be *nontransferable*. That is, an individual could not transfer the same response to another different individual. On the other hand, *nonprimary* relations involve transferable responses between individuals who are responding only to limited aspects of one another. For example, a non-primary relationship exists between a salesperson and a customer; each behaves in a routinized way, and the "role" behavior of each is easily transferable to any number of other individuals.

nontransferable responses

Second, primary relations impose *no boundaries on topics* deemed suitable for discussion. Virtually all issues constitute fair game for consideration. This is certainly not the case in the nonprimary relation, where topical boundaries are defined, if only implicitly. A salesperson is not expected to offer the buyer amateur psychological counseling, for example.

The third major characteristic of primary relations is that *personal satisfaction* is the most important goal of the relationship. Individuals enter into primary relationships for the purposes of personal growth, development, satisfaction, and any other relevant personal needs.

Considering two of the major features of primary relations—responses to whole persons and unbounded discussion topics—friction between individuals in primary groups is very likely to occur. There are far greater opportunities for and probabilities of conflicting beliefs, opinions, and attitudes, inducing feelings of tension between interacting group members.

Primary groups—and primary relations—are especially important in the study of consumer behavior, because these are the groups that may exert the most influence on the purchase patterns of members. Since primary relations typically involve face-to-face interaction, the opportunity to influence members both directly and explicitly is great in primary groups. And since there are no boundaries on topics of discussion, primary groups can influence purchase decisions for a wide variety of product categories.

How Groups Are Formed   Before we discuss the ways in which primary groups actually influence consumers' decisions, we may find it helpful to consider the underlying structure of groups. The processes of group influence are quite subtle, and understanding the reasons group members are attracted to one another enables us to gain a greater appreciation of the pressures exerted by groups on their members.

A classic theory of **group formation** was proposed by T. M. Newcomb, whose major premise is that likes attract. That is, people who have similar attitudes will be more likely to form friendship bonds than people who have different attitudes. Newcomb believes that individuals have a certain view of their situation or environment, and that they also have a need to find support for their views. (Recall that this is consistent with the cognitive-consistency approach of attitude theorists.) Newcomb terms this need for support from others **consensual validation.**

Newcomb points out that when strangers meet, they initially send out messages to discover one another's attitudes about various objects, events, or ideas. Relationships, according to Newcomb, are most likely to occur when (1) individuals have mutual positive feelings for one another and (2) they share the same attitude, positive or negative, toward a particular attitude object. This is especially true when the attitude object is highly important to both individuals.[3]

The main thrust of Newcomb's argument is that people form relationships with others who share basically the same attitudes and beliefs. We would expect that the more similar the beliefs and attitudes of group members, the more support members receive for those beliefs and attitudes, and the more **cohesive** the group will be. Correspondingly, the more cohesive the group, the more susceptible members will be to group influence.

group cohesion

Group Influence on Consumer Behavior

From the point of view of consumer decision-making, members of more tightly-knit and cohesive groups should exhibit greater similarity in their purchase behavior and preferences than members of less cohesive groups. This premise was supported by a study of small primary groups by Witt,[4] who found that the similarity of brand choice among group members increases with greater group cohesiveness. The study also found that as individuals gained knowledge of the brand choices of other group members, the overall similarity of brand choice increased. This finding supports Newcomb's notion of *consensual validation:* As others' preferences become known, group members (who already have similar attitudes) provide additional cognitive support, thereby strengthening friendship bonds.

However, Witt also found that group cohesiveness alone does not explain the process of influence, because products are not all equally susceptible to group influence.[5] For products characterized by a high level of social involvement (such as cigarettes and beer), similarity of members' brand choices increases with increasing group cohesiveness. That is, the more cohesive the group, the more likely members are to select the same brand of high social-involvement products. But group cohesiveness is not as important a factor in the choice of low social-involvement goods (such as deodorant). For these products, members' choices of products appear to be unrelated to the level of group cohesiveness.[6] Group influence, then, appears to be related to both the symbolic nature of the product and the cohesiveness of the group.[7]

In another study of group influence on consumer behavior, Moschis[8] used Festinger's theory of social comparison[9] to try to explain the influence process. Moschis wondered why people identify with and are influenced by some groups rather than others. The theory of social comparison posits that people compare themselves with others on a number of characteristics. Individuals identify with a specific group when they perceive a high degree of **co-orientation** or similarity with group members on various characteristics. (Note that Festinger's notion of co-orientation parallels Newcomb's view that individuals are attracted to people similar to themselves.)

social comparison

co-orientation

Moschis' empirical study of consumer choice behavior investigated group influence on women selecting cosmetics. He found that co-orientation of members was positively related to group influence. Specifically, as the individual's co-orientation with group members increased, she was more likely (1) to have a need to seek information from group members, (2) to perceive the group as a highly credible source of information, and (3) to be influenced by the group.

Moschis holds that his findings provide new information for managers. First, the theory of social comparison relates to diffusion theory by shedding light on the speed of diffusion. Innovations are diffused most quickly when potential adopters share a high degree of co-orientation about the new product. More interpersonal communications maximize personal influence. Second, the theory of social comparison relates to source credibility. Traditional thinking is that an audience evaluates a communicator's credibility only on the basis of his or her expertise. But source credibility, such as that found within groups, also appears to be related to co-orientation. Notions of co-orientation as well as expertise may help television advertisers in creating effective commercials.

The conclusion for consumer behavior is that much purchase influence is exerted in groups, and the influencers are basically similar to those whom they influence. The groups that exert the most influence on consumer choice are very cohesive, with members sharing a high level of co-orientation. Group influence differs across products, however, with products characterized by high social involvement being most susceptible to influence.

REFERENCE GROUPS

So far we have been concerned mainly with small primary groups. Now, we broaden our perspective to incorporate all types of groups in the consumer's environment. As we have seen, not all groups exert the same amount of influence or have the same relevance for an individual member. While some groups are extremely influential in determining an individual's judgments, beliefs, and behavior, other groups exert minimal, if any, influence. Sociologist Herbert Hyman coined the term **reference group** to refer to those groups which do have the ability to modify or reinforce an individual's attitudes.[10]

point of reference

Hyman's definition of a reference group was that it was one which serves as a *point of reference* that individuals use in order to compare themselves with others and to form judgments about their solutions to problems. For example, members of a high school class can evaluate their own "success" in light of the achievements of other members of the class at their class reunions.

Hyman's notion of the reference group has been expanded to incorporate two other dimensions.[11] Reference groups can also serve as groups to which individuals *aspire to belong*. An example is the upwardly mobile family that models its behavior and attitudes on the behavior and attitudes of members of a higher social class. The third dimension of a reference group is that it can act as a group whose *norms or standards* for behavior are adopted by the

normative perspective

individual, and whose *perspectives* the individual adopts in interpreting the environment. Thus, if an individual internalizes the standards of a reference group, his or her activities—including consumption activities—will be in accord with these standards. The notion that a reference group has a perspective, then, has behavioral implications. Members' actions are affected by the group's perspective. Shibutani has pointed out that primary groups are the most important groups for most individuals, although larger social groups (such as social class or ethnic groups) can also set standards for an individual's behavior.[12]

The individual may have multiple reference groups, and, importantly, he or she does not necessarily have to be an actual member of all of these groups. This notion, which was proposed by Sherif,[13] points to the fact that individuals can attempt to identify with some reference groups *psychologically*.

multiple reference groups

One study of psychological identification investigated the influence exerted by socially distant reference groups, using the term *socially distant* "to describe that relationship between the potential influence recipient and the reference group characterized by the absence of regular interaction."[14] Results showed that the more favorably individuals perceive the members and activities of the socially distant reference group, the more they will be influenced by that group.

The idea that individuals need not be actual members of a reference group is extremely important for consumer behavior in a mass society.[15] Advertising campaigns often ask consumers to assume the perspective and adopt the underlying behavior of groups to which they will never belong. Movie stars and athletes, for example, are regularly used in advertising appeals, and consumers are encouraged to adopt their product attitudes and preferences.

So far, we have treated reference groups as groups with which individuals positively identify. But reference-group influence is not always positive. A distinction can be drawn between aspirational and dissociative groups. An **aspirational group** is one to which an individual wishes to belong, either as a bona fide member or at least psychologically. Conversely, a *dissociative group* is one with which an individual does not wish to be associated. For instance, families who have moved from working-class to middle-class status may view working-class consumption as an indication of how not to consume. These families may consciously avoid purchasing products or brands that they believe have a working-class image.

aspirational versus dissociative groups

In summary, a *reference group* is a group that influences a consumer's choice behavior. It can be a primary group or a broader group, such as social class. Individuals need not be actual members of all their reference groups. Identification with the reference group can be either aspirational or dissociative—an important distinction, since it emphasizes the fact that reference groups exert different types of influence on members.

Types of Influence

Reference groups do not always have the same type of influence on members. Deutsch and Gerard proposed an interesting distinction between *normative social influence,* influence to conform to the expectations of others, and *infor-*

mational social influence, influence to accept information contributed by others as evidence of reality.[16] This classification corresponds closely to Bauer's typology of psychosocial and problem-solving games,[17] which is developed in Chapter 16. Bauer's notion of the psychosocial game is equivalent to Deutsch and Gerard's concept of normative social influence, in which individuals conform to group norms and standards in order to gain some type of status or other reward. Similarly, the problem-solving game parallels informational social influence. In this case, information gained from others is used as a reference point for assessing events or objects.

Expanding this typology, Park and Lessig suggest that reference groups exert three different types of influence:

1. **Informational influence.** Reference groups are regarded as highly credible sources of information (similar to Deutsch and Gerard's *informational influence*).
2. **Utilitarian influence.** Reference groups exert pressure to comply with group norms (similar to Deutsch and Gerard's *normative influence*).
3. **Value-expressive influence.** Even in the absence of obvious pressure, individuals comply with group norms because they are personally motivated to do so, either to bolster their own egos or because they have positive affect toward (liking for) the reference group.[18]

Park and Lessig found that the three types of influence did indeed operate on consumers. An additional finding emerged from the research. Of the two groups of respondents in the study—housewives and students—the students were consistently more susceptible to reference-group influence, regardless of the *type* of influence. As Park and Lessig point out, this finding is very important for students of consumer behavior, since research studies are often conducted using a student sample. Although the cause of this greater susceptibility is not discussed in the study, it is possible that their student samples could be characterized by a higher level of co-orientation than other population groups. Park and Lessig's results are congruent with Moschis' finding that as an individual's co-orientation with group members increases, he or she is more likely to be influenced by the group.[19]

The three types of reference-group influence can be used as the basis for advertising various products.[20] In an advertisement based on informational influence, the information provided by the reference group in the advertisement is seen as enhancing the consumer's knowledge. The advertisement in Exhibit 17–1, for example, states that pharmacists (a credible group to provide information on drugs) recommend a particular over-the-counter drug.

A utilitarian advertising appeal capitalizes on the consumer's motivation to avoid punishment or to gain a reward or success. Advertisements based on this appeal may show, for example, *appropriate* behavior for husbands or wives, or the appropriate beer for a real he-man to drink. Exhibit 17–2 makes the point that Michelob light beer is an appropriate drink for both men and

EXHIBIT 17–1
REFERENCE-GROUP INFORMATIONAL INFLUENCE

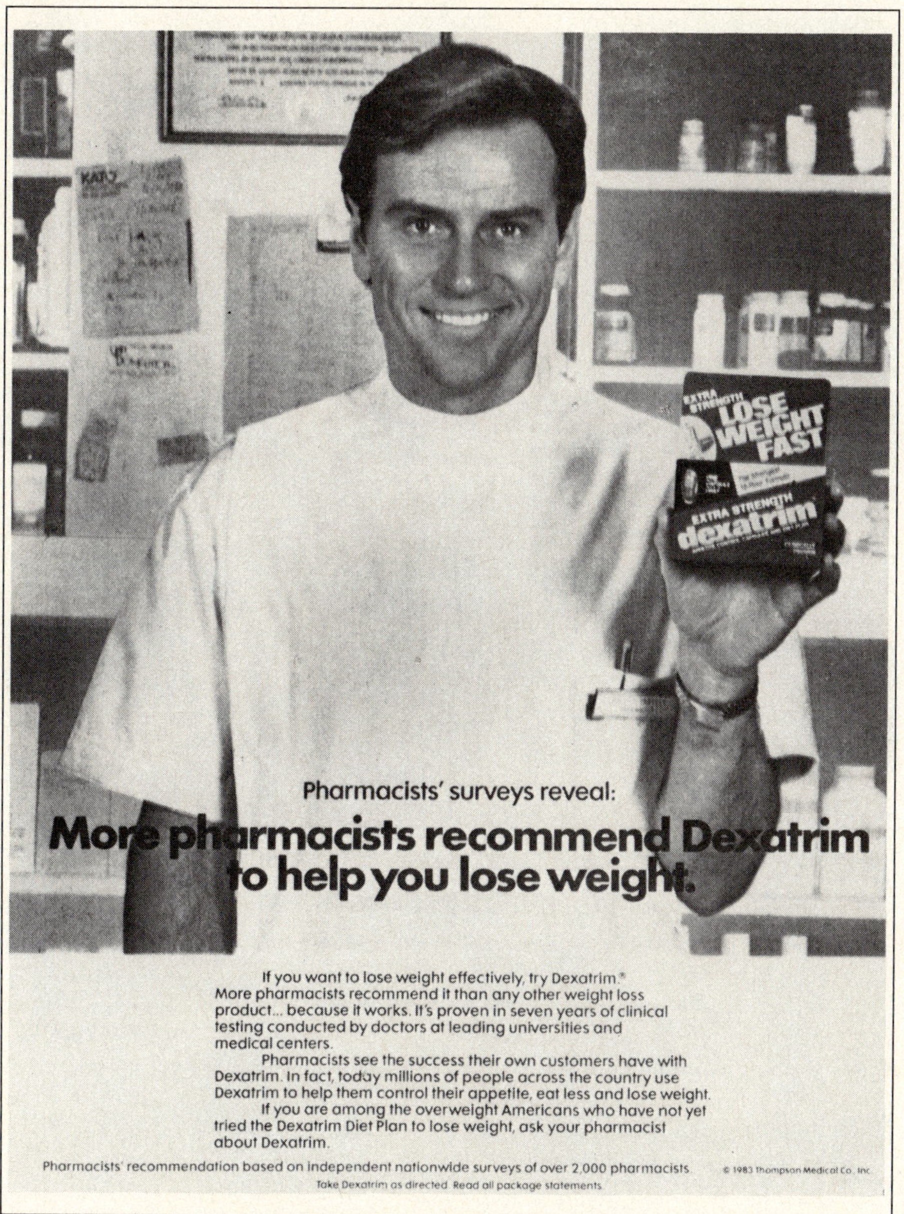

EXHIBIT 17–2
REFERENCE-GROUP UTILITARIAN INFLUENCE

women who are active and, presumably, concerned about their weight and physical fitness.

Finally, advertisements incorporating a value-expressive function suggest that product use will enable consumers to express themselves or bolster their egos by identifying with the reference group depicted in the ad. The advertisement for Polo cologne shown on p. 332 is an example from a value-expressive campaign.

Product and Brand Differences

It has long been recognized that not all products are equally susceptible to reference-group influence. Bourne originally suggested that influence varies with the "conspicuousness" of a good.[21] There are two aspects of conspicuousness. The first relates to the *exclusivity* of a good. If everyone owns a particular item, then no matter how visible it is, it is not conspicuous. The second aspect is that conspicuous goods must be *seen or identified by others*.

product conspicuousness

A study by Bearden and Etzel expands Bourne's framework. They use Bourne's notion of exclusivity as the basis for differentiating between necessities (which nearly all consumers own) and luxuries (which are characterized by a measure of exclusivity). The notion that conspicuous goods must be seen and identified by others is taken to refer to *where* an item is consumed—in public or in private.

> A public *product is one that other people are aware you possess and use. If they want to, others can identify the brand of the product with little or no difficulty.*
>
> A private *product is one used at home or in private at some location. Except for your immediate family, people would be unaware that you own or use the product.*[22]

Combining the **public/private** dimension with the **luxury/necessity** dimension, Bearden and Etzel generate the two-by-two matrix in Exhibit 17–3. Four categories of goods result, each subject to a different degree and type of reference-group influence. Product purchase influence is relevant for the luxury/necessity dimension: groups exert strong influence to purchase luxuries and only weak influence to purchase necessities. Brand purchase influence affects the public/private dimension, with strong influence on the brands of publicly consumed goods and weak influence on brands of privately consumed items. Thus, the four groups of products subject to reference-group are as follows.

1. *Publicly Consumed Luxury*
   luxury = strong product influence
   public = strong brand influence

2. *Privately Consumed Luxury*
    luxury = strong product influence
    private = weak brand influence

3. *Publicly Consumed Necessity*
    necessity = weak product influence
    public = strong brand influence

4. *Privately Consumed Necessity*
    necessity = weak product influence
    private = weak brand influence

Exhibit 17–3 has a number of managerial implications. If a consumer good can be identified on the luxury/necessity and public/private dimensions, different advertising strategies are suggested. For example, for privately consumed necessities, advertising should emphasize product attributes like quality, price, and so on, and should attempt to capitalize on group identification if reference-group influence is in force.

GROUP CONFORMITY

We have been discussing how reference groups exert pressure on members to conform. But we haven't yet considered the effectiveness of groups in exacting this compliance. In other words, how much conformity do members of groups actually exhibit? It is to this topic that we now turn our attention.

The Social Psychological Outlook

values

Before we discuss group conformity, it will be helpful to review the concepts of values and beliefs. In Chapter 14, *values* were defined as general orientations toward a system of abstract and concrete objects. *Values* are cultural goals; they are salient symbolic concepts representing the "good," the "moral," and the "worthwhile." For example, an important value of American society is said to be the *achievement ethic*. While the majority of groups subscribe to culturally accepted values, some groups, like street gangs or charismatic religious sects, challenge the existing system by adopting values at variance with the status quo.

beliefs

Groups are also characterized by a belief system. In Chapter 11, we defined a *belief* as the relatively stable cognitions and perceptions an individual holds about a given object. Beliefs are narrower than values; they generally pertain to specific objects, while values pertain to much broader categories or classes of objects.

norms

Social norms are related to values and beliefs. *Norms* are societal rules or guidelines that define acceptable conduct for achieving values and supporting beliefs. Norms flow from the values they support and simultaneously serve to reinforce these values by lending credence to them. Using the example of the achievement value, a specific norm is the legal requirement that children attend school until the age of sixteen. Norms are highly specific guidelines for behavior compared with values and beliefs.

Underlying the influence process is the notion that every group exerts pressure on the individual to **conform** to its particular ideology—its belief systems, values, and norms. For beliefs and values, this pressure is not usually coercive. Most individuals join groups that have beliefs and values compatible with their own. In addition, the beliefs and values of a group tend to be self-reinforcing. As group members are exposed to each other and to sim-

EXHIBIT 17–3

COMBINING PUBLIC-PRIVATE AND LUXURY-NECESSITY DIMENSIONS WITH PRODUCT AND BRAND PURCHASE DECISIONS

	NECESSITY Weak reference group influence on product (−)	**LUXURY** Strong reference group influence on product (+)
PUBLIC Strong reference group influence on brand (+)	**Public Necessities** Influence: Weak product and strong brand Examples: wristwatch, automobile, man's suit	**Public Luxuries** Influence: Strong product and brand Examples: golf clubs, snow skis, sailboat
PRIVATE Weak reference group influence on brand (−)	**Private Necessities** Influence: Weak product and brand Examples: mattress, floor lamp, refrigerator	**Private Luxuries** Influence: Strong product and weak brand Examples: home video game, trash compactor, icemaker

SOURCE : William O. Bearden and Michael J. Etzel (1982), "Reference Group Influence on Product and Brand Purchase Decisions," *Journal of Consumer Research*, 9 (Sept.), p. 185.

ilar experiences and expectations, their original adherence to the values and beliefs of the group is strengthened.

Unlike the pressure to conform to group values and beliefs, the pressure to conform to group norms tends to be highly coercive. Each member is expected to behave in accordance with group rules and norms, even when those norms have not been made explicit, but rather are learned from communication of expectations among group members. As a general rule, the norms of formal groups are more clearly and explicitly defined than the norms of informal groups. For example, in a formal work group, a set of rules and expectations may be imposed on workers, and specified performance extracted from them, with severe sanctions (reprimand or dismissal) if they fail to perform accordingly. On the other hand, the norms of an informal group may require nothing more than a willingness to converse, avoid argument, and initiate interaction. An additional difference is that the scope of the norms of formal groups tends to be confined to the behavior of the members while they are actually interacting in the group. Conversely, informal group norms can be much broader and more pervasive, including, for instance, implicit guidelines on how to dress, decorate the home, or rear children.

The power of the group to influence its members to conform has been demonstrated in two classic social-psychological experiments. The first, conducted by Sherif, brought together subjects in small groups and asked them to announce their judgments of the distance and direction a small point of light appeared to move in a dark room. Actually, the light was stationary, but because of a physiological process called the *autokinetic effect*, the light actually appeared to be moving in a random manner to all members of the group. In the autokinetic effect, any dim visual stimulus that lacks a spatial frame of reference appears to move in a random manner. The apparent movement may be due to minor tremors that exist in the eye. The experimental results indicated that even though subjects initially differed in their judgments of movement, they converged on a common norm. This is an example of conformity resulting from informational social influence; individuals regarded one another as credible sources of information and hence created a mutually agreed upon norm. When the group was dispersed and individual judgments made again, the subjects held to the established group norm.[23]

The second experiment demonstrating the power of the group was conducted by Solomon Asch, who brought together small groups of subjects who were asked to match the size of a line on one card to one of three lines on another.[24] When individuals made the judgments alone, virtually no errors were made. In the group situation, however, Asch used confederates who deliberately announced wrong answers. Under the pressure of being the only group member giving the correct response, naive subjects often conformed to obviously incorrect group judgments. Interestingly, when just one of the confederates supported the judgments of the naive subject, the incidence of conformity to the rest of the group decreased dramatically. The extent of conformity depended on the size of the group, but on the average, minority subjects accepted misleading majority decisions in 37 percent of selections. Only thirteen of the fifty critical subjects made no errors; fifteen went along with the erroneous majority six or more times, with an average of 3.84 errors.

Obviously, not all group situations will evoke the same degree of conformity from members. In general, there are three factors that affect conformity. The first is the clarity of the stimulus involved. Typically, the more ambiguous the stimulus, the more members are open to group influence on their judgments. For instance, members may be more susceptible to group influence for the purchase of an innovative product, such as a word processor, than for an established product, such as a self-correcting typewriter. The product benefits and features of various word processors may not be as clearly defined at the outset of the search process. Thus, group members would be quite receptive to group influence.

clarity of stimulus

The second factor that affects conformity is the amount of power a group has to sanction members for nonconformity. The more power held by the group, the more members conform. An extreme example is the military, to which members conform virtually immediately and totally. Religious orders have similar sanctioning power. Note, however, that both the military and religious orders are characterized by an extremely high level of group cohesiveness. The effectiveness of sanctions is heightened by group cohesiveness, since it is difficult for the individual member to gain rewards outside of the group.

group sanctioning power

Finally, conformity is also influenced by the degree to which an individual wishes to belong to the group. The more members identify with group values and with other group members, the more they conform. For example, fraternities and sororities are able to exact a great deal of conformity from members and prospective members.

degree of identification

Conformity in Purchase Behavior

A number of experiments focusing on conformity have been conducted on consumer topics. One of the first was conducted by Kurt Lewin during World War II, during an attempt to change meat consumption patterns to less desirable but more plentiful cuts, such as kidneys and sweetbreads.[25] In this study, two experimental conditions were employed. In one, housewives heard a lecture on the benefits of the foods; in the other, a discussion was instituted. The same information was relayed in both cases. Results gathered at a later date showed that 32 percent of the participants in the discussion used the unfamiliar cuts, compared with only 3 percent of the individuals who heard the lecture. The explanation given for this considerable divergence is that, in the discussion situation, a group was formed as the individuals interacted with one another. Group processes thus came into play to reinforce the normative behavior desired.

In an experiment similar to that of Asch, Venkatesan found that in a consumer decision-making situation in which product characteristics were hard to evaluate objectively, consumers accepted information provided by peers.[26] Group respondents were asked to choose the "best" suit of clothes among three identical suits that were said to have quality differences. When confederates of the researcher announced a choice, the naive subject then chose that suit in a majority of the cases. However, when the confederates suggested that they were selecting a suit just to "go along" with the first person who answered, the effect of group pressure was eliminated, and the subject perceived the confederates as conforming rather than as having definite opinion. Subjects either remained indifferent or chose a different suit as the "best." Thus, people may not conform as long as they do not feel pressured to conform. This situation presented students with ambiguous, competing stimuli (the three identical suits), similar to the situation facing consumers for many relatively nondifferentiated products. It is not surprising that they turn to other consumers and rely on group standards in making consumption decisions.

In another study, Stafford presented consumers with identical, competing, and ambiguous stimuli.[27] Stafford identified in advance small informal groups of consumers who were individually asked to select a loaf of bread from four identical loaves marked with different letters of the alphabet. Selections were made over the course of eight weeks. Stafford's hypotheses were that informal groups would exert influence toward conformity of brand preferences; that the degree of such influence would be related to group cohesiveness (the attractiveness of the group to the members); and that group leaders would be most influential in the formulation of brand preferences. He found that "the informal groups had a definite influence on their members toward conformity behavior." Group cohesiveness did not appear significant in determining brand conformity, however. Informal group leaders did not have the hypothesized brand-preference influence.

type of product

These negative results could be due to the particular product (bread) Stafford studied. In fact, a more recent article refines Stafford's contention that reference groups influence members toward conformity by pointing to inherent differences in the *types of products* subject to group influence.[28] Ford and Ellis note that Robertson[29] suggests that products that are low in visibility, complexity, and perceived risk are not subject to group influence. Yet this is exactly the case with Stafford's test product, bread. More visible or complex products may be more susceptible to group influence.

The results of Venkatesan's and Stafford's studies have been elaborated by other researchers. For example, Burnkrant and Cousineau integrated the findings of these studies with the notions of normative versus informational social influence.[30] They note that both Venkatesan and Stafford asked respondents to select the most preferable object from among a set of identical objects, but that the respondents could not adequately evaluate either the bread (Stafford) or the suits (Venkatesan) simply by looking at them. Given this condition, it is reasonable to expect that people will use the stated opinions of others as informational cues. Burnkrant and Cousineau investigated people's ratings of coffee—which could actually be tasted and then evaluated on the basis of experience. Respondents in a control group as well as in an experimental group were asked to rate the coffee from "the worst I've ever tasted" to "the best I've ever tasted." In the control group, individuals ranked the coffee individually, with no group pressure exerted upon them. In the experimental group, subjects were led to believe that others before them had rated the coffee favorably; in this case, they evaluated the coffee *more* favorably than the control group did.

Burnkrant and Cousineau point out that prior research suggested that the opinions of others constitute a group norm (or expectation), and that normative social influence was exerted. But, in this study,

> *it appears that, after observing others evaluate a product favorably, people perceive the product more favorably themselves than they would have in the absence of this observation. They use the evaluations of others as a basis for inferring that the product is, indeed, a better product.*[31]

As we pointed out in our discussion of Sherif's study of the autokinetic effect,[32] the opinions of others, then, constitute *informational* social influence. Burnkrant and Cousineau suggest that in ordinary shopping situations consumers purchase brands which are favorably evaluated by others—not to conform to a group norm, but in order to assure themselves that they are indeed selecting a good product.

GROUP BEHAVIOR AND MARKETING STRATEGY

There are two types of approaches to the development of marketing strategy which capitalize on the concept of reference groups. These are (1) utilizing the primary group to facilitate sales and (2) incorporating nonprimary group membership as an incentive for prospective buyers.

The Group as Facilitator of Sales

We have seen that primary relations, that is, face-to-face interactions with nontransferable responses to all facets of another's personality, form the basis of primary groups. Also, members of a primary group tend to share the same values, which are reinforced by shared group norms. The sharing of values and norms is not unexpected, since primary groups are generally composed of individuals who have similar attitudes. Finally, to insure group solidarity, groups exact conformity from members. Taken as a whole, the primary group provides an ideal climate for the acceptance of certain products and services, given that the product or service is first approved of by selected influential group members.

Perhaps the company that has capitalized most on the structure of primary reference groups is Avon Products. The company directly employs district managers. It is the responsibility of the district managers to recruit and hire representatives—commonly known as Avon "ladies," (some of whom are men, albeit a small minority). Historically, each Avon lady, who works on a complete commission basis, has been given a special number of homes in her own neighborhood as an exclusive territory. At present, she receives 100 households, but in the past, when fewer individuals sought these positions, the number has been as high as 200.

The result for Avon is that representatives typically share the same life style and attitudes as their customers. But the Avon lady is more knowledgeable about cosmetics and fashion, and thus acts as an opinion leader for her customers. The customer feels pressure to conform to the attitudes and behavior fostered by the representative, namely, to be more attractive, take greater time and care with appearance, and so on.

The Avon system of neighborhood representatives has changed somewhat in response to the greater number of women in the workforce. Whereas selling to peers in the office was once frowned upon, Avon now has a group of "industrial" representatives who sell in their offices or factories.

One benefit Avon gains from this structure is that marketing research can often be conducted on Avon representatives, who constitute a willing and easily recruitable set of respondents. Representatives are assumed to be quite similar to their customers in their overall opinions and preferences, making research results generalizable to the entire population of customers without great risk.

There are numerous other firms that utilize primary groups as a component of selling. Tupperware employs a group of representatives whose responsibility is to organize and attend Tupperware "parties." The representative demonstrates Tupperware's entire product line at the party, which is typically composed of a group of friends or acquaintances who have been gathered together by their group leader. The group leader is offered product incentives if a specified number of party attendees agree to hold additional Tupperware parties in the future. Thus, a powerful type of peer pressure is established.

Some companies have parties at which provocative undergarments, nightgowns, and sex aids are sold. Once again, a company representative visits the home of an individual who has invited a group of friends to attend the gathering. An additional benefit for these companies is that the reference group acts to legitimatize the purchase of sexually-oriented items and provides a private (nonstore) venue in which purchases may occur.

Another example of the impact of reference groups on consumer behavior is the Girl Scouts of America, who annually sell cookies. Girl Scouts typically approach members of family and neighborhood groups, who feel pressure to buy as a result of primary relations not only with the individual scout, but also with her parents. Primary relations also act as an impetus for making donations to charities. Both the Heart Fund and the Multiple Sclerosis Society utilize neighborhood volunteers to solicit funds from members of informal neighborhood groups, believing the additional personal pressure to donate is an effective tool in increasing giving.

Finally, the sale of health insurance to individual employees through their places of employment is an interesting example of the role of groups. Insurance vendors are able to offer corporations, hospitals, universities, and other large organizations health insurance at lower rates than are ordinarily available to individuals. The employer organization then provides health insurance as an employee benefit. Two aspects of group dynamics are operating. First, the insurance vendor uses the corporate group to facilitate sales. A large number of policies is gained by approaching the one group. Second, the insured employees agree to conform to the norms established by the supplier. The scope of the policy, the specific deductible required, and the terms of payment (direct to health provider or reimbursement, after payment, to employee) are typically not open to negotiation. Although the employee may be able to obtain more favorable conditions on any of these specific aspects of insurance, he or she forgoes this opportunity in order to obtain the overall benefit of participation in a group plan.

Group Membership as an Incentive

The examples we have just discussed each used an existing reference group as an impetus for purchase. The fact that one is a group member entails certain role responsibilities. Being invited to and accepting an invitation to attend a Tupperware party, for example, constitutes a tacit agreement—if not to purchase, then at least to consider purchase.

A different role can be played by groups in the process of buyer behavior. The marketer can offer the prospective buyer membership in a group, membership that entails certain rights, privileges, or responsibilities. Offering membership for sale differs in principle from capitalizing on existing reference groups. Where membership is the product, a solitary individual with no current relationships with group members may seek inclusion in the group.

This is relevant in two types of marketing situations: The first entails *nominal* memberships and the second *committed* memberships. In the case of nominal memberships, the individual joins a group solely to gain access to the **nominal memberships** rights or benefits offered by the group. For example, the major airlines have long had frequent-traveler clubs which may be joined for a fee. Pan American's Clipper Club, TWA's Ambassador Club, and American Airlines' Admiral's Club, for instance, offer members personalized services and travel advantages. Similarly, work groups and college alumni groups sometimes offer reduced-price travel packages, and group buying plans offer members discounts on a variety of goods. One such plan available to employees of certain corporations is Consumer Cause, Inc. If an individual wants to buy, say, an automobile or videotape recorder or microwave oven, he or she simply provides specific information about the model, style, and options to Consumer Cause or one of its subsidiaries, which, because of its mass purchasing power, is able to provide the good at a discounted price.

These examples entail only nominal group membership, in that the individual is not required to develop any primary relations with other group members, and need not accept any group values. In fact, in many cases group norms and values are not operative. There is no real pressure toward conformity, in behavior or beliefs, placed upon the members of such groups.

committed memberships

In the second type of marketing situation, group membership acts as an incentive: the prospective member agrees to accept and comply with explicitly defined group values and norms in order to affect some type of behavior modification. Two well known examples are Weight Watchers and Alcoholics Anonymous. In the case of Weight Watchers, individuals who join perceive themselves as being overweight. They agree to adhere to a set of norms not only governing food consumption and preparation, but also dictating attendance at regular meetings, "public" weigh-ins, and so on. The norms are followed specifically to achieve a group value—normal weight.

Alcoholics Anonymous has the same basic structure, in which the individual agrees to abide by group norms (abstinence) in order to achieve the shared value. The group value is not only sobriety; it covers many aspects of life (health, family well-being, avoidance of drunk driving, and so on) that are negatively affected by alcoholism. One real difference between AA and Weight Watchers is that a number of offshoot groups have emerged from AA. Alanon, for instance, assists the spouses of alcoholics, and Alateen is geared to the children of alcholics. The alcoholic need not attend AA for his or her spouse and children to join these related groups, which attempt to assist individuals in coping with the alcoholic's norm- and value-violating behaviors.

There are numerous other groups, such as Smoke Enders and Gamblers Anonymous, which can be instrumental in inducing behavior modification. Each of these groups attempts to provide a set of clear-cut norms that individuals can follow in order to achieve a mutually valued goal. A critical feature of such organizations is that they are able to provide group pressures toward conformity, which may not be present in the individual's outside environment.

SUMMARY

A group differs from a random collection of people. In general, the members of a group have common needs and goals, share a set of social relationships, and interact over time. We can differentiate between formal groups (which have defined structures and defined functions) and informal groups (which are loosely organized).

Of particular importance for consumer behavior is the primary group, which is characterized by face-to-face interaction. Members of these groups have primary relations, which have three components: responses are to whole persons rather than to facets of people; there are no boundaries on topics considered suitable for discussion; and the goal of personal satisfaction is paramount. Given the nature of interaction and relationships, primary groups exert direct influence on members' purchase decisions in a wide variety of product categories. The influence of nonprimary groups is more restricted.

The process of group formation illustrates group members' tendency to share similar attitudes and beliefs. The greater this similarity, the more cohesive primary groups tend to be. Studies of consumer behavior have shown that as group cohesiveness increases, the similarity of brand choice increases. However, this influence differs for different types of products. Symbolic products are more susceptible to group influence than are nonsymbolic products.

Reference groups are also of relevance to consumer behavior. Individuals identify with reference groups; they interpret and evaluate themselves, others, and the environment from the group's point of view. The concept of the reference group is broader than that of the primary group: reference groups include primary groups and larger groups, such as social class. Individuals need not be bona fide members of all their reference groups. In fact, psychological affiliation is sufficient.

Reference groups exert various types of influence on members. One typology suggests that influence can be informational (the group is perceived as a reliable source of information), utilitarian (the group exerts normative influence on members to comply with its standards), or value-expressive (individuals comply with group standards to enhance their egos).

Group influence on the purchase of different types of goods also varies. In general, groups exert more influence on the purchase of luxuries than necessities, and more influence on brand selection of publicly consumed goods than on privately consumed goods. Combining these two dimensions suggests that publicly consumed luxuries are subject to the most reference-group influence (product and brand), and that privately consumed necessities are subject to the least. Privately consumed luxuries (product influence only) and publicly consumed necessities (brand influence) are subject to an intermediate degree of reference-group influence.

Underlying the concept of group influence is the notion of conformity. All groups demand a level of conformity from their members to ensure their survival. Both social-psychological and consumer-behavior experiments have demonstrated the ability of groups to exact conformity from members.

Understanding the structure and functioning of groups can assist managers in the development of marketing strategies. If managers are aware that different goods are subject to different types of group influences, these influences can be used as the basis of advertising and promotional campaigns. For some products, existing groups can be used to facilitate sales. For other products or services, group membership can act as an incentive to purchase.

KEY CONCEPTS

formal group	co-orientation	value-expressive
informal group	reference group	influence
primary group	aspirational group	public versus private
group formation	dissociative group	products
consensual validation	informational influence	luxuries versus
group cohesiveness	utilitarian influence	necessities
		conformity

DISCUSSION QUESTIONS

1. How does purchase influence exerted by a formal group differ from purchase influence exerted by an informal group?
2. What are the major features of primary relations, and why are they important in the study of consumer behavior?
3. How would the influence process which operates in a highly cohesive, primary group differ for the purchase of (a) an automobile, (b) a lawnmower, and (c) alcoholic beverages?
4. What are the main aspirational reference groups influencing the purchase behavior of students? Of housewives? Of business executives?
5. Distinguish between the influence of (a) values and (b) norms on consumer behavior. Provide examples of each.
6. For what types of products would (a) informational influence, (b) utilitarian influence, and (c) value-expressive influence be most appropriate?
7. What are the different factors affecting conformity? Do these factors differ for durable versus nondurable goods? For high-involvement versus low-involvement goods?
8. Recommend general strategic guidelines for the marketing of (a) public necessities, (b) private necessities, (c) public luxuries, and (d) private luxuries.

NOTES

1. Michael S. Olmsted (1959), *The Small Group* (New York: Random House), p. 21.
2. C. H. Cooley (1962), *Social Organization* (New York: Schoken). Originally published in 1909.
3. T. M. Newcomb (1961), *The Acquaintance Process* (New York: Holt, Rinehart & Winston).
4. Robert E. Witt (1969), "Informal Social Group Influence on Consumer Brand Choice," *Journal of Marketing Research,* 6 (Nov.), pp. 473–77.
5. Robert E. Witt (1969).
6. Robert E. Witt and Grady D. Bruce (1970), "Purchase Decisions and Group Influence," *Journal of Marketing Research,* 7 (Nov.), pp. 533–35.

7. Robert E. Witt and Grady D. Bruce (1972), "Group Influence and Brand Choice Congruence," *Journal of Marketing Research*, 9 (Nov.), pp. 440–43.

8. George P. Moschis (1976), "Social Comparison and Informal Group Influence," *Journal of Marketing Research*, 13 (Aug.), pp. 237–44.

9. Leon Festinger (1954), "A Theory of Social Comparison Process," *Human Relations*, 7, pp. 117–40.

10. H. H. Hyman (1942), "The Psychology of Status," *Archives of Psychology*, 38, No. 269.

11. Very instrumental in broadening the definition of reference groups was R. K. Merton and A. Kitt (1950), "Contributions to the Theory of Reference Group Behavior," in *Continuities in Social Research: Studies in the Scope and Method of "The American Soldier,"* ed. R. K. Merton and P. F. Lazarsfeld (Glencoe, Ill.: Free Press), pp. 40–105.

12. Tamotsu Shibutani (1955), "Reference Groups as Perspectives," *American Journal of Sociology*, 60 (May), pp. 560–69. This article contains an excellent discussion of reference groups in general, particularly in light of their third function.

13. M. Sherif (1953), "The Concept of Preference Groups in Human Relations," in *Group Relations at the Crossroads*, ed. M. Sherif and M. O. Wilson (New York: Harper), pp. 203–31.

14. A. Benton Cocanougher and Grady D. Bruce (1971), "Socially Distant Reference Groups and Consumer Aspiration," *Journal of Marketing Research*, 8 (Aug.), pp. 379–83.

15. James E. Stafford and A. Benton Cocanougher (1977), "Reference Group Theory," in *Selected Aspects of Consumer Behavior*, ed. Robert Ferber (Washington, D.C.: GPO), Ch. 16, pp. 316–80.

16. M. Deutsch and Harold B. Gerard (1955), "A Study of Normative and Informational Social Influences Upon Individual Judgement," *Journal of Abnormal and Social Psychology*, 51, pp. 624–36.

17. Raymond A. Bauer (1967), "Source Effect and Persuasibility: A New Look," in *Risk Taking and Information Handling in Consumer Behavior*, ed. Donald F. Cox (Boston: Harvard Business School), pp. 559–78.

18. C. Whan Park and V. Parker Lessig (1977), "Students and Housewives: Differences in Susceptibility to Reference Group Influence," *Journal of Consumer Research*, 4 (Sept.), pp. 102–9.

19. George P. Moschis (1976).

20. V. Parker Lessig and C. Whan Park (1978), "Promotional Perspectives of Reference Group Influence: Advertising Implications," *Journal of Advertising*, 7, pp. 41–47.

21. Francis S. Bourne (1958), "Group Influence in Marketing and Public Relations," in *Some Applications of Behavioral Research*, ed. R. Likert and S. P. Hayes (Basil, Switzerland: UNESCO).

22. William O. Bearden and Michael J. Etzel (1982), "Reference Group Influence on Product and Brand Purchase Decisions," *Journal of Consumer Research*, 9 (Sept.), pp. 183–94.

23. M. Sherif (1952), "Group Influences upon the Formation of Norms and Attitudes," in *Readings in Social Psychology*, ed. G. E. Swanson, T. M. Newcomb, and E. L. Hartley (New York: Holt, Rinehart & Winston), pp. 249–62.

24. Solomon Asch (1951), "Effects of Group Pressure upon the Modification and Distortion of Judgments," in *Groups, Leadership and Men*, ed. H. Guetzkow (Pittsburgh: Carnegie Press).

25. Kurt Lewin (1947), "Group Decisions and Social Change," in *Readings in Social Psychology*, ed. T. M. Newcomb and E. L. Hartley (New York: Holt, Rinehart & Winston), pp. 330–44.
26. M. Venkatesan (1966), "Consumer Behavior: Conformity and Independence," *Journal of Marketing Research*, 3 (Nov.), pp. 384–87.
27. James E. Stafford (1966), "Effects of Group Influences on Consumer Brand Preferences," *Journal of Marketing Research*, 3 (Feb.), pp. 68–72.
28. Jeffrey D. Ford and Elwood A. Ellis (1980), "A Reexamination of Group Influence on Member Brand Preference," *Journal of Marketing Research*, 17 (Feb.), pp. 125–32.
29. Thomas S. Robertson (1971), *Innovative Behavior and Communication* (New York: Holt, Rinehart & Winston), Ch. 8.
30. Robert E. Burnkrant and Alain Cousineau (1975), "Informational and Normative Social Influence in Buyer Behavior," *Journal of Consumer Research*, 2 (Dec.), pp. 206–15.
31. Burnkrant and Cousineau (1975), p. 214.
32. M. Sherif (1953).

18 Family Behavior

Since approximately three out of four Americans live together as members of a family group, the question of how consumer behavior processes occur in families is important in the formulation and implementation of marketing strategies for consumer products and services. In spite of this self-evident proposition, marketers often target individuals, since the actual purchase of many goods—especially nondurables—is carried out by a single person. Moreover, syndicated market-research services, such as Target Group Index, Nielsen, and Simmons, all report data by individual-consumer characteristics (although some variables, like "household size," are presumably surrogates for family variables).

We have all observed family consumption behavior in process. For example, husbands and wives shop together as they purchase durable goods or even clothing for one spouse or the other. Consumption decisions in families may also involve children, especially for food products. Such observations, however, tell us little about the underlying dynamics of family buying and the motives, interests, and strategies of individuals in the family group. It might be, for example, that the wife wants to buy a home video system. Although her husband may have no interest in the purchase, he may display apparent interest in one video system or another as part of a strategy of "giving in" on this purchase in order to be able to dictate terms for the purchase of an automobile.

The composition and function of family groups are being affected by social changes such as the high rate of divorce and the changing roles played by husbands and wives in response to trends such as increased participation of women in the work force. From the marketing manager's perspective, it is possible to target families as consumption units, but the changing nature of American family life requires careful analysis in order to make effective strategy decisions. Consider the following examples of strategic actions marketers may employ to target family groups.

- *Pricing strategies might center around family plans (airline fares and motel prices).*
- *Product strategies might include a company's decision to diversify into amusement parks or "family" restaurants.*
- *Promotion strategies might include media decisions to appeal to entire families or to separate family members. For example, toy companies continually assess whether to target children or parents, and decisions must be based on some understanding of toy-buying decisions in the family unit.*

The major strategic issues facing marketing managers center around when to conceptualize the family as a consuming unit (that is, for what kinds of products and services) and how to do it. Should separate strategies be designed for different family members? Or, should one campaign target the entire family or a sub-unit of the family?

In this chapter, we assess behavioral concepts that are pertinent to questions such as these. We begin by defining family groups—a seemingly straightforward matter until you consider the many social changes affecting living patterns today. Consequently, we also note the many recent demographic and lifestyle changes that affect the formation and functioning of family groups. Next, we assess the kinds of consumer decisions that occur in families, the variables influencing those decisions, and the processes that characterize them. Finally, we take a look at family consumer behavior from a cross-cultural perspective.

THE CHANGING NATURE OF AMERICAN FAMILIES

At the outset, it is important to assess the changes that have occurred in the nature of American families during this century. Some of these changes have affected patterns of consumer behavior: *what* things are purchased, the *rate* at which they are purchased, and *how* they are purchased.

To begin with, some scholars feel that the very concept of **family** has changed. Consider, for example, how one sociologist defines a "family."

> [A family is] *a set of persons, related to each other by blood, marriage, or adoption, and constituting a social system whose structure is specified by familial positions and whose basic societal function is replacement.*[1]

This definition reflects traditional sociological perspectives on the **family of orientation** (that is, the family one is born into) and the **family of procreation** (that is, the family that is begun by marriage). Sociologists also distinguish the **nuclear family,** meaning parents, children, and offspring who live together, from the **extended family,** which includes all other relatives. Many changes, such as cohabitation, group living arrangements, and the rise of single-parent families suggest the possibility of expanding such traditional sociological definitions for purposes of assessing consumer-behavior patterns.

Family Formation and Role Development

The origins of the *family of procreation* involve one of the most important "consumer behaviors" men and women will ever experience: partner selection. This process is depicted in Exhibit 18–1. Across the stages from *meeting* to *partnership love,* individuals experience both *feelings* (and emotions) and *thinking.* Note that the first two stages involve egocentric thinking, as each prospective partner internally sizes up the prospective partner. As attachment develops, the period of *mutual revelation* occurs, as couples discuss and evaluate each other's values and behavior. In time, couples may begin to sort out **role specialization** *(planning partnership),* which might include ideas about how they will engage in consumer behavior as a couple.

When the couple begins to live together, further role developments occur. These changes are shown in a model of role changes that occur in families, in Exhibit 18–2. In this model, individuals are seen as *ego centered* as they begin the partner-selection process, reflecting the kinds of *thinking* processes in the first two stages of the model in Exhibit 18–1. After marriage, the couple is highly *pair centered.* This probably means that many purchases will involve joint decision-making, since couples may feel normative pressure to make decisions together, and because they have not had the time and experience to sort out who should be responsible for what kinds of purchases (role specialization). With the arrival of children, the nuclear family has begun, and the unit is highly *family centered;* after the children move on, the partners can again become *pair centered,* although their needs, and their processes of

EXHIBIT 18–1
MARRIAGE-PARTNER SELECTION

	Feeling	Thinking
1. Meeting	Attraction Comfortable	Interesting Good looking
2. Getting Acquainted	Liking Happy, comfortable Stimulated, interested	Applying standards of class, ethnicity, religion, education, surface behavior
3. Developing Attachment	Affirmed Fulfilled Desire to be close Caring	Mutual revelation Discussion and approval of values, behavior
4. In Love	Esteemed Cherished Interdependent Constant awareness Heightened desire for closeness and physical intimacy	Mental intimacy Heightened communication Trying out roles Planning partnership
5. Partnership Love	As a pair Care, respect, responsibility	Mutual commitment Knowledge

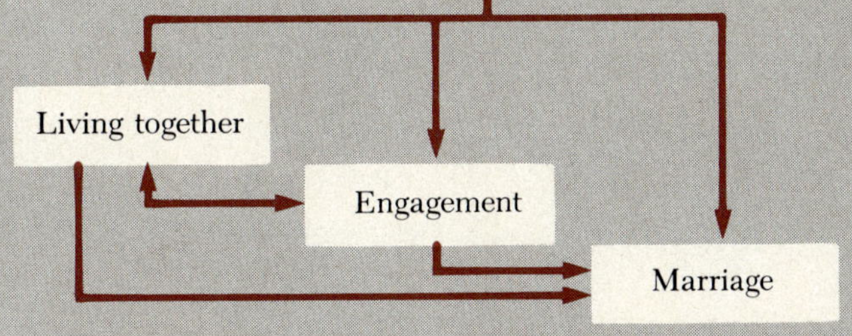

Living together → Engagement → Marriage

SOURCE: Laura S. Smart and Mollie S. Smart (1980), *Families—Developing Relationships* (New York: Macmillan), p. 180.

EXHIBIT 18–2
ROLE CHANGES AS FAMILIES DEVELOP

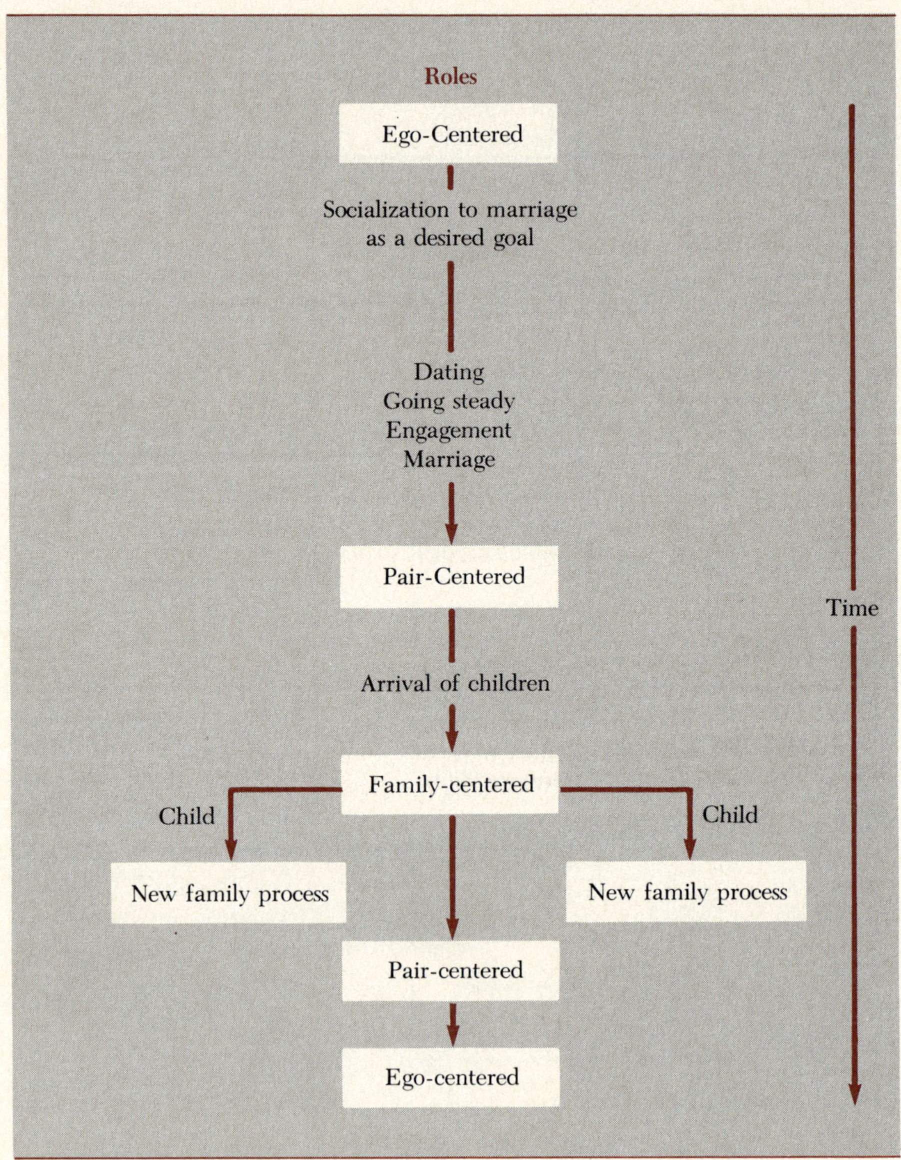

SOURCE: Sylvia Clavan (1969), "The Family Process: A Sociological Model," *Family Coordinator*, 18 (Oct.), pp. 312–17.

consumer behavior, are probably quite different from those of the early years of their marriage. By this time, the partners doubtless have well established roles relating to consumer behavior, and little communication will be necessary for each partner to communicate his or her product desires, since these will be well understood after many years of marriage or partnership. Finally, if divorce or death occurs, the remaining partner is again *ego centered.*

Over the course of an individual's life cycle, needs for products and services vary markedly, as Exhibit 18–3 shows. Individuals in the bachelor stage obviously have very different needs from individuals who are newly married, beginning a family, and so forth. Some of these consumption patterns are examined in more detail in Exhibit 18–4.

Consuming food at home peaks when people are between 35 and 44 and again when they are over 65. Probably very different factors are at work: individuals in the 35–44 age category are likely to have the expense of children at home or in college, while people over 65 simply lack the discretionary income (and the social occasions) for meals outside the home. Home furnishings decline, and then rise again when people retire, perhaps reflecting renewed interest in "nesting." Conversely, clothing purchases increase slightly, then decrease linearly with age. The proportion of the family budget spent for vehicles decreases, probably because vehicle purchases require a sizable proportion of a young (under 25) person's income, and interest in (and need for) vehicles declines with age.

Demographic and Lifestyle Changes

Recent developments suggest the need to broaden the concept of *family* to reflect increasing numbers of unmarried, separated, or divorced American adults.* For example, about 12 percent of white children and 40 percent of black children live with only one of their parents (usually the mother), reflecting the fact that about four in ten marriages in the U.S. end in divorce.[2] Moreover, while couples living together without formal marriage still make up only about 1 percent of U.S. households, such living arrangements would constitute a "family" for marketing purposes, since some joint purchasing undoubtedly occurs (for however brief a period.[3]

---

*Perhaps the broadest conceptualization of a family would result from using as a measure of a *household* any set of persons living together in some way that involves interdependence. The main objection to so broad a definition is that the concept of *family* should be reserved for primary groups—that is, very important associations characterized by interpersonal intimacy. The usual meaning of *family* includes some notion of kinship. In order to distinguish the family concept from closely related concepts discussed in Chapter 17, "Group Behavior," and Chapter 19, "Organizational Buying Behavior," we generally take *nuclear family* to include some notion of kinship in this chapter. But it should be kept in mind that many of the concepts in this chapter are quite relevant to decision-making in other types of social groups.

In Chapter 14, we reviewed several interrelated demographic trends that have important implications for the nature of families in America. For example, later marriages, smaller families, and more closely-spaced children result in a more condensed length of time parents must devote attention (and expenditures) to children compared with earlier generations, and a longer time when couples can engage in activities "on their own."[4] For marketing, such demographic changes imply that products and services can be targeted to young couples who have more time and money available to spend as a couple. Demographic changes have resulted in a much more fragmented market of

EXHIBIT 18–3
CONSUMPTION PATTERNS OVER THE FAMILY LIFE CYCLE

Bachelor stage; young single people not living at home	Newly married couples; young, no children	Full nest I, youngest child under six	Full nest II; youngest child six or over six	Full nest III; older married couples with dependent children
Few financial burdens. Fashion opinion leaders. Recreation oriented. Buy: Basic kitchen equipment, basic furniture, cars, equipment for the mating game, vacations.	Better off financially than they will be in near future. Highest purchase rate and highest average purchase of durables. Buy: Cars, refrigerators, stoves, sensible and durable furniture, vacations.	Home purchasing at peak. Liquid assets low. Dissatisfied with financial position and amount of money saved. Interested in new products. Like advertised products. Buy: Washers, dryers, TV, baby food, chest rubs and cough medicine, vitamins, dolls, wagons, sleds, skates.	Financial position better. Some wives work. Less influenced by advertising. Buy larger sized packages, multiple-unit deals. Buy: Many foods, cleaning materials, bicycles, music lessons, pianos.	Financial position still better. More wives work. Some children get jobs. Hard to influence with advertising. High average purchase of durables. Buy: New, more tasteful furniture, auto travel, non-necessary appliances, boats, dental services, magazines.

SOURCE : William D. Wells and George Gubar (1966), "The Life Cycle Concept in Marketing Research," *Journal of Marketing Research* (Nov.), pp. 355–65.

families than once was the case. Note, for example, the comparisons of population distributions across the "usual" flow and the "recycled flow" of family structures in a modernized conception of the *family life cycle* shown in Exhibit 18–5. The inclusion of structures with "divorced parent with children" reflects important changes that have occurred in family relationships in recent years.

It is interesting to contrast consumer behavior among contemporary family units with that of previous generations—that is, to compare consumption patterns of the family of *procreation* with the family of *orientation*, and then with

Empty nest I; older married couples, no children living with them, head in labor force	**Empty nest II; older married couples, no children living at home, head retired**	**Solitary survivor, in labor force**	**Solitary survivor, retired**
Home ownership at peak. Most satisfied with financial position and money saved. Interested in travel, recreation, self-education. Make gifts and contributions. Not interested in new products. Buy: Vacations, luxuries, home improvements.	Drastic cut in income. Keep home. Buy: Medical appliances, medical care, products which aid health, sleep, and digestion.	Income still good but likely to sell home.	Same medical and product needs as other retired group; drastic cut in income. Special need for attention, affection, and security.

the previous, "grandparent" generation. One study examined the purchasing behavior of these three generations, comparing the relative medians of durable goods accumulated by each generation over the years of marriage.[5] As Exhibit 18–6 shows, the "children" (newly-marrieds) had purchased about thirteen different types of durable goods before their tenth year of marriage, while their parents took almost thirty years of marriage to acquire the same median number of goods, and the grandparents, forty years. While these findings reflect the fact that grandparents purchased goods that were not available in the early years of their marriage, the study also notes that the "newly

EXHIBIT 18–4
PROPORTION OF ANNUAL FAMILY BUDGET SPENT ON SELECTED ITEMS, BY AGE OF HEAD OF HOUSEHOLD

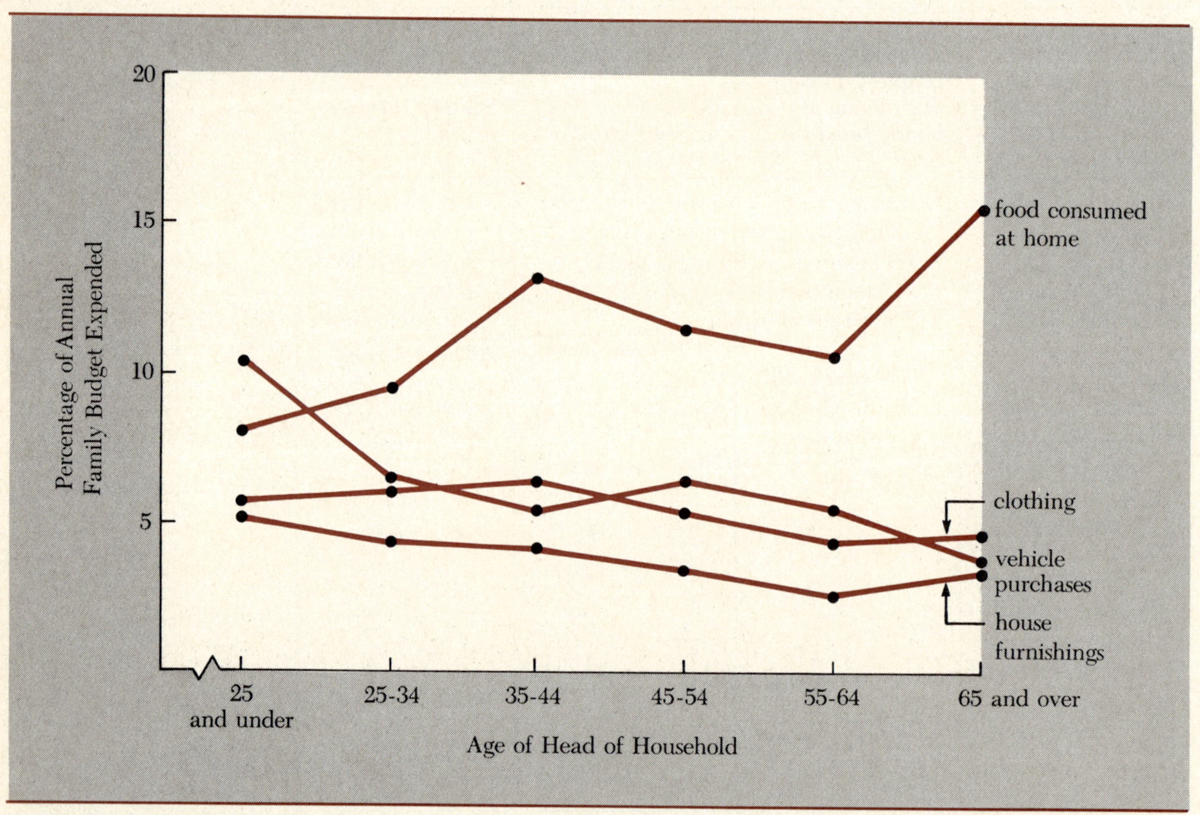

SOURCE: Based on "Consumer Expenditure Survey Series, 1973" (1976), U.S. Dept. of Labor, Bureau of Labor Statistics, Rpt. 455–2 (Washington, D.C.: GPO), Table 4b.

EXHIBIT 18–5
MODERNIZED FAMILY LIFE-CYCLE FLOWS

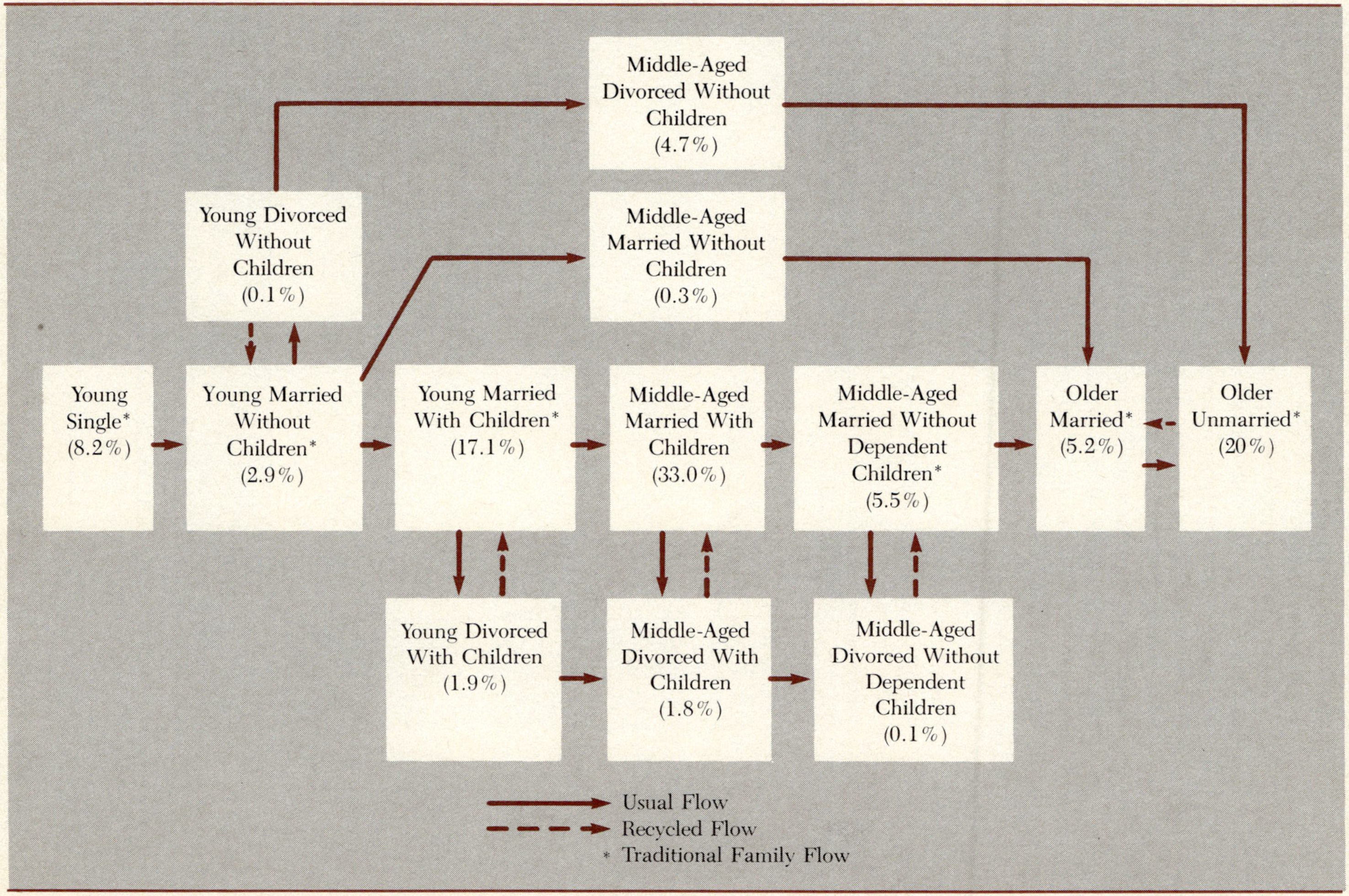

SOURCE: Patrick E. Murphy and William A. Staples (1979), "A Modernized Family Life Cycle," *Journal of Consumer Research*, 6, p. 17.

married" children purchased more goods, at a faster rate, than their parents and grandparents.

These findings, together with the demographic changes we have already discussed, suggest fundamental changes in attitudes and lifestyles among American families. Many observers have suggested that American family structures are becoming less formal and hierarchical than in earlier years, when power centered around the father. Marketing observers and sociologists suggest that married women have demanded and obtained more equal participation in the range of joint decisions marriage partners must make, and that they have become more "tough-minded" in their intrafamily negotiating. As one sociologist put it, there are "virtually no nonnegotiable issues among

EXHIBIT 18–6
SIZE OF INVENTORY BY YEAR OF MARRIAGE AND GENERATION

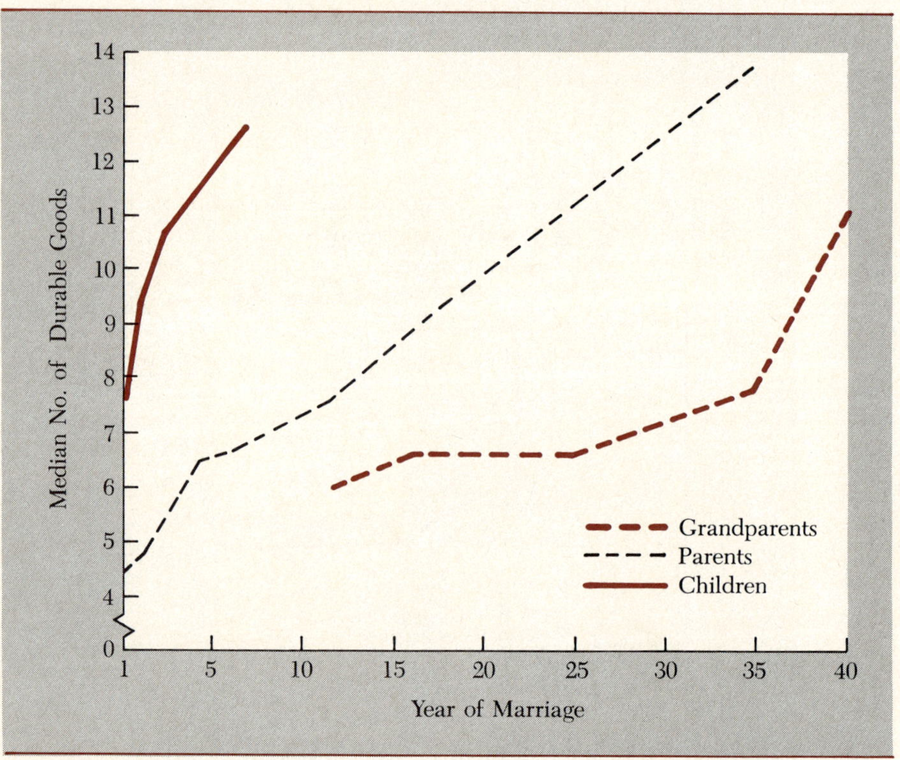

SOURCE: Reuben Hill (1971), *Family Development in Three Generations* (Cambridge, Mass.: Schenkman).

modern marriages."[6] Employed married women ("workwives") have been found to have greater autonomy and to feel more independent in many consumption decisions, and to use traditional advertising media (especially television) less than their unemployed counterparts.[7]

Writing of nuclear families, one sociologist suggests that "democratization" of American families can be traced to four factors: (1) a decline of cultural and institutional support for an autocratic family structure—for example, the declining influence of those religious institutions that may have stressed the notion that fathers should control the behavior of other family members; (2) increasing urbanization and industrialization, permitting more opportunities for women to work and to form friendship groups outside of the immediate family environment; (3) greater median educational attainment, resulting in more questioning of traditional ideas of family structure; and (4) increased exposure of parents to "democratizing" child-rearing literature.[8]

On the last point, Bronfenbrenner sees major changes in the way parents are rearing their children.[9] He notes that parents encourage their children to be expressive, rather than to be "seen and not heard." In a more permissive environment and with earlier responsibilities, children may be exerting more influence on family consumer decisions. Moreover, children may have more independence—and obtain it at an earlier age—in their own consumption behavior. We examined this topic in more detail in Chapter 7.

In summary, the traditional family is changing. While the majority of American families are still "nuclear," and marriage and family patterns are not undergoing *radical* changes, broad social trends—such as late marriages and the increasing numbers of working women—are affecting patterns of marriage, child-bearing, and child-rearing. Attitudes and lifestyles are changing, with the result that simplistic or traditional conceptualizations of "the family" are no longer sufficient for marketers as they design and implement strategies. In addition to the increasing diversity in the structure of family relationships, the processes characterizing consumption decisions in families have become more diverse. We discuss the nature of these processes in the next section.

CONSUMER DECISION-MAKING IN FAMILIES

Models of Family Consumption Decisions

Conceptualization of the kinds of consumption decisions that occur in family groups is useful. One view of family decisions suggests a distinction between financial and nonfinancial decisions. As Exhibit 18–7 indicates, both types of decisions are affected by family *developments* (such as the arrival of children, change in job or location, and so forth) and larger economic and political events (such as periods of high inflation or recession). Family developments have implications for the family's objectives, while economic and political events have a major impact on the family unit's available resources. The unit's attitudes affect both types of decisions.

Another perspective on family processes is provided by examining the dynamics of power relationships between husbands and wives. One notion is that the **least interested partner** has the least to lose in a relationship. Therefore, that partner has more power than the more highly involved partner, who has much to lose if the partnership breaks up. For example, the husband may have more power if his wife perceives that it is easier for the man to leave the family and live alone, or with someone else, than it is for her. One author calls this possible state of affairs the **law of personal exploitation,** in that the person who is less involved and who has less at stake can demand more from the other for continuing to participate.[10]

Wolfe suggests that the occupational experience and success of each marriage partner are important predictors of who will hold most of the power in a family. Based on an early (1959) study, he concludes that,

least interested partner

law of personal exploitation

EXHIBIT 18–7

A MODEL OF FINANCIAL AND NONFINANCIAL DECISIONS IN FAMILIES

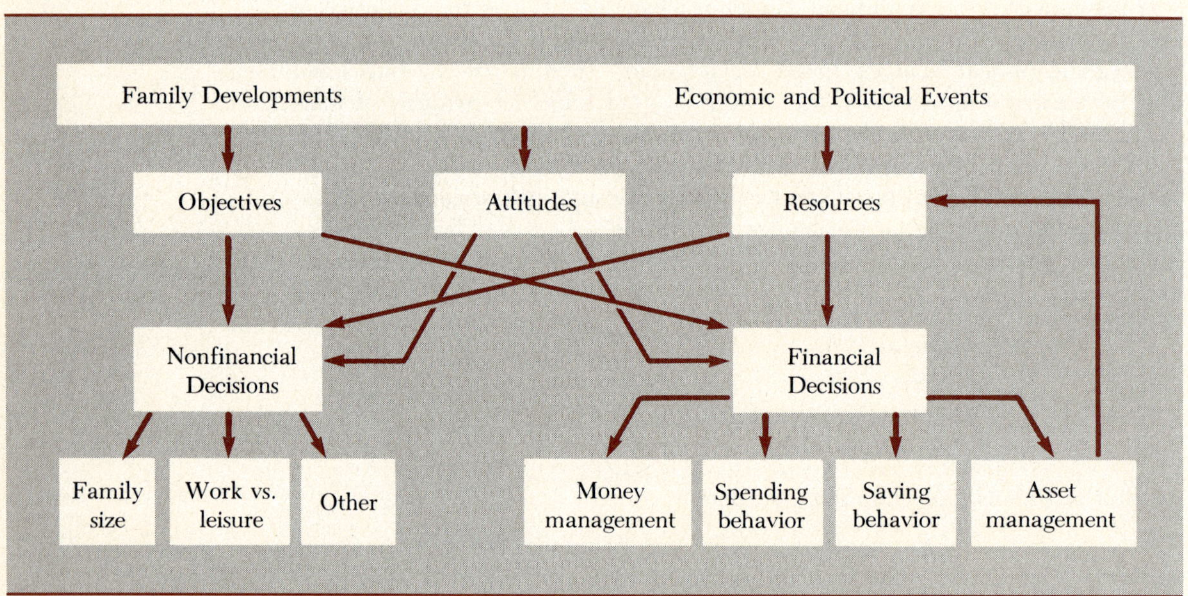

SOURCE: Robert Ferber (1973), "Family Decision Making and Economic Behavior," in *Family Economic Behavior: Problems and Prospects*, ed. E. B. Sheldon (Philadelphia: Lippincott), p. 31.

1. Husbands who achieve success and prestige on their jobs exercise more authority in their homes than do those who are not so successful. In higher socioeconomic strata, husbands tend to be more dominant; in the lower strata, it is the wives;
2. Wives who are at work, or who have worked outside the home, have more authority in the family than wives who have never worked outside the home;
3. Control of the family's finances is in the hands of the dominant figure in the family; and
4. The relative power of the wife increases with age.[11]

Viewed from the perspective of the 1980s, one wonders whether conclusions 1 and 3 would hold today. In "upscale" families both partners may work, for

EXHIBIT 18–8
PERCEPTUAL MAP (hypothetical) OF DEGREES OF PURCHASE INVOLVEMENT OF HUSBAND AND WIFE

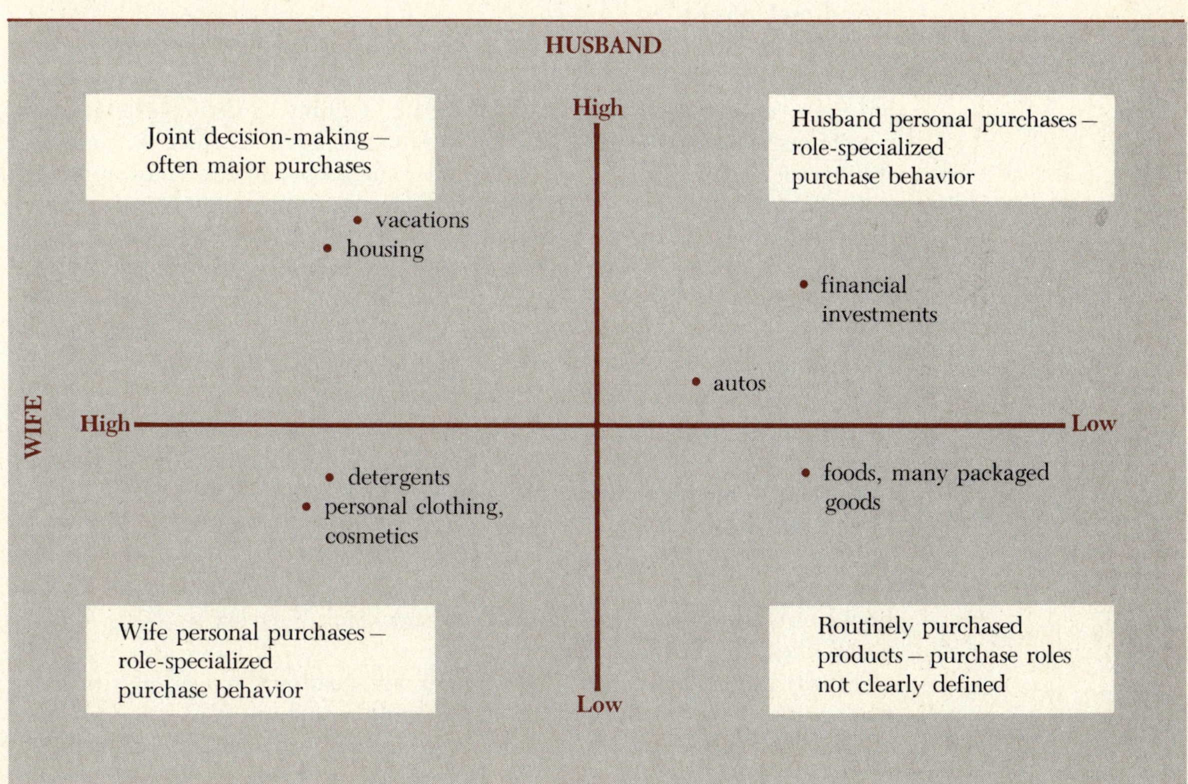

example. Dual-income families and trends toward greater education among both husbands and wives may make tenuous the assertion that dominance flows to the partner who "controls finances."

A final conceptualization of family buying decisions is provided by distinguishing between decisions in two-person families (husband and wife) and those in nuclear families (husband, wife, and offspring). Exhibit 18–8 shows a perceptual map portraying the degrees of involvement of husband and wife in purchase decisions. The quadrants reflecting high involvement of one spouse and low involvement of the other indicate two kinds of purchases: (1) purely personal purchases, in which the item purchased is likely to be consumed by the purchaser, and that occur with little or no involvement or influence of the other spouse and (2) "role specialized" purchases of products or services to be jointly consumed, but involving only one spouse in the purchase. The other quadrants reflect high or low involvement of both partners. High-involvement decision-making occurs for major purchases, whereas low-involvement decision-making occurs for routinely purchased products for which neither partner has strong preferences and purchase roles are not clearly established. For example, one partner may buy a snack food or soft drink on an experimental basis, without regard for the other partner's perceived preferences.

DMU
CU

Note that Exhibit 18–8 characterizes couples without children—either early in the family life cycle, before they have children, or later in the family life cycle, after the children have left home. Exhibit 18–9 suggests a similar map to characterize purchase decisions in nuclear families. Here we represent the decision-making unit (**DMU**) as one dimension and the consuming unit (**CU**) as the other. The DMU and the CU range from one individual to all family members. The area in the middle of the map represents decision-making or consumption of some subgroup within the family, such as the husband and wife, or one spouse and some of the children. Often, the husband-wife subgroup acts as the DMU but the entire family is the consuming unit. At other times, the entire family may decide on a purchase affecting every family member—such as what fast food restaurant to patronize.

The upper quadrants represent instances in which one individual—most often the wife or husband—acts as the DMU, purchasing something for another family member. This role-specialized behavior characterizes a wife's buying her husband something he has requested, for instance. The upper quadrants also suggest instances of **passive dictation**—in which the individual making the purchase may know from experience the other person's favorite brand of coffee or the family's favorite soft drink.[12] Overt requests for purchase, then, are not necessary.

passive dictation

Finally, some purchases in the upper left quadrant are simply personal, made without the involvement of other family members.

Such perceptual maps are useful in indicating just who is involved in the decision-making process and who is involved in actual consumption. They may also be useful in suggesting relative frequencies of *kinds* of family consumption decisions. For example, husbands and wives jointly make decisions affecting the entire family far more frequently than, say, a mother and child make a decision to buy something that will be consumed by the father (see the lower left quadrant). The latter type of decision would likely be confined to purchases like gifts, while the former type would cover a wide range of purchases.

These maps suggest many issues that require deeper analysis of family consumption behavior: (1) How do the kinds of decisions portrayed in each perceptual map vary from family to family? The purchase of an automobile may be exclusively the domain of the husband in one family, but may involve the husband, wife, and children in another, for example; (2) How do the kinds of decisions within a family change over time? and (3) Is it valid to classify decisions in terms of relative degrees of involvement, since different family

EXHIBIT 18–9

PERCEPTUAL MAP (hypothetical) OF DEGREES OF PURCHASE INVOLVEMENT IN NUCLEAR FAMILY UNITS

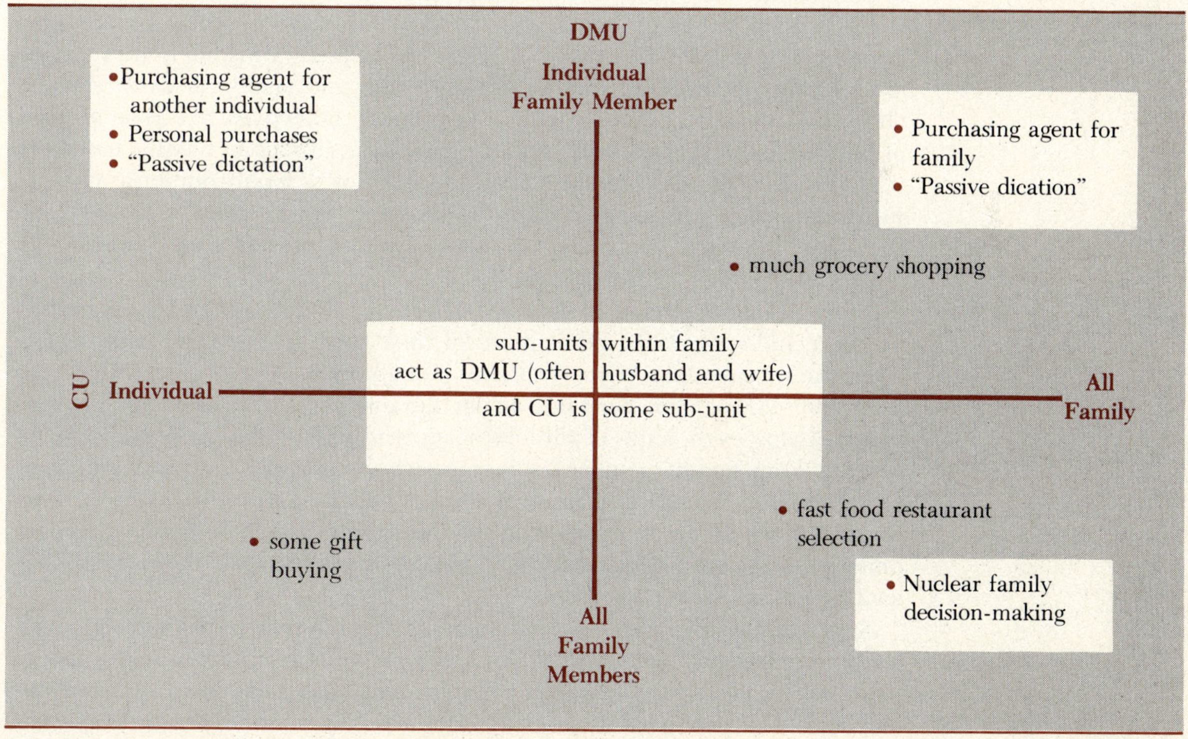

members may have varying degrees and kinds of involvement over the course of the DMP? Such issues require analysis of the processes characterizing family buying decisions and the variables affecting them.

Family Consumption Processes

Family consumption processes refers, broadly, to the activities in which family members engage—either separately or jointly—that result in a purchase. The process may begin with perception of a need and proceed through stages of information search, product and brand evaluation, and so forth, until a purchase occurs. Such purchase decision stages are discussed in many chapters in this book—dealing with consumer cognitions, communication processes, and organizational buying behavior. The difference here is that we focus on family members who are involved in different ways in different parts of the decision-making process. Some of the DMP rests with individual family members who have the time or resources to gather certain types of information; or the entire family may shop together, actively discussing or negotiating a purchase. Salespeople in a shoe store, for example, need to be aware of the DMU and the DMP involved when a family group visits the store. Fast food restaurants show their awareness by providing fast service and low prices to appeal to parents, and diversions for children.

The major variables influencing family consumption processes are portrayed in Exhibit 18–10. At the broadest level, family consumption processes are affected by variables such as demographics and family life-cycle stage.[13] Other variables are economic conditions, family objectives, the type of good or service being considered, and the purchase situation. Family members may also feel different pressures from the same or different reference groups. For example, a husband may favor a "prestige" car in order to impress his friends at the club, while his wife may prefer an economy car because she feels it will project a thrifty image.[14]

More specific personal variables affect family consumption processes. These include members' perceptions of their roles in the DMP and of how other family members perceive them. For example, the husband may consider himself the "decider" in a major durable-good purchase, but his wife (and perhaps even some of the offspring) may have different perceptions of his role. Each family member has various criteria to apply to a purchase, goals to accomplish, brand- and product-related beliefs, and attitudes toward aspects of the purchase. Depending on the extent to which family members differ in their criteria, goals, beliefs, and attitudes, there is the potential for conflict in the DMP.

Such conflictful situations are fundamentally different from those in which family members are jointly deciding and no conflict exists or in which family members have clearly designated roles and independence in decision-making.[15] The processes themselves may involve joint decisions, role specialization, and various individual strategies over the DMP. We will examine these processes later in this chapter.

While many variables other than those portrayed in Exhibit 18–10 may be involved in family consumption processes, those portrayed are of considerable importance. Consider, for example, the different kinds of roles that family members might play. Parsons and Bales suggested that women play an **expressive** (or "socio-emotional") role, reflecting concern for symbolic and affective aspects of purchases; men, on the other hand, play an **instrumental** (or "task-oriented") role, being more involved with the actual decision and its implementation.[16] These role designations may have been more appropriate for the 1950s than for the 1980s and, in any case, would seem to be restricted

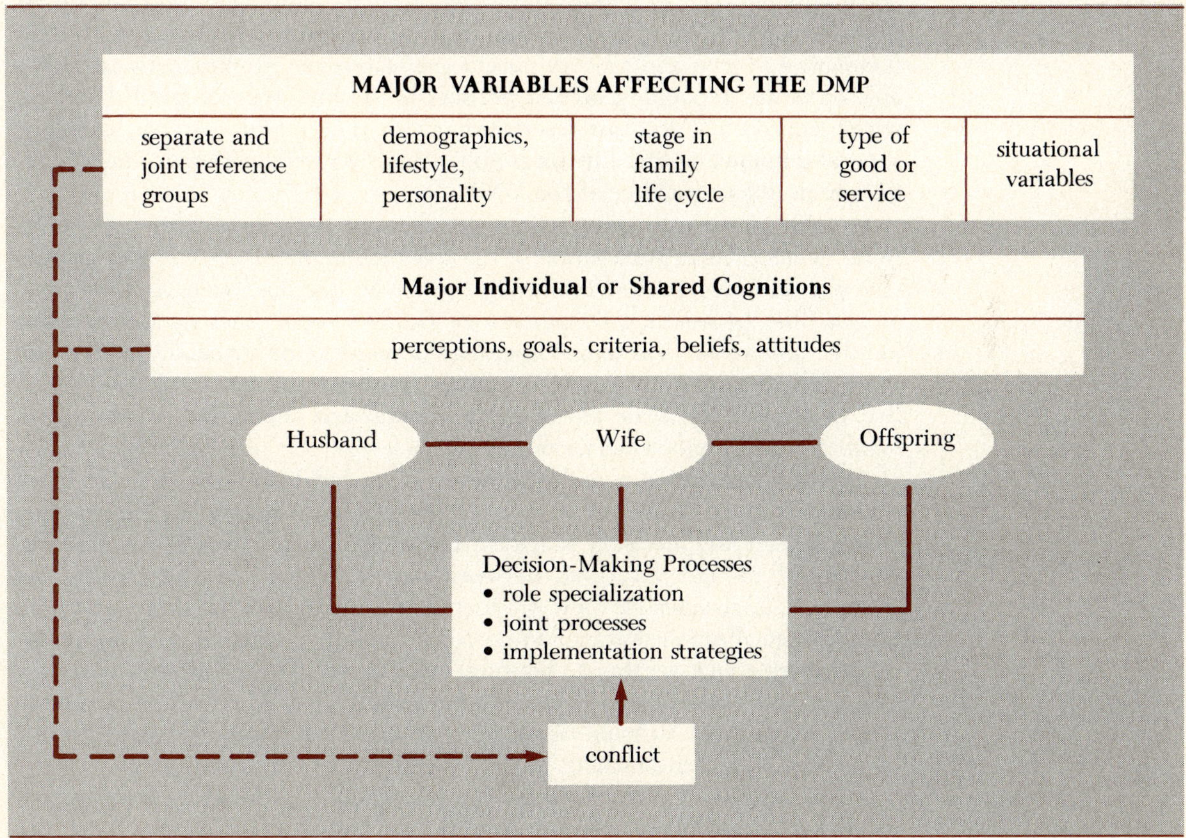

to the American culture. Other researchers have noted that women play instrumental roles in developing societies.[17]

Another view of roles within families conceives of one spouse or the other as the "family financial officer" (**FFO**), responsible for planning and implementing the family unit's financial affairs. In a study of newly married couples,[18] it was found that immediately after marriage, spouses perform the FFO function jointly, probably reflecting the normative view that they *should* engage in many activities together. Over time, the FFO role gravitates to one marriage partner or the other—most often the wife. Somewhat different patterns of expenditures occur depending on whether the FFO is the husband or the wife. For example, husbands are more likely to invest the family's assets in real estate and negotiable securities.

The FFO notion raises the question of who has the power to make consumption decisions in families. Early studies attempted to characterize families as either "husband-dominant" or "wife-dominant" on the basis of survey questions about perceived amounts of influence in various purchases reported by each spouse. Between the mid-1950s and the mid-1970s there were some apparent shifts—for example, toward less husband-dominance and more joint decision-making about automobiles and (perhaps surprisingly) greater wife-dominance in food and grocery purchasing. However, studies show considerable variation depending on the product or service, type of family, and research approach.[19] A major reservation about such unidimensional studies of spousal influence is that husbands and wives may exert different kinds of influence at different stages of the DMP.

A study of seventy-three urban, upper-class Belgian couples provides a more detailed conceptualization of the roles family members can play in specific purchase decisions.[20] Twenty-five purchase decisions were first classified syncratic decisions as *syncratic* (more than 50 percent of families report making the decision jointly), *autonomic* (less than 50 percent of families), or husband or wife *dominant*. The resulting triangle (Exhibit 18–11) shows the spread of the twenty-five decisions. The scale along the horizontal axis shows the percentage of families reporting joint decision-making.

This study also examines the influence of husband versus wife across three stages of the DMP: *problem recognition* (stage 1), *search for information* (stage 2), and *final decision* (stage 3). These changes are depicted in Exhibits 18–12 and 18–13. Note that, between stages 1 and 2 (Exhibit 18–12), the magnitude of changes for most products is not great, but that there is a trend toward specialization (autonomic decision-making) as couples seek to gather information about vacations, housing, and so on. Several items, including TV/stereo, car, and housing upkeep tend toward husband influence, while the wife-dominant and husband-dominant decisions do not vary between the first two stages of decision-making.

A very different pattern emerges when couples move from information-gathering to making the final decisions: As Exhibit 18–13 shows, there is a

EXHIBIT 18–11
MARITAL ROLES IN TWENTY-FIVE DECISIONS

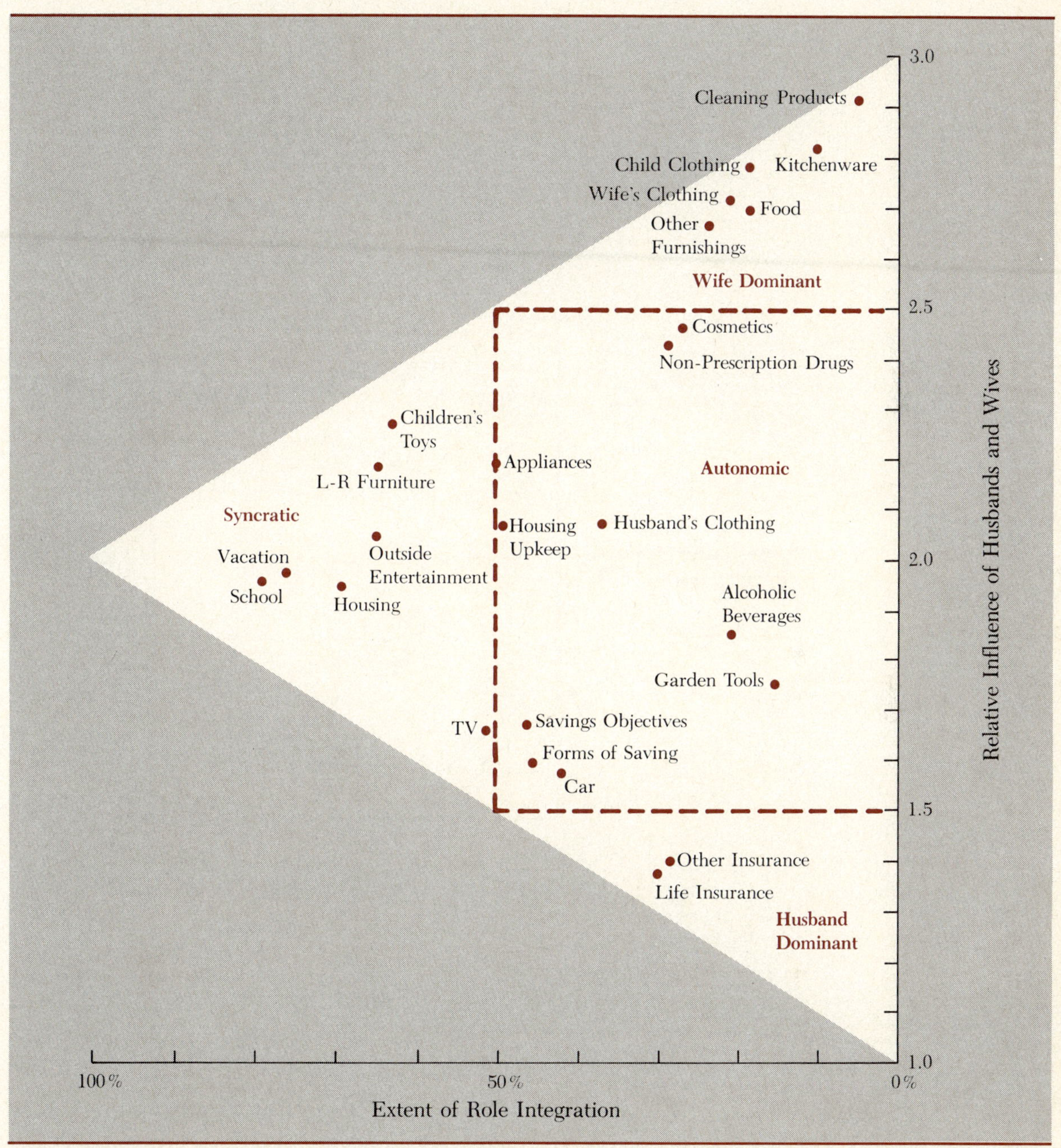

SOURCE: H. L. Davis and B. P. Rigaux (1974), "Perception of Marital Roles in Decision Processes," *Journal of Consumer Research*, 1 (June), p. 54.

EXHIBIT 18–12
CHANGES IN MARITAL ROLES BETWEEN PROBLEM-RECOGNITION STAGE AND INFORMATION-SEARCH STAGE

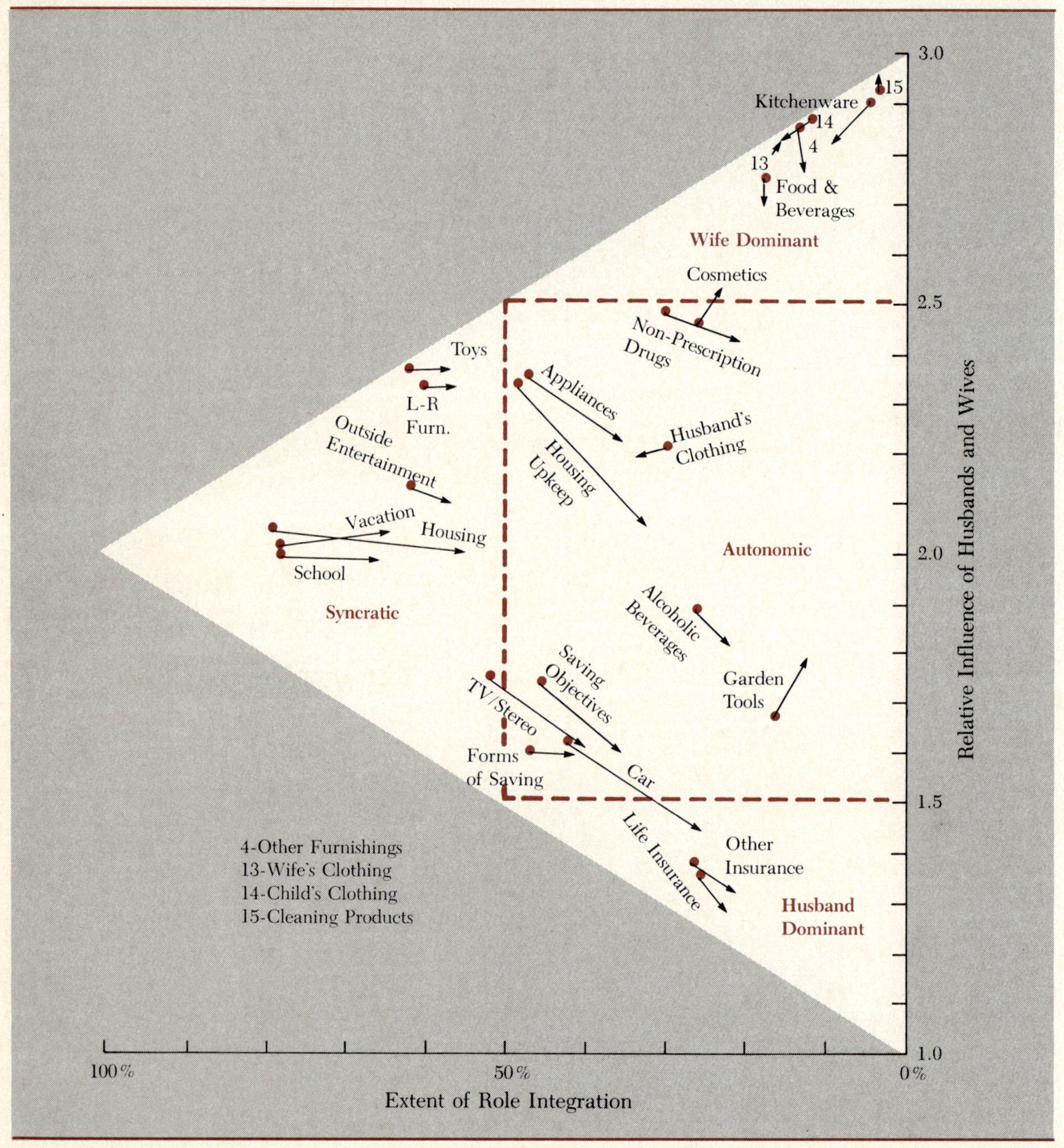

SOURCE: H. L. Davis and B. P. Rigaux (1974), "Perception of Marital Roles in Decision Processes," *Journal of Consumer Research*, 1, p. 56.

marked shift over many product categories toward syncratic decisions. In spite of these shifts, sixteen of the twenty-five decisions (64 percent) remain in the same decision categories across the three stages. For some products, changes occur in two of the three stages. For example, while purchases such as garden tools, alcoholic beverages, and nonprescription drugs remain in the autonomic pattern, other purchases move from autonomic in the first two phases to syncratic for the final decision. These include housing upkeep, household appliances, husband's clothing, and savings. The most variation occurs for automobile purchases, moving from autonomic for problem recognition, to husband-dominant for information search, to syncratic for the final decision.

This research rather clearly shows that role specialization and degree of spousal influence vary not only by product category, but also by tasks within the overall decision-making process.

Purchase Strategies

What kinds of strategies do spouses employ in order to achieve consumption goals as they interact in the decision-making process? A first consideration is whether family members agree about the goals of consumption or not. Disagreement may result in conflict. In fact, conflict may arise over many aspects of a purchase decision:

- conflict about goals ("Will the purchase satisfy our needs?");
- conflict about the brand being considered ("Is this the right product or brand for us?"); and
- conflict over the purchase process ("Who should be doing what as we evaluate this product?" "Should we buy it now or wait until later?").

Mechanisms for Dealing with Conflicts

Families may adopt **normative mechanisms** for preventing family conflict and **instrumental mechanisms** for resolving conflicts, when and if they do arise.[21] The term *normative mechanism* refers to standard practices families adopt to avoid conflicts, while *instrumental mechanism* refers to actions specifically taken to solve conflicts.

Normative Mechanisms   Normative mechanisms include the following:

1. *Avoidance of probable sources of conflict.* Just as many states require couples to wait between the time of applying for a marriage license and the wedding date in order to provide time for each partner to reconsider, families may delay a purchase or schedule it for long-term consideration. Such delaying tactics may help to avoid conflict. Often the rationale for delay may be depersonalized, as when couples decide they cannot buy something

EXHIBIT 18–13
CHANGES IN MARITAL ROLES BETWEEN INFORMATION-SEARCH STAGE AND FINAL DECISION

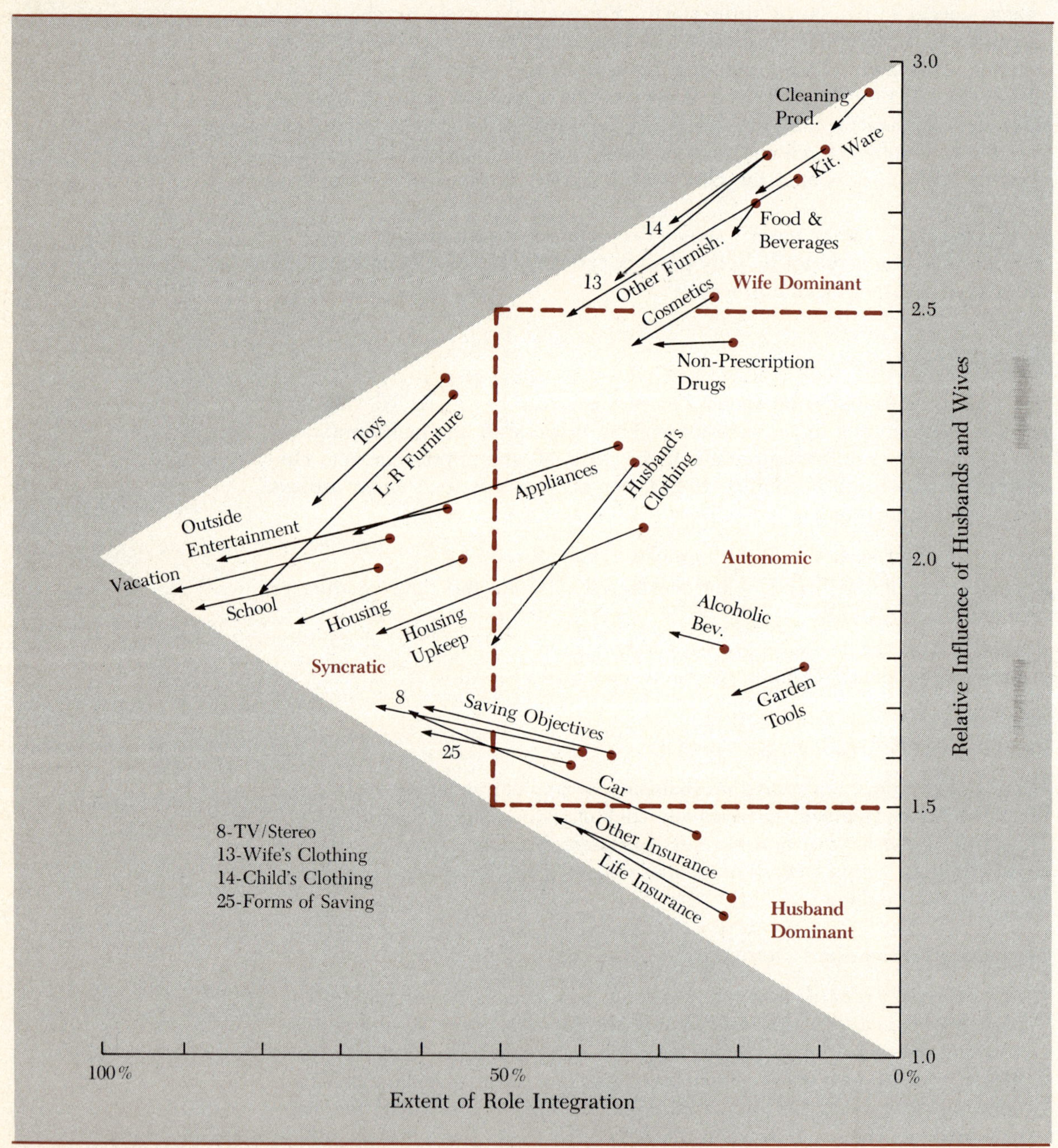

SOURCE: H. L. Davis and B. P. Rigaux (1974), "Perception of Marital Roles in Decision Processes," *Journal of Consumer Research*, 1, p. 57.

now "because of the budget." In the extreme, family members may dictate that something will never be considered for purchase ("we'll never get a home video game") as a means of "permanently" avoiding conflict.

2. *Allocation of rights and duties to particular roles.* As we have seen, families may allocate *authority* to one member in purchasing decisions. The allocation may be more or less explicit and is highly dependent on the kind of product or service being considered (as Exhibits 18–11 and 18–12 show); it is also influenced by the family's demographic and lifestyle characteristics. For example, decision-making in families with working wives differs from that in more "traditional" families.

   Allocation of *responsibilities* to one family member is another way families avoid conflict ("that's your father's decision, and his say is final"). Sometimes such allocation is simply a means of taking advantage of unequal distributions of skills and interests among family members. For example, fathers may consult their teenage sons about automobile purchases, believing the sons to have knowledge of cars.

3. *Equality of treatment within the family.* Some families establish a norm of "equal treatment" among family members. In consumer behavior, "equal treatment" may mean promising one sibling that he or she can choose the fast food restaurant on the family's next trip, but this trip's decision belongs to another sibling. Most often, such normative mechanisms are age-related, as in telling a young sibling that he or she will be able to stay up until 10 P.M. when the youngster is ten years old.

Instrumental Mechanisms   When conflicts do arise, families may adopt certain instrumental mechanisms for resolving them. Among these are the following:

1. *Increased facilities for family satisfaction.* A family might decide to purchase two toys of the same type in order to resolve conflicts that arise between children over "ownership" of toys. As families move through the life cycle and role relationships among family members change, they may even buy a new home or add an addition to the current home in order to provide privacy and increased space for family members.

2. *Priority systems.* The budget provides a good tool for avoiding conflicts by setting priorities among purchases, and it can also help to resolve conflicts. For example, one family member can use the budget as a reason to veto a purchase that might be highly desired by another family member.

3. *Increasing autonomy of family members.* Some conflictful situations may arise because individuals within the family feel they do not have enough freedom to make purchases. Perhaps the most obvious example is the teenager who wishes to spend his or her allowance without considering parents' wishes.

Implementing Strategies

Some ways in which family members actually carry out purchase strategies are described in Exhibit 18–14.[22] The strategies listed can occur under two conditions: with **consensus** among relevant family members about the goals of consumption or with the goal of **accommodating** the conflicting wishes of family members.

Strategies When Family Members Agree About Goals   When there is consensus, family members simply need to complete the purchase transaction in the most efficient way. The following are illustrative strategies:

1. *Role structure strategies*, in which one family member is assigned the task of carrying out the purchase. Other family members may contribute to the decision by providing advice, gathering some information, and so forth, but the transaction is seen as one family member's responsibility.
2. *Budget strategies*, which involve carrying out the purchase within the constraint imposed by the family budget. As we have seen, the budget can be a means of avoiding or resolving conflict. It can also facilitate decision-making when family members agree on goals. When a family agrees that a new stereo should be purchased, for example, the family "controller" can

EXHIBIT 18–14
ALTERNATIVE DECISION-MAKING STRATEGIES

Goals	Strategy	Ways of Implementing
"Consensus" Family Members Agree About Goals	Role Structure	"The Specialist"
	Budgets	"The Controller"
	Problem-Solving	"The Multiple Purchase"
"Accommodative" Family Members Disagree About Goals	Persuasion	"The Irresponsible Critic" "Feminine Intuition" "Shopping Together" "Coercion" "Coalitions"
	Bargaining	"The Next Purchase" "The Impulse Purchase" "The Procrastinator"

SOURCE : Harry L. Davis (1976), "Decision Making Within the Household," *Journal of Consumer Research* (March), pp. 255–64.

further clarify the agreement—and focus the shopping effort—by insisting that the budget allows for a maximum expenditure of $500.

3. *Problem-solving strategies*, even when family members agree on consumption goals. When problems arise during the DMP, family members may agree to discuss the problem, to consult outside sources of information for advice, to make multiple purchases instead of one in order to satisfy more than one family member, and so forth.

From a marketing perspective, consensus situations are surely preferable to accommodative ones, since the marketing effort can be devoted to promotion of the particular brand or type of good or service being considered. For example, if family members all wish to take a vacation together at the seashore, then competitors for their vacation dollars who fall within the family's agreed upon requirements can compete with each other, instead of trying to build primary demand for their particular resort areas.

The marketing effort is considerably more difficult when family members disagree about goals. In such cases, marketers may either segment the market to target family units or sub-units who agree about goals, or they may adopt a strategy that stresses that their particular product or service can meet everyone's needs. For example, Club Med positions its various resorts to different segments. Some resorts are positioned as the perfect spot for young singles who desire a liberating but carefree midwinter vacation, while others are positioned as the perfect place for families. On the other hand, Atlantic City resorts proclaim that they are the perfect spots for families, since the parents can gamble while the kids can enjoy the boardwalk. Nearby resorts, such as Stone Harbor and Margate, N.J., segment their marketing efforts to appeal to families who seek a quiet, "together" time.

Strategies When Family Members Disagree About Goals

1. *Persuasion strategies* include impugning the disagreeing family member's competence or motives ("the irresponsible critic"), appealing to "special" competence ("feminine intuition"), attempting to co-opt other family members while shopping together, and outright coercion ("you'd better get your hair cut, or there will be no allowance this week"). Finally, some family members may form a coalition in order to persuade another family member to go along. For example, it is not unusual for one spouse and one offspring (or two or more offspring) to join ranks in order to force the purchase of a new puppy!

2. *Bargaining strategies* involve trade-offs among conflicting family members. For example, a couple might decide to purchase a freezer this year with the understanding that next year they will purchase a new car. A particularly devious bargaining strategy is to excuse a conflictful purchase on the basis of "impulse" ("I couldn't help myself when I saw all those puppies").

And parents may try to stall the purchase of a child's favorite—but not very nutritious—breakfast cereal by appealing to poor memories ("I forgot it this time").

This typology of strategies is suggestive of the kinds of ways family members might carry out consumption, both when goals are agreed upon and when they are not. Purchases are rarely totally consensual or accommodative, and any single purchase might have aspects about which family members agree and other aspects about which they disagree. The framework is useful for attempting to capture the intrafamily dynamics leading up to purchase.

Marketers would do well to continually assess the extent to which customers within market segments agree or disagree about consumption goals. Many marketing programs simply assume that family members agree on goals. For example, some hotels in New York City promote heavily-discounted room rates for weekend nights, reflecting lower demand from businesspeople, who normally travel during the week. The hotels promote "New York Fling" weekends and stress that children under twelve can stay free. Such promotions to family groups imply that families agree that it would be nice to have a weekend at a good New York hotel and to save money. But what if family members disagree about goals? The promotions might be more effective if they created different packages to appeal to different segments. Subsegments of the "family" market may be more likely to agree about goals.

It seems clear that diagnosing consumer decisions within families requires marketers to go beyond simplistic assessments of relative amounts of power possessed by husbands and wives. The DMU and the DMP within total family units must be considered, as well as the strategies and nature of decision-making that occur over a family's life cycle.

FAMILY DECISION-MAKING: INTERNATIONAL PERSPECTIVES

With the exception of Davis and Rigaux's study of husband-wife decision-making, which was conducted among Belgian families, most of the research that forms the basis of our understanding of "family decision-making" has been conducted in America. As marketers increasingly seek to develop markets in different countries, they must question the extent to which our American-based knowledge can be generalized to other countries and cultures. Some aspects of human behavior can indeed be considered "basic," in that they occur and operate in similar ways in different cultural contexts. For example, principles of learning theory (Chapter 9), cognitive information-processing (Chapters 5 and 6), and children's cognitive development (Chapter 7) have been found to occur and operate relatively independently of national boundaries. The same would not seem to be true of families.

Anyone who has traveled in other countries has noticed differences in family structure and processes. Families in some countries seem to be more "traditional" in that the husband works while the wife stays home and tends to the house and the children; extended families of husband-wife, offspring, and grandparents often live together under one roof. Such observations have been documented in "ethnographic" or "participant-observer" studies in which researchers have actually lived with families in order to observe their behavioral patterns thoroughly and systematically.[23]

From a study of families in ten nations, one sociologist has suggested four family types, roughly corresponding to different stages of societal development. These family types are as follows:

1. *Patriarchy*, in which family life generally revolves around the father's authority, across social strata. India is cited as a prime example.
2. *Modified patriarchy*, in which the husband is still generally the most powerful family member, but some egalitarian norms emerge among better-educated, upper social-strata groups. Greece and Yugoslavia are cited as examples.
3. *Traditional egalitarianism*, in which power differences in families are achieved, not ascribed. For example, as women in some countries achieve goals that are felt to be important to the society—such as higher levels of education and income—they achieve greater power in the society and in their family groups. The United States and West Germany are examples.
4. *Egalitarianism*, in which there is the greatest degree of felt equality between husband and wife and the greatest sharing of power between the marriage partners. Examples cited include Denmark and Sweden.[24]

One study examined husband-wife decision-making patterns in five nations for seven types of purchases, including groceries, furniture, savings, automobiles, and insurance.[25] Two nations (Gabon and Venezuela) were considered to be in the patriarchal and modified patriarchal stages of development; the United States, the Netherlands, and France were considered to be in the latter two stages. The results are shown in a "correspondence analysis" (perceptual map format) in Exhibit 18–15. The researchers found statistical support for their hypotheses that decision-making patterns would vary between countries in the first two stages (patriarchal and modified patriarchal societies) and in the second two stages (traditional egalitarianism and egalitarian). They also found more syncratic decisions in the latter two societies and more husband-dominant decisions in the first two. In Exhibit 18–15, the horizontal axis shows greater incidence of syncratic decisions in the U.S., France, and Holland, and more autonomous decisions in Gabon and Venezuela.

Across societies, purchasing groceries is largely a wife's activity, while purchasing insurance and automobiles is largely a husband's. Savings is more or less in the middle of the map. Note that vacations, appliances, furniture, and, to some extent, savings, tend to be joint decisions in almost all of the countries. However, in Gabon and Venezuela decisions about appliances, savings, furniture, and vacations tend to be made more autonomously than in other countries; vacations and furniture are husband-oriented; and savings and appliances are wife-oriented.

EXHIBIT 18–15
PERCEPTUAL MAP OF SPOUSAL INFLUENCE ON PURCHASING DECISIONS IN THE UNITED STATES, FRANCE, HOLLAND, VENEZUELA, AND GABON

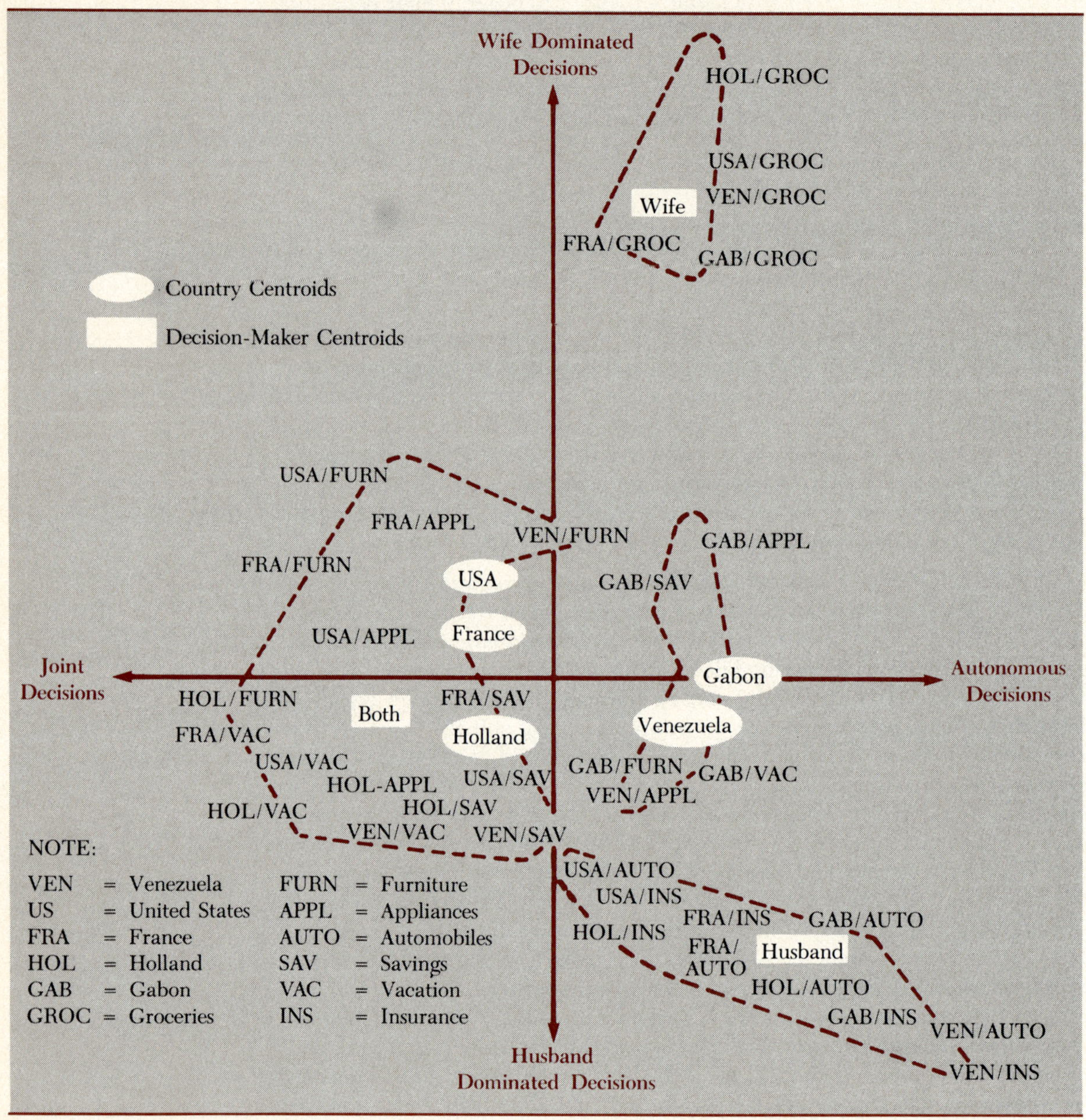

SOURCE: Robert T. Green, Jean-Paul Leonardi, Jean-Louis Chandon, Isabella C. M. Cunningham, Bronis Verhage, and Alain Strazzier (1983), "Societal Development and Family Purchasing Roles: A Cross-National Study," *Journal of Consumer Research*, 9 (March), pp. 436–42.

This study does not examine differences in spousal influence across various stages of the DMP, as did the study of Belgian households; moreover, the study does not begin to represent complete array of countries along the conceptual dimensions from traditional to egalitarian. Nonetheless, the results provide a useful, if tentative, examination of family consumer decision-making in other countries.

Many marketing programs have failed to transcend national borders because marketers have paid too little attention to cultural and family differences that exist between countries. Recently, for example, Campbell Soup gave up its attempt to introduce canned soups in Brazil because most women in that country are expected to make soup "from scratch."[26] Using a canned soup would be viewed as a failure to perform the traditional homemaking role. In another example of failure to understand the nature of families in their cultural context, an American company introduced in Great Britain a breakfast cereal with a picture of an "All-American"-looking youngster on the package. But the product was not well received by the British, who have a more formal and traditional view of children.[27]

SUMMARY

In this chapter, we have examined the nature of consumption decisions which occur in family units. While most marketers would probably agree that decision processes in families are important determinants of product and brand selection, individual family members are most often targeted as markets, a reflection of the nature of most market research data and the difficulty of developing valid and reliable measures of intrafamily influence patterns.

While there are no radical shifts in marriage formation and family life, there are some trends which have implications for consumption behavior. Among these are the tendency for families to form later, to be smaller, and to include two working heads of households, and lifestyle changes affecting husband-wife and parent-offspring relationships.

We have reviewed various conceptualizations of family decision-making and have proposed two models to account for (1) the degree of involvement in decisions by husbands and wives and (2) the composition of the DMU (decision-making unit) and the CU (consuming unit) in nuclear families. We have also examined the *processes* of decision-making. It is inadequate simply to assess degree of husband and wife "power," since the assessment may oversimplify the nature of the process ("power" is a complex variable) and it does not account for changes in influence over the stages of the DMP. The study by Davis and Rigaux provides support for the proposition that spousal influence varies depending on the stage of the DMP.

Beyond family decision-making processes, we have reviewed strategies family members might employ to accomplish their consumption goals. We distinguish between two broad sets of strategies—those employed when family members agree about goals and those employed when they do not. To avoid and resolve conflict, various normative and instrumental mechanisms may be utilized within families.

Finally, we have examined family consumption decision-making in various cultures. Interestingly, there were few extreme differences from family consumption decision-making in our culture. The variation we do find across cultures seems related to the degree of development of the culture, from traditional to egalitarian.

KEY CONCEPTS

family	**DMU**	**consensus vs.**
family of orientation	**CU**	**accommodative**
family of procreation	**passive dictation**	**goals**
nuclear family	**expressive and**	**ethnographic studies**
extended family	**instrumental roles**	**family types**
role specialization	**autonomic processes**	patriarchal
family life cycle	**syncratic processes**	modified patriarchy
FFO	**normative mechanisms**	traditional
least interested	**instrumental**	egalitarianism
partner	**mechanisms**	egalitarian
law of personal		
exploitation		

DISCUSSION QUESTIONS

1. How might the patterns of influence between husbands and wives regarding consumer behavior change over the course of their marriage?
2. Consider the following products. Describe possible family decision-making scenarios for their purchase by a middle-aged couple.

liquor	washing machine	power tools
men's underwear	automobile	women's fur coat
	living room furniture	

3. What are the most important changes in the nature of American families? What are the implications for consumer behavior?
4. How might the trend toward working women affect family decision-making?
5. Discuss the major limitations in the following study design: A researcher plans to give husbands and wives (separately) in the same household a list of products and services. The husband or the wife will check one space on a 4-point scale, to indicate the degree of his or her influence on the purchase.
6. What kinds of conflict might arise in a family about consumption, and how might families resolve conflicts?
7. Describe the major strategies by which one spouse or the other might obtain desired products or services.
8. What are the major dimensions distinguishing consumption decision-making in American households from those in other countries?

NOTES

1. Robert F. Winch (1971), *The Modern Family* (New York: Holt, Rinehart & Winston), 3rd ed.

2. For a more complete discussion, see Alan C. Kerckhoff (1976), "Patterns of Marriage and Family Formation and Dissolution," *Journal of Consumer Research* (March), pp. 261–72.

3. For a more complete discussion of unmarried couples, see Larry Wortzel (1977), "The Young Adult Consumer: An Introduction and Overview," Cambridge, Mass.: Marketing Science Inst., report 77–118 (Dec.).

4. U.S. Bureau of the Census, *Current Population Reports,* Series P–20, no. 349. More detail on trends such as these is in Kerckhoff (1976).

5. Reuben Hill (1970), *Family Development in Three Generations* (Cambridge, Mass.: Schenkman).

6. John Scanzoni (1977), "Changing Sex Roles and Emerging Directions in Family Decision Making," *Journal of Consumer Research* (Dec.), pp. 185–89.

7. Suzanne H. McCall (1977), "Meet the 'Workwife,' " *Journal of Marketing* (July), pp. 55–65.

8. Glen Elder, Jr. (1962), "Structural Variations in the Child-Rearing Relationships," *Sociometry,* 25, pp. 241–62.

9. Urie Bronfenbrenner (1958), "Socialization and Social Class through Time and Space," in *Readings in Social Psychology,* ed. Eleanor E. Macoby, Theodore M. Newcomb, and Eugene L. Hartley (New York: Holt, Rinehart & Winston), pp. 400–425.

10. Robert F. Winch (1971), pp. 334–35.

11. Donald M. Wolfe (1959), "Power and Authority in the Family," Ch. 7 in *Studies in Social Power,* ed. Dorwin Cartwright (Ann Arbor: Univ. of Michigan Press), pp. 99–117. See also Robert O. Blood, Jr., and Donald M. Wolfe (1965), *Husbands and Wives: The Dynamics of Married Living* (New York: Free Press).

12. William F. Wells (1966), "Children as Consumers," in *On Knowing the Consumer,* ed. Joseph Newman (New York: Wiley), pp. 138–45.

13. See Donald Hempel and Lewis Tucker (1980), "Issues Concerning Family Decision Making and Financial Services," in *Advances in Consumer Research,* ed. Jerry Olson, Vol. 7 (Assn. for Consumer Research), pp. 216–20. See also Donald Hempel (1975), "Family Role Structure and Housing Decisions," in *Advances in Consumer Research,* ed. M. J. Slinger (Assn. for Consumer Research), pp. 71–80; Robert Ferber and Lucy Lee (1974), "Husband-Wife Influence in Family Purchasing Behavior," *Journal of Consumer Research* (June), pp. 43–50.

14. E. Bott (1955), "Urban Families: Conjugal Roles and Social Networks," *Human Relations,* 8, pp. 345–84.

15. See Arch Woodside (1972), "Dominance and Conflict in Family Purchasing Decisions," *Proceedings,* Association for Consumer Research, pp. 650–59. See also John P. Spiegel (1957), "The Resolution of Role Conflict Within the Family," in *The Patient and the Mental Hospital,* ed. Milton Freenblatt, Daniel J. Levinson, and Richard H. Williams (New York: Free Press of Glencoe), pp. 545–64 and Robert O. Blood, Jr. (1960), "Resolving Family Conflicts," *Journal of Conflict Resolution,* 4, 2, pp. 209–19.

16. Talcot Parsons and R. F. Bales (1955), *Family, Socialization and Interaction Process* (Glencoe, Ill.: Free Press).

17. J. Aronoff and W. D. Crano (1975), "A Re-examination of the Cross-Cultural Principles of Task Segregation and Sex Role Differentiation in the Family," *American Sociological Review,* 40 (Feb.), pp. 12–20.

18. Robert Ferber and Lucy Lee (1974).

19. See H. Sharp and P. Mott (1956), "Consumer Decisions in the Metropolitan Family," *Journal of Marketing* (Oct.), pp. 149–56; E. H. Wolgast (1958), "Do Husbands or Wives Make the Purchasing Decisions?" *Journal of Marketing* (Oct.), pp. 151–58; Robert Ferber and Lucy Lee (1974); and Robert Ferber and F. Nicosia (1972), "Newly Married Couples and Their Asset Accumulation Decisions," in *Human Behavior in Economic Affairs: Essays in Honor of George Katona,* ed. B. Strumpel, J. N. Morgan, and E. Zahn (San Francisco: Jossey-Bass and Amsterdam: Elsevier), pp. 161–87.

20. Harry L. Davis and B. P. Rigaux (1974), "Perception of Marital Roles in Decision Processes," *Journal of Consumer Research* (June), pp. 51–63. This study was replicated with a sample of 60 high-income families in the U.S., and results generally confirm the Belgian findings. See E. H. Bonfield (1977), "Perception of Marital Roles in Decision Processes: Replication and Extension," *Proceedings,* Association for Consumer Research.

21. Blood and Wolfe (1965).

22. Harry L. Davis (1976), "Decision-Making Within the Household," *Journal of Consumer Research* (March), pp. 255–60.

23. For excellent examples, see Herbert J. Cans (1962), *The Urban Villagers* (New York: Free Press) and Lee Rainwater, R. Coleman, and G. Handel (1959), *Workingman's Wife* (New York: Oceana Publications).

24. See Hyman Rodman (1970), "Marital Power and the Theory of Resources in Cross-Cultural Context," *Journal of Comparative Family Studies,* 1, pp. 50–67 and (1967), "Marital Power in France, Greece, Yugoslavia and the United States: A Cross-National Discussion," *Journal of Marriage and the Family,* 29, pp. 320–4.

25. Robert T. Green, Jean-Paul Leonardi, Jean-Louis Chandon, Isabella C. Cunningham, Bronis Verhage, and Alain Strazzier (1983), "Societal Development and Family Purchasing Roles: A Cross-National Study," *Journal of Consumer Research,* 9 (March), pp. 436–42. See also Susan P. Douglas (1979), "A Cross-National Exploration of Husband-Wife Involvement in Selected Household Activities" (Cambridge, Mass.: Marketing Science Inst.), Rpt. 79–103 and Denise B. Kandel and Gerald S. Lesser (1972), "Marital Decision-Making in American and Danish Urban Families," *Journal of Marriage and the Family,* 34, 1 (Feb.), pp. 145–52.

26. "Campbell Soup Fails to Make It to the Table" (1981), *Business Week* (Oct. 12), p. 66.

27. David A. Ricus, Jeffrey S. Arpan, and Marilyn Y. Fu (1975), *International Business Blunders* (Columbus, Ohio: Grid Publishing).

19 Organizational Buying Behavior

Organizational buying behavior *is a term used to describe the processes by which formal administrative groups—organizations—make consumption decisions. Most often, the focus is on large industrial companies, but the term also applies to nonprofit institutions, retailing firms, and government agencies, all of which engage in the process of buying as organizations.*

Organizational buying behavior is a sub-area of the general topic of **industrial marketing.**[1] *This term refers to marketing activities between firms in which the buying firm procures goods to be used in the manufacture of other goods. That is, goods and services are sold to other business firms, rather than to ultimate consumers. Many firms engage in both consumer and industrial marketing, but their organizations for each type of marketing are quite different because of the different characteristics and needs of these markets.*

By better understanding how buying decisions are made within organizations, the marketing manager can better design and implement effective strategies for industrial markets; conversely, as buying organizations study their procurement (buying) procedures and the influences on them, they may become more efficient and effective "consumers" of industrial products and services. The stakes are high for both industrial sellers (**vendors**) *and industrial buyers (customers). For the vendor, an individual customer may represent a significant proportion of revenue, since industrial marketers generally have far fewer customers than consumer goods marketers. Moreover, the primary promotional vehicle for industrial marketers is the sales force, and personal sales calls are extremely expensive (about $178 per call, according to one estimate).*[2]

For the customer, the topic of organizational buying behavior is no less important. Typically, buying decisions take weeks or months, requiring the effort of many people in the organization. Furthermore, buying firms are interested in assessing their decision-making processes to make them more cost-efficient. Finally, quality, delivery times, and many other factors are of crucial importance since purchased goods are used in the manufacture of the buying company's products.

In this chapter, we first distinguish between "organizational buying behavior" and "consumer behavior," noting the key differences between the buying processes involved. Next we examine decision-making processes in organizations, how the processes differ for different kinds of buying tasks, and the roles individuals perform in buying decisions. Finally, we focus on the most crucial part of the organizational buying process: what happens when buyer and seller sit down to negotiate, that is, buyer-seller interaction.

ORGANIZATIONAL BUYING BEHAVIOR VERSUS CONSUMER BEHAVIOR

How different is organizational buying behavior from individual consumer behavior? First, it is important to realize that "organizations" do not make buying decisions—people within organizations do. It does not follow, however, that the same concepts that apply to individual consumer behavior can simply be reapplied to individuals as they engage in consumer behavior as part of their jobs. The organizational context influences buying behavior; the "whole is greater than the sum of its parts." The behavior of individuals involved in making purchases within an organization is qualitatively different from their behavior as individual consumers, both because the *kinds* of things being purchased are different and because the buying context is markedly different. Exhibit 19–1 summarizes some of the differences between organizational buying behavior and individual consumer behavior.

Consumer market and buyer characteristics differ markedly from organizational ones. As we have noted, organizational buying occurs within the con-

EXHIBIT 19–1
DIFFERENCES BETWEEN ORGANIZATIONAL AND CONSUMER BUYING BEHAVIOR

A. *Characteristics of Organizational Markets*
   1. Smaller number of customers
   2. Larger purchase orders
   3. Derived demand (as opposed to original demand)
   4. Joint demand with other products and services

B. *Characteristics of Organizational Buying*
   1. More technically qualified and professionally trained buyers
   2. Multiple buying influences and contingencies
   3. Committee buying decisions
   4. Multiple vendors to spread risk
   5. Reciprocity relationships
   6. Communication and buying information often formally channeled
   7. Often very explicit criteria
   8. Usually much longer time period for decision-making processes
   9. Needs greater interpersonal contact (personal selling function is critical)

SOURCE : Jagdish Sheth (1983), from an oral presentation to AT&T.

text of industrial marketing, which is characterized by fewer customers and much larger purchase orders than in consumer markets. Industrial markets are also characterized by *derived demand* to a greater degree than consumer markets; for example, if the demand for trucks increases, then manufacturers of truck parts will face increased demand.

derived demand

Buyers in industrial markets are technically qualified and professionally trained, often holding positions in their firms such as "Vice-President for Procurement" or "Purchasing Agent." These people specialize in buying. Organizational buying is characterized by multiple influences and constituencies, frequently resulting in buying decisions being made by committees. In contrast, consumer buying often simply involves buying a product or service for personal consumption. Industrial buyers often use multiple vendors to spread the risk of an interruption of supply because of a strike, quality control problem, or other such problem. In using multiple vendors the buying company also encourages competition. In consumer buying, on the other hand, individuals may change brands but they wield little power over sellers since any one consumer is a relatively small influence on the seller. Finally, industrial marketing often involves reciprocal relationships (in which a vendor and buyer buy from each other), an important element in marketing negotiations.

Communication normally flows through formal channels within organizations; in consumer markets communication is informal and often implicit. For example, we saw in Chapter 18 that because mothers learn their children's brand preferences over time, no direct communication is necessary for the child to obtain his or her favorite brands (the "passive dictation" phenomenon). In contrast, organizational buying decisions are often based on explicit criteria—specifications.

Organizational buying decisions take place over a longer period of time than most consumer ones, reflecting the complexity of the decision-making process and the greater risk involved in most industrial purchases.

Finally, organizational decision-making requires a great deal of personal sales contact, whereas consumer decision-making is most often influenced by mass communication, such as advertising. Factors such as large order size, small number of customers, and the need to customize many transactions, mean that organizational buying behavior is often influenced by the sales force. In fact, the salesperson is usually the key.

CHANGING VIEWS OF ORGANIZATIONAL BUYING BEHAVIOR

Views of organizational buying behavior have changed dramatically over the last fifty years, coinciding with the changes in views of consumer behavior discussed in Chapter 1. In particular, studies of group behavior and social systems in the 1950s and 1960s have markedly changed our conceptions of organizational buying behavior.[3] Nonetheless, the sheer volume of consumer-behavior research shows clearly that most of the effort has focused on individual consumer behavior. Note, for example, that of the twenty-three chapters in this book, only this one focuses specifically on organizational buying behavior.

There would seem to be two primary reasons for the imbalance in buying-behavior research. First, because there are so many individuals and factors involved in organizational decisions, organizational buying behavior is more difficult to study than individual consumer behavior. The second reason is related to the differences between consumer and industrial markets. The "mass" nature of markets for consumer goods and services allows the manager to aggregate individuals into segments and to use nondirective marketing approaches for each segment. Indeed, this is the only economical method for dealing with the large number of buyers who comprise consumer markets. In industrial markets, on the other hand, there are fewer organizational buying units, and marketing approaches must be tailored to each by the salesperson. Therefore, generalities across buyers are fewer than in consumer marketing.

Our views of organizational buying behavior have changed over the years, as marketers have become more rigorous in formulating marketing strategies for industrial markets. Exhibit 19–2 summarizes views of organizational buying behavior over several eras and their implications for how salespeople should "behave." The earliest views of organizational buying were that it was highly **rational**—the result of careful, fully-informed decisions, in which personal factors were not important, and price and quality were paramount. The roots of this view are in the dominant behavioral discipline in those early years: *economics*, with its "classical" concepts of rationality and assumptions of decision-making under conditions of full and perfect information. The salesperson was seen as simply an "animated catalogue" for the selling of the organization's products—and an order taker. Thus, the key characteristic of a good salesperson was technical knowledge.

With the growing acceptance of Freud's notions in the late 1920s and 1930s, the view of organizational buying behavior mirrored the marked changes in the view of individual consumer behavior. That is, just as advertising in that period shifted from long copy and "rational" appeals to shorter copy and emotional appeals, we also began to view organizations as responsive to emotional appeals. Thus, the era of the salesperson as **music man** began—the kind of character epitomized by Willie Loman in Arthur Miller's play *Death of a Salesman*. Dedication, motivation, and a good sales pitch promised sales effectiveness. Sales jobs acquired a paradoxical "professional" status—*paradoxical* in that salespeople devoted themselves to their careers, but received little of the respect normally ascribed to professionals. Salespeople were viewed as competent and motivated, but also as insincere and manipulative, employing any and all manner of guile and persuasion to succeed.

With the postwar era came the view of multiperson, multilevel decisions within companies and the resulting need for sellers to employ "team selling" in order to match individuals in both the selling and the buying organization in expertise, background, and level of responsibility. For example, companies formed "national account" teams that might include engineers, systems specialists, and service personnel, in addition to a sales specialist (the account executive or the manager). Such teams have counterparts in buying organizations, and the concept of national account management has stimulated efforts to sell integrated systems of goods and services rather than individual items.

The most recent view of organizational buying behavior casts the salesperson as the **problem solver.** Salespeople must be thoroughly familiar not only with the customer's organization, but with that organization's customers as well, in order to appreciate the complexities faced by the customer. For example, a salesperson for a company selling copying machines must be familiar with each account's customer base—the customer groups for small copying centers versus large copying centers, or for downtown locations versus college

EXHIBIT 19–2

HISTORICAL VIEWS OF ORGANIZATIONAL BUYING BEHAVIOR AND SALESPERSON BEHAVIOR

Era	Organizations Were Perceived As . . .	Salespeople Were Perceived As . . .	Underlying Model
"Rational Buyers" (up to 1930s)	Unidimensional, buying according to product-based, strict criteria	"Order-Takers"; "animated catalogue"	Economics: concept of rationality
"Music Man Era" (1930s to World War II)	Quite rational, but open to persuasion; personal relationships between buyers and salesperson crucial	Canned sales presentations; "sell the sizzle, not the steak"	Emerging Freudian concepts, "irrationality"
Team-Selling Era (post World War II to late 1970s)	Complex, multi-individual, multilevel decision-making units (DMUs)	"Team Sellers"	Based on concepts of decision-making unit (DMU) and decision-making processes (DMP)
"Problem Solver" (1980s)	Complex, multi-individual, multilevel decision-making units, in increasingly competitive situations in which customer relations are crucial	"Problem-Solvers"	Contemporary notions of identifying fully with customers, and understanding their market-related problems

EXHIBIT 19–3
PURCHASE OF CAPITAL EQUIPMENT PROCESS CHART

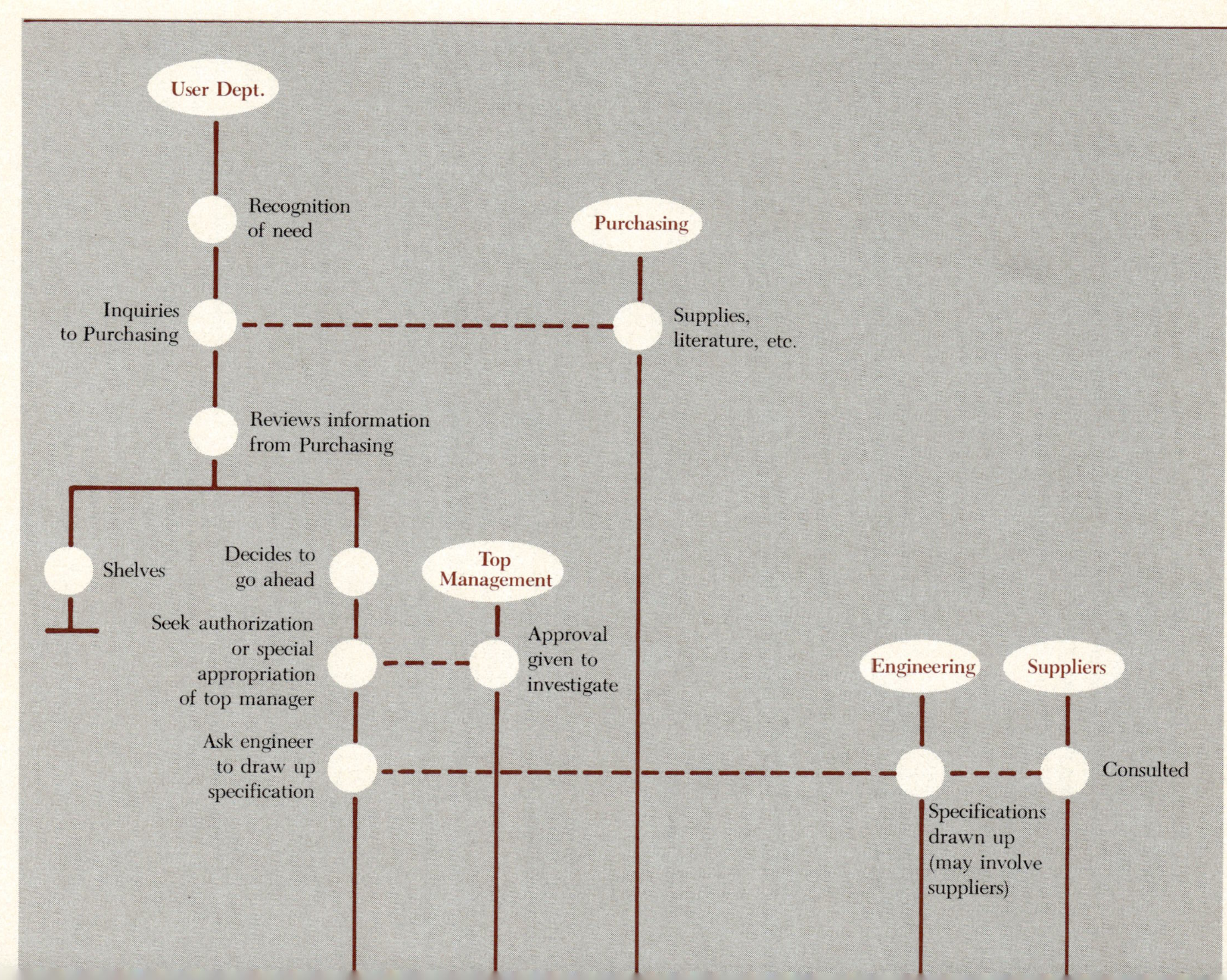

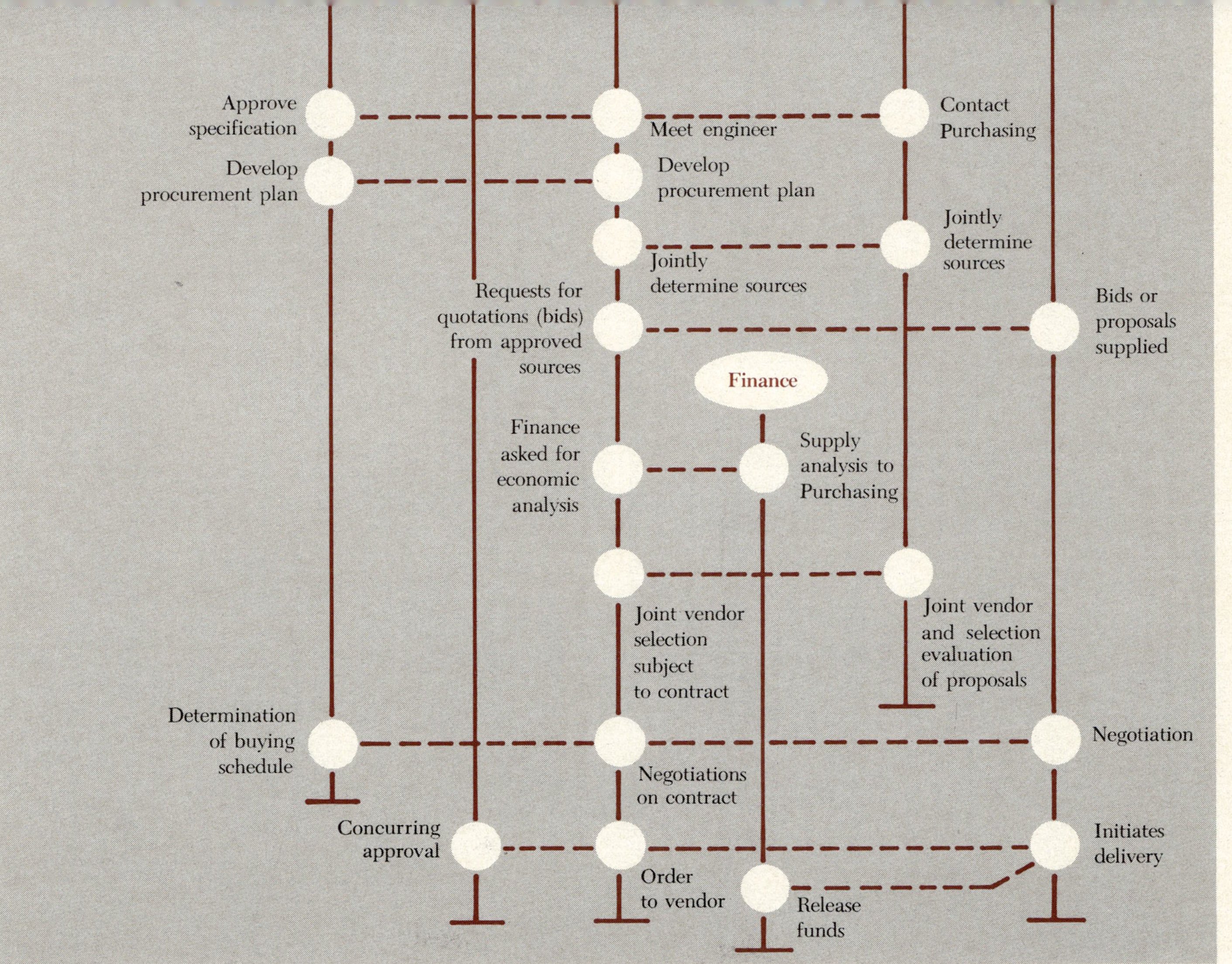

SOURCE: Joel Steckel and John O'Shaughnessy (1983), "Measuring Power in the Organizational Buying Center," oral presentation, Columbia Univ. Business School.

locations. Although each copying center may have similar equipment needs, the salesperson must know the particular problems of each and show sensitivity to them in order to maximize the possibility of sales success.

PICTORIAL MODELS OF ORGANIZATIONAL BUYING BEHAVIOR

Pictorial models of the organizational buying process can be useful for identifying individuals and activities. The process chart in Exhibit 19–3, for example, shows the interactions and decisions involved in the purchase of capital equipment. This model provided its authors with a useful starting point for their broad, quantitative study of how power can be conceptualized and measured in industrial purchases. By themselves, however, pictorial models have limited usefulness, for several reasons.

First, such models apply to only one purchase decision; we cannot be sure whether a similar pattern would characterize another firm's capital-equipment purchase, or whether the same firm would exhibit the same kind of pattern at a different time or for comparable kinds of equipment. Although a good industrial salesperson is able to draw such models for each sales situation, he or she would need to go beyond pictorial models to understand the relative importance of individuals and what factors underlie such power differences. Finally, because such models do not cover the time frame of the decision and the factors that were evaluated by different individuals, they provide no true guidance for the marketing manager who may be trying to market capital equipment. In short, such models are descriptive, but not prescriptive, and there are even serious deficiencies in what is described.

CONCEPT-BASED MODELS OF ORGANIZATIONAL BUYING BEHAVIOR

In contrast to pictorial models, conceptual models are useful because they enable us to generalize across situations, suggesting key factors to consider when examining any organizational decision.

Behavioral Theory of the Firm

Although not focused on purchase decision-making, an early conceptual model which greatly aided our understanding of organizational buying behavior is Cyert and March's **behavioral theory of the firm,** which examines how organizations (1) set goals, (2) form expectations, (3) search for information, and (4) make choices.[4]

Their theory consists of four interrelated concepts. The first, *quasi-resolution of conflict*, is based on the notion that there is latent conflict among goals in organizations. Several methods are used to manage or reduce conflict. For example, the problem of selecting a vendor might be broken down into subproblems and handled by different parts of the organization (Cyert and March call this "local rationality"). The second concept, *uncertainty avoidance*, suggests that organizations try to control the environment in their negotiations with potential vendors. This could involve short-term contract negotiations, for example. The third concept is *problemistic search*, in which individuals in organizations seek information, beginning with the most familiar sources and progressing to less familiar ones, until an acceptable course of action is found. Finally, *organizational learning*, indicates that organizations learn from each experience of problem-solving. For example, they may learn to adapt future goals to reflect success or failure in the past problem-solving exercise or they might adopt "attention rules," (that is, they learn to become more selective in information-seeking).

Although Cyert and March's model is extremely useful in positing central concepts for understanding decision-making within firms, it is limited to interaction between individuals within the firm. There is no concern with the extent and nature of competitive influences, various marketing stimuli, and the broader influence of environmental forces.

An Organizational Buying Behavior Model

A more recent theory that includes these influences is that of Webster and Wind.[5] Their model of organizational buying behavior is described in Exhibit 19–4. The model is composed of four parts: (1) the *buying center*, which calls attention to "task" and "nontask" related activities and interaction among individuals involved in the decision; (2) as a subpart of the buying center, the actual *decision-making process* as it is carried out; (3) the *external environment*, including marketing stimuli and broad constraints (such as technological, legal, and social limitations) as well as organizational constraints (such as the quality and quantity of individuals involved in buying decisions, time available, and so forth); and (4) the *nature of buying responses*, including communication (such as information search and negotiation) and actual purchase activities.

Webster and Wind's model is particularly useful since it points out three key dimensions of organizational buying behavior:

1. environmental and organizational constraints,
2. the decision-making process (DMP) itself, and
3. the decision-making unit (DMU) or buying center.

Environmental and Organizational Constraints　　Webster and Wind identify six major *environmental constraints* on organizational buying behavior. First are *physical factors*, such as climate and geographical location of the firm relative to suppliers and customers. Second are *technological influences*, such

EXHIBIT 19–4
AN ORGANIZATIONAL BUYING BEHAVIOR MODEL

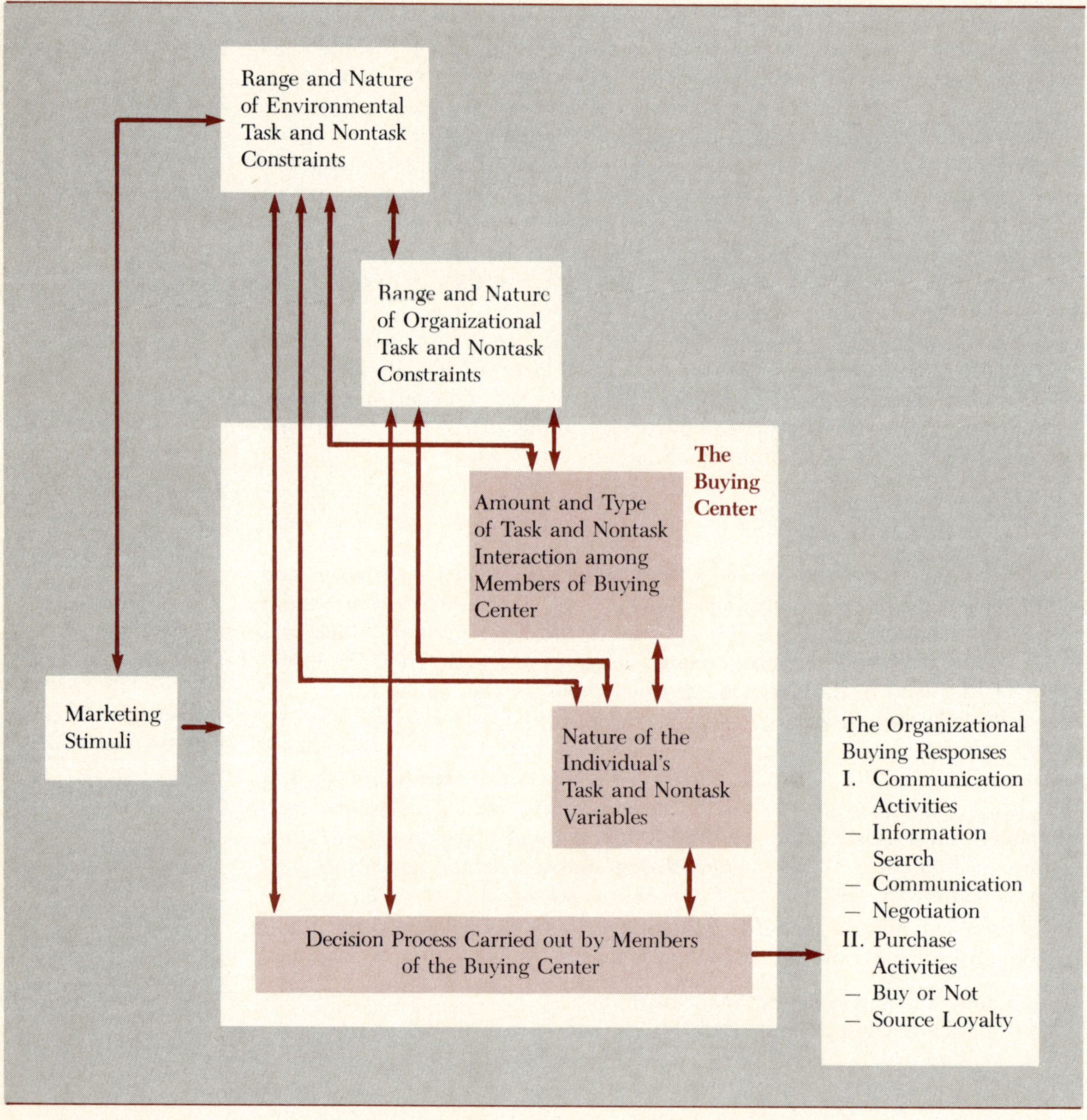

SOURCE: Frederick E. Webster, Jr., and Yoram Wind (1972), *Organizational Buying Behavior* Englewood Cliffs, N.J.: Prentice-Hall), p. 30.

as the rapidly changing environments affecting innovative high-tech firms versus the more stable environments of mature industries. Third are *economic factors*, such as high interest rates (that can be particularly hard on industries such as housing). Finally, *political*, *legal*, and *cultural* factors can also affect the buying behavior of organizations.

To appreciate the impact of such environmental forces, consider firms that are particularly sensitive to changes in the customer environment. For example, toy manufacturers must carefully monitor trends in the birth rate, a demographic factor that indicates primary market size, but that also relates to broad social and lifestyle changes. These companies must also monitor changes in technological and cultural aspects of the environment. Increasingly sophisticated electronic toys are possible, but should a firm invest in research and production facilities for such toys? What will be the impact of changes in the birth rate? Equally important, might there be changes in the social environment which lessen demand for such toys—for example, local ordinances and public concern with children's "addiction" to electronic games?

Organizational constraints are reflected in the firm's establishment of procurement rules or relatively invariate procedures to be followed in the purchase of goods and services. Such rules are an attempt to reduce uncertainty (see Cyert and March's behavioral theory of the firm). Although organizational constraints may serve to systematize the buying process, such procedures are not always appropriate. For instance, the procurement rules for purchasing materials that have long been used by a company (such as sheet steel in the automotive industry) may not be appropriate as a company seeks to purchase a material it has not used before—for example, an automobile manufacturer purchasing electronic components for an electronic ignition system.

Decision-Making Processes and Decision-Making Units   While the environment exerts powerful influences on a firm's buying processes, and organizational constraints mediate those processes, the actual dynamics of organizational buying behavior are represented by the decision-making processes (DMP) and the individuals involved—the decision-making unit (DMU). These dimensions of organizational buying behavior, along with a third dimension, the buying situation, are portrayed in Exhibit 19–5.

Decision-making processes are characterized with a generalized problem-solving model, beginning with some kind of recognized need or problem, progressing through information-gathering, information evaluation, and, finally, to choice (buying from a particular vendor). Decision-making processes vary with the time over which they occur and the degree of specificity of the steps involved. Some firms have highly structured DMPs, while others have less formalized procedures.

The DMP may vary with the nature of the buying task—which can range from a simple reorder of a good or service that has been routinely purchased for some time to the purchase of something for the first time. Between these two extremes are other possibilities: for example, a firm may be upgrading its equipment—say, computers—from one generation to the next. This process has led to a strategy called *migration* that is used by some suppliers. The computer manufacturer encourages customers to migrate from one generation of equipment to the next, so that they will not be lost to a competitor.

EXHIBIT 19–5
THE BUYING CENTER: DECISION STAGES BY ROLES AND BUYING SITUATIONS

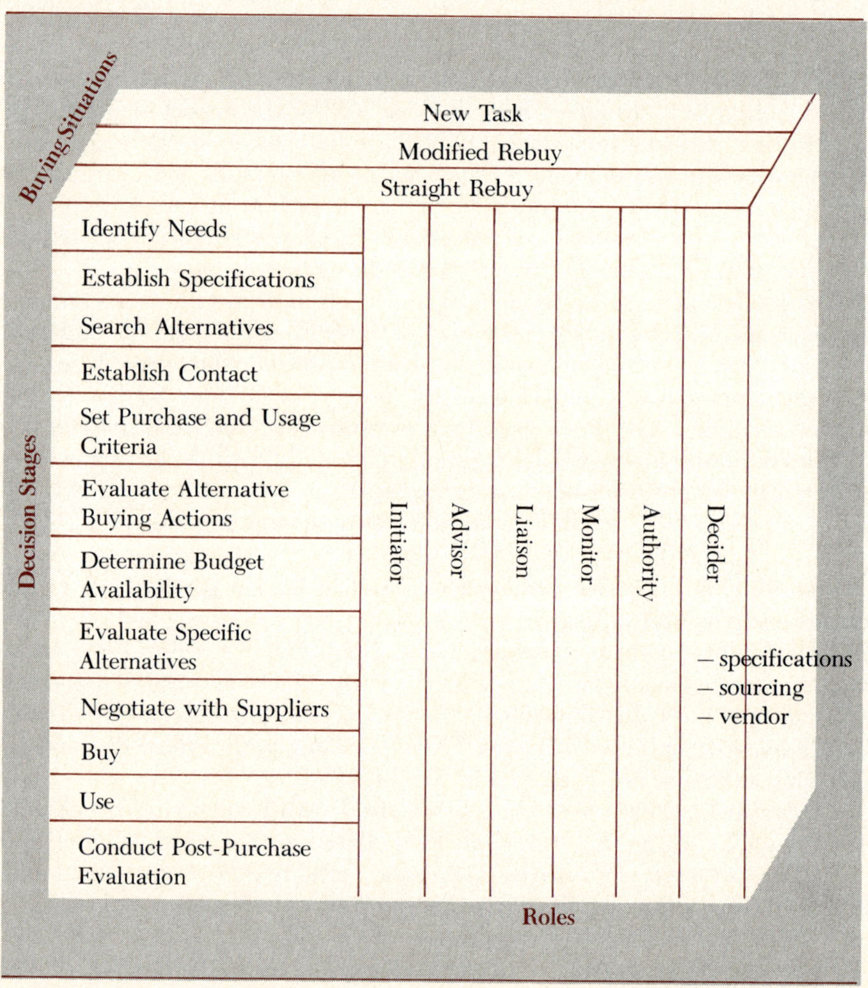

SOURCE: Based on Frederick E. Webster, Jr., and Yoram Wind (1972), *Organizational Buying Behavior* (Englewood Cliffs, N.J.: Prentice-Hall). Role designations are suggested in John O'Shaughnessy (1977), "Aspects of Industrial Buying Behavior Relevant to Supplier Account Strategies," *Industrial Marketing Management*, 6 (1), pp. 15–22.

One dimension of the model in Exhibit 19–5 delineates these three buying situations: (1) *new tasks*, (2) *modified rebuys*, and (3) *straight rebuys*.[6] In the earlier example involving the automobile company, the purchase of sheet steel was a straight rebuy and the purchase of electronic ignitions was a new buying task. Modified rebuys are purchases that are related to previous use of products, but that represent significant changes in the type of material purchased—as in the example of a company's purchase of successive generations of computers.

Consider, for example, the case of a manufacturer of pumps and controls used in drilling for oil. Several years ago, the Canadian government opened up vast areas in the north for oil exploration. Major oil companies deemed such exploration too risky, so small "wildcat" firms formed the primary customer base for the pump and control manufacturer. For a few years, the company enjoyed impressive sales, since its standardized line, technical support staff, and knowledgeable salespeople were precisely what the small customers needed as they purchased the company's equipment—a relatively new task for most of them. As time passed, however, new, specialized competitors gained significant market shares, and the company wondered what had gone wrong. The answer lay in the changing nature of the buying task, reflecting increases in customer sophistication, and, therefore, different product needs. What had been new buys became routine rebuys and modified rebuys as customers became more experienced and knowledgeable. Instead of a standardized line of equipment, customers needed special-purpose pumps and controls, and instead of technical expertise from the selling company, they wanted better prices. The selling company did not realize that the buying criteria had changed, and that the change had important implications for their product line, sales force, and marketing program.

Marketing managers can gain considerable insight into organizational buying behavior when they consider the interrelationship of the buying situation and the DMP, as shown in Exhibit 19–5. For example, a firm's progression through the stages may be very rapid for straight rebuys; in fact, stages may be skipped altogether as a firm routinely reorders some product or service. For modified rebuys or new tasks, however, the DMP may take several weeks or even months. From the selling firm's perspective, the most complex selling tasks are those in the initial stages of the DMP, for modified rebuys or new tasks. In these cases, the salesperson must work with the customer in order to carefully define the customer's needs. The simplest selling tasks are those in the opposite corner of the model: working with companies to establish ordering procedures for straight rebuys.

Some firms make their DMPs very specific and communicate them both internally and externally. Internal communication of the DMP helps individuals in the buying organization to operate under a single set of procedures. As we have seen, such formalization is an attempt to reduce uncertainty as to buying tasks. External communication of the DMP clarifies procedures for potential vendors. For example, government agencies issue **RFPs** (Requests for Proposals), which specify the quantity and quality of materials or services needed and the steps that will be followed in the procurement process.

Formal or publicized DMPs are the exception rather than the rule, however, especially in smaller companies. Consequently, vendors must attempt to characterize the DMP so that marketing efforts are most appropriate for the particular type of the decision. Miscalculating the DMP can be disastrous. For example, if a salesperson attempts to help a company define its problems and needs (the first step in Exhibit 19–5), but the company has progressed beyond that stage and is searching for alternatives (the third step), then the marketing strategy is inappropriate. The salesperson is likely to lose credibility, since he or she has misjudged the DMP.

Even when a company publicizes its DMP, the selling firm's marketing manager must plan and execute strategies and personal selling tactics based on an assessment of the "real" DMP, since formal ones are often not followed.

Some companies require their salespeople to hypothesize the steps in a customer's DMP and to identify individuals who may be involved in the DMU, estimating the degrees of influence each will exert over the course of the DMP.

Simultaneous Scanning Versus Sequential Evaluation

Another conceptualization of a DMP is based on the overall, implicit strategy a firm pursues in its buying. For example, a firm might attempt to "simultaneously scan," or "array and review," the range of potential vendors, or to first rank them and then proceed through a "sequential evaluation" in order to select one.[8] The two overall strategies are depicted in Exhibit 19–6. In **simultaneous scanning** an organization evaluates potential suppliers A through D at the same time, and each of them has an approximately equal chance of being selected. This strategy is thought to occur when

1. total dollar expenditure is high,
2. probability of suppliers not meeting specifications is moderate to high,
3. major risk is perceived in paying a premium price, and
4. adequate management resources are available.

In **sequential evaluation,** one firm (A) has a strong likelihood of being selected; however, if it cannot meet specifications or is rejected for some other reason, the buying organization will proceed through vendors B, C, and D sequentially, until one is found that satisfies buying needs. This strategy is thought to occur when

1. total dollar expenditure is low,
2. probability of supplier failing to meet specifications is low,
3. major risk is perceived in interruption of supply, and
4. management resources available to choose among suppliers are limited.

It would seem likely that sequential-evaluation buying processes characterize straight rebuys, at least as long as the buyer is satisfied with the usual supplier. These processes also occur when one firm is clearly predominant in a market, and secondary firms would be chosen only under unusual circumstances. Conversely, simultaneous-scanning processes are likely when a firm is buying services and equipment for the first time, and several good potential suppliers are available.

As examples of these overall kinds of decision-making processes, consider the changes that have occurred over the years in the marketing of mainframe computers and telecommunications equipment. In the early days of both industries, one firm dominated each market: IBM in mainframe computers and AT&T in telecommunications. Both firms probably enjoyed the results of sequential-evaluation processes, since they were by far the dominant vendors in each industry. However, largely as a result of antitrust activities and rapid technological development, formidable competitors have arisen for both firms, which have probably shifted buyers' strategies to sequential evaluation.

Profound changes have also occurred in customer decision-making processes over the course of the product life cycles for these products. For example, a company's first purchase of a mainframe computer probably involves many individuals within the company, including the president, financial offi-

EXHIBIT 19–6
SEQUENTIAL EVALUATION VERSUS SIMULTANEOUS SCANNING STRATEGIES

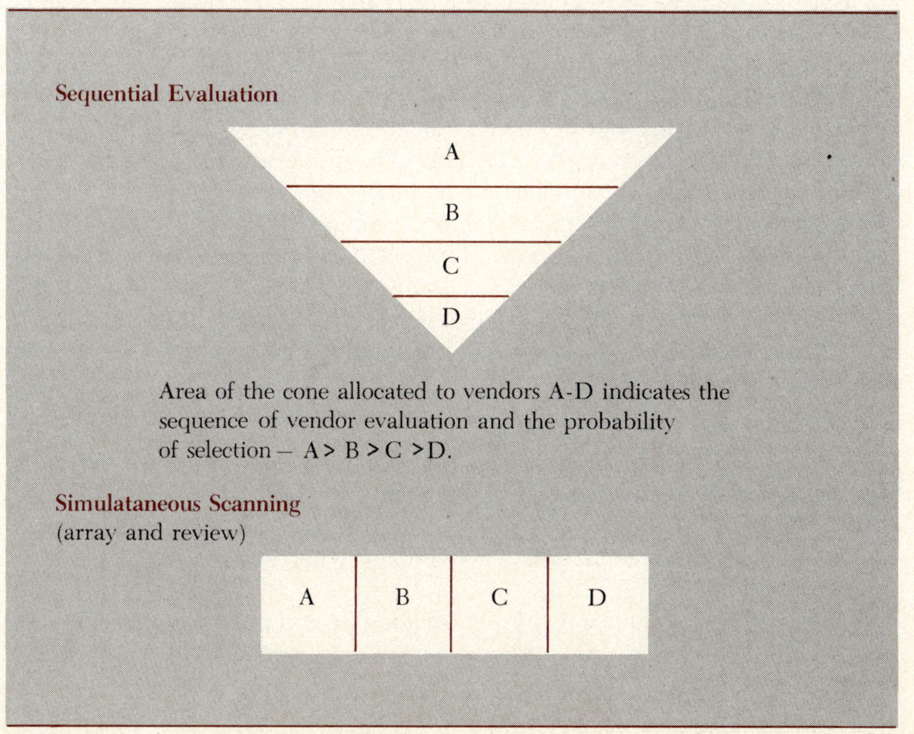

cers, and so forth. Over time, however, as data-processing personnel are hired and the technology and its applications become more familiar, subsequent purchases are likely to become more specialized, involving fewer people, with criteria focused on the needs of these specialists.[9]

Thus, for both AT&T and IBM, the rise of competition and changes in customer behavior have changed their relatively comfortable positions. Customers who are relatively experienced in buying computers and telecommunications equipment will probably array and review vendors, whereas relatively young companies or those that have not extensively used computers or advanced telecommunications systems before will probably use sequential evaluation, beginning with the industry giants.

The Decision-Making Unit or the *Buying Center*

The DMU consists of all individuals who have some significant input to a buying decision. In Exhibit 19–5, these individuals are portrayed by roles. At first glance, it would seem easy to identify the individuals in these roles according to their job titles. It seems obvious, for example, that the purchasing agent plays a dominant role in buying decisions. For costly goods the financial vice-president or even the president may provide key inputs.

Although "job titles" can be useful to a salesperson beginning to approach a particular customer, this method of identifying the DMU may indicate nothing about the kinds of input various individuals provide throughout the buying process. Job titles may not tell us, for example, who wields the greatest power or who acquiesces to others at key points in the DMP.

A better way to understand the DMU is to identify individuals who are involved according to the *roles* they actually play. Webster and Wind suggest five key roles often present in organizational buying: *users, influencers, buyers, deciders*, and *gatekeepers*.[10] Gatekeepers, for example, are often purchasing agents, who may not play an important decision-role in the buying process, but who have the crucial role of directing salespeople to the "right" people and who often keep the flow of information going between individuals during the decision-making process. The decider and the buyer may be the same individual, but sometimes the decision is made by one individual (such as the financial vice-president) and implementation of the decision is left to a buyer (such as an office manager).

The following is another conceptualization of roles within the DMU:[11]

1. *Initiators*. These people start the ball rolling by indicating a need for a product or service. In the pictorial model of a purchase for capital equipment (Exhibit 19–3), the initiator is someone in a user department, such as research and development or production, who recognizes a product or service need.
2. *Advisors*. These people provide information over the course of the DMP. In Exhibit 19–3 these people appear to be primarily in the engineering department.

users

influencers

buyers

deciders

gatekeepers

3. *Liaisons*. These people can be individuals who provide for the flow of information within the buying firm or who are the main points of contact with possible vendors. In Exhibit 19–3, considerable liaison activity exists between purchasing and engineering, but the main points of contact with suppliers is through the engineering department.
4. *Monitors*. These people ensure that the process continues toward procurement. In Exhibit 19–3 they appear to be in the user department and in purchasing.
5. *Authorities*. These are people who have some expertise or other type of power over the course of the DMP. Note in Exhibit 19–3 that top management merely gives approval to investigate and concurring approval. Different kinds of authority are evident: finance provides authority for economic analysis, while the user department approves specifications drawn up by the engineering department.
6. *Deciders*. These people are involved in either (a) deciding on the specifications needed, (b) specifying the type of sourcing required (for example, single or multiple sources of supply), and (c) specifying the particular vendor. Note in Exhibit 19–3 that the user department decides only on the buying schedule, while purchasing negotiates the contract; purchasing and engineering jointly select and evaluate proposals from suppliers.

Identification of the roles played by members of the DMU is a difficult task, particularly as salespeople assess new prospects; while companies may have similarities, no two—even within the same industry—are exactly alike in their DMU composition. The purchasing agent may exert considerable influence in one company, but not much influence at all in another. The task is even more difficult for the following reasons: (1) Individuals may exert their role-influences only at certain points in the decision-making process. Thus, marketing efforts directed at the influencer may be critical in the early stages of the process, but not important later. (2) An individual may play more than one role—particularly in the case of small companies. (3) The domain of influence may not be adequately reflected in the traditional role designations. For example, Wind and Robertson investigated the purchase of innovative radiology equipment by various hospitals.[12] Building on previous theorizing by Likert,[13] they identified *linking pin* roles, which denote individuals who exert leadership and influence in their own group within an organization and who also maintain effective membership and influence in higher levels within the organization. For example, the chief radiologist may exert great influence in his or her department, but may also influence financial managers within hospitals (who are most likely to be concerned with costs) and top hospital administrators (who may be most concerned with satisfying the board of directors). Obviously, the domains of influence of such individuals—the linking pins—make them crucial targets for marketing efforts, and it would be a serious error to assume that a person such as a chief radiologist was interested only in technical aspects of the new equipment.

KEY DIMENSIONS OF SALESPERSON-BUYER INTERACTION

The importance of **personal selling** to firms marketing to organizational customers is reflected in the enormous costs associated with training and maintaining a "professional" sales force. Grikscheit estimates that $60 billion is spent annually on the personal selling effort,[14] whereas Kotler puts the figure at $32 billion on personal selling and $21 billion on advertising (in the late 1970s).[15] The relative differences in these expenditures are confirmed in a survey of 476 companies.[16] Another source estimates that the average cost of an industrial sales call in 1981 was $178—an increase of 30 percent from the 1979 total of $137.[17]

Sales call costs vary by industry, with the highest costs in chemicals, electronics, and fabricated metals industries, and lowest costs in the drug and medicine and instruments industries.[18]

Weitz stresses the need to understand what makes for successful personal selling when he observes that one third of industrial salespeople account for almost two thirds of the orders received by companies. Personal selling is of paramount importance in industrial marketing, since customized product-programs must be designed for individual accounts. Yet, choosing a "good" salesperson is not an exact science. Each of the following is a stereotype of good selling:

> *Good salespeople are born that way. If you find a good one, he or she can sell anything to anybody.*
>
> *A good product sells itself. All the salesperson has to do is to make a reasonable presentation of its performance and its benefits.*
>
> *If you train people well, and provide them with good selling techniques, they can succeed, even in spite of a poor product.*
>
> *All that really matters is the personal relationship between the buyer and the seller. A good salesperson always picks up the tab, and, frankly, kisses the buyer's ________!*

Although instances can be found in support of each stereotype, none is correct in all circumstances. In fact, all four views are probably wrong, since they place all of the burden on the salesperson's native selling ability and skill at interpersonal ingratiation, or on the product and on sales training. Obviously, the best salespeople would combine all four of these dimensions and many others.

Applying Behavioral Concepts to Personal Selling

The earliest attempts to apply knowledge of human behavior to personal selling came in the form of prescriptions or rules which salespeople could use across selling situations. These were sometimes called *road maps to sales suc-*

cess, since they offered a series of steps salespeople could follow leading to a sale: for example, always ask for the sale, meet objections with questions, and so forth. Most of these rules presumed a one-way flow of influence from salesperson to buyer, with little or no regard for two-way processes that occur as salespeople interact with buyers.

Some early attempts to select "good" salespeople were based on personality tests, which measured characteristics such as empathy, forcefulness, and sociability. Other attempts concentrated on demographic and situational factors associated with sales success, such as age, education, intelligence, and sales experience, as well as product knowledge and training. The results were remarkably inconsistent, with some studies finding positive relationships between these variables and salesperson performance and others finding none.[19]

Gradually, interest arose in exploring interactive processes to provide a stronger basis for salesperson selection and training.[20] An early example is the well-known "sales grid" of Blake and Mouton, a framework for classifying individuals on two dimensions: concern for the customer and concern for the sale.[21]

sales grid

A similar and more familiar framework is shown in Exhibit 19–7. Here individuals are classified as one of four types based on their scores on paper-and-pencil personality tests and their performance in sales exercises. The two dimensions in this case are *assertiveness* and *responsiveness*, similar to Blake and Mouton's dimensions.

In addition to questions of reliability and validity about such approaches, the strategic question about them is, what does one do with this kind of information? Would a salesforce manager assign a *driver* to work with an account in which his or her main contact would be an *analytic*? Do "opposites attract," or do "birds of a feather flock together"?

Schemes that classify salespeople on such dimensions as assertiveness, responsiveness, concern for the sale, and so forth, have some uses, but it is difficult to use this information in designing and implementing sales strategies. Moreover, there are conceptual and measurement difficulties associated with such classification procedures: do salespeople *always* display the predispositions which are measured? *Should* they do so for optimal sales performance? Such questions led researchers and managers to search for other behavioral concepts, more closely linked to the actual interpersonal encounters which occur in salesperson-buyer interaction.

One stream of research has attempted to infer the processes occurring in the salesperson-buyer "dyad" or two-person unit by examining the importance of similarities between salespeople and buyers.[22] Research in other contexts has consistently demonstrated that similarity is causally related to liking, perhaps because individuals who are relatively similar have common bases of experience and a greater pool of things to discuss than highly dissimilar people.[23] Such interaction with similar others may prove easier and more rewarding than the often awkward interactions between highly dissimilar people.

Studies in marketing contexts confirm the similarity-liking relationship and have found positive relationships between customer-salesperson similarity and sales success. Many dimensions of similarity appear to be involved: backgrounds, physical characteristics, and personality needs, and subjective measures. And customers who are sold tend to *perceive* the salesperson as more like themselves than do customers who aren't.[24]

Sometimes customer-buyer similarity is more important than apparent expertise in achieving sales. In a study of this subject, a salesperson in a hard-

EXHIBIT 19–7
TYPES OF SALES BEHAVIORS

<table>
<tr><td colspan="2" align="center">RESPONSIVE/CONTROL</td></tr>
<tr>
<td>

Analytical

"Serious, exacting people who tend to be low in assertiveness but high in control of emotions; they often gather facts, ask questions, and study data seriously"

Examples: Eric Sevareid, Ralph Nader

</td>
<td>

Driver

"Strong-willed, serious people who usually tell others what they think but not what they feel"

Examples: Barbara Walters, Charles Bronson, Dan Rather,

</td>
</tr>
<tr>
<td>

Amiable

"Supportive, dependable people who display feelings openly and are more interested in being agreeable than in asserting needs and desires"

Examples: John Denver, Dinah Shore

</td>
<td>

Expressive

"Assertive, dramatic people who tend to make their thoughts, feelings, and requirements known and openly express emotions"

Examples: John McEnroe, Robin Williams

</td>
</tr>
<tr><td colspan="2" align="center">EMOTE/NON-RESPONSIVE</td></tr>
</table>

ASK/NON-ASSERTIVE (left axis)   TELL/ASSERTIVE (right axis)

SOURCE: David Merrill and Robert H. Reid (1981), *Personal Styles and Effective Performance* (Radnor, Penn.: Chilton Books). Quotations and examples are from "Careers: A Matter of Style," *Washington Post* (Aug. 24), C5.

ware store was trained to use one of two approaches whenever his customer was interested in buying paint: he portrayed himself either as an expert or simply as having painting problems and needs similar to the customer's.[25] Greater sales success was achieved with the similarity approach.

Other studies have examined another aspect of similarity: how closely salespeople and customers agree on their definitions of "ideal" sales behaviors. The degree of agreement is a measure of **role consensus.** In one study, customers also rated their particular salesperson's actual performance.[26] The difference between ideal and actual performance refers to the customer's **expectation level.** It was found that role consensus was unrelated to salesperson effectiveness, but that expectation level was related to the number of competitors customers use: the closer the salesperson comes to meeting the customer's expectations, the fewer the competitors used.

role consensus

expectation level

The kinds of research we have just reviewed move far beyond earlier studies and frameworks based on one or two personality dimensions of salespeople. More recent contributions have focused explicitly on interactive concepts. For example, Weitz builds on leadership research in social psychology in his *contingency framework* for sales effectiveness across different kinds of selling interactions.[27] Sales effectiveness, according to Weitz, is contingent on four major factors: (1) the behavior of the salesperson in customer interactions, (2) the salesperson's resources, (3) the customer's buying task and (4) the customer-salesperson relationship. Some of the elements subsumed by each of these factors are indicated in Exhibit 19-8. This framework integrates the kinds of dimensions suggested in the earlier discussion of salesperson stereotypes, that is, it is not *just* the salesperson's behavior, nor is it *just* the personal relationship between buyer and seller, nor the product and the salesperson's knowledge of it. Rather, *all* of these factors combine to influence ultimate effectiveness.

Weitz expands on his contingency framework with his **ISTEA sales process model** (see Exhibit 19-9). ISTEA is an acronym for the five elements of his model: impression formation, strategy formulation, transmission, evaluation, and adjustment. Weitz describes the kinds of activities within each stage.

> *In the first activity, the salesperson combines information gained through past experience with information relevant to the specific interaction to develop an impression of the customer. The salesperson can derive information about the target customer by examining past experiences with the target customer and other customers, by observing the target customer during an interaction, and by projecting himself into the target customer's decision-making situation.*
>
> *In the second activity, the salesperson analyzes his impression of the customer and develops a communication strategy which includes an objective for the strategy, a method for implementing the strategy, and specific message formats. The objective of the strategy is defined in another section as the specific cognitive element to which the messages are directed.*

Having formulated the strategy, the salesperson transmits the messages to the customer. As the salesperson delivers the messages, he evaluates their effects by observing the customer's reactions and soliciting his opinions. On the basis of these evaluations, the salesperson can make adjust-

EXHIBIT 19–8
A CONTINGENCY MODEL OF SALESPERSON EFFECTIVENESS

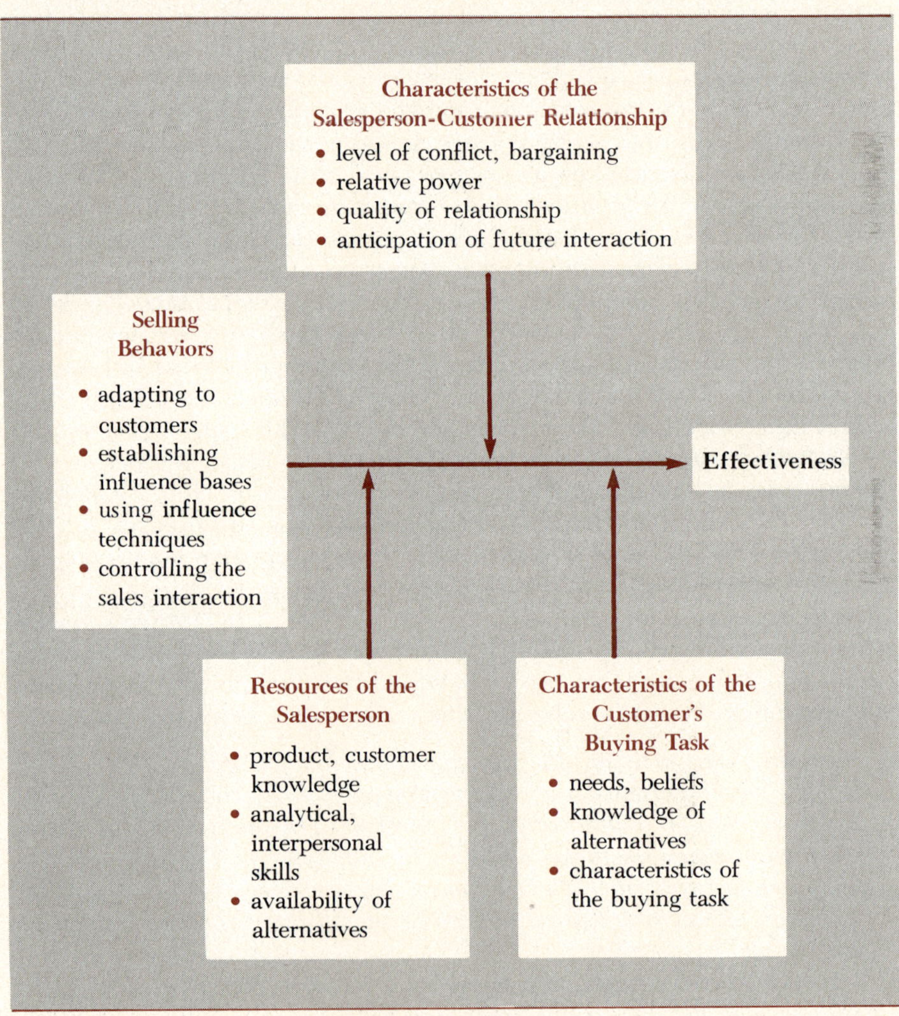

SOURCE: Barton A. Weitz (1981), "Effectiveness in Sales Interactions: A Contingency Framework," *Journal of Marketing*, 45 (Winter), p. 90.

ments by either reformulating his impression of the customer, selecting a new strategic objective, or changing the method for achieving the strategic objective, or the salesperson can continue to implement the same strategy.

For Weitz, the key concepts seem to be *empathy* and *adaptability*—the abilities to monitor the customer's leanings, feelings, and reactions, and to adapt to them on a moment-by-moment basis in sales interactions. In initial research on his model, Weitz found that variations in abilities during the two initial stages—impression formation and strategy formulation—account for 20 percent of the variance in actual field sales performance. These findings seem to corroborate Grikscheit's earlier findings, which show that more effective salespeople understood more of the feedback from customers, especially non-verbal cues.[28] Moreover, they were better able to summarize customer feedback consistently and to pick responses more appropriate for the prospect than less effective salespeople.

empathy

adaptability

Finally, other approaches to salesperson effectiveness stress the importance of combinations of variables. For example, Walker, Churchill, and Ford sug-

EXHIBIT 19–9
***ISTEA* SALES PROCESS MODEL**

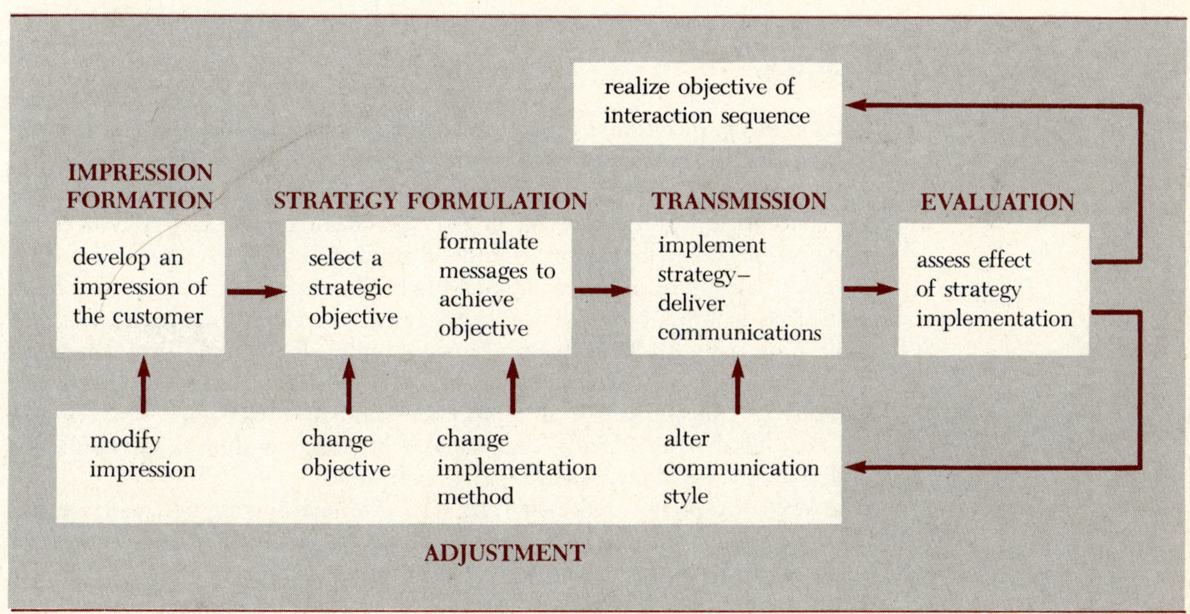

SOURCE: Barton A. Weitz (1978), "Relationship Between Salesperson Performance and Understanding of Customer Decision Making," *Journal of Marketing Research*, 15 (Nov.), p. 502.

gest that a salesperson's motivation level, aptitude, and role perceptions are crucial.[29] *Role perceptions* reflect dyadic behavior; the concept involves allocation of effort across a salesperson's account and products, a perception of the role the salesperson is to play, and a strategy for dealing with each account. In this model, role behaviors may remain relatively fixed over time, as salespeople develop and maintain characteristic styles. However, allocation of effort and account strategies should be modified to the extent that salespeople learn to utilize feedback to modify their behaviors. Computerized models have been utilized to help salespeople with the allocation of time. One such model is CALLPLAN, whose progenitor, Leonard Lodish, reports that salespeople using the model averaged 8 percent higher sales than salespeople not using the model.[30]

In summary, the behavioral concepts used to help increase personal selling effectiveness have progressed from the early unidimensional "rules" and attempts to hire "natural" salespeople based on personality test results. Clearly, as Capon, Holbrook, and Hulbert point out, such efforts reflected a greatly oversimplified model of personal selling.[31]

More recent research has focused on a two-way model of interpersonal communication, such as that proposed by Weitz. The most promising aspect of these models is the stress on the salesperson's abilities to monitor the sales encounter, adapting his or her behavior accordingly.

SUMMARY

The topic of organizational buying behavior is critically important to companies that sell to other organizations. It is more difficult to conduct research on organizational buying behavior than on individual consumer behavior, because more people are involved in decision-making processes and because generalizations about behavior are difficult to derive.

Conceptualizations of organizational buying behavior have progressed from simple ideas of firms buying on purely economic criteria to complex ideas of organizations as multi-level decision-making units. Paralleling these changing views of organizational buying behavior is the changing conceptualization of the industrial salesperson, from simply an "animated catalogue" and "order-taker" to a highly-trained individual capable of understanding the dynamics of complex decision-making in customer organizations.

The key concepts for understanding organizational buying behavior are the DMP, or decision-making process; the DMU, or decision-making unit; and the nature of the buying task. The DMP is best viewed as a series of implicit or explicit steps an organization takes, from recognizing the need for a product or service to selecting a vendor. The DMU is best viewed as the group of individuals who play some role over the course of the buying process. The nature of the buying task powerfully affects the DMU and the DMP, since, for example, the resources needed to purchase a good or service for the first time are quite different from those needed for a straight rebuy.

In contrast to consumer marketing, industrial marketing requires considerable interpersonal contact between seller and buyer; sales involve large amounts of money and risk and customizing for individual customers is necessary. Consequently, personal selling is a considerably more important component of the marketing mix than in consumer marketing. Today considerable attention is being paid to the nature of salesperson-buyer interaction. The resulting conceptualizations stress the need for salespeople to be adaptive in sales interactions.

KEY CONCEPTS

simultaneous scanning
sequential evaluation
DMU
DMP
industrial marketing
rational buyer
"music man" era
new tasks
modified rebuys
straight rebuys

problem-solver
flow chart models
behavioral theory of
   the firm
buying center
RFP
DMU roles
salesperson-buyer
   dyad

role perceptions and
   consensus
customer expectations
ISTEA sales process
   model
users
influencers
buyers
deciders
gatekeepers

DISCUSSION QUESTIONS

1. Under what circumstances is a buying organization likely to use multiple buying sources? A single source? Use various concepts from this chapter in explaining your answers.
2. Contrast the relative roles of various forms of promotion in consumer and industrial marketing. What behavioral concepts are useful in assessing differences?
3. What factors do you feel led to changing views of customers from the "rational buyer" era to the "problem-solving" era?
4. Of what use are flow-chart models? What are their limitations?
5. What behavioral factors distinguish new buys, modified rebuys, and straight rebuys?
6. What would you say to a salesperson who complained that the only reason he or she can't sell a good or service to a customer firm is that "the price is too high"?
7. Why have "sales aptitude" tests, and other personality-based tests, been poor predictors of salesperson performance?
8. With what kind of customers would you pair a young, aggressive male salesperson? An older, philosophical salesperson?

NOTES

1. See E. Raymond Corey (1976), *Industrial Marketing: Cases and Concepts*, 2nd ed. (Englewood Cliffs, N.J.: Prentice-Hall).
2. U.S. Bureau of Labor Statistics (1981), *Monthly Labor Review*, June; see also McGraw-Hill Research (undated), Laboratory of Advertising Performance, no. 8013.6.
3. Among the "classic" early studies of organization behavior: Amitai Etzioni (1961), *A Comparative Analysis of Complex Organizations: On Power, Involvement and Their Correlates* (New York: Free Press); Peter Blau (1955), *The Dynamics of Bureaucracy* (Chicago: Univ. of Chicago Press); and David L. Sills (1957), *The Volunteers* (New York: Free Press).
4. Richard M. Cyert and James G. March (1963), *A Behavioral Theory of the Firm* (Englewood Cliffs, N.J.: Prentice-Hall).
5. Frederick E. Webster, Jr. and Yoram Wind (1972), *Organizational Buying Behavior* (Englewood Cliffs, N.J.: Prentice-Hall), p. 30.
6. Patrick J. Robinson, Charles W. Faris, and Yoram Wind (1967), *Industrial Buying and Creative Marketing* (Boston: Allyn & Bacon).
7. This example is drawn from Jean-Marie Choffray and Gary L. Lillien (1980), "Industrial Market Segmentation by the Structure of the Purchasing Process," *Industrial Marketing Management*, 9, pp. 331–42.
8. See Richard N. Cardozo (1968), "Segmenting the Industrial Market," *Proceedings*, Fall Conference, American Marketing Assn.; see also Richard N. Cardozo and James W. Cagley (1971), "Experimental Study of Industrial Buying Behavior," *Journal of Marketing Research* (Aug.), pp. 329–34.
9. F. Stewart DeBruicker and Gregory L. Summe (1973), "The Experienced Customer Phenomenon," working paper, The Wharton School, Univ. of Pennsylvania.
10. Frederick E. Webster, Jr. and Yoram Wind (1972).
11. John O'Shaughnessy (1977), "Aspects of Industrial Buying Behavior Relevant to Supplier Account Strategies," *Industrial Marketing Management*, 6 (1), pp. 15–22.
12. Yoram Wind and Thomas S. Robertson (1982), "The Linking Pin Role of the Organizational Buying Center," *Journal of Business Research*, 10, pp. 169–84.
13. Rensis Likert (1961), *New Patterns of Management* (New York: McGraw-Hill).
14. Gary M. Grikscheit (1973), "An Experimental Investigation of Persuasive Communication in Selling," *Proceedings*, Conference, American Marketing Assn., pp. 261–67.
15. Philip Kotler (1976), *Marketing Management: Analysis, Planning and Control*, 3rd ed. (Englewood Cliffs, N.J.: Prentice-Hall).
16. Jon G. Udell (1972), *Successful Marketing Strategies in American Industry* (Madison, Wis.: Mimir Publishers).
17. See note 2. Other detailed information on salesforce costs is contained in "1980 Survey of Selling Costs" (1980), *Sales and Marketing Management* (Feb. 25).
18. "1980 Survey of Selling Costs (1980).
19. See S. N. Stevens (1958), "The Application of Social Science Findings to Selling and the Salesman," in *Aspects of Modern Management*, Management Report no. 15, (New York: American Management Assn.) pp. 85–94; Ronald P. Illet and Allan L. Pennington (1967), "Customer and Salesman: The Anatomy of Choice and Influence in a Retail Setting," in *Science, Technology and Marketing*, ed. R. M. Haas, Proceedings of the Fall, 1966, Conference of the American Marketing Association, Chicago, pp. 598–616. A good review of this stream of research is in James C. Cotham, III (1970), "Selecting Salesmen: Approaches and Problems," *MSI Business Topics* (Winter), pp. 64–72.
20. See, for example, Franklin B. Evans (1963), "Selling as a Dyadic Relationship," *American Behavioral Scientist*, 6, 9 (May), pp. 76–79; A. G. Woodside and William J. Davenport (1974), "The Effect of Salesman Similarity and Expertise on Consumer Purchasing Behavior," *Journal of Marketing Research* (May), pp. 198–202; Frederick E. Webster, Jr. (1968), "Interpersonal Communication and Salesman Effectiveness, *Journal of Marketing* (July), pp. 7–13; Richard W. Olshavsky (1973), "Customer-Salesmen Interaction in Appliance Retailing,"

Journal of Marketing Research (May), pp. 208–12; and David T. Wilson (1975), "Dyadic Interaction: An Exchange Process," in *Advances in Consumer Research,* ed. B. Anderson, (Assn. for Consumer Research), pp. 384–97.

21. Robert R. Blake and Jane S. Mouton (1970), *The Grid for Sales Excellence: Benchmarks for Effective Salesmanship* (New York: McGraw-Hill).

22. Much research on this topic and related ones is reviewed in Harry L. Davis and Alvin J. Silk (1971), "Behavioral Research on Personal Selling: A Review of Some Recent Studies of Interaction and Influence Processes in Sales Situations," working paper (Cambridge, Mass.: Marketing Science Inst.), Apr.

23. Evans (1963). See also M. S. Gadel (1964), "Concentration by Salesmen on Congenial Prospects," *Journal of Marketing* (Apr.), pp. 64–66. A good review of the similarity-attraction hypothesis is Donn Byrne (1969), "Attitudes and Attraction," in *Advances in Experimental Social Psychology,* ed. Leonard Berkowitz, 4 (New York: Academic Press), pp. 35–89.

24. Evans (1963).

25. Timothy C. Brock (1965), "Communicator-Recipient Similarity and Decision Change," *Journal of Personality and Social Psychology* (June), pp. 650–54.

26. Henry L. Tosi (1966), "The Effects of Expectation Levels and Role Consensus on the Buyer-Seller Dyad," *Journal of Business* (Oct.), pp. 516–29.

27. Barton A. Weitz (1981), "Effectiveness in Sales Interactions: A Contingency Framework," *Journal of Marketing,* 45 (Winter), pp. 85–103.

28. Gary M. Grikscheit (1973).

29. Orville C. Walker, Jr., Gilbert Churchill, and Neil M. Ford (1977), "Motivation and Performance in Industrial Selling: Existing Knowledge and Needed Research," *Journal of Marketing Research* (May), pp. 156–68.

30. Leonard Lodish (1971), "CALLPLAN: An Interactive Salesman's Call Planning System," *Management Science,* Part II, 18 (Dec.), pp. 25–40.

31. Noel Capon, et al. (1972), "Persuasive Effects of Sales Messages Developed from Interaction Process Analysis," *Journal of Business Administration,* 4, pp. 69–77.

PART

IV

Socio-Cultural Theories and Applications

20 Social Class and Sociographic Segmentation

In American society, the social classes to which individuals belong depend on a number of factors, including occupation, education, income, and area of residence. These classes form the basis of the social stratification system.

Social class is an important concept in the study of consumer behavior, because consumption patterns are often directly related to class. Individuals who identify with a particular social class, such as the middle class or the working class, tend to have similar values and life styles. Lifestyle defines the types of interests and activities—and hence expenditures—that predominate among members of a social class. Individuals from different social classes tend to purchase different types of products, to expose themselves to different media, to patronize varying types of retail outlets, and to have different levels of price sensitivity. For all these aspects of marketing, an understanding of social class can assist managers in developing strategies specifically geared to the preferences, needs, and habits of each social-class market segment.

In this chapter we first define social class and discuss the class structure of American society and the behavioral and attitudinal differences characterizing the various classes. Next, we consider social-class measurement and the specific relationship between social class and income. Finally, we address the issue of sociographic (social-class) segmentation and the effects of social class on elements of the marketing mix.

DEFINITION OF SOCIAL CLASSES

Variations in people's wealth, power, and prestige form the basis of the **social stratification system** of our society. *Social class* refers to an individual's position within the stratification system. Social class is of interest to marketers because consumption patterns are often directly related to class. On the concept of social class and its impact on consumption, the following has been said:

> *Class membership is total. This means that a person's class is related to . . . one's total social experience. This extends from income, prestige, and education to lifestyle and culture. With respect to consumption, this means that . . . standards of taste, consumption aspirations, consumption rituals, shopping patterns, and decision-processes are closely related to class membership.*[1]

Social classes are characterized by four important properties. First, they are *hierarchical.* That is, relative to one another, they are ordered. Members of higher social classes have greater wealth, power, and prestige than members of the lower social classes. Second, members of social classes are *homogeneous in behavior.* That is, they share similar values, beliefs, and consumption patterns. This characteristic is especially important for marketers, since individuals belonging to a particular social class tend to buy similar types of goods, in the same types of stores, and are exposed to the same types of media. Third, social classes are said to *restrict social interaction between classes.* The great majority of people with whom individuals interact socially are members of their own social class. As we pointed out in Chapter 17, "Group Behavior," individuals are influenced in decision-making mainly by members of their primary groups. Thus, interpersonal influence tends to be limited by social-class boundaries. The fourth important property of social classes is that they are *multi-dimensional.* That is, social class is not determined solely by occupation, income, education, or area of residence. Instead, it is a multi-dimensional, composite variable which is correlated with numerous component variables.

The one variable with which social class is most highly correlated is occupation, which is in turn highly correlated with education and income. The prestige of occupations has been studied extensively by sociologists. Exhibit 20–1 shows the prestige rankings for a list of several occupations from physician (highest prestige) to street sweeper (lowest prestige), based on research in fifty-five countries. The prestige ratings of various occupations have remained quite stable in the United States over time. Obviously, prestige ratings of scientific occupations have increased somewhat with the increased importance of science in society. But in general, occupational prestige, like social class, is a relatively stable phenomenon.

Within the United States we have been generally reluctant to admit the existence of a class order. It has been part of our heritage to dismiss visible

social stratification system

hierarchical

homogeneous in behavior

restrict social interaction

multi-dimensional

symbols of ascribed (in other words, inherited) status, such as titles of nobility, and to minimize belief in class distinctions. Yet a class hierarchy or *social-stratification system* seems to be characteristic of all societies. The relevant issue is really not whether a class order exists in the United States, but rather, the form that it takes.

In examining a particular social stratification system, a paramount concern is the level of fluidity or rigidity within that system. This is usually measured in terms of the degree of *social mobility* which a system allows, that is, movement upward or downward in social class. A further measure is the extent to which social-class placement is based on *ascribed* (that is, inherited) or on *achieved* (that is, earned) status. The system in the United States is more fluid than those in other highly industrialized societies, although some rigidity exists because of unequal distribution of opportunities.

social mobility

ascribed versus achieved status

EXHIBIT 20–1
SELECTED INTERNATIONAL OCCUPATIONAL PRESTIGE RATINGS

Occupation	Prestige Rating	Occupation	Prestige Rating
Physician	78	Farmer	47
University professor	78	Electrician	45
Lawyer, trial lawyer	71	Insurance agent	45
Head of large firm	70	Office clerk	43
Engineer, civil engineer	70	Garage mechanic	43
Banker	67	Shopkeeper	42
Airline pilot	66	Typist, stenographer	42
High school teacher	64	Policeman	40
Pharmacist	64	Tailor	40
Armed forces officer	63	Foreman	39
Clergyman	60	Carpenter	37
Artist	57	Plumber	34
Teacher, primary teacher	57	Sales clerk	34
Journalist	55	Mail carrier	33
Accountant	55	Driver, truck driver	33
Civil servant, minor civil servant	54	Barber	30
Professional nurse, nurse	54	Shoemaker, repairer	28
Building contractor	53	Waiter	23
Actor	52	Janitor	21
Bookkeeper	49	Servant	17
Traveling salesperson	47	Street sweeper	13

SOURCE: Donald J. Treiman (1977), *Occupational Prestige in Comparative Perspective* (New York: Academic Press), Appendix A.

SOCIAL CLASS IN AMERICA

Sociologists have studied social class in considerable depth. As we will see, the basic structure of the social stratification system in the United States has remained quite stable over time.

Class Structure

From the 1940s through the early 1980s, the most commonly used and accepted social stratification system, based on the pioneering work of sociologist W. Lloyd Warner,[2] divided the United States into the six social classes shown in Exhibit 20–2. These classes may be described as follows.

1. *The upper-upper class* is the aristocracy of birth and wealth, the social register in a community. These are the locally prominent families with at least second- or third-generation wealth. They are very aware of their "position" in society.
2. *The lower-upper class* is composed of families who more recently acquired wealth. The members of this social class are known as the "nouveau riche." Although they may be wealthier than members of the upper-upper class, they are not fully accepted socially. These families are headed by highly successful professionals, high-salaried top executives, or owners of large businesses.
3. *The upper-middle class* is composed of professionals and managers. They emphasize "careers," with family life traditionally revolving about the advancement of the husband's career. Members of this social class are highly visible in community affairs, and a disproportionate number of community leaders are upper-middle class members.

EXHIBIT 20–2
WARNER'S SOCIAL CLASS SYSTEM

Social Class	Membership
Upper-upper	Aristocracy
Lower-upper	New Rich
Upper-middle	Professionals and managers
Lower-middle	White-collar workers
Upper-lower	Blue-collar workers
Lower-lower	Unskilled laborers

SOURCE : W. Lloyd Warner, Marcia Meeker, and Kenneth Eells (1949), *Social Class in America* (Chicago: Science Research Associates).

4. *The lower-middle class* is composed of white-collar office workers, small-business proprietors, and some highly skilled blue-collar workers. In contrast to the career emphasis of the upper-middle class, an emphasis on the home characterizes the lower-middle class. Individuals tend to be very conscious of having a "nice" home in a "respectable" neighborhood. Members of this class correspond most closely to the term "the average American." They are law-abiding citizens who believe in traditional values and goals.

5. *The upper-lower class* is the working class of blue-collar workers, including some skilled tradesmen, semiskilled tradesmen, and the composite of workers who essentially earn a living with their hands. Union membership is common, and a core value is security. Social interactions are more limited than those of the higher social classes, being confined primarily to relatives and immediate neighbors.

6. *The lower-lower class* consists of the unskilled workers in society, the unemployed, and the "disreputables." Frequently, these individuals live in slums.

Warner's six-class depiction of American society retained popularity, in both the sociological and the consumer-behavior literature, for nearly four decades. However, given the social and demographic trends of the 1980s, the applicability of Warner's typology to the current-day social system may be limited. Two more recent analyses of our social structure provide an updated perspective. Coleman and Rainwater[3] and Gilbert and Kahl[4] have independently suggested that there are three basic divisions in American society—*Upper, Middle,* and *Lower.* Each of these major classes is further divided, as shown in Exhibit 20–3.

Upper, Middle, and Lower

As Coleman points out in a comparison of the two views, despite their somewhat different orientations, each scheme assigns approximately the same proportion of the population to each division.[5] While the Coleman-Rainwater typology retains a basic similarity to Warner's early categorization, the Gilbert-Kahl approach explicitly incorporates the notion of capitalism. In fact, Gilbert and Kahl maintain that the capitalist class, which accounts for 1 percent of the population, controls about half of the country's wealth.

Comparing the two updated hierarchies with Warner's original version, it is interesting to note that there are more similarities than differences. Both retain Warner's fundamental distinction between the upper (monied) class and the upper-middle (career) class. But the newer hierarchies group the upper-middle class with the upper class—an important idea for managers, since

> *. . . the motives and goals in consumption of most mass-marketed products do not necessarily differ significantly between these three substrata of Upper Americans: it is only when you get into luxury goods and services, or specialty items, that differences in lifestyle and consumption behavior between these three levels become of great interest to marketers—then, of course, it is critical to divide these people by social rank for separate consideration.*"[6]

EXHIBIT 20–3

TWO RECENT VIEWS OF THE AMERICAN STATUS STRUCTURE

The Gilbert–Kahl New Synthesis Class Structure:[a] A situations model from political theory and sociological analysis	The Coleman–Rainwater Social Standing Class Hierarchy:[b] A reputational, behavioral view in the community study tradition

Upper Americans

The Capitalist Class (1%)—Their investment decisions shape the national economy; income mostly from assets, earned/inherited; prestige university connections

Upper Middle Class (14%)—Upper managers, professionals, medium businessmen; college educated; family income ideally runs nearly twice the national average

Middle Americans

Middle Class (33%)—Middle level white-collar, top level blue-collar; education past high school typical; income somewhat above the national average

Working Class (32%)—Middle level blue-collar; lower level white-collar; income runs slightly below the national average; education is also slightly below

Marginal and Lower Americans

The Working Poor (11–12%)—Below mainstream America in living standard, but above the poverty line; low-paid service workers, operatives; some high school education

The Underclass (8–9%)—Depend primarily on welfare system for sustenance; living standard below poverty line; not regularly employed; lack schooling

Upper Americans

Upper-Upper (0.3%)—the "capital S society" world of inherited wealth, aristocratic names

Lower-Upper (1.2%)—The newer social elite, drawn from current professional, corporate leadership

Upper-Middle (12.5%)—The rest of college graduate managers and professionals; life style centers on private clubs, causes, and the arts

Middle Americans

Middle Class (32%)—Average pay white-collar workers and their blue-collar friends; live on "the better side of town," try to "do the proper things"

Working Class (38%)—Average pay blue-collar workers; lead "working class life style" whatever the income, school background, and job

Lower Americans

"A lower group of people but not the lowest" (9%)—Working, not on welfare; living standard is just above poverty; behavior judged "crude," "trashy"

"Real Lower-Lower" (7%)—On welfare, visibly poverty-stricken, usually out of work (or have "the dirtiest jobs"); "bums," "common criminals"

[a]Abstracted by Coleman from Dennis Gilbert and Joseph A. Kahn (1982). "The American Class Structure: A Synthesis," Chapter 11 in *The American Class Structure: A new Synthesis* (Homewood, Ill.: Dorsey Press).

[b]This condensation of the Coleman-Rainwater view is drawn from Chapter 8, 9, and 10 of Richard P. Coleman and Lee P. Rainwater, with Kent A. McClelland (1978). *Social Standing in America: New Dimensions of Class* (New York: Basic Books).

SOURCE: Richard P. Coleman (1983), "The Continuing Significance of Social Class to Marketing," *Journal of Consumer Research*, 10 (Dec.).

Both of the newer views also retain Warner's separate divisions of white-collar middle class and blue-collar working class. But the updated versions group these two classes as Middle Americans. As Coleman points out, the incomes and political philosophies of these groups are quite similar, although their lifestyles and values still differ considerably. The updated typologies share the new feature of differentiating between two subclasses of the lower class: those who are usually employed and self-supporting and those who depend on government support.

Since Warner's initial work with social class, it appears that subtle shifts in the orientations of the classes rather than dramatic social reorganization have occurred, demonstrating an "impressive thematic continuity from one generation and era to the next."[7]

Characteristics of Members of Social Classes

The underlying assumption of social-class analysis is that placement within a social class reflects consistencies in values, lifestyle, and behavior—including consumption behavior. Before we look at the differences in consumption behavior exhibited by members of the various social classes, we shall consider some broader attitudinal and behavioral differences to illustrate how social-class membership influences numerous aspects of living.

Child Rearing   Parent-child relationships differ across social class. In a key article in the literature of sociology, Kohn demonstrates that

> . . . *middle-class parental values differ from those of working-class parents; that these differences are rooted in basic differences between middle-class and working-class conditions of life; and that the differences in values have important consequences for their relationships with their children.*[8]

The two major differences in child-rearing practices concern goals parents set for children and methods of controlling/disciplining children. Middle-class parents want their children to be happy, sharing, cooperative, eager to learn, loving, and self-controlled. In contrast, working-class parents want their children to be neat, clean, obedient, respectful, and pleasing to adults. Middle-class parents stress self-direction and self-discipline. They punish children not only for actions, but also for the intentions underlying actions. Withholding of love is the primary means of punishment. On the other hand, parents from the working-class emphasize adherence to "rules" (rather than self-direction), and punishment is based on the consequences of actions. Physical punishment (spanking) is far more prevalent than punishment via emotional means.

Social-class differences also exist in the use of language with children. Elkin and Handel suggest that "Insofar as social classes use language differently they are organizing their realities differently."[9] Middle-class parents use more complex structure and syntax, making possible a more subtle grasp of reality

("I'd rather you made less noise"). Working-class parents use less complex sentences and less abstraction ("Be quiet").

The end results of differences in parent-child relationships are that middle-class children grow up to be more self-disciplined and to have a greater ability to delay gratification, that is, to postpone rewards for the sake of obtaining greater rewards in the future. Attending college is an example of delayed gratification, since the student postpones the opportunity to earn a salary for four years or more in order to gain professional qualifications that will be beneficial in the future. Working-class adults are more physically oriented, more prone to immediate gratification, and somewhat more literal in their perception of the world.

Attitudes Toward Illness Another social-class related issue (of some concern to health-care providers) is that members of the lower social classes utilize medical services less often and instead rely more on lay opinion. In reviewing research on the health-care practices of consumers, Wortzel summarizes the research evidence that people of different social classes have different views and attitudes toward illness.

> *. . . lower-class people tended to be apprehensive about illness and to be relatively ignorant with respect to their bodies and bodily functions. They also evidence considerable ignorance about illness, and about types of medical treatment. They tended to view the physician as something of a mystic, whose skills were arcane, incomprehensible, and above questioning. The upper-class patient . . . evidenced much more sophistication with respect to illness. This patient tended to view the physician much more as a colleague.*[10]

Religion and Politics Members of different social classes have different religious and political affiliations. Exhibit 20–4 presents a profile of religious groups in terms of occupational status and education level. Within the Protestant grouping, for example, the Congregational sect appears to be particularly high in social class whereas fundamentalists are likely to be low. Social class is also associated with political behavior: in one study, rich whites were almost four times as likely to be Republicans as poor whites, and a positive linear relationship was found between income and identification with the Republican party.[11]

Mobility Another difference in orientation among the various social classes is illustrated in Coleman's report of a sample of 1,000 residents of Houston, Dayton, and Rochester, asked to indicate where their nearest relative lived.[12] The results showed that 55 percent of lower-class and 45 percent of working-class members lived within one mile of a parent, sibling, in-law, grandparent, or other relative. In contrast, only 19 percent of middle-class and 12 percent of upper-class respondents lived this close to kin. Additionally, members of the working-class were far more likely to depend on their relatives for economic, social, and personal advice. As Coleman states, "this emphasis on family ties has been only one sign, moreover, of how much more limited—and different—working-class horizons are, socially, psychologically, and geographically, than middle-class. In almost every respect a parochial view characterizes this blue-collar world."[13] This fundamental difference, noted by Rainwater et al. over twenty years ago, continues to apply, and is reflected in the consumer behaviors of the members of the working- and middle-classes. For example, middle-class members tend to travel more frequently and to place more long-distance telephone calls than their working-class counterparts.

SOCIAL-CLASS MEASUREMENT

Having identified the various social classes, we shall now discuss various techniques that may be used to obtain the social-class rankings of members of our society.

EXHIBIT 20–4
SOCIAL CLASS PROFILES OF AMERICAN RELIGIOUS GROUPS

Religious Group	Median Occupational Status[a]	Median School Years Completed
Protestant	45.3	12.0
Congregational	82.7	16.5
Episcopal	59.9	13.0
Presbyterian	60.3	13.5
Methodist	45.0	12.1
Lutheran	42.9	12.0
Baptist	28.6	11.4
Church of Christ	23.3	11.5
Other fundamentalist	26.4	11.0
Roman Catholic	43.2	12.0
Eastern Orthodox	55.0	12.6
Jew	65.0	15.7
No preference; other	55.0	12.1
Average	45.2	12.0

[a]The current occupation of the respondent was first coded into the six-digit detailed occupation-industry code of the U.S Bureau of the Census and then recoded by computer to the two-digit code of Duncan's Index of Socioeconomic Status.

SOURCE: Edward O. Laumann (1969), "The Social Structuring of Religious and Ethnoreligious Groups in a Metropolitan Community," *American Sociological Review*, 34 (Apr.), pp. 182–97.

Approaches to Measurement

There are three approaches to the measurement of social class: the subjective approach, the reputational approach, and the objective approach.

The **subjective approach,** which is also known as the *perception measurement approach,* involves individuals in rating themselves in terms of their social class. Richard Centers, who did the original work in support of this approach, argues that class consciousness as indicated by this self-designation method is a very powerful predictor of behavior, because people will behave in accordance with their self-perceptions.[14]

A drawback of the subjective approach is that we cannot assume that all respondents perceive and interpret each social class in the same way. The middle class may well represent different things to different people; two individuals, both of whom state they are members of the middle class, may actually be quite heterogeneous in their values and behavior.

The second commonly used system of evaluating social class is the **reputational approach.** This method relies on intensive interviews with informants in a community in order to assign individuals to a particular social class. The reputational approach, developed by W. Lloyd Warner and his associates, is predicated on the idea that reputation or participation in the community is the key to social-class placement.[15] A more recent application of this "evaluated-participation" method is the exhaustive research by Coleman and Rainwater, who intensively interviewed informants in both Kansas City and Boston in order to document the social stratification systems of those cities.[16]

The reputational approach is an appropriate technique to use when the key informants (a) are familiar with those people they are evaluating and (b) can be assumed to be evaluating others on the basis of similar criteria. But practically speaking, measuring social class by using this technique is costly and time-consuming.

For marketing purposes, an objective approach to social-class measurement is feasible. The **objective approach** entails measuring "objective" criteria such as income, occupation, or education. These individual measures are then weighted and combined into a composite measure of social class.

There are a number of objective approaches, each of which includes slightly different criteria. Warner developed an objective classification scheme based on four indicators—*occupation, source of income, residential area,* and *type of dwelling.*[17] Each indicator is rated on a seven-point scale, where a rating of *1* represents highest status, and *7,* lowest status. The ratings are then weighted and combined as shown.

Criteria	*Weight*
Occupation	Rating $\times$ 4
Source of Income	Rating $\times$ 3
Residential Area	Rating $\times$ 3
Dwelling Type	Rating $\times$ 2
Social Class Score	$\Sigma(\text{Rating}_i \times \text{Wt}_i)$

subjective approach

reputational approach

objective approach

Warner's index

An alternative approach is Hollingshead's index, which consists of weighted ratings of *occupation, education,* and *dwelling area.*[18] In both the Warner and Hollingshead indices *occupation* receives the heaviest weighting, consistent with the belief held by most sociologists that occupation is the leading correlate of social class.

The objective-measurement approach is the one most frequently used to assess the social-class rankings of consumers. Collection of ratings data is relatively straightforward and unambiguous.[19]

Measurement Issues and Developments

A major issue in sociology and consumer behavior is whether or not the variables included in the traditional Warner and Hollingshead indices still constitute social class in today's world. One deficiency of these scales is that in assessing a family's social class, they incorporate only the husband's occupation and/or education. The social-class contribution of the wife is not considered relevant. Smith and Yokum refer to this as the **"husband only" fallacy.**[20] When these scales were developed, the majority of American households consisted of a nuclear family composed of a breadwinner husband and a homemaker wife. At that time, the family's social class was derived from the husband's occupation and income. But today's situation is dramatically different, with more and more women entering the paid work force.

Some researchers have begun to include the wife's status characteristics in determining the family's social class. Coleman provides an illustration of a social-class index incorporating the occupation of the household head, area of residence, total family income, and the educational levels of both husband and wife.[21] A different approach is suggested by Smith and Yokum, who argue for a combined husband-wife measure, in which the social class of the family is weighted in the direction of the spouse who has more relative influence in the particular purchase-decision being studied.[22] As more and more women enter the work force and contribute to their household income, it seems only logical that the wife's status characteristics are taken into account for social-class measurement.

A related measurement issue concerns the relevance of other variables in social class. For example, Smith and Yokum suggest that since individuals learn a great many of their consumption patterns as children, their social-class backgrounds could well influence their purchasing habits as adults. In a very thorough study, Nock and Rossi investigated how a family's social status was affected by a number of variables: husband's and wife's occupations and educations, family ethnicity and race, and the occupations and educational levels of the fathers of the couple. The only ascribed characteristic, that is, *unearned* characteristic, that had an effect was the fathers' occupations; and this was the least important characteristic. The achieved characteristics of the couple were most important in determining their social status. In line with traditional thinking, the contribution of the husband outweighed that of the wife, but, according to Nock and Rossi,

> . . . the husband alone is clearly not responsible for family prestige. As a matter of fact, his achievements were found to contribute only a maximum of 50% to overall family standing. The wife, through her occupation and education, makes sizeable and significant contributions to the social standing of the household, potentially contributing as much as 40% to the overall evaluation.[23]

Even as social-class measurement is refined further, a remaining issue is that of the classification of nonfamilies, such as one-person households and single-parent families. Although this problem is yet to be solved, consumer-behavior researchers are aware of the issue, as we have seen in Chapter 14, "Demographics and Values."

SOCIAL CLASS AND CONSUMER BEHAVIOR

As we have seen, social classes exhibit consistencies in values, lifestyle, and other aspects of behavior. We might, then, expect certain consistencies in consumption behavior. This is not to suggest that social class will discriminate between Maxwell House and Folgers' buyers, or Ford and Chevrolet buyers, but it may well discriminate between buyers of Maxwell House and imported Colombian coffee beans, or between buyers of Ford and Mercedes.

For products and services that allow people to make distinctions in lifestyle, social class may allow meaningful segmentation. Social-class segmentation suggests different product, pricing, channel, and promotional programs in line with the specific characteristics, need-value systems, and media patterns of each social class.

Such **sociographic segmentation** may actually be superior to income or demographic segmentation. The following model is posited.

$$\text{social class} \rightarrow \text{values} \rightarrow \text{lifestyle} \rightarrow \text{consumption patterns}$$

In other words, social class is associated with different value systems (for example, placing high value on education) which lead to different consumption patterns (for example, to attend college or to buy books). In contrast, there is less reason to expect any consistency in values or lifestyle on the basis of income alone, since there is no identification or consciousness attached to income level.

Social Class and Income

The distinction between social class and income level deserves emphasis. Social class cannot be directly inferred from income, despite the fact that a significant relationship exists. Income varies quite widely within a given social-class level and is not monotonically related to status. In a review of the social-stratification literature, Haug points out the frequent social class-income discrepancy:

> *The high standing of college professors is obviously not produced by high income . . . some categories of blue-collar workers earn considerably more than white-collar workers, the well-publicized claim that New York street sweepers take home $17,000 a year or more than most school teachers, being a case in point.*[24]

Yet, even though street sweepers and school teachers sometimes earn equivalent incomes, society does not accord these individuals equal social prestige; indeed their social-class rankings are quite different. We would expect their consumption patterns to be quite different as well. But is this always the case? Is social class always a better prediction of consumption patterns than income?

Social Class or Income?

The early research on social class suggested that social class is an extremely valuable segmentation variable, explaining numerous differences in purchasing patterns exhibited by members of higher or lower classes.[25] But in 1965, Carman generated results which indicated that both income and stage in the family life cycle were superior to social class in predicting ownership of large household appliances.[26] In support of Carman's research, Myers, Stanton, and Haug determined that income was a superior predictor for seventy-nine of the ninety-three products they researched.[27] Myers and Mount obtained similar results for thirty-two of their thirty-six selected products.[28]

Rich and Jain reported limited support for the superiority of social class over income in predicting some (but not all) aspects of shopping behavior.[29] Whereas women from different classes had different reasons for enjoying shopping (lower-class women liked acquiring products, and upper-class women enjoyed spending time in pleasant store environments), all classes were equally likely to use friends as reference groups.

Matthews and Slocum initially supported social class over income.[30] They reported that social class was a good predictor of motivation for using credit cards: members of higher social classes were more likely to use credit cards for convenience, whereas lower social-class shoppers used them as a means of gaining extra credit to make installment purchases. Their later research, however, tempered this result by stating that income was an equally good predictor of behavior.[31]

One attempt to integrate income and social class began when Coleman proposed that a distinction be drawn between the **overprivileged** and the **underprivileged** members of a social class.[32] Overprivileged members have an income greater than the median for their class. The underprivileged have an income below the class median. Coleman used this distinction to explain

overprivileged versus underprivileged

purchasing patterns for the automobile market: the overprivileged members of all social classes accounted for a disproportionate number of luxury cars, and the underprivileged for a disproportionately large number of compact cars. Later research by Peters supported the relevance of this distinction, once again for the automobile market.[33]

More recently, Hugstad's analysis of spending patterns found some support for the use of the overprivileged/underprivileged concept in explaining expenditure patterns beyond the automobile market.[34] Overprivileged members of their social classes accounted for a great proportion of the total expenditure for some products (including alcohol, clothing, and education), but not for others (including tobacco, major appliances, and food both at and away from home). Hugstad concludes that more research is needed before a definite conclusion about the efficacy of the overprivileged/underprivileged concept in explaining expenditure patterns can be drawn.

Hisrich and Peters provided a new insight into the relationship between income, social class, and buyer behavior.[35] They too conclude that income is a better predictor when the dependent variable is ownership of a product or *use versus nonuse*. Social class, however, is superior when the *frequency* of use is the dependent variable. For example, whereas income may predict whether consumers *ever* drink imported wine with dinner, regular consumption of imported wine with dinner is predicated on lifestyle, and hence on social class.

After a hiatus of several years, a new consensus regarding the income-social class debate appears to be emerging. As Coleman says, the time has come to

> *put aside the question of which is the better variable, income or class. The proper question for marketers to ask instead is:* How *does social class affect use of income in the marketplace? This should be asked with the broadest possible "how"—meaning "why"—coupled with the subjunctive "when" and the quantitative "how much."*[36]

It is precisely this approach that Schaninger has adopted in his study of a large number of consumer goods.[37] Schaninger states that the social-class/income debate was often fueled by studies that looked at limited—and different—aspects of consumer behavior. He states that *both* are valuable segmentation variables, sometimes alone and sometimes combined. The key is to match individual product classes with their proper segmentation variable.

Schaninger found that *social class is a superior segmentation variable* for food and convenience items, beverages, shopping behavior, and television viewing.[38] In other words, social class explains differences in these aspects of consumption better than income does. For example, members of the lower classes consume more frozen, canned, and prepared convenience food entrees, snack foods, and sandwich components. On the other hand, members of the middle and upper social classes consume more ground coffee, frozen juice, and imported wines, and fewer sweet beverages.

Schaninger's results indicate that *income is superior to social class as a segmentation variable* for major-appliance ownership and for the consumption of soft drinks, mixers, and hard liquor. In-home consumption of these "low-cost 'luxury' items" is influenced by a family's ability to afford them rather than by social class values.

Schaninger also reports that "the combination of social class and income is generally superior for product classes that are highly visible, serve as symbols of social class or status within class, and require either moderate or substantial expenditure."[39] Among such product classes are make-up, clothing, automobiles, and television sets. For these products, we must look not only at social class, but also at income level within social class. For example, relatively underprivileged women in the upper middle class are more likely to purchase low-priced dresses. Also, *overprivileged* and *underprivileged* differences were reported for automobiles, lending some support for Peters' earlier findings. Finally, television ownership varies by income within each social class. Higher income members of the upper-lower and lower-lower classes own the largest number of television sets and of color sets; high income lower-middle and upper-middle class families follow. Upper-class families own the fewest television sets, and the fewest color sets.

In summary, to evaluate the impact of social class on consumption behavior and to assess the relative efficacy of income and social class on variations in consumer behavior, it is best to adopt a product-by-product approach. Since products differ markedly in their levels of involvement, in the risk involved in their purchase, and in their frequency of purchase, it seems logical that the impact of social class on their purchase differs as well.

SOCIAL CLASS AND MARKETING STRATEGY

Social class can be used as a segmentation variable for numerous products and services. Identifying sociographic segments can assist managers in four areas of marketing strategy: product policy, advertising and promotion, pricing policies, and selection of channels of distribution.

Product/Service Differences in Consumption

Social class can be related to consumer selection of products or services. In some cases, a particular sociographic segment accounts for the consumption of an entire product category. In other cases, the product or service can be consumed by a range of social classes, with certain brands or types differentiated by price level and image, appealing mainly to one social-class segment. Finally, although the same product may be used by members of different social classes, the motivation underlying use varies by class.

Exclusive Product Category   For a number of product categories, managers can identify their target market as consisting of a single social class. Knowledge of this class's demographic and lifestyle characteristics can guide decision-making for advertising, promotion, channels of distribution, and pricing. Manufacturers of china, silver, ski equipment, and golfing equipment can quite confidently define their market as "upscale" in social class, where *upscale* refers to *Upper Americans,* that is, the top 14 or 15 percent of Americans as defined by Coleman et al.[40] and Gilbert and Kahl.[41] The markets for air travel, real estate, and financial investments are similarly composed of Upper Americans. By contrast, a number of products and services, including bowling, bus travel, and plastic dinnerware, appeal to lower social-class markets.

Certain foodstuffs also appeal exclusively to a particular social class. For example, buyers of caviar and pâté de foie gras are members of higher social classes. The high cost combined with the relatively sophisticated learned tastes preclude lower-class interest.

Category Segmentation   Some products or services are consumed by members of all social classes, but various brands in the product category appeal to different social classes. For such products, the manager should identify the specific sociographic segment to which his or her brand appeals.

Scotch whisky, for example, spans a wide range from locally produced brands (generally unadvertised, except through value promotions) to the top of the line, with brands such as Chivas Regal. Downscale buyers, concerned primarily with price, purchase local brands. At the other end of the scale, despite the fact that very few people can actually differentiate between brands on the basis of taste tests, consumers buy the symbolism associated with premium-priced, prestige brands.

Similarly, marketers of products such as watches, furniture, and automobiles select a competitive social-class segment, and position their products accordingly. A low-priced Timex watch provides its wearer with the correct time, just as an expensive Piaget watch does. But the difference in symbolic meaning is enormous.

Furniture provides an interesting example, since members of the various social classes differ not only in where they buy but also in how they buy. Lower-class consumers typically walk into a furniture store or mass merchandisers's outlet where they purchase matched sets of living-room furniture that can be delivered within the week. Middle-class consumers are more likely to buy living-room furniture one piece at a time, purchasing from a number of different department stores or specialty furniture stores. The furniture must often be ordered, and is delivered after four to six weeks. Buyers from the upper classes often have their furniture custom designed. Working through an interior decorator, they choose fabrics separately from furniture styles. In fact, fabrics often are not sold by the same dealer from whom the furniture is purchased. Neither long delays in delivery nor high prices are a deterrent.

The marketing of new automobiles is another example of product-category segmentation. Alfred P. Sloan, chairman of General Motors in the twenties, first developed automotive market segmentation across a range of offerings. As General Motors was created from a group of hitherto independent companies, Sloan had to integrate the various makes and models. By the early 1930s, he had succeeded in creating five basic brands, from Chevrolet to Cadillac, each with a distinctive identity and corresponding price. In time, a "loaded" Chevrolet would cost more than a "stripped" Pontiac. But impressions created among the buying public over the years, reinforced by advertising, still contribute to today's consumers' perceptions of each GM car.

Motivation for Product Usage   Social class has a definite influence on the motivation underlying usage of some goods and services. For example, members of the lower classes perceive credit cards as a form of easily available credit, using them to purchase durable goods and necessities. In contrast, upscale consumers see credit cards as a convenience, using them to purchase luxury goods, like restaurant meals, for example.[42] Additionally, the frequency of use of credit cards is higher among upscale consumers.[43]

Carrying segmentation further, American Express and Diners Club, for instance, require stiff annual fees, high incomes, and in-depth credit checks before an applicant can "qualify." And American Express targets its Gold Card to an even smaller segment. Positioned for the top 5 percent of consumers in the United States, the Gold Card is a visible symbol of success. American Express has identified a small but lucrative market segment whose motivation for usage is not only the convenience generally desired by upscale consumers, but the differentiation from other holders of prestige credit cards created by this visible symbol.

The field of personal investment and cash management provides another example of differences in consumer motivations. Investment, once the province of the upper social classes, has become of interest to the middle class. The growth of two-income families and the overall increase in income levels has also created a need for money management. Whereas the upper classes seek effective management of their considerable estates and continued investments, the middle classes, faced with burgeoning home, lifestyle, and educational expenses, need financial planning assistance. E. F. Hutton has begun offering financial planning services for young executives who wish to invest their present income while simultaneously paying mortgages and insurance premiums, saving for their children's college education, and planning for retirement. For middle-class members, the motivation for use of financial planning services is security. For the upper classes, it is sustaining and tracking a portfolio of investments.

A similar example was found in the gold and silver boom markets of late 1979 and early 1980. Traditionally, gold had been the cornerstone of investments, characterized by high stability. The upper classes viewed gold as a long-term investment. When the prices of gold and silver began to escalate dramatically, new investors—often from the lower social classes—began buying the precious metals hoping to latch onto a fast moving upward market and to "get rich quick." When barbers and waiters joined bankers and executives in the gold rush, the market crashed. In general, the new investors from lower social classes suffered the greatest losses. Upper Americans, with their longer-term orientation, knew when to withdraw from the market.

Advertising and Promotion

Differential response to advertising media can be documented by social class. Generally, print media—especially magazines—tend to reach higher social classes than broadcast media, but this generalization must be qualified by content or programming and time of day. For example, the early-evening television audience has a heavier working-class composition, and the late-evening audience has a heavier middle-class composition. Preferred content of television programming also varies by social class. Levy found that the lower classes favored quiz shows, westerns, and late-night movies, and that higher classes favored dramatic presentations and late-night shows.[44] Fashion, travel, and literary magazines are more often found in middle-class homes. *Town and Country* and *The New Yorker* are directed toward readers from the upper classes. In contrast, sports, outdoor, and romance magazines are more often found in working-class homes. Thus, the marketer can reach a fairly well specified social-class audience by judicious media selection, matching the desired market profile with the media profile.

In the development of advertising campaigns, the content of the actual appeal varies by product category according to social class. As we have already noted, the middle classes tend to use more complex language structure than the working classes. One result of this is that members of the middle class tends to think more symbolically than members of the lower class, who are more literal. Advertising directed toward the higher social classes is often highly symbolic, containing very little detail. The advertisement in Exhibit 20–5 and the Chivas Regal advertisement on page 333 use product display and only *very brief* copy to underscore major messages. In the Chivas Regal ad, not even the entire product name is visible.

In contrast, advertisements for, say, Greyhound, are factual, literal, reassuring, and more likely to be based on a specific product attribute—"Take the bus, and leave the driving to us." Similarly, typical advertisements for U-Haul trailers appeal to people who need to move on a reduced budget. These advertisements tend to discuss many attributes and specific details of moving (such as safety and ways to save money), and no symbolic imagery is incorporated into the ad. Moving companies that direct their advertising toward more upscale consumers (like Allied Van Lines and Nationwide) stress the competence of their staff and the resulting concern for the consumer who is moving. They discuss very few specific attributes of the companies.

Price Consciousness and Pricing Policies

Social class influences the manner in which consumers view price and approach buying decisions. Members of the lower classes are more likely to equate price with quality. This, combined with low self-confidence in making

EXHIBIT 20–5
ADVERTISEMENT USING PRODUCT DISPLAY

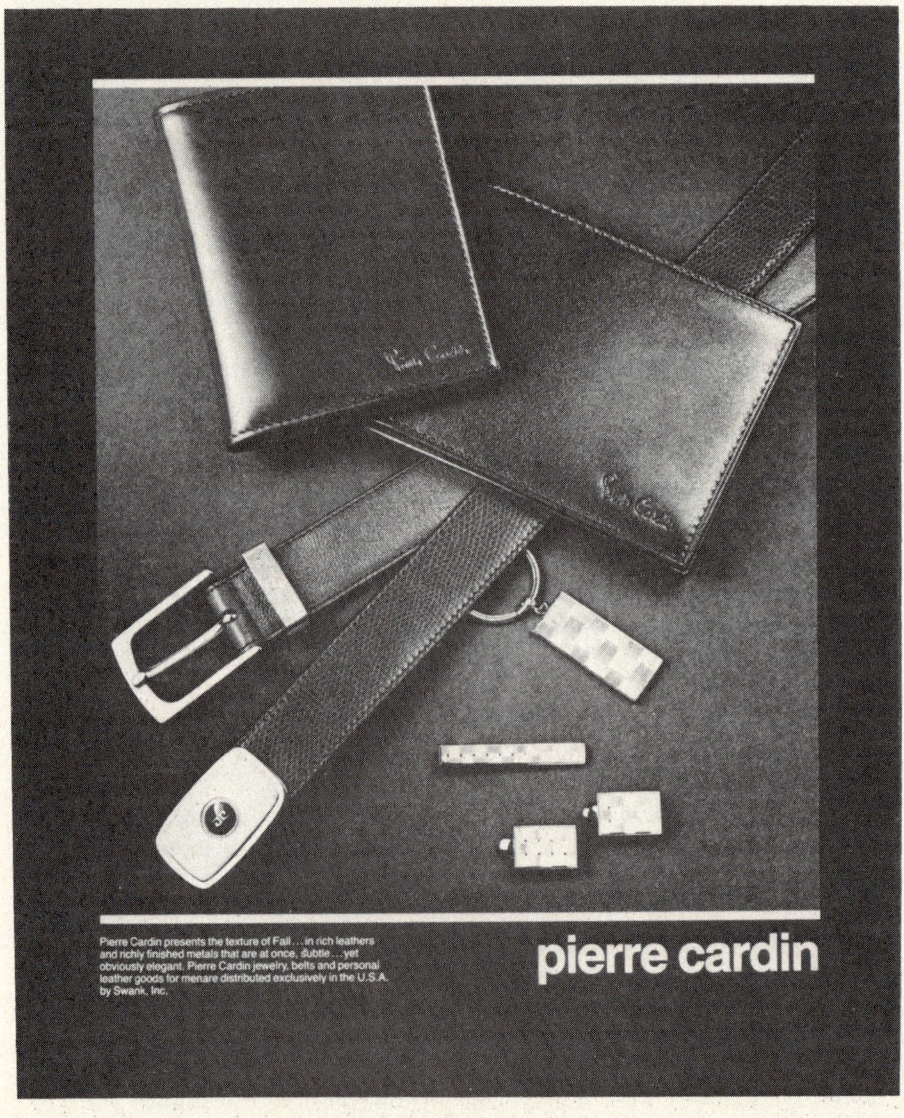

quality comparisons among brands, leads to a great tendency to purchase the more costly national brands.[45]

Upper-class buyers are more willing to spend their money on symbolic goods and services—like dining in prestigious restaurants, designer clothing, and travel abroad. Cosmetics for the higher social classes tend to have a comparatively higher mark-up than cosmetics for the lower social classes. This is due partially to more expensive packaging, but it also capitalizes on the typical view that for high-involvement, symbolic goods, product price reflects product efficacy. Similary, the cost of manufacturing a Cadillac is greater than for a Chevrolet—but not as much, proportionally, as the difference between the retail prices of the cars. Consumers who purchase Cadillacs pay a premium for the symbolism attached to this tangible good.

We can offer a tentative interpretation of the relationship between social class and pricing: the prestige brands and symbolic, high-involvement goods that are usually positioned for the upper classes are characterized by higher mark-ups than brands at the nonprestige end of the product category. Members of the upper classes are willing to spend their money for the symbolism. For low-involvement, nonsymbolic goods, mark-ups are not as variable across all brands in a product category. The costlier nationally branded products tend to appeal to lower-class downscale consumers, who are more likely to perceive a price-quality relationship.[46]

Channels of Distribution

Social classes may also affect retail shopping patterns. In a sense this is obvious: the clientele of Saks Fifth Avenue is of a higher social class than that of Sears. A number of studies have shown that lower-class consumers are more likely to shop in discount stores. But it has been suggested that social class affects shopping patterns for only certain product categories.[47] Prasad found that for products of low social risk, such as tools or appliances, consumers across social-class levels held relatively similar attitudes toward patronizing discount stores. For products of high social risk, however, such as women's clothes, consumers in the upper social class held significantly less favorable attitudes toward discount stores.[48] Prasad concludes that

> . . . *consumers in the higher socioeconomic strata are more likely to exhibit "patronage mix" tendencies, probably preferring to patronize the more conventional department stores and specialty stores for the purchase of products with higher social risk, but favorably predisposed to patronize the discount stores for a vast number of other products that may be characterized as of low social risk.*[49]

Mail-order catalogues, which once were the typical means of reaching downscale, rural buyers, have recently undergone a marked transformation. More and more mail-order companies are appealing to members of the middle and upper social classes. For example, the Spiegel catalogue, traditionally targeted to working-class consumers, has attempted to change its positioning to appeal to the middle class. A print advertising campaign shows svelte models and speaks of "The New Spiegel."

A final trend is "off-price" outlets, such as Loehmann's, Marshall's, and T. J. Maxx, that carry upscale merchandise at discount prices. It seems likely that these stores would appeal to the underprivileged members of each social class. We can infer that shoppers at, say, Loehmann's, feel social pressure to purchase more upscale merchandise, but lack adequate finances to buy in traditional upscale stores.

SUMMARY

The social classes to which individuals belong form the basis of the social stratification system. Social class is an important concept for managers because the members of each social class share common values and lifestyles, and often exhibit similar patterns of buyer behavior.

Recent studies of the American social structure posit three basic classes—Upper, Middle, and Lower. The Upper class is composed of very wealthy individuals (both "old money" and the nouveau riche) and successful professionals and managers. Middle Americans are either white-collar employees or members of the blue-collar working class. Lower Americans are divided into two groups—low paid workers who are usually employed and individuals who rely on government support.

Members of the various social classes differ in their child-rearing practices, attitudes toward illness, religious and political preferences, and mobility. The lower classes tend to be more traditional and parochial than the higher classes.

Three approaches to social-class measurement are the subjective self-report, the reputational method, and the objective method. The objective approach, which rates families on such criteria as occupation, income, and place of residence, is the most commonly used method in consumer research. Although traditional measurement relied solely on the husband's characteristics, more recent methods incorporate the wife's contributions to her family's social-class standing.

The differences in the orientations of classes form the basis for sociographic segmentation of the market. An especially rich understanding of sociographic segments results when the effects of social class and income are considered jointly.

Social class can be used as a segmentation variable in the development of product-positioning strategies. An understanding of social class can also help managers in the selection of media and distribution channels, and in determining pricing levels for various products and brands.

KEY CONCEPTS

social stratification
  system
occupational prestige
social class structure
  Upper Americans
  Middle Americans
  Lower Americans

Warner system
  upper-upper
  lower-upper
  upper-middle
  lower-middle
  upper-lower
  lower-lower
social mobility
subjective
  measurement

reputational
  measurement
objective measurement
relationship of social
  class and income
underprivileged versus
  overprivileged
sociographic
  segmentation

DISCUSSION QUESTIONS

1. Why is *occupation* the variable that contributes the most to an individual's social class?
2. How has the social-class structure of the United States changed since Warner's pioneering work? What are the major differences and similarities?
3. What are the major differences characterizing the various social classes?
4. Discuss the major problems in measuring social class.
5. What is the relationship between income and social class? When should a manager use each as a segmentation variable?
6. Discuss the concept of underprivileged versus over-privileged members of a social class. In general, how would the buyer behavior of these groups differ for symbolic luxury products?
7. Given the differences in parent-child relationships, how would the purchase-decision processes differ for Upper Americans, Middle Americans, and Lower Americans for (a) children's clothing, (b) toys, and (c) child-oriented foods, such as cereals and cookies?
8. Select a product for which the market is particularly amenable to sociographic segmentation. Discuss the major advertising, pricing, and distribution differences induced by social class.

NOTES

1. Robert N. Mayer (1978), "Exploring Sociological Theories by Studying Consumers," *American Behavioral Scientist*, 21 (March/Apr.), p. 603.
2. W. Lloyd Warner and Paul S. Lundt (1941), *The Social Life of a Modern Community* (New Haven, Conn.: Yale Univ. Press).
3. Richard P. Coleman and Lee P. Rainwater, with Kent A. McClelland (1978), *Social Standing in America: New Dimensions of Class* (New York: Basic Books).
4. Dennis Gilbert and Joseph A. Kahl (1982), *The American Class Structure: A New Synthesis* (Homewood, Ill.: Dorsey Press).

5. Richard P. Coleman (1983), "The Continuing Significance of Social Class to Marketing," *Journal of Consumer Research*, 10 (Dec.).

6. Richard P. Coleman (1983).

7. Richard P. Coleman (1983).

8. M. L. Kohn (1963), "Social Class and Parent-Child Relationships: An Interpretation," *American Journal of Sociology*, 68 (Jan.), pp. 471–80.

9. Frederick Elin and Gerald Handel (1972), *The Child and Society* (New York: Random House).

10. Lawrence H. Wortzel (1975), "The Behavior of the Health Care Consumer: A Selective Review," in *Advances in Consumer Research*, ed. Beverlee B. Anderson, Vol. 3 (Assn. for Consumer Research), p. 299.

11. W. H. Form and J. Huber (1971), "Income, Race, and the Ideology of Political Efficacy," *Journal of Politics*, 33 (Aug.), pp. 659–88.

12. Richard P. Coleman (1983).

13. Lee P. Rainwater, Richard P. Coleman, and Gerald Handel (1959), *Workingman's Wife: Her Personality, World, and Life Style* (New York: Oceana Press), pp. 27–28.

14. Richard P. Centers (1952), "The American Class Structure: A Psychological Analysis," in *Readings in Social Psychology*, ed. C. E. Swanson, et al., 5th ed. (New York: Holt, Rinehart & Winston), pp. 299–311.

15. W. Lloyd Warner, Marcia Meeker, and Kenneth Eells (1949), *Social Class in America* (Chicago: Science Research Associates).

16. Richard P. Coleman and Lee P. Rainwater, with Kent A. McClelland, (1978).

17. W. Lloyd Warner, Marcia Meeker, and Kenneth Eells (1949).

18. August B. Hollingshead (1949), *Elmtown's Youth: The Impact of Social Class in Adolescents* (New York: Wiley).

19. Unfortunately, a major problem with different objective measures is that class placements using different instruments often are not highly correlated. A thorough treatment of this subject may be found in Luis V. Dominguez and Albert L. Page (1981), "Use and Misuse of Social Stratification in Consumer Behavior Research," *Journal of Business Research*, 9, pp. 151–73.

20. Terence A. Smith and J. Thomas Yokum (1981), "Extensions of the Basic Social Class Model Employed in Consumer Research," in *Advances in Consumer Research*, ed. Kent Monroe (Assn. for Consumer Research).

21. Richard P. Coleman (1983).

22. Terence A. Smith and J. Thomas Yokum (1981).

23. Steven L. Nock and Peter H. Rossi (1978), "Ascription Versus Achievement in the Attribution of Family Social Status," *American Journal of Sociology*, 84 (Nov.), p. 588.

24. Marie R. Haug (1977), "Measurement in Social Stratification," in *Annual Review of Sociology*, ed. Alex Inkeles, 3 (Palo Alto, Cal.: Annual Reviews), p. 53.

25. See, for example, Pierre Martineau (1958), "Social Classes and Spending Behavior," *Journal of Marketing*, 23, pp. 121–41 and S. J. Levy (1966), "Social Class and Consumer Behavior," in *On Knowing the Consumer*, ed. J. W. Neuman (New York: Wiley), pp. 146–60.

26. James M. Carman (1965), *The Application of Social Class in Market Segmentation*, Inst. of Business and Economic Research, Univ. of California at Berkeley.

27. James H. Myers, Roger R. Stanton, and Arne F. Haug (1971), "Correlates of Buying Behavior: Social Class vs. Income," *Journal of Marketing*, 35 (Oct.), pp. 8–15.

28. James H. Myers and John F. Mount (1973), "More of Social Class vs. Income as Correlates of Buying Behavior," *Journal of Marketing*, 37 (Apr.), pp. 71–73.

29. Stuart A. Rich and Subhash C. Jain (1968), "Social Class and Life Cycle as Predictors of Shopping Behavior," *Journal of Marketing Research*, 5 (Feb.), pp. 41–49.

30. Herbert Lee Matthews and John W. Slocum, Jr. (1969), "Social Class and Commercial Bank Credit Card Usage," *Journal of Marketing*, 33 (Jan.), pp. 71–78.

31. John W. Slocum, Jr., and Herbert Lee Matthews (1970), "Social Class and Income as Indicators of Consumer Credit Behavior," *Journal of Marketing*, 34 (Apr.), pp. 69–74.

32. Richard P. Coleman (1960), "The Significance of Social Stratification in Selling," in *Marketing: A Maturing Discipline*, ed. Martin L. Bell (Chicago: American Marketing Assn.), pp. 171–84.

33. William Peters (1970), "Relative Occupational Class Income: A Significant Variable in the Marketing of Automobiles," *Journal of Marketing*, 34 (Apr.), pp. 74–77.

34. Paul S. Hugstad (1981), "A Re-examination of the Concept of Privilege Groups," *Journal of the Academy of Marketing Science*, 9 (Fall), pp. 399–408.

35. Robert D. Hisrich and Michael P. Peters (1974), "Selecting the Superior Segmentation Correlate," *Journal of Marketing*, 38 (July), pp. 60–63.

36. Richard P. Coleman (1983), p. 55.

37. Charles M. Schaninger (1981), "Social Class Versus Income Revisited," *Journal of Marketing Research*, 18 (May), pp. 192–208.

38. Charles M. Schaninger (1981).

39. Charles M. Schaninger (1981), p. 207.

40. Richard P. Coleman and Lee P. Rainwater, with Kent A. McClelland (1978).

41. Dennis Gilbert and Joseph A. Kahl (1982).

42. Joseph T. Plummer (1971), "Life Style Patterns and Commercial Bank Credit Card Usage," *Journal of Marketing*, 35 (Apr.), pp. 35–41.

43. H. Lee Matthews and John W. Slocum (1969) and John W. Slocum and H. Lee Matthews (1970).

44. S. J. Levy (1966).

45. M. Ross (1965), "Uptown and Downtown," *American Sociological Review*, 30, pp. 255–59.

46. M. Ross (1965).

47. Stuart A. Rich and Subhash C. Jain (1968).

48. V. Kanti Prasad (1975), "Socioeconomic Product Risk and Patronage References of Retail Shoppers," *Journal of Marketing*, 39 (July), pp. 42–47.

49. V. Kanti Prasad (1975), p. 47.

21 Subcultures and Subcultural Marketing

*Within a culture as complex and heterogeneous as that in the United States, there is a great diversity of people and backgrounds. The term **subculture** refers to a category of people who share a sense of identification that is distinguishable from that of the total culture.*

The heterogeneity of the United States is reflected in the multiplicity of races, national origins, religions, social classes, and regions that make up the country. Each of these "subcultures" has identifiable values which may affect its members' behavior.

*In a strict sense, anthropologists might insist that a subculture exists only if it possesses a distinct **social heritage**, separate from the dominant culture, and if it transmits this heritage intergenerationally (from generation to generation) through the socialization of its children. Thus, for example, it might be agreed that the Amish (see Exhibit 21–1)—who adhere to their Old World ways, such as manner of dress and refusal to use electricity—constitute a subculture, but it is often debated whether there is a black subculture. There would seem to be almost as much diversity among blacks as among whites, and blacks apparently adhere to the dominant values and behaviors of the total culture of the United States.*

The richness of the subculture concept may be lost, however, if we adhere strictly to a formal definition of subcultures based on the transmission of a shared social heritage. For our purposes we will find it more valuable to use a relatively open definition, such as that of David Arnold, who defines subculture as,

> *. . . a subdivision of a national culture, composed of a combination of factorable social situations such as class status, ethnic background, regional and rural or urban residence, and religious affiliation, but forming in their combination a functioning unity which has an integrated impact on the participating individual.[1]*

This relaxed definition, which is more in line with the common use of the term, does not necessarily imply a consistent socialization experience from generation to generation. It allows us to speak of a black subculture or a Hispanic subculture to the extent that the component elements of that aggregate have some impact on individual behavior. Thus, whether there is a black heritage that is distinct and separate from the dominant U.S. heritage is debatable, but there does seem to be a black subculture to the extent that a combination of factors exists that leads to some consistent impact on the individual.

In this chapter we examine the effect of subcultures on consumer behavior. We then turn to an in-depth analysis of the two largest subcultures in the United States—black and Hispanic. We discuss the implications of subcultures for marketing strategy and marketing program design throughout.

SUBCULTURAL IMPACT ON CONSUMER BEHAVIOR

The impact of subcultures on consumer behavior may be quite direct or even *prescriptive*, in that it can define appropriate and inappropriate behavior. This is most often the case for religious subcultures (such as the Amish), who may have rules regarding the use of alcohol, foods, medical services, or clothing. Generally, however, subcultural influence works more indirectly by af-

EXHIBIT 21–1
THE AMISH SUBCULTURE: VALUES AND CONSUMPTION PATTERNS

The Amish are a religious subculture concentrated in Pennsylvania and Ohio. They have chosen to live their lives within a closed social system, and their faith dictates an adherence to stability rather than change. Here are some of their values and the consumer-behavior consequences.

Values	Consumption Patterns
Averse to change and progress	Mode of transportation still the horse-drawn carriage
	Old-fashioned wood or coal stoves used for cooking and heating
	No electricity, radio, television, or modern appliances
Self-sufficient	Grow their own food
	Make their own clothing
A strict code of church discipline (the ORDNUNG)	Code dictates clothing styles:
	• styles never change
	• hem lines are constant
	• women wear black bonnets and dark colored, full-length dresses with white aprons (if unmarried) or black aprons (if married)
	• men wear black suits and black hats in winter, straw hats in summer
Pacifist	Do not wear buttons on clothing because of their military origins

SOURCE: Based, in part, on James A. Warner and Donald M. Denlinger (1969), *The Gentle People: A Portrait of the Amish* (New York: Grossman).

fecting people's **values**—for example, the value placed on achievement or on charity—which then has a bearing on the goods and services that people consume.

The Jewish subculture is an example of how ethnicity affects values and, indirectly, consumer behavior. A particularly dominant value communicated by the Jewish subculture, according to Hirschman, is the need for achievement. This is transmitted intergenerationally to Jewish children by exposure to education and experiences which stimulate their upward mobility. Upon reaching adulthood, the individual will have internalized these values, and will then seek to advance and achieve on a self-motivated basis.

The thesis of the need for achievement was tested by Hirschman in research with Jewish and non-Jewish samples. She found the following distinguishable consumer behavior profiles, which are assumed to result from the value placed on achievement.

- Jews are exposed to more information sources during childhood (like magazines and special training and instruction) than non-Jews are.
- Jews are exposed to more mass-media information sources as adults than non-Jews are.
- Jews are more innovative (buy more new products) than non-Jews do.
- Jews exert more opinion leadership for new products than non-Jews do.[2]

These results are suggestive rather than definitive, but support the thesis that the values of a subculture may have an impact on consumer behavior.

Further research has found ethnic variations in leisure activities. For example, Protestant and Catholic consumers are more oriented toward solitary athletic activities than Jewish consumers are. In contrast, Jewish consumers prefer leisure activities providing more companionship or greater sensory stimulation (making love, eating) than Protestants or Catholics do. Jewish consumers are also more oriented to fun/pleasure activities.[3] Again, the research is exploratory but suggestive of distinguishable patterns of subcultural consumer behavior.

subcultural effects The general model that we shall use, as in Chapter 20, on social class, shows that subcultural identification leads to the acceptance of a set of values which influences lifestyle, which is reflected in media behavior, shopping behavior, and consumption behavior.

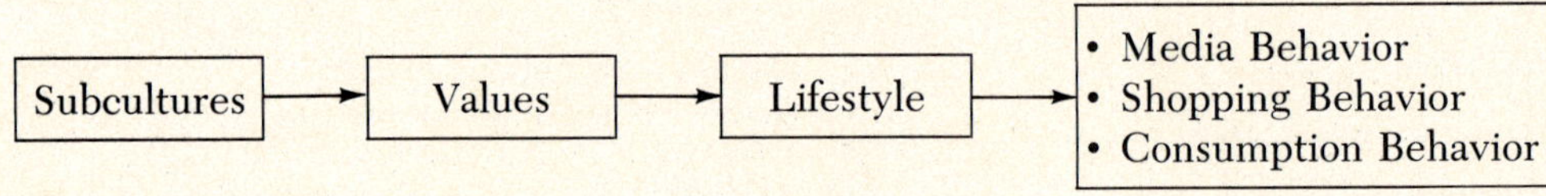

There is not, however, such a direct causal link from subculture to behavior, except in relatively extreme cases, such as the Amish subculture. Instead, most people belong to multiple subcultures—religious, racial, national, and social—and are subject to conflicting values. An individual's behavior is ultimately a compromise among the total set of values to which he or she is exposed, as well as a function of personality and other psychological variables.

Subcultures also have different *levels of impact* for an individual. The degree of influence is a function of the individual's strength of identification and interaction with a particular subculture. In fact, we refer to *strong ties* when the person has a high level of identification with a subculture, and *weak ties* when identification and interaction are low. For some people, being Catholic may be a strong tie and have a major bearing on the conduct of one's life, whereas for other Catholics, the religious affiliation may be a weak tie and of little consequence.

strong ties/weak ties

Of course, by their very nature some religions are more demanding than others, requiring a strong tie if membership is to be maintained. It is in these cases that the flow from values to behavior is most direct. The Mormon religion and fundamentalist Christian sects, for example, tend to demand a strong tie and acceptance of a unique set of values—with direct consequences for consumption. Mormons, for example, abstain from alcohol and coffee. Christian Scientists do not believe in the value of medicines or physicians.

The impact of a subculture on consumer behavior should be assessed not only for members of that subculture but also for the total population. For example, many subcultural products, like Mexican food or kosher wine, diffuse to the total population. Exhibit 21–2 suggests four separate categories of subcultural impact and marketing strategies.

EXHIBIT 21–2
SUBCULTURAL IMPACT AND MARKETING STRATEGIES

		PRODUCT	
		Subcultural	**Non-Subcultural**
POPULATION SEGMENT	**Subcultural**	**Specialized** 1 | 3 **Idiosyncratic** Specialized subcultural products marketed to a particular subculture	Mass-market products directed to a particular subculture
	Non-Subcultural	**Diffused** 2 | 4 **Mass Market** Subcultural products that diffused beyond the original subculture	Mass-market products marketed to the total population

Specialized

This category includes specialized subcultural products and services to be marketed to members of a particular subculture. Examples are cosmetics for blacks, kosher foods for Jews, religious bookstores for members of certain denominations, or specialized services for the aged subculture.

Some products may be unique to a subculture, meeting the particular

EXHIBIT 21–3
CLOTHING ARTIFACTS OF THE "PREPPY" SUBCULTURE

SOURCE: *Preppy Handbook* (1980), Lisa Birnbach, illustration by Oliver Williams (New York: Workman), pp. 98–99.

needs of that market segment. These needs may arise from physiological variables—complexion, hair, and so forth—or symbolic variables—religious symbols and artifacts or peer group symbols, such as clothing. The *Preppy Handbook*, for example, lightheartedly suggests a unique manner of dressing for the individual who identifies with the "preppy" subculture (see Exhibit 21–3).

The marketing implications are quite clear. There may be opportunities to sell a unique inventory of products and services to members of certain subcultures.

Diffused

This category includes subcultural products that are marketed beyond the original subculture. Many products that at one time are unique to a subculture diffuse beyond the subculture to other segments of the population. Recognizing the wider appeal of these products can yield the marketer a key opportunity. The following are some examples of subcultural services or products that are successfully marketed beyond the subculture.

- Chinese cuisine, woks
- Mexican restaurants
- Manischewitz wine (originally targeted to Jews and now sold mainly to nonJews—see Exhibit 21–4).

Idiosyncratic

This category includes mass-market products that are directed to particular subcultures. There are three possible scenarios here.

In the first scenario a firm with a mass-market product, such as Pepsi, also runs *subcultural advertising*—in black or Spanish-language media, for example. The basic assumption is that by appealing directly to a subculture, the brand will gain greater acceptance and achieve a higher market share in that subculture. Perhaps because of such subcultural emphasis, Colgate toothpaste, for example, has a much higher market share among Hispanics than it has for the total population.

In the second scenario a mass-marketed product has higher usage within a particular subculture even without any deliberate marketing effort to create that higher usage. Later in this chapter we suggest that black consumers use proportionately more of some products, such as rice and evaporated milk, than whites. Can such differences be explained in terms of subcultural values and lifestyle, or are they just random occurrences? Is there anything about being black that encourages higher levels of consumption of evaporated milk? We would not think so and instead would attribute this difference to an income-level effect or some other such factor.

Similarly, an individual brand may find that it has a higher market share among members of a particular subculture. For example, Kool cigarettes sell better to blacks than to whites. Again, is there any *subcultural* reason for this phenomenon or is this mainly an accidental variation? It may be that the Kool advertising campaigns struck a more resonant chord among blacks than whites. To our knowledge, however, the company was not seeking to gain greater acceptance among blacks. Of course, when marketers find that a product has higher use in a particular subculture, they may then wish to direct separate campaigns to that subculture in order to reinforce this pattern, as Kool subsequently has done.

In the third scenario a brand of mass-market product or service is explicitly marketed to a subculture. For example, Jewel Foods Stores in the Chicago

EXHIBIT 21–4
A SUBCULTURAL PRODUCT THAT HAS DIFFUSED BEYOND THE ORIGINAL SUBCULTURE

"Everything in this country is sweet," says Chet Moss heatedly. "Your baby food is sweet. Chocolate ice cream is sweet. You bring people up like that and then *you* (he points accusingly at the *Forbes* reporter) want them to drink a dry white wine? Forget about it."

As head of operations at about $60 million (sales) Monarch Wine Co., Inc., Brooklyn-based makers of sweet Manischewitz kosher wines, Moss is not exactly an unbiased observer. . . . Our question about how it was able to do that when Americans were apparently switching to dry white wines has obviously struck a raw nerve. From all sides, the owner-managers of Monarch—Leo Star, president; Meyer Robinson, general manager; Marshall Goldberg, chairman of the management committee; Cliff Adelson, sales director; and operations chief Moss—respond by going on the offensive.

"The truth of the matter is that if you're in an upward-mobility group, it is chic to be dry," Adelson concedes in the deep, hoarse voice of a Damon Runyon character. "You're not going to go to J. G. Melon's (a bistro on New York's Upper East Side) and order sweet wine. But you and your group represent *zilch* population-wise!"

"You tell me that people drink dry?" asks Goldberg socratically. "What is the largest-selling imported wine in the United States? Did you ever taste Lambrusco? Sweet, right? Do you know how many cases of that they sell? Would you believe 19 million cases a year?"

On goes the argument: people standing, shouting across the table, interrupting, good-naturedly haranguing the *Forbes* reporter on a topic of vital, visceral interest to Monarch. The interview, barely ten minutes old, has degenerated into something out of a Marx Brothers movie, with several of the firm's rabbis, bewildered by all the commotion, playing walk-on parts. . . .

. . . Last year Monarch (it licenses the name "Manischewitz" from the B.

area once converted a number of their stores in black neighborhoods, calling them *Lucky Star* stores. The plan was to appeal more directly to blacks by advertising, by the use of all-black employees, and by modifying the store design in line with black color preferences. This experiment, however, failed. Soul Brothers Scotch whisky, another example of directing a mass-market product explicitly to blacks, also met with minimal acceptance.

The merits of subcultural brands or stores are not very obvious to consumers, unless there is a unique subcultural consumption pattern, as for cosmetics. Otherwise, members of all subcultures want the same benefits: clean supermarkets, for example, that are well stocked with good meats and produce and that have good service; or good-tasting Scotch with lots of status attached. Furthermore, there may even be a resentment if subcultural brands or stores are perceived as not as good as those for the mass market.

Manischewitz kosher food company) shipped over 13 million gallons of wine, every drop of it prepared under the most stringent rabbinical supervision (*kasbruth*) and certified to be kosher for Passover. Today Monarch is the ninth-largest winery in the U.S. . . .

. . . The image of the Manischewitz wine brand, according to advertising director Hal Balk, is that of "a stodgy, ethnic sweet wine for old Jewish folks." At one time there was some truth to that image. Years ago Monarch's typical customer was the head of a Jewish household who bought the wine for Passover. . . .

. . . Monarch's clientele is no longer predominantly Jewish. In fact, over 85% of sales are to non-Jews. Manischewitz wines are exported to 30 countries, in many of which Jews constitute a miniscule minority. For years Manischewitz has been the number one imported wine in Puerto Rico, outselling fine Spanish wines 2-to-1. The day *Forbes* visited Monarch, two containers were being loaded aboard a ship bound for the Republic of Cameroon. Meyer Robinson delights in reading letters sent by satisfied Gentile customers from, for example, Moose Jaw, Saskatchewan. "I don't have to tell you that there probably aren't many of our Jewish brethren up there in Moose Jaw," he observes.

In fact, Monarch's clientele is no longer predominantly white: 60% of sales are to blacks. According to a survey conducted for the company by Simmons, a syndicated national survey that provides consumer information, the typical Manischewitz wine drinker today is black, is a blue-collar worker, is in the lower-middle income bracket and lives in a large city. . . . "So you can't just think of a bunch of people sitting around the Passover seder table (as your image of the wine)," says Goldberg.

SOURCE: From Steven Flax (1981), "Let Them Keep Laughing," *Forbes* (Sept. 28), pp. 84–85.

Mass Market

This category includes mass-market products marketed to the total population. This final strategy obviously lacks any subcultural considerations. In general, however, subcultures must be taken into account in the design of marketing programs—especially the black subculture (some 11.5 percent of the population) and the Hispanic subculture (some 6.4 percent of the population). At a minimum, it must be determined whether the media mix for advertising should include black and Hispanic media in the total plan. Black or Hispanic advertising executions (using black or Hispanic models in the advertising or using Spanish language) should also be considered.

THE BLACK AND HISPANIC SUBCULTURES

The two largest subcultures in the United States are black and Hispanic. These subcultures must be considered in the design of almost all marketing programs because of their size and high rate of population growth.

Numerous other bases for subcultural segmentation exist, since the United States is rich in its diversity. Most other countries are much more homogeneous on such factors as race, national origin, and religion. This diversity of subcultures in the United States offers marketing opportunities for products and services tailored to specialized subcultural needs. Examples of subcultural segmentation by age and life cycle are discussed in Chapter 18, on family behavior, and by region in Chapter 14, on demographics and values. In the remainder of this chapter, we will focus on the black and Hispanic subcultures.

Demographic Profiles

The black population constitutes 11.7 percent of the total population of the United States and is projected to reach 12.2 percent by 1990; the Hispanic population is 6.4 percent of the total and is projected to grow to 7.0 percent by 1990. Both subcultures are young, with median ages considerably below that of the white population, and both subcultures have average family sizes considerably larger than that of the white population (see Exhibit 21–5).

Blacks and especially Hispanics are more likely to live in metropolitan areas than whites are. Education levels are highest for whites, followed by blacks, and then Hispanics. Median family income is highest among whites, followed by Hispanics, and then blacks. Exhibit 21–5 provides details on these variables.

A Note on Hispanics

There is considerable debate as to the size and definition of the **Hispanic subculture** in the United States. Our data (Exhibit 21–5) are based on Census reports, in which Hispanics are those who classified themselves as of Spanish origin. There are also some Hispanics who are black. Some estimates place the size of the Hispanic subculture at over 20 million (in contrast with the Census estimate of 14.6 million), or an increase to 8.5 percent of the total population.[4] The larger estimate compensates for underrepresentation of illegal Hispanic aliens in the Census.

EXHIBIT 21–5

DEMOGRAPHIC PROFILES OF MAJOR SUBCULTURES IN THE UNITED STATES: 1980 CENSUS

Characteristics	Subculture		
	Blacks	**Hispanics**[a]	**Whites**
Population[b]	26.5 million	14.6 million	188.3 million
Population Percent: 1980	11.7%	6.4 %	83.1%
Projected Population Percent: 1990[c]	12.2%	7.0%	80.8%
Median Age[b]	24.9 years	23.2 years	31.3 years
Average Family Size[d]	3.8	3.9	3.3
% of Population in Metropolitan Areas[e]	75.1%	85.3%	65.0%
Median Education[f] (years of school completed by those 18 and over)	12.1	11.3	12.5
Median Family Income[g]	$12,618	$14,711	$20,840

[a]Hispanics in the 1980 Census are those who classified themselves in one of the Spanish-origin categories—*Mexican, Puerto Rican, Cuban,* or *Other Spanish/Hispanic.* Hispanics in the 1970 Census classified themselves as *White* in 93 percent of cases, but in the 1980 Census, only 56 percent reported their race as *White* and 40 percent reported *Other.*

[b]Total U.S. population for 1980 is reported at 226.5 million. Totals here are larger since Hispanics are also included in *White* and *Black* categories. U.S. Bureau of the Census (1981), *1980 Census of Population, Supplementary Reports,* PC 80-S1-1, "Age, Sex, Race, and Spanish Origin of the Population by Regions, Divisions, and States: 1980," (Washington, D.C.: GPO), p. 3.

[c]Reid T. Reynolds, Bryant Robey, and Cheryl Russell (1980), "Demographics of the 1980s," *American Demographics,* 2 (Jan.), pp. 16–17.

[d]U.S. Bureau of the Census (1979), *Current Population Reports,* Series P-20, No. 340, "Household and Family Characteristics: March 1978," (Washington, D.C.: GPO), pp. 10–13.

[e]U.S. Bureau of the Census (1979), pp. 53–59.

[f]U.S. Bureau of the Census (1980), *Current Population Reports,* Series P-20, No. 356, "Educational Attainment in the United States: March 1978 and 1979, (Washington, D.C.: GPO), pp. 24–27.

[g]U.S. Bureau of the Census (1980), *Provisional Estimates of Social, Economic and Housing Characteristics: 1980,* PHC80-S1-1 (Washington, D.C.: GPO), p. 36.

The Hispanic population in the United States is actually drawn from a number of distinct heritages. The major countries of origin are Mexico (some 60 percent of U.S. Hispanics), Puerto Rico (some 15 percent), and Cuba (some 6 percent). A number of other countries account for the remainder of our Hispanic population.[5] Hispanics who immigrated to the United States from Latin America and the Caribbean represented 36 percent of all immigrants in the period 1951–77, replacing Europeans as the most prominent group.[6] The U.S. Hispanic population is the fifth largest Spanish-speaking population in the world, ahead of those in such countries as Peru, Venezuela, and Chile.[7]

The Hispanic subculture in the U.S. has a marked regional profile. Some 60 percent of Hispanics are concentrated in the Southwest (Arizona, New Mexico, and Texas) and in California. However, the top five metropolitan markets are (1) New York—Puerto Rican heritage, (2) Los Angeles—Mexican heritage, (3) San Antonio—Mexican heritage, (4) Miami—Cuban and Central American heritage, and (5) San Francisco—Mexican heritage.

Subcultural Heterogeneity

A major caveat in any discussion of subcultures is that none of them is characterized by overall uniformity. Neither the black nor the Hispanic subculture, for example, is homogeneous in values and lifestyles.

There is perhaps as much diversity in the black as in the white subcultures. People are young or old, affluent or poor, from large families or small, and educated or uneducated. Their values, lifestyles, and consumer-behavior patterns reflect their life situation. Older blacks are likely to have values different from younger blacks, and blacks who have achieved managerial and professional status find the lower-class black value system to be as alien as do their white counterparts. As with other markets, then, it is necessary to *segment* the black market—rather than to group the 26.5 million people of the subculture into a single market that is not uniform or homogeneous.

The large number of countries of origin of the Hispanic subculture suggests considerable heterogeneity, raising the question of whether these subgroups can be appealed to in the same manner. The National Association of Spanish Broadcasters adheres to the view (perhaps self-serving) that the similarities far outweigh the differences.

> *. . . U.S. Hispanics share basic cultural values and traditions that have much more to do with being Hispanic than with being from any single Hispanic country. The U.S. Hispanic population embraces a close family orientation, the extended family not being uncommon. As an entity, U.S. Hispanics also adhere to a strong Catholic tradition as one of their most salient cultural characteristics. These shared cultural traits have much greater impact on shaping behavior, attitudes and perceptions than the individual history of a specific country of origin.*[8]

In a review of the Hispanic market, it is suggested by the J. Walter Thompson Advertising Agency that there is a Spanish "character."

All Spanish speaking Americans, of any ethnic group, have in common some basic traits: a conservative nature, close family ties and relationships, a high ethnic awareness, a strong Roman Catholic religious identification, great regard for self sufficiency, the "Work" ethic, reliance on personal trust and loyalty to person or institution, and language.[9]

Whether such a character is uniform across the Mexican, Puerto Rican, and Cuban populations is debatable but worth investigating. The J. Walter Thompson report further elaborates: "The lines of national/ethnic origin today are not as sharply drawn as they once were. What is of a greater importance is the individual's economic status."

Ethnicity Versus Income

A further caveat is the importance of not confounding ethnicity and income. For example, because of the lower overall income level of the black population, it is easy to attribute characteristics to blacks that are actually attributable to all low-income people—whether black, white, or Hispanic.

The confounding of race and income is a common mistake. The key question here is whether a particular observed pattern is due to being, for example, black or simply due to income. If it is reported that blacks consume more canned beans than whites, for example, it is logical to ask whether this has anything to do with being black or whether it is the effect of low income, since black family income is lower than white. We must, then, *control for income* if we want to know whether blacks consume any more canned beans than whites. If we look at blacks with an income level of, say, $10,000 and whites with the same income level, is there any difference in the consumption of beans? When analysts control for income, many supposed black and white consumption differences either disappear or are much less pronounced than originally thought.

SUBCULTURAL MOTIVATIONS

A basic dichotomy in subcultural motivations is the preference for **cultural integration** versus the preference for **cultural distinctiveness.** How much, for example, do blacks or Hispanics desire assimilation and integration compared with how much they desire a separate identity and maintenance of a distinct social heritage? The perspective on subcultural motivations has changed in the past fifteen years, from an emphasis on cultural integration to an emphasis on cultural distinctiveness. This has been reflected particularly in the literature on the motivations of black consumers.

The dominant view of the consumer behavior of blacks in the 1960s and early 1970s was that it was based on a desire for cultural integration. It was assumed that blacks wanted to be like whites and that they consumed in a manner which reflected a desire for assimilation into the total culture. One observer, for example, stated that blacks "attempt to surround themselves with symbols of whiteness."[10] Similarly, research by Bauer and Cunningham stressed that blacks are "fighting to attain full membership in American society," and that they use consumption of a socially visible nature as a means of showing that they have arrived. In particular, when Bauer and Cunningham divided blacks into *strivers* and *nonstrivers* (that is, according to "desire to get ahead"), they found that the strivers were more likely to accept values that are characteristic of the white community. Furthermore, the consumer behavior of black strivers was closer to that of whites.[11]

This desired-assimilation view assumes an essentially negative black self-identity and a preference for identification with whiteness. Recent research on black self-esteem, however, shows that it is not lower than white self-esteem.[12] We obviously need to update our conceptions of the motivations that drive black consumers. The desired-assimilation viewpoint may still represent the motivations of some black consumers, but certainly not of all. It is a limited (if not biased) viewpoint.

The alternative view of consumer motivation in the black subculture is that it is based on a preference for cultural distinctiveness. Blauner suggests the following change in black perspective.

> *During the 1960s the Black communities of the nation became increasingly concerned with their culture. Afro-Americans aggressively substituted their own ethnic alternatives for dominant standards of beauty, behavior and value, many of which were rejected as 'white'. . . . Although the emphasis on blackness was largely a project of the younger generation, it pervaded the group as a whole and affected the entire society.*[13]

The preference for cultural distinctiveness seems to vary by subculture and by segment within the subculture. The Hispanic subculture, for example, must be considered in terms of its national components, such as Mexican-Americans, Puerto Ricans, and Cuban-Americans. Within each component there is variation on preference for cultural distinctiveness. The Mexican-American subculture, for example, is characterized by a large segment that prefers to be called "Chicano" and has a high need for cultural identity.[14] Within the Jewish subculture, there is a significant percentage of people who are interested in being defined as Jewish and who want to be communicated to as Jews via Jewish media.[15]

Preferences for cultural integration and for distinctiveness both exist within subcultures. Some segments of a subculture may desire assimilation into the general culture, and some may prefer separatism. Yet, both integration and distinctiveness may occur simultaneously within a segment. People may seek integration in some areas and distinctiveness in others. The two motivations should not be thought of as mutually exclusive.

Cultural Exclusion

Consumer behavior may be affected also by **cultural exclusion**—not so much the desire for distinctiveness but the inability to achieve integration. The literature on the **subculture of poverty** as popularized by Oscar Lewis is particularly relevant here.[16] He proposed that blacks, Hispanics, and other economically disadvantaged groups are trapped by their environment, lacking the opportunity to break out and to move upward socially.

This perspective underlies research that suggested that the **poor pay more** for goods and services. Exhibit 21–6 presents an abstract of David Caplovitz's classic work on the ghetto marketplace based on his research in Spanish Harlem. Caplovitz presented compelling evidence that the poor were trapped by their lack of mobility and were exploited by the inner-city merchants and peddlers who charged more for goods and services than residents in suburban (mainly white) areas were paying.[17] Further research has supported many of Caplovitz's findings, although the poor do not always pay more since many supermarkets maintain a single pricing policy, and many poor people are mobile and able to reach mass-distribution outlets.[18]

A basic dilemma is that it costs merchants more to do business in ghetto areas, placing upward pressures on prices.[19] Additionally, such areas are infrequently served by modern supermarkets and mass merchandisers. As Sturdivant has noted,

> *One of the cruelest ironies of our economic system is that the disadvantaged are generally served by the least efficient segments of the business community. The spacious, well-stocked, and efficiently managed stores of America's highly advanced distribution system are rarely present in the ghetto. . . . Instead their shopping districts are dotted with small, inefficient 'mom and pop' establishments. . . .*[20]

The thesis of the subculture of poverty raises the basic question of whether consumer-behavior patterns are a function of the *environment* (in this case, the environment of the poverty subculture) or whether they are a function of *income* (and would change if higher income were achieved). Lewis believes that the subculture of poverty is self-perpetuating.

> *Once it comes into existence it tends to perpetuate itself from generation to generation because of its effect on the children. By the time slum children are age six or seven they have usually absorbed the basic values and attitudes of their subculture and are not psychologically geared to take advantage of changing conditions or increased opportunities which may occur in their lifetime.*[21]

This view suggests that poverty is more than a state of income deprivation and represents an intergenerational subculture with its own values and lifestyle. In order to understand the consumer-behavior patterns of the poor, it would be necessary to study these patterns from the subcultural perspective.

EXHIBIT 21–6
THE GHETTO MARKETPLACE

THE MERCHANT AND THE LOW-INCOME CONSUMER

The dilemma of the low-income consumer lies in these facts. He is trained by society (and his position in it) to want the symbols and appurtenances of the "good life" at the same time that he lacks the means needed to fulfill these socially induced wants. People with small incomes lack not only the ready cash for consuming major durables but are also poorly qualified for that growing substitute for available cash—credit. Their low income, their negligible savings, their job insecurity all contribute to their being poor credit risks. . . .

Not having enough cash and credit would seem to create a sufficient problem for low-income consumers. But they have other limitations as well. They tend to lack the information and training needed to be effective consumers in a bureaucratic society. Partly because of their limited education and partly because as migrants from more traditional societies they are unfamiliar with urban culture, they are not apt to follow the announcements of sales in the newspapers, to engage in comparative shopping, to know their way around the major department stores and bargain centers, to know how to evaluate the advice of salesmen—practices necessary for some degree of sophistication in the realm of consumption. . . .

The key to the marketing system in low-income areas lies in special adaptations of the institution of credit. The many merchants who locate in these areas and find it profitable to do so are prepared to offer credit in spite of the high risks involved. Moreover, their credit is tailored to the particular needs of the low-income consumer. All kinds of durable goods can be obtained in this market at terms not too different from the slogan, "a dollar down, a dollar a week." The consumer can buy furniture, a TV set, a stereophonic phonograph, . . . if not for a dollar a week then for only a few dollars a week. In practically every one of these stores, the availability of "easy credit" is announced to the customer in both English and Spanish by large signs in the windows and sometimes by neon signs over the doorways. . . .

Although credit charges are now regulated by law, no law regulates the merchant's markup on his goods. East Harlem is known to the merchants of furniture and appliances in New York City as the area in which pricing is done by "numbers." We first heard of the "number" system from a woman who had been employed as a bookkeeper in such a store. She illustrated a "one number" item by writing down a hypothetical wholesale price and then adding the same figure to it, a 100 per cent markup. Her frequent references to "two number" and "three number" prices indicated that prices are never less than "one number," and are often more.

The system of pricing in the low-income market differs from that in the bureaucratic market of the downtown stores in another respect: in East Harlem there are hardly any "one price" stores. In keeping with a multi-price policy, price tags are conspicuously absent from the merchandise. The customer has to ask, "how much?," and the answer he gets will depend on several things. If the merchant considers him a poor risk, if he thinks the customer is naive, or if the customer was referred to him by another merchant or a peddler to whom he must pay a commission, the price will be higher. . . .

As for the merchandise sold in these stores, the interviewers noticed that the furniture on display was of obviously poor quality. Most of all, they were struck by the absence of well-known brands of appliances in most of the stores. . . . This results in the irony that the people who can least afford the goods they buy are required to pay high prices relative to quality, thus receiving a comparatively low return for their consumer dollar. . . .

But although the merchants are ready to exploit the naivete of their traditionalistic customers, it is important to point out that they also cater to the customer's traditionalism. As a result of the heavy influx of Puerto Ricans into the area, many of these stores now employ Puerto Rican salesmen. The customers who enter these stores need not be concerned about possible embarrassment because of their broken English or their poor dress. On the contrary, these merchants are adept at making the customer feel at ease, as a personal experience will testify.

> *Visiting the area and stopping occasionally to read the ads in the windows, I happened to pause before an appliance store. A salesman promptly emerged and said, "I know, I bet you're looking for a nice TV set. Come inside—we've got lots of nice ones." Finding myself thrust into the role of customer, I followed him into the store and listened to his sales pitch. Part way through his talk, he asked my name. I hesitated a moment and then provided him with a fictitious last name, at which point he said, "No, no—no last names. What's your first name? . . . Ah, Dave; I'm Irv. We only care about first names here." When I was ready to leave after making some excuse about having to think things over, he handed me his card. Like most business cards of employees, this one had the name and address of the enterprise in large type and in small type the name of the salesman. But instead of his full name, there appeared only the amiable, "Irv."*

The merchant starts from the premise that most of his customers are honest people who intend to pay but have difficulty managing their money. Missed payments are seen as more often due to poor management and to emergencies than to dishonesty. The merchants anticipate that their customers will miss some payments and they rely on informal controls to insure that payments are eventually made. . . . Should the customer miss an occasional payment or should he be short on another, the merchant considers this a normal part of his business. . . .

In sum, a fairly intricate system of sales-and-credit has evolved in response to the distinctive situation of the low-income consumer and the local merchant. It is a system heavily slanted in the direction of a traditional economy in which informal, personal ties play a major part in the transaction. . . .

The system is not only different from the larger, more formal economy; in some respects it is a "deviant" system in which practices that violate prevailing moral standards are commonplace. . . . The basic function of the low-income marketing system is to provide consumer goods to people who fail to meet the requirements of the more legitimate, bureaucratic market, or who choose to exclude themselves from the larger market because they do not feel comfortable in it. . . .

SOURCE: From David Caplovitz (1967), *The Poor Pay More* (New York: Free Press), pp. 12–30.

By contrast, of course, many authors believe that the poor do not constitute a self-perpetuating subculture and that it is a lack of income that determines consumer-behavior patterns. If income were increased, then consumer-behavior patterns would also change. In fact, Lewis himself was not very willing to posit that a subculture of poverty exists in the United States (most of his work was done in Puerto Rico and Cuba), because of our advanced technology, high literacy rates, pervasive mass media, and high aspiration levels.

Other researchers, such as Rossi and Blum, have directly disputed the idea of a poverty subculture.

> *There is little firm evidence for the existence of a "culture of poverty" which marks off the very poor as distinctively different from SES (socio-economic status) levels immediately above them. The poor appear to be quantitatively rather than qualitatively different.*[22]

These researchers and others, such as Valentine, see the behavior of the poor as an adaptation to existing conditions, and not the result of the transmission of a set of values and a poverty heritage.[23] This position is also taken by Liebow in his analysis of street-corner life among lower-class black males. His overall conclusion is that,

> *The street-corner man does not appear as a carrier of an independent cultural tradition. His behavior appears not so much as a way of realizing the distinctive goals and values of his own subculture, or conforming to its models, but rather as his way of trying to achieve many of the goals and values of the larger society, of failing to do this, and of concealing his failure from others and from himself as best he can.*[24]

As such, Liebow would argue that there is not a self-perpetuating subculture of poverty nor a separate set of values divergent from the mainstream of society.

No single theory will account for the values and motivations of an entire subculture—especially subcultures as large and diversified as the black or Hispanic populations in the United States. The diversity within subcultures by demographic, personality, and attitudinal factors suggests the inappropriateness of any one conception of consumer motivation.

SUBCULTURAL CONSUMPTION PATTERNS

We now turn to the effects of subcultures on consumer behavior. Subcultural consumption has been examined mainly for blacks and, to a lesser extent, for Hispanics. Other subcultures have not received much attention in the consumer-behavior literature, with the exception of some research on the Jewish subculture.[25] The following discussion, therefore, is focused to a large extent on the black subculture.

Usage of Product Categories

At the product-category level, the differences between the consumption patterns of whites and nonwhites are small. Exhibit 21–7 shows that nonwhites consume slightly more in some product categories and slightly less in others, but that the differences are slight—a maximum of 3.4 percent. The exhibit suggests, for example, that nonwhites consume slightly more food, alcohol, tobacco, clothing, accessories, jewelry, and housing, but slightly less in transportation, medical care, and personal business than whites.

The limited range of differences leads to the conclusion that the similarities between white and nonwhite consumption patterns far outweigh the differences. For broad product categories, race would not seem to be a significant predictive factor.

EXHIBIT 21–7
COMPARISON OF WHITE AND NONWHITE EXPENDITURES, 1973

Overspending[a]—Nonwhite More Than White	
Food, alcohol, and tobacco	3.4%
Clothing, accessories, and jewelry	2.3%
Housing	1.2%
Personal	0.5%
Household operation	0.3%
Total overspending	7.7%
Underspending[a]—Nonwhite Less Than White	
Transportation	−3.3%
Medical care expenses	−1.9%
Personal business	−1.3%
Recreation	−0.7%
Private education	−0.5%
Total underspending	−7.7%

[a]The terms *overspend* and *underspend* are not intended as an evaluation but are used for comparing nonwhite to white spending. The term *white* describes the members of the Caucasoid division of mankind; the term *nonwhite* describes persons of all races other than white. In the United States, 90% of the nonwhite population is black.

SOURCE: Based on Frederick D. Sturdivant (1981), "Minority Markets and Subcultural Analysis," in *Perspectives of Consumer Behavior*, ed. Harold H. Kassarjian and Thomas S. Robertson, 3rd ed. (Glenview, Ill.: Scott, Foresman), p. 437.

Usage Within Product Categories

Consumption of products within categories sometimes differs across subcultures. Exhibit 21–8, for example, is a breakdown of the product category of groceries, showing products that blacks and Hispanics use heavily and those that they use lightly. Blacks, for example, are heavy users of rice and evaporated milk but light users of dishwashing detergent and salad dressing. Hispanics are heavy users of fruit nectar, malt liquor, and baby food, but light users of dog food and diet soft drinks. It is important to note, however, that these data do not control for income; some of the patterns may be associated primarily with lower average income rather than with subculture. Furthermore, for all grocery products the similarities across subcultures are greater than the differences.

Brand Preferences

For the individual marketing manager, a key question is whether there are subcultural differences among brand preferences. For example, Kool cigarettes has a higher market share among blacks (14.2 percent) than among whites (3.8 percent).[26] Colgate toothpaste has a 72 percent share of the Hispanic market in New York versus a 32 percent share of the nonHispanic market—perhaps because it has advertised in Spanish media.[27]

The marketing manager must know the relative share of his or her brand across subcultures before attempting to increase the brand's share in multiple subcultures. To do so, it is important to consider subcultural media and the possibility of separate advertising appeals. Exhibit 21–9, for example, shows the subcultural market shares for instant-coffee brands in New York City. The major differences suggest the need to think subculturally in building total market share.

Brand Loyalty

There is some evidence that both black and Hispanic consumers favor national brands more than do white consumers. Blacks and Hispanics are also more brand loyal than whites. These conclusions were developed for the black subculture in the 1970s[28] but have been reaffirmed for both the black and Hispanic subcultures in the 1980s.[29] The validity of these conclusions, however, depends considerably on the segment within the subculture and the particular product category being considered.

Innovativeness

Level of innovativeness (new-product purchases) may vary by subculture as a function of subcultural interests. For example, research by Dalrymple, Robertson, and Yoshino found that blacks were more innovative for new clothes,

EXHIBIT 21–8
BLACK AND HISPANIC GROCERY-PRODUCT CONSUMPTION

Products with Heavy Usage Among Blacks		Products with Light Usage Among Blacks	
Product	Use Index	Product	Use Index
Rice and rice dinners	215	Dishwashing detergent	57
Evaporated milk	187	Salad dressing and mayonnaise	80
All-purpose flour	153	Prepared soups	82
Salad and cooking oils	140	Regular coffee	86
Toilet soaps	126	Prepared puddings	87
Strained baby foods	117	Canned tuna	87
Tomato paste	116	Dry cereals	87
Tea bags	115	Cake mixes	89
Catsup	111	Table syrups	92
Paper towels	108	Frozen prepared dinners	94
Instant tea	105	Foil and plastic wraps	95

Products with Heavy Usage Among Hispanics		Products with Light Usage Among Hispanics	
Product	Use Index	Product	Use Index
Canned spaghetti	456	Dog food	40
Fruit nectar	376	Diet soft drinks	41
Malt liquor	226	Frozen vegetables	56
Baby food	203	Decaffeinated coffee	60
Powdered drinks	189	Salad dressing	61
Beer	134	Cat food	72
Soft drinks	127	Yogurt	77
Ground coffee	121	Tuna	83
Tomato paste	118	Lunch meats	85
White bread	112	Frozen dinners	86

SOURCES: Data for blacks are based on A. C. Nielsen Co., in Thayer C. Taylor (1977), "Blacks: Two Distinct Markets in One," in *Sales and Marketing Management* (Dec. 12), p. 35. Data on Hispanics are for New York and are based on (1980), *U.S. Hispanics—A Market Profile*, ed. Antonio Guernico (New York: National Association of Spanish Broadcasters and Strategy Research Corporation), pp. 102–3.

whites for new food products, and Japanese-Americans for new appliances.[30] Bauer and Cunningham also have found that blacks are more innovative for new clothing styles.[31] Recent research by Hirschman has suggested that the characteristics of black and of white innovators are somewhat different. For example, white innovators participate more in formal groups and organized social activities.[32]

Family Decision-Making

Reflective of the somewhat more matriarchal structure of the black family, some research has suggested that females are likely to be more dominant in purchase decisions in black families than in white families.[33] Further research is necessary to sort out the differences between families with a female head of household (more prevalent in black families) and families with both a husband and wife present. Family-decision processes will obviously vary between such families. The somewhat more patriarchal structure of the Hispanic family, in contrast, suggests the possibility that Hispanic males are more dominant in family purchase decisions than are males in nonHispanic white families. No evidence has been collected to support such a hypothesis, however.

EXHIBIT 21–9

SUBCULTURAL MARKET SHARES FOR INSTANT COFFEE IN NEW YORK CITY

	Percent of Homes with Each Brand[a]			
	Total Market	Black	Hispanic	Jewish
Maxwell House	28.5%	20.1%	14.5%	56.0%
Sanka	26.3	19.6	7.2	50.5
Taster's Choice	10.5	7.5	1.7	13.3
Nescafé	8.6	6.6	2.1	12.4
Maxim	7.0	3.4	0.9	17.4
Brim	5.7	1.4	1.3	13.5
Folgers	3.4	2.0	2.1	3.9
Yuban	3.4	0	0.4	13.3
Bustelo	2.0	0	11.1	0

[a]Only the major brands are shown, so the table totals are not 100%. Data are for Jan.–Feb., 1982.

SOURCE: Joseph Jacobs Organization, Inc. (1982), Jan.–Feb., New York.

REACHING SUBCULTURES: THE ROLE OF MEDIA

Marketers are very interested in ways of reaching different subcultures. In particular, they want to know the role of specialized media aimed exclusively at particular subcultures.

For most products the best way to reach a subculture is through advertising in the mass media, since these media are attended to across almost all subcultures. Specialized subcultural media may then be used to supplement mass media and to achieve greater advertising coverage. Specialized media may also be used to convey a slightly different message or a message more compatible with subcultural interests and preferences. Blacks may, for example, prefer black models and symbols; Hispanics may prefer Hispanic models and symbols. Examples of advertisements directed to blacks using *Ebony* magazine and to Hispanics using *Miami Mensual* magazine are shown in Exhibit 21–10 for Pontiac. The advertising message is the same but the models

EXHIBIT 21–10
SUBCULTURAL EXECUTIONS OF AN ADVERTISING CAMPAIGN TO REACH BLACKS AND HISPANICS

and sports represented are different: football, to appeal to blacks, and soccer, to appeal to Hispanics.

The Hispanic subculture, in particular, may require more specialized advertising efforts because of its language. Spanish is spoken in over 80 percent of Hispanic households. Hispanics use Spanish-language media considerably more, for example, than blacks use black media—undoubtedly because of the Spanish-language preference of many Hispanics. The relative concentration of Hispanics in a limited number of metropolitan areas and the concordant concentration of Spanish media in these areas leads to an efficient means of reaching Hispanics.[34]

Mass media and mass-media advertising, however, may not adequately *represent* American subcultures, particularly blacks and Hispanics. Television programming underrepresents ethnic subcultures.[35] Similarly, mass-media advertising underrepresents the black subculture in terms of the percentage of black actors used. According to Kassarjian blacks now appear more often in advertising, and in more favorable roles than they once did, but still not in proportion to their population percentage.[36]

Marketers are also interested in both black and white reaction to integrated advertising. It appears that integrated advertising is effective in appealing to both blacks and whites. For example, early research on this question by Barban found that blacks evaluated both integrated and black-model-only advertisements rather similarly. His results also "revealed a decidely *favorable* white response" to integrated advertisements.[37]

Research on advertising by Szybillo and Jacoby varied the level of integration on a continuum ranging from four blacks and zero whites to zero blacks and four whites. Their results indicated that integrated advertising was more effective among blacks when it suggested equality (that is, two blacks and two whites) than when it suggested tokenism (one black and three whites).[38]

Other research has generally confirmed the effectiveness of integrated advertising. It may be concluded that blacks prefer truly integrated advertisements (not token integration) and that whites do not react negatively to integrated advertisements.[39]

Media Strategy

The specific media strategy to use in advertising to subcultures depends on the classification of products and subcultures, as shown earlier in Exhibit 21–2. For each category a different media strategy is appropriate.

1. *Specialized*—specialized products for a subculture. If, for example, the product is cosmetics for the black subculture, then the media selected should be for the black-only market.
2. *Diffused*—subcultural products that have diffused beyond the subculture. A product such as Parks sausages, which started as a black-owned brand

directed to blacks, in time went to the mass market. The media mix for advertising changed from black-only, adding mass media directed to the total population.

3. *Idiosyncratic*—mass-market products directed to a subculture. In this category a product, such as Kool cigarettes, may have a history of selling disproportionately to members of a subculture, such as blacks. The media mix selected for advertising Kools, then, should include a high proportion of black media. In the Hispanic market brands such as Colgate toothpaste and Chef-Boy-Ar-Dee have achieved high Hispanic brand shares through separate Spanish-language media expenditures. Another example is Pathmark supermarkets, whose campaign calls its stores *La Bodega Grande* in Spanish-language advertising. Pathmark is building on the image of a bodega—a small friendly neighborhood store—for its large supermarkets.

4. *Mass Market*—mass-market products directed to the total population. For these products the advertising media mix includes mainly mass media. However, even here some subcultural media could be used to insure that subcultural consumers are receiving the message—particularly Spanish-speaking consumers.

SUMMARY

Subcultures, that is, categories of people who share a distinguishable sense of identification separate from the total culture, add another level of explanation for consumer behavior. The salience of a subculture for the individual varies, and most Americans belong to multiple subcultures based on race, religion, national origin, and social class. The impact of a subculture on consumer behavior is a function of the individual's level of identification with the subculture and the uniqueness of the subculture's values. Consumer behavior is also affected by the degree to which members of a subculture seek cultural integration versus cultural distinctiveness.

In some cases, such as the Amish subculture, values and lifestyle may be highly differentiated from that of the dominant culture, leading to a quite distinct pattern of consumer behavior. For most subcultures, however, the subcultural effects on consumer behavior are more indirect and mediated by many other factors.

A useful paradigm for designing subcultural marketing strategy is based on whether a product is unique to a subculture or not and whether it has diffused beyond the subculture or not. The model suggests different marketing and advertising approaches.

In this chapter we have focused particularly on blacks and Hispanics, two very large U.S. subcultures. Examination of these subcultures reveals a number of characteristic consumer-behavior patterns, such as level of innovativeness, family decision-making processes, and levels of brand loyalty.

Within some product categories, consumption differs and brand preferences vary across subcultures. Some of these differences, however, are due to lower average-income levels rather than to subculture, and, in general, the similarities across subcultures are usually greater than the differences.

Subcultures also affect advertising strategy. For subcultural products advertising media and appeals will be highly targeted. Even for nonsubcultural products, however, it is often advisable to use media to appeal directly to specific subcultures. This is particularly important in the Hispanic subculture because of the preference for the Spanish language.

KEY CONCEPTS

subculture	Hispanic subculture	cultural distinctiveness
social heritage	desired assimilation	"poor pay more"
values	subculture of poverty	cultural exclusion
black subculture	cultural integration	strong ties/weak ties

DISCUSSION QUESTIONS

1. What is meant by a *subculture*? Name several subcultures to which you belong.
2. The Hispanic subculture in the United States is composed of people of several different national origins—Mexico, Puerto Rico, Cuba, and others. Can a subcultural marketing program be designed for the total Hispanic population or are separate marketing programs by national origin necessary?
3. One disturbing aspect of the "subculture of poverty" is that poor people often pay more for goods and services. What are some of the reasons that the poor pay more? Is it true that the poor always pay more?
4. Discuss the preference for cultural *integration* versus cultural *distinctiveness* among members of a subculture. Are these motivations mutually exclusive? How would these motivations affect consumption behavior?
5. Apply the four-cell subcultural marketing matrix to a subculture with which you are familiar. Give examples of specialized, diffused, idiosyncratic, and mass-market products and services.
6. Would you recommend creating separate subcultural brands—for, say, detergents or facial tissue? Why or why not?
7. Why is it important not to confound ethnicity and income?
8. Conduct a content analysis of prime-time television. What percentage of commercials is integrated (black and white actors and actresses)? What percentage uses blacks only? What percentage uses Hispanics? What can you conclude?
9. Take a drive through a "poverty" area of a city. How would you characterize the retail structure? Are large national chains present? What can you conclude?

NOTES

1. David O. Arnold (1970), *The Sociology of Subcultures* (Berkeley, Cal.: Glendasary Press).
2. Elizabeth C. Hirschman (1981), "American Jewish Ethnicity: Its Relationship to Some Selected Aspects of Consumer Behavior," *Journal of Marketing,* 45 (Summer), pp. 102–10.
3. Elizabeth C. Hirschman (1982), "Ethnic Variation in Leisure Activities and Motives," working paper, Institute of Retail Management, Graduate School of Business, New York University.
4. J. Walter Thompson, Inc. (1980), *Advertising to the Hispanic Consumer* (New York: J. Walter Thompson). For a more complete view of Hispanic Demographics, see A. J. Jaffe, Ruth M. Cullen, and Thomas D. Boswell (1980), *The Changing Demography of Spanish Americans* (New York: Academic Press).
5. National Association of Spanish Broadcasters and Strategy Research Corporation (1980), *U.S. Hispanics—A Market Profile,* ed. Antonio Guernico (New York: Natl. Assn. of Spanish Broadcasters).
6. Natl. Assn. of Spanish Broadcasters (1980), p. 12.
7. Natl. Assn. of Spanish Broadcasters (1980), p. 22.
8. Natl. Assn. of Spanish Broadcasters (1980), p. 39.
9. J. Walter Thompson (1980), p. 18.
10. H. A. Bullock (1961), "Consumer Motivations in Black and White," *Harvard Business Review,* 39, p. 96.
11. Raymond A. Bauer and Scott Cunningham (1970), *Studies in the Negro Market* (Cambridge, Mass.: Marketing Science Inst.), p. 62.
12. Judith R. Porter and Robert E. Washington (1979), "Black Identity and Self Esteem," in *Annual Review of Sociology,* ed. Alex Inkeless, et al. (Palo Alto, Cal.: Annual Reviews), pp. 53–74.
13. Robert Blauner (1972), *Racial Repression in America* (New York: Harper & Row), p. 124.
14. Alan R. Andreasen (1979), "Disadvantaged Hispanic Consumers: A Research Perspective," pp. 3–19 and Luis V. Dominguez (1979), "The Hispanic Market: A Primer on Characteristics and Research Needs," pp. 20–30, both in *Proceedings of the 2nd National Symposium on Hispanic Business and Economy in the United States,* ed. Leonardo Rodriguez and Luis Aranda (Miami: Florida Intl. Univ.).
15. Personal correspondence with Richard A. Jacobs, President of Joseph Jacobs Organization, Inc., a firm specializing in Jewish and subcultural marketing, Aug. 2, 1982.
16. Oscar Lewis (1966), *La Vida* (New York: Free Press).
17. David Caplovitz (1967), *The Poor Pay More* (New York: Free Press).
18. Charles S. Goodman (1968), "Do The Poor Pay More?" *Journal of Marketing,* 32 (Jan.), pp. 18–24.
19. Alan R. Andreasen (1978), "The Ghetto Marketing Life Cycle: A Case of Underachievement," *Journal of Marketing Research,* 15 (Feb.), p. 24.
20. Frederick D. Sturdivant (1981), "Minority Markets and Subculture Analysis," in *Perspectives in Consumer Behavior,* ed. Harold H. Kassarjian and Thomas S. Robertson, 3rd ed. (Glenview, Ill.: Scott, Foresman), p. 433.
21. Oscar Lewis (1966), p. xiv.
22. P. H. Rossi and Z. D. Blum (1967), "Social Stratification and Poverty," a paper presented at the Annual Meeting of the Sociological Research Association in San Francisco.
23. C. A. Valentine (1968), *Culture and Poverty* (Chicago: Univ. of Chicago Press).
24. E. Liebow (1967), *Tally's Corner: A Study of Negro Streetcorner Men* (Boston: Little, Brown), p. 222.
25. Elizabeth C. Hirschman (1981), pp. 102–10.
26. Simmons Market Research Bureau (1979), "Tobacco Products and Photography," *The 1979 Study of Media and Markets, P-15* (New York: Simmons), pp. 50–64.
27. J. Walter Thompson (1980), p. 50.

28. Raymond A. Bauer and Scott Cunningham (1970) and Carl M. Larson and Hugh G. Wales (1973), "Brand Preferences of Chicago Blacks," *Journal of Advertising Research*, 13 (Aug.), pp. 15–21.
29. Alphonzia Wellington (1981), "Traditional Brand Loyalty," *Advertising Age* (May 18), p. S–2. Natl. Assn. of Spanish Broadcasters (1980), p. 101.
30. Douglas J. Dalrymple, Thomas S. Robertson, and Michael Y. Yoshino (1971), "Consumption Behavior Across Ethnic Categories," *California Management Review*, 14 (Fall), pp. 65–70.
31. Raymond A. Bauer and Scott Cunningham (1970).
32. Elizabeth C. Hirschman (1980), "Black Ethnicity and Innovative Communication," *Journal of the Academy of Marketing Science*, 8 (Spring), pp. 100–119.
33. Douglas J. Dalrymple, Thomas S. Robertson, and Michael Y. Yoshino (1971).
34. For a discussion of Hispanic media, see Antonio Guernica (1982), *Reaching the Hispanic Market Effectively* (New York: McGraw-Hill).
35. George Comstock and Robin E. Cobbey (1979), "Television and the Children of Ethnic Minorities," *Journal of Communication*, 29 (Winter), pp. 104–15.
36. Waltraud M. Kassarjian (1973), "The Role of Blacks in Mass Media," *Journalism Quarterly*, 50 (Summer), pp. 285–91, p. 305.
37. Arnold M. Barban (1969), "The Dilemma of 'Integrated' Advertising," *Journal of Business*, 42 (Oct.), p. 496.
38. George J. Szybillo and Jacob Jacoby (1974), "Effects of Different Levels of Integration on Advertising Preference and Intention to Purchase," *Journal of Applied Psychology*, 59, pp. 274–80.
39. Ronald F. Bush, Joseph F. Hair, Jr., and Paul J. Solomon (1979), "Consumers' Level of Prejudice and Response to Black Models in Advertisements," *Journal of Marketing Research*, 16 (Aug.), pp. 341–45.

22 Culture and Multinational Marketing

Culture *refers to the social heritage of a people. It is composed of characteristics and practices shared by members of a society, including, among other things, values, language, and beliefs. Culture provides the basis for our interaction both with other members of society and with the environment.*

The effects of culture may vary from country to country, but the impact is always there. Knowledge and acceptance of a culture and its symbolism strengthen the marketer's position, both at home and abroad.

Unfortunately, our cultural myopia has sometimes limited our ability to market overseas effectively. J. William Fulbright has insightfully commented on our cultural naiveté and our linguistic poverty. He says, for example,

> When we go abroad, we tend to cluster in hotels and restaurants where English is spoken. The attitudes and information we pick up are conditioned by those natives—usually the more affluent—who speak English. Our business dealings are conducted through interpreters.[1]

Indeed, we are often oblivious to differences in cultural expectations and meanings. According to Fulbright,

We like to think of ourselves as friendly, yet we prefer to be at least three feet or an arm's length away from others. Latin Americans and Middle Easterners like to come closer and touch, which makes Americans uncomfortable.

More and more firms are becoming involved in cross-cultural marketing efforts. Over half of Coca-Cola's business, for example, is conducted overseas. IBM, Revlon, The Ford Motor Company, General Foods, and Time, Inc., are extensively involved in overseas operations. Similarly, foreign firms such as Toyota, Panasonic, and Unilever are making inroads into the American marketplace. If a corporation is to succeed in developing foreign markets, it is imperative that management investigate, understand, and respond to the unique cultural environments of its target countries.

In this chapter we discuss the influence of culture on consumer behavior, expectations, and needs. We begin with an examination of the types of structural differences that characterize various cultures, and then discuss some of the ways in which cultural variations can affect elements of the marketing mix and the development of marketing strategy.

CROSS-CULTURAL ANALYSIS

A framework for the analysis of world cultures can be based on three major dimensions: demographic, organizational, and normative. The **demographic dimension** refers to a society's composition, in terms of such variables as the age, income, and education distributions of the population. Demographic characteristics are especially important for companies either seeking new countries in which to market their current product lines or developing new products for specific foreign markets. The **organizational dimension** of a society refers to the structure of its cultural institutions, including social classes and family units. The ways in which individuals interact and, hence, do business, are conditioned by the rules inherent in social institutions. The third important societal dimension—the **normative**—refers to the culture's value system, including its economic and religious philosophies. Planned product introductions, advertising and promotional campaigns, and potential distribution channels must not violate cultural norms, and can be accurately evaluated only from the point of view of the host country's normative system.

Demographic Dimension: Product Marketing Opportunities

demographic profile

A major consideration in multinational marketing is the demographic profile of a nation. Opportunities for the sale of products and services depend on factors such as the disposable income of a nation, the population level, the degree of urbanization, birth rate, and so forth. The diversity of societies on the demographic dimension is illustrated in Exhibit 22–1. Multinational marketers must consider these factors in their decisions about what markets to enter and what marketing programs to use. For example, demand for luxury products requires relatively high levels of per-capita income (as in Switzerland and the United States). Or, to take another example, the use of print advertising requires a high literacy level, although even high literacy is not a sufficient condition in a country with a low population density and a relatively low degree of urbanization. If print media cannot be widely distributed, print advertising may be precluded.

Many American marketers have not marketed aggressively overseas because of the sheer size and opportunity of our own market. Even though Australia, for example, is an obvious country into which an American marketer might expand, consider that the population of Australia is only 15 million, compared to over 200 million in the United States. An American firm might well decide that its resources are better utilized in attempting to gain an additional 1 percent share of the American market than in attempting to capture, say, 50 percent of the Australian market.

Organizational Dimension: Doing Business

The organizational structure of a country is the second major dimension that influences the nature of marketing overseas. It is sometimes useful to simplify by thinking in terms of "ideal types." Robert Redfield proposes a distinction between folk society and modern industrial society.[2] In **folk society**, life centers around the family, and behavior is based on custom and tradition. In modern **industrial society**, many functions are transferred from the family to other societal institutions, and customs and traditions are often not allowed to hinder progress. In general, it appears that traditional (folk) societies are characterized by an extended-family pattern, whereas modern societies are characterized by a conjugal (father, mother, children) family pattern.

The individual's relationship to a society and its organizational structure may differ quite markedly from country to country, with a resulting effect on modes of interaction. Davis has noted, for example, that both North Americans and Latin Americans have a strong sense of individuality, but that this means something quite different for each.[3] The North American bases his or her notion on *equality;* individuality is considered to have its best chance to flourish when each person has equal rights and opportunities. "Paradoxically," says Davis, "it is his belief in his very sameness, vis-a-vis others, that makes

folk society versus industrial society

EXHIBIT 22-1
DEMOGRAPHIC VARIABLES IN SELECTED COUNTRIES

	India	Chile	Ghana	Japan	Iraq	Switzer-land	United States
Population (thousands)[a]	643,000	10,880	10,650	114,850	12,350	6,310	203,235
Population Density[b] (per square mile)	506.6	37.2	115.6	799.0	73.5	395.8	57.5
Population Growth[c] (%)	2.2	1.9	2.8	1.3	3.4	0.3	0.8
Urbanization[d] (% in urban areas)	20.0	76.0	32.0	72.0	51.0	55.0	74.0
Life Expectancy (years) (male-female)	41.9–40.5	60.5–66.0	41.9–45.1	72.1–77.3	57.6–57.4	70.3–76.2	68.7–76.5
Infant Mortality (per 1000 births)	122	55.6	156	9.3	108.1	10.7	15.1
Literacy (% of adults)	33.4	88.1	30.2	97.8	24.2	99.0	99.0
Per Capital Income[e]	$150	$1,050	$580	$4,910	$1,390	$8,880	$7,890

[a]Est. 1978, except U.S., 1970.

[b]Est. 1978, except U.S., 1970.

[c]Annual rate of increase, 1970–77.

[d]Figures for 1970. These are not strictly comparable, because the countries define urban areas differently.

[e]In U.S. dollars (1976).

SOURCES: Harold H. Kassarjian and Thomas S. Robertson (1981), *Perspectives in Consumer Behavior,* 3rd ed. (Glenview, Ill.: Scott, Foresman), p. 481. Data from *Information Please Almanac* (1979), 33rd ed. (New York: Viking); *The Statesman's Year-Book—1979/1980* (1978), 115th ed. (New York: St. Martin's); *Statistical Yearbook, 1977* (1978) (Paris: UNESCO); *Demographic Yearbook* (1978) 29th ed. (New York: United Nations); and *World Tables—1976* (1976) (Baltimore: International Bank for Reconstruction and Development/World Bank).

him distinct and defines his individuality." The Latin American, in contrast, views individuality in terms of *uniqueness*. According to Davis, calling a Latin American the "equal" of anyone else would be an insult, since an individual cannot be equal to others if he or she is unique.

group interaction

The basic conceptual distinctions noted by Davis lead to differences in group interaction and functioning. In North America, the group is the place where individuality is suppressed and the cooperative spirit is stressed. Teamwork is perceived to be vital to progress, and, as Davis notes, it is felt that "people who do not work well in groups represent a threat to both the stability and progress of our society." In Latin America, on the other hand, the group tends to function as a haven for individuality and exists "as a protective environment, a sanctuary in which the unique identity of each individual is valued, supported, and enhanced, rather than absorbed and assimilated into a single group identity." Davis cites the charter of a group of Latin American students who formed an association: the first sentence states that they had "come together to act as individuals in forming this association."

In Japan, to look at another country, the functioning of groups is different from that in both the United States and Latin America. Group activity is seen primarily as a means of sharing responsibility. If anything should go wrong, "the prospect of individual shame is lessened or at least shared by all the members," according to Weingand.[4] This is frequently frustrating to American business people marketing in Japan, since finding the decision maker when decisions are shared is difficult, and authority and responsibility are somewhat diffuse.

decision-making

The process of making business decisions in Japan seems to follow a different pattern from that in the United States. The period of time leading to the decision is long by American standards, and the decision seems to flow "up" the organization. In the United States, faster decisions are generally made, and the process is more likely to reflect a "top down" pattern. Nevertheless, the time before decisions are implemented may be equivalent since in Japan all managers are in agreement by the time a decision is finally made, whereas in the United States, the process of gaining the commitment of middle- and lower-level management is likely to begin after the decision is made.

Even seemingly similar societies, such as the United States and Australia, tend to differ in some structural aspects. A recent report by Exxon indicated that friction in business interactions often arises between Americans and Australians.[5] Whereas Americans are oriented to achieving agreement on decisions as quickly and as smoothly as possible, Australians tend to eschew quick agreement. They tend to believe in their own points of view so strongly that they find it difficult to compromise. Additionally, on both the personal and business levels, they enjoy dissension and argument; they interpret a strong, noncompromising opponent as a better friend or associate than one who compromises his or her position. The strong opponent is seen as one who is honest enough to express a dissenting opinion, and also strong enough to resist pressure to conform.

When a firm decides to enter foreign markets, it is important that executives have a good understanding of the organizational dimension of the society. The presumption that all other cultures are organized along similar lines to that of the home country can result not only in marketing failures, but also in the alienation of local business people and consumers.

Normative Dimension: Culturally Approved Attitudes and Behaviors

The third factor which affects overseas marketing is the normative dimension of a culture. To understand its impact, we must first differentiate between cultural values and norms. **Values** are widely accepted beliefs that certain goals, activities, objects, or emotions are personally and socially worthwhile. The emphasis on achievement fostered in American society, for example, is a cultural value. It grew from the Protestant ethic, which sanctions hard work and frugal living. Thus, Benjamin Franklin advised his readers in *Poor Richard's Almanac* as follows:

> *How much more than is necessary do we spend in sleep! Forgetting that "the sleeping fox catches no poultry, and that there will be sleeping enough in the grave." . . . If we are industrious, we shall never starve; for . . . "at the working man's house hunger looks in, but dares not enter."*[6]

Although these thoughts no longer fully represent the American position, the social heritage handed down to us has been affected by the Protestant ethic.

Values tend to be nontangible and abstract, and they do not offer any specific guidelines for behavior. But they do provide the basis for **norms,** which define acceptable behavior. In American society, for example, the rule that children attend school until they are sixteen years old is a norm derived from the achievement value.

Norms may be quite general or very specific. A general norm in almost all cultures is the prohibition against murder, which is affiliated with the value for the sanctity of life. A more situation-specific norm involves the starting and stopping work times companies designate for their employees. The normative dimension is also reflected in a society's rituals, customs, and practices. In the following examples we can see some cross-cultural differences in everyday customs:

> *. . . while in the United States bringing a bottle of wine for the host at a dinner party is likely to please, in France, such a gift would be considered an insult to the host's choice of wine.*[7]

> *The sturdy handshake is very much a part of the American cultural repertory. Yet in the Middle East the visitor receives a flaccid or "dead fish" handshake which he may associate with femininity or unfriendliness. To the Arab the hearty grasp is a sign that the American has more brawn than brains.*[8]

A multinational marketer must understand such cultural practices, accept them, and reflect them in the conduct of business.

cultural values

norms

general versus specific norms

social customs and practices

Mauser relates an amusing business-related anecdote about a difference in normative expectations between Japanese and Americans. He points out that the Japanese do not mix humor with serious business discussions. Many Americans, however, ignore this norm in dealing with the Japanese. Mauser writes of a Japanese translator informing his audience (in Japanese) of this American custom prior to a speech given by an American. Each time the American speaker made jokes, the translator informed his audience that a laugh was in order. The courteous audience obliged, and the speaker was delighted that (at last!) here was a translator who could handle humor.[9]

The normative dimension in business in foreign markets is also reflected by the fact that consumers evaluate various products, brands, and services in terms of their cultural values and norms. Efforts to persuade women in India to utilize birth-control methods, for example, have proved largely unsuccessful. Partly because of the extremely high rate of infant mortality, women believe that it is necessary to have many children to ensure that some do survive. Arguing that fewer births would enable Indian parents to have greater resources per child, thus decreasing the mortality rate, contradicts the cultural heritage and the value system of Indians, who have not widely adopted birth-control procedures. Given the Indian government's highly visible advertising campaign, some change has been affected in recent years. But the process of change has been very slow, demonstrating the high degree of stability inherent in the normative dimension.

Over time, it is possible to change some cultural objections to certain products or services. One of the strongest examples of such a change is the American attitude toward Japanese products. After World War II and into the early 1960s, a product that was "made in Japan" was perceived as inferior, not durable, and poorly made. Today, Japanese goods represent extremely high quality, durability, and technical excellence.

THE BEHAVIORAL SCIENTIST'S VIEW OF CULTURE

Culture refers to the social heritage of a people. It is the distinctive lifestyle of a society, representing its particular adaptation to its environment and its design for living. The noted anthropologist Ralph Linton described culture as ". . . the configuration of learned behavior and results of behavior whose component elements are shared and transmitted by the members of a particular society."[10] E. B. Tylor, often regarded as the father of cultural anthropology, views culture more simply as ". . . that complex whole which includes knowledge, beliefs, art, morals, law, customs and any other capabilities and habits acquired by man as a member of society."[11] Writing more recently, Peterson suggests that contemporary thought sees culture as consisting of four basic elements: norms, values, beliefs, and expressive symbols. And, Peterson says, "While the culture concept has been greatly elaborated [since Tylor's definition], it has not been fundamentally changed."[12]

Culture is the broadest concept that anthropologists and sociologists use when studying different societies. Understanding the effect of culture on consumer behavior involves examining four aspects of culture.

1. Culture is *symbolic*. Words, objects, products, and actions are not neutral, but often have very important emotional meanings.
2. Culture is *pervasive*. It permeates every aspect of life. It is often very

EXHIBIT 22–2
ADVERTISEMENT SHOWING A PRODUCT'S BENEFITS

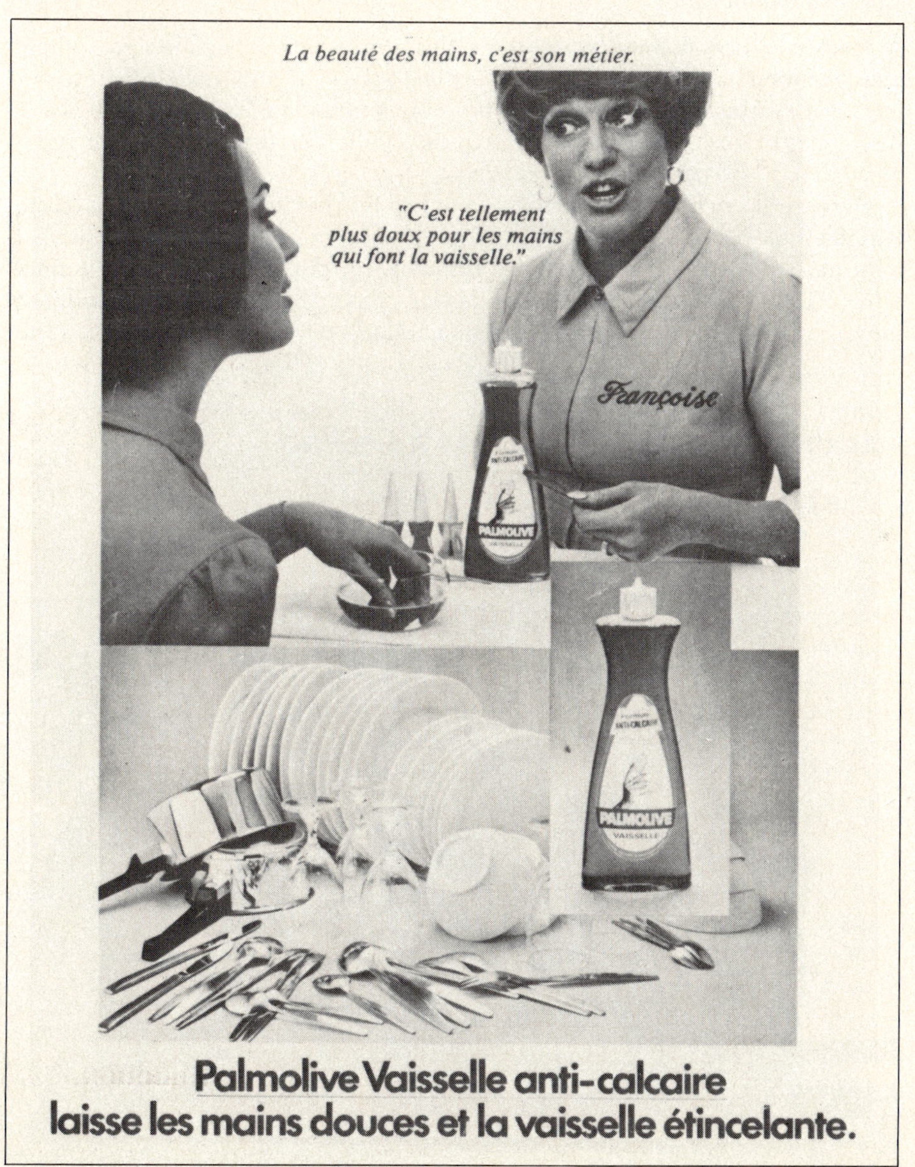

difficult to identify cultural influences, because we are so surrounded by and absorbed in them.

3. Cultural values and norms are *transmitted from generation to generation.* Values and norms define numerous aspects of acceptable behavior.
4. Culture and *language* are integrally connected. Language is not only a tool that we use for expression, but also a dynamic force that can sometimes shape reality.

Cultural Symbolism

symbols

A *symbol* can be defined as anything that represents or signifies something else. Symbols may be words—the word *newspaper* represents a concrete object. But symbols may also be events, actions, drawings, and so forth. When discussing culture, anthropologists typically differentiate between two types of symbols, *referential* and *expressive.*

referential symbols

expressive symbols

Referential symbols are denotative, that is, they represent and indicate tangible objects. The words *table* and *toothpaste* are referential symbols that indicate certain objects. **Expressive symbols,** on the other hand, are connotative. They represent not only an object or act, but they also provide an indication of the meanings and emotions attached to the object or act. The

EXHIBIT 22–3
ADVERTISEMENT USING A PRODUCT AS A SYMBOL

word *physician*, for instance, denotes an individual who practices medicine, but it also connotes a good deal more about an individual, including the facts that he or she is well-educated and financially secure and has a particular lifestyle.

Consumer behavior is influenced by the symbolism of culture. Products, brands, and services are cultural symbols which may be either referential or expressive. Low-involvement goods such as radio batteries, light bulbs, and commodities in general are referential. But automobiles, clothing, china, and home furnishings are expressive symbols, connoting qualitative information about a consumer's preferences, attitudes, and lifestyle. The purchase of a product that is also an expressive symbol means far more to an individual than the purchase of a referential, low-involvement good.

Advertisers implicitly use the distinction between referential and expressive goods in the development of appropriate advertising campaigns. Since image is not an important factor for referential products, a sound advertising approach stresses an obvious advantage of a product over competitors. The advertisement in Exhibit 22–2 illustrates the strategy of advertising a product's benefits. Even students who speak no French can appreciate the benefits being promoted: Palmolive's gentleness and cleaning effectiveness. The advertisement for Chivas Regal Scotch in Exhibit 22–3 uses a different strat-

egy. Notice that no particular trait is mentioned. Rather, Chivas Regal is used as a symbol that differentiates one man from a group of homogeneous "others."

Perhaps the advertising campaign that most strongly capitalized on expressive symbolism was the series of ads in the 1930s for the luxurious Duesenberg automobile. In each ad, there appeared a single, elegantly dressed man or woman, seated in a library or on the deck of a boat, or standing in front of a large stately home (see Exhibit 22–4). No car was pictured in the ad. A caption simply read, "He drives a Duesenberg" or "She drives a Duesenberg." No other copy was in the advertisement.

Product meaning and advertising approaches are not the only elements of the marketing mix affected by cultural symbolism. Product price has an obvious cultural significance, with higher price often taken as an indicator of higher quality. A more subtle example of cultural symbolism involves consumer perception of various channels of distribution. From the early 1900s to the end of the 1960s mail order was popular primarily among mass merchandisers such as Sears, Roebuck and Montgomery Ward, and was focused primarily at rural lower-income markets. As shopping centers and retailing reached out into the more rural areas, mail order became more specialized. Nonetheless, it was still not widely used for the sale of prestige goods, and consumers' perceptions of mail order were largely conditioned by former associations with "downscale" merchandise. The introduction of the prestigious Horchow catalogue in the early 1970s contributed strongly to the elevation of mail-order as a prestigious channel of distribution.

Cultural Pervasiveness and Ethnocentrism

Culture influences every aspect of the life of a society. It pervades all human activity from art and literature to technology to bodily adornment and perceptions of physical attractiveness. Culture dictates appropriate attitudes, preferences, and beliefs on every aspect of life. Culture has even been shown to affect individuals' emotional responses.[13] The very **pervasiveness** of culture has two ramifications for a society. First, culture is taken for granted. Individuals are not aware that their values, customs, and preferences are socially conditioned. Second, most individuals tend to be *ethnocentric*, that is, they believe that their culture and way of life are qualitatively superior to other, foreign, cultures.

ethnocentricity

Individuals who are ethnocentric are said to be **culture bound.** When a culture-bound person learns of the beliefs, practices, or experiences of a new culture, **culture shock** often occurs. *Culture shock* is the feeling of basic confusion and frustration that results when one's fundamental "truths" are questioned.

culture bound

culture shock

The concept of ethnocentricity has direct application to consumer behavior. For example, in a study of how American and Japanese consumers perceive products "made in" Japan and "made in" the United States, Narayana found that American consumers perceive American products to be of higher quality than Japanese products. Correspondingly, Japanese consumers believe Japanese products to be superior.[14] Another study questioned consumers in Finland about their attitudes toward the products and marketing practices (such as advertising) of eight different countries.[15] Respondents were most favorably

EXHIBIT 22–4
ADVERTISEMENT CAPITALIZING ON EXPRESSIVE SYMBOLISM

disposed toward both products and practices of Finland. Sweden and West Germany followed. Japan, the United States, and England were ranked next, and France and Russia were last.

In both of these studies, consumers demonstrate their ethnocentrism by enhancing the familiar products and marketing activities and devaluating the foreign and unfamiliar. Ethnocentrism is not necessarily a negative phenomenon, because it gives rise to cultural identity and feelings of patriotism and loyalty. As such, ethnocentrism is found in all societies. The challenge for the multinational firm is to develop a philosophy of **cultural relativism,** that is, acceptance of foreign cultures and beliefs without judgment. When marketers attempt to enter foreign markets without real understanding of the cultures, differences can act as a barrier. Cultural ethnocentricity of overseas consumers may inhibit them from trying new products or new approaches that differ from the indigenous, "best" approach.

Cultural Values and Norms

As you saw in Chapter 7, culture is passed from generation to generation through the socialization process. During socialization, children learn the fundamental values and norms of the culture, from the culture's point of view. In other words, *socialization* is the process through which individuals are inducted into a culture.

It is important to understand the relationship between values and consumer behavior. Values broadly define the activities, beliefs, products, and services that are socially acceptable. Thus, consumers' tastes for certain types of products are culturally transmitted. The impact of culture on consumption of alcoholic beverages in three European countries is revealed in Exhibit 22–5. Consistent with their stereotypes, Germans consume the most beer per capita, and the French consume the most wine. Hard liquor consumption is highest among Swedes, followed by Germans. Of course, cultural stereo-

EXHIBIT 22–5
ANNUAL ALCOHOLIC BEVERAGE CONSUMPTION IN EUROPE (per capita)

	Beer (liters)	Wine (liters)	Spirits (liters)
France	44.9	135.1	1.8
Germany	148.5	30.1	7.4
Sweden	61.0	9.1	8.0

SOURCE: Euromonitor (1977), "Consumer Europe," *Market Research Great Britain,* 17 (Oct.), p. 27.

types and folklore can be deceiving. Chinese visitors to this country are surprised to learn that we attribute chop suey to the Chinese, just as some Northern Italians express surprise that we consider pizza to be an Italian food staple.

Values influence more than consumers' tastes for particular products. They can influence the decision-making process itself. For example, the structure of family decision-making differs across societies holding different values. Rodman proposes that the division of marital power in decision-making depends on (a) the relative resources (income, education, occupational status) each partner brings to the relationship, and (b) the cultural or subcultural expectations about the division of marital power.[16] Using these dimensions, Rodman suggests four types of societies:

1. *Patriarchy*—traditional societies in which men have great authority in all segments of society;
2. *Modified Patriarchy*—more modern societies in which patriarchal family norms still operate, but in which equalitarian norms have taken hold for the upper strata of society;
3. *Transitional Equalitarianism*—societies in which equalitarian norms are in the process of replacing patriarchal norms for all strata; and
4. *Equalitarian*—societies characterized by an established sharing of power between husbands and wives.

Rodman's approach is interesting because it provides a mechanism to link cross-national differences in buyer behavior with the underlying values and social structures that generate those differences. Patriarchical societies, for example, are characterized by husband dominance in consumer decision-making, while at the other extreme, joint decision-making is the norm in equalitarian societies.

This is not to say that all cultures differ dramatically in their values or social structures. In a study of German, English, and French women, Boote examines the importance of twenty-nine values in the three countries by having consumers rate each value from *very important* to *not at all important*.[17] While the samples show some marked differences, they also show strong similarities. For example, "having a familiar routine" was a value ranked differently by the three samples: It was ranked as *very important* by the Germans, *moderately important* by the English, and *unimportant* by the French. On the other hand, all three samples agreed that "having expensive looking possessions" was *not at all important*. Overall, Boote found more similarities than differences among the three samples.

Language and Culture

Language plays two roles in society, both of which have significance for consumer behavior. First, language is the tool people (including advertisers) use to express ideas, feelings, and needs. As individuals take their cultures for granted, so do they take their language for granted. The second, and perhaps more subtle, role of language in society is that it is the mechanism through which culture is transmitted from generation to generation. Culture is *learned*, and the very structure of language can influence the content of what is learned.

Language and Advertising   A key issue in multinational marketing is the extent to which an advertising campaign can be standardized across cultures. Weichmann reports that advertising tends to be more decentralized than other marketing functions and that advertising strategy of American and European multinational firms varies from country to country more than other aspects of the marketing program.[18] Dunn reports that the proportion of American firms using the same advertisements in both the United States and in other countries actually declined in the 1970s.[19] McDonald's fast foods are an interesting example of American products that are relatively uniform worldwide, but for which the advertising focuses on somewhat different benefits. In Australia, McDonald's uses the theme,
At McDonald's we've got it all.

In Germany,
McDonald's, eating with enjoyment.

In Japan,
McDonald's does it with taste.

And in Holland, known for frugality, the theme is,
McDonald's restaurants—unusually good for your money.[20]

Many advertising campaigns simply do not translate well, although a few do. The Marlboro campaign runs almost unchanged throughout the world, and, in fact, began appearing on television in the People's Republic of China in 1979 in its familiar cowboy format.[21] The Marlboro advertisement on p. 336 has appeared in Japanese print media. Dunn reports that Coca-Cola's "Things go better with Coke" proved transferable, but that "It's the real thing" was difficult to use in many markets.[22] There are many failures in translation. Dunn also reports that "Body by Fisher" became "Corpse by Fisher" in some translations within Europe, and that Pepsi's "Come alive" became "Come out of the grave."

Where there is any potential problem with language, back-translation is **back-translation**   recommended.[23] *Back-translation* involves having one translator (or a group of translators) translate an advertising message from its original language to the new one, and a different translator (or group) translate back to the original language. This process, especially if it is repeated a number of times, helps to ensure that the intended conceptual meaning of the message is indeed captured.

Language and the Transmission of Culture   Language plays an integral role in the transmission of culture because we use language to express our thoughts and beliefs. Since we take language very much for granted, largely because we seem to be able to express all the thoughts, beliefs, and attitudes that we have, we do not see language placing any limits on our ability to communicate.

Linguists Benjamin Whorf and Edward Sapir, however, have a very different view of language.[24] They maintain that the *structure* of language influences and constrains the manner in which individuals perceive their world. The **Whorf-Sapir hypothesis** holds that an individual's perceptions, understandings, and relationships are shaped and determined by the structure of language. A relatively straightforward example of this effect is the contrast between our view of snow and Eskimos' view. Whereas we use the word *snow* to refer to all types of snow, Eskimos have distinct words to refer to icy snow, slushy snow, falling snow, hard-packed snow, and so forth.[25] The Whorf-Sapir hypothesis says that the very structure of the Eskimo language enables Eskimos to differentiate various types of snow so keenly.

One study of consumers has discussed cross-national differences and language. Examining a wide range of family activities, Douglas found substantial similarity in the roles played by husbands and wives in Chicago, London/Glasgow, Paris, Quebec, and Brussels.[26] Where differences in the relative involvement of husbands and wives did occur, patterns varied with the *language* spoken: English-speaking respondents differed from those who spoke French. Douglas suggests that the cultural trend toward egalitarian relationships between the sexes underlies this difference. The Anglo-Saxon cultures appear more accepting of egalitarianism than the Latin cultures.

structure of language

Whorf-Sapir hypothesis

THE IMPACT OF CULTURE ON ELEMENTS OF THE MARKETING MIX

Culture often has a direct influence on consumer characteristics and behavior and, correspondingly, on the elements of the marketing mix. We now turn our attention to an examination of differences in product meaning, pricing behavior, and the distribution structure in various societies.

Product Meaning

The culture in which a person lives affects consumption patterns. In the broadest sense, cultural values position products in a social milieu, and a given product can have different meanings in different societies. For example, discussing the current scene in Germany, one observer concludes that Mercedes can barely produce enough cars to meet the demand from dentists in Beverly Hills, but that, "Owning a Mercedes [in Germany] is tacky, a statement of self-satisfaction and complacency—it's being a butter-and-eggs man; it's having a big gut; and it's absolutely the wrong image. . . ."[27]

The social meanings attached to a product within a culture are critical in assessing how likely a product is to be accepted. In many countries, for example, it is considered demeaning for people of high status to engage in any form of manual labor. Hired laborers are, therefore, common, and the introduction of do-it-yourself products and even appliances meets social resistance.

Plummer questioned samples from various cultures about views on the use of deodorant and on housekeeping.[28] Exhibit 22–6 shows the percentages of the samples agreeing with the relevant statements. It is evident that there are marked differences in the extent to which the various cultures stress personal hygiene and stress housecleaning. Especially interesting are the differences in levels of agreement for both statements among respondents from the United States, United Kingdom, and Australia—three cultures that are often presumed to be quite homogeneous.

Pricing Behavior

Pricing is often bound to a society's economic philosophy and the degree of price control (a societal norm) that philosophy exerts on business firms. In Japan, for example, the government plays a far greater role in consumer issues—including pricing. Indeed, government regulation of pricing is far more common—and culturally approved—than in the United States.

The use of price as a means of competition is not as important in many countries as in the United States. Resale-price maintenance, for example, ef-

EXHIBIT 22–6

CULTURAL DIFFERENCES: USE OF DEODORANTS AND HOUSEKEEPING

"Everyone should use a deodorant."	agreement	"A house should be dusted and polished three times a week."	agreement
United States	89%	Italy	86%
French Canada	81	United Kingdom	59
English Canada	77	France	55
United Kingdom	71	Spain	53
Italy	69	Germany	45
France	59	Australia	33
Australia	53	United States	25

SOURCE: Joseph T. Plummer (1977), "Consumer Focus in Cross-National Research," *Journal of Advertising*, 6 (Spring), pp. 10–11.

fectively limits the discounting of national brands in Britain. Spain, among many other countries, fixes the prices of raw materials. The pricing of consumer items in Spain also seems fairly rigid.

On the other hand, the one-price system is less common in some countries than in the United States. In fact, bargaining is often an institutionalized societal norm and an important part of a culture's way of life. For example, Fayerweather writes of a Peruvian woman and her bushel of corn:

> When a visitor offered to buy the whole bushel early in the morning for a relatively high price, she refused. Although she had to earn a living, the satisfaction of spending a day in the market haggling with an assortment of buyers over the purchase of small fractions of her bushel was equally, if not more, important to her.[29]

Distribution Structure

As a general rule, distribution structures tend to become less fragmented as a country experiences greater economic growth. But this is not always the case. France, for example, has a much more fragmented retail structure than the United States, and small shops survive even as supermarkets and hypermarkets (large-scale general merchandise stores) spread. There are still separate shops for fish, dairy, pastries, meat, coffee, and many other food products, and the small merchant has shown considerable resilience in the face of large-scale retailing. Small stores apparently meet a real need for French consumers, whether because of traditional French values for food preparation or as a communication channel for the community.

In an analysis of French and American consumption of new convenience foods, Douglas concludes that the lower French usage of these products is in large part due to the prevalence of small stores that do not have shelf space to stock such items.[30] The conclusion is that the fragmented retail structure contributes to a lag in the adoption of new convenience products. However, as Douglas acknowledges, the causality may be the reverse, and differences in the retail environment may reflect differences in consumer values and attitudes. Does the retail structure slow new convenience food acceptance or is it the interest in more traditional fresh products that perpetuates the existing small-scale retail structure?

One of the most mysterious distribution structures to many American marketers is the Japanese system. As described by Shimaguchi, Japanese distribution channels "comprise a small business . . . embedded in Japanese beliefs, attitudes, as well as other social relationships."[31]

Tsurumi traces the failure of some American firms in the Japanese market to their lack of understanding of and adaptation to the Japanese distribution system.[32] Japan is characterized by *multilayered* distribution channels for mass-consumed products such as food and packaged goods, drugs, toiletries, and small appliances. Three, four, or even seven layers of wholesalers intervene between the manufacturer and the final retailer. This system was developed as an efficient way to serve a market in which consumers have relatively low incomes and small living quarters, and rely on public transport. As a result of these characteristics, consumers make frequent (often daily) shopping trips and buy small amounts. Dependence on public transport means consumers patronize local merchants. These numerous local merchants lack the financial and managerial resources to carry large inventories. They receive frequent, small shipments of goods from another layer of subwholesalers, who are in turn supplied by still another layer of wholesalers. Tsurumi points out that successful American firms have adapted to this system, which depends on personal relationships. In discussing Smith, Kline's successful entry, Tsurumi says,

> *In order to service such a delicate, organic entity as Japanese distribution channels, Smith, Kline & French's sales representatives make daily contacts with wholesalers and key retail outlets. Most representatives live in the same cities as the wholesalers; they attend the morning gathering of the wholesalers' sales forces and participate in the wholesalers' regular recreational events and evening parties. They also make regular calls to retail outlets and become closely acquainted with these store owners. In addition, SK&F's executives and president frequently call on wholesalers and cultivate close personal ties with the wholesaler executives. These visits by high level executives of the manufacturing firm confirm vividly the importance they attach to special relationships with their wholesaler customers.*"[33]

Exhibit 22–7 shows Pepsi-Cola's use of a river launch in Bangkok to get their product to consumers. As Pepsi points out, innovative distribution channels are a key to successful marketing in Far Eastern markets.

THE EFFECT OF CULTURE ON CORPORATE STRATEGY: AVON'S APPROACH IN JAPAN

Although the cultures of Japan and the United States differ dramatically in many respects, a thorough understanding of the role played by culture in the determination of consumer needs and preferences has facilitated Avon's success in the Japanese market. In Japan, cultural forces exert an identifiable influence on product lines, product size, distribution, and motivational and promotional decisions.

Product Lines

Skin-care products (cleansers, moisturizers, and toners, for example) constitute Avon's largest product category in Japan. In the United States, in con-

EXHIBIT 22–7
AN INNOVATIVE DISTRIBUTION CHANNEL

SOURCE: Annual Report (1980), PepsiCo, Inc.

trast, makeup outsells skin-care products by a considerable margin. Cultural factors can shed light on some of the reasons for this difference.

The United States is an action-oriented, impatient society. When Americans have needs or problems, they attempt to find solutions as quickly as possible. When an American woman wants to look attractive, she applies makeup and receives an immediate payoff. American women have always been eager to purchase makeup, but they have been reluctant to buy skin-care items. Avon management suggests that this trait has a cultural basis, namely that the *benefits* of using skin-care products are not immediate. Correspondingly, if an American woman has a skin blemish, she covers it with makeup (immediate payoff). In contrast, the Japanese have historically been a patient society. They believe that events do not occur spontaneously, but that they evolve slowly over time. In Japan, endurance is a prized cultural value. The Japanese woman's attitude toward skin care is affected by this cultural trait. Japanese women make skin care into a ritual, using six to eight products, morning and night, to cleanse, tone, and moisturize their skin. Japanese girls begin to use skin-care products around the age of fifteen, but not makeup, and throughout their lives they are concerned with maintaining their basically beautiful skin.

A second culturally explainable difference is that the American woman is far more likely to buy many brands of cosmetics. She may use Avon eye shadow, Revlon mascara, and Estée Lauder lipstick. But the Japanese woman tends to use only one brand. She perceives skin care (like history and time) as a whole. Mixing brands would constitute fragmentation of the whole.

Of course, not all differences in product preferences in Japan—or in other cultures—are the result of cultural variations. Physiological differences, for example, can play a role. Japanese men tend to have coarse hair, and to keep it in place they use heavy hair tonics and gels that are generally unavailable in the United States. Similarly, the color of the Japanese woman's complexion is confined to a fairly narrow range. Avon thus has a smaller range of makeup colors in Japan, but within that range there are more subtle variations in shades.

Product Size

Japan is approximately the same size, geographically, as the state of California. Yet it has a population of over 100 million—approximately half the population of the United States. The population density of Japan is 799.0 (per square mile), contrasted with 57.5 in the United States. Because of the population density, Japanese housing units tend to be smaller and to have less storage space than American ones.

Correspondingly, Avon's products for the Japanese market are smaller than those for the American market. But the physical limits on space in Japan are reinforced by cultural expectations. There is a popular Japanese saying:

"Nothing is better than too many." Having too much of anything is considered ostentatious and impolite. "Extra large" simply doesn't sell well in Japan.

Distribution

In Japan, calling door-to-door is considered rude, and no prestigious product would be sold in this way. The connotations of rudeness have a historical basis. During the Shogunate period of the fifteenth century, the powerful Tokagawa successfully ruled the Japanese by discouraging geographic mobility and simultaneously developing spy networks within the stable populations of towns. Individuals who, for any reason, failed to comply with Tokagawa's dictates against mobility became known as "floating weeds," that is, rootless. The floating weeds would either beg or sell wares, door to door.

Today, the Japanese Avon "lady" does not call on her neighbors door-to-door in the manner of her American counterpart. Rather, she approaches only five or six of her most intimate friends and relatives—as compared with the more than twenty customers of the American Avon representative. Thus, Avon's customer-to-salesperson ratio in Japan is much smaller than in any of the other countries in which Avon operates.

Sales Incentives

In the United States, the Avon representative responds well to monetary rewards. In addition, periodic special prize incentives are revealed at sales meetings. Sales supervisors (known as district managers) may encourage their representatives to "sell x bottles, make x dollars, and win custom lingerie," for example.

But in Japan, the Avon representative hasn't enough customers to enable her to earn a large profit. More important culturally, she is unwilling to submit herself to the "shameful" practice of aggressively selling a product to her friends. The Japanese rationale in selling? "Smell this beautiful fragrance. Don't you wish to share it with your friends?"

Incentives for the Japanese Avon representative are therefore more subtle. The sales meeting itself is first and foremost a *social* encounter—a good place for the representative to meet friends and also to learn more about making herself more attractive. Another incentive is that Avon representatives are able to purchase products themselves at a discount.

Promotion

Japanese women perceive themselves as being more homogeneous in their appearance than white occidental women are. They see themselves as having the same skin tones, the same facial bone structure, and basically black hair.

They see Caucasian women as having more varied hair and eye colors and skin tones.

In sales brochures, Avon finds that it is more effective to use Caucasian models for makeup—allowing a Japanese woman to see a wide variety of special effects more easily. Interestingly and understandably, however, Japanese women prefer Japanese models in promotions of skin-care products. It is reassuring for them to know that Avon's skin-care products are "right" for Japanese skin.

SUMMARY

An analysis of culture provides the basis for developing international marketing strategies. A thorough cross-cultural analysis examines the demographic, organizational, and normative dimensions of each foreign market a multinational corporation considers entering. The *demographic dimension* refers to a population's age, income, and education distributions, and to factors such as the literacy rate and degree of urbanization. The *organizational dimension* refers to the structure of society and cultural institutions: social classes, family units, and business networks are included. The *normative dimension* refers to the cultural values held by the society. These values have a direct influence on the manner in which members of a society perceive products, advertising, and so forth.

The field of consumer behavior owes much of its fundamental understanding of culture to cultural anthropology and sociology. Behavioral scientists have discussed a number of aspects of culture that are particularly relevant to consumer behavior: cultural symbolism, cultural pervasiveness, cultural values, and the relationship between language and culture. As *symbols*, products, brands, and services often have subtle yet specific cultural meanings that vary cross-nationally. Marketers must take a culture's symbolic order into account in developing strategic plans. Besides being symbolic, culture is *pervasive:* It influences every aspect of life. Members of a cultural group tend to become culture bound and ethnocentric, believing their culture to be superior to others, and evaluating foreign beliefs and practices from the point of view of their own beliefs. Successful multinational firms, however, adopt an attitude of *cultural relativism,* accepting foreign cultures nonjudgmentally.

Cultural *values and norms* are integrally related to buyer behavior. Values and norms can influence consumers' tastes for particular products, the structure of the decision-making process, and other aspects of buyer behavior, such as brand loyalty and the perception of risk.

Cultural anthropologists have also studied the relationship between *language and culture*. Language is doubly relevant to advertising outside a firm's own culture. *Back-translation* of advertising messages can help to ensure that the translation is correct. Language also plays a role in the transmission of culture. The Whorf-Sapir hypothesis suggests that the structure of language restricts individuals' perceptions and relationships. We are unaware of these limitations, since our language seemingly allows us to express all our ideas and emotions.

Culture can have an impact on elements of the marketing mix. Product positioning, pricing decisions, and distribution structures are sensitive to cultural variations.

KEY CONCEPTS

ethnocentricity
cross-cultural analysis
  demographic
    dimension
  organizational
    dimension
  normative dimension
folk society
industrial society

values
norms
goal orientations
cultural symbolism
  referential
    symbolism
  expressive
    symbolism

cultural pervasiveness
  culture bound
  culture shock
cultural relativism
socialization
Whorf-Sapir
  hypothesis

DISCUSSION QUESTIONS

1. Considering the demographic information provided in Exhibit 22–1, choose the most promising markets (countries) for each of the products listed below.
   - Frozen vegetables
   - Magazines
   - Compact cars
   - Fine china

   What other information would be needed to supplement the demographic data in each case?

2. Describe the various roles played by the demographic, organizational, and normative dimensions of buyer behavior. Does any one of these three dimensions influence consumer behavior more than the others? Explain.

3. Ethnocentricity is an element of cultural pervasiveness. How does it affect the multinational marketer?

4. In general, what types of products are more likely to be characterized by cultural symbolism? What general marketing guidelines would you suggest for highly symbolic goods?

5. How can advertisements show cultural relativism?

6. If you were a brand manager for disposable diapers, investigating the possibility of expanding into foreign markets, what cultural considerations would you take into account?

7. How does culture affect the design of the marketing mix?
8. Select two foreign companies or products that you believe have been highly successful in your country and two that have been less successful. Compare and contrast the marketing strategies used for product positioning, distribution, and pricing.

NOTES

1. J. William Fulbright (1979), "We're Tongue-Tied," *Newsweek* (July 30), p. 15.
2. Robert Redfield (1956), *Peasant, Society, and Culture* (Chicago: Univ. of Chicago Press).
3. Stanley M. Davis (1969), "U.S. versus Latin America: Business and Culture," *Harvard Business Review*, 47 (Nov./Dec.), pp. 88–98.
4. R. E. Weingand (1963), "Department Stores in Japan," *Journal of Retailing*, 39 (Fall), pp. 31–35, 52.
5. Exxon Eastern Organization (1980), *Australian and American Cultures: Similarities, Differences, Difficulties,* unpublished report (Houston).
6. Benjamin Franklin (1806), *The Complete Works of the Late Dr. Benjamin Franklin* (London: J. Johnson and Co.), pp. 454–55.
7. Susan P. Douglas and Bernard Dubois (1977), "Looking at the Cultural Environment for International Marketing Opportunities," *Columbia Journal of World Business*, 12 (Winter), pp. 102–9.
8. L. Stessin (1975), "Bracing for the Arab World's Culture Shock," *New York Times* (Feb. 2), p. F–7.
9. Ferdinand F. Mauser (1977), "Losing Something in the Translation," *Harvard Business Review*, 55, 4 (July/Aug.), pp. 14, 163–64.
10. Ralph Linton (1937), "One Hundred Percent American," *American Mercury*, 40 (Apr.), pp. 427–29.
11. E. B. Tylor (1891), *Primitive Culture* (London: John Murrary), p. 1.
12. Richard A. Peterson (1979), "Revitalizing the Culture Concept," *Annual Review of Sociology*, 5, pp. 137–66.
13. Thomas D. Kemper (1981), "Social Constructionist and Positivist Approaches to the Sociology of Emotions," *American Journal of Sociology*, 87, pp. 336–62.
14. Chem L. Narayana (1981), "Aggregate Images of American and Japanese Products: Implications on International Marketing," *Columbia Journal of World Business*, 16 (Summer), pp. 31–35.
15. John R. Darling (1981), "The Competitive Marketplace Abroad: A Comparative Study," *Columbia Journal of World Business*, 16 (Fall), pp. 53–62.
16. Hyman Rodman (1972), "Marital Power and the Theory of Resources in Cross Cultural Context," *Journal of Comparative Family Studies*, 1, pp. 50–67.
17. Alfred S. Boote (1982–83), "Psychographic Segmentation in Europe," *Journal of Advertising Research*, 22 (Dec./Jan), pp. 19–25.
18. U. S. Weichmann (1974), "Integrating Multinational Marketing Activities," *Columbia Journal of World Business*, 9 (Winter), pp. 17–24.
19. S. Watson Dunn (1976), "Effect of National Identity on Multinational Promotional Strategy in Europe," *Journal of Marketing*, 40 (Oct.), pp. 50–57.
20. Ron Butler (1980), "A Hamburger That's Devouring the World," *Philadelphia Inquirer* (Feb. 3), p. 5G.
21. K. Erlich (1979), "Advertising in China," *China Business Review*, 6 (July/Aug.), pp. 10–12.
22. S. Watson Dunn (1976).
23. Richard W. Brislin (1970), "Back-Translation for Cross-Cultural Research," *Journal of Cross-Cultural Psychology*, 1 (Sept.), pp. 185–216.
24. Edward Sapir (1929), "The Status of Linguistics as a Science," *Language*, 5, pp. 207–14.

25. Benjamin Whorf (1956), *Language, Thought, and Reality* (New York: Wiley), p. 216. (First published 1940.)

26. Susan P. Douglas (1979), *A Cross-National Exploration of Husband-Wife Involvement in Selected Household Activities*, Marketing Science Institute Report No. 79–103 (Cambridge, Mass.: Marketing Science Inst.).

27. J. Vinocur (1979), "German Burden of Wealth: A Hunt for Status Symbols," *New York Times* (May 3), p. A-12.

28. Joseph T. Plummer (1977), "Consumer Focus in Cross-National Research," *Journal of Advertising*, 6 (Spring), pp. 5–15.

29. J. Fayerweather (1965), *International Marketing* (Englewood Cliffs, N.J.: Prentice-Hall).

30. Susan P. Douglas (1978), "Cross National Comparisons and Consumer Stereotypes," in *European Business in International Business* (Amsterdam: North Holland), pp. 263–81.

31. M. Shimaguci (1978), *Marketing Channels in Japan* (Ann Arbor, Mich.: U.M.I. Research Press).

32. Yoshi Tsurumi (1982), "Managing Consumer and International Marketing Systems in Japan," *Sloan Management Review*, 24 (Fall), pp. 41–50.

33. Yoshi Tsurumi (1982), p. 45.

23 Consumerism, Social Policy, and Consumer Satisfaction

The term **consumerism** is a broad one, generally referring to activities having to do with "consumer welfare," and involving consumers, legislative activities and agencies, and businesses. To some, consumerism and consumer welfare mean dissatisfaction with specific business practices, or even general dissatisfaction with the free enterprise system. To federal and state legislatures and government agencies, they mean laws and regulations affecting a broad spectrum of business practices, from deceptive advertising to antitrust violations. To businesspeople, consumerism means the need for corporate responsibility, and underscores the importance of carefully evaluating virtually every corporate action from production to manufacturing and from marketing practices to the firm's investment portfolio.

In any case, consumerism seems best defined as a social movement, which some have likened to the development of labor unions, or to the development of other movements, such as student rights, farm workers, and American Indians. In the same way that labor unions and companies negotiated the nature of their exchange relationship in the American labor movement, our definition of consumerism focuses on the rights and obligations of consumers and marketers whenever they are involved in exchange transactions, including prepurchase and postpurchase activities, as well as the activities of the transaction itself. Finally, this notion of consumerism involves other parties to the exchange: government agencies and legislatures, and consumer-movement leaders, or "consumerists," such as Ralph Nader.

In this chapter, we examine the relationship between consumer-behavior theories, concepts, and research findings, and consumerism. As an area of research, consumer behavior has the potential to be useful to the four groups involved in consumerism: ultimate consumers, consumerists, government entities, and marketers.

We begin by describing the sociological, governmental, and business dimensions to consumerism. Then we assess consumer behavior's potential role in the consumerism movement, and assess the field's inputs to consumerism issues.

The breadth and scope of consumerism are reflected in Exhibit 23–1. Virtually every area of business activity may be linked to some consumerism issues. In many cases, particular consumer groups have positioned themselves as particularly concerned with a specific issue—for example, Action for Children's Television is an international group that seeks improvements in programming and advertising affecting child audiences. Other groups, such as "Nader's Raiders," raise issues across a broad range of consumerism issues.

Consumerism is often associated with such recent concerns as those triggered by Rachel Carson's investigations into pollution,[1] Ralph Nader's initial concerns with automobile safety,[2] Robert Choate's attacks against "empty calories" in breakfast cereals advertised to children,[3] and President Kennedy's four freedoms for consumers: to be safe, to be informed, to choose, and to be heard.[4]

EXHIBIT 23–1
EXAMPLES OF CONSUMERISM ISSUES RELATED TO VARIOUS BUSINESS ACTIVITIES

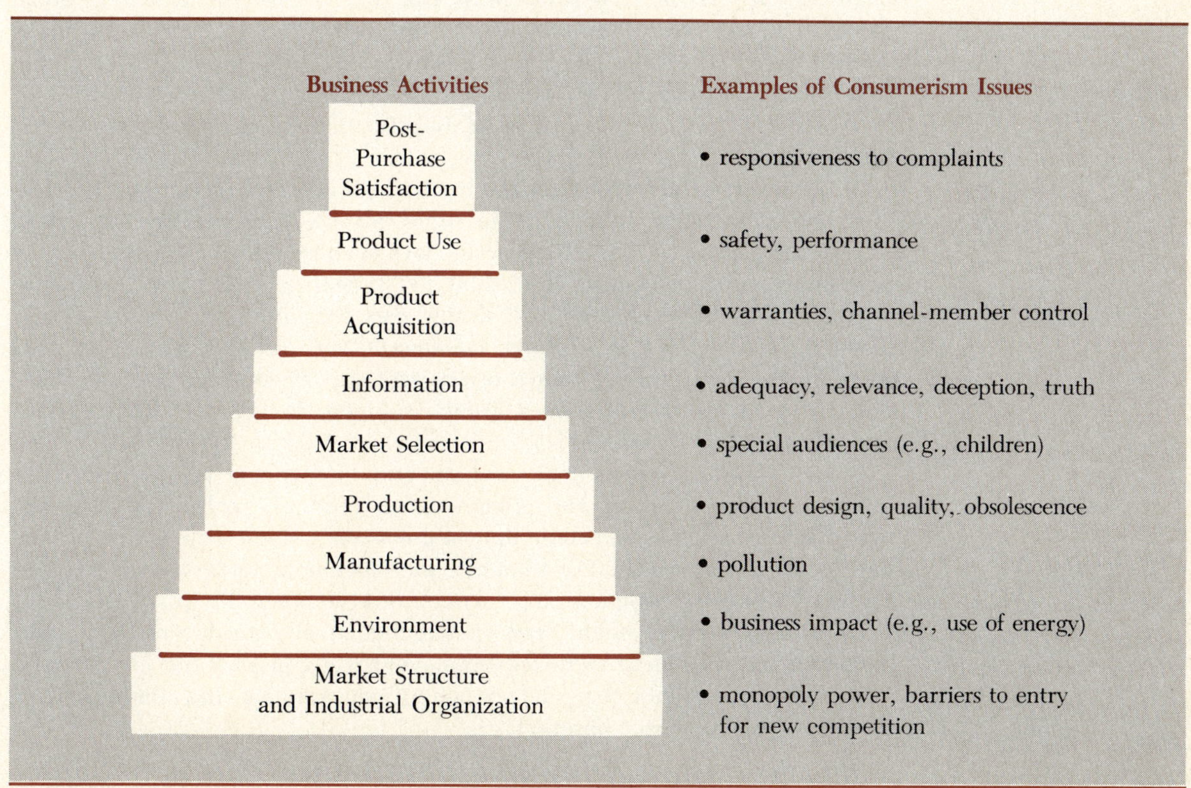

Sociological Dimension

As a *sociological* phenomenon, consumerism's roots may be traced to Upton Sinclair's early exposés of seamy conditions in American industries. His book *The Jungle*[5] is credited with compelling Congress to pass early "consumer protection" laws providing for meat inspection. By the depression era of the late 1920s and 1930s, and into the World War II era, the consumer movement usually took the form of educating consumers to budget carefully, invest in savings, and so forth.[6]

social movement

By the 1960s and 1970s, consumerism had emerged as a social movement, with broad concerns and diverse objectives. As Bloom and Greyser observe:

> *Conditions were right for the movement. The increased complexity of products, the broadening of self-service channels and depersonalization of shopping, the growth of consumer services (of which consumers have more difficulty in judging quality), the broader availability of the "material things of life" to those with newly expanded discretionary buying power, and other factors—all combined to create strong "consumer demand" for ideas and actions that would help the public obtain a better deal in the marketplace.*[7]

During those years, the consumerism movement achieved some significant victories, such as the Magnuson-Moss Bill (which gave the Congress broad power to address consumer complaints), the establishment of the Consumer Product Safety Commission, and truth-in-lending legislation. However, the proportion of pro-regulation votes has declined, and anti-regulation votes have increased in the U.S. House of Representatives from the 92nd to the 96th Congress.

In the era of deregulation, beginning under President Carter and accelerating under President Reagan, some argue that the consumerism movement is following a kind of product life cycle. Two such models for the life cycle of social movements are shown in Exhibit 23–2. Both models portray a waning of broad public interest, although Kotler sees consumerism issues gradually becoming institutionalized through *managerial* and *bureaucratic* stages over time.[8] Kotler also suggests that consumerism may become increasingly fragmented as specialized consumer groups compete for support from various market segments.

Downs' model suggests that consumerism movements progress through stages of great enthusiasm and militancy, but suddenly realize that progress toward achieving goals will come only at great cost, which societal institutions may be unwilling to bear. For example, the movement against advertising on children's television programming encountered the possibility that withdrawal of advertising support might lead to a reduction of Saturday morning programming aimed at child audiences—an event many parents did not desire!

There is little doubt that the potency of consumerism has diminished in the 1980s. As one writer observes:

> *The return swing of the pendulum . . . was just as rapid and unexpected. Specific industries—insurance, breakfast cereals, advertising, tobacco,*

*medicine, began to spend serious money on candidates. Consumerists, be-
cause they had attacked on so broad a front, unified their enemies. Um-
brella trade associations like the Chamber of Commerce and the Business
Roundtable were able to exploit wider misgivings about too much government. . . . Things got so silly that Representative Marty Russo of Illinois
could claim with a straight face that the funeral cost-disclosure rule would
reduce productivity.*[9]

EXHIBIT 23–2
ALTERNATIVE MODELS OF THE LIFE CYCLE OF A SOCIAL MOVEMENT

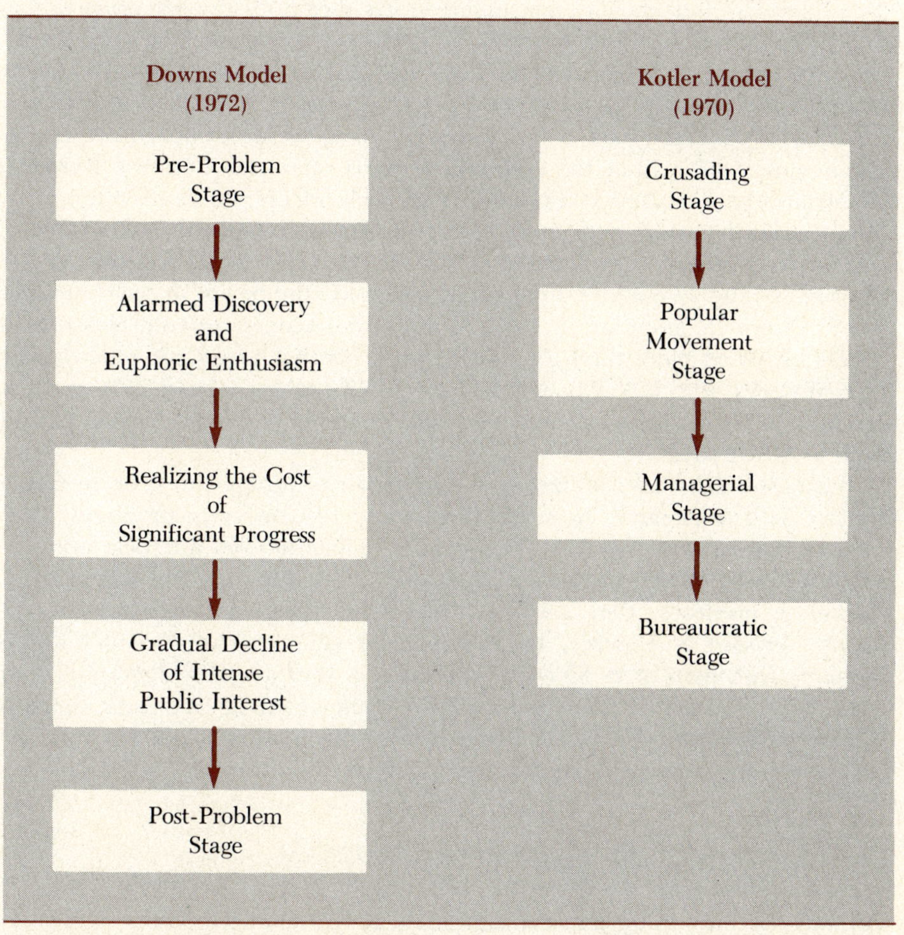

SOURCE: Adapted from Paul N. Bloom and Stephen A. Greyser (1981), "Exploring the Future of
Consumerism," working paper no. 81-102 (Cambridge, Mass.: Marketing Science Inst.), July,
p. 4. Models are proposed by Anthony Downs (1972), "Up and Down with Ecology—the 'Issue-
Attention Cycle,' " *The Public Interest*, 28 (summer), pp. 38–50 and Philip Kotler (1971), "The
Elements of Social Action," *American Behavioral Scientist* (May/June), pp. 691–717.

Governmental Dimension

As a *governmental* phenomenon, consumerism resulted in new laws, establishment of federal regulatory agencies, and the strengthening of existing agencies at the federal and state levels. For example, sixteen federal agencies in the area of consumer safety and health experienced total budget increases of 105 percent (from $1.3 billion to $2.7 billion) in the period of intense consumerism activity from 1974 to 1979.[10] In the deregulation era of the 1980s, these budgets have been sharply curtailed.

Business Dimension

As a *business* phenomenon, consumerism has meant greater attention to virtually all areas of business practice. In particular, companies have bolstered existing industry self-regulatory bodies, such as Underwriters Laboratories in the electrical industry, to assure product standards. New mechanisms for voluntary self-regulation have been established, such as the Children's Advertising Review Unit within the National Council of Better Business Bureaus. Companies have expanded the number of public affairs positions within firms to more closely monitor consumer and governmental concerns and activities.

Voluntary recall of products is increasing, perhaps largely because of the Consumer Product Safety Commission, which has the power to order product recalls. Since its founding in 1973, to 1981, the agency ordered about 1830 recalls involving more than 108 million products that posed potential danger to consumers. The U.S. Food and Drug Administration issued 2568 product recalls (mostly for labeling and medicine quantity problems) in the period from 1978 to 1981.[11]

Businesses have also utilized new marketing techniques to keep in direct contact with consumers, in order to be more responsive to problems. One such technique is the use of 800 numbers. Some 106,000 numbers are currently used by 60,000 businesses. Although these 800 numbers are used for marketing purposes, they are also used for responding to consumer complaints. Procter & Gamble, for example, provides one of several toll-free numbers with each of its fifty-nine products. A staff of eighty-five employees handles an average of 1200 calls daily.[12] While relatively few calls concern product complaints, the mechanism provides the company with a system for close communication and monitoring of consumer satisfaction.

CONSUMER BEHAVIOR AND CONSUMERISM

Perhaps the only thing that consumerists, government regulators, and marketers can agree about is that more information would be useful in dealing with issues raised by consumerism. However, various types of information are needed for different kinds of consumerism issues. For example, *economic analyses* are most useful in addressing issues of market structure and possible barriers to new competition. As a case in point, the Federal Trade Commission used economic research in its inquiry into possible barriers to entry in the breakfast-cereal market.[13] The allegation was that the market structure, of a few large firms accounting for the majority of advertising and market shares, might impede the entry of new firms into the market. For other issues, such as those involving the environment or manufacturing and production activities, data are most often sought to measure industry compliance with standards—such as those for air quality and product design.

The concepts, theories, and research data resulting from the study of consumer behavior are particularly pertinent to the top five areas portrayed in Exhibit 23–1. As we shall see in this chapter, consumer-behavior research has helped to illuminate issues such as marketing impacts on special audiences (especially the poor, the elderly, and children). These concepts and data have contributed to programs dealing with product information disclosures such as warnings on labels and informative package inserts. The study of consumer behavior has generated concepts and data related to marketing information—in particular, evidence concerning how consumers process information in making product and brand choices, and what kinds of information are most useful in making decisions (see Chapters 4 and 5).

Types of Consumer-Behavior Research for Consumerism Issues

Many types of consumer-behavior research are relevant to consumerism issues. The earliest traditions of research in the field borrowed concepts from basic behavioral disciplines and applied them to consumption phenomena. For example, findings from studies of message-source credibility in social psychology and communications research have been applied to decisions regarding what kind of spokesperson to use in advertising messages. Such research can be useful in consumerism debates. For example, source-credibility research was used to assess the allegation that a particular actor's endorsement of a low-caffeine coffee might deceive some consumers since the actor portrayed a physician on a popular, prime-time television series. Some argued that the source effect was so strong that some consumers might believe the actor's assertions represented a medical endorsement. Early source-credibility research provided an empirical basis for examining the advertising and a conceptual basis for assessing the alleged communication processes. However, more specific studies, using the particular advertising in question, would be required to calibrate the precise effects of the actor's endorsement.

In recent years, consumer-behavior researchers have begun to design studies that are directly related to consumerism issues. The increase in such studies reflects the increasing interest of consumer-behavior researchers in these areas, as well as the receptivity of those involved in consumerism issues to the concepts, theories, and empirical findings emanating from the field of consumer behavior. For example, some researchers have investigated consumerism implications of marketing practices affecting particular market segments, including the urban poor[14] and children.[15]

Who can use consumer-behavior concepts and findings, and in what way? Exhibit 23–3 identifies the four parties to consumerism issues, and suggests some ways the field of consumer behavior can be useful. For legislators and government-agency officials, the concepts and research of consumer behavior can help to identify problems and to describe and explain underlying behavioral processes. For example, the Federal Trade Commission, with its limited staff and financial resources, must continually choose which deceptive advertising cases to pursue. Such choices must be based on the apparent severity of the suspected deception, the likelihood of accomplishing the FTC's objective, and the costs and benefits to consumers. Consumer-behavior research

EXHIBIT 23–3
CONSUMER BEHAVIOR RESEARCH AND ITS USERS

Uses of Consumer-Behavior Research Pertaining to "Consumerism" Issues	How Consumer-Behavior Research Can Be Useful
Government Legislators and Agencies (such as the Federal Trade Commission)	• identify problem areas (such as product safety and deceptive marketing practices) • describe and explain underlying patterns of consumer behavior (such as responses to advertising claims)
Marketers	• understand dimensions of consumer satisfaction and dissatisfaction with marketers' products and services • describe underlying consumer behavior patterns to guide marketing activities (such as advertising execution and product design)
Consumer Movement Leaders	• to identify problem areas • to document arguments • to better understand relevant behavioral phenomena
Ultimate Consumers	• to become more effective and efficient in marketplace transactions by better understanding consumer-behavior patterns

can help by pinpointing problem areas through consumer responses to advertising.

Marketers can find consumer analysis helpful in dealing with consumerism as they seek to understand consumer satisfaction and dissatisfaction with their products and services. Moreover, consumer analysis can guide marketing activities by answering questions about how consumers interpret advertising claims, how they use various products, and so on.

Finally, consumer movement leaders and ultimate consumers may benefit from consumer-behavior research. Consumerists can better document their arguments and gain greater understanding of various aspects of consumer behavior. For example, Action for Children's Television has extensively documented its petitions and legal complaints with references to research on television advertising's effects on children. Ultimately, consumers themselves should be helped by becoming more efficient and effective in their consumption behavior. Such "consumer education" may develop rapidly in the future, as consumer-behavior researchers turn increasingly to applied topics.

Difficulties in Applying Consumer Behavior to Consumerism Issues

Despite the potential value of consumer-behavior concepts, theories, and research to be useful to the various parties to consumerism, there are significant problems. Most parties agree that "more data are needed" to assess and resolve issues—regarding both the extent and nature of problem areas, and the costs versus the benefits of possible solutions. However, they want very different kinds of data, and want to use consumer-behavior information in very different ways. These differences stem from three underlying problems:

- Differences in approaches to consumerism issues and conflict resolution;
- Differences in underlying values; and
- Poorly defined issues and/or off-target approaches to research.

Differences in Approaches to Consumerism Issues The parties to consumerism issues are guided by self-interest. They are less interested in full and objective research on an issue than they are in findings that support their position and objectives. While such biases may be inherent in any disputes and negotiations, the problem is intensified by the advocacy mode of litigation in American courts, where many consumerism battles are waged. For example, until recently, evidence from consumer-behavior research was rarely used in litigation involving consumerism issues because the courts viewed empirical-research evidence, based on data from samples of consumers, as "hearsay"—unsupportable evidence which is inadmissable in courts. In our legal system, testimony on consumerism issues was based primarily on case law—that is, on legal precedents that were set in earlier, similar cases. To the extent that other testimony was used, it was obtained from expert witnesses, usually psychologists or psychiatrists, who based their testimony on clinical experience. Over time, however, the courts have ruled that data from empirical studies is admissable. The consumerism movement has been a major impetus toward expanding the nature of evidence used in litigation.[16] For example, over the course of this century, consumer inputs (including direct testimony from consumers as well as survey evidence and other forms of empirical research) have increased from 4 percent to over 50 percent of the categories of evidence in FTC deliberations.[17]

The parties to consumerism controversies sometimes have little interest in consumer-behavior research, preferring to use publicity, proxy fights, or other approaches that avoid objective and systematic analyses of patterns of consumer behavior.

In some cases, consumer data are desired only to document and describe a particular phenomenon, such as the incidence and severity of accidents associated with a product. In other cases, more explanatory data are desired. For example, a consumer group may want information about how different individuals respond to comparative claims made in an advertisement.

Differences in Underlying Values   A second major problem is the differences in the values of the parties to consumerism controversies. Conflicting values often reduce the usefulness of consumer-behavior information, since empirical data are not relevant to values, unless individuals are willing to change values on the basis of such data. But such open-mindedness is not characteristic of many consumerism debates. For example, the FTC has maintained that if 5 to 10 percent of persons exposed to advertising are deceived or misled, it might initiate action against the advertiser. Advertisers have maintained that the 5 to 10 percent level is too low and that most forms of mass communication, including newscasts and programming, as well as advertising, generate similar and even higher levels of miscomprehension. The American Association of Advertising Agencies commissioned a study to investigate the relative levels of miscomprehension for various types of mass-communication content. The results suggest that between one fourth and one third of all material broadcast over commercial television is miscomprehended by viewers. Advertising and programming excerpts were miscomprehended at similar levels, and levels were even higher for televised editorials and local newscasts.[18]

Even though these findings are consistent with the results of other studies, and with the concept of selective attention and the low-involvement nature of television viewing (see Chapters 5 and 10), they were attacked on several grounds. The nature of the test used to measure miscomprehension was questioned, as was the **external validity** of the findings—that is, the extent to which the laboratory results would hold under real-world conditions.[19] Perhaps more importantly, in spite of the acknowledged limitations of the study, many may use the results to argue for a less stringent FTC standard for assessing problems regarding miscomprehension of advertising, whereas others may still favor the more stringent 5 to 10 percent criterion. The data themselves cannot resolve issues of values.

Poorly Defined Issues and Off-Target Research   The third barrier to consumer behavior's utility in consumerism disputes stems from the interacting problems of poorly defined issues and approaches to research that may not be consistent with the needs of the parties to consumerism controversies. Consumerism issues are often specified more in terms of emotions and values than as empirical issues that may be submitted to objective analysis.

One manifestation of these problems is the incomplete statement of issues, as when an effect is alleged without a cause. In the controversy over advertising and children, for example, it is sometimes simply alleged that "children cannot understand commercials." On the other hand, some consumerists may allege causes without specific effects—for example, "premium offers are unfair." Such poorly delineated issues provide little guidance for the consumer-behavior researcher for structuring analyses and investigations. What mechanisms are thought to impede children's understanding? What effects are thought to occur as a result of exposure to advertising containing premium offers? In the absence of such specification, and to some extent because the use of consumer-behavior research in consumerism disputes is fairly recent, research is often "off the mark," in that it fails to be fully relevant to the needs and desires of parties to consumerism issues. For example, in the area of advertising to children, several content analyses have simply assessed the frequency with which different kinds of advertising appear on television at different times.[20] Such descriptive research may be useful only as an objective assessment of the occurrence of types of advertising; it does nothing to explore the effects of various types of advertising on children.

Issues may be interrelated and confounded, adding to the difficulty of understanding what types of consumer-behavior input would be useful. For example, a major proposal of some consumer groups is to eliminate advertising aimed at child audiences for products containing certain amounts of sugar. From the consumerist's point of view, such a proposal has a high probability of acceptance, since it might gain the support of groups opposed to advertising, as well as health-related groups opposed to sugar consumption. However, from the point of view of the consumer-behavior researcher, the issue is not clear—does it concern advertising's effects on children, a particular type of advertising, or possible detrimental effects of sugar in the products themselves?

To summarize, consumer behavior concepts and theories, and data from empirical studies can be useful to consumerism issues in several ways:

- by identifying potential problem areas (for example, descriptive research on the nature and severity of injuries from product use);
- by providing an empirical basis for assessing issues (for example, examining processes by which consumers evaluate comparative claims in advertising

or assessing the nature of children's responses to television commercials); and

- by assessing the efficacy of proposed solutions to consumerism problems (for example, research that evaluates consumer responses to information disclosures on package labeling).

The usefulness of consumer research in specifying and assessing consumerism issues depends on the extent to which issues are specified for empirical analysis, the willingness of parties to controversies to separate value positions from empirical issues, and the diligence of the consumer-behavior researcher to design and carry out research that is pertinent to specific policy needs.

APPLYING CONSUMER BEHAVIOR TO CONSUMERISM ISSUES: TWO CASES

Consumer-behavior concepts, theories, and data have been useful in consumerism issues, despite the problems we have just discussed. Although many forces were at work in the consumerism issues we review here (such as political influences, lobbying, and so forth), the field of consumer behavior provided useful input in (1) Federal Trade Commission (FTC) actions to regulate advertising and (2) information disclosure requirements—that is, what amounts and types of information should be disclosed to consumers, and in what form?

EXHIBIT 23–4
MAJOR ISSUE AREAS IN CONSUMERISM CONTROVERSIES

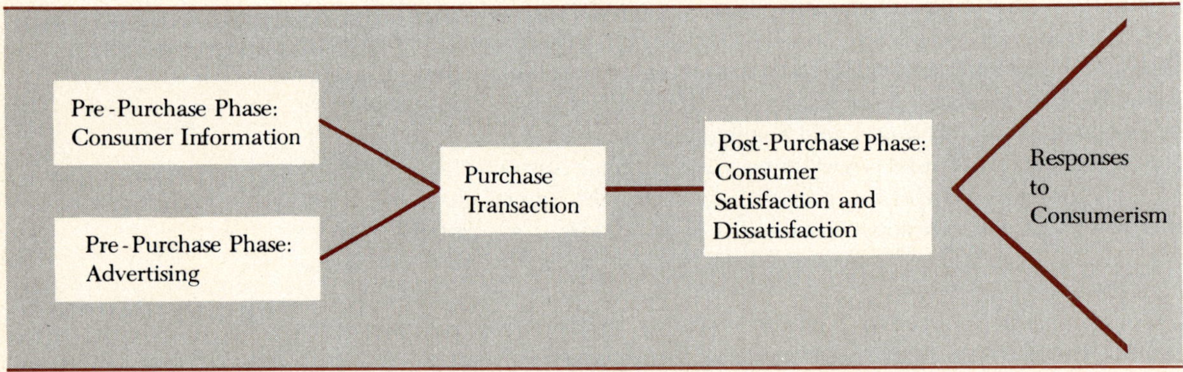

SOURCE: David A. Aaker and George S. Day (1978), *Consumerism*, 3rd ed. (New York: Free Press). The model is derived from the outline of chapters in this book.

These two issues may be conceptualized in terms of the major areas of consumerism issues portrayed in Exhibit 23–4. They both pertain to *Pre-Purchase* activities: the availability of product information and the impact of advertising on consumers. The *Purchase Transaction* area involves issues such as product standards (for example, whether generic prescription drugs are equivalent to branded drugs), ecological problems (for example, the costs and benefits of bills requiring cash deposits on product containers), and, at the macro level, market-structure constraints on product choice (antitrust issues).

pre-purchase

purchase transaction

The *Post-Purchase* area involves consumerism issues arising from warranties and service, product safety and liability, and consumer satisfaction. In recent years, consumer-behavior researchers have turned their attention to defining the dimensions underlying consumer satisfaction and dissatisfaction, assessing the nature of consumer complaints, and developing adequate measures of consumer satisfaction and dissatisfaction. We discuss these areas later in this chapter.

post-purchase

CASE 1: THE FTC'S PROGRAMS TO REGULATE ADVERTISING

The original charge of the Federal Trade Commission, established in 1914, was to "prohibit unfair methods of competition," but the Wheeler-Lea Act of 1939 extended its powers to include regulation of "unfair, deceptive, and misleading" commercial acts. The FTC cannot propose or pass laws, and technically, it cannot "punish" offenders (for example, by levying monetary fines). It can hold hearings and prohibit practices found to be "unfair, deceptive and misleading."

For many years, the FTC focused mainly on antitrust issues, and when it did pursue cases of fraudulent selling and misleading advertising, the agency's targets were often local companies. When it did take on major national advertisers, its procedures were so slow as to be ineffective.*

In recent years, the FTC has become considerably more active and timely in pursuing major cases of questionable advertising. Spurred by a critical report by the American Bar Association, and the appointment of an energetic chairman (Myles Kirkpatrick) by President Nixon, the agency held hearings on "Modern Advertising Practices" in 1972. At these informational hearings, the business community, the legal profession, and consumer groups aired their attacks on and defenses of advertising. An implicit objective of the hear-

---

*For example, in 1959, the FTC charged Bristol-Meyers, manufacturers of Rapid-Shave shaving creme, with deception because an advertisement purported to show the softening power of the product by a demonstration involving "shaving sandpaper." In fact, since sandpaper did not hold up well in the commercial, the company's advertising agency glued grains of sand on plexiglass. The FTC issued a cease-and-desist order, but appeals through the federal courts delayed ultimate disposition of the case for six years—long after the deceptive advertising campaign was history.[21]

ings was to provide a framework for possible regulation of advertising. The breadth of opinion about how advertising works was sought because the FTC is composed primarily of economists and lawyers, rather than marketers and behavioral scientists who could bring their perspectives to bear on Commission actions.

Subsequent FTC actions with respect to advertising are reflected in increased concern expressed in public attitudes. For example, a recent national survey indicates that 9 percent of Americans believe that *all* television advertising is *seriously* misleading, 37 percent think *most* of it is seriously misleading, and 39 percent think *some*. Comparable figures for newspaper and magazine advertising are 4 percent *(all)*, 24 percent *(most)* and 50 percent *(some)*.[22]

advocacy system

trade regulation rules

The FTC proceeds in essentially two ways: (1) the **advocacy system** and (2) issuance of **trade regulation rules** (TRRs). In the traditional advocacy system (case-by-case approach), findings for or against a particular advertiser in a particular case become the precedent for similar cases. *TRRs* refer to broad prohibitions across all marketers within an industry.

The FTC has traditionally had five weapons at its disposal:

1. *Letter of Compliance*—an informal arrangement that merely involves a written promise to discontinue a practice that the FTC has disputed.
2. *Stipulation*—a recorded public action that stops short of a courtroom hearing; can be used as evidence in future hearings, but does not constitute admission of guilt.
3. *Consent Order*—a short-cut settlement after a formal complaint has been issued; still does not constitute admission of guilt.
4. *Cease-and-Desist Order*—a finding of guilt after a hearing; may be appealed to any Federal Court of Appeals.
5. *Publicity*—all complaints are publicized in news releases; the longer a case is contested, the more publicity is likely.

Increasingly, the FTC is relying on issuance of trade regulation rules (TRRs) that can prohibit general practices, without waiting for specific cases. But even though the great majority of FTC actions stop short of actual cases, when advertisers and the FTC do lock horns in a case it is first heard before an administrative-law judge, whose primary mission is to compile a record. He or she renders a finding, which can be accepted or rejected by the full five-person Commission. TRR hearings, on the other hand, are held before a hearing examiner, who is an FTC employee. Both findings from cases and TRR hearings can be appealed by respondents (advertisers) in federal courts.

Once the Commission began to receive inputs beyond those of lawyers and economists, information about marketing practices and consumer behavior led to two major developments—and to new remedies for questionable advertising that are firmly rooted in behavioral notions of consumer information processing. The most important of these remedies are discussed below.

Advertising Substantiation

In 1971, the Commission announced a program requiring **substantiation** of explicit or implicit claims in advertising, both to deter advertisers from making unsubstantiated claims, and to help consumers make more "rational" buying decisions. Explicit claims must be supported by objective tests. In the Firestone case, for example, "persons with skill and expertise in the field conduct the test and evaluate its results in a disinterested manner using testing procedures generally accepted in the profession which best insure accurate results."[23] More difficult, of course, is determining whether a claim is **puffery,** or whether it involves an implicit claim for which there is no reasonable basis for substantiation. (Consider, for example, "Milwaukee's finest beer" or "the best handling compact car.")

puffery

A second development reflecting the FTC's increasing scope of concern is in the area of **uniqueness claims.** Even substantiated claims may not be used if (unsupported) uniqueness is implied by an advertisement. For example, Wonder Bread advertised that it "helps build strong bodies twelve ways." While technically true, every bread apparently contributes to growth in much the same way.[24]

uniqueness claims

The FTC proposed some remedies for false, deceptive, or misleading advertising. One such remedy is **affirmative disclosure,** which was proposed both through the Commission and through "Truth in Advertising" legislation. Essentially, affirmative disclosure shifts the burden of proof of advertising claims to the advertiser. Opponents of affirmative disclosure argue that it would be costly to perform all the tests necessary to support claims fully, and these costs would be passed on to consumers. Moreover, they argue, affirmative disclosure will inhibit advertisers from making much more than platitudinous statements, to avoid possible entanglements.

affirmative disclosure

Corrective Advertising

The Commission has often threatened, and occasionally invoked, **corrective advertising** to correct past deception. Essentially, advertisers are required to devote some portion of the advertising budget over some defined time period to corrective advertising. In the Profile bread case, for example, the company (Continental Baking) was ordered to devote 25 percent of its advertising budget for one year to messages refuting the earlier alleged impression that the bread has fewer calories per ounce. (While initial results showed heightened awareness of the bread during the year the corrective advertising ran, sales eventually dropped 20 percent.[25])

The FTC has not frequently used the corrective-advertising weapon, perhaps because it raises so many legitimate questions. How much time and money should be spent, on what kind of messages? In fact, one advertiser publicized the results of four independent tests that it felt refuted FTC contentions of deception. The headline read:

> *If every motorist used Chevron with F–310 for 2,000 miles, air pollutants would be reduced by thousands of tons in a single day. The Federal Trade Commission doesn't seem to think that's significant. We think it is.*

In the parlance of communications research, such a headline is a **refutational-inoculation** message, that is, a message that *forewarns* (innoculates) readers against *counter* (refutational) messages that might be forthcoming. Such messages have been shown to blunt the effects of corrective advertising—as it did in the Chevron case.[26]

Another example of an advertiser's response to an FTC corrective-advertising order is shown in the text of STP's "corrective" ad, in Exhibit 23–5. The "advertisement" was run in business-oriented publications such as *Barron's* and *Business Week*. The choice of media may have missed many users of STP, and the language of the ad may be corrective only in a technical-legal sense, rather than in actually correcting consumer perceptions.

In more recent cases the FTC has turned to consumer research in order to determine whether or not a false impression has been corrected. In the case against Hawaiian Punch, for example, the Commission required the company to provide correct information about the amount of fruit juice actually in the drink. With a behavioral scientist's input, and the consent of the company and Commission, the company agreed to run advertising until the correct information was conveyed (measured by telephone survey) to 67 percent of all consumers, 80 percent of all fruit-drink purchasers, and 95 percent of Hawaiian Punch buyers.

Consumer Behavior and the FTC's Advertising Initiatives

One can search for the basis of these FTC trends by examining the legalistic definitions and findings in FTC decisions over the years. However, the continuing controversies surrounding advertising suggest that legal precedents alone are not sufficient to resolve consumerism issues involving "false, misleading, or deceptive" advertising. For example, defining *deceptive advertising* is difficult indeed—a matter of interpretation which, in an FTC's lawyer's view, can only evolve as a result of various cases and rulings.

The FTC clearly takes into account the "credulous" and the "naive," not just the "average," consumer in determining what is deceptive. Moreover, the FTC judges the entire advertisement, not just individual statements or parts of the message, to capture the overall tendency or capacity of an ad to mislead (actual *behavior* based on deception is not required). And the FTC shows increasing concern in its decisions with failure to disclose information and with ambiguous statements. The latter refer often to *puffery,* an acceptable advertising practice that has two general forms:

1. subjective statements about a product's quality ("the finest. . . .") and
2. exaggeration to the point of outright spoof (the "Jolly Green Giant").

FTC NOTICE

As a result of an investigation by the
Federal Trade Commission into certain allegedly
inaccurate past advertisements
for STP's oil additive, STP Corporation
has agreed to a $700,000 settlement.
With regard to that settlement,
STP is making the following statement:

It is the policy of STP to support its advertising with objective information and test data. In 1974 and 1975 an independent laboratory ran tests of the company's oil additive which led to claims of reduced oil consumption. However, these tests cannot be relied on to support the oil consumption reduction claim made by STP.

The FTC has taken the position that, in making that claim, the company violated the terms of a consent order. When STP learned that the test data did not support the claim, it stopped advertising containing that claim. New tests have been undertaken to determine the extent to which the oil additive affects oil consumption. Agreement to this settlement does not constitute an admission by STP that the law has been violated. Rather, STP has agreed to resolve the dispute with the FTC to avoid protracted and prohibitively expensive litigation.

The *models of consumer behavior* that guide FTC initiatives have apparently changed over the years. The two most important features of these implicit FTC "models" have been the *assumption of rationality,* and the *view of consumer information processing* reflected in Commission actions.

At one time the FTC seemed to view all consumers as "rational" men and women, in economic-theory terms. Consumers were thought to seek, find, and use all pertinent information in all consumer decisions. But consumer research has clearly shown that people are highly selective in seeking and using information, and that their patterns of information gathering and processing vary with type of consumer decision and among consumers (see Chapters 4 and 13).

The second important feature of the Commission's early model of consumer behavior is its view of how consumers process information.[27] First, an implicit notion behind the view is that *more information is better.* The view ignored consumers' varying needs and desires for information, the environment in which information is used, and the information gained through word-of-mouth influence and actual product experience. The frequent failure of consumer-education campaigns attest to the variety in need for information and the limitations of consumer information processing.

The Commission's early models also showed a *lack of concern with message quality and content.* The implicit belief seems to have been that if something is said in plain English, the message will "get through" to all consumers. Advertisers, fund raisers, politicians, and others have all found that messages do not always penetrate awareness, much less result in the intended effect. This lack of concern has affected both the Commission's selection of cases and its evaluation of corrective advertisements.

Finally, consumers were thought to *process information in a uniform way.* Consumer research, however, has shown that not all consumers want the same information and that the value of information to different consumers depends in part on when it is available. For example, some consumers may want information about the availability of products or services—during the initial phases of decision-making, while others may want more focused information—at different stages.

Industry Responses to Trends in Advertising Regulation

Increasingly, farsighted marketers are taking a hard look at appropriate strategies for marketing in response to consumerism issues. Many marketers feel that a good many of the consumerist thrusts, and FTC actions, are desirable because they discourage questionable advertising. They are adopting a proactive posture, rather than a reactive one. Some companies, for example, have dramatically expanded their advertising screening committees to include not only legal and marketing staff, but behavioral scientists, consumer representatives, and others, from various disciplines. Companies are also testing consumer response to advertising *before* it is actually run, both to anticipate problems and possibly modify campaigns, and because evidence gathered *before* possible FTC actions is more compelling than tests conducted after cases have been initiated.

Marketers and individuals within the FTC have begun to bring a behavioral perspective to bear within the Commission. Behavioral scientists now help to shape policy decisions, as well as influence the nature of acceptable evidence within TRR hearings and within case proceedings.

CASE 2: INFORMATION-DISCLOSURE REQUIREMENTS

Consumer behavior has also had input to the consumerism controversy involving "information disclosures." This issue concerns how much of what kinds of information should be disclosed—in what form—to segments of consumers, and with what objectives? Many consumerists have argued that, simply, "more information is better," while marketers have frequently taken the position that too much information may confuse and even mislead consumers. For example, the Pharmaceutical Manufacturers Association fought a proposed rule that would have mandated that advertising for antacids containing high amounts of sodium include verbal and/or visual warnings to consumers on low-sodium diets. The trade association's position was that such advertising might frighten all consumers, and so inhibit sales, and that persons on such diets are predisposed to read warning labels on package inserts (where the relevant information already appeared).

Given the microeconomics notion that consumers use all possible information, in order to make "rational" decisions, the idea that "more information is better" has found many supporters. The consumer's "right to know" was one of President Kennedy's four "consumer freedoms." Moreover, consumer-behavior concepts and research seem to support the essential notion, since consumer information processing involves "selective exposure" (consumers use information they see as relevant and pay less attention to information seen as irrelevant).

But conceptualizations of "information overload" (see Chapters 4 and 5) suggest a problem. Moreover, as Day points out, the specific objectives of proposed information-disclosure requirements are not clear:

> *. . . there is seldom agreement among proponents as to whether new requirements should simply enhance the consumer's "right to know," improve the quality of products and competition, facilitate value comparisons, enable buyers to better match products and needs and thus increase purchase satisfaction, or pursue broad education aims such as creating general public interest in nutrition or sensitivity to energy conservation.*[28]

One early study purported to show that increasing information on product packages tends to produce beneficial effects upon the consumer's degree of satisfaction but confusion regarding product selection: "In other words, our subjects felt better with more information, but actually made poorer purchase decisions."[29] This provocative study was attacked on several grounds, and reanalysis showed a reversal of the original conclusion of dysfunctional effects from increasing information.[30]

Subsequent studies focused on consumer uses of information pertaining to

EXHIBIT 23–6
RECENT OR PROSPECTIVE INFORMATION DISCLOSURE REQUIREMENTS
(illustrative, not comprehensive)

Type of Disclosure	Implemented in Past Five Years[a]	Probable in the Future[b]
1. Comparative prices	Truth in lending Unit pricing Automobile list prices	Prescription prices Truth in life insurance Costs of operation of appliances and automobiles Truth in consumer leasing
2. Comparative performance and efficiency	Nutrition labeling of food products Lumen and life data for bulbs Stereo amplifier power output Octane labeling Automobile performance (vehicle stopping distance, acceleration and passing ability, and tire reserve load)	Automobile gas mileage Appliance energy consumption and comparative efficiency Appliance performance Tire mileage, stopping ability, and high speed resistance to heat Carpet and upholstery wear characteristics Quality grade labels for food products Sun-screen efficacy of suntan preparations Standards of drug efficacy Detergent efficacy Vocational school drop-out rate
3. Ingredients (including additives)	Cosmetics Food Liquor Phosphate content of detergents	Labeling of fat content in food Presence of pesticides Pigment content of paint Labeling to explain purpose of food ingredients and additives

specific disclosure requirements. In an important review of these studies, Aaker and Day summarize recent or prospective information on disclosure requirements (Exhibit 23–6) and the evidence of effects of various information-disclosure requirements (Exhibit 23–7).

Mazis also summarizes studies evaluating specific disclosure programs.[31] He notes that many information-disclosure programs actually fail to expose consumers to information or to make them aware of information disclosures.

Type of Disclosure	Implemented in Past Five Years[a]	Probable in the Future[b]
4. Life/Perishability	Open dating of foods	Appliance durability and life Expiration dates for drug potency Automobile damage susceptibility and repair costs
5. Warnings/Clarifications	Cigarette health hazards Lack of efficacy of vitamins Flammability (children's sleepwear)	Flammability of cellular plastic insulation
6. Form and usage of product, terms of contract, and warranties	Size standards (e.g., TV screens and refrigerators) Truth in warranties and service contracts Tire construction and load rating	Standards specifying amount of product to use (e.g., detergents) Care labeling for clothing Terms of land sales contracts Truth in imports (country of origin) Truth in savings (interest payments) Disclosure of manufacturer, packer, and distributor of food products Net and drained weights of canned and frozen food

[a]Many of the disclosure requirements in this column will be the subject of future legislation designed to extend coverage (especially from state to federal jurisdictions) or clarify implementation problems. Some are primarily in existence as voluntary industry standards motivated by the threat of government involvement.

[b]As of the second quarter of 1975, none of these requirements had been implemented federally although serious proposals were being considered in virtually all cases.

SOURCE: David A. Aaker and George S. Day (1978), *Consumerism*, 3rd ed. (New York: Free Press), p. 131.

Mazis further notes that consumers sometimes receive information at the wrong time. The insurance cost-disclosure package that informs people of the total costs of insurance protection, for example, reaches the buyer only after a policy is purchased and delivered.

In summary, consumer-behavior concepts have played a key role in shaping information-disclosure policies. However, the area is as complex as the underlying phenomenon of consumer-information processing. Continued research concerning these underlying processes, as well as research evaluating the efficacy of current disclosure programs, will shape such policies in the future.

EXHIBIT 23–7
EVIDENCE OF EFFECTS OF SELECTED INFORMATION DISCLOSURE REQUIREMENTS (unless noted, proportions refer to entire sample)

	Disclosure Requirement	
Effect	**Nutrition Labeling**	**Unit Pricing**
1. Awareness of information	26% saw label	60% to 70% awareness of concept
2. Comprehension of information	16% understood label	50% understood meaning of concept
3. Confidence in judgments	—	—
4. Satisfaction	—	—
5. Claimed use of information (one or more times)	9% used labels at least once	30% to 50% used in a buying decision
6. Impact on behavior (a) self-report	—	5% to 38% of claimed users said some element of a shopping trip was influenced
(b) other evidence	—	—

SOURCE: George S. Day (1976), "Assessing the Effects of Information Disclosure Requirements," *Journal of Marketing*, 40 (Apr.).

CONSUMER SATISFACTION AND DISSATISFACTION

In recent years, many consumer-behavior researchers have turned their attention to questions of the nature, causes, and effects of **consumer satisfaction and dissatisfaction (CS/D).**[32] Increasing interest in this area stems, in part, from the proliferation of consumerism issues in the 1960s and 1970s. Is it possible that consumerism reflects some general phenomenon of dissatisfaction, and, if so, what changes in products, consumers, marketing, or other factors have led to this dissatisfaction?

The concept of consumer satisfaction is central to economic models of mar-

	Disclosure Requirement	
Truth in Lending	**Buying Guide Tags (small appliances)**	**Open Dating**
57% of all credit buyers noticed	50% noticed tag	65% noticed
35% correctly reported interest rate on a recent purchase	—	36% knew that the pull date was used
54% felt better knowing rates and charges	—	—
—	—	Higher degree of satisfaction with freshness
10% of all credit buyers used in last durables purchase	28% found tag helpful	39% used open dating on one or more products during last trip
—	—	50% reduction in report of spoiled food
Negligible relationship of knowledge and shopping behavior, choice of credit source, or decision to use cash or credit	No evidence of effect on pattern of sales for specific models	—

ketplace behavior (see Chapter 13), and the concept and related ones are often specified in formal models of consumer behavior. For example, *satisfaction* is specified in most consumer-behavior models, as are other concepts related to satisfaction, such as consumer motivations and expectations.[33] From a more general perspective, the study of CS/D may be viewed as a central mission of the field of consumer behavior. If the objective of studying consumer behavior is to increase our understanding and abilities to predict patterns of buying behavior, then the study of CS/D is central, to the extent that satisfaction and dissatisfaction play a major role in determining consumer behavior. Some argue that the broader mission is not only to understand and predict buying behavior, but also to offer normative suggestions for making it a more effective and efficacious activity for consumers.

From a corporate perspective, Stokes surveyed food marketers and found that about 60 percent of them had "no idea" of the actual consumer-dissatisfaction rate (based on the frequency of complaints received from consumers).[34] Managers point to increasing sales and profits of the firm as the best measure of satisfaction. As Howard and Hulbert observe:

> . . . *they have been too easily disposed to accept sales dollars, market share or profits as a substitute for the yardstick of true consumer satisfaction.*[35]

Concepts and measures of CS/D would be useful in a number of areas. Hunt notes that many major policy programs proceed without careful measures of CS/D relating to either the problems underlying the policy, or the programs proposed to solve the problems. He points to the policymakers at the Federal Energy Administration as an example:

> [They] *are attempting to allocate and reduce the use of various types of energy. The various public comments by agency personnel lead to the impression that the policymakers would prefer to reduce the energy use with minimum decrease in consumer satisfaction. Granting that energy use must be curtailed, the goal is to bring about that curtailment with minimum burden to consumers. Yet there is no measure of consumer satisfaction and no underlying conceptualization or theory which these policy makers can turn to in their decision-making. So they make their decisions based on their best judgement, hoping all works out well.*[36]

Hunt has also identified the need to conceptualize and measure CS/D with respect to information-disclosure requirements. He notes that the FTC has made far-reaching decisions in the area of nutritional labeling on the *assumption* that such labeling will increase consumer satisfaction:

> *Since there is no CS/D measure, the program initiators can claim any degree of success they want for the programs, i.e., not knowing where they started, where they are going, or whether they got there, it is one expert's*

opinion against another's as to whether consumer satisfaction was increased or decreased by the programs.[37]

Complaining Behavior

One approach to CS/D is to assess *complaining* behavior, which may be viewed as a manifestation—though not necessarily representative—of consumer dissatisfaction. The National Council of Better Business Bureaus receives about 6.4 million inquiries or complaints in a given year. About one quarter of these (1.5 million) are genuine complaints. About 85 percent of these are resolved, mostly through referral to the company involved.

Landon suggests the following model of consumer complaint behavior.[38]

Complaint Behavior = f (dissatisfaction, importance,
benefit from complaining,
personality)

As with most models of consumer behavior, the objective is to organize and synthesize what is presently known, to conceptualize relationships between variables, and to indicate gaps in our knowledge. Landon explicates each of the components of his model: *Dissatisfaction* is a function of the discrepancy between consumer expectations and actual perceived benefits. Some reduction of dissatisfaction may occur as cognitive dissonance operates. That is, consumers rationalize or assimilate the discrepancy in order to reduce the psychological discomfort of dissatisfaction.

Importance is a function of product cost, search time, well-being associated with the product, and ego involvement. Increasing "amounts" of these variables are related to greater perceived importance of the purchase and to possible dissatisfaction, and, therefore, to complaining behavior.

The *benefit from complaining* is a function of the expected payoff minus the cost of complaining. In turn, each element of this cost-benefit tradeoff is a function of other factors.

Expected Payoff from = f (importance, nature of defect)
Complaining
Expected Cost of = f (firm's image, complaining
Complaining   experience, and nature of defect)

For example, Landon thinks that consumers are more likely to complain if the firm has a reputation for products of high quality (*firm's image* variable). The nature of a product's defect may influence the expected payoff from complaining because product performance may be "instrumental"—thought of as the seller's problem—or it may be "expressive"—seen by consumers as their own problem. For example, the instrumental performance of clothing involves its durability and quality, while the expressive performance involves a "psychological" level of performance—how the user responds to the clothing.

Finally, Landon's model suggests that complaining behavior may be related to an individual's *personality* and personal characteristics. Many studies have found that consumer activism is an "upscale" phenomenon. That is, consumer activists are likely to have higher levels of education and income. Moreover, activism tends to increase with family size. The tendency to activism increases up to the age of forty-four, but then tends to decline.

In a more general sense, complaining behavior may be related to the nature of attributions consumers make regarding product failures. It has been found that consumers who attribute product failure to *external* causes (the failure is the fault of the retailer or manufacturer) are more likely to complain than consumers who attribute failure to *internal* ones (it was my fault for buying it).[39] One study even found that the likelihood of complaining is not related to product performance.[40] Instead, it is related to personal characteristics and "internal" factors—how the product is experienced and used. These results suggest that marketers cannot rely on complaints to gauge the degree of satisfaction or dissatisfaction with their products. Rather, more systematic means of gathering information about CS/D are required, such as ongoing surveys. The findings also suggest that performance and information standards must be vigorously enforced; otherwise consumers who are not very vocal— who are not likely to be complainers—may be vulnerable to exploitation.

A final issue in the area of CS/D concerns the nature of the phenomena themselves. It may be that consumer satisfaction and consumer dissatisfaction are different phenomena, rather than opposite ends of the same dimension. If this is true, it does not follow that consumers who are not dissatisfied are therefore satisfied, and vice versa. As one researcher put it:

> *Appearance would affect satisfaction and price would act on dissatisfaction. Improved appearance would never reduce dissatisfaction; a quantum increase in appearance accompanied by a small increase in price (a much better value in conventional terms) would increase dissatisfaction. Similarly, a price cut, no matter how deep, could not increase satisfaction which should only be affected by design improvements.*[41]

If two factors are involved, then the often stated marketers' goal of "maximizing consumer satisfaction" should be replaced by two separate but related goals: maximizing satisfaction and minimizing dissatisfaction.

SUMMARY

We have assessed the relationship between consumer-behavior concepts, theories, and research and "consumerism" issues. Consumerism has sociological, governmental, and business dimensions. Many of the issues reviewed in this chapter reflect consumerism in America, but they are also observed in other countries.

The field of consumer behavior is well positioned to provide useful input to consumerism issues by identifying problem areas and providing baseline data, by fostering greater understanding of consumption phenomena (such as information-processing and consumer satisfaction and dissatisfaction), and perhaps ultimately by helping consumers become more effective and efficient in their buying behavior. The major barriers to effective consumer-behavior contributions to consumerism issues are the different approaches to conflict resolution among the parties to the issues, different value positions, and the difficulty of specifying issues for consumer-behavior analysis on the one hand, and the difficulty of undertaking research that is useful in assessing or implementing consumer policy decisions on the other hand.

We have examined two specific consumerism areas—advertising regulation and information-disclosure requirements—that have benefitted from consumer-behavior inputs, but in different ways. In the case of advertising regulation, consumer-behavior contributions regarding consumer reactions to advertising have helped the FTC expand its understanding of how advertising works beyond traditional "rational man" notions derived from economic theory. FTC initiatives in this area now reflect the behavioral notions of *selective exposure* and *information processing*. Similarly, the advertising substantiation programs, and especially the corrective advertising programs of the FTC, have advanced beyond arbitrary notions of "correction" to assessment of altered perceptions of advertising claims through consumer research.

Consumer-behavior research has been used in information-disclosure programs from truth-in-lending to nutritional labeling. Hierarchical notions of consumer selection, evaluation, and use of product information have guided some of these efforts, or at least provided benchmarks by which to assess the degree to which consumers use different forms of information in different product decisions.

An emerging area of consumer-behavior research is consumer satisfaction and dissatisfaction. This research explores the phenomena of CS/D and the sources of varying degrees of satisfaction and dissatisfaction, as well as the characteristics of individuals associated with varying types and degrees of CS/D.

KEY CONCEPTS

consumerism	consumer	affirmative disclosure
external validity	satisfaction/dis-	corrective advertising
value issues	satisfaction (CS/D)	refutational-inoculation
empirical issues	advocacy system	messages
information disclosure	trade regulation rules	puffery
advertising substan-	uniqueness claims	self-regulation codes
tiation program		and guidelines

DISCUSSION QUESTIONS

1. Using behavioral concepts from this chapter and from other parts of this book, assess the following proposals from the point of view of a consumer advocate and then from the point of view of someone opposed to the advocate.
   - Requiring a listing of the top fifteen ingredients in all advertising for processed food products
   - Encouraging comparative advertising
   - Banning television advertising addressed to children under eight years of age
2. "Consumerism is a cyclical phenomenon—extremely important one year, and on the back-burner the next." Discuss.
3. Why have the courts and regulatory agencies relied primarily on "expert witnesses" rather than on consumer-behavior research in proceedings on consumerism issues?
4. What could consumer-behavior researchers do to increase the utility of behavioral concepts and research in consumerism areas?
5. What advice would you give the Federal Trade Commission regarding information disclosure requirements? What kinds of practices would you advocate, and what kinds of practices would you discourage? What behavioral concepts regarding consumers underlie your answers?
6. Recalling concepts from earlier chapters, what behavioral concepts are relevant to the area of consumer satisfaction and dissatisfaction? In what way are they relevant?
7. Should marketers rely on consumer complaints in order to assess levels of consumer satisfaction and dissatisfaction? Why or why not?
8. Conduct a content analysis of prime-time television commercials. As a consumer advocate, critique this advertising. As a marketing executive, defend it.

NOTES

1. Rachel Carson (1962), *Silent Spring* (Boston: Houghton Mifflin).
2. Ralph Nader (1966), *Unsafe at Any Speed* (New York: Pocket Books).
3. Robert Choate (1970), Consumer Subcommittee of the Senate Commerce Committee, *Hearing on Dry Cereals*, 91st Cong., 2nd sess. (Washington, D.C.: GPO), ser. 72, at pp. 21–129, 270. See also Choate and Debevoise (1975), "How to Make Trouble: Battling the Electronic Baby-sitter," *Ms. Magazine* (Apr.), p. 91.
4. For discussion, see "Consumer Advisory Council: First Report" (1963), Executive Office of the President (Washington, D.C.: GPO), Oct.
5. Upton Sinclair (1906), *The Jungle* (New York: Doubleday, Page).
6. An excellent historical overview is Ralph M. Gaedeke (1970), "The Movement for Consumer Protection: A Century of Mixed Accomplishments," *University of Washington Business Review*, 29, 3 (Spring), pp. 31–40.
7. Paul N. Bloom and Stephan A. Greyser (1981), "Exploring the Future of Consumerism," working paper no. 81-102 (Cambridge, Mass.: Marketing Science Inst.), July, p. 4.
8. Philip Kotler (1971), "The Elements of Social Action," *American Behavioral Scientist* (May–June), pp. 691–717.
9. Quoted in "Is Consumerism Dead?" (1982), Editorial Notebook, *New York Times* (Nov. 22).
10. Center for the Study of American Business (1979), Washington University, St. Louis, Mo.
11. Quoted in "Voluntary Recall of Products is Increasing" (1981), *New York Times* (Oct. 17).
12. Quoted in "Ringing Up Sales" (1982), *Newsweek* (June 14), pp. 65–66.
13. Paul D. Scanlon (1970), "Oligopoly and 'Deceptive' Advertising: The Cereal Industry Affair," *Antitrust Law & Economics Review*, 3, 3 (Spring). Reprinted (abridged version) in David A.

Aaker and George S. Day (1978), *Consumerism: Search for the Consumer Interest,* 3rd ed. (New York: Free Press), pp. 321–31.

14. A good overview is Leonard L. Berry (1972), "The Low Income Marketing System: An Overview," *Journal of Retailing,* 48 (Summer), pp. 44–61.

15. Scott Ward (1972), "Effects of Television Advertising on Children and Adolescents," in *Television and Social Behavior, Vol. 4: Television in Day to Day Life: Patterns of Use,* ed. E. Rubinstein, G. Comstock, and J. Murray (Washington, D.C.: Dept. of Health, Education and Welfare), pp. 432–51.

16. Gary C. Gerlach (1972), "The Consumer's Mind: A Preliminary Inquiry into the Emerging Problems of Consumer Evidence and the Law," working paper (Cambridge, Mass.: Marketing Science Inst.).

17. Gary C. Gerlach (1972).

18. J. Jacoby, W. D. Hoyer, and D. A. Sheluga (1980), *The Miscomprehension of Televised Communication* (New York: American Assn. of Advertising Agencies). A summary of the results is J. Jacoby and W. D. Hoyer (1982), "Viewer Miscomprehension of Televised Communication: Selected Findings," *Journal of Marketing,* 46, 4 (Fall), pp. 12–27.

19. See Gary T. Ford and Richard Yalch (1982), "Viewer Miscomprehension of Televised Communication—A Comment," *Journal of Marketing,* 46, 4 (Fall), pp. 27–32; Richard W. Mizerski (1982), "Viewer Miscomprehension Findings are Measurement Bound," *Journal of Marketing,* 46, 4 (Fall), pp. 32–35; and David C. Schmittlein and Donald G. Morrison (1982), "Measuring Miscomprehension for Televised Communications Using True-False Questions" (Philadelphia: Center for Marketing Strategy Research), The Wharton School, University of Pennsylvania.

20. Earle F. Barcus (1971), "Saturday Children's Television," unpublished paper (Newton, Mass.: Action for Children's Television), (July).

21. See Laurence P. Feldman (1976), *Consumer Protection: Problems and Prospects* (St. Paul, Minn.: West) and Ray O. Werner (1978), "The 'New' Supreme Court and the Marketing Environment 1975–1977," *Journal of Marketing* (Apr.), pp. 56–62.

22. "Consumerism at the Crossroads" (1977), survey conducted for Sentry Insurance (Cambridge, Mass.: Marketing Science Inst.).

23. National Dynamics, et al. (1971), 3, *Trade Reg. Rep.,* par. 19, 653.

24. ITT Continental Baking Co., et al. (1971), 3, *Trade Reg. Rep.,* par. 19, 539.

25. William Wilkie (1973), "Research on Counter and Corrective Advertising," paper presented to Advertising and the Public Interest Conference, American Marketing Association, Washington, D.C. (May), p. 9.

26. H. Keith Hunt (1973), "Effects of Corrective Advertising," *Journal of Advertising Research,* 13 (Oct.), pp. 15–24.

27. For an extended discussion of these issues, see William Wilkie and David Gardner (1974), "The Role of Marketing Research in Public Policy Decision-Making," *Journal of Marketing,* 38, 1 (Jan.), pp. 38–47.

28. George S. Day (1976), "Assessing the Effects of Information Disclosure Requirements," *Journal of Marketing,* 40 (Apr.), pp. 42–52. Reprinted (abridged) in David A. Aaker and George S. Day (1978), pp. 130–46.

29. See Jacob Jacoby, D. E. Speller, and C. A. Kohn (1974), "Brand Choice Behavior as a Function of Information Load," *Journal of Marketing Research,* 11 (Feb.), pp. 63–69; Jacoby, et al. (1973), "Brand Choice Behavior as a Function of Information Load: Study II" (Purdue Paper in Consumer Psychology no. 131); and Jacob Jacoby (1975), "Consumer Reaction to Information Displays: Packaging and Advertising," in *Advertising and the Public Interest,* ed. Sal Divita (Chicago: American Marketing Assn.).

30. See J. O. Summers (1974), "Less Information is Better?" *Journal of Marketing Research,* 11 (Nov.) and William Wilkie (1974), "Analysis of Effects of Information Load," *Journal of Marketing Research,* 11 (Nov.).

31. Michael B. Mazis (1982), "Effectiveness of Required Information Disclosures to Consumers," in *Consumerism and Beyond: Research Perspectives on the Future Social Environment,* Report no. 82-102, pp. 75–78. (Cambridge, Mass.: Marketing Science Inst.).

32. An excellent overview is H. Keith Hunt (1977), "Consumer Satisfaction and Dissatisfaction: Perspectives and Overview," Report no. 77-112 (Cambridge, Mass.: Marketing Science Inst.).

33. John Howard and Jagdish Sheth (1969), *The Theory of Buyer Behavior* (New York: Wiley).

34. Raymond C. Stokes (1974), "Consumer Complaints and Consumer Dissatisfaction," speech before Food Update Conference, The Food and Drug Law Institute (Apr.), Phoenix, Ariz.

35. John Howard and J. Hulbert (1973), *Advertising and the Public Interest* (Chicago: Crain Publications).

36. H. Keith Hunt (1977), pp. 4–5.

37. H. Keith Hunt (1977), p. 5.

38. E. Laird Landon (1977), "A Model of Consumer Complaint Behavior," in *Consumer Satisfaction, Dissatisfaction, and Complaining Behavior*, ed. Ralph Day, Symposium Proceedings, School of Business, University of Indiana, Bloomington, Indiana (Apr. 20-22).

39. Marjorie Wall, Lois E. Dickey, and Wayne Talarzyk (1977), "Predicting and Profiling Consumer Satisfaction and Propensity to Complain," in *Consumer Satisfaction, Dissatisfaction, and Complaining Behavior*.

40. John Howard and J. Hulbert (1973).

41. R. Neil Maddox (1981), "Two-Factor Theory and Consumer Satisfaction: Replication and Extension," *Journal of Consumer Research,* 8 (June), pp. 97–102.

Acknowledgments

CREDITS FOR CHARTS AND GRAPHS

Chapter 1
EX 1–2, From Reuben Hill (1970), *Family Development in Three Generations* (Cambridge, Mass.: Schenkman Publishing Company, Inc.), p. 154. Reprinted by permission.

EX 1–3, Yoram J. Wind, PRODUCT POLICY, © 1982, Addison-Wesley, Reading, Massachusetts. Page 87, Exhibit 4–12. Reprinted with permission.

Chapter 3
EX 3–4, R. Strahan and K. Gerbasi (1972), "Short, Homogeneous Versions of the Marlow-Crowne Social Desirability Scale," *Journal of Clinical Psychology*, 28 (Apr.), p. 192. Reprinted by permission.

Chapter 7
EX 7–3, Scott Ward and Daniel B. Wackman, page 137, NEW MODELS FOR MASS COMMUNICATION RESEARCH, edited by Peter Clarke. Copyright © 1973 by Sage Publications, Inc. Reprinted by permission.

EX 7–4, Scott Ward and Daniel B. Wackman, page 139, NEW MODELS FOR MASS COMMUNICATION RESEARCH, edited by Peter Clarke. Copyright © 1973 by Sage Publications, Inc. Reprinted by permission.

EX 7–6, Scott Ward, Daniel B. Wackman, and Ellen Wartella, page 68, HOW CHILDREN LEARN TO BUY: THE DEVELOPMENT OF CONSUMER INFORMATION PROCESSING SKILLS. Copyright © 1977 by Sage Publications, Inc. Reprinted by permission.

EX 7–7, Scott Ward, Daniel B. Wackman, and Ellen Wartella, page 69, HOW CHILDREN LEARN TO BUY: THE DEVELOPMENT OF CONSUMER INFORMATION PROCESSING SKILLS. Copyright © 1977 by Sage Publications, Inc. Reprinted by permission.

Chapter 8
EX 8–1, From PATTERNS OF DISCOVERY by Dr. Norwood R. Hanson, 1958. Rerpinted by permission of Cambridge University Press.

EX 8–5, Flying Tiger Line Marketing Research, 1978. Used with permission.

EX 8–6, Reprinted by permission of the Harvard Business Review. An exhibit from "New Ways to Measure Consumers' Judgments" by Paul Green and Yoram Wind (July/August 1975). Copyright © 1975 by the President and Fellows of Harvard College; all rights reserved.

Chapter 9
EX 9–3, Walter R. Nord and J. Paul Peter (1980), "A Behavior Modification Perspective on Marketing," *Journal of Marketing*, 44 (Spring), p. 42. Published by the American Marketing Association, and reprinted by permission.

Chapter 10
EX 10–5, Based on Alan Sawyer and Scott Ward (1977), "Carry-over Effects in Advertising Communication: Evidence and Hypotheses from Behavioral Science," in *Cumulative Advertising Effects: Sources and Implications*, ed. Darral Clarke, Report 77-111 (Cambridge, Mass.: Marketing Science Inst.). Reprinted by permission.

EX 10–8, H. A. Zielske (1959), "The Remembering and Forgetting of Advertising," *Journal of Marketing*, 23, pp. 239–43. Published by the American Marketing Association, and reprinted by permission.

Chapter 11

EX 11–5, Robert J. Holloway (1967), "An Experiment on Consumer Dissonance," *Journal of Marketing,* 31 (Jan.), p. 40. Published by the American Marketing Association, and reprinted by permission.

EX 11–6, Alvin A. Achenbaum (1966), "Knowledge Is a Thing Called Measurement," in *Attitude Research at Sea,* ed. Lee Adler and Irving Crespi (New York: American Marketing Assn.), p. 113. Reprinted by permission.

EX 11–7, Data from "The Adult Toy Buyer" by Bureau of Advertising, A.N.P.A. (1967). Reprinted by permission of Newspaper Advertising Bureau, Inc. Cited in F. S. DeBruicker and S. Ward (1980), CASES IN CONSUMER BEHAVIOR (Englewood Cliffs, N.J.: Prentice-Hall, Inc.) page 53.

EX 11–7, Data collection for "Ocean Spray" sponsored by Ocean Spray Cranberries, Inc. Reprinted by permission of the Harvard Graduate School of Business Administration. Copyright © by the President and Fellows of Harvard College; all rights reserved.

Chapter 12

EX 12–3, from "Activities, Interests, and Opinions" by William D. Wells and Douglas J. Tigert from JOURNAL OF ADVERTISING RESEARCH, Volume 11, August 1971. Copyright © 1971 by the Advertising Research Foundation. Reprinted by permission.

EX 12–4, Joseph T. Plummer (1974), "The Concept and Application of Life Style Segmentation," *Journal of Marketing,* 38 (Jan.), pp. 33–37. Published by the American Marketing Association, and reprinted by permission.

EX 12–6, William D. Wells, Arthur D. Beard, "Personality and Consumer Behavior," in CONSUMER BEHAVIOR: Theoretical Sources, edited by Scott Ward, Thomas S. Robertson, © 1973 p. 195. Adapted by permission of Prentice-Hall, Inc., Englewood Cliffs, New Jersey.

Chapter 13

EX 13–7, Reprinted by permission of Elsevier Science Publishing Company, Inc. from "Indicators of Consumer Behavior: The University of Michigan Surveys of Consumers" by Richard T. Curtin in PUBLIC OPINION QUARTERLY, Volume 46, page 348. Copyright © 1982 by The Trustees of Columbia University.

EX 13–9, Based on Vernon Smith, Arlington W. Williams, W. Kenneth Bratton, and Michael G. Vannoni (1982), "Competitive Market Institutions: Double Auctions vs. Sealed Bid-Offer Auctions," *American Economic Review,* 72 (March), p. 62. Reprinted by permission.

Chapter 14

EX 14–6, Reprinted by permission of the Harvard Business Review. Excerpt from "What every marketer should know about women" by Rena Bartos (May, June 1978). Copyright © 1978 by the President and Fellows of Harvard College; all rights reserved.

Chapter 15

EX 15–5, Johan Arndt (1967), "The Role of Product-Related Conversation in the Diffusion of a New Product," *Journal of Marketing Research,* 4 (Aug.), p. 293. Published by the American Marketing Association, and reprinted by permission.

EX 15–8, Thomas S. Robertson (1971), *Innovative Behavior and Communication* (New York: Holt, Rinehart & Winston), p. 50. Reprinted by permission.

EX 15–9, Reprinted by permission of Frank M. Bass, "A New Product Growth for Model Consumer Durables," MANAGEMENT SCIENCE, Volume 15, Number 5, January, 1969. Copyright © 1969 The Institute of Management Sciences.

EX 15–11, Based on Thomas S. Robertson (1971), *Innovative Behavior and Communication* (New York: Holt, Rinehart & Winston), pp. 100–101. Reprinted by permission.

EX 15–11, Reprinted with permission of Macmillan, Inc. from DIFFUSION OF INNOVATIONS, Third Edition, by Everett M. Rogers. Copyright © 1962, 1971, 1983 by The Free Press, A Division of Macmillan Publishing Company, Inc.

Chapter 16

EX 16–3, James S. Coleman, Elihu Katz, and Herbert Menzel (1966), *Medical Innovation: A Diffusion Study* (Indianapolis: Bobbs-Merrill), p. 75. Reprinted by permission.

Chapter 17

EX 17–3, William O. Bearden and Michael J. Etzel (1982), "Reference Group Influence on Product and Brand Purchase Decision," *Journal of Consumer Research*, 9 (Sept.), p. 185. Reprinted by permission.

Chapter 18

EX 18–1, Reprinted with permission of Macmillan Publishing Company from FAMILIES: DEVELOPING RELATIONSHIPS, Second Edition, by Laura S. Smart and Mollie S. Smart. Copyright © 1980 by Macmillan Publishing Company, Inc.

EX 18–2, From "The Family Process: A Sociological Model" by Sylvia Clavan in THE FAMILY COORDINATOR, October, 1969. Copyright © 1969 by the National Council on Family Relations, 1219 University Avenue Southeast, Minneapolis, Minnesota 55414. Reprinted by permission.

EX 18–3, William D. Wells and George Gubar (1966), "The Life Cycle Concept in Marketing Research," *Journal of Marketing Research* (Nov.), pp. 355–65. Published by the American Marketing Association, and reprinted by permission.

EX 18–5, Patrick E. Murphy and William A. Staples (1979), "A Modernized Family Life Cycle," *Journal of Consumer Research*, 6, p. 17. Reprinted by permission.

EX 18–6, Reuben Hill (1971), *Family Development in Three Generations* (Cambridge, Mass.: Schenkman Publishing Company, Inc.). Reprinted by permission.

EX 18–11, EX 18–12, EX 18–13, H. L. Davis and B. P. Rigaux (1974), "Perception of Marital Roles in Decision Processes," *Journal of Consumer Research*, 1 (June), pp. 54, 56, 57. Reprinted by permission.

EX 18–14, Harry L. Davis (1976), "Decision Making Within the Household," *Journal of Consumer Research* (March), pp. 255–64. Reprinted by permission.

EX 18–15, Robert T. Green, Jean-Paul Leonardi, Jean-Louis Chandon, Isabella C. M. Cunningham, Bronis Verhage, and Alain Strazzier (1983), "Societal Development and Family Purchasing Roles: A Cross-National Study," *Journal of Consumer Research*, 9 (March), pp. 436–42. Reprinted by permission.

Chapter 19

EX 19–8, Barton A. Weitz (1981), "Effectiveness in Sales Interactions: A Contingency Framework," *Journal of Marketing*, 45 (Winter), p. 90. Published by the American Marketing Association, and reprinted by permission.

EX 19–9, Barton A. Weitz (1978), "Relationship Between Salesperson Performance and Understanding of Customer Decision Making," *Journal of Marketing Research*, 15 (Nov.), p. 502. Published by the American Marketing Association, and reprinted by permission.

Chapter 20

EX 20–1, Donald J. Treiman (1977), *Occupational Prestige in Comparative Perspective* (New York: Academic Press), Appendix A. Reprinted by permission.

EX 20–3, Richard P. Coleman (1983), "The Continuing Significance of Social Class to Marketing," *Journal of Consumer Research*, 10 (Dec.). Reprinted by permission.

Chapter 21

EX 21–9, Joseph Jacobs Organization, Inc. (1982), Jan.-Feb., New York. Reprinted by permission.

Chapter 22

EX 22–6, Joseph T. Plummer (1977), "Consumer Focus in Cross-National Research," *Journal of Advertising*, 6 (Spring), pp. 10–11. Reprinted by permission.

Chapter 23

EX 23–6, From "Assessing the Effects of Information Disclosure Requirements" by George S. Day from JOURNAL OF MARKETING, 40, April 1976. Published by the American Marketing Association, and reprinted by permission.

EX 23–7, George S. Day (1976), "Assessing the Effects of Information Disclosure Requirements," *Journal of Marketing*, 40 (Apr.). Published by the American Marketing Association, and reprinted by permission.

CREDITS FOR LITERARY SELECTIONS

Chapter 3

EX 3–3, from Mason Haire (1950), "Projective Techniques in Marketing Research," *Journal of Marketing*, 14 (Apr.), pp. 649–56. Published by the American Marketing Association and reprinted by permission.

Chapter 10

EX 10–4, from "Miller Lite's Ads Best Liked, But Aren't the Most Efficient" by Bill Abrams in THE WALL STREET JOURNAL, March 3, 1983. Reprinted by permission of The Wall Street Journal. Copyright © 1983 by Dow Jones & Company, Inc. All Rights Reserved.

EX 10–6, from " 'Ring Around the Collar' Ads Irritate Many Yet Get Results" by Bill Abrams in THE WALL STREET JOURNAL, November 4, 1982. Reprinted by permission of The Wall Street Journal. Copyright © 1982 by Dow Jones & Company, Inc. All Rights Reserved.

Chapter 14

EX 14–2, adapted from Carole B. Allan (1981), "Measuring Mature Markets," *American Demographics* (March), pp. 13–17. Reprinted with permission from American Demographics, © March 1981.

EX 14–4, from Bernie Whalen (1983), "The Nine Nations of North America," *Marketing News* (Jan. 21), p. 18. Published by the American Marketing Association, and reprinted by permission.

Chapter 16

EX 16–1, "K-Mart Has a Little Trouble Killing Those Phantom Snakes from Asia" by Charles W. Stevens in THE WALL STREET JOURNAL, October 20, 1981. Reprinted by permission of The Wall Street Journal. Copyright © 1981 by Dow Jones & Company, Inc. All Rights Reserved.

Chapter 21

EX 21–4, from Steven Flax (1981), "Let Them Keep Laughing," *Forbes* (Sept. 28), pp. 84–85. Reprinted by permission.

EX 21–6, reprinted with permission of Macmillan, Inc. from THE POOR PAY MORE by David Caplovitz. Copyright © 1963, 1967 by The Free Press, a Division of The Macmillan Company.

CREDITS FOR PHOTOGRAPHS AND ILLUSTRATIONS

Chapter 3

EX 3–1, GRIN AND BEAR IT by George Lichty © 1971 Field Enterprises, Inc. Courtesy of Field Newspaper Syndicate.

EX 3–2A, from Rorschach, PSYCHODIAGNOSTIK. Verlag Hans Huber Bern. Copyright © 1921 (renewed 1948).

EX 3–2B, reprinted by permission of the publishers from Henry A. Murray, THEMATIC APPERCEPTION TEST, Cambridge, Mass.: Harvard University Press, Copyright © 1943 by the President and Fellows of Harvard College, © 1971 by Henry A. Murray.

Chapter 5
EX 5–2, courtesy of Perception Research Services.

Chapter 8
EX 8–3, pictorial history of Betty Crocker reproduced with the permission of General Mills, Inc.

Chapter 9
EX 9–4, interactive imagery and non-interactive imagery copyright by the American Psychological Association. Reprinted/Adapted by permission of the publisher and the authors.

Chapter 11
EX 11–2, advertisement for *Fortune*, Copyright 1983 Time Inc.

Chapter 14
EX 14–5, advertisement for Charlie Reprinted Courtesy of Revlon.

EX 14–7A, "My daughters, the doctors" © 1981 International Telephone and Telegraph Corporation.

EX 14–7B, advertisement for Gerber Used by permission; Gerber Products Company.

Chapter 17
EX 17–1, advertisement for Dexatrim Reprinted Courtesy of Thompson Medical Company, Inc.

EX 17–2, advertisement for Michelob Reprinted Courtesy of Anheuser-Busch.

Chapter 21
EX 21–3, "Prep Persona" © 1980 by Lisa Birnbach. Reprinted from THE OFFICIAL PREPPY HANDBOOK by permission of Workman Publishing, New York. Illustration by Oliver Williams.

Chapter 22
EX 22–3, advertisement for Chivas Regal, permission granted by Joseph E. Seagram & Sons, Inc.

EX 22–8, courtesy of PepsiCo, Inc.

p. 323, advertisement for Perdue chicken, reprinted with permission.

p. 325, advertisement for Lip-Smackers, reprinted with permission of BONNIE BELL, INC.

p. 326, advertisement for Grand Marnier, Carillon Importers Ltd., New York, NY.

p. 327, advertisement for Sanka. SANKA is a registered trademark of General Foods Corporation. Advertisement reprinted with permission of General Foods Corporation.

p. 328, advertisement for Ferrari, reprinted with permission.

p. 330, advertisement for Charlie, reprinted with permission of Revlon.

p. 333, advertisement for Chivas Regal, permission granted by Joseph E. Seagram & Sons, Inc.

p. 334, advertisement for EF Hutton, reprinted with permission.

p. 336, advertisement for Marlboro, reprinted with permission of Philip Morris Incorporated. Use of this advertisement was in no way prompted or solicited by Philip Morris. Neither Philip Morris nor any of its employees or agents have made nor is it intended that they will make any payment to the authors of any kind in connection with their use of this advertisement.

Product/Company Index